Happy Anniversary

To Mother

Nov. 1977

From John &
Stella

D0966296

An AMERICAN HERITAGE Guide

# HISTORIC HOUSES
## of
# AMERICA
*Open to the Public*

BY THE EDITORS OF
AMERICAN HERITAGE
The Magazine of History

EDITOR IN CHARGE
BEVERLEY DA COSTA

INTRODUCTION BY
MARSHALL B. DAVIDSON

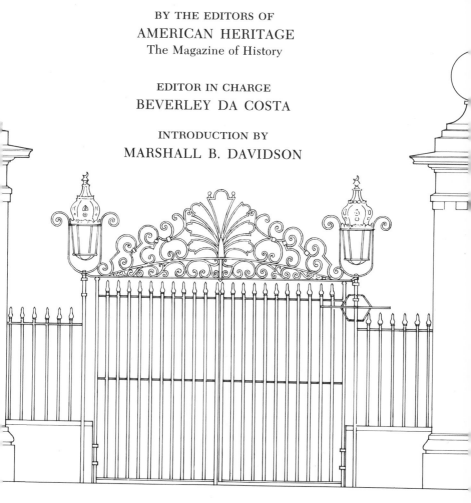

PUBLISHED BY American Heritage Publishing Co., Inc. New York

## Staff for this Book

EDITOR IN CHARGE
Beverley Da Costa

ASSOCIATE EDITORS
Audrey N. Catuzzi
Susan E. Green

ART DIRECTOR
Philip Lief

COPY EDITOR
Kathleen Fitzpatrick

PICTURE EDITOR
Maureen Dwyer

## American Heritage Publishing Co., Inc.

PRESIDENT AND PUBLISHER
Paul Gottlieb

EDITOR-IN-CHIEF
Joseph J. Thorndike

SENIOR EDITOR, BOOK DIVISION
Alvin M. Josephy, Jr.

EDITORIAL ART DIRECTOR
Murray Belsky

GENERAL MANAGER, BOOK DIVISION
Andrew W. Bingham

Library of Congress Catalog Card Number:
79-149725
International Standard Book Number:
07-001135-4

# INTRODUCTION

Each of the houses listed in this Guide represents, both literally and figuratively, a landmark in the history of American life; each stands witness to this country's heritage in some way that claims our interest; and each is open to the public all or some part of the year, as indicated. Some that are included are notable because of their associations with one or more historic personages, or with memorable historic events that gave special meaning to the American experience. The house of Paul Revere in Boston, for instance, is an inseparable element in our appreciation of that almost fabulous patriot and craftsman. Other houses have been selected principally because the character of the buildings in themselves helps us to understand the development of an American way of life and the formation of American culture over the course of more than three centuries. In their design and construction the trim buildings of Samuel McIntire of Salem and Charles Bulfinch of Boston have much to say about Yankee rectitude and forthrightness, of disciplined good taste and competence. More often than not all these features, historical associations along with architectural interest, are present in a single structure, as they are in such abundant measure in notable establishments like Thomas Jefferson's Monticello, for example, at once so studiously and exquisitely designed and so intimately related to the story of American independence and American democracy. In any case, the houses here listed can often tell us more about intimate aspects of the past than can be read in all the books of history, and we cherish them accordingly.

Every region of the land, every state of the union — from Maine and Florida to Alaska and Hawaii — has preserved such tangible evidence of what the past of this country has contributed to the present. The greatest number and the most venerable examples of historic American houses are, naturally, to be seen in those areas that were earliest settled, particularly along the Atlantic seaboard. Mount Vernon is the most illustrious example of a home that is steeped in tradition and rich in association of important interest to anyone concerned with the American past. Beyond that, thanks to the devoted and knowing care Washington gave to every detail of the plan, design, decoration, and furnishing of his house and estate, Mount Vernon also epitomizes the household arts in America over the decades when Americans were struggling for their freedom and establishing their identity among the nations of the world. Washington was a tireless and gracious host — he referred to his home as a "well-resorted tavern" — and many of those who crossed the Atlantic to report on the new republic got their most lasting and significant impression from a visit to Mount Vernon.

However, as the following pages testify, there are many hundreds of other houses, built earlier or later than Mount Vernon, and more or less elaborate than that hallowed structure, that are also eminently worthy of our attention—homes of the great and the not so great, homes of the wealthy and the not so wealthy, homes of infinitely varied character in which, taken together, we can find the texture and color of American life throughout the breadth of the land and the history of its people.

Over the years America has probably produced more different styles of buildings, from log cabins and sod huts to country mansions and city "palaces," than any other nation in the same span of time. That fact is testimony to the rich fabric of American life as it developed from elementary beginnings in the seventeenth century to the complex and sophisticated society of recent years. It is testimony also to the many different strands of tradition, brought here sometimes from far places, that have been woven into the American adventure in living. Still further, it is testimony to the enormous diversity of the land itself and the nature of its abundant resources, which have led the builder and planner to meet the exigencies and opportunities of local and regional circumstances in special ways in separate places. To witness this variety one has only to compare the neat, snug, eighteenth-century clapboard structures of the Connecticut River Valley with the spacious mansions that line the James River in Virginia, or the city streets of Charleston—or, indeed, the adobe dwellings of New Mexico and California. The Santa Barbara house of Captain Horatio Gates Trussell provides one beguiling instance of the way the disparate traditions that fed the mainstream of American building sometimes mingled and fused into expressions of decided local character. Trussell, a down-Easter who came to California in the 1850s, lived in an adobe house typical of the area. However, when a shipwreck off the Santa Barbara coast supplied the necessary materials, he incorporated timber additions to his home reminiscent of the frame constructions of New England. It survives as an early example of a gradual adaptation of native Spanish-American tradition to Eastern habits and practices.

The editors believe that what follows is the most complete listing of houses of historic interest and open to the public that has been published to date. There are, to be sure, innumerable other structures of equivalent interest that are privately owned and that can be visited only by personal invitation. Where there is a concentration of such homes, as in Charleston, South Carolina, Newport, Rhode Island, and certain other communities, mention is made of the fact that these can at least be admired and studied in passing.

To compile such a list is a risky venture for, unfortunately, almost every day sees the destruction of some treasured landmark, either by fire, neglect, or demolition. In the late 1930s and early 1940s a compendious list of twelve thousand outstanding examples of American architecture was first published under the direction of the National Park Service, as the Historic American Buildings Survey. By 1966 almost half those structures had already been destroyed—and the toll continues to mount. Hardly more than a year ago, as one poignant example, the Dodge House in Los Angeles, designed in 1916 by the architect Irving Gill and considered one of the fifteen most significant houses in the entire history of American architecture, was bulldozed overnight, even while an impressive number of American and foreign students, with architects, historians, various state and local authorities, and desperately hopeful citizens struggled for its preservation. The loss was complete and final, and nothing of comparable interest or importance has replaced it.

In compiling the present list the editors have received touching messages from those who care deeply about such matters. Answering our inquiries about the Haumont House in Broken Bow, Nebraska, a correspondent wrote: "Have no regular hours. Come when you want to. They tell us that this is the only two-story sod house still standing in the United States. The house is in poor condition. No one seems interested in restoring this place so 1971 will probably be the last year for the house." As we go to press the house still stands; by the time these words reach the reader it may not.

Without the earnest co-operation of many individuals, historical and preservation societies, and other organizations—local, state, and national— it would have been flatly impossible to attempt the compilation that follows. Our gratitude to countless persons and groups who have helped to produce this Guide can be only partially acknowledged (see pp. 318–20). A total reckoning of those who have contributed to these pages would be a small volume in itself. The conversations and correspondence with all our informants would be a separate, intimate history of our country, the gist of which, however, is here included. With full recognition of all the help that has been provided, the editors remain responsible for any inadvertent errors that may have escaped their attention. M.B.D.


In order to include all the houses open to the public we have had to abbreviate organizational names, titles, and geographical locations. No local chapter names or "inc." have been given for the organizations operating the houses. As the entrance fees are often very nominal or by personal donation, these have not been listed. The "open" hours refer to local time schedule and since these are occasionally subject to change, we suggest you check beforehand to avoid any inconvenience. Special arrangements for group tours are not mentioned, but groups can usually be accommodated by prior appointment.

The date the house was first built immediately follows the name; any other dates represent a significant addition or alteration to the structure or style of the house. The cut-off period for inclusion in this Guide is in the 1920s. Military posts, universities, battlefields, parks, et cetera, are mentioned if there are private residences open to the public on the grounds. Since the Indians built the first housing in America, some of the most important ruins are also included. Finally, the symbol ■ preceding many of the entries indicates the house is listed in *The National Register of Historic Places* (as of December, 1970) and/or is operated by the National Park Service. B.D.C.

# BUILDING STYLES 1640s–1880s

*Medieval – peaked gables*

*Medieval saltbox*

*Early Georgian – gambrel roof*

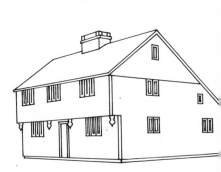

*High Georgian – hip roof*

*Federal*

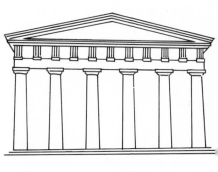

*Greek Revival*

*Cape Cod cottage*

*Monterey adobe*

*Gothic Revival*

*Italian or Tuscan villa*

*High Victorian*

*Queen Anne*

## BIRMINGHAM

### ARLINGTON, 1842
**331 Cotton Ave, SW**
Frame Greek Revival plantation house built onto an earlier one by Judge William S. Mudd. Used in 1865 by Gen. James H. Wilson as headquarters; during the brief Union occupation a "spy," poetess Mary Gordon Duffee, hid in the attic. Period furnishings; relics of the War Between the States; museum of great Alabama women; mementos of Elyton, the town which predated Birmingham
*Operated by Ala. State Fair Authority. Open weekdays 9-5, Sun. 1-6*

*Arlington*

## CAMDEN

### WHITE COLUMNS, 1859
White frame Greek Revival-style house. The present owners are heirs to part of the estate of J.M.W. Turner, English landscape painter. Many of the artist's sketches and engravings are on display. The house is furnished with antiques.
*Operated by Mrs. Lois A. Starr, owner. Open spring and summer: daily 1-6. Winter: by appointment*

## DEMOPOLIS

### ■ BLUFF HALL, 1832
**405 N Commissioners Ave**
Mansion is built in Greek Revival style of brick covered with plaster. It is located on White Bluff on the Tombigbee River—landing site of Napoleonic exiles who founded Demopolis in 1818. Built by Francis Strother Lyon, a lawyer, who became a member of both the U.S. and the Confederate congresses. The unusual and interesting house features are the drawing room's columns and pilasters, the transverse hall and carriage entrance,

the ceiling ornamentation in the dining room and entrance hall, and the ante-bellum kitchen.
*Operated by Marengo Co. Historical Soc. Open Sun. 2-5 and by appointment*

### GAINESWOOD, 1842
**805 S Cedar St**
Two-story stone-and-stucco Greek Revival mansion, with elements of the Adam style, designed and built by Gen. Nathan B. Whitfield. Distinctions of the house are its mirrored ballroom, a round-galleried bedroom, twin dining and music rooms with domed ceilings, and ornamental plaster.
*Operated by Ala. Dept. of Conservation. Open weekdays 9-4, Sun. 1-4; closed Mondays, Christmas, and New Year's Day*

## EUFAULA

### SHEPPARD COTTAGE, 1837
**East Barbour Street**
Simple pioneer cottage, one of Eufaula's oldest; home of Dr. Edmund Sheppard, who came here with other settlers from Tidewater, New Jersey, hoping to develop an oyster industry. Houses Eufaula Chamber of Commerce
*Operated by Eufaula Heritage Assn. Open during business hours*

### SHORTER MANSION, 1906
**340 N Eufaula Ave**
Outstanding Greek Revival mansion, with Corinthian columns, ornate frieze, and balustraded roof, built by Eli Sims Shorter and Wileyna Lamar Shorter. Furnished with Federal-style antiques and Oriental rugs and porcelains. Now houses the Eufaula historical museum and is headquarters for the April Eufaula Pilgrimage
*Operated by Eufaula Heritage Assn. Open Mon. and Fri. 10-12, 1-4*

### ■ THE TAVERN, 1836
**105 Riverside Dr**
Two-story, columned Greek Revival structure originally known as Irwinton Inn and built to accommodate the river traffic on the Chattahoochee. Used as a Confederate hospital during the War Between the States; restored
*Operated by Cowikee Educational and Cultural Foundation. Open by appointment*

*The Tavern*

## FLORENCE

### COURTVIEW (ROGERS HALL), 1855
**Court Street**
A two-and-a-half-story red brick house with a classic portico supported by four white columns across the front. The open front gallery is enclosed by a wrought-iron railing, behind which French doors open into a wide center hall. Built for George Washington Foster, a wealthy planter, the house now serves as a student and faculty social center.
*Operated by Florence State University. Open during school sessions: daily 8–5*

### ■ OSCAR KENNEDY HOUSE, about 1820
**303 N Pine St**
One-and-a-half-story Federal house with later additions, one of the earliest Federal-style structures in the Tennessee Valley region. The red brick load-bearing walls are 13 inches thick; inside the original woodwork is still intact. Now used as offices for the local housing authority
*Operated by Florence Housing Authority. Open during business hours*

### POPE'S TAVERN, 1811
**203 Hermitage Dr**
Brick structure with veranda stretching full length of the front and supported by poplar columns. Originally built as a stage stop and tavern, the building was bought in 1874 by Frank G. Lambeth and thereafter was the home of the Lambeth family. It is furnished with antiques, and many Civil War relics are displayed.
*Operated by Florence Historical Board. Open Tues.–Sat. 9–12, 2–5, Sun. 2–5*

### W. C. HANDY HOUSE, about 1870
**Marengo and College Streets**
Three-room log cabin simply furnished with pieces over 100 years old and displaying mementos of W. C. Handy, Negro musician and composer who in 1914 wrote "St. Louis Blues"
*Operated by Florence Historical Board. Open Tues.–Sun. 9–5*

## GREENSBORO

### MAGNOLIA GROVE (HOBSON MEMORIAL), 1835–38
**1002 Hobson St**
Ante-bellum mansion that is the birthplace and ancestral home of Adm. Richmond Pearson Hobson, Spanish-American War hero. It contains the original antique furnishings as well as historic relics and curios brought from foreign countries by Adm. Hobson.
*Operated by Miss Margaret Hobson, caretaker. Open Mon.–Sat. 9–12, 2–5, Sun. 2–5*

## MOBILE

### ■ FORT CONDE-CHARLOTTE HOUSE, early 1700s
**104 Theater St**
Two-story brick house covered with smooth stucco, painted white. Four columns support a porch across the front; another four support the roof. Fort Conde was the name during the French occupation, which ended with the Treaty of Paris (1763). The British gained control of the territory and renamed the fort in honor of England's Queen Charlotte, wife of George III. Spain captured Mobile in 1780 and ruled there until 1813, when American troops took the fort. In 1820 it was made into an imposing residence by Jonathan Kirkbridge. Each room is furnished to represent a period of Mobile's history.
*Operated by Soc. of Colonial Dames. Open Jan. 3–Mar. 26: Mon.–Fri. 1–4. Mar. 27–Apr. 16: Mon.–Sat. 10–1, 2–5, Sun. 1–5. Apr. 17–May: Mon.–Fri. 1–4; may be closed temporarily because of tunnel construction under Mobile River*

## OAKLEIGH, 1833–38
### 350 Oakleigh Place

Classical revival house with raised one-story portico designed and built, with locally made brick and hand-hewn lumber, by James W. Roper, a successful businessman, and named for the many beautiful giant oaks surrounding it. Period furniture, family portraits, parlor doors with original silver-plated door knobs, and an unusual collection of memorabilia of Mobile's Mardi gras are on display. *Operated by Historic Mobile Preservation Soc. Open Sept.–July: Mon.–Sat. 10–4, Sun. 2–4. August: by appointment; closed July 4th, Labor Day, Christmas, and New Year's Day*

### ■ RAPHAEL SEMMES HOUSE, about 1856
### 802 Government St

Greek Revival house purchased in 1871 by the citizens of Mobile as a home for Adm. Raphael Semmes in grateful recognition of his outstanding accomplishments and loyalty to Mobile. Two parlors are furnished and used as a small chapel; the other rooms are reserved for church use. *Operated by First Baptist Church. Open by appointment*

## MONTGOMERY

### FALCONER HOUSE, about 1840
### 428 S Lawrence St

A white frame cottage with white fretwork on the porch. Only the front double parlors and hall are original; the remainder of the house has been rebuilt as it was. It now serves as the visitors' information center for the city of Montgomery; gift shop on premises. *Operated by Young Women's Christian Organization. Open daily 9–4*

### FIRST WHITE HOUSE OF THE CONFEDERACY, about 1825
### Corner of Washington and Union Streets

Simple, white frame two-story house occupied by Jefferson Davis when he became President of the Confederacy. Contains original Davis furniture and relics of the War Between the States. *Operated by White House Assn. Open daily 9–4:30; closed Christmas and New Year's Day*

Fort Conde-Charlotte House

Oakleigh

First White House of the Confederacy

### GOVERNOR'S MANSION, 1907–8
### 1142 S Perry St

Greek Revival mansion originally designed by architect Weatherly Carter for Robert F. Ligan, Jr., and made the executive residence in 1950. Four towering Corinthian columns and graceful ironwork balustrades ornament the façade; interiors feature neoclassic plasterwork, flooring of handsome parquetry and Alabama marble, and a grand central staircase. The furnishings are fine Victorian reproductions made in Alabama. *Operated by State of Ala. Open Mon.– Fri. 9–5:30*

## GREIL HOUSE, about 1854 and 1900
### 305 S Lawrence St
Originally built as a stucco-over-brick Italianate villa by John Dickerson, it was later changed, around 1900, to the neoclassic style by the addition of six columns to the façade. It served as the residence of John Gill Shorter, governor of Alabama from 1861 to 1863. Now Junior League headquarters *Operated by Junior League of Montgomery. Open Mon.–Fri. 9–5 and by appointment*

## MURPHY HOUSE, 1851
### 22 Bibbs St
Greek Revival mansion built by wealthy cotton factor and member of the city water board John H. Murphy. The façade is brick covered with stucco and has six Corinthian columns. The double parlor, which served as a ballroom, is being restored with period furnishings; other rooms are offices. *Operated by Montgomery Water Works and Sanitary Sewer Board. Open Mon.–Fri. 8–5; closed holidays*

## SHAW HOUSE COMPLEX, 1850s
### 230 N Hull St
Three ante-bellum houses in proximity showing great architectural diversity: *Ordeman-Shaw House* (1851), a stucco-over-brick Italianate villa with restored dependencies open as a house museum with period furnishings; *Dewolf-Cooper House* (about 1855), a frame modified Gothic cottage serving as the information center; and *Campbell-Holtzclaw House* (1852), a frame Greek Revival cottage not yet open. *Operated by Landmarks Foundation of Montgomery. Open Tues.–Sat. 10–4, Sun. 1:30–4:30*

## TEAGUE HOUSE, 1848
### 468 S Perry St
Brick, Greek Revival house designed by architect Berry Owens. It was used as headquarters by "Wilson's Raiders" when that Union outfit occupied Mont-

gomery during the War Between the States. House served as private residence of Teague family from 1889 to 1955, when it was purchased by Alabama State Chamber of Commerce; Empire and early Victorian furnishings *Operated by Ala. State Chamber of Commerce. Open weekdays 10–12, 1–3; closed holidays*

# MOULTON VICINITY

## PIONEER HOUSE, 19th century
Authentic pioneer cabin, furnished with household goods and implements actually used by homesteaders, reflects the rugged life of early settlers. Moonshine still in yard *Operated by Pioneer House Museum. Open daily 7–6*

# SELMA

## STURDIVANT HALL, 1853
### 713 Mabry St
Brick-and-marble Greek Revival mansion, designed by a cousin of Robert E. Lee, has had three private owners of wealth and even before its 1957 restoration was in fine condition. It has notable plasterwork in ceiling friezes. An interesting feature is a spiral staircase which leads from the third floor to the eight-windowed widow's walk. Chippendale, Hepplewhite, and Empire furnishings *Operated by the Sturdivant Museum Assn. Open daily 9–12, 2–4, Sun. 2–4*

# TUSCALOOSA

## FRIEDMAN HOME, 1835
### 1010 Greensboro Ave
Two-story Greek Revival-style house with six square pillars across the front veranda, which has a small balcony. Home was built by Alfred Battle, early merchant and planter. It has been the home of Virginia Tunstall Clay Clopton, author of *Belle of the Fifties*, and poet Robert Loveman. Empire and Victorian furnishings *Operated by Tuscaloosa Co. Preservation Soc. Open Sun. 2–5 and by appointment*

## GORGAS HOME, 1829
### University of Alabama Campus
The first permanent building of the University of Alabama campus. Built

by English architect Nickols as the college dining hall. In 1840 the building became a private residence. It is distinguished by the two curving stairways and wrought-iron rails leading to the second-story porch. The house is named for Gen. Josiah Gorgas, Confederate chief of ordnance, who lived here as president of the university in the 1880s, and his son Gen. William Crawford Gorgas, who served as Surgeon General of the U.S. armed forces in World War I. He is best known for conquering yellow fever during the construction of the Panama Canal.
*Operated by Gorgas Memorial Board. Open weekdays 10–12, 2–5, Sun. 3–5*

*Gorgas Home*

## JEMISON HOME–FRIEDMAN LIBRARY, 1862
**1305 Greensboro Ave**
Italian villa-style house built by Robert Jemison, legislator, prominent merchant, and stagecoach inn operator, with all interior walls of brick. Distinctions are its fine moldings, paneling, and marble mantels.
*Operated by Tuscaloosa Co. Library. Open daily*

## OLD TAVERN (WILSON HOME), 1827
**Capitol Park**
Two-story brick house with French-style balcony. Onetime home of John Gayle, governor of Alabama (1831–35); then a stagecoach inn, and later a residence of the Wilson family. In 1966 the building was moved from Broad Street to Capitol Park and extensively restored. Furnished with local museum items and 19th-century furniture
*Operated by Tuscaloosa Co. Preservation Soc. Open Tues.–Sun. 2–5*

## SWAIM HOME, 1835–36
**2111 14 St**
Two-story Greek Revival structure, with 16 Ionic columns extending around three sides, built by Alexander Dearing, pioneer merchant in Alabama. In 1865 it was invaded by the Federal forces. Interior features circular stairway, elaborate friezes, black Italian marble mantels; Victorian furnishings
*Operated by S. G. Swaim family. Open by appointment*

## TUSCUMBIA

### ■ BIRTHPLACE OF HELEN KELLER (IVY GREEN), 1820
**300 W North Common**
Frame house built by Helen Keller's grandfather and a nearby smaller building where Miss Keller was born. The blind and deaf child was taught an alphabet code with which she learned to read, write, speak, and "hear" others. Both houses contain furniture and mementos associated with Miss Keller's amazing career. Grounds planted with 150-year-old boxwoods; scene of annual summer theater presentation of *The Miracle Worker*, based on Miss Keller's childhood. The pump at which Helen learned her first word remains as it was then between the main house and the outdoor kitchen.
*Operated by Helen Keller Property Board. Open Mon.–Sat. 8:30–4:30, Sun. 1–4:30; closed Christmas and New Year's Day*

## TUSKEGEE

### ■ THE OAKS, 1896–99
**Tuskegee Institute**
This three-story brick house was the home of Booker T. Washington, founder of Tuskegee Institute. It was the home of the Washington family until the death of his widow, Mrs. Margaret Murray Washington, in 1925 when the property was purchased by the institute to be established as a shrine to the memory of the great educator. The major portion of the building is now used as offices. However, Dr. Washington's den has been preserved with his original furnishings.
*Operated by Tuskegee Institute. Open daily 8–12, 1–4*

# EAGLE

■ **EAGLE HISTORIC DISTRICT on the Yukon River at the mouth of Mission Creek**
Located in the heart of the Yukon gold region, Eagle served as a fur-trading post and supply center for gold-mining operations in the 1890s on the upper Yukon. It was here that Judge James Wickersham established the first U.S. court in the interior. Old Fort Egbert ruins may be seen.

# JUNEAU

**GOVERNOR'S HOUSE, 1912**
Built by the Federal government as the residence for the territorial governor of Alaska, this house was turned over to the new state in 1959 and continues to be the governor's residence. *Operated by State of Alaska. Open on special occasions*

**HOUSE OF WICKERSHAM, 1899**
Home of Judge James Wickersham, historian and pioneer judge who went to Alaska to establish the first courts and government in the interior. Judge Wickersham was also sent to clean up the great gold scandal at Nome in 1901. One of the largest collections of Alaskana—diaries and early artifacts dating back to Russian-American days —may be viewed. *Operated by Alaska Airlines. Open daily 11:30–7:30*

# KODIAK

■ **BARANOF-ERSKINE HOUSE, between 1792 and 1799; 1870; 1912 Main and Mission Streets**
The oldest Russian colonial building extant in the U.S. Alexander Baranof, overseer of a Russian fur company, moved his headquarters here in 1792 when a tidal wave swept over his settlement at Three Saints Bay. During the 1870s red cedar was brought by ship from California to sheathe the log timbers of the original structure. In 1912 the house became known as the Erskine House, after W. J. Erskine, who remodeled the house for his family. Antiques and Russian relics disposed of in 1948. Now operated as a museum *Operated by Kodiak and Aleutian*

*Islands Historical Soc. Open summer: daily 10–3. Winter: Wed., Fri., Sat., Sun. 1–3*

*Baranof-Erskine House*

# SKAGWAY

■ **SKAGWAY HISTORIC DISTRICT, 1897 Head of Taiya Inlet on Lynn Canal**
Skagway is the largest existing example of an Alaskan frontier mining town. It was settled as a result of gold discoveries on the upper Yukon and in the Klondike region. There are about 100 buildings still standing, including the railroad depot, saloons, hotels, and the Federal court building, which is now a museum named the "Trail of '98." Skagway is the northernmost point of the protected Inside Passage and the southern terminus of the White Pass and Yukon Railway, which operates all year.

# WRANGELL

**TRIBAL HOUSE OF THE BEAR, 1834 Shakes' Island**
Replica of the community house built by Tlingit Indians, a group of seafaring tribes inhabiting the southern coast of Alaska and northern British Columbia. The house is constructed of red cedar planks and timbers fitted together by tongue and groove and wooden pegs. Ancient carvings in the house and surrounding totem poles, some 200 years old, painted with tribal designs are featured. *Operated by Wrangell Chamber of Commerce. Open daily*

## CAMP VERDE VICINITY

■ **MONTEZUMA CASTLE NATIONAL MONUMENT, 13th or 14th century**
**Arizona Route 79**
A tract of 521 acres containing the remains of prehistoric cliff dwellings cut into the sandstone. The best-preserved of its type, the "castle," a five-story structure of adobe brick, was built by Pueblo Indians in a natural cave high in the cliffs. It was a home and fortress for about 20 families.
*Operated by National Park Service.*
*Open—Visitors' center—summer: 7–7.*
*Rest of year: 8–5*

## CHINLE

■ **CANYON DE CHELLY NATIONAL MONUMENT, 348–1300**
**one mile east of Chinle**
Within the canyon four periods of Indian culture may be seen—the Basketmakers, or early Anasazi, who constructed houses over a dug-down floor; the Pueblos, or later Anasazi, responsible for the apartment-style homes in caves or rock shelters; the Hopi Indians, also a Pueblo people, who occupied the canyons sometime after the 1300s; and the present-day Navajos, who have their summer homes here and who use the canyon floor for farming and grazing. Principal ruins of the area are White House, Antelope House, Standing Cow, and Mummy Cave.
*Operated by National Park Service.*
*Open—Visitors' center—summer:*
*8–6. Winter: 8–5*

*Canyon de Chelly*

## CLARKDALE VICINITY

■ **TUZIGOOT NATIONAL MONUMENT, about 1125–1450**
**two miles east of Clarkdale**
Hilltop pueblo of 110 clustered rooms, about 500 feet long and 100 feet across. A museum nearby houses the complete collection of artifacts recovered during excavations.
*Operated by National Park Service.*
*Open daily 8–5*

## COOLIDGE VICINITY

■ **CASA GRANDE RUINS NATIONAL MONUMENT, about 1000–1450**
**Arizona Route 87**
Four-story tower of packed earthen walls built over 600 years ago by Indian farmers of the Gila River Valley. A remarkable example of the construction techniques of the early American Indian, it served as an observation tower and apartment house.
*Operated by National Park Service.*
*Open daily 8–5*

## FLAGSTAFF VICINITY

■ **WALNUT CANYON NATIONAL MONUMENT, about 100–1200**
**U.S. Route 66**
Remains of over 300 small cliff dwellings of prehistoric Indians built in recesses along canyon walls
*Operated by National Park Service.*
*Open daily 8–5*

■ **WUPATKI NATIONAL MONUMENT, about 1000–1215**
**U.S. Route 89**
Prehistoric pueblos built by groups of farming Indians. Nearly 800 sites are located within the boundaries of the monument.
*Operated by National Park Service.*
*Open daily 8–5*

## GANADO

■ **HUBBELL HOUSE, 1900–1915**
**Hubbell Trading Post National Historic Site, Arizona Route 264**
One of the most noted trade centers of the Navajo Indian Reservation, the home of Don Lorenzo Hubbell is the oldest surviving post of its kind.

Hubbell was one of the first to encourage the Navajo weavers and silversmiths to trade their products. The home displays Indian crafts and paintings and depicts the history of the Southwest and the life of a trader's family.
*Operated by National Park Service. Open daily 8-6*

## JEROME
■ **JEROME HISTORIC DISTRICT**
**on U.S. Route 89A**
Now almost a ghost town, this was one of the great copper-mining centers in the world by 1907. Much of its original appearance and atmosphere is retained by the frame buildings built on stilts and its narrow, steep streets. The *James H. Douglas Mansion*, in the Jerome State Historic Park, is open daily 8-5 as a mining museum.

## MOCCASIN
■ **WINSOR CASTLE, 1870-71**
**Pipe Springs National Monument**
Monument to the Mormon pioneers responsible for the exploration, settlement, and development of this part of · the Southwest. Buildings are original though extensively restored, and their furnishings have been collected from neighboring communities. The fort, originally called "Winsor Castle," is typical of the Mormon forts built in the Utah Territory. It served as a ranch house until 1923, when it became a national monument.
*Operated by National Park Service. Open daily 8-5*

## NOGALES VICINITY
**PETE KITCHEN MUSEUM, 1860**
**U.S. Highway 89**
Replica of the famed old ranch in Arizona, built like a fort, in which the rugged settler Pete Kitchen held out against hostile Apaches through the 1860s and 1870s. Now operated as a museum with Spanish furniture and armor from the days of the conquistadors. Mission relics, paintings, and the 1584 Guadalupe *retablo* may be seen in the adjacent Kino Chapel.
*Operated by Col. Gil Procter. Open Tues.-Sun. 10-5; closed Christmas*

## PHOENIX VICINITY
**PIONEER ARIZONA**
**Interstate Highway 17**
Reconstructed pioneer village with 23 completed buildings re-creating life in Arizona during the 1870s and 1880s. Youth camping facilities available
*Operated by Pioneer Ariz. Foundation. Open summer: daily 9-sunset. Winter: daily 9-5*

■ **PUEBLO GRANDE RUIN,**
**12th century**
**East Washington Street**
An ancient Indian pueblo and archaeological site museum. Exhibits pertaining to life of Hohokam Indians. Reference library
*Operated by City of Phoenix. Open Mon.-Fri. 9-5, Sun. 1-5; closed major holidays*

## PRESCOTT
**OLD GOVERNOR'S MANSION**
**[SHARLOT HALL MUSEUM], 1864**
**400 W Gurley St**
Sturdy log house built for John N. Goodwin, Arizona's first territorial governor. It served as his home and office, the state capitol, and the military commandant's headquarters until 1867. Now a museum; Indian artifacts, Victorian furnishings, and articles representative of the first white settlers are exhibited. Also on the grounds is the first house built in Prescott, *Old Fort Misery*, a two-room log cabin. In this house lived the first lawyer of the area, John Howard. Many original furnishings may be seen.
*Operated by Prescott Historical Soc. Open Mon.-Sat. 9-12, 1-5, Sun. 1-5. Nov. 15-May 15: closed Mon.*

## ROOSEVELT VICINITY
■ **TONTO NATIONAL**
**MONUMENT, 1100-1400**
Most accessible of many prehistoric cliff dwellings preserved here. Occupied by the Salado Indians
*Operated by National Park Service. Open—Visitors' center—daily 8-5*

## TOMBSTONE
■ **TOMBSTONE HISTORIC**
**DISTRICT**
In the 1880s Tombstone was a boom

town, well known for its lawlessness. It was the site of the famous gun battle between the Earp and Clanton clans at the OK Corral in 1881. Boothill Graveyard, at the city limits, contains the graves of nearly 200 notorious characters. Also of interest in Tombstone are several museums devoted to the history of the town—the Wyatt Earp Museum, containing memorabilia of the Earp family; the Tombstone Courthouse (1882), displaying relics of early Tombstone; and the Bird Cage Theater (1881), once a lusty honky-tonk, with its original furnishings and interior preserved intact.

## TONALEA

■ **NAVAJO NATIONAL MONUMENT, 13th century**
**60 miles northeast of Tuba City**
Surrounded by the Navajo Indian Reservation, the largest and most intricate of the state's known cliff dwellings are preserved here. There are three areas, each with a pueblo ruin.
*Operated by National Park Service. Open—Visitors' center—daily 8–5*

## TUCSON

**CHARLES O. BROWN HOUSE (THE OLD ADOBE PATIO), 1850s; 1876; 1888**
**40 West Broadway**
Example of the southern Arizona-Sonora style of architecture which evolved on this frontier. The home of Charles O. Brown, a highly enterprising gentleman who, as a youngster, traveled from Illinois to Texas and on to the California gold fields. He settled in Tucson in 1858 at the age of 28. In 1868 Brown purchased an adobe house on Jackson Street, and he added to it over the years, sparing no expense either in the construction costs or the furnishings. Restored, with a restaurant and specialty shops.
*Operated by Arizona Pioneers' Historical Soc. Open daily 10–9*

**EDWARD NYE FISH HOUSE, 1868**
**208 N Main St**
Edward Nye Fish was a wealthy merchant and politician in Tucson, having migrated from Barnstable, Massachusetts, by way of the California gold

fields and a general merchandising business in San Francisco and Sacramento. The house he built on Main Street was decorated in the latest fashion, complete with English Victorian furniture and Brussels carpets, and was a social center of the city.
*Operated by Tucson Art Center. Open by appointment*

**HIRAM S. STEVENS HOUSE, about 1860**
**212 N Main St**
In 1864 Stevens, a wealthy merchant, married Petra Santa Cruz, from Sonora, and shortly thereafter they moved into this house on Main Street. Stevens was active in the commercial and political life of the area, and their home became one of the social centers of the town. In 1874 Stevens acquired the house adjoining his, and the two houses were incorporated to form the present complex.
*Operated by Tucson Art Center. Open by appointment*

## WHITERIVER VICINITY

■ **KINISHBA RUINS, about 1250–1350**
**15 miles west of Whiteriver**
Large pueblo which could have housed up to 1,000 Indians. It consists of two large and seven small buildings. A rectangular building with two enclosed courtyards represents an architectural plan typical of this region during the late 13th and early 14th centuries. The inhabitants of this pueblo were a blend of Mogollon and Anasazi ancestry.
*Operated by University of Ariz. Open daily 8–5*

## YUMA

**OLD SANGUINETTI HOUSE (CENTURY HOUSE AND GARDENS), about 1870**
**248 Madison Ave**
Adobe structure, enlarged after 1885, the home of Eugene F. Sanguinetti, one of Yuma's early merchants. The house is now furnished as an Arizona Territory home with exhibits depicting the early history of Yuma.
*Operated by Yuma Co. Historical Soc. Open Oct.–May: Tues.–Sat. 2–5; closed holidays*

# CAMDEN

## CHIDESTER HOUSE (STAGECOACH HOUSE), 1848
### 926 Washington St, NW

Large 11-room house built by Peter McCallum. Col. John T. Chidester, a native New Yorker, and his wife moved into the house about 1857. During the years the Chidesters' five sons were growing up the house was a major stop for the stagecoach on its way to Georgia, Alabama, and Mississippi. It was the first house in Camden to have papered walls, a cookstove, and sewing machine. The furniture, most of which is original, was bought by the colonel in New Orleans and shipped by flatboat to Camden.
*Operated by Ouachita Co. Historical Soc. Open Tues.–Sun. 9–4; closed holidays*

# CONWAY

## GREATHOUSE HOME, about 1830
### Faulkner County Court Yard

Constructed of cypress logs at "Cross Roads," about 25 miles north of Little Rock, and moved here in 1965; built by Daniel Greathouse, whose family moved from Lancaster, Pennsylvania, to Virginia, Kentucky, and on to Arkansas. The house has been extensively restored and furnished with local items of the mid-19th century.
*Operated by Faulkner Co. Historical Soc. Open spring and fall: 9–12 and by appointment*

# EMMET

## ARKLA VILLAGE
### U.S. Route 67

A re-created mid-1800 frontier town. Saddlery, furniture, pony- and horse-drawn vehicles are manufactured here by methods similar to those of the 19th century.
*Operated by Arkla Village. Open daily 9–5*

# EUREKA SPRINGS

## HATCHET HALL (CARRY NATION'S LAST HOME), 1883
### 31 Steel St

Built as a boarding house in the early days of Eureka Springs and purchased by Carry Nation in 1908. She lived here the last three years of her life operating the boarding house and a school. Hatchet Hall is now operated as a memorial to the zealous crusader against alcohol and tobacco.
*Operated by Hatchet Hall Museum. Open daily 9:30–5; closed Sun. during summer*

# FAYETTEVILLE

## HEADQUARTERS HOUSE (TEBBETTS HOUSE), about 1853
### 118 E Dickson St

Low white frame house combining Georgian and Greek Revival styles. Built by Jonas M. Tebbetts, a lawyer, judge, and member of the state legislature. Judge Tebbetts and his family were forced to leave Arkansas during the Civil War because of his notoriety as a Union man. The house was the headquarters of Federal troops in 1863. Holes made by Confederate musket balls are visible in the interior woodwork. Antique furnishings
*Operated by Washington Co. Historical Soc. Open June–Oct: Tues.–Sun. 2–4*

# HOT SPRINGS

## WILDWOOD, 1884
### 808 Park Ave

Modified Queen Anne-style house built by Prosper Ellsworth, a pioneer physician active in standardizing qualifications to practice medicine. The interiors are unique — 15 rooms of different shapes (none square) with hand-carved and hand-rubbed native woods, stained-glass windows, and furnishings dating to the period of the house and earlier.
*Operated by Mr. and Mrs. Tom Ellsworth, owners. Open Mon.–Sat. 10–4, Sun. 1–5; closed Dec.–Feb.*

# LITTLE ROCK

## ARKANSAS TERRITORIAL CAPITOL RESTORATION, 1820–40
### East Third and Cumberland Streets

These 12 buildings in a half-block area re-create the appearance of Little Rock in the early 19th century. Included are *Conway House* (1830), home of Elias Nelson Conway, fifth

**ARKANSAS**

governor of the state; *Noland House* (1830), home of Lt. C. F. M. Noland, who delivered the first Arkansas constitution to Washington, D.C.; *Woodruff Group* (1824), home, print shop, and kitchen built by William E. Woodruff, founder of the *Arkansas Gazette*, oldest paper west of the Mississippi. *Operated by State of Ark. Open Apr.– Sept: Tues.–Sat. 9:30–5, Sun., Mon. 1–4:30. Rest of year: Tues.–Sat. 10– 4:30, Sun., Mon. 1–4:30; closed Easter, Thanksgiving, Christmas Eve, Christmas, and New Year's Day*

*Villa Marre*

## PIKE-FLETCHER-TERRY MEMORIAL, 1840
**411 E Seventh St**
Imposing two-story ante-bellum residence built for Albert Pike, soldier, explorer, lawyer, and author. The house was purchased by Capt. John Fletcher in 1889; his son John G. Fletcher, Arkansas poet, spent his boyhood here. Private residence
*Operated by Mrs. David D. Terry, owner. Open Tues., Thurs. 2–5*

## TRAPNALL HALL, 1843
**423 E Capitol Ave**
Restored ante-bellum house built by Frederick W. Trapnall, a prominent Little Rock citizen, from plans said to have been prepared by Gideon Shyrock, a famous Kentucky architect. The house had undergone numerous alterations over the years and suffered a serious fire in 1916. This structure was the pilot project in the restoration of the Quapaw Quarter and has now regained its simple classic design.
*Operated by Junior League of Little Rock. Open Mon.–Fri. 10–4 by appointment*

## ■ VILLA MARRE, 1881
**1321 Scott St**
Restored Italianate-style mansion with dormer windows and mansard roof. The house was built by Angelo Marre, a wealthy saloonkeeper, who had come to America from Italy in 1854 at the age of 12. Arkansas' first three-term governor, Jeff Davis, lived in the house in 1901–2 while he was governor. Victorian furnishings
*Operated by Mr. James W. Strawn, Jr., owner. Open Mon.–Fri. 9:30–11:30, 1:30–4:30; closed holidays*

## MAGNOLIA

### FROG LEVEL, 1852
**Frog Level Road**
Well-preserved ante-bellum house with a two-story portico. Southern antiques, family and community furnishings, and historical papers may be seen.
*Operated by Mary Woodward, owner. Open Tues. 10–5*

## NORFORK

### MAJ. JACOB WOLF HOUSE, 1809
**Route 5, 14 miles east of Norfork**
Two-story log house, probably the oldest such structure in the state, built by Major Wolf, who came to Arkansas as an Indian agent shortly after the Louisiana Purchase. It served as the first courthouse in Arkansas and as one of the first post offices in the state. Collection of early furnishings and assorted utensils exhibited
*Operated by Elna M. Smith Foundation. Open Mon.–Sat. 12–4, Sun. 2–6*

## PINE BLUFF

### DU BOCAGE HOUSE, 1866
Two-story classical revival house built by Judge Joseph W. Bocage, who was born in the West Indies of French parentage. Reared in North Carolina, Bocage came to Arkansas while in his teens. He first studied medicine but later switched to the practice of law and became the state's attorney general under Gov. Archibald Yell, 1840– 44. The house has been restored and furnished.
*Operated by Optimist Club of Pine Bluff. Open Thurs., Sat. 1–4, Sun. 2–6*

## POTTSVILLE

■ **POTTS INN, 1850–56**
Built by Kirkbride Potts, this ante-bellum structure, besides being the family home, served as a coach station on the Butterfield Overland Mail Route between Memphis and Fort Smith. It was also the first post office in the area. The builder's heirs occupied the house until 1970. To be restored and furnished
*Operated by Pope Co. Historical Foundation. Hours to be determined*

## WASHINGTON

**AUGUST H. GARLAND HOUSE, 1836**
Restored one-story house of classical revival style built by Simon T. Sanders. Augustus H. Garland married Virginia Sanders here in 1853, and they lived in the house until his career in state and national politics dictated they move to the state and national capitals. Garland was a Confederate congressman and senator, governor of the state,
U.S. senator, and Attorney General under Grover Cleveland.
*Operated by Pioneer Washington Foundation. Open daily 9–4*

**BLOCK-CATTS HOUSE, 1828–32**
One of the oldest two-story houses standing in Arkansas. The house was built by Abraham Block, whose slaves cut virgin timber and dressed it by hand. The Catts family owned the house from 1904 to 1957.
*Operated by Pioneer Washington Foundation. Open daily 9–4*

**GRANDISON D. ROYSTON HOUSE, about 1830**
One-story frame house built by Gen. Royston, a prosecuting attorney in the Arkansas Territory and a delegate to the first state constitutional convention, which framed the constitution under which Arkansas was admitted to the Union in 1836. The house was built in the Greek Revival period; it is one of the finest remaining houses in this area.
*Operated by Pioneer Washington Foundation. Open daily 9–4*

## ANAHEIM

**MOTHER COLONY HOUSE, about 1858**
**414 N West St**
First frame home in Anaheim, the residence and office of George Hansen when he was laying out the pre-planned community in 1858 and 1859. Moved to its present site by the Daughters of the American Revolution and furnished as a house museum by descendants of early Anaheim residents; in 1953 it was deeded to the city. A California historical landmark
*Operated by Anaheim Public Library. Open Wed. 3–5*

## ARCADIA

**LOS ANGELES STATE AND COUNTY ARBORETUM**
**301 N Baldwin Ave**
The 127-acre botanical garden, across the road from the famous Santa Anita racetrack, is all that remains of the original 13,000-acre Rancho Santa Anita. On the grounds are three
state historical landmarks: *Hugo Reid Adobe* (about 1840), built by the Scottish owner of the rancho, with the adobe walls, reed roof, and enclosed patio representative of California's transition period from Mexican to U.S. jurisdiction. Authentically furnished by the Soc. of Colonial Dames, with pieces brought from the Atlantic seaboard and the Orient; *Baldwin Cottage* (about 1875), a Queen Anne cottage that ranch owner E.J. "Lucky" Baldwin—fabulous mining king—used as a guesthouse and art gallery. Mr. Baldwin's coach barn, fully restored, is part of this complex; The Santa Fe Depot of Santa Anita, the third landmark, was recently moved from its original location to the arboretum.
*Operated by Los Angeles State and Co. Arboretum. Open daily 8–6:30; closed Christmas*

## BAKERSFIELD

**PIONEER VILLAGE, 1868–1910**
**3801 Chester Ave**
An outdoor museum on 12 acres with

over 30 structures representing a typical frontier community in central California. The residences range from the *Sheepherder's Cabin* (1906) and *Barnes Log Cabin* (1867) to the *Weller Ranch House* (1890) and *William Howell Residence* (1891). Period furnishings
*Operated by Kern Co. Museum. Open Mon.–Fri. 8–3:30, Sat., Sun., holidays 12–3:30*

## BELMONT

### ■ WILLIAM C. RALSTON HOME, about 1854; 1866–68
**College of Notre Dame Campus**
Originally built by Count Aconetto Cipriani, this elaborate villa was expanded to 88 rooms by financier William C. Ralston, "the man who built San Francisco." The foyer is a replica of the Palm Court at the old Palace Hotel in San Francisco, and the famous ballroom is fashioned after the Hall of Mirrors at Versailles. The furnishings are antiques of the late 19th century.
*Operated by Sisters of Notre Dame de Namur, College of Notre Dame. Open Tues. 3–4:30, Sat. 10–11:30, and by appointment*

## BRIDGEPORT VICINITY

### ■ BODIE HISTORIC DISTRICT
**Bodie State Historic Park**
One of the most significant mining ghost towns of the West because of its more than 100 surviving buildings. Its history is typical of the strike, boom, and decline cycle of the western mining communities.
*Operated by Calif. Dept. of Parks and Recreation. Open daily 8–5*

## CALABASAS

### LEONIS ADOBE, 1845; 1879
**23537 Calabasas Rd**
Adobe ranch house of the late Mexican period remodeled by giant Basque pioneer Miguel Leonis into a gracious two-story Monterey-style mansion with Victorian fretwork balcony. Speaking little Spanish or English, the colorful Leonis acquired a small empire of land and livestock in the San Fernando Valley; his marriage to the wealthy Indian widow Espiritu Chujilla greatly increased his holdings. Furnishings of

the 1880 period; family pieces
*Operated by Leonis Adobe Assn. Open Wed., Sat., Sun. 1–4, and by appointment*

## CHICO

### BIDWELL MANSION, 1865–68
**525 Esplanade**
Stately mansion of pink stucco with chocolate trim in the Tuscan villa style designed by architect H.W. Cleveland for California pioneers Gen. and Mrs. John Bidwell. Containing 26 rooms on three levels with broad verandas, marble fireplaces, and costly furnishings, it was a center of western hospitality. It became a school after Mrs. Bidwell's death and in 1964 a state historic monument.
*Operated by Calif. Dept. of Parks and Recreation. Open daily 9–5*

*Bidwell Mansion*

## CHINO VICINITY

### YORBA-SLAUGHTER ADOBE, 1850–53
**Pomona-Rincon Road**
Built by Raimundo Yorba with Indian labor, this is a good example of rancho adobe construction prevalent in California during the days of Mexican sovereignty. When the Butterfield stages passed the house (1859–63), the Yorbas furnished relay teams. Bought in 1868 by Fenton Slaughter, a Mexican War veteran, it was restored by his daughter and furnished with the original family pieces in 1928, thus creating an authentic museum of the rancho period. A state historical landmark
*Private. Open by appointment*

## COLOMA

### ■ MARSHALL GOLD DISCOVERY STATE HISTORIC PARK
**near Placerville, in El Dorado County**

At 7:30 A.M. on the morning of January 24, 1848, James Wilson Marshall picked up some bright objects from the tailrace of Sutter's Mill and shouted: "Boys, I believe I have found a gold mine!" Today about 70 per cent of the town of Coloma is included in the state park dedicated to that historic strike. Along with museums, stores, a replica of the sawmill, et cetera, are several old houses of that era, including *Marshall's Cabin, Thomas House,* and *Claussen House.* The park also offers hiking, fishing, and picnicking facilities.
*Operated by Calif. Dept. of Parks and Recreation. Open daily 8–5*

## COLUMBIA

### ■ COLUMBIA HISTORIC DISTRICT, 1850s
#### Columbia State Historic Park
A restored gold rush town in the heart of the famed Sierra Nevada gold belt with over 40 structures, including miners' cabins, schoolhouse, saloon, church, jailhouse, courthouse, fandango hall, smithy, firehouse, period stores, et cetera. There are several business concessions in the park for gifts and refreshments, as well as a summer repertory theatre group.
*Operated by Calif. Dept. of Parks and Recreation. Open daily 8–5*

## ENCINO

### LOS ENCINOS RANCHO
#### 16756 Moorpark St
A state historical monument, this five-acre area, once part of the 4,460-acre Encino Rancho, has warm springs, a guitar-shaped lake, and three historic buildings: *Reyes Hut,* a stone hut built about 1797 by Francisco Reyes, onetime mayor of Los Angeles; *Osa Adobe,* a nine-room house, similar to the mission-type, built by Vincente de la Osa in 1849; *Garnier Home,* a two-story limestone house in French provincial style built about 1867 by Eugene Garnier, who engaged in extensive sheepherding. As early as 1858 the rancho became a station for the Butterfield stage line. The Garnier house is shown without furnishings.
*Operated by Calif. Dept. of Parks and Recreation. Open daily 9–5; closed Christmas and New Year's Day*

## EUREKA

### CARSON HOUSE, 1889
#### 202 M St
Victorian home with colorful exterior which William Carson built directly across the street from his now-famous mansion as a wedding gift for his son, J. Milton Carson. It was used as a rooming house for many years until its restoration in 1964. Its beautifully refurbished Victorian interiors now house an antique shop, restaurant, and business offices.
*Operated by Robert Madsen, realtor. Open during business hours*

*Carson Mansion*

### CARSON MANSION [INGOMAR CLUB], 1884–85
#### Second and M Streets
An elaborate late Victorian mansion designed by the Newsom Brothers, architects, for lumber baron William Carson. The Carson sailing fleet brought lumber from many foreign lands, and the fantastic mansion was constructed by the employees of the Carson sawmill. It is now a privately owned businessman's organization.
*Operated by Ingomar Club. Open by appointment*

## FRESNO

### MARTIN THEODORE KEARNEY MANSION, 1898–1903
#### Kearney Park
Turn-of-the-century Edwardian mansion designed by Willis J. Polk for one of the wealthiest landowners in the San

Joaquin Valley. Now a house museum shown with the original furnishings. The former Kearney carriage house is a fire-fighting museum.
*Operated by Fresno Co. Historical Soc. Open Wed.–Sun. 2–5*

## GLENDALE

### CASA ADOBE DE SAN RAFAEL, about 1864
1330 Dorothy Dr
Hacienda-type adobe home built by Tomas Sanchez, first sheriff of Los Angeles, on part of the Rancho San Rafael—the original land grant of 36,403 acres made in 1784 by King Charles III of Spain to Jose Maria Verdugo. The property changed hands many times over the years until in 1935 it was dedicated as a city park. House partially furnished with historic articles
*Operated by Glendale Parks and Recreation Div. Open Mon.–Fri. by appointment*

## GLEN ELLEN VICINITY

### ■ JACK LONDON RANCH, 1905
Jack London State Historical Park
The state park includes 49 acres of the original 130-acre Beauty Ranch of Jack London, significant literary figure of the early 20th century, and his wife, Charmian. The ruins of *Wolf House*, his elaborate home destroyed by fire immediately after construction, and the *House of Happy Walls*, erected by London's widow in 1919 and now a museum, and his grave can be visited along the hiking trail.
*Operated by Calif. Dept of Parks and Recreation. Open daily 10–5*

## GRASS VALLEY

### LOLA MONTEZ HOUSE, 1850s
Walsh and Mill Streets
Modest cottage of the beautiful Countess of Lansfeld, the famous dancer Lola Montez, where she lived in retirement from 1852 to 1854. Her friendships with the great included George Sand, Alexandre Dumas (père), Victor Hugo, Alphonse Lamartine, and Franz Liszt. Her soirees, mainly for the benefit of the younger miners, became the talk of the area.
*Private. Open daily 9–5*

## JENNER

### ■ FORT ROSS COMMANDER'S HOUSE, 1812
Fort Ross State Historic Park
Log building of original Russian construction corresponding directly to the 1812 descriptions of the "Old Manager's Home." Double-sided fireplace may well be the original; the sturdy wood joinery was more like that of boatbuilding than carpentry. Within the stockade are several restored buildings from the period. Fort Ross was the largest single Russian trading center south of Alaska.
*Operated by Calif. Dept. of Parks and Recreation. Open daily 9–5*

## LA PUENTE

### JOHN A. ROWLAND HOME, 1855; 1897
16021 E Gale Ave
Two-story brick mansion, with large porches front and back, built on the great La Puente Rancho for Charlotte Gray Rowland by her husband, the co-leader of the Rowland-Workman party, first wagon train settlers in southern California (1841). The attic was used as a dormitory for Indian girls who worked on the ranch. In 1897 the house was stuccoed, a kitchen was added, and other "modern" improvements were made. The original black walnut furniture brought around the Horn in the 1850s may be seen.
*Operated by La Puente Valley Historical Soc. Open Wed. 1–4, first Sun. of every month 1–4*

## LONG BEACH

### ■ LA CASA DE RANCHO LOS CERRITOS, 1844
4600 Virginia Rd
Cited by the Dept. of Interior "as a magnificent example of a courtyard Ranch House in which the Monterey Colonial style is compared with the traditional Spanish Mexican plan." The ranch house—of adobe brick baked on the grounds and redwood beams from the forests near Monterey, resting on a foundation of fired brick brought around the Horn by sailing ships—was built by Don Juan Temple as headquarters of his vast cattle

ranch. After 1866 Flint, Bixby and Co. purchased the ranch for sheep raising, and Jotham Bixby and his family lived here between 1866 and 1881. Descendant Llewellyn Bixby restored the house in 1930 with period furnishings relating to the time the first Bixbys lived in it. Large outdoor courtyard
*Operated by Long Beach Public Library. Open Wed.–Sun. 1–5; closed holidays*

## LOS ANGELES

### AVILA ADOBE, 1818
**14 Olvera St**
On a restored street of Mexican shops, the Avila Adobe, built by onetime mayor of the pueblo Francisco Avila, is the oldest residence in Los Angeles. Only one seven-room wing remains of the original 18-room house; the two-and-one-half-foot-thick walls show remnants of the original cottonwood beams. Furnishings donated by old California families
*Operated by El Pueblo de Los Angeles. Open daily 10–5*

### CHARLES F. LUMMIS HOUSE (EL ALISAL), 1898
**200 E Ave 43**
Native stone home of the transplanted New England author C. F. Lummis (1859–1928), who was the leader of the southwestern regional school of writing. He was also the founder of Southwest Museum, the Landmarks Club, Sequoia League, and the Southwest Archeological Soc. One room is a museum of Indian artifacts; native plants and flowers in the garden
*Operated by City of Los Angeles. Open daily 9–5*

*El Alisal*

### HALE HOUSE, about 1898
**3800 N Homer St, Highland Park**
Flamboyant late Victorian frame house with fish-scale shingles, plaster-cast ornaments, ornate brick chimneys, and a corner turret crowned by a giant copper fleur-de-lis. Interiors feature original gaslight fixtures, hardwood paneling, and hand-carved wood ornamentation. Moved to Heritage Square in 1970 and now being restored
*Operated by Cultural Heritage Foundation. Restoration in progress*

*Hale House*

### HOLLYHOCK HOUSE, 1918–20
**4808 Hollywood Blvd, Barnsdall Park**
The first residence in the L.A. region designed by Frank Lloyd Wright and an outstanding example of his genius in fitting a building to its site. All the structures in Barnsdall Park, an 11-acre hilltop site, were designed by Wright for Aline Barnsdall, who envisioned the area as a major cultural center for the performing arts. The master plan never reached fruition, and in 1927 Miss Barnsdall deeded the entire property to the city for art and recreational purposes. The two-story house suggests a Mayan influence and incorporates an abstract motif of the hollyhock in the cast concrete on both exterior and interior. A romantic house, each room looks out on an intimate garden or pool; in fact, there

CALIFORNIA

was once a reflecting pool in front of the fireplace. Some of the original furnishings designed by Wright may still be seen. Under restoration
*Operated by City of Los Angeles Recreation and Parks Dept. Open for special functions*

*Hollyhock House*

## PICO ADOBE, 1840s
**10940 Sepulveda Blvd, Mission Hills**
Two-story adobe brick building, plastered and set on a fieldstone foundation, probably originally part of the San Fernando Mission and the home of Eulogio de Celis in rancho days. After being enlarged it was the home of Romulo Pico, son of Andres Pico—the brother of the last Mexican governor, Pío Pico. Now restored and a state historical landmark
*Operated by San Fernando Valley Historical Soc. Open Tues.–Fri. 10–12, 1–4, Sat., Sun. 12–5*

## MARTINEZ

■ **JOHN MUIR HOUSE, 1882–83**
**4202 Alhambra Ave**
Late Victorian 17-room frame mansion with a cupola at the peak of the roof built by Dr. John Strentzel, father-in-law of John Muir (1838–1914), famed naturalist, author, scientist, and "Father of the National Park System." The exterior is restored to the post-earthquake period of 1906–14, and the interiors are furnished with examples of the period. The property is a national historic site with the 1849 *Vincente Martinez Adobe* under restoration.
*Operated by National Park Service. Open daily for tours; closed Thanksgiving, Christmas, and New Year's Day*

## MONTEREY

### CASA AMESTI, 1834; 1846
**516 Polk St**
Two-story adobe house built by Don

Jose Amesti for his daughter; considered one of the best early California adobes. The original structure of two rooms and an attic was enlarged in 1846. The architectural details reveal eastern influence, even though the basic redwood log-adobe construction is characteristic of early California.
*Operated by Old Capital Club of Monterey for the National Trust. Open Fri. afternoons*

■ **LARKIN HOUSE, 1830s**
**STEVENSON HOUSE, 1838**
**CASA GUTIERREZ, 1841**
**Monterey State Historic Monument**
The state has preserved nine buildings and sites that were part of the history of early California in Monterey; three houses are open to the public. Larkin House, designed and built by Thomas Oliver Larkin, became the pattern for the "Monterey" style of architecture. The attractive two-story adobe building, with hip roof, balcony, and veranda, became the consulate when Larkin was appointed the first and only U.S. consul to Mexico in Monterey from 1844 to 1848. Many of the furnishings are original Larkin items. Stevenson House, a two-story adobe, was built for Don Rafael Gonzales, the first administrator of customs of Alta California. In 1846 pioneer Frenchman Juan Girardin and his wife, Manuela Perez, became the owners and took in roomers, one of whom was Robert Louis Stevenson, who stayed there during the autumn of 1879. Restored and furnished as a home of the 1870s, it has several rooms devoted to Stevenson memorabilia. On a lot granted him by the municipality, Joaquin Gutierrez and his wife, Josefa, built Casa Gutierrez, an adobe typical of that of the average citizen in Monterey during the Mexican period.
*Operated by Calif. Dept. of Parks and Recreation. Open daily 10–5*

*Larkin House*

■ OLD TOWN HISTORIC DISTRICT

Sixty years after Juan Rodríguez Cabrillo first sighted the California coast, Sebastián Vizcaíno landed at Monterey Bay in 1603 and named it in honor of the viceroy of New Spain. It was not until 1769–70, however, that Spain was able to start colonization with the founding of the mission at San Diego and the mission and presidio of Monterey. In 1821 Mexico obtained her independence from Spain, and during the 25 years the Mexican flag flew over Monterey the town expanded beyond the old presidio walls and seafaring men from New England modified the old Spanish colonial style. Visitors were charmed by the picturesque beauty of the old pueblo. Although many of the old buildings have disappeared, fine examples of this heritage are preserved for the enjoyment of all.

## NEWHALL

**WILLIAM S. HART HOME, 1925–28**
**24151 N Newhall Ave**
Spanish-style home of the famous motion picture actor, who called it "La Loma de Los Vientos." Bill Hart willed his ranch and dream castle, with his western art collection and furnishings, to the county to be maintained as a public park. The residence, old ranch house, and outbuildings may be seen on conducted tours.
*Operated by Los Angeles Co. Dept. of Parks and Recreation. Open Tues.–Sun. 10–5; closed Thanksgiving, Christmas, and New Year's Day*

## OAKLAND

■ **JOAQUIN MILLER HOUSE (THE ABBEY), 1886**
**Joaquin Miller Road**
Three one-room frame structures connected to form a single unit, each room with a shingled peak roof; home of the "Poet of the Sierras," first major poet of the western frontier. Here Miller wrote "Columbus" and other poems; he lived here until his death in 1913.
*Operated by City of Oakland. Open by appointment*

## PACIFICA

**SANCHEZ ADOBE, 1842–46**
**Linda Mar Boulevard**
Two-story adobe with Monterey-style porches built by Don Francisco Sanchez on an 8,926-acre tract in the San Pedro Valley—land granted by Gov. Juan B. Alvarado. By the age of 37 Don Francisco was the mayor of San Francisco, a position he held repeatedly. Furnishings of the mid-1800s
*Operated by San Mateo Co. Parks and Recreation Comm. Open Wed.–Sun. 10–12, 1–4*

## PACIFIC PALISADES

**WILL ROGERS HOUSE, early 1900s**
**14253 Sunset Blvd**
Ranch home of the famous actor and "cracker-barrel philosopher" Will Rogers, who lived here from 1928 to 1932. Within the house are trophies, works of art, and curios collected by the humorist. The 186-acre ranch is a state historic park, with the original stable, corrals, riding ring, roping arena, and trails laid out by Rogers.
*Operated by Calif. Dept. of Parks and Recreation. Open daily 8–5; closed Thanksgiving, Christmas, and New Year's Day*

## PASADENA

**DAVID B. GAMBLE HOUSE, 1908**
**4 Westmoreland Place**
Best preserved and most complete work of the internationally known architectural firm of Greene and Greene. It embodies the highest level of the California bungalow style and is one of the finest examples of the American Craftsman movement. Beautifully sculptured in wood, with projecting rafters, open sleeping porches, hand-shaped heavy beams supporting overhanging eaves, and shingle-clad exterior stained to soft greens to blend with the landscape. Interiors are carried out in various hand-rubbed woods. The furnishings were designed by the architects as an integral part of the whole. Now houses the Greene and Greene library
*Operated by University of S. Calif., School of Architecture and Fine Arts. Open Tues., Thurs. 11–4, second Sun. of Apr. and Oct.*

CALIFORNIA

## PETALUMA VICINITY
### ■ PETALUMA ADOBE, 1836
Casa Grande Road
Huge two-story adobe ranch house with balcony, largest adobe in northern California; headquarters of Gen. Mariano Guadalupe Vallejo's 66,000-acre Petaluma Rancho, on which grazed thousands of cattle and horses. Hundreds of acres were devoted to wheat, fruit, and vegetables. Indians rode the vast range as vaqueros and worked the fields. Restored as a state historic monument; period furnishings
*Operated by Calif. Dept. of Parks and Recreation. Open daily 10–5*

*Petaluma Adobe*

## POMONA
### ADOBE DE PALOMARES, 1850–54
491 E Arrow Highway
A 13-room adobe home with cloth ceiling and shake roof, the second one built by Don Ygnacio Palomares on the Rancho San Jose he owned jointly with Don Ricardo Vejar. The *casa* became a popular regional rendezvous as well as a station on the San Bernardino stage route. Restored, with authentic pieces of the old Spanish period, including precious heirlooms donated by the descendants of the early families
*Operated by Historical Soc. of Pomona Valley. Open Tues.–Sun. 2–5; closed Thanksgiving and Christmas*

## RED BLUFF
### WILLIAM B. IDE ADOBE, about 1850
Adobe Road
Old adobe home and outbuildings, built by the leader of the Bear Flag revolt at Sonoma in 1846, on the Rancho de la Barranca Colorada—Red Bluff Ranch—the site where the California-Oregon Trail crossed the Sacramento River. The ranch is now a state historical monument set up as a memorial to pioneer W. Brown Ide.
*Operated by Calif. Dept. of Parks and Recreation. Open daily 8–5*

## REDDING VICINITY
### OLD SHASTA
Highway 299
Located six miles west of Redding in the rolling foothills, this historic town is a reminder of the early gold rush days of 1848. On Shurtleff Hill stands the fine old residence erected in 1851 by Dr. Benjamin Shurtleff, pioneer physician; Main Street has a row of brick ruins that was once the longest row of brick buildings in the state. Only the courthouse is restored and open to the public. A state historic monument
*Operated by Calif. Dept. of Parks and Recreation. Open daily 9–5*

## ROSAMOND
### BURTON'S TROPICO GOLD CAMP, about 1880–1900
Route 1
A gold-mining camp consisting of authentic old buildings moved here from nearby sites for preservation. It includes homes, bars, stores, an assay office, schoolhouse, and museum. Adjacent is an open gold mine and mill.
*Operated by Burton's Tropico Gold Mine and Mill Tours. Open Oct.–June: Thurs.–Mon. 9:30–4*

## SACRAMENTO
### GOVERNOR'S MANSION (GALLATIN HOUSE), 1877–78
16 and H Streets
Victorian Gothic frame mansion built for Albert Gallatin, a local hardware merchant, by U.M. Reese from designs by architect Nathaniel D. Goodell. In 1887 it was purchased by dry goods merchant Joseph Steffens (father of journalist and social reformer Lincoln Steffens), who sold it to the state in 1903. Gov. George Pardee was the first of 13 governors to live here, the last being Gov. Ronald Reagan, who lived here during the first part of 1967

though the building had been determined unsafe for occupancy as early as 1941. The furnishings range from the period of the 1870s to the present. *Operated by Calif. Dept. of Parks and Recreation. Open daily 10–5*

*Governor's Mansion*

### ■ OLD SACRAMENTO HISTORIC DISTRICT, 1849–50

The original business district of the river port of Old Sacramento has a larger number of buildings dating from the gold rush period than any other major city, for this city emerged as the major distribution and transportation center for the gold mines in the Mother Lode country of the Sierra Nevada.

### STANFORD-LATHROP MEMORIAL HOME, 1857; 1872
### 800 N St

Two-story brick home made into a four-story-high Victorian mansion in 1872 by Leland Stanford. It served as an unofficial gubernatorial mansion during his term in office (1861–63) and F.F. Low's (1863–67). In 1899 Stanford's widow, Jane Lathrop Stanford, gave the building to the Roman Catholic diocese of Sacramento as a home for dependent children, which it still is today. Several of the rooms on the main floor have been restored and furnished with original pieces.
*Operated by Sisters of Social Service. Open by appointment*

### SUTTER'S FORT STATE HISTORICAL MONUMENT, 1839
### 2701 L St

The restored and reconstructed fort of sun-dried adobe bricks built in 1839 by John Sutter, born of Swiss parents in Germany in 1803. He called his 48,000-acre land grant New Helvetia in honor of his former homeland. With the help of Indians he built his fort to guard his territory, raised livestock, and developed agriculture. During the conquest of California, the American flag was raised over the fort in July, 1846. The property passed out of Sutter's hands shortly after the discovery of gold in 1848. Among the restored buildings are: *Sutter's Quarters*, the central building, Indian guardrooms, a blacksmith shop, and a bastion and dungeon.
*Operated by Calif. Dept. of Parks and Recreation. Open daily 10–5; closed Thanksgiving, Christmas, and New Year's Day*

## SAN DIEGO

### ■ CASA DE ESTUDILLO, 1827–29
### MACHADO-STEWART ADOBE, 1830
### Old Town San Diego State Historic Park

There are four remaining original adobe houses in the Old Town site, two of which are restored and open. Casa de Estudillo is a one-story, 12-room adobe built around a beautiful patio, with Spanish tile roof and supporting oak beams laced together with leather thongs; home of Jose Maria Estudillo, onetime commandant of San Diego. For years the house was mistakenly called "Ramona's Marriage Place" because some of the scenes in Helen Hunt Jackson's romantic novel *Ramona* were set in Old Town. The Machado-Stewart Adobe is the oldest extant adobe structure in Old Town. This two-room house was built by *Señor* Machado, a corporal in the San Diego company, and lived in for many years by his daughter Rosa Machado and her husband, Jack Stewart. Both houses were furnished with handsome antiques by the Soc. of Colonial Dames. The *Casa de Bandini* and *Machado Adobe* will be restored.
*Operated by Calif. Dept. of Parks and Recreation. Open daily 10–5*

## CASA DE LOPEZ [THE CANDLE SHOP], 1835
### 3890 Twiggs St

Built by Francisco Lopez, who called it *"La Casa Larga,"* or Long House, because a room was added each time the family increased in size. The model for the priest Father Antonio Ubach in Helen Hunt Jackson's novel *Ramona* lived in the east end of the house. This old Mexican family home is now a business establishment.
*Operated by The Candle Shop. Open during business hours*

## CASA DE PEDRORENA
## [MANUEL'S RESTAURANT], 1838
### 2616 San Diego Ave

Original adobe built by the Spaniard Don Miguel de Pedrorena, with 24-inch-thick walls, a frame peak roof, and window frames brought from Spain by sailing ship around Cape Horn. The patio, sheltered by high adobe walls, contains many rare and lovely plants and is used for alfresco dining; in the indoor dining room the original exposed ceiling beams may be seen.
*Operated by Manuel's Restaurant. Open daily 11–11*

## DERBY-PENDLETON HOUSE, 1851
### 1962 Harney St

The forerunner of the modern-day prefab, an outstanding small Greek Revival home built in 1851 in Portland, Maine, disassembled and shipped around the Horn to San Diego, and reassembled that same year by Juan Bandini as a wedding gift to his daughter Dolores and Charles Johnson. A two-room adobe kitchen building was erected behind the house and later joined to it to form the present seven-room building. It later served as the home of Lt. George H. Derby, Army engineer, and Capt. George Pendleton, county clerk. Original furnishings of the 1860s period
*Operated by Historical Shrine Foundation. Open June–Sept: Wed.–Sun. 10–4:30. Oct–May: Wed.–Sun. 12:30–4:30*

## JESSE SHEPARD HOUSE ("VILLA MONTEZUMA"), 1880s
### 1925 K St

Eclectic Victorian mansion, with a central tower surmounted by a Moorish dome, built for the musician Jesse Shepard. In the elaborate interiors may be found a repertoire of high Victorian design—polished redwood walls, Lincrusta Walton ceilings, art glass windows, tiled and pedimented fireplaces, et cetera. Now being restored as a historic house museum and cultural center
*Operated by San Diego Historical Soc. Restoration in progress*

## THOMAS WHALEY HOUSE, 1856
### 2482 San Diego Ave

Noted for its beauty of proportion and excellence of detail, a two-story Greek Revival home built by Thomas Whaley, pioneer merchant and civic leader; believed to be the oldest remaining brick structure in southern California. Whaley made his own bricks and seashell plaster but brought the white cedar flooring and doors and window glass by ship from New York. At various times the house served as the county courthouse, a Sunday school and church, city hall, dairy, mortuary, and theater. Restored and furnished with authentic pieces of the 1850s and 1860s from other early San Diego homes
*Operated by Historical Shrine Foundation. Open June–Sept: Wed.–Sun. 10–4:30. Oct.–May: Wed.–Sun. 12:30–4:30*

*Thomas Whaley House*

## SAN FRANCISCO
## OCTAGON HOUSE, about 1861
### 2645 Gough St

Unique eight-sided house, one of five in early San Francisco, built by William G. McElroy. The eight sides of concrete and plaster have clapboard facing. Moved to its present site and restored by California Soc. of Colonial Dames, who use it as their headquarters. Although the house is Victorian,

the furniture, china, and silver are of the colonial period.
*Operated by Soc. of Colonial Dames. Open first Sun. and second and fourth Thurs. of every month 1–4*

*Whittier Mansion*

## SCHUBERT HALL, 1905
**2209 Pacific Ave**
Built for John D. Spreckels, Jr., as a wedding present from his father, this baroque-style house is constructed of wood and stucco with turn-of-the-century ornamentation over the windows, which also incorporate handsome iron grillwork. Now serves as a library for the nearby historical society
*Operated by Calif. Historical Soc. Open Tues.–Sat. 10–4*

## WHITTIER MANSION, 1895–96
**2090 Jackson St**
Red sandstone Richardsonian mansion with columned portico and massive pediment above between two huge towers. Built for merchant William Frank Whittier from a design by Edward R. Swain, this was one of the first town houses in California to be constructed of stone on a steel framework. Now serving as headquarters of the California Historical Soc.; features elegantly carved interior paneling and some Victorian furnishings
*Operated by Calif. Historical Soc. Open Tues.–Sat. 10–4*

## SAN JOSE VICINITY

### ■ NEW ALMADEN, 1824
**County Route G8**
An old mining town, the site of the first mercury deposits discovered in North America. The mines, now inactive, were essential to the processes used during the boom days of the California Mother Lode and the Nevada Comstock Lode. There are several wood and adobe buildings dating from this period still extant.

## SAN JUAN BAUTISTA

### ■ CASTRO ADOBE, 1840–41
### ZANETTA COTTAGE, 1850s
### ZANETTA HOUSE (PLAZA HALL), 1868
**San Juan Bautista State Historic Park**
Facing the old plaza are: Castro Adobe, two stories with red tile roof and full-length balcony, first the home of Gen. Jose Maria Castro—prefect of the northern district and then commander of all Spanish military forces in California—and later occupied by the Patrick Breen family, survivors of the ill-fated Donner party; Zanetta Cottage, first home of the Zanettas and later occupied by their daughter Victoria. Beautiful flower gardens and Spanish orchards dating back to the mission period surround the historic buildings; Zanetta House, constructed of adobe brick from an old mission home for unmarried Indian girls. Angelo Zanetta—professional restaurateur and hotelkeeper—used the first floor as his private residence and the second for public meetings.
*Operated by Calif. Dept. of Parks and Recreation. Open daily 8–5*

### ■ SAN JUAN BAUTISTA PLAZA HISTORIC DISTRICT
Remaining almost unchanged since the days of the dons, this historic community was built around the Mission San Juan Bautista (1797), largest in the California chain of missions. The old plaza was originally the site of bullfights, fandangos, and general festivities. Surrounding the plaza are old buildings dating from mission days to the era of American settlement.

## SAN LUIS OBISPO

### DALLIDET ADOBE, 1853
**Pacific and Toro Streets**
A state historical landmark, this charming old adobe dwelling was built by a French vintner, Pierre Hyppolite Dallidet, and was occupied by his family for a century. In 1953 Paul Dal-

lidet gave it to the historical society. Restored as a house museum and furnished with the original family pieces *Operated by San Luis Obispo Co. Historical Soc. Open May–Oct: Sun. 1–4:30*

## SAN RAFAEL

### IRA COOK HOUSE, 1879
**Boyd Park**
Victorian house with gingerbread trim featuring interiors with Carrara marble fireplaces and plaster ceiling decorations. Three of the rooms are devoted to historical exhibits pertaining to Marin County; the remainder of the house is used by the park gardener, who maintains the 17-acre park.
*Operated by Marin Co. Historical Soc. Open Wed., Sat., Sun. 2–5*

## SAN SIMEON

### LA CUESTA ENCANTADA, begun 1919
**Hearst San Simeon State Historical Monument**
Set against the Santa Lucia mountains on a coastal knoll overlooking the sea is "The Enchanted Hill," the 123-acre estate of William Randolph Hearst (1863–1951), head of a vast publishing, ranching, and mining empire. Three palatial guesthouses in Mediterranean Renaissance style were completed before work was begun in 1922 on the fabled mansion *La Casa Grande*. The 137-foot-high Hispano-Moresque structure is constructed of poured reinforced concrete—the main part faced with Utah limestone—and was designed by Hearst and Miss Julia Morgan, a distinguished Berkeley architect. Twin towers patterned after those of a Spanish cathedral top the imposing castle; the 100 rooms serve as a display area for furniture, antiques, and a valuable art collection. The Neptune Pool, one of two swimming pools on the estate, is set off by a classical temple façade. White marble statues at the edges of the pool and Etruscan-style colonnades at each end complete the concept. Among the exotic landscaping and terraced gardens imported wildlife still roam freely and can be seen on the five-mile ride to the crest.
*Operated by Calif. Dept. of Parks and Recreation. Open daily for tours only*

*San Simeon*

## SANTA BARBARA

### COVARRUBIAS ADOBE, 1817
**715 Santa Barbara St**
An L-shaped adobe built for Domingo Carrillo, whose daughter married Jose Maria Covarrubias in 1838; their descendants occupied the house for over a century. Dating from the mission period, it was undoubtedly constructed by Indian labor; the Indian "river of life" design is carved into the solid doors. Restored, it retains the original adobe walls, high ceilings, and 55-foot-long *sala* but is unfurnished. A state historical monument
*Operated by Los Rancheros Visitadores. Open by appointment*

### FERNALD HOUSE, 1862
**414 W Montecito St**
Victorian house of sanded brick with Gothic bracketed gables and wide verandas built by cabinetmaker Roswell Forbush, an American who came to Santa Barbara in pueblo days, for the prominent Judge Charles Fernald, originally of North Berwick, Maine. The interior woodcarving shows the artistry of the cabinetmaker. When the judge served as mayor of the city, the house was the center of much official entertaining. Lovely period furnishings, some original
*Operated by Santa Barbara Historical Soc. Open Sun. 1:30–4:30*

### TRUSSELL-WINCHESTER ADOBE, 1854
**412 W Montecito St**
Capt. Horatio Gates Trussell, a Maine

Yankee, came to California in the 1850s on the first steamboat to enter Santa Barbara harbor. When the *Winfield Scott* was shipwrecked off the coast in 1853, Capt. Trussell incorporated the salvaged timbers in the wooden wings of his house. The central portion is of sun-dried adobe bricks in the California tradition, but the architectural line and details reflect an eastern colonial reserve that identifies the building with the transition period when adobe construction was being superseded by wood frame construction. Lovely paintings and period furnishings, many brought from the East around the Horn; surrounding flower garden and fruit orchard. A state historical landmark
*Operated by Santa Barbara Historical Soc. Open Sun. 1:30–4:30*

## SANTA ROSA

### ■ LUTHER BURBANK HOUSE AND GARDENS, 1883
**Santa Rosa Avenue**
Three-acre site — including gardens, original greenhouse, house, and stable — where the internationally known horticulturist lived and worked for 40 years. Burbank's pioneering experiments with thousands of plants produced many important cultivated varieties of flowers, vegetables, grains, grasses, and fruits. He is buried at the foot of the towering cedar of Lebanon he planted more than 60 years ago.
*Operated by Santa Rosa Junior College. Open daily*

## SOLEDAD VICINITY

### RICHARDSON ADOBE (LOS COCHES RANCHO), 1843
**U.S. Route 101**
William Brunner Richardson, a native of Baltimore, built this adobe house on the rancho (8,994.2 acres) granted to his wife, Maria Josefa Soberanes de Richardson, by the Mexican government in 1841. This was the site of Capt. John C. Frémont's encampment in 1846 and 1847. Later used as a stage station and post office, the adobe was given to the state in 1958. A state historic monument
*Operated by State of Calif. Open daily 9–5*

## SONOMA

### LACHRYMAE MONTIS (VALLEJO HOME), 1852
**Sonoma State Historic Park**
The 20-acre estate of Gen. Mariano Guadalupe Vallejo, founder of Sonoma, named for the abundant springs on the hillside. The picturesque Victorian house, a redwood frame structure with adobe bricks within the walls for insulation, stands at the end of a long tree-flanked lane. It has a steeply pitched roof with dormer windows, a large Gothic second-story window, and carved ornamental eaves. A Swiss chalet houses Vallejo relics; lovely surrounding gardens
*Operated by Calif. Dept. of Parks and Recreation. Open daily 10–5*

*Vallejo Home*

### ■ SONOMA PLAZA
An eight-acre plaza, the largest in California, laid out by Gen. Vallejo in 1835 and scene of the dramatic Bear Flag revolt in 1846. Facing the plaza is a portion of the site of the general's *Casa Grande*, the Indian residence and kitchen which served it, and the soldiers' barracks; all maintained as a state historic park. Nearby is San Francisco Solano Mission (1823), the last and most northerly of the 21 Franciscan missions of Alta California and the only one established by the Mexicans.

## SUSANVILLE

### ROOP'S FORT, 1854
**75 N Weatherlow St**
Log cabin with shake roof built by Isaac N. Roop, pioneer prospector in the area. Stronghold called Fort Defiance during the so-called "Sagebrush War" (1864), a boundary dispute over the California-Nevada line

*Operated by Lassen Co. Historical Soc. Open daily*

## VENTURA

### OLIVAS ADOBE, 1840s
**Olivas Park Drive**
Two-story adobe hacienda, with balconies front and back in the Monterey style, built by Don Raimundo Olivas on his Rancho San Miguel beside the Santa Clara River. His first small adobe is incorporated into the patio's walls, which enclose a beautiful garden. Restored by the city of San Buenaventura and furnished with lovely antiques donated by pioneer families
*Operated by Ventura Co. Open daily*

## VISALIA

### TULARE COUNTY MUSEUM
**27000 Mooney Blvd**
A pioneer village of authentic old buildings of Tulare County moved for preservation to the Mooney Grove site, remnant of a great oak forest that once covered the Kaweah River delta. There are three houses; the *Log Cabin* (about 1854), one of the oldest houses in the county, built by Isaac Harmon on his ranch on Elbow Creek; *Cramer House* (about 1863), built by Jacob Cramer on the north fork of the Tule River; *Emken House* (1890), typical large ranch house built by Robert G. Rogers near Woodville. Among the other exhibits are a school, jailhouse, and shops.
*Operated by Tulare Co. Museum. Open daily 9–5*

## WHITTIER

### PIO PICO MANSION, about 1830
**6003 Pioneer Blvd**
Two-story home—originally 33 rooms with adobe walls, gabled roof, and wooden floors and shutters—of the last Mexican governor of California, Pío Pico, and his beautiful wife, *Doña Maria*. On the more than 8,000 acres of Rancho Paso de Bartolo, which he affectionately called El Ranchito, the hacienda was the center of social and political life for many years. Almost half the house was swept away in the San Gabriel River flood of 1866. The remaining portion of 16 rooms and beautiful gardens has been restored

as a state historical monument.
*Operated by Calif. Dept. of Parks and Recreation. Open daily 9–5*

## WILMINGTON

### GEN. PHINEAS BANNING HOUSE, 1864
**Banning Manor Park, 401 M St**
A 30-room Victorian frame mansion, with a cupola on the roof, reminiscent of Delaware colonial residences; built by the founder and leading businessman of Wilmington, Gen. Banning. Located in the center of a 20-acre park and shown with some original antique furnishings and paintings
*Operated by Los Angeles Dept. of Recreation and Parks. Open Mar. 28–Oct. 10: Sun. 1–4:30*

## YOSEMITE

### ■ PIONEER YOSEMITE HISTORY CENTER, 1852–1915
**Yosemite National Park**
A pioneer village consisting of various cabins of logs, one- and two-story buildings, and cabins of sawed boards collected from various locations in the park; moved to Wawona and restored in the 1960s. The homesteader cabins represent the period of the 1880s and 1890s, when hundreds of acres were homesteaded and patented. Village includes a covered bridge, art gallery, wagon shop, and Wells Fargo office.
*Operated by National Park Service. Open June 15–Sept. 10: daily 10–5*

## YUCAIPA

### SEPULVEDA ADOBE, 1842
**32183 Kentucky St**
Two-story adobe ranch house, the oldest in San Bernardino Co., built by Diego Sepulveda, who sold it to Mormon colonists in 1851. Finally it was sold in the 1860s to Texas cattleman John Dunlap, whose family retained possession until 1954. Only the three downstairs rooms are open, with furnishings of the Sepulvedas brought from Spain around Cape Horn in 1802 and late 19th-century furnishings of the Dunlap period. A state historical monument
*Operated by San Bernardino Co. Open Tues.–Sun. 1–5*

## CENTRAL CITY
### ■ CENTRAL CITY HISTORIC DISTRICT
Colorado's first major gold strike was made here in 1859; town of log cabins and tents quickly sprang up, but most were destroyed in an 1874 fire. Many Victorian buildings remain from boom days after the fire, including the *Teller House* (1872), considered the epitome of frontier elegance for a hotel, and the opera house (1878), still in use.

## COLORADO SPRINGS
### McALLISTER HOUSE, 1873
**423 N Cascada Ave**
Home of Maj. Henry McAllister, who came to Colorado at the request of Gen. William Palmer, the founder of Colorado Springs. Bricks for the house had to be transported from Philadelphia since there were no suitable ones made nearby. Restored and shown with original furnishings
*Operated by Soc. of Colonial Dames. Open Tues.–Sun. 10–5*

## CORTEZ VICINITY
### ■ MESA VERDE NATIONAL PARK
Hundreds of spectacular prehistoric cliff dwellings and mesa-top pit houses and pueblos inhabited from about the first century A.D. until about 1300. Among the best-preserved sites are *Cliff Palace*, a village of more than 200 rooms and 23 kivas, and *Far View House*, a large mesa-top pueblo. Included in the 52,000-acre park is the Chapin Mesa Museum, with exhibits of Indian history and arts and crafts.
*Operated by National Park Service. Open June 21–Sept. 9: daily 7:45–7:30. Sept. 10–June 20: daily 8–6*

*Cliff Palace, Mesa Verde*

## CRIPPLE CREEK
### ■ CRIPPLE CREEK HISTORIC DISTRICT
Among the world's largest gold fields; holds the U.S. record for single-year production with $25 million in 1901. Fires in 1906 destroyed most of the many dance halls, saloons, and gambling houses for which the town was famous. Among the extant buildings are the railroad depot, now a museum, and the old headquarters of the Western Federation of Mines.

## DENVER
### ■ GOVERNOR'S MANSION, 1905–8
**400 E Eighth Ave**
Four-story, 27-room brick mansion built by pioneer Walter Cheesman and purchased in 1926 by Claude Boettcher, who furnished the house with fine European antiques and his extensive art collection. In 1960 the Boettcher Foundation donated the mansion with its furnishings for use as the governor's residence.
*Operated by State of Colo. Open May–Oct: Tues. 12:30–4:30*

*Governor's Mansion*

## FAIRPLAY
### SOUTH PARK CITY
**Fourth and Front Streets**
A reconstructed pioneer and mining village featuring many restored and furnished buildings, including a newspaper office, drugstore, gold mine, and general store
*Operated by South Park Historical Foundation. Open May 15–Labor Day: daily 9–7. Sept.–Oct. 15: daily 9–5*

**COLORADO**

## FORT COLLINS

### ANTOINE JANIS CABIN, 1844
**219 Peterson St**
Log cabin with shake roof and pole ceiling built by French trapper Antoine Janis; the first dwelling built in Colorado north of the Arkansas River. Now part of the Pioneer Museum, which features an extensive gun collection and other items of local history
*Operated by City of Fort Collins. Open Tues.–Sun. 1–5; closed holidays*

## GEORGETOWN

### HAMILL HOUSE, begun 1867
**Argentine and Third Streets**
Frame Victorian house, considered one of the finest of the mining era, begun by Joseph Watson, who later lost his fortune; purchased and completed by William Hamill, prospector and state senator. Hamill's descendants lived here until 1914; the house features the family's carved walnut furnishings with gold and silver trim and camel's hair wallpaper.
*Private. Open June–Sept: daily 8–6*

## GEORGETOWN-SILVER PLUME

### ■ GEORGETOWN-SILVER PLUME HISTORIC DISTRICT
Second most important mining area in Colorado; from 1864 to 1939 over $90 million in gold, silver, lead, copper, and zinc was produced here. Georgetown Loop Historic District, featuring a railroad and some early mines, is being developed through this country famous for its spectacular scenery. Among the historic buildings that remain are Georgetown's *Maxwell House*, built 1880, and the Hotel de Paris, built 1875.

## GREELEY

### ■ MEEKER MUSEUM, 1871
**1324 Ninth Ave**
Originally a four-room sod-and-adobe house, with brick rear section added later; built by Nathan Cook Meeker, leader of a colony that founded Greeley in 1870. Meeker named the town for Horace Greeley and built his home to give the community a sense of permanency. Restored in 1959 and furnished with some of the Meeker family's possessions
*Operated by City of Greeley. Open Mon.–Fri: 1–5*

## LAS ANIMAS

### THE BOGGS HOUSE, 1866
Home of Thomas Boggs, who conducted the first successful irrigation project in this area in 1866; he and his partners cultivated 1,000 acres of land. The house is still a private residence.
*Operated by the Noel Kerr family. Open by appointment*

### KIT CARSON MUSEUM, 1876
**225 Ninth St**
The old jail and house serve as part of this museum of local history. A restored period bedroom, living room, and trapper's corner are featured. Other exhibits pertain to the early cattle industry and local Indians.
*Operated by Pioneer Historical Soc. of Bent Co. Open Memorial Day–Labor Day: daily 1:30–5*

## LEADVILLE

### ■ DEXTER CABIN, 1879
**912 Harrison Ave**
"The only mid-Victorian cabin in America" served as hunting lodge and exclusive poker club for James V. Dexter, ardent sportsman and banker. Interior of rough-hewn cabin is decorated in Victorian elegance with Lincrusta-Walton wall coverings, Persian rugs, and floors of narrow planks of alternating dark and light woods. The restored cabin also features a fully equipped period kitchen.
*Operated by State Historical Soc. of Colo. Open summer: daily 9–12, 1–5*

*Dexter Cabin*

36

### ■ HEALY HOUSE, 1878
**912 Harrison Ave**

This 13-room frame Victorian house recalls halcyon days of Colorado miners; built by August Meyer and from 1888 to 1936 owned by Dan Healy and his descendants. Elegant "gay nineties" furnishings include hand-carved black walnut and mahogany furniture, diamond-dust mirrors, and stained-glass windows.
*Operated by State Historical Soc. of Colo. Open June 1–Oct. 15: daily 9–12, 1–5*

*The House with the Eye*

### ■ LEADVILLE HISTORIC DISTRICT

For a time this was the country's leading silver camp; between 1879 and 1889 nearly $136 million in silver was mined here. The area also produced major quantities of gold, lead, zinc, and other metals. Many buildings, including the Tabor Opera House, opened in 1879, have been preserved.

### TABOR HOUSE, 1877
**116 E Fifth St**

Two-story frame house with bargeboard trim built by silver king H. A. W. Tabor and his wife Augusta, later the subjects of a national scandal. The Tabors entertained ex-President and Mrs. Ulysses S. Grant here in 1880. Restored as a museum in the 1950s
*Operated by Mr. and Mrs. Walter Larson. Open daily 8–8*

*Healy House*

### THE HOUSE WITH THE EYE, 1879
**127 W Fourth St**

Nine-room frame house with hand-carved gingerbread trim; built by French-Canadian carpenter for his bride. Most noteworthy is the stained-glass window shaped like an eye in the gable; taken from the Colorado state seal, it represents the all-seeing eye of God. Furnished with items of Leadville's history, including a "Molly Brown" bedroom, a miner's kitchen, and dining room. A carriage house has been added to display sulkies, buggies, a fire wagon, and other horse-drawn vehicles.
*Operated by George and Mary B. Cassidy. Open May 30–Labor Day: daily 10–6*

### PLEASANT VIEW

### ■ LOWRY PUEBLO RUINS, about 1050
**nine miles west of U.S. Route 160**

The ruins of a great kiva and three-story pueblo of about 40 rooms and eight small kivas; built by the Anasazi Indians on the ruins of pit houses constructed by Indians of an earlier culture. The pueblo housed 50 to 100 people and with the great kiva was probably a religious center. The upper floors of the pueblo were restored in the 1960s.
*Operated by Bureau of Land Management, San Juan office, Montrose District. Open daily*

## PUEBLO

### ROSEMOUNT, 1891
**419 W 14 St**

Three-story mansion of brick, covered with rose-colored stone, with Vermont marble pillars, built by John Albert Thatcher, pioneer merchant and banker. Interior of 37-room mansion features fresco ceilings, hand-carved banisters, and Victorian furnishings. Thatcher's heirs donated the mansion to the Pueblo Metropolitan Museum in 1968.
*Operated by Pueblo Metropolitan Museum Assn. Open May 30–Labor Day: Tues.–Sat. 9–5, Sun., holidays 2–5. Sept.–May: Tues.–Sun. 2–5*

## SILVERTON

### ■ SILVERTON HISTORIC DISTRICT

Once a booming mining town in the southwestern San Juan basin; important in the development of the Rocky Mountain area. Among the interesting buildings that remain from mining days are the Grand Imperial Hotel, built 1882, and the gold-domed courthouse, built 1907.

## STEAMBOAT SPRINGS

### TREAD OF PIONEERS MUSEUM, about 1910
**Oak and Fifth Streets**

Turn-of-the-century house built by architect Ernest Campbell. Now a museum of local history with displays of mining, pioneer homemaking, and other areas of local interest; also, the museum features a fine collection of early skis
*Operated by Tread of Pioneers Historical Comm. Open May–June: daily 4–8. July–Aug: daily 1–9*

## TELLURIDE

### ■ TELLURIDE HISTORIC DISTRICT

Short-lived but very productive mining town; claims were first made in 1875. The town grew after a railroad was built to it in 1890. Among the turn-of-the-century buildings that remain are the city hall, built in 1883, and the opera house, which was built about 1900.

## TRINIDAD

### ■ BACA HOUSE, 1869
**Main Street and Interstate Highway 25**

Plain two-story adobe home of Don Felipe Baca, wealthy rancher and freighter and one of the area's first settlers; occupied by the Baca family into the 1920s. In the rear is a one-story adobe building that housed families of the Baca workers. Now a pioneer museum with exhibits that emphasize the local Spanish heritage
*Operated by State Historical Soc. of Colo. Open May 15–Oct. 15: daily 9–5*

*Baca House*

### BLOOM MANSION, 1882
**Main Street and Interstate Highway 25**

Ornate Victorian brick mansion with native sandstone trim and mansard roof built for Frank G. Bloom, pioneer merchant, banker, and cattleman. Restored and shown with period furnishings; surrounded by a Victorian garden featuring 80 varieties of roses and native wildflowers
*Operated by State Historical Soc. of Colo. Open May 15–Oct. 15: daily 9–5*

## VICTOR

### LOWELL THOMAS BOYHOOD HOME, 1897
**225 S Sixth St**

Large turn-of-the-century house where author and broadcast journalist Lowell Thomas spent his boyhood years. Shown with the original furnishings and many of Thomas' personal effects
*Private. Open May 30–Labor Day: daily 10–5*

## ANSONIA

### THE MANSFIELD HOUSE, 1672
**33 Jewett St**
Weathered saltbox, one of oldest houses in area, resided in by the venerable Rev. Richard Mansfield for 72 years, 1748–1820, during which time he was rector of St. James Church, Derby. Parlor contains personal items and furniture of the Mansfield family
*Operated by Derby Historical Soc. Open by appointment*

## BRIDGEPORT

### ■ CAPT. JOHN BROOKS HOUSE, 1788
**199 Pembroke St**
Excellent example of unusual style of Connecticut architecture of the period, the half house, built by Revolutionary War Capt. Brooks and birthplace of his son John II, prosperous steamboat captain and twice mayor of Bridgeport. Unusual plank-wall construction and curved hood over front door. Now under restoration and open to public in June of 1971 with much of original furniture, china, and glass
*Operated by Museum of Art, Science, and Industry. Open Tues.–Sun. 2–5*

## BRIDGEWATER

### "THE CAPTAIN'S HOUSE," mid-19th century
**Main Street**
Plain frame dwelling of Capt. William D. Burnham around 1850. Completely restored and relocated to house collection of local historical society
*Operated by Bridgewater Historical Soc. Open May–Sept: Sat. afternoons*

## BRISTOL

### MILES LEWIS HOUSE, [AMERICAN CLOCK & WATCH MUSEUM], 1801
**100 Maple St**
Post-Revolutionary mansion built by Miles Lewis, now housing the only museum devoted exclusively to the history of American horology
*Operated by American Clock & Watch Museum. Open Apr.–Oct: Tues.–Sun. 1–5*

## CLINTON

### STANTON HOUSE, about 1790
**63 E Main St**
Fine 18th-century home of three generations of Stantons, built on site of home of the Rev. Abraham Pierson, first president of Yale. Replica of country store operated in one of ells
*Operated by Hartford National Bank. Open May–Nov: Tues.–Sun. 2–5 or by appointment*

## COLCHESTER

### FOOTE HOUSE, 1702
**The Green**
Tiny, one-room gambrel-roofed house of the early 18th century moved from its original foundation and restored. Now maintained as a house museum
*Operated by Daughters of the American Revolution. Open by appointment*

## COLEBROOK

### UNDERWOOD HOUSE (SEYMOUR INN), 1816
**Colebrook Center**
White clapboard Federal building, built by William Underwood as a wedding present for his daughter, Mrs. Rufus Seymour. Now operated as museum for local history
*Operated by Colebrook Historical Soc. Open May 15–Sept. 15: Sat., Sun., holidays 2–5*

## COS COB

### BUSH-HOLLEY HOUSE, about 1685
**39 Strickland Rd**
A 17th-century house renovated in the 18th century; a center for many young artists and writers of national importance in the early 20th century. Fine early American furnishings
*Operated by Greenwich Historical Soc. Open Tues.–Sun. 2–4*

## COVENTRY

### ■ NATHAN HALE HOMESTEAD, 1776
**South Street**
Built by Deacon Richard Hale, father of the patriot; fine ten-room mansion of the period, lived in by Hale family until 1832. Completely restored and furnished with Hale family memorabilia
*Operated by Conn. Antiquarian &*

Landmarks Soc. Open May 15–Oct. 15: daily 1–5

## DANBURY

**ST. JOHN HOUSE, 1750**
**BARNUM HOUSE, 1780**
**43 Main St**
Two 18th-century houses now operated as museums with period rooms ranging from early colonial to late Victorian. Frequent demonstrations of colonial arts and crafts
*Operated by Danbury Scott-Fanton Museum. Open Tues., Thurs., Sat. 2–5*

## DARIEN

**BATES-SCOFIELD HOMESTEAD, about 1737**
**45 Old Kings Highway**
House museum open to the public as an example of 18th-century local architecture and furnishings
*Operated by Darien Historical Soc. Open Wed., Thurs. 2–4, Sun. 2:30–4:30*

## DEEP RIVER

**OLD STONE HOUSE, 1840**
**South Main Street**
Stone house built for Deacon Ezra Southworth and his bride. Original tin roof replaced and other alterations made in 19th and 20th centuries. Many items relating to local Connecticut River history on exhibit
*Operated by Deep River Historical Soc. Open Thurs. afternoons in summer and by appointment*

## EAST HADDAM

**GILLETTE CASTLE, 1914–19**
**Gillette Castle State Park**
Granite 24-room castle in medieval style built by famous actor William Gillette. All the interior woodwork is hand-hewn southern white oak; all the ingenious locking devices on the doors were designed by the owner. Grandiose living room suggests a stage setting
*Conn. State Park and Forest Comm. Open June–Oct: daily 11–5*

## EAST LYME

■ **THOMAS LEE HOUSE, about 1660**
**Shore Road**
Saltbox-type frame structure built by Thomas Lee II, added to in 1695 and again in 18th century; restored in 20th century. Lived in by the family for 250 years; furnishings reflect the growth of a family over this span
*Operated by East Lyme Historical Soc. Open June–Sept: Tues.–Sun. 12–5*

## ESSEX

**PRATT HOUSE, mid-18th century**
**20 West Ave**
An unrestored house of the mid-18th century that has on exhibit the well-known Griswold collection of American furniture and furnishings
*Operated by Soc. for the Preservation of New England Antiquities. Open by appointment*

## FARMINGTON

**HILL-STEAD MUSEUM, 1900**
**Farmington Avenue**
Beautiful mansion built for Mr. and Mrs. Alfred A. Pope, designed by famous architect Stanford White and their daughter Theodate, who married ambassador John W. Riddle. The Riddles left their remarkable collection of Impressionist paintings and exquisite furnishings in trust to be maintained as a museum.
*Operated by Trustees of Hill-Stead Museum. Open Wed., Thurs., Sat., Sun. 2–5*

■ **STANLEY-WHITMAN HOUSE, 1664**
**37 High St**
One of finest examples of a 17th-century frame dwelling in New England with great center chimney, steeply pitched roof, and framed overhang ornamented by carved pendants. Completely furnished with rare early American pieces
*Operated by Farmington Museum. Open Apr.–Nov: Tues.–Sat. 10–12, 2–5. Dec.–Mar: Fri., Sat. 10–12, 2–5*

*Stanley-Whitman House*

## GREENWICH

### PUTNAM COTTAGE, before 1729
**243 E Putnam Ave**
White frame structure built by Timothy Knapp, served as Knapp Tavern, from which in 1779 Gen. Israel Putnam made his daring escape from the approaching redcoats. Has undergone several renovations; now equipped with 18th- and 19th-century period furnishings
*Operated by Daughters of the American Revolution. Open Mon., Thurs., Fri., Sat. 10–5*

## GUILFORD

### HENRY WHITFIELD HOUSE, 1639
**Whitfield Street**
Built for the Rev. Henry Whitfield; oldest stone dwelling in New England, served as fort, church, and meeting hall for early settlers. Restored in 20th century as a state historical museum and furnished with appropriate 17th-century antiques
*Operated by State of Conn. Open Apr.– Oct: 10–5. Nov.–Mar: 10–4; closed Mon. and Dec. 15–Jan. 15*

*Henry Whitfield House*

### ■ HYLAND HOUSE, 1660
**Boston Street**
Typical 17th-century house, built by George Hyland; lean-to added about 1720 by Ebenezer Parmelee to create saltbox shape. Here Parmelee made the first town clock in America for the church steeple; furnished in style of Pilgrim century
*Operated by Dorothy Whitfield Soc. Open June 15–Sept: Tues.–Sun. 11–5*

### ■ THOMAS GRISWOLD HOUSE, 1735
**161 Boston St**
Classic example of 18th-century saltbox; built by Griswold family, whose descendants lived there until 1958. Exhibits include Guilford town artifacts and early farm utensils and blacksmith shop in barn museum
*Operated by Guilford Keeping Soc. Open Apr.–Nov: Tues.–Sun. 11–5*

## HADDAM

### THANKFUL ARNOLD HOUSE, 1795–1810
**Haddam Green**
A medium-sized family house built in three sections between 1795 and 1810 for Joseph Arnold and his wife Thankful, a direct descendant of John and Priscilla Alden. Now furnished with period pieces
*Operated by Haddam Historical Soc. Open June–Sept: Sat., Sun. 2–5*

## HAMDEN

### JONATHAN DICKERMAN HOUSE, 1770
**Mt. Carmel Ave**
Simple, red 18th-century dwelling built by Jonathan Dickerman II; period furnishings now on display
*Operated by Hamden Historical Soc. Open summer: Sat., Sun. 2–5 and by appointment*

## HARTFORD

### ■ HARRIET BEECHER STOWE HOUSE, 1871
**73 Forest Ave**
Victorian home, combining elements of the rustic cottage and Gothic villa, of the famous author and her husband, Prof. Calvin Stowe, from 1873 to 1896. The house has been faithfully restored to this period, and the Stowe family furniture is on display; the restoration of the kitchen was based on *The American Woman's Home* by Mrs. Stowe and her sister Catherine Beecher.
*Operated by Nook Farm–Stowe-Day Foundation. Open Tues.–Sat. 10–5, Sun. 2–5; closed holidays*

### ■ MARK TWAIN HOUSE, 1874
**351 Farmington Ave**
An unusual red brick house designed

by Edward T. Potter for the famous author in the Victorian style. Noteworthy interiors by Louis C. Tiffany. Restored with Clemens family furniture and memorabilia on display
*Operated by Nook Farm–Mark Twain Memorial. Open Tues.–Sat. 10–5, Sun. 2–5; closed holidays*

### ■ SAMUEL COLT HOUSE (ARMSMEAR), 1857
**80 Wethersfield Ave**
Eclectic Victorian mansion somewhat like an Italian villa but with Turkish domes and pinnacles built by Samuel Colt, inventor of the Colt revolver and munitions manufacturer. Now occupied as a residence for retired Episcopal churchwomen
*Operated by Trustees of The Colt Bequest. Open by appointment*

## LEBANON

### ■ GOV. JONATHAN TRUMBULL HOUSE, 1740
**The Common**
Frame home built by Capt. Joseph Trumbull; birthplace of his son Gov. Jonathan Trumbull and scene of the latter's vital activities in the cause of independence. Also birthplace of the builder's grandson, the celebrated painter John Trumbull. Period furnishings on display
*Operated by Daughters of the American Revolution. Open May – Nov: Tues.–Sat. 1–6*

## LITCHFIELD

### ■ LITCHFIELD HISTORIC DISTRICT, late 18th century
**neighboring the Village Green**
One of New England's best surviving examples of a late 18th-century town built around a green. Today, Litchfield still has 15 frame houses dating from that period.

### OLIVER WOLCOTT, JR., HOUSE, 1799; 1817
**South Street**
Two-story house with gable ends built by Elijah Wadsworth and soon purchased for Oliver, Jr., who enlarged it in 1817. The interior has been altered many times; little is left of interest except the original ballroom with clas-

*Mark Twain House*

*Armsmear*

*Litchfield village street*

sical trim. Now contains offices, a library, a music room, and study
*Operated by Wolcott Library and Historical Soc. Open library hours*

## ■ TAPPING REEVE HOUSE AND LAW SCHOOL, 1772–74
**South Street**
First law school in U.S., at the side of Judge Reeve's house, built by Moses Seymour. Fine furnishings exhibited with memorabilia of the many nationally prominent graduates
*Operated by Litchfield Historical Soc. Open May 15–Oct. 15: daily 11–12, 2–5; closed Wed.*

## MADISON
### NATHANIEL ALLIS HOUSE, 1739
**Boston Post Road**
Original one-story frame building built by Nathaniel Allis II, to which second story and more rooms added at later dates. Fine furnishings
*Operated by Madison Historical Soc. Open June 15–Sept. 15: Tues.–Sat. 10–5*

## MANCHESTER
### CHENEY HOMESTEAD, about 1780
**106 Hartford Rd**
Originally a Cape Cod style farmhouse built by Timothy Cheney, farmer and clockmaker, and added to over the years to accommodate a growing family. Seven of the rooms on exhibit with fine antique furnishings, including a set of Chippendale chairs
*Operated by Manchester Historical Soc. Open Thurs., Sun. 1–5; closed holidays*

## MERIDEN
### ■ ANDREWS HOMESTEAD, 1760
**424 W Main St**
Typical Connecticut saltbox with lean-tos at the rear, built by Moses Andrews. Now maintained as a museum
*Operated by Meriden Historical Soc. Open Sun. 2–5 and by appointment*

## MIDDLETOWN
### ■ ALSOP MANSION, 1838
**301 High St**
Greek Revival mansion built by Rich-
ard Alsop IV and believed to have been designed by architect Ithiel Towne. Trompe-l'oeil statues on façade and interior decorations in oil on plaster are unique in American domestic architecture. Now used as Davison Art Center; furnished with fine antiques
*Operated by Wesleyan University. Open Mon.–Fri. 9–5, Sat. 9–12, 1–4, Sun 2–5; closed weekends during college vacations*

### DAVISON HOUSE, 1845
**327 High St**
Gothic Revival house built of local brownstone by Duane Barnes, who quarried every stone of the cottage himself. The house was described by A.J. Downing in his *Cottage Residences* as one of the most artistic residences in the country at that time and was visited by Charles Dickens. Several pieces of Gothic furniture
*Operated by Wesleyan University. Open as infirmary*

### GEN. MANSFIELD HOUSE, 1807
**Main Street**
Brick town house built by Samuel and Catherine Livingston Mather, whose daughter married Gen. Joseph King Fenno Mansfield. They lived the balance of their lives in this house which has rich associations with the Civil War period. Period furnishings
*Operated by Middlesex Co. Historical Soc. Open Wed. 3–5 and by appointment*

### ■ RUSSELL HOUSE, 1828; 1860
**High Street**
Outstanding Greek Revival stucco mansion, probably designed by architect Ithiel Towne for sea captain Samuel Russell, who made his fortune in the China trade. Six Corinthian columns supporting classical portico; original 22 rooms expanded to 42 when north wing added in 1860. Now used as Honors College
*Operated by Wesleyan University. Open Sept.–June: Mon.–Fri. 9–5, weekends by appointment*

## MILFORD
### COL. STEPHEN FORD HOUSE,
**early 18th century**
**142 W Main St**
Impressive 18th-century house first

operated as a licensed tavern in 1710. Features the original taproom with furnishings of the period
*Private. Open Mon.–Sat. 10–5*

## EELLS-STOW HOUSE, 1684
**34 High St**
Simple 17th-century dwelling, built by Samuel Eells, which has undergone several alterations; antique furnishings and town documents on display
*Operated by Milford Historical Soc. Open June–Sept: Tues.–Sun. 2–5*

## MOODUS

### AMASA DAY HOUSE, 1816
**On the Green**
Country house showing transition from Federal to Greek Revival style, built by Julius Chapman; still has original stencil designs on front stairs, upstairs hall, and two floors. Lived in by Amasa Day from 1843 to 1896. Seven museum rooms restored with Day family heirlooms of the early 19th century
*Operated by Conn. Antiquarian & Landmarks Soc. Open May 15–Oct. 15: daily 1–5*

## MYSTIC

### DENISON HOMESTEAD, 1717
**Pequot-Sepos Road**
Mansion built in 1717 on site of original "mansion hous" built by Capt. George Denison, commander of Connecticut troops in King Philip's War. Now restored in successive periods to show how 11 generations lived their daily lives
*Operated by Denison Soc. Open June–Sept: Tues.–Sun. 1–5*

### MYSTIC SEAPORT VILLAGE, 19th century
**Greenville Avenue**
Re-creation of a 19th-century New England coastal village on a 37-acre site with nearly 60 museum buildings, including craft shops, a tavern, and historic ships permanently berthed. Some of the dwellings illustrating different periods and styles are the *Samuel Buckingham House* (1768), *Edwards House* (about 1815), and *Thomas Greenman House* (1840).
*Operated by Marine Historical Assn. Open daily 9–5; closed Thanksgiving and Christmas*

## NEW CANAAN

### HANFORD-SILLIMAN HOUSE, about 1764
**33 Oenoke Ridge**
Fine Georgian house built by Stephen Hanford, Revolutionary soldier. Later, home of Silliman family for more than two centuries; many fine antiques
*Operated by New Canaan Historical Soc. Open Sun., Mon., Tues., Thurs. 2–5*

### ■ JOHN ROGERS STUDIO, 1877
**10 Cherry St**
Frame studio residence of 19th-century sculptor John Rogers; contains representative collection of Rogers Groups
*Operated by New Canaan Historical Soc. Open Sun., Mon., Tues., Thurs. 2–5*

## NEW HAVEN

### ■ JAMES DWIGHT DANA HOUSE, 1849
**24 Hillhouse Ave**
Stucco house, representing transition style between austere Greek Revival and exotic eclecticism, designed by Henry Austin for J.D. Dana, one of leading 19th-century American scientists
*Operated by Yale University. Open as Yale Statistics Dept.*

### ■ OTHNIEL C. MARSH HOUSE, 1875–80
**360 Prospect St**
Beautifully cut red sandstone mansion designed by J. Cleveland Cady for O.C. Marsh, America's first professor of paleontology. With its fine botanical gardens crowning the hill in the fashionable part of town, it marks a high tide of the affluent society of its day.
*Operated by Yale University. Open as School of Forestry*

### PARDEE-MORRIS HOUSE, 1685; 1779
**325 Lighthouse Rd**
First dwelling on the site, built by Eleazar Morris, burned by the British in 1779. Amos Morris then reconstructed house on original foundations and stone walls; further alterations made in 19th century. Period furnishings on display

Operated by New Haven Colony Historical Soc. Open May–Oct: Mon.–Fri. 10–5, Sun. 2–5

## NEW LONDON

### ■ DESHON-ALLYN HOUSE, 1829
**613 Williams St**
Granite Federal house, with Palladian window above front door, built for Capt. Daniel Deshon, prosperous whaling master. Outstanding furniture and accessories of the period
*Operated by Lyman-Allyn Museum. Open by appointment*

### ■ HEMPSTED HOUSE, 1678; 1728
**11 Hempstead St**
Built by Joshua Hempsted, son of one of founders of New London; 17th-century frame dwelling added to in 1728; lived in until 1937 by Hempsted heirs. Restored, with furnishings and atmosphere of Pilgrim century
*Operated by Conn. Antiquarian & Landmarks Soc. Open May 15–Oct. 15: daily 1–5*

*Hempsted House*

### SHAW MANSION, 1756
**11 Blinman St**
Stone mansion built for Capt. Nathaniel Shaw, who engaged dispossessed Acadians from Nova Scotia to quarry the stone from his land. Partially burned by British in 1781; considerably altered in 19th century. Period furnishings on display
*Operated by New London Co. Historical Soc. Open Tues.–Sat. 1–4*

## NEW MILFORD

### KNAPP HOMESTEAD, 1815
**1 Old Albany Post Rd**
Old frame house now used as a museum by the local historical society.

Knapp family furnishings; collections of glass, china, silver, portraits, etc.
*Operated by New Milford Historical Soc. Open Wed., Sat. 2–5*

## NORWALK

### ■ LOCKWOOD-MATTHEWS MANSION, 1868
**295 West Ave**
Outstanding granite mansion built by LeGrand Lockwood, president of New York Stock Exchange, and designed by Detlef Lienau. Extremely elegant carved and inlaid interiors; now a museum of the city of Norwalk
*Operated by Junior League of Stamford-Norwalk. Open Sun. 1–5 and by appointment*

*Lockwood–Matthews Mansion*

## NORWICH

### DR. JOHN D. ROCKWELL HOUSE, 1818
**42 Rockwell St**
Gray stone house built by Maj. Joseph Perkins, with later additions, and lived in by his grandson, Dr. Rockwell, for many years. Fine period furnishings on display
*Operated by Daughters of the American Revolution. Open summer: Wed. 2–5 and by appointment*

### LEFFINGWELL INN, 1675
**348 Washington St**
Originally built by Stephen Backus in 1675, this excellent restoration clearly shows the early practice of joining two small houses to make a mansion and then adding ells. During Revolution Thomas Leffingwell's "publique house" was local center for patriots. Rare items on display in museum
*Operated by Soc. of Founders of Norwich. Open summer: Tues.–Sun. 10–12:30, 2–5. Winter: Sat., Sun. 2–4*

CONNECTICUT

## LITTLE PLAIN HISTORIC DISTRICT

This district includes all the residences around Little Plain and Huntington parks and reflects the accumulation of wealth in the 18th and 19th centuries resulting from great activity in shipping, manufacturing, and trade.

### ■ NATHANIEL BACKUS HOUSE, 1750
44 Rockwell St

Frame home built by Nathaniel Backus, descendant of one of the founders of Norwich. Now moved from original site to serve as a museum
*Operated by Daughters of the American Revolution. Open summer: Wed. 2–5 and by appointment*

## OLD LYME

### FLORENCE GRISWOLD HOME, 1817
Post Road

Outstanding Greek Revival house designed by Samuel Belcher. In 1900 Miss Florence Griswold formed a summer colony of prominent American artists who painted some of their finest works on the doors throughout the first floor of the house. Many fine antiques and a rare china collection on display
*Operated by Lyme Historical Soc. Open June–Sept: Tues.–Sun. 2–5*

*Florence Griswold House*

## SHARON

### GAY-HOYT HOUSE, 1775
Main Street

Rare brick Connecticut dwelling built by Ebenezer Gay, prominent resident in early Sharon. Many exhibits—furniture, costumes, guns, farm tools, town records, etc.

*Operated by Sharon Historical Soc. Open Mon.–Sat. 10–5*

## SIMSBURY

### CAPT. ELISHA PHELPS HOUSE, 1771; 1879
800 Hopmeadow St

This gambrel-roof frame structure originally built by Capt. Phelps has been lived in continuously by members of his family. It was used as a hotel and tavern in the 19th century; in 1879 a Victorian-style rear ell replaced the older one. Now houses fine collection of historical objects
*Operated by Simsbury Historical Soc. Open Apr.–Nov: Wed., Sat. 1–4*

## SOUTH GLASTONBURY

### WELLES-SHIPMAN HOUSE, 1755
912 Main St

Fine frame two-story house built by Thomas Welles; furnished with 18th-century antiques
*Operated by Historical Soc. of Glastonbury. Open May 25–Sept. 7: Sun.*

## STAMFORD

### ■ HOYT-BARNUM HOUSE, about 1690
713 Bedford St

A simple farmhouse, now the oldest structure in downtown Stamford. Collections of period dolls, costumes, and farm tools
*Operated by Stamford Historical Soc. Open Tues.–Fri. 1–5*

## STRATFORD

### CAPT. DAVID JUDSON HOUSE, 1723
Academy Hill

Substantial 18th-century clapboard house built by Capt. Judson; furnished as comfortable dwelling of its day. The adjoining museum features exhibits from all periods of Stratford history.
*Operated by Stratford Historical Soc. Open Mar.–Nov: Wed., Sat., Sun. 11–5*

## SUFFIELD

### DR. ALEXANDER KING HOUSE, 1764
Main Street

Frame dwelling built by Dr. King,

leader in the community; completely furnished with examples from 17th to 19th centuries
*Operated by Suffield Historical Soc. Open May–Nov: Wed. 2–4*

**HATHEWAY HOUSE, 1760; 1795 Main Street**
Main part of house built by Oliver Phelps; north wing, added in 1795, contains fine Adam-style plasterwork and four original French hand-blocked wallpapers of 1780s by Reveillon. Recently restored with period furnishings
*Operated by Conn. Antiquarian & Landmarks Soc. Open May 15–Oct. 15: daily 1–5*

*Hatheway House*

## TORRINGTON

**HOTCHKISS-FLYER HOUSE, 1900 192 Main St**
Turn-of-the-century mansion designed by William H. Allen for politician Orsamus R. Flyer. Richly furnished in period style
*Operated by Torrington Historical Soc. Open by appointment*

## WALLINGFORD

**NEHEMIAH ROYCE HOUSE, 1672 538 N Main St**
Frame saltbox, the earliest home in town built two years after its settlement. Restored and modern kitchen and bathroom added; used as a guesthouse. Original beams, latches, diamond-studded batten door, horizontal feather paneling; period furnishings
*Operated by The Choate School. Open by appointment*

**SAMUEL PARSONS HOUSE, 1759; 1855 180 S Main St**
Red, gambrel-roofed colonial dwelling built for Samuel Parsons; small ell added in 1855. Once a tavern and coach stop between New York and Boston, now maintained as a museum
*Operated by Wallingford Historical Soc. Open Sun. 2–5 and by appointment*

## WATERFORD

**HARKNESS MANSION, 1904 Harkness Memorial Park**
Limestone manor in Italian style built for Edward Stephen Harkness; now houses collection of bird paintings by Rex Brasher
*Operated by State of Conn. Open June–Sept: daily 10–6*

## WEST HARTFORD

**■ NOAH WEBSTER BIRTHPLACE, 1700–1720 227 S Main St**
Frame saltbox, typical of farm family of modest means, where the famous lexicographer was born in 1758. Containing only five rooms and simply furnished in mid-18th-century style; also Noah Webster's books and manuscripts on display
*Operated by Noah Webster House Foundation. Open Mon.–Fri. 10–4*

## WETHERSFIELD

**■ BUTTOLPH–WILLIAMS HOUSE, about 1692 Broad and Marsh Streets**
Fine 17th-century frame house with overhang, built by David Buttolph and called a "Mansion House." Restored in 1947 to original form with outstanding period furnishings. "Ye Greate Kitchin" considered to be most complete 17th-century kitchen in New England
*Operated by Conn. Antiquarian & Landmarks Soc. Open May 15–Oct. 15: daily 1–5*

**ISAAC STEVENS HOUSE, 1788–89 215 Main St**
Plain, well-proportioned frame country house built by Stevens for his bride.

Family furnishings on display and museum relating to children
*Operated by Soc. of Colonial Dames. Open May–Oct: Mon.–Sat. 10–4, Sun. 1–4. Nov.–Apr: Mon.–Sat. 10–4*

■ **JOSEPH WEBB HOUSE, 1678; 1752**
**211 Main St**
Distinguished Georgian frame house with great historic interest. In May of 1781 General Washington and Count de Rochambeau spent five days there in conference planning the Yorktown campaign. Fine period interior furnishings, including rare flock wallpaper hung in honor of the general's visit
*Operated by Soc. of Colonial Dames. Open May 15–Oct. 15: Mon.–Sat. 10–4, Sun. 1–4. Oct. 16–May 14: Mon.–Sat. 10–4*

*Joseph Webb House*

■ **SILAS DEANE HOUSE, 1766**
**203 Main St**
Unique 18th-century mansion built by the patriot Silas Deane; with elaborate staircase and entrance hall. Now being restored and furnished in elegant period style
*Operated by Soc. of Colonial Dames. Open by request at Webb House*

## WILTON

**LAMBERT HOUSE, 1724**
**150 Danbury Rd**
Striking colonial dwelling built by David Lambert and lived in by his descendants until the 20th century. Now used as cultural and educational center; furnished with antiques
*Operated by Wilton Historical Soc. Open Tues–Fri. 1:30–5; closed Aug.*

## WINDSOR

**LT. WALTER FLYER HOUSE, about 1640 and 1765**
**96 Palisado Ave**
Early structure built by one of town's first settlers, Lt. Flyer; gambrel-roof

section added in 18th century. A portion once used as a store and town's first post office; now houses possessions of local historical society
*Operated by Windsor Historical Soc. Open Feb.–Dec: Tues.–Sun. 10–2, 1–5; closed holidays*

**LOOMIS HOMESTEAD, 1639–40**
**Batchelder Road**
Frame homestead originally built by Joseph Loomis during the years 1639 and 1640 and added to in later years by the eight successive generations of the family over a span of three centuries. Splendid example of the development of the American rural house. Furnished with the Loomis family heirlooms
*Operated by The Loomis Institute. Open by appointment*

■ **OLIVER ELLSWORTH HOMESTEAD, 1740; about 1785**
**778 Palisado Ave**
Fine central-hall house with original woodwork and paneling; Oliver Ellsworth, third Chief Justice of U.S., added the ell about 1785. Beautiful furniture, tapestry, silver, and china
*Operated by Daughters of the American Revolution. Open May–Oct: Tues.–Sat. 1–6*

## WINSTED

**SOLOMON ROCKWELL HOUSE, 1813**
**225 Prospect St**
Fine Federal mansion, sometimes called "Solomon's Temple," built by Solomon Rockwell, prosperous iron manufacturer. Attractive furnishings, paintings, items of local interest
*Operated by Winchester Historical Soc. Open June 15–Sept: Tues.–Sat. 2–5*

## WOODBURY

**THE GLEBE HOUSE, 1690; 1750**
**Hollow Road**
A 17th-century frame house enlarged about 1750; associated with Samuel Seabury, elected Bishop of Connecticut in 1783, and called the birthplace of American Episcopacy
*Operated by Seabury Soc. for the Preservation of Glebe House. Open Sun., Tues. 1–5, Wed.–Sat. 11–5; closed holidays*

## DOVER

### GOVERNOR'S MANSION, about 1790
Lovely three-story house of red brick in Flemish bond built by Charles Hillyard on land given to his great-grandfather by William Penn. Restored as the governor's mansion in 1966 and shown with fine period antiques from the Delaware, Delmarva Peninsula, and southeastern Pennsylvania areas
*Operated by Del. Dept. of Administrative Services, Div. of State Buildings. Open Tues. 1–5*

## DOVER VICINITY

### ■ JOHN DICKINSON MANSION, 1740
**Kitts Hummock Road**
A two-and-a-half-story house with Flemish bond façade built on the plantation of Samuel Dickinson; gutted by fire in 1804 and rebuilt with a brick kitchen wing. Famous as the home of Samuel's son John Dickinson, known as the "Penman of the Revolution" for his many writings in favor of the Revolutionary cause
*Operated by Del. Dept. of State. Open Tues.–Sat. 10–5, Sun. 1–5*

## LEWES

### BURTON-INGRAM HOUSE, about 1800
Two-and-a-half-story shingle house with a small lean-to wing. Restored
*Operated by Lewes Historical Soc. Open Memorial Day–Labor Day: Sat. 2–5*

### PLANK HOUSE, about 1700
Small structure of long wooden planks dovetailed at the corners; believed to be the oldest building in the area. Interior indicates it was used as a home.
*Operated by Lewes Historical Soc. Open Memorial Day–Labor Day: Sat. 2–5*

## MILFORD

### PARSON THORNE MANSION, 1730–35; 1750
**501 NW Front St**
Oldest part of this brick plantation house with connected wings is the one-room rear section built by Joseph Booth; the front section was added about 1750. The house is named for the Anglican clergyman Sydenham Thorne, one of the founders of Milford. Restoration began in 1962; when completed the house will be fully furnished with period pieces.
*Operated by Milford Historical Soc. Open by appointment*

## NEW CASTLE

### AMSTEL HOUSE, about 1780
**2 E Fourth St**
Three-story Dutch house of brick laid in Flemish bond; the home of Delaware's seventh governor, Nicholas Van Dyke. Scene of a wedding in 1784 at which George Washington was a guest. Now historical society headquarters featuring colonial furnishings
*Operated by New Castle Historical Soc. Open Mon., Tues., Thurs.–Sat. 11–5; closed holidays*

### ■ NEW CASTLE HISTORIC DISTRICT
Founded by the Dutch in 1651, New Castle has retained much of its early architecture. Along The Strand, the city's cobbled main street, many fine town houses, some dating from 1679, still stand. On New Castle Day, the third Saturday in May, many historic homes are open to the public.

### OLD DUTCH HOUSE, about 1690
**Third Street on the Village Green**
Small Dutch house of brick with low pent eaves; believed to be the oldest house in the state. Restored and furnished with Dutch colonial pieces
*Operated by New Castle Historical Soc. Open Apr.–Nov: daily 11–4*

## NEW CASTLE VICINITY

### BUENA VISTA, 1846
**U.S. Route 13**
Two-story brick house built by John M. Clayton, U.S. senator and Secretary of State under Zachary Taylor, for whose Mexican War victory the house is named. Clayton's great-nephew Clayton Buck, governor of Delaware, added a wing in 1930. Furnishings are mainly from the Empire period.
*Operated by Del. Dept. of Administrative Services. Open Tues.–Sat. 10–5, Sun. 1–5*

## ODESSA

■ **CORBIT-SHARP HOUSE,**
**1772–74**
**Main and Second Streets**
One of the finest Georgian houses in
the Delaware Valley; built for William Corbit by Robert May, a master
builder. Two-and-a-half-story brick
house with hipped roof, carved cornices, and Chinese lattice roof deck
was restored by H. Rodney Sharp
after he acquired it in 1938. He then
furnished it with fine antiques and
donated it to Winterthur Museum.
*Operated by Henry Francis du Pont*
*Winterthur Museum. Open Tues.–Sat.*
*10–5, Sun. 2–5; closed major holidays*

**WILSON-WARNER HOUSE, 1740;**
**1769**
**Main Street**
Two-story Georgian brick house with
main section added on to a 1740 wing;
built for prosperous merchant David
Wilson. Owned by his descendants
until 1830 and reacquired by his great-
granddaughter in 1902. Furnishings
are mainly 18th-century pieces
*Operated by Henry Francis du Pont*
*Winterthur Museum. Open Tues.–Sat.*
*10–5, Sun. 2–5; closed major holidays*

## SMYRNA

**ALLEE HOUSE, about 1753**
**Dutch Neck Cross Road**
Pre-Revolutionary brick farmhouse
now a museum with antiques
*Operated by Del. Dept. of State, Div.*
*of Historical and Cultural Affairs.*
*Open Sat., Sun. 2–5*

**BELMONT HALL, 1689; about 1750**
**Route 13**
Front section of Georgian brick house
built by Thomas Collins was added on
to a previously constructed portion.
Collins was president of Delaware
when the state ratified the Constitution in 1787.
*Private. Open by appointment*

**THE LINDENS, before 1725**
Dutch colonial brick house with a
gambrel roof built by a colonial miller;
the wooden wing was added in the
middle 1800s. Also on the grounds is
the *Plank House,* an early log cabin.
*Operated by Duck Creek Historical*
*Soc. Open daily 10–5*

*Eleutherian Mills*

## WILMINGTON

■ **ELEUTHERIAN MILLS, 1803;**
**1805; 1853**
**Greenville**
Stately Georgian-style mansion with
small Palladian dormer windows and
twin double chimneys; built by
Eleuthère Irénée du Pont near the site
of the powder mills he founded. Two-
story mansion of buff-colored stucco
over local stone has an 1805 wing addition and a two-story piazza, added in
1853. Furnished with early American,
Federal, and Empire pieces; occupied
by the family until 1958. Other buildings open to the public on the 185-
acre site include the first offices and
early mills.
*Operated by Eleutherian Mills-Hagley*
*Foundation. Open late Apr.–early*
*June, Mid-Sept.–late Oct: Tues.–Sat.*
*9:30–4:30, Sun. 1–5*

## WINTERTHUR

**WINTERTHUR, 1839**
Originally the home of Mrs. J. A.
Biderman, great-aunt of Henry Francis
du Pont. In 1927 du Pont began to
install in the house woodwork taken
from early American East Coast homes
to be demolished. Now nearly 200
rooms are furnished with fine antique
pieces showing the growth of American decorative arts from 1640 to 1840.
The house is set on 60 acres with
formal gardens. Reservations are
needed for a complete tour; ten rooms
in the reception area can be seen without prior arrangement.
*Operated by Henry Francis du Pont*
*Winterthur Museum. Open–House:*
*Tues.–Sat. 9:30–4. Gardens: Apr.–*
*June, Sept. 15–Oct: Tues.–Sat. 9:30–*
*4; both closed major holidays*

## ALVA BELMONT HOUSE [NATIONAL WOMAN'S PARTY], about 1799–1800
### 144 B St, NE

Original "manor house" built on the site of Lord Baltimore's land grant, now Capitol Hill. The house was enlarged by Robert Sewall about 1800 and then rebuilt by him after it was burned by the British in 1814. It was the residence of Albert Gallatin, Secretary of Treasury under Madison. *Operated by National Woman's Party. Open daily 2–4*

## ■ CALDWELL-MONROE HOUSE [ARTS CLUB OF WASHINGTON], 1802–6
### 2017 I St, NW

Built by Timothy Caldwell, this Federal town house served briefly as the Executive Mansion after burning of the White House in 1814. It was the home of James Monroe before and during his first months of Presidency and in subsequent years of such dignitaries as Charles Francis Adams and Gen. Silas Casey. Notable interiors *Operated by Arts Club of Washington. Open Mon.–Sat. 9–5; closed national holidays*

## ■ CHRISTIAN HEURICH MANSION [COLUMBIA HISTORICAL SOC.], 1892–94
### 1307 New Hampshire Ave, NW

Gabled and turreted Victorian brownstone residence of Christian Heurich, a successful German-immigrant brewer, designed by John G. Meyers. Interiors and furnishings are a museum of their period—the end of the 19th century. *Operated by Columbia Historical Soc. Open Mon., Wed., Sat. 2–4; closed national holidays*

## ■ DECATUR HOUSE [NATIONAL TRUST FOR HISTORIC PRESERVATION], 1818–19
### 748 Jackson Place, NW

Red brick mansion of the Federal era designed by Benjamin H. Latrobe for Stephen Decatur, victorious naval commander of the War of 1812. It has been the home of many Washington notables, including Henry Clay and Martin Van Buren. Interiors restored and furnished *Operated by National Trust. Open daily 10–5; closed Christmas*

## DUMBARTON HOUSE [SOC. OF COLONIAL DAMES], 1799–1805
### 2715 Q St, NW

Federal-style mansion begun by Samuel Jackson, originally facing the city at the end of Q Street. The house was moved in 1915 to allow extension of the street. Restored in 1931; notable interiors with fine colonial furnishings; typical Georgetown garden of 1800 *Operated by Soc. of Colonial Dames. Open Sept.–June: Mon.–Sat. 9–12; closed holidays*

## DUMBARTON OAKS, 1801
### 1703 32 St, NW

Built by William H. Dorsey, an orphans' court judge, the original structure was in the Georgian style. Over the years it has been extensively altered and extended. In 1944 the international meeting leading to the formation of the United Nations was held here. Now a museum of Byzantine and early Christian art and a center for medieval studies. Formal gardens *Operated by Harvard University. Open—House: Tues.–Sun. 2–5. Gardens: daily 2–5; both closed July–Labor Day and national holidays*

*Dumbarton Oaks*

## ■ FREDERICK DOUGLASS HOME (CEDAR HILL), about 1855
### 1411 W St, SE

Home of Frederick Douglass, the self-educated former slave who rose to prominence as an abolitionist leader, lecturer, and writer. His two-story brick home, which overlooks the Anacostia River, is presently being restored as a museum. *Operated by National Park Service. Restoration in progress*

## FREDERICK DOUGLASS TOWN HOUSE [MUSEUM OF AFRICAN ART], 1870s
### 316 A St, NE

The first home in D.C. of Frederick

Douglass. The house serves as a museum, with collections of traditional African sculpture, 19th- and 20th-century Afro-American art, and selected examples of 20th-century Western art reflecting African influence. Douglass' study re-created, with documents, photographs, and memorabilia
*Operated by Frederick Douglass Institute. Open Mon.–Fri. 10–5:30, Sat., Sun. 2–5:30*

■ **GEORGETOWN HISTORIC DISTRICT**
Established 1751, incorporated into D.C. 1871. Exclusive residential area with narrow tree-lined streets; many fine restored houses, most from Federal and Georgian periods; quaint shops; site of Georgetown University

■ **LAFAYETTE SQUARE HISTORIC DISTRICT**
**borders Pennsylvania Ave between Madison and Jackson Places and extends through H St, NW**
Site selected by George Washington for a public park and later named for the Marquis de Lafayette. Flanking the park were the District's most select residential streets, and a few of the fine town houses remain. Historic buildings on Madison and Jackson Places are being refinished for use as Federal offices but may be viewed from the exterior.

**LARZ ANDERSON HOUSE
[SOC. OF THE CINCINNATI], 1904
2118 Massachusetts Ave, NW**
Stately town residence built by Larz Anderson, III, the U.S. ambassador to Japan from 1912 to 1913. Mr. Anderson's collection of Oriental art is on display. The interiors are particularly noteworthy, as is the society's museum of the Revolution exhibited throughout the rooms.
*Operated by Soc. of the Cincinnati. Open Tues.–Sun. 2–4; closed national holidays*

■ **THE OCTAGON HOUSE
[AMERICAN INSTITUTE OF ARCHITECTS], 1798–1800
1741 New York Ave, NW**
Designed for Col. John Tayloe of

Mount Airy, Virginia, by Dr. William Thornton, the original architect of the national Capitol, the house is actually in the shape of a hexagon, with a semicircular tower at the corner entrance. Gen. George Washington was responsible for Tayloe's selecting the Federal city for his town house. The residence of President Madison after the White House was burned by the British, the Treaty of Ghent, officially ending the War of 1812, was signed here in 1815. Now a museum of architecture and the allied arts
*Operated by American Institute of Architects. Open Mon.–Fri. 8:30–5*

■ **OLD STONE HOUSE, 1765
3051 M St, NW**
One of the oldest structures in D.C., begun by Christopher Layhman, a cabinetmaker, and finished by his widow. Over the years it was used by various commercial establishments and underwent much mutilation and defacement. From 1958 to 1959 it was restored and furnished with authentic and replica furniture typical of the 18th-century home. Craft demonstrations held
*Operated by National Park Service. Open Tues.–Sat. 10–12; closed national holidays*

■ **PENNSYLVANIA AVENUE NATIONAL HISTORIC SITE
Pennsylvania Avenue, from Capitol Hill to the White House**
Pierre L'Enfant laid this street out in 1791 as the shortest distance between the Capitol and the Executive Mansion. It has been the ceremonial route of the nation and witness to its triumphs and tragedies. Traveling this route have been Presidents following their inaugurations, funeral processions of Presidents and national leaders, and victory processions signaling the close of four major wars.

■ **PETERSEN HOUSE (HOUSE WHERE LINCOLN DIED),
about 1849
516 10th St, NW**
A modest, brick, row house opposite Ford's Theater (which is now a museum of Lincolniana) was being used as a rooming house in 1865 when Lincoln died there in a small bedroom

on the first floor. Memorabilia connected with the last hours of Lincoln's life are exhibited.
*Operated by National Park Service.*
*Open daily 9–12; closed Christmas*

■ **THE WHITE HOUSE, 1792–1800**
**1600 Pennsylvania Ave, NW**
The residence of the President of the U.S. since John Adams, the building was designed by James Hoban in the classical revival style. It was burned by the British in 1814 and rebuilt by Hoban from 1815 to 1817. Extensively renovated, enlarged, and remodeled during the Truman administration. Excellent collection of historic furnishings and Presidential memorabilia; selected rooms open to the public
*Operated by National Park Service.*
*Open Tues.–Sat. 10–12; closed national holidays*

*The White House*

■ **WOODROW WILSON HOUSE, 1915**
**2340 S St, NW**
Neo-Georgian home of Woodrow Wilson after his retirement from the Presidency in 1921. Original furnishings; collection of World War I memorabilia; special exhibits
*Operated by National Trust. Open June–Sept. 14: daily 10–5. Sept. 15–May: daily 10–4; closed Christmas*

## CROSS CREEK

■ **MARJORIE KINNAN RAWLINGS HOUSE, late 19th century**
**State Road 325**
Three separate wooden buildings connected by porches and bridgeways form this typical "cracker" farmhouse, home of Marjorie Kinnan Rawlings, who was awarded the Pulitzer Prize in 1939 for her classic *The Yearling*. Shown with Mrs. Rawlings' furnishings; much of the surrounding land is now a public park
*Operated by State of Fla. Dept. of Natural Resources. Open Tues.–Sun. 9–6*

## ELLENTON

■ **GAMBLE MANSION, 1842–45**
**U.S. Route 301**
Two-story mansion with wide double verandas on three sides supported by 18 columns; built of bricks and plaster made from sand, lime, and sugar. Mansion on the plantation of Robert Gamble, soldier and banker; here Judah P. Benjamin, Confederate Secretary of State, took refuge at the end of the Civil War. Contains many Civil War relics. Nearby are the ruins of Gamble's sugar mill.

*Operated by Fla. Dept. of Natural Resources, State Parks. Open daily 9–5*

## FORT GEORGE ISLAND

■ **KINGSLEY PLANTATION HOUSE, after 1804**
**Kingsley Plantation State Park**
This 14-acre park contains the oldest plantation house in Florida, a two-story white frame house built either by Zephaniah Kingsley or John Houstoun McIntosh, from whom he purchased the plantation in 1817. Nearby is a small house made of tabby – a building material combining lime, shell, stone, and water – built by a previous owner about 1798. Known as "Anna Jai's," this house is named for Kingsley's African wife, the daughter of a Senegal chief. The plantation house is furnished with period pieces.
*Operated by Fla. Dept. of Natural Resources, State Parks. Open daily 9–12, 1–5*

## FORT MYERS

**THOMAS A. EDISON HOME, 1886**
**2341 McGregor Blvd**
Large house designed for tropical living; prefabricated in Maine and shipped to Florida as the winter home of Thomas Edison. The 13-acre estate features the inventor's huge botanical

garden, where he conducted many experiments—including research for new sources of rubber—and his office-laboratory, where many of his inventions are exhibited.
*Operated by City of Fort Myers. Open daily 9–4; closed Christmas*

## KEY WEST

### AUDUBON HOUSE, about 1830
**205 Whitehead St**
Charming frame house with a second-story veranda built by Capt. James Geiger. In 1832 John James Audubon lived here while painting the Florida wildlife. Restored in 1962 and shown with furnishings from the late 18th and early 19th centuries. On display is a complete edition of the double elephant folios of *Birds of America*.
*Operated by Mitchell Wolfson Family Foundation. Open daily 9–12, 1–5*

*Audubon House*

### ■ ERNEST HEMINGWAY HOME AND MUSEUM, 1851
**907 Whitehead St**
Two-story house built in the architectural style popular in New Orleans, where the original owner, Asa Tift, lived. From 1931 to 1940 this was Hemingway's home; here he wrote many of his most famous novels, including *To Have and Have Not*. Owned by the Hemingway family until 1961; shown with some of the author's furnishings and mementos
*Private. Open daily 9–5*

## MIAMI

### ■ VIZCAYA, 1914–16
**3251 S Miami Ave**
Luxurious palace built for industrialist James Deering in the style of an Italian Renaissance palazzo. Furnished with fine period antiques, textiles, and sculpture. Ten-acre estate features landscaped grounds, formal gardens, reflecting pools, and statuary. Now a museum of decorative arts
*Operated by Metropolitan Dade Co. Park and Recreation Dept. Open daily 10–5, Wed. 10–10; closed Christmas*

*Vizcaya*

## PALM BEACH

### WHITEHALL, 1900–1902
**Whitehall Way**
Large mansion of Standard Oil partner and Florida land developer Henry

*Whitehall*

54

Morrison Flagler; built by architects Carrère and Hastings in a Spanish motif with ground-floor rooms situated around a large indoor court. Interiors and furniture designed by William P. Stymus, Jr., of the prominent New York firm Pottier & Stymus. After many years as a hotel the mansion was converted to a museum and opened in 1960. Much of the original furniture and many works of art were reacquired. *Operated by Henry Morrison Flagler Museum. Open Tues.–Sun. 10–5; closed Christmas*

## PENSACOLA

### DOROTHY WALTON HOUSE, 1810
**221 E Zarragossa St**
White clapboard house reflects Louisiana French style with apron roof, high loft, and front and back verandas. Home of Dorothy Walton, widow of George Walton, a signer of the Declaration of Independence. Deeded to the city and moved to present site in 1966. Directly to the rear is the two-room *Moreno Cottage*, built in 1879 as a honeymoon cottage for a Spanish patriarch for one of his 27 children. *Operated by Historic Pensacola Preservation Board. Open May–Oct: daily 10–5*

### DORR HOUSE, 1871
**Adams and Church Streets**
Victorian house with high ceilings and rift pine floors reflects city's lumber boom years. Built for Clara Barkley Dorr, widow of a prominent citizen. Furnished with Victorian pieces *Operated by Pensacola Heritage Foundation. Open May–Aug: Tues.–Sun. 9:30–4:30*

### LEE HOUSE, 1866
**Alcaniz and Main Streets**
Post-Civil War house built by William Franklin Lee, engineering officer for the Confederacy. Moved to the present site in 1967 and now being restored *Operated by Pensacola Realtors Assn. Under restoration*

### ■ PENSACOLA HISTORIC DISTRICT
First permanent settlement of the city was made by the Spanish in 1698 with the establishment of a military outpost. Although the city was at various times Spanish, French, British, and American, the historic district retains the flavor of the "old city" of the first Spanish settlement. Fort San Carlos, a semicircular brick fortification built by the Spanish, is still standing.

### QUINA HOUSE, 1821
**204 S Alcaniz St**
Typical Gulf Coast architecture, featuring a double chimney in the center of the apron roof, which is supported by four hand-hewn round columns. Built by Italian-born apothecary Desiderio Quina, Sr; shown with furnishings and an herb garden. The Quina house (1845) next door is an art gallery. *Operated by Pensacola Historical Preservation Soc. Open May–Sept: Sat., Sun. 10:30–4*

## ST. AUGUSTINE

### ARRIVAS HOUSE, about 1720
**46 St. George St**
One of a complex of 18th-century homes belonging to the Avero family. Headquarters of the local restoration commission, which also operates the *De Mesa House* (about 1750), a small coquina dwelling with period furnishings on display. *Operated by Historic St. Augustine Preservation Board. Open Mon.–Sat. 9–5, Sun. 10–5*

### FATIO HOUSE, about 1798
**20 Aviles St**
Two-story house of coquina, a soft shell limestone, with red tile roof; built by Andreas Ximenes in the style of the second Spanish occupation, dating from 1783. Separate kitchen contains the only extant stone bake oven in the city. Furnished with Spanish furniture, items of local history *Operated by Soc. of Colonial Dames. Open Jan.–May 15: Thurs. 10–4*

### ■ FERNANDEZ-LLAMBIAS HOUSE, before 1763
**31 St. Francis St**
Originally a one-story coquina-and-tabby house of the Spanish colonial period and later enlarged to two stories. Occupied by settlers of Minorcan descent after 1777 and later by the Llambias family. Restored and shown with period pieces, including furnishings typical of the Minorcans *Operated by City of St. Augustine. Open first Sun. of each month 2–4*

**OLD SPANISH TREASURY [DR. PECK HOUSE], after 1702; 1837**
**143 St. George St**
Two-story house with first floor of stone built after 1702, when fire destroyed the original house built here for the Spanish royal treasurer. Purchased in 1837 by Dr. Silas Peck, who added the wooden second story; owned by his descendants until 1932. Furnished with 19th-century pieces; treasury room features Spanish treasure chest and collection of old coins
*Operated by St. Augustine Woman's Exchange. Open Mon.–Sat. 9–5*

■ **THE OLDEST HOUSE, after 1703**
**14 St. Francis St**
Built on a site occupied since the late 1500s, the house has thick coquina walls, a second story of wood, and a hipped roof. Shown with Spanish furnishings and a garden typical of the Spanish period. Adjacent is *the Tovar House* (before 1763), a museum with period furnishings and other items of local history.
*Operated by St. Augustine Historical Soc. Open daily 9–5:45*

*The Oldest House*

**RODRIGUEZ-AVECO-SANCHEZ HOUSE, 1702**
**52 St. George St**
Little stone house built by Antonio de Avero; now houses a collection of old toys from around the world
*Operated by Museum of Yesterday's Toys. Open daily 9–5*

■ **ST. AUGUSTINE HISTORIC DISTRICT**
The oldest city in U.S., first settled by the Spanish as a military base in 1565. By 1598 the street system, town plaza, and marketplace had been established. A restoration project is under way to return the old city to its colonial appearance.

**ZORAYDA CASTLE, 1885**
**83 King St**
A replica of the Alhambra in Granada, Spain; built of coquina and concrete by architect Franklyn W. Smith. Now a museum featuring an outstanding collection of European, Middle Eastern, and Oriental antiques
*Operated by Zorayda Castle. Open daily 9–6*

## ST. PETERSBURG

**GRACE C. TURNER HOUSE, 1918**
**3501 Second Ave, S**
Florida bungalow-type house; now a museum featuring Victorian furnishings. Next door is the Haas Museum, with many early American exhibits.
*Operated by St. Petersburg Historical Soc. Open Tues.–Sun. 1–5*

## SARASOTA

**CA'D'ZAN, 1925–26**
**5401 Bay Shore Rd**
Venetian Gothic *palazzo* modeled after the façade of the *Doge's Palace* in Venice; designed by architect Dwight James Baum for circus magnate John Ringling. The rose-cream stucco mansion with glazed terra cotta accents features a two-and-a-half-story inner court, spectacular grounds, and lavish furnishings.
*Operated by The Ringling Museums. Open Mon.–Fri. evgs. 9–10, Sat. 9–5, Sun. 1–5*

## TALLAHASSEE

**GOVERNOR'S MANSION, 1907**
**700 N Adams St**
Two-story frame Greek Revival mansion occupying a square block serves as the governor's residence. Renovated in 1957, the mansion is furnished with antiques mainly from the Queen Anne period.
*Operated by State of Fla. Open by appointment*

# ALBANY

## CAPTAIN SMITH HOUSE, 1860
**516 Flint Ave**
First brick house to be built in Albany, the bricks being hauled by mule wagons from Macon. Restored, the house now serves as a museum.
*Operated by Albany Area Museum. Open Mon.–Fri. 9–12, 2–5*

# ATHENS

## EDWIN KING LUMPKIN HOUSE, 1848
**973 Prince Ave**
Restored stuccoed house with a wide veranda across the front; lacy ironwork of French-Spanish flavor adorns the exterior. In January, 1891, Mary B. T. Lumpkin organized the world's first garden club in the parlor of the house.
*Operated by Young Harris Memorial Methodist Church. Open by appointment*

## FOUNDERS MEMORIAL GARDENS, 1857
**375 S Lumpkin St**
Built as a professor's home, the original kitchen and smokehouse are still standing. The house is restored and furnished with period pieces and is now state headquarters of the Garden Club of Georgia. Gardens designed and built to honor founding of the world's first garden club in Athens
*Operated by Garden Club of Ga. Open Mon.–Fri. 10–4 and by appointment*

# ATLANTA

## SWAN HOUSE [ATLANTA HISTORICAL SOC.], 1928
**3099 Andrews Dr, NW**
Italian Renaissance-style house designed by Philip Shutze, *Grand Prix de Rome* winner, for Samuel Inman. Antique furnishings, historical collections, manuscripts, and pictures
*Operated by Atlanta Historical Soc. Open Mon.–Fri. 10–3, Sun. 1–3:30*

## TULLIE SMITH HOUSE (SWAN HOUSE ESTATE), about 1835
**3099 Andrews Drive, NW**
Two-story clapboard house (with a pitched gable roof), one of the earliest in the Atlanta area. Moved from its original site, the Tullie Smith House

is to become a museum depicting early life in the Atlanta vicinity.
*Operated by Atlanta Historical Soc. Restoration in progress*

## ■ WREN'S NEST (JOEL CHANDLER HARRIS HOUSE), about 1880–85
**1050 Gordon St, SW**
Gray frame Victorian house of irregular shape, numerous gables, and fancy scrollwork, the home of the creator of *Uncle Remus and Brer Rabbit* and other folk tales. Harris named the house for a wren that built its nest in his mailbox (he built another to avoid disturbing her). Original editions of his works, personal possessions, and letters are displayed.
*Operated by Joel Chandler Harris Memorial Assn. Open Mon.–Sat. 9:30–5, Sun. 2–5*

# ATLANTA VICINITY

## STONE MOUNTAIN PLANTATION
**Stone Mountain Memorial Park, U.S. Route 78**
Several ante-bellum buildings moved from various parts of the state to re-create a self-sustaining plantation complex. The *Dickey House*, or "big house," which was built in the 1840s at Dickey, Georgia, is especially noteworthy. It was occupied by descendants of the original owners until it was bought and moved here in 1961; furnishings are of the 18th century. The *Kingston House*, built in 1845, represents an overseer's house, although when it was built it was the main house on a several-hundred-acre plantation near Kingston, Georgia. Another structure, the *Thornton House*, is part of the plantation complex although it is of an earlier period, about 1790. This is one of the few remaining 18th-century houses in Georgia.
*Operated by Stone Mountain Land. Open June–Labor Day: daily 10–9. After Labor Day–May: 10–5:30*

# AUGUSTA

## ■ MACKAY HOUSE (WHITE-HOUSE), about 1760
**1822 Broad St**
Restored house, famous for the battle fought here in 1780 between British

forces, under Col. Thomas Brown, and Revolutionary forces, under Col. Elijah Clarke, of Augusta. After the battle 13 patriots were hanged from the stairway. Furnished with 18th- and early 19th-century pieces; the second floor serves as a museum of the Revolution, with exhibits appropriate to the southern involvement in the war.
*Operated by Ga. Historical Comm. Open Apr.–Sept: daily 10–5:30. Oct.– Mar: daily 10–5*

*Mackay House*

## MEADOW GARDEN (GEORGE WALTON HOUSE), before 1800
**2216 Wrightsboro Rd**
Late 18th-century plantation "plain-style" white clapboard house of one and one-half stories. Associated with George Walton, a signer of the Declaration of Independence. Furnishings include a rocking chair used by George Washington.
*Operated by Daughters of the American Revolution. Open daily by appointment*

## WARE'S FOLLY [GERTRUDE HERBERT INSTITUTE OF ART], 1818
**506 Telfair St**
Georgian-style house with Adam influence which now houses the Gertrude Herbert Institute of Art with offices and galleries. Original cost of $40,000; one room furnished
*Operated by Gertrude Herbert Institute of Art. Open Mon.–Fri. 10–5*

## CALHOUN VICINITY

■ **NEW ECHOTA, 1825**
**Georgia Route 225, three miles east of Calhoun**
A project is under way to reconstruct and/or restore the various buildings of the Cherokee capital of 1825. New Echota was named for Chota, an "old beloved town," in Tennessee. Of the buildings reconstructed is the Print Shop, where the Cherokees established a national press and newspaper in 1826. Another is the Court House, where the Cherokee supreme court met to hear cases appealed from Cherokee circuit and district courts. The home of Samuel A. Worcester, who came to New Echota in 1827 as a missionary sent by the American Board of Commissioners for Foreign Missions, is also here.
*Operated by Ga. Historical Comm. Open May–Oct: daily 9–5:30. Nov.– Apr: daily 9–5*

## CARROLLTON

■ **BONNER-SHARP-GUNN HOUSE, 1844**
**West Georgia College Campus**
Greek Revival-style house (originally a farmhouse) with a two-story portico. The house has served as a dormitory, dean's residence, faculty residence, and offices. It is currently being used as a center for student affairs.
*Operated by West Ga. College. Open Mon.–Fri. 8–5 and by appointment*

## COLUMBUS

■ **COLUMBUS HISTORIC DISTRICT**
The historic district of Columbus includes 20 blocks and nine partial blocks of the original plan of the city, which was first surveyed in 1828. The district contains about 612 structures, ranging from Georgian cottages to Greek Revival and Gothic Revival homes and buildings.

**RANKIN HOUSE, mid-19th century**
**1440 Second Ave**
Brick house with iron grillwork on the lower veranda; valued at $18,000 in 1898 and considered the finest in Columbus. The house was built by James Rankin, member of a family prominent in the cultural, economic, and social life of the city. The first floor is restored as a house museum; furnishings are of the 1850–70 period.
*Operated by Historic Columbus Foundation. Open Mon.–Fri. 10–4*

■ **WALKER-PETERS-LANGDON HOUSE, 1828**
**716 Broadway**
Restored one-story Federal-style cottage, clapboarded, with brick foundation and chimneys. Originally built by the wealthy Walker family, it remained in the possession of their descendants until 1967. Now a house museum
*Operated by Historic Columbus Foundation. Open Mon.–Fri. 10–4*

## CRAWFORDVILLE

■ **LIBERTY HALL (ALEXANDER H. STEPHENS HOME), 1834**
**Georgia Route 12**
Ante-bellum home of the Vice President of the Confederacy, Alexander Stephens, one of the South's great statesmen, U.S. congressman, and Georgia's governor. Stephens came here to live and study law in 1834 and purchased the property in 1845 when the owner died; he remodeled the house in the seventies. It has been restored, and furnishings include Victorian period pieces, many of Stephens' belongings, and reproductions. Now part of the Alexander H. Stephens Memorial State Park
*Operated by Ga. Dept. of State Parks. Open Tues.–Sun. 9–5*

## INDIAN SPRINGS

**INDIAN CHIEF WILLIAM McINTOSH HOME, completed 1824**
**Route 23**
Two-story frame house, with handmade brick chimneys, built by the chief of the Creek nation. The treaty between the Creek nation and the Federal government, ceding to the whites the lands west of the Flint River to the Mississippi, was signed here. Furnished in the period of the house; collection of Indian artifacts
*Operated by Atlanta Museum. Open Mar.–Nov: daily 9–5*

## JEKYLL ISLAND

**JEKYLL ISLAND VILLAGE**
Exclusive winter resort for American millionaires from 1899 to 1942. Nine "cottages" once belonging to the Rockefellers, Goulds, Morgans, Vanderbilts, Pulitzers, and Astors may be visited. The Rockefeller cottage is being restored as a museum.
*Operated by Jekyll Island State Park Authority. Restoration in progress*

## LA GRANGE

**BELLEVUE, before 1854**
**204 McLendon Ave**
Stately Greek Revival mansion, the home of Benjamin Hill, member of the Georgia legislature. Although against secession, he felt he had to support the Confederacy, and Jefferson Davis and other important Confederates were visitors here. After the war he became a U.S. congressman and later a senator. Interior of the house noted for spacious rooms, walnut stairway, and black Carrara mantels
*Operated by La Grange Women's Club. Open by appointment*

## LUMPKIN

**BEDINGFIELD INN, 1836**
**Town Square**
Plantation "plain-style" house with Greek Revival-style details. Built by Dr. Bryan Bedingfield, it was the center of commercial and community activity during the 19th century. It served as an inn, stagecoach stop, and private residence. Restored as a stagecoach stop of the 1830s
*Operated by Stewart Co. Historical Soc. Open Sat. 9–5, Sun. 1–5, and by appointment*

**WESTVILLE HISTORIC DISTRICT**
**one-half mile from Lumpkin**
Westville is operated as a 19th-century farm village, with quilting, pottery, brick masonry, carpentry, and blacksmithing performed as they were in the 1850s. The village is being reconstructed on a 58-acre tract of land with 40 buildings planned and 18 already developed. Only restored original buildings and homes are used.
*Operated by Westville Historic Handicrafts. Open Wed.–Sat. 11–5, Sun. 1–5*

## MACON

**HAY HOUSE, 1855–60**
**1934 Georgia Ave**
Mr. William B. Johnston, a wealthy

GEORGIA

merchant, and his bride returned from their honeymoon in Italy to build this 24-room brick mansion of modified Italian Renaissance design. Most of the materials used were imported from that country, and the mansion's interior boasts 19 Carrara marble mantels, frescoed ceilings, crystal chandeliers, and mahogany and rosewood paneling. Art treasures, period furniture, tapestries, lavish floor coverings and decorations are in profusion throughout. *Operated by P. L. Hay Foundation. Open Tues.–Sat. 10–5, Sun. 2–5*

*Hay House*

### OLD CANNON BALL HOUSE, 1853
**856 Mulberry St**
Ante-bellum Greek Revival-style mansion built by Judge Asa Holt. It has been known as the Cannon Ball House since, according to tradition, it was struck by a cannon ball during a battle in 1864. Restored and furnished with antiques dating to the ante-bellum period
*Operated by United Daughters of the Confederacy. Open Tues.–Sun. 2–5*

### MIDWAY

### MIDWAY COLONIAL MUSEUM,
**18th century**
**U.S. Route 17**
Raised cottage-style house, typical of those built on the coast in the 18th century. The museum, founded in 1754, contains furnished rooms, a library, and numerous exhibits revealing the history of the Midway community.
*Operated by Ga. Historical Comm. Open May–Oct: Tues.–Sat. 10–5:30, Sun. 2-5:30. Nov.–Apr: Tues.–Sat. 10–5, Sun. 2–5*

### MILLEDGEVILLE

### ■ OLD GOVERNOR'S MANSION, 1838
**Clark Street**
This fine classical revival mansion was based on the designs of Andrea Palladio. It served as the executive mansion of eight successive Georgia governors until the capital was moved to Atlanta in 1868. After 1890 it was the home of the presidents of Georgia State College for Women. English Regency, French Empire, and American Federal furnishings
*Operated by Ga. College at Milledgeville. Open Tues.–Sat. 10–4, Sun. 2–5*

### SANFORD HOUSE, 1820
**West Hancock and North Jackson Streets**
Federal or plantation "plain-style" house with a two-story portico and an open veranda across the back. Operated as an inn in its earliest days; the Sanford family moved here after 1850. The Old Capitol Historical Soc. purchased the house in 1966 and moved it from its original site here.
*Operated by Old Capitol Historical Soc. Restoration in progress*

### MILLEN VICINITY

### JONES PLANTATION, 1762; 1770; 1847
**Georgia Route 7**
Rambling plantation house (with Greek Revival and Victorian additions), which may be the oldest in Georgia lived in continuously by the family that built it. Numerous weathered outbuildings remain on the property, including a blacksmith shop and a dining room.
*Private. Open by appointment*

### ROSWELL

### BARRINGTON HALL, 1842
**U.S. Route 19, north of Atlanta**
Magnificent Greek Revival-style building built by pioneer textile manufacturer and founder of Roswell, Barrington King. Fluted Doric columns grace the exterior as well as the interior hallway. The house contains original antique furnishings and Civil War documents.
*Operated by Miss Katherine Simpson. Open by appointment*

# SAVANNAH

## DAVENPORT HOUSE, between 1815 and 1820
### 324 E State St, Columbia Square

Excellent example of late Georgian colonial architecture, built by Isaiah Davenport, son of the noted English potter. The elliptical double stairway, with its delicate wrought-iron banisters and beautiful fan-lighted doorway, enhances the severe simplicity of the house. Badly neglected as the city expanded outward, the house has been restored to its original elegance. Furnishings include heirlooms of the Davenport family and feature a collection of antique china.

*Operated by Historic Savannah Foundation. Open Mon.–Sat. 10–5*

## LOW HOUSE [COLONIAL DAMES HOUSE], about 1848
### 329 Abercorn St

Andrew Low, an Anglo-American cotton merchant, built this Victorian house of stuccoed brick, with wrought-iron railings on the front and side balconies. Jalousied porches, reflecting West Indian influence, overlook a brick-walled garden in the rear. The Girl Scout movement was founded in this house in 1912 by Juliette Gordon Low, the daughter-in-law of Andrew Low. Well-proportioned rooms, with elaborately decorated ceilings and carved woodwork; furnishings in keeping with the style of the house

*Operated by Soc. of Colonial Dames. Open Mon.–Sat. 10:30–5; closed national holidays*

## OWENS-THOMAS HOUSE, 1816–19
### 124 Abercorn St on Oglethorpe Square

This imposing mansion is considered by some authorities to be the finest architectural example of the English Regency style in America. Designed by 21-year-old architect William Jay in 1816, a year before he came to this country from England, and built for Richard Richardson, a wealthy merchant-banker from New Orleans. George Welchman Owens purchased the house in 1830 after Richardson lost his fortune in the depression that began in 1820. The Owens family owned and occupied the house for 120 years. Now a house museum furnished with American and English antiques

*Operated by Telfair Academy of Arts and Sciences. Open Sun., Mon. 2–5, Tues.–Sat. 10–5; closed September*

*Owens-Thomas House*

## ■ SAVANNAH HISTORIC DISTRICT
### bounded by Bay, East Broad, Gwinett, and West Broad Streets

Significant area of the city which retains much of the original plan of James Oglethorpe, founder of Georgia and of Savannah, its first settlement. Many buildings of architectural merit built between 1816 and 1825 by William Jay, the English architect, may be seen.

## ■ WAYNE-GORDON HOUSE (JULIETTE GORDON LOW BIRTHPLACE), 1818
### 10 Oglethorpe Ave, E

Elegant English Regency-style house designed by William Jay of London, who was now practicing his art in Savannah and Charleston. Built for James Wayne, who later became a congressman and an associate justice of the U.S. Supreme Court. Wayne sold the property to William Gordon I in 1831. When his second daughter, "Daisy," was to be married in 1886 to William M. Low, William Gordon II added a piazza and top floor, designed by N.Y. architect Detlef Lienau, a founder of the American Institute of Architects. Juliette ("Daisy") Gordon Low was born in the house, and it is now a museum dedicated to her and to the Girl Scouts of the U.S.A., which she founded in 1912. Furnishings of the house are Gordon family pieces and antiques of the period of the house.

*Operated by Girl Scouts of the U.S.A. Open Mon.–Sat. 9–4:30, Sun. 2–4:30; closed Thanksgiving, Christmas, and New Year's Day*

**GEORGIA**

## SPRING PLACE

■ **CHIEF VANN HOUSE, 1804–5**
**U.S. Route 76**
Restored Federal-style mansion built
by James Vann, son of a Scottish trader
and a Cherokee. Vann's son, Joseph,
and his family were forced to move
west with the dispossessed Cherokee
tribe when the Federal government
confiscated their lands in 1834. A
handsome building, the bricks, nails,
and hinges are said to have been hand-
wrought on the property. Interior
features are an elaborately carved,
cantilevered stairway and hand carving with the Cherokee rose a pre-
dominating motif. Many relics of the
Vann family are on exhibit.
*Operated by Ga. Historical Comm.
Open Apr.–Sept: daily 10–5:30. Oct.–
Mar: daily 10–5*

## THOMASVILLE

■ **LAPHAM-SCARBOROUGH
HOUSE, about 1885**
**626 N Dawson St**
Three-story Victorian mansion with
two octagonal bays separated by an
octagonal porch. Built at a time when
Thomasville was known as a resort
center for wealthy northerners; plans
are to open the house as a museum
depicting late Victorian life
*Operated by Ga. Historical Comm.
Restoration in progress*

## TOCCOA

■ **TRAVELERS REST (JARRETT
MANOR), 1775–84**
**U.S. Route 123, six miles east of Toccoa**
Large, two-story frame house built by
Major Jessie Walton, whose family
was massacred by Indians; it then
passed to Devereaux Jarrett, whose
descendants owned the property until 1955. The hand-hewn clapboards
have never been painted, and the
building is said to be the oldest in
northeast Georgia. It served for many
years as a fort, stagecoach inn, and
post office but has now been restored.
Among its furnishings is the register
signed by prominent guests.
*Operated by Ga. Historical Comm.
Open May–Oct: Tues.–Sat. 9–5:30,
Sun. 2–5:30. Nov.–Apr: Tues.–Sat.
9–5, Sun. 2–5*

## VALDOSTA

**THE CRESCENT (COL. WILLIAM
S. WEST HOUSE), 1898**
**904 N Patterson St**
Built by Col. West, a lawyer, lumberman, and U.S. senator, this semicircu-
lar-shaped mansion, with its Ionic
columned portico, was saved from destruction in 1951 by a house-to-house
campaign that raised enough money
to purchase it. Now restored to its
original splendor, it serves as one of
the South's finest garden centers.
*Operated by Valdosta Garden Club.
Open Fri. afternoon*

## WASHINGTON

■ **BARNETT-SLATON HOUSE
[WASHINGTON-WILKES
HISTORICAL MUSEUM], 1835–36**
**308 E Robert Toombs Ave**
Built by Albert Gallatin Semmes, this
rambling 18-room frame house has
been enlarged over the years; it has
13 doors that open to the outside.
Civil War relics and Ku Klux Klan
regalia of the Reconstruction era are
exhibited; mid-1800s furnishings
*Operated by Ga. Historical Comm.
Open winter: Mon.–Wed., Fri., Sat.
9–5, Sun. 2–5. Summer: Mon.–Wed.,
Fri., Sat. 9–6, Sun. 2–6*

**THE CEDARS, 1793; about 1803**
**201 Sims St**
A 20-room villa-style mansion, the
oldest part of which was built by Anthony Poulain, a French *émigré* whose
son was Lafayette's personal physician. Francis Colley lived here from
1838 to 1859, and his descendants
have occupied the house to the present
time. Victorian furnishings
*Operated by Mrs. M. S. DeVaughn and
Mrs. W. R. Latimer, owners. Open by
appointment*

## WAYNESBORO

**WAYNESBORO HISTORICAL
MUSEUM, before 1850**
**U.S. Route 25 at Waynesboro**
Restored ante-bellum house with ex-
hibits commemorating the early his-
tory of Burke County, one of Georgia's
original counties
*Operated by Ga. Historical Comm.
Open Tues.–Sat. 9–5, Sun. 2–5*

# ISLAND OF HAWAII
## HILO

### LYMAN HOUSE, 1839; 1854
### 276 Haili St

Two-story frame house with wide verandas built by the Rev. and Mrs. David Belden Lyman, who came to Hawaii in 1832 as part of the fifth group of missionaries sent out from Boston. The original steep thatch roof was replaced in 1854 by a galvanized iron roof from England supported by hand-hewn native timbers; the floors and doors are of uneven-width planks of native koa. Occupied by the Lyman family for 90 years, it is now a memorial museum that vividly pictures the way of life of the early Hawaiians and the missionaries. Many Polynesian, Oriental, and New England artifacts on display
*Operated by Lyman House Memorial Museum. Open Mon.–Sat. 10–4, Sun. 1–4*

*Lyman House*

## KAILUA VILLAGE

### HULIHEE PALACE, 1837–38; 1884
### Alii Drive

Two-story vacation residence built of coral mortar, lava rock, ohia and koa wood; originally the home of John Adams Kuakini, brother of Queen Kaahumanu – the favorite wife of King Kamehameha I. King Kalakaua acquired it for his "Summer Palace" in 1884; he stuccoed the exterior, plastered the interior, and widened the verandas. Now maintained as a museum preserving mementos of old Hawaiian life, such as the Hawaiian feather cape, as well as period furnishings and portraits
*Operated by Daughters of Hawaii. Open Mon.–Fri. 9–4, Sat. 9–12*

# ISLAND OF KAUAI
## HANALEI VILLAGE

### WAIOLI MISSION HOUSE, 1836–37

Rev. W. P. Alexander laid up the sandstone chimney himself on the mission house after living in a grass house for two years with his wife and small son. The Edward Johnsons came as schoolteachers and together with the Alexanders planted sugar cane and cotton to help pay for a school, church, and bell. The Old Waioli Church (1841), with long sloping roof and wide eaves, was restored in 1921 together with the old home, and both were then opened to the public.
*Operated by Waioli Hawaiian Church. Open when caretaker is on premises*

# ISLAND OF MAUI
## LAHAINA

### ■ LAHAINA HISTORIC DISTRICT

As the former capital of Maui, Lahaina was intermittently the residence of Hawaiian kings. It was also a center of activity for American missionaries, who left important architectural influences. But it was most prominently associated with the American whaling industry in the Pacific, a trading activity that influenced the Americanization and subsequent annexation of Hawaii. It still preserves the atmosphere of a mid-19th-century seaport.

### THE REV. DWIGHT BALDWIN HOUSE, 1834; 1840; 1849
### Town Square

Standing on the town square facing the harbor is the sturdy coral-and-stone home with hand-hewn timbers of missionary-physician the Rev. Baldwin, formerly of Durham, Connecticut. Lahaina was a major whaling port, and the Baldwins were involved in the mighty struggles between commercial and religious forces to gain the support of the royalty. As a practicing doctor the reverend helped save the islands from the great smallpox epidemic of 1853. The home has been restored (with furnishings of the 1850s) as a tribute to the community service of the New England missionaries.
*Operated by Lahaina Restoration Foundation. Open daily*

## WAILUKU

### "HALE HOIKEIKE" (BAILEY HOME), 1833–50
Iao Road
A stone structure, the two earlier sections of which were built by the pastor of the Wailuku Church, Jonathan Greene. In 1842 and then in 1850 Edward Bailey, principal of the Wailuku Female Seminary and later operator of a sugar mill, who became well known as a landscape painter, added a connecting section and the entire third floor. It is now a museum, with rooms devoted to displays from different periods of Maui's history, including artifacts from Hawaii's royal and missionary periods as well as from the stone-age culture prior to the arrival of the white man, such as shell and stone implements.
*Operated by Maui Historical Soc. Open Mon.–Sat. 10–3:30*

## ISLAND OF OAHU

## HONOLULU

### E. FAXON BISHOP HOME, [COMMUNITY CHURCH OF HONOLULU], before 1902
234 Nuuanu Ave
An irregular-plan Victorian home, with Georgian architectural features executed in wood, built in the Nuuanu Valley by the Bishop family. In recent years this lovely old building has been remodeled to serve as the temporary home of two small colleges; now it houses a church.
*Operated by Community Church of Honolulu. Open by appointment*

### FRED L. WALDRON HOME, [BAPTIST STUDENT CENTER], 1905
2042 Vancouver Dr
Large Edwardian home built in the Manoa Valley by merchant Fred L. Waldron. The building retains its exterior integrity despite remodeling for student housing; it features an undulating façade with a wealth of detail, including a central projecting section topped by a pediment, elaborate scrollwork, and Palladian windows. Inside, the fanciful glass lights, handsome central hall with Corinthian pilasters, and finely turned newels on

the staircase attest to its former grandeur.
*Operated by University of Hawaii. Open by appointment*

### ■ IOLANI PALACE, 1879–82
364 S King St
Stone Italian Renaissance-style palace with double porticoes on all four sides, the only royal palace in the U.S., constructed by King Kalakaua on the site of an earlier Iolani Palace. The original design by T.J. Baker was changed several times by the subsequent superintendents C.S. Wall and Isaac Moore. Used as a royal residence by Kalakaua and then by his sister Queen Liliuokalani until the monarchy was overthrown in 1893. It has been the seat of governmental authority for the provisional government, the Republic of Hawaii, the Territory of Hawaii, and now the State of Hawaii. On the grounds still stand Kalakaua's coronation pavilion, now the bandstand, and the rebuilt Iolani barracks.
*Operated by State of Hawaii. Open during office hours*

*Iolani Palace*

### ■ MISSION HOUSES, 1821–41
King and Kawaiahao Streets
Sent by the American Board of Commissioners for Foreign Missions from Boston in 1819 by way of Cape Horn, the pioneer company of 14 American missionaries and five children landed in Hawaii in 1820. Just beyond the Kawaiahao Church are the three mission houses that served as their homes: *Oldest Frame House* (1821), the oldest of its kind in the Islands—its timbers were cut and fitted in Boston—replaced the original grass houses on the site and sheltered many of the early

missionaries. *Printing House* (1841) was built of coral blocks as a two-room bedroom annex to the frame house. It was believed to be the early printing house, and a replica of the original 1820 Ramage press turns out copies of the mission tracts. *Chamberlain House* (1831), built of native coral blocks and white pine from Maine, served as a storehouse for mission goods and as a home for the business agent Levi Chamberlain. Furnishings and memorabilia of the missionary pioneers on exhibit
*Operated by Hawaiian Mission Children's Soc. Open Mon.–Fri. 9–4, Sat., holidays 9–1; closed Thanksgiving, Christmas, and New Year's Day*

## QUEEN EMMA SUMMER PALACE (HANAIAKAMALAMA), about 1847
**2913 Pali Highway**
Lovely white frame house with large rooms and wide veranda—originally built by American merchant and minister to the Hawaiian Kingdom (1869–77) Henry A. Peirce—used by gracious Queen Emma (1836–85), consort of King Kamehameha IV, as a cool summer retreat and social center. Restored as a museum devoted to the artifacts of this beloved royal couple; antique furnishings
*Operated by Daughters of Hawaii. Open Mon.–Fri. 9–4, Sat. 9–12*

## ROBERT LOUIS STEVENSON'S GRASS HOUSE, 1880s
**3016 Oahu Ave**
Grass shack that was once the property of Hawaiian royalty. Here the famed author made his home in 1880 for six months as the guest of Princess Kaiulani. The grass roof is replaced every four years, and period artifacts are on display.
*Operated by Waioli Tea Room. Open daily 8–4*

## WALTER F. DILLINGHAM HOME (LA PIETRA), 1921
**2933 Poni Moi Rd**
Stucco Mediterranean mansion, with red tile roof and ceramic tile floors, on the slopes of Diamond Head overlooking Waikiki Beach; designed by Chicago architect David Adler for the prosperous descendant of an early missionary family. Set in lovely gardens, this composite of several Italian villas is built around a central court lined with arcades. Interiors have been extensively renovated to serve its present purpose as a girls' school.
*Operated by Hawaii School for Girls. Open Mon.–Fri. 8–4, weekends by appointment*

*La Pietra*

## WASHINGTON PLACE, 1846
**320 S Beretania St**
Large two-story colonial mansion, the official governor's residence since 1922, originally built by American sea captain John Dominis, who disappeared on a trading voyage to China in 1847. His wife rented a suite of rooms to the American commissioner Anthony TenEyck, who established the U.S. legation there and in 1848 officially named it "Washington Place," in honor of George Washington's birthday. The captain's son, John Owens Dominis, married Lydia K.P. Kapaakea, who later became Queen Liliuokalani. Upon her retirement from public life the queen lived in state at Washington Place receiving visitors from around the world. After her death in 1917 the property was purchased by the Territory of Hawaii to serve as the executive mansion, which it has remained from 1922 to the present.
*Operated by State of Hawaii. Open on special occasions*

## KANEOHE

### VILLAGE OF ULU MAU
Replica of an old Hawaiian village where islanders demonstrate examples of early arts and crafts
*Operated by Village of Ulu Mau. Open daily 9:30–4:30*

## BOISE

### COSTON AND PEARCE CABINS, 1863
**Julia Davis Park**
These two pioneer cabins were built the year Idaho was organized as a separate territory. I.N. Coston's cabin, made of driftwood held together with pegs, and Ira B. Pearce's cabin, made of logs transported by oxen from the mountains, were both moved from their original sites to the park. An adobe house, built in the 1860s, has recently been moved to the park. Although none of the structures are open to the public, plans are being made to restore and furnish them.

### GOVERNOR'S HOUSE, 1914
**1805 N 21 St**
Two-story frame house in use as the governor's residence since 1947. This ten-room house will soon be replaced by a more elaborate dwelling.
*Operated by State of Idaho. Open by appointment*

### ■ MOORE-DE LAMAR HOUSE, 1879
**807 Grove St**
Large brick house, topped by a mansard roof, built by Christopher W. Moore, banker and businessman. In 1891 Joseph R. De Lamar, millionaire friend of President Benjamin Harrison, purchased the house, which was converted into a hotel in 1905. Called the De Lamar Hotel, it can be viewed from the outside.

*Moore-De Lamar House*

## LEWISTON

### LUNA HOUSE MUSEUM, about 1910
**310 Third St**
This turn-of-the-century stucco house stands on the site of the Luna House, a long-gone pioneer hotel and courthouse. The present museum, which takes its name from the old hotel, features a collection of articles of local historical interest.
*Operated by Luna House Historical Soc. Open Tues.–Sat. 1–5, Sun. 2–4*

## LEWISTON VICINITY

### ■ Spalding Memorial Park
**11 miles east of Lewiston**
In 1836 the Rev. Henry Spalding established a settlement here among the Nez Perce; he built a church and school, ran a gristmill, and operated a printing press. The log cabin, which houses a fine collection of Indian exhibits, is said to have been built by him but probably dates from a later era. This park is one of the sites in Nez Perce National Historical Park.
*Operated by National Park Service*

## MOSCOW

### WILLIAM J. McCONNELL HOUSE, 1881–86
**110 S Adams St**
William J. McConnell, Idaho's first senator and third governor, built this house. In 1966 Dr. Frederic Church of the University of Idaho, Moscow, willed the house to the county for use as a museum and meeting place. The museum features furnishings from 1871 to the World War I era.
*Operated by Latah Co. Pioneer Historical Museum Assn. Open by appointment*

## NAMPA

### CLEO'S FERRY MUSEUM, 1862
**311 14 Ave, S**
This adobe house was in use for 58 years as the home of the ferry master who operated his boat across the Snake River at Walter's Ferry. It was also used as a hotel for travelers. Restored and now used as a museum, with antique furnishings and other displays
*Operated by Cleo Swayne. Open by appointment*

## ARCOLA
### ROCKOME GARDENS, 1920
**Route 2**
Simple, two-story frame house constructed by the Amish. It was occupied until 1963, when the house was restored and furnished to represent how the Amish people live. Interesting rockwork and flower gardens, an Indian museum, and a blacksmith and harness shop may also be seen.
*Operated by Rockome Gardens. Open May-Oct: 10-5*

## AURORA
### WILLIAM TANNER HOME, 1856–57
**Oak Avenue and Cedar Street**
A 17-room Victorian mansion built by William Tanner, an early settler and merchant, and occupied by his descendants until 1934. The house now serves as a museum, with two rooms, the parlor and a bedroom, displayed as they were originally. Exhibits include pioneer portraits, early furniture, Indian artifacts, and a collection of local historical material.
*Operated by Aurora Historical Museum. Open Wed., Sun. 2–4:30, and by appointment*

## BISHOP HILL
### ■ BISHOP HILL HISTORIC DISTRICT, 1846
Communal settlement established by a group of Swedish religious dissenters led by Erik Janson, who emigrated from Sweden following a break with the established church. The community prospered for a brief period, until internal squabbling led to the murder of Janson. After several years of mismanagement by trustees and religious disagreement among the members of the community, the venture split into factions, and by 1861–62 the idea of communism was abandoned. The Old Colony Church, built in 1848, has an outstanding collection of early American primitive paintings.

## BLOOMINGTON
### DAVID DAVIS MANSION, 1870–72
**100 E Monroe St**
A two-story Victorian mansion of yellow brick designed by the architect Alfred H. Piquenard for Judge David Davis, a close friend of Abraham Lincoln. Notable features include a three-story mansard-roofed tower over the main entrance, generously proportioned rooms and halls, elaborate stencil-painted wall decorations, and eight Italian marble fireplaces. On the grounds are a small formal garden, stables, carriage houses, and other outbuildings of the Davis farm.
*Operated by Ill. State Historical Library. Open Tues.–Sun. 1–5; closed Thanksgiving, Christmas, and New Year's Day*

## CAHOKIA
### CAHOKIA COURTHOUSE STATE MEMORIAL, about 1737
**off Route 3, south of East St. Louis**
Pioneer house of vertical log construction, the oldest private dwelling in the state, built by Jean Baptiste Saucier. Having served as a home for half a century, it was purchased in 1793 for use as a courthouse and jail. In 1904 the building was dismantled and moved to St. Louis, Missouri, for display at the Louisiana Purchase Exposition. After the fair it was moved to Jackson Park in Chicago, and finally, in 1938, it was moved back to its original site and reconstructed on its old foundations. On display are artifacts found during excavation.
*Operated by State of Ill. Open daily 9–5; closed Thanksgiving, Christmas, and New Year's Day*

*Cahokia Courthouse*

## CAIRO
### ■ MAGNOLIA MANOR (CHARLES A. GALIGHER HOUSE), 1869–72
**2700 Washington Ave**
Italianate house built by merchant

Charles A. Galigher. This show place, which was the scene of a reception for President and Mrs. Ulysses S. Grant in 1880, was built at a time when Cairo expected to surpass Chicago as an industrial center. The house is furnished with Victorian antiques, some of which are original to the house.
*Operated by Cairo Historical Assn. Open daily 9–5*

## CARMI

### ROBINSON-STEWART HOUSE, about 1814
**110 N Main Cross St**
One of the oldest structures in the state, this was originally a log cabin of two rooms and a loft. It was built by John Craw and served as a courthouse for several years. Later it was the home of Gen. John M. Robinson, a U.S. senator from 1830 to 1841, and during the period of his residence clapboard siding and wings were added to the house. Now restored with early 19th-century furnishings, some of which were brought from the East when Gen. Robinson was serving in the Senate.
*Operated by White Co. Historical Soc. Open Mon.–Fri. 1–4, Sat. 9–4*

*Lincoln Log Cabin*

## CHARLESTON VICINITY

### LINCOLN LOG CABIN STATE PARK
**between Illinois Routes 16 and 121**
Some 86 acres contain the reconstructed, furnished cabin of Thomas and Sarah Bush Johnston Lincoln, Abraham Lincoln's father and stepmother, as well as their graves at nearby Shiloh cemetery and *Moore House*, home of Lincoln's stepsister, Mrs. Ruben Moore. This house now serves as a museum.
*Operated by Ill. Dept. of Conservation. Open—Lincoln Log Cabin: daily*

*9–5. Moore House: summer: daily 9–5 and by appointment*

## CHICAGO

■ **ALBERT F. MADLENER HOUSE, 1902**
**4 West Burton St**
Severe, cubical town house designed in the tradition of a Florentine *palazzo* by Richard E. Schmidt for the Madlener family. The interior is restored and remodeled.
*Operated by Graham Foundation for Advanced Studies in the Fine Arts. Open by appointment*

### CHICAGO HISTORICAL SOC.
**North Avenue at Clark Street**
Replica of a two-room French trader's home of the period from 1723 to 1765, with rare furnishings from the French provinces. The gallery across the front of the house is an architectural feature brought from Haiti, where the ships stopped on the way to New Orleans.
*Operated by Soc. of Colonial Dames. Open Mon.–Sat. 9:30–4:30, Sun. 12:30–5:30*

### FRANK LLOYD WRIGHT HOUSE AND STUDIO, 1889–95
**951 Chicago Ave**
House in which Frank Lloyd Wright and his wife lived for several years. The house was built over a period of six years and shows the development of Wright's architectural style during this period. This is one of the only two Wright houses open to the public in Chicago; tours conducted by students
*Operated by Mr. and Mrs. Clyde W. Nookers, owners. Open Wed.–Sat. 10–5*

■ **FREDERICK C. ROBIE HOUSE, 1908–9**
**5757 Woodlawn Ave**
Prairie-style house designed by Frank Lloyd Wright and considered to be one of his finest earlier designs. The Robie house is the forerunner of the modern split-level dwelling. It now houses the Adlai E. Stevenson Institute of International Affairs.
*Operated by Adlai E. Stevenson Institute of International Affairs. Open by appointment*

### ■ HULL HOUSE, 1856
**800 S Halsted St, on Chicago Circle**
Two-story brick building built by Charles Hull, a Chicago businessman. The structure was converted into a settlement house by Jane Addams, pioneer social worker and the first American woman to win the Nobel Prize for peace. Restored; memorabilia of Jane Addams and her awards exhibited
*Operated by University of Ill. Foundation. Open Mon.–Fri. 9–5, Sat. 10–3, Sun., holidays 12–4*

### ■ JOHN J. GLESSNER HOUSE, 1886
**1800 S Prairie Ave**
A 35-room Romanesque-style house, the only remaining building in Chicago built by Henry H. Richardson and considered to be one of his finest works. A museum, library, and information center on Chicago architecture are now maintained by the Chicago School of Architecture Foundation in the building.
*Operated by Chicago School of Architecture Foundation. Open Tues., Thurs., Sat. 10–2*

### ■ PULLMAN HISTORIC DISTRICT, 1880s
A grandiose experiment in town planning initiated by George M. Pullman, inventor and manufacturer of the Pullman sleeping car. A group of experts were hired to build a model settlement within the municipality of Hyde Park for the employees of Pullman's plant. In 1894 the Illinois supreme court found that the company was exceeding its rights in leasing houses to its workers, and the cottages and apartments passed into private ownership. There are many fine old houses and public buildings still standing to give evidence of the proprietary utopia that briefly flourished here.

## ELLIS GROVE VICINITY

### ■ PIERRE MENARD HOUSE, about 1802
**Fort Kaskaskia State Park**
Situated at the foot of the hill on which Fort Kaskaskia stood is this beautiful example of a large French colonial Louisiana-type plantation house, the only surviving example in the area.

*Pierre Menard Home*

Many original furnishings exhibited.
*Operated by Ill. Dept. of Conservation. Open daily 9–5; closed Thanksgiving, Christmas, and New Year's Day*

## EVANSTON

### CHARLES G. DAWES HOUSE, 1894
**225 Greenwood St**
Home from 1909 to 1951 of Gen. Charles Gates Dawes, winner of the Nobel Prize for peace and Vice President of the U.S. under Calvin Coolidge. The house now contains exhibits pertaining to Evanston history and is the headquarters of the Evanston Historical Soc. and the Junior League.
*Operated by Northwestern University. Open Mon., Tues., Thurs., Fri. 1–4:30, Sat. 9–12; closed holidays*

### ■ REST COTTAGE (FRANCES WILLARD HOUSE), 1865
**1730 Chicago Ave**
Victorian Gothic cottage built by Josiah and Mary Willard, parents of Frances E. Willard, world-famed educator, advocate of woman suffrage, and crusader for temperance and social reforms. It was due to the publicity attending her efforts against the social evils of liquor that the temperance movement attained national significance. The house is furnished with many of Miss Willard's belongings and serves as the headquarters of the National Woman's Christian Temperance Union, of which she was the president.
*Operated by National Woman's Christian Temperance Union. Open Mon.– Fri. 9–12, 1:30–4:30, Sat., Sun., holidays by appointment*

## FREEPORT

### "BOHEMIANA" (OSCAR TAYLOR HOME), 1857
**1440 S Carroll Ave**
Victorian mansion, Italianate in feel-

ing, built by Oscar and Malvina Taylor. Their grandson donated the house to the Stephenson County Historical Soc., and it now serves as a museum. On the grounds is an arboretum containing an extensive variety of old large trees. A farm museum and blacksmith shop may also be seen.
*Operated by Stephenson Co. Historical Soc. Open Fri.–Sun. 1:30–5; closed national holidays*

## GALENA

### DOWLING HOUSE, 1826
**Main and Diagonal Streets**
Built by pioneer merchant John Dowling, this handsome stone structure, the oldest house standing in Galena, served as a dwelling and trading post for the lead miners who rushed here in the 1820s to strike it rich. The house has been restored and furnished to represent its original use as a residence and trading post.
*Operated by Ralph G. Benson. Open Apr. 15–Oct: daily 9–6*

### ■ GALENA HISTORIC DISTRICT
Some of the finest period architecture of the Middle West may be found in Galena. Many pre-Civil War mansions and five century-old churches remain. There are conducted tours through Galena's historic homes the second weekend in June and the last weekend in September.

### ORRIN SMITH HOUSE, 1852
Imposing brick residence built by Orrin Smith, a river boat captain in the heyday of river boating in the Galena area. Now a private residence, restored and furnished in the period
*Operated by Mr. George Funke, owner. Open June–Oct: daily 9–5*

### ■ ULYSSES S. GRANT HOME, 1859
**511 Bouthillier St**
Bracketed two-story Italianate house purchased by several private citizens for Grant when he returned to Galena as a war hero in 1865. He lived here until 1867, when he became Secretary of War, and again from 1879 to 1881, when he moved to New York. The house has been restored, and much of the furniture exhibited belonged to

the Grant family. The china and silver was used by the Grants when they occupied the White House.
*Operated by Ill. Dept. of Conservation. Open daily 9–5; closed Thanksgiving, Christmas, and New Year's Day*

*Ulysses S. Grant Home*

## GALESBURG

### CARL SANDBURG BIRTHPLACE, about 1875
**331 E Third St**
Typical one-story wood frame workingman's cottage with three rooms. The Lincoln Room, an exhibition area slightly larger than the main building, was added to the rear of the cottage in 1949. In the yard stands a red granite boulder inscribed "Remembrance Rock," beneath which Sandburg's ashes are buried.
*Operated by Carl Sandburg Birthplace Assn. Open Mon.–Sat. 9–12, 1–5, Sun. 1–5; closed Thanksgiving, Christmas, and New Year's Day*

## GRAND DETOUR

### ■ JOHN DEERE HOUSE, 1836
**John Deere Historic Site, off Illinois Route 2**
One-and-a-half-story clapboard house furnished in the style of the 1830s. A chimney, fireplace, and front porch were added to the house in 1920. John Deere, a country blacksmith, invented and manufactured a steel plow, which helped to open the West to agricultural development.
*Operated by John Deere Historic Site. Open May–Oct: daily 9–5*

## HIGHLAND PARK

### HIGHLAND PARK HISTORICAL SOC., 1871
**326 Central Ave**
Brick Victorian house, now headquar-

ters of the Highland Park Historical Soc. The house has several period rooms, a museum, a library, and offices of the society.
*Operated by Highland Park Historical Soc. Hours to be determined*

### STUPEY LOG CABIN, 1847
**1700 block of St. Johns Ave**
Restored one-and-a-half-story structure furnished in the period of 1850
*Operated by Highland Park Historical Soc. Open Sun. 1–5*

## KANKAKEE

### DR. A.L. SMALL HOME, 1855
**Small Memorial Park, Eighth Avenue and Water Street**
Native limestone home of Dr. A.L. Small, a prominent Kankakee citizen. The house is accented by wide porches and eaves supported by scroll brackets. Period furnishings, some original to the house
*Operated by Kankakee Co. Historical Soc. Open Sat., Sun. 2–5, and by appointment; closed national holidays*

## NAUVOO

### ■ NAUVOO HISTORIC DISTRICT, about 1840
Headquarters and principal town of the Mormons before their violent expulsion from Illinois, which began in 1844 with the murder of Joseph Smith, the church's founder and leader. The Mormon exodus, which took them finally to the site of Salt Lake City, Utah, was one of the most dramatic events in the history of American westward expansion. Among the dozen or more Mormon buildings of the 1840s at Nauvoo are the *Joseph Smith*

*Wilford Woodruff House*

*Homestead,* the first Nauvoo home of the Smith family; *Mansion House,* the last residence of Joseph Smith; and the *Heber C. Kimball House,* home of the man who headed the first Mormon mission to Great Britain.
*Operated by Nauvoo Restoration. Open daily 8–6*

## PETERSBURG

### EDGAR LEE MASTERS MEMORIAL MUSEUM, about 1850
**Eighth and Jackson Streets**
Small frame house, the home during the 1870s of the author famous for his *Spoon River Anthology.* Masters also wrote several biographies, the most controversial being *Lincoln – The Man.* The house has been restored and furnished with family pieces.
*Operated by Edgar Lee Masters Museum Board. Open May 15–Sept. 15: Tues.–Sun. 1–5*

### LINCOLN'S NEW SALEM STATE PARK
**Illinois Routes 97 and 123**
Reconstructed pioneer village of New Salem, home of Abraham Lincoln from 1831 to 1837. Some 23 cabins, including shops, school, sawmill, and the Rutledge Tavern, have been reproduced. Nearby is the New Salem Carriage Museum, which exhibits a rare collection of early American horse-drawn vehicles.
*Operated by Ill. Dept. of Conservation. Open Apr. 15–Oct. 15: daily 8:30–5*

## PEORIA

### FLANAGAN HOUSE, 1837
**942 NE Glen Oak Ave**
Built by Judge John C. Flanagan, this pink brick house with lacy grillwork on the verandas houses an antique carpenter shop, a collection of gowns and accessories, and furnishings of the pre-Civil War era.
*Operated by Peoria Historical Soc. Open Sat., Sun. 2–5, and by appointment*

### MORRON HOUSE, 1862; 1865
**1212 W Moss Ave**
Victorian house with gray shingles and white trim. Furnished elegantly with mid-Victorian pieces. The Harry

L. Spooner Library, with its vast collection of items related to early Peoria history, occupies the second floor.
*Operated by Peoria Historical Soc. Open Tues.–Fri. 2–5, Sun. 2–5*

## QUINCY

### ■ JOHN WOOD MANSION, 1835
**425 S 12 St**
Greek Revival house built by John Wood, one of Quincy's first settlers and an early Illinois governor. The furnished interiors reflect the life of Gov. Wood and the ante-bellum life of Illinois. Fine architectural details. The house is now a public museum.
*Operated by Historical Soc. of Quincy and Adams Co. Open Tues.–Fri. 10–12, 2–5, Sat., Sun. 2–5*

## RIVERSIDE

### ■ RIVERSIDE LANDSCAPE ARCHITECTURAL DISTRICT, 1860s
Occupying densely wooded park land, Riverside was one of the earliest preconceived residential communities in this country. Frederick Law Olmsted and Calvert Vaux, the landscape designers of New York's Central Park, were commissioned in 1866 to plan an ideal Chicago suburb. A total of $1.5 million was spent in the establishment of the village.

## ROCKFORD

### ERLANDER HOME MUSEUM, 1871
**404 S Third St**
First brick house in Rockford, built with materials entirely from the Rockford area. The house was built by John Erlander and occupied by the Erlander family until recent years.
*Operated by Swedish Historical Soc. of Rockford. Open Sun. 2–5 and by appointment*

### TINKER SWISS COTTAGE, 1865
**411 Kent St**
Robert Tinker, onetime mayor of Rockford, was a world traveler and collector of rare objects. After his travels in Switzerland he returned home to build this house; he faithfully followed sketches he had made of Swiss chalets. Now restored, with the priceless antiques and curios he collected throughout his travels on exhibit
*Operated by Tinker Swiss Cottage Assn. Open Wed., Thurs., Sat., Sun. 2–5, and by appointment*

## SALEM

### WILLIAM JENNINGS BRYAN MUSEUM, 1852
**408 S Broadway**
House in which "The Commoner" was born in 1860. Built by his father, Judge Silas Bryan, the house now serves as a museum and contains many personal effects of the famous prosecuting attorney of the Scopes trial. John T. Scopes, indicted for teaching evolution in his classes in Dayton, Tennessee, was also born in Salem.
*Operated by City of Salem Historical Comm. Open daily 10–5*

*Abraham Lincoln's Home*

## SPRINGFIELD

### ■ ABRAHAM LINCOLN'S HOME [LINCOLN HOME STATE MEMORIAL] 1839; 1856
**420 S Eighth St**
This is the only house Abraham Lincoln ever owned. He purchased it in 1844 for $1,500 from the rector who had married him to Mary Todd in 1842. Originally a cottage of one and one-half stories, Mrs. Lincoln had the house enlarged in 1856 to a full two stories. The Lincolns lived in this house from 1844 to 1861, except during his term in Congress. Three Lincoln sons were born in the house, and one died here. Much of the original furniture has been returned over the

past few years, and this has been used as a nucleus in restoring the house as nearly as possible to its appearance while the Lincolns lived here.
*Operated by Ill. Dept. of Conservation. Open daily 9–5; closed Thanksgiving, Christmas, and New Year's Day*

■ **EDWARDS PLACE**
**700 N Fourth St**
The oldest house in Springfield, former home of Benjamin S. Edwards, a prominent lawyer and contemporary of Abraham Lincoln. The house is furnished in the 19th-century style and houses a collection of paintings.
*Operated by Springfield Art Assn. Open Tues.–Sun. 2–5*

**GOVERNOR'S MANSION, 1855**
**Jackson Street**
A 28-room white brick Victorian mansion situated on a landscaped knoll three blocks from the state capitol. Many changes have been made in the house over the years, the most noticeable being the replacement of the cupola and low gabled roof by a mansard roof. Records indicate that the Lincolns were frequent guests at the mansion.
*Operated by State of Ill. Open Wed. 9–5*

**VACHEL LINDSAY HOME,**
**about 1830**
**603 S Fifth St**
Home of the poet Vachel Lindsay, with displays of his original manuscripts and drawings. Period furnishings
*Operated by Vachel Lindsay Assn. Open June–Sept: daily 9–5. Oct.–May: by appointment*

## WHEATON

**CANTIGNY (COL. ROBERT R. McCORMICK HOUSE), 1896; 1932; 1936**
**115 Winfield Rd**
The home of the eccentric late editor and publisher of the Chicago *Tribune*, a lifelong military enthusiast. On his 500-acre estate, which is now a war memorial, instead of the usual tree-lined malls there are tanks and field artillery, a war library, and a half-size replica of the memorial statue of Normandy Beach. Various patriotic ceremonies are held on the estate during the year.
*Operated by Cantigny War Memorial. Open May–Sept: daily 9–5. Oct.–Apr: 10–4*

## AURORA

**HILLFOREST, 1852–56**
**213 Fifth St**
Built by Thomas Gaff, a leading Ohio Valley industrialist, this mansion is basically Italian Renaissance in type though independent in character.

*Hillforest*

Sometimes called the "steamboat mansion" because of its verandas and wrought-iron balconies offering views of the Ohio River. Restored, with Victorian furnishings
*Operated by Hillforest Historical Foundation. Open Apr.–Dec: Tues.–Sun. 1–5*

## BELMONT

**T.C. STEELE STATE MEMORIAL**
**Indiana Route 46, near Nashville**
Estate containing 211 acres on which the originator of the Brown County Art Colony, Theodore Clement Steele, had his home (not open to the public) and studios. Many of his canvases are displayed in the studios (times below).
*Operated by Ind. Dept. of Conservation. Open summer: daily 8:30–5:30. Winter: Tues.–Sun. 9–12, 1–5*

## BLOOMINGTON

**ANDREW WYLIE HOUSE, 1835**
Second and Lincoln Streets
Brick house built by Andrew Wylie, the first president of Indiana University. Interiors and hand-carved woodwork are distinctive.
*Operated by Ind. University. Open Wed., Fri. 1:30–5*

## BROOK VICINITY

**HAZELDON (GEORGE ADE HOME), 1904**
Indiana Route 16, east of Brook
Home of George Ade, author, humorist, and playwright. Ade became internationally famous for his *Fables in Slang* and had three plays running simultaneously on Broadway in the early 1900s. William Howard Taft launched his successful campaign for the Presidency of the U.S. in a nationwide rally at Hazeldon in 1908. Restored with much original furniture, mementos, and trophies belonging to George Ade
*Operated by George Ade Memorial Assn. Open by appointment*

## CAMBRIDGE CITY

**HUDDLESTON HOUSE, 1839**
Road 40, 15 miles west of Richmond
House which served as an old stagecoach stop during the middle of the 19th century. To be restored and opened to the public in the near future as a house museum
*Operated by Historic Landmarks Foundation of Ind. Open by appointment*

## COLUMBIA CITY

**THOMAS R. MARSHALL HOME, before 1877**
108 W Jefferson St
Home of Thomas R. Marshall, governor of Indiana from 1909 to 1913, when he became Vice-President of the U.S. under Woodrow Wilson. Marshall served as Vice-President for two terms, through World War I. The house now serves as a museum, with furnishings and mementos of the Marshall family and Whitley County.
*Operated by Whitley Co. Historical Soc. Open Sun. 2–5 and by appointment*

## CRAWFORDSVILLE

**LANE PLACE, 1845**
212 S Water St
Fine old house built by Col. Henry S. Lane, governor of Indiana and U.S. senator during the Civil War. Exhibits of household belongings of Lane, early pioneer objects, dolls and children's furniture, and Lincoln items
*Operated by Montgomery Co. Historical Soc. Open May–Oct: Tues.–Sun. 1:30–4:30. Nov.–Apr: Tues.–Sun. 1–4*

## CROWN POINT

**OLD HOMESTEAD, 1847**
227 S Court St
Quaint white clapboard house built by pioneer Wellington A. Clark. The house, surrounded by pine cuttings and flowers, remained in the Clark family until 1965, when a granddaughter willed the property to the city with the stipulation it be opened to the public. Period furnishings
*Operated by City of Crown Point. Open by appointment*

## FORT WAYNE

**THOMAS SWINNEY HOMESTEAD, 1844; 1875**
1424 W Jefferson St
Originally a one-and-a-half-story Greek Revival-style house, one of the oldest in Fort Wayne, begun by pioneer agriculturist and financier Col. Thomas Swinney. Altered in the Victorian era with the addition of another story, a wing, and a front veranda. The building now serves as a museum, with collections of glassware, primitive paintings, Indian relics, and a Victorian parlor patterned after photographs of the Swinney homestead in the 1880s.
*Operated by Allen Co.–Fort Wayne Historical Museum. Open Tues.–Fri. 10–5, Sat., Sun. 1–5; closed holidays*

## FOUNTAIN CITY

■ **LEVI COFFIN HOUSE, 1827**
115 N Main St
Federal-style two-story brick house of Levi Coffin, often called the "president" of the Underground Railroad for runaway slaves. His house served as a depot in the early years. Coffin

began work for the freedmen after the issuance of the Emancipation Proclamation and assisted in forming the English Freedmen's Aid Soc., which contributed over $100,000 to the newly freed Negroes.
*Operated by Wayne Co. Historical Soc. Open Feb. 15–Dec. 15: Tues.–Sun. 1–5*

## GENEVA

### LIMBERLOST CABIN, 1895
**Sixth and Williams Streets**
Two-story, 14-room home of Gene Stratton Porter, the authoress who made this part of the country famous. Some of her furnishings and photographic works are here. Garden landscaped by Mrs. Porter
*Operated by Ind. Dept. of Conservation. Open summer: daily 8:30–5:30. Winter: Tues.–Sun. 9–12, 1–5*

## GREENFIELD

### JAMES WHITCOMB RILEY HOME, before 1849
**300 W Main St**
Birthplace of James Whitcomb Riley, the "Hoosier poet." The house has been restored and contains many of his belongings. Nearby is Riley Memorial Park, named in honor of the noted poet, and within the park is "The Old Swimmin' Hole," made famous by his verses.
*Operated by James Whitcomb Riley Old Home Soc. Open May–Oct: Mon., Tues., Thurs.–Sat. 10–5, Wed. 12–5, Sun. 1–5*

### LOG HOUSE, 19th century
**James Whitcomb Riley Memorial Park**
Located in the southeast corner of Riley Park, this old log house served as a jail and residence and is now a museum.
*Operated by Hancock Co. Historical Soc. Open by appointment*

## INDIANAPOLIS

### ■ BENJAMIN HARRISON HOME, 1874–75
**1230 N Delaware St**
Bracketed, Italianate home built by Benjamin Harrison, 23rd President of the U.S. and grandson of William Henry Harrison, ninth U.S. President. It was here in the back parlor of the house that Benjamin Harrison ac-

cepted his party's nomination on July 4, 1888. Ten of the original 16 rooms have been restored and contain much of Harrison's original furnishings.
*Operated by Arthur Jordan Foundation. Open Mon.–Sat. 10–4, Sun. 12:30–4; closed Christmas–New Year's Day*

### IRVINGTON BENTON HOUSE, 1873
**312 S Downey Ave**
Stately two-story brick house of French mansard design with a picturesque tower entrance and tall linteled windows. This ten-room house, situated on a wooded lot, was for 20 years the home of Allen R. Benton, president of Butler University. Restored and furnished as a cultural, historical, social, and civic center for community use
*Operated by Irvington Historic Landmark Foundation. Open by appointment*

### GOVERNOR'S MANSION, 1924
**4343 N Meridian St**
Buff-colored brick house built by the president of the Stutz Motor Car Company. Two years later it was sold to Mr. and Mrs. J.H. Trimble, from whom the state bought the house in 1945. This is the fifth home Indiana has provided its governors.
*Operated by State of Ind. Open by appointment and on special occasions*

*James Whitcomb Riley Home*

### ■ JAMES WHITCOMB RILEY HOME, 1872
**528 Lockerbie St**
Italianate house in which the famous poet lived as a paying guest the last

23 years of his life. The owners, Maj. and Mrs. Charles L. Holstein, were friends of Riley's, as was Mrs. Holstein's father, John R. Nickum, who built the house. It is of solid brick with a stone foundation and slate roof. Interior woodwork of solid hardwoods is hand-carved and there are Italian and Vermont marble fireplaces throughout. Furnished as it was when Riley lived here; poet's memorabilia displayed
*Operated by James Whitcomb Riley Assn. Open Tues.–Sat. 10–4, Sun. 12–4*

### MORRIS-BUTLER HOUSE, 1859–62
**1204 N Park Ave**
French mansard-type house built by John D. Morris, a Kentuckian whose family moved to Indianapolis a year after it became the capital city. The house is of soft-clay brick with a five-story central tower. In 1879 Noble Chase Butler, clerk of the U.S. district court, purchased the house, and the Butler family lived here until 1958. Now restored, the house serves as a residence as well as a museum of Victorian furnishings.
*Operated by Historic Landmarks Foundation of Ind. Open by appointment*

### THOMAS A. HENDRICKS HOUSE, 1830; 1851; 1857
**1526 S New Jersey St**
Picturesque house situated in a quiet residential section on the south side of the city. Indications are that the earliest portion of the house was built about 1830, but the main part of the building was erected by Hervey Bates, the first sheriff of Marion County, in the 1850s. Thomas A. Hendricks, Indiana's 16th governor and Vice-President of the U.S. under Grover Cleveland, lived here from 1865 to 1872.
*Operated by Miss Lois Hagedorn, owner. Open by appointment; closed Jan.–Mar.*

### TOLL HOUSE, 1850s
**4702 N Michigan Rd**
Simple frame house which served as a post office, country store, and tollhouse on the wilderness road linking Lake Michigan with the Ohio River. Now restored; furnishings provided by the Soc. of Colonial Dames
*Operated by Harrell Foundation. Open by appointment*

## JEFFERSONVILLE

### HOWARD NATIONAL STEAMBOAT MUSEUM, 1892
**1101 E Market St**
A collection of steamboat pictures, models, furniture, and equipment and a library of material on the steamboat era are housed in this 22-room Gothic mansion.
*Operated by Howard National Steamboat Museum. Open Apr.–Nov: daily 10–4:30*

## KOKOMO

### ELWOOD HAYNES MUSEUM, 1914
**1915 S Webster St**
One of the first American automobiles was invented in Kokomo in 1893 by Elwood Haynes. Now a museum, the house contains industrial exhibits and memorabilia of the inventor's life as well as his 1904, 1925 automobiles.
*Operated by City of Kokomo. Open Tues.–Sat. 1–4, Sun. 1–5*

## LAFAYETTE

### MOSES FOWLER HOME, 1851–52
**909 South St**
English Gothic-style house built by Moses Fowler, a wealthy businessman, landowner, farmer, and banker. The house is one of the few dwellings remaining from the days when Lafayette was a small but lusty river town—a shipping center before the "iron horse" made its appearance. Now serving as a museum; collections include porcelains, paintings, firearms, Indian artifacts, and furniture.
*Operated by Tippecanoe Co. Historical Assn. Open Tues.–Sun. 1–5; closed holidays*

*Moses Fowler Home*

## LA PORTE

### AMES-PATON HOUSE, 1842
**Waverly Road**
New England-type house built by Capt. Charles Ames, a native of West Bridgewater, Massachusetts. It was occupied by the Ames family for almost a century. The house is situated on a wooded plot with an 1838 barn and another house built in 1856 in the Greek Revival style.
*Operated by Maurice E. Paton, owner. Open June–Aug: Sat. 1–5 by appointment*

## LOGANSPORT

### LONG HOUSE
**1004 E Market St**
Two-room carriage house with paintings by early Indiana artists, historical documents, a fine lusterware collection, and a research library
*Operated by Cass Co. Historical Soc. Open Tues.–Sat. 1–5, first Sun. of each month, open house*

## MADISON

### JAMES F.D. LANIER HOUSE, 1844
**First Street**
Stately classical revival-style mansion built by the architect Francis Costigan for James F.D. Lanier, a lawyer, clerk in the Indiana House of Representatives, businessman, and banker. Lanier is credited with advancing the state about $1,040,000 during two early financial crises, and his mansion, on the banks of the Ohio River, was one of the most pretentious structures in the Middle West.
*Operated by Ind. Dept. of Natural Resources. Open daily 9–5; closed Mon. during winter*

*James F. D. Lanier Home*

### JEREMIAH SULLIVAN HOUSE, 1818
**Second and Poplar Streets**
Brick Federal-style house built by Jeremiah Sullivan, who emigrated from Virginia to Madison at the age of 23. Within three years of his arrival he was elected a member of the Indiana legislature, and from 1836 to 1846 he was a judge of the supreme court of Indiana. The house is furnished with many fine pieces, some of which are said to have been brought from Virginia in 1818.
*Operated by Historic Madison. Open May–Nov: Tues.–Sat. 10–4:30*

### SHREWSBURY HOUSE, 1849
**301 W First St**
Classical revival-style house designed by Francis Costigan for Capt. Charles Shrewsbury. Considered to be one of the remarkable architectural monuments of the Old Northwest of the affluent period of the 1850s. Grand in scale, with templelike rooms and Greek columns, 16-foot ceilings, and a notable freestanding staircase to the third floor. Now restored and open as a museum and antique shop
*Operated by Mr. and Mrs. John T. Windle, owners. Open Mar.–Dec: daily 9–5 and by appointment*

## MITCHELL

### SPRING MILL VILLAGE
**Spring Mill State Park, Indiana Route 60, three miles east of Mitchell**
Historical restoration of a frontier trading post founded before 1850. Buildings restored or reconstructed are a gristmill, sawmill, hatshop, post office, bootshop, stillhouse, and apothecary shop.
*Operated by Ind. Dept. of Natural Resources. Open daily 9–5*

## NEW ALBANY

### CULBERTSON MANSION, 1868
**914 E Main St**
Built by W.S. Culbertson, merchant prince, financier, banker, and philanthropist, this fabulous Victorian mansion cost over $120,000 before it was finished. The 26-room structure rises three stories to a mansard roof fringed by a three-foot-high iron fence. The

interiors include a vestibule and reception hall with 18-foot filigree-edged ceilings, a three-story staircase of finely carved mahogany and rosewood, and a ballroom. Restored, with fine furnishings of the Victorian period
*Operated by Historic New Albany. Open Mar.–Nov: Tues.–Sun. 1:30–4:30*

*Culbertson Mansion*

**SCRIBNER HOUSE, 1814**
**State and East Main Streets**
The oldest house in New Albany, built by Joel Scribner and his wife, Mary Bull Scribner, who were among the town's first settlers. The house was purchased in 1917 from a granddaughter of the builder and restored. Much of the original furniture has been replaced in the house, and it now serves as D.A.R. headquarters of the Piankeshaw Chapter.
*Operated by the Daughters of the American Revolution. Open by appointment*

## NEW ALBANY VICINITY

**OLD YENOWINE HOMESTEAD, 1840**
**5118 State Rd 64**
Brick farmhouse built by Daniel Yenowine; the bricks were made on the site, and the timber was cut from surrounding forest. Interior woodwork is superior to that of most backwoods farmhouses of this period. The house

still serves as the residence of the builder's granddaughter.
*Operated by Clara Yenowine Nichols, owner. Open by appointment*

## NEW CASTLE

**WILLIAM GROSE HOME, 1870**
**614 S 14 St**
Once the home of Gen. William Grose, this building now houses the museum of the Henry County Historical Soc., with exhibits of pioneering tools and household items and a portrait gallery of early Hoosiers.
*Operated by Henry Co. Historical Soc. Open Mon.–Sat. 1–4:30*

## NEW HARMONY

**FAUNTLEROY HOUSE, early 19th century**
Harmonist frame house in which the Minerva Soc. (the first women's club with a written constitution) was founded by Constance Owen Fauntleroy. Furnished with many interesting and historical items
*Operated by Ind. Dept. of Natural Resources. Open summer: daily 8:30–5:30. Winter: Tues.–Sun. 9–12, 1–5*

**HARMONIST MUSEUM HOUSE, 1815**
The only restored Rappite dwelling in New Harmony. Collection of Rappite relics and early pioneer-style furnishings as well as some pieces of original Harmonist furniture
*Operated by Soc. of Colonial Dames. Open May–Oct: Tues.–Sat. 10–12, 1–5, Sun., holidays 1–5*

**■ NEW HARMONY HISTORIC DISTRICT**
Site of the Rappite colony settled by followers of Father George Rapp in 1815. About 35 Rappite buildings remain. In 1825 Welsh reformer Robert Owen purchased the community for his short-lived experimental colony aimed at educational and scientific reforms.

## NEW TRENTON

**ALDIANNE, about 1810**
**Chappelow Road, Far Away Acres Reservation**
Possibly the oldest log house in the Ohio River Valley. Restored and fur-

nished, this structure represents the better homes of pioneer days.
*Operated by Vernon and Gladys Welker, owners. Open Apr. 15–Oct. 15: daily 10–5 and by appointment*

## NOBLESVILLE

### CONNER PRAIRIE PIONEER SETTLEMENT AND MUSEUM (WILLIAM CONNER HOMESTEAD), 1823
**Indiana Route 37A**
Original structures as well as reconstructions comprise this pioneer settlement. The William Conner home was the first brick building in the New Purchase area of central Indiana. Conner was a leading figure in the transition of the region from Indiana Territory to statehood.
*Operated by Earlham College. Open May, Sept., Oct: Sat., Sun. 1–5. June 8–Labor Day: Tues.–Sat. 11–5, Sun. 1–5, and by appointment*

*William Conner Homestead*

## PERRYSVILLE

### LOG BUILDINGS, mid-19th century
**off Indiana Route 63, three miles west on Indiana Route 32**
Log buildings and blacksmith shop with displays of Indian relics, stuffed birds and animals, tools, stone forge and bellows. Collections of farm implements and antique cars and trucks may also be seen.
*Operated by Norman Lewis Skinner, Jr., owner. Open by appointment*

## ROCKPORT

### LINCOLN PIONEER VILLAGE
**City Park**
Reconstructed village, surrounded by a stockade, consisting of 18 log buildings, including a museum of early

transportation and pioneer items
*Operated by City of Rockport. Open daily 8–5*

## ROME CITY

### GENE STRATTON PORTER HOME, 1914
**Gene Stratton Porter State Memorial**
**Indiana Route 9**
Constructed of Wisconsin cedar logs, this two-story structure was designed and built by Mrs. Porter, popular Hoosier authoress and photographer.
*Operated by Ind. Dept. of Conservation. Open summer: daily 8:30–5:30. Winter: Tues.–Sat. 9–12, 1–5*

## RUSHVILLE

### JOHN K. GOWDY HOME, 1888
**619 N Perkins St**
Home of John K. Gowdy, consul general in Paris under President William McKinley. Now a museum, with several furnished rooms and exhibits relating to early county history
*Operated by Rush Co. Historical Soc. Open Sun. 12–5 and by appointment*

## SALEM

### JOHN HAY BIRTHPLACE, 1824
**106 S College Ave**
Small brick house in which John Hay, lawyer, statesman, and literary figure, was born. Hay began his career as assistant secretary to President Lincoln and went on to become Assistant Secretary of State, ambassador to Great Britain, and Secretary of State. The house has been restored and furnished with period pieces.
*Operated by Washington Co. Historical Soc. Open daily 1–5*

## TERRE HAUTE

### ■ EUGENE V. DEBS HOUSE, 1885
**451 N Eighth St**
Two-story frame house, home of the founder of industrial unionism in the U.S. Debs was a leader of the Pullman strike in Chicago in 1894 and was arrested and sentenced to six months' imprisonment. He became the leader of the Social Democratic Party of America and was the Socialists' candi-

date for President five times between 1900 and 1920.

*Operated by Eugene V. Debs Foundation. Open Sun. 2–4 and by appointment*

*Eugene V. Debs House*

## HISTORICAL MUSEUM OF THE WABASH VALLEY, 1868; 1876
**1411 S Sixth St**

The original front part of this structure was the residence of William H. Sage, a local baker and confectioner. The middle section was built in 1876 by Henry Robinson, a prominent businessman. Purchased in 1905 by Clemens Nagel, the house remained in the Nagel family until 1957. It now serves as a museum, with exhibits of 18th- and 19th-century documents, furniture, and other historical items.

*Operated by Vigo Co. Historical Soc. Open Wed. 2–4, Sun. 2–5*

## PAUL DRESSER BIRTHPLACE, before 1859
**First and Farrington Streets**

Two-story house, restored and faced with brick, in which Paul Dresser, brother of Theodore Dreiser, was born in 1859. During the "gay nineties" Paul Dresser was one of the most successful songwriters of Tin Pan Alley. "On the Banks of the Wabash," for which he became famous, was adopted as Indiana's state song in 1913.

*Operated by Vigo Co. Historical Soc. Open Apr.–Oct: Wed., Sun. 2–4, and by appointment*

# VINCENNES

## ■ GROUSELAND (WILLIAM HENRY HARRISON HOME), 1804
3 W Scott St

Residence of William Henry Harrison from about 1804 to 1812, while he was territorial governor of Indiana. A defender of white settlement of the West, Harrison met the Indian leader Tecumseh here in 1811, and from here, the same year, he launched his campaign against the Indians, which ended with the Battle of Tippecanoe and scattered Tecumseh's followers. After serving in Congress for several years, William Henry Harrison became the ninth President of the U.S.

*Operated by Daughters of the American Revolution. Open daily 9–5; closed Thanksgiving, Christmas, and New Year's Day*

*Grouseland*

# WINCHESTER

## CARRIE GOODRICH HOUSE, about 1838
**416 S Meridan St**

Square, brick two-story house built by Carrie Goodrich, an uncle of James P. Goodrich, onetime governor of Indiana. Furnishings are of the period and earlier, including a large bed belonging to Goodrich which had been built within one of the rooms. Collection of glass bottles, farm tools, and household utensils

*Operated by Randolph Co. Historical Soc. Open spring–fall: Sun. 1–5 and by appointment*

## AMANA VICINITY

■ **AMANA VILLAGES, 1850s-70s**
Seven "old world" villages founded by the Community of True Inspiration, a German religious sect that emigrated from Europe to Iowa in 1855. The *Amana Heim* in Homestead and the *Christian Haus Antique Museum* in main Amana, two typical early dwellings, have been restored and furnished. For further information contact Ox Yoke Inn, Amana.

## BENTONSPORT

**MASON HOUSE, 1846**
**five miles east of Keosauqua**
Two-and-a-half-story modified Georgian-style building of 21 rooms; originally built as a hotel and partially converted to a home in 1857 by Louis J. Mason. Located in a once-bustling steamboat town on the Des Moines River; now the state's ghost town, with less than 100 full-time residents. Restored and furnished with the original Mason family furniture
*Operated by Herbert and Burretta Redhead, owners. Open Apr.–Oct: daily 9–6*

## CLERMONT

**MONTAUK, 1874**
Red brick-and-limestone Victorian mansion built by Iowa's 12th governor, William Larrabee. The 80-acre farm, outbuildings, and mansion have been preserved as they were during Larrabee's lifetime. The house, shown with the original furnishings, was lived in until recently by the governor's daughter.
*Operated by Historical Gov. Larrabee Home. Open May 30–Oct: daily 10–5*

## COUNCIL BLUFFS

■ **GRENVILLE M. DODGE HOUSE, 1869**
**605 Third St**
This 14-room Victorian brick house with mansard roof and French windows was built for Gen. Grenville M. Dodge, chief engineer of the Union Pacific Railroad. Interiors feature walnut woodwork and Italian marble fireplaces. Restored and shown with period furnishings, including some of Dodge's personal artifacts
*Operated by City Park Comm. Open Tues.–Sat. 10–5, Sun. 2–6; closed Jan.*

*Grenville M. Dodge House*

## DAVENPORT VICINITY

**CODY McCAUSLAND HOUSE, 1851**
**Route 61**
Typical mid-19th-century Iowa homestead, built by Isaac Cody; the boyhood home of his famous son, "Buffalo Bill." Frame addition built by the McCausland family, Cody relatives who bought the house. Restored and partially furnished with period pieces
*Operated by Soc. of Colonial Dames. Open daily 10–5*

## DES MOINES

**SALISBURY HOUSE, 1923-28**
**4025 Tonawanda Dr**
This replica of King's House in Salisbury, England, was built by Carl and Edith Weeks. It represents different architectural styles from the 13th to the mid-17th century and is constructed of limestone, flint, and brick. Set on 11 acres; with original furnishings
*Operated by Iowa State Education Assn. Open by appointment*

## DUBUQUE

**HAM HOUSE, 1840-57**
**2241 Lincoln Ave**
Beautiful Gothic Revival mansion of native limestone, with river captain's lookout tower, built by Mathais Ham, early Iowa businessman and prominent citizen. Now a historical museum, with four of the 23 rooms furnished

with Victorian pieces. Also on the grounds are a one-room schoolhouse, a caboose, and the first log cabin built in Iowa.
*Operated by Dubuque Historical Museum. Open May 30–Labor Day: Tues.–Sun. 12:30–4:30*

## FORT DODGE

### FORT DODGE HISTORICAL MUSEUM
**U.S. Route 20**
An exact replica of the fort built here in 1850 to protect the early settlers from roving bands of Indians; the museum features exhibits of dolls, guns, pioneer and Indian relics, other items of local history, and an 1891 schoolhouse.
*Private. Open May 15–Oct: daily 9–8*

### VINCENT HOME, 1871–79
**824 Third Ave, S**
Three-story house of "soft" brick with a mansard roof and tall narrow windows on the first floor; a brick kitchen wing replaced the original wooden one in 1901. Built by James Swain, a prominent early settler, and owned and occupied by the Vincent family from 1879 to 1970.
*Operated by Young Women's Christian Assn. Hours to be determined*

## IOWA CITY

### PLUM GROVE, 1844
**727 Switzer Ave**
Simple, seven-room house of locally made red brick, built by Iowa's first territorial governor, Robert Lucas. Restored in 1940; furnished with period pieces. Wild plum trees have been planted so that the grounds are as they were when Lucas lived there.
*Operated by Iowa State Conservation Comm. Open May–Nov. 15: Tues.–Sun. 1–5*

## MARSHALLTOWN

### SUSIE SOWER HISTORICAL HOUSE, 1860
**North Second Avenue**
Large brick house with gingerbread trim and a covered porch; bought by George Sower in 1870 and occupied by his descendants until the death of Susie Sower in 1952. It has been restored and furnished with typical midwestern period pieces. There are also on display some Indian artifacts.
*Operated by Historical Soc. of Marshall Co. Open by appointment*

## MOUNT PLEASANT

### HARLAN HOUSE, 1860s
**122 N Jefferson St**
Mid-19th-century home of James A. Harlan, U.S. senator and Secretary of the Interior under President Lincoln. Lincoln's eldest son, Robert Todd, married Mary Harlan, and their three children spent many summers here. Restored and furnished with some original pieces and Lincoln memorabilia. The height marks of the President's grandchildren can still be seen where they were originally marked on the front door.
*Operated by Iowa Wesleyan College. Open by appointment*

## MUSCATINE

### LAURA MUSSER ART GALLERY AND MUSEUM, 1908
**1314 Mulberry Ave**
A 22-room mansion built by pioneer lumberman Peter Musser and the home for many years of his daughter Laura. A music room was added in 1921 to accommodate a 731-pipe player organ, which is still operative. Since 1966 a museum with changing art exhibits and extensive gardens; furnished with many of the family's pieces
*Operated by Laura Musser Art Gallery and Museum. Open Tues.–Sun. 2–5, Tues., Thurs. evgs. 7–9*

## OSKALOOSA

### NELSON HOMESTEAD PIONEER FARMS, 1852
**Glendale Road**
Two-story farmhouse built of native lumber and bricks fired at a local kiln. Now a museum in a complex featuring an 1856 barn. During September demonstrations are given of pioneer crafts, including spinning, weaving, and candle dipping.
*Operated by Mahaska Co. Historical Soc. Open May 12–Oct. 12: Tues.–Sat. 10–5, Sun. 1–5*

## PELLA

### WYATT EARP BOYHOOD HOME, 1849
### 507 Franklin St

Wyatt Earp lived in this two-story brick house from 1850 to 1864, when his family joined a wagon train to California. The east half of the house is restored with period furnishings; the west half is a museum featuring antiques of the town's Dutch founders. Also on the grounds is a restored pioneer log cabin.
*Operated by Pella Historical Soc. Open Mon.–Fri. 9–11:30, 1–4:30*

## SALEM

### LEWELLING QUAKER SHRINE, 1840–45
### West Main Street

Six-room sandstone house built by Henderson Lewelling and used as a "station" for escaping slaves on the Underground Railroad. Lewelling, a noted horticulturist, is credited with discovering the "Bing" cherry. Restored house is shown with early pioneer furniture and utensils
*Operated by Lewelling Quaker Shrine Board of Trustees. Open Apr.–Oct: Sun. 1–5, weekdays by appointment*

## SIBLEY

### H.K. ROGERS HOMESTEAD, 1871
### Sibley Park

Originally a one-room frame cabin. Log extensions have been built around the cabin to house the museum. Exhibits include ammunition from the Civil War to World War II, china, farm equipment, and period furnishings in the Rogers homestead.
*Operated by Osceola Co. Historical Soc. and the City of Sibley. Open May–Aug: Sun. 2–5*

## SIOUX CITY

### PEIRCE MANSION, 1890
### 2901 Jackson St

A 21-room mansion, with walls of South Dakota quartzite, built for local realtor John Peirce, who was forced to sell it in 1894 because of a financial depression. Later a residence hall for nurses and since 1961 a museum featuring historical exhibits

*Operated by Sioux City Public Museum. Open Tues.–Sat. 9–5, Sun. 2–5*

*Peirce Mansion*

## SPILLVILLE

### BILY CLOCK EXHIBIT, before 1893

Two-story brick house where Anton Dvořák spent the summer of 1893; here he composed his "American Quartette" and did final work on the "New World Symphony." Since 1947 the building has housed an unusual collection of hand-carved clocks.
*Operated by Town of Spillville. Open May–Oct: daily 8:30–5:30*

## STORM LAKE

### HALVER ELLERTON DAHL LOG CABIN, before 1871
### East Lakeshore Drive

Log cabin typical of those built by late 19th-century Scandinavian homesteaders. Originally built in Rembrandt, Iowa, by Halver Ellerton Dahl.
*Operated by Buena Vista Historical Soc. Open May 30–Labor Day: Sun. 2–5*

## TABOR

### HISTORIC REV. JOHN TODD HOUSE, 1853

House of native lumber with hand-hewn walnut beams; a "station" on the Underground Railroad and headquarters of John Brown and the Free Kansas Fighters. Rifles were stored here and shipped to Harpers Ferry prior to Brown's famous raid. Restored

and furnished with period pieces
*Operated by Tabor Historical Soc.
Open summer: Sun. 1–5 and by
appointment*

## WATERLOO

### RENSSALAER RUSSELL HOUSE, 1861
**520 W Third St**
Lovely Victorian house of red brick
with white trim, topped by a cupola.
Built by a local businessman and occupied by his descendants until 1964,
when the house was restored to its
original period. Furnished with early
Victorian pieces
*Operated by Assn. for the Preservation
of the Renssalaer Russell House. Open*

*Feb.–May, Oct.–Nov: Sun. 1:30–4.
June–Sept: Wed. 1:30–4*

## WEST BRANCH

### ■ HERBERT HOOVER NATIONAL HISTORIC SITE
Two-room frame cottage, built about
1870, where Herbert Hoover was born
in 1874; restored and shown with
some of the original furniture. Also
included in the historic site are the
Presidential library and museum, a
replica of Hoover's father's blacksmith shop, a Quaker meetinghouse,
and the graves of the former President
and his wife.
*Operated by National Park Service.
Cottage open daily 8–5*

## ABILENE

### DWIGHT D. EISENHOWER HOME, 1870
**201 SE Fourth St**
Boyhood home of Dwight D. Eisenhower maintained as it was at the time
of his mother's death in 1946. Part of a
complex including a museum of his
personal effects, the Presidential library, and his grave site
*Operated by Eisenhower Foundation.
Open daily 9–5; closed Christmas*

*Dwight D. Eisenhower Home*

## ARGONIA

### SALTER HOUSE, 1884
Home of Mrs. Susanna Madora Salter,
elected the first woman mayor in U.S.
in 1887. Restored and furnished; his-

torical society headquarters featuring
18th-century household items
*Operated by Argonia and Western
Sumner Co. Historical Soc. Open May
–Sept: daily 2–5 and by appointment*

## ATHOL

### HOME ON THE RANGE CABIN, 1872
Small log cabin where homesteader
Dr. Brewster Higley wrote the words
to "Home on the Range." After a well-
publicized national copyright fight
established Dr. Higley as the official
author of the words, his cabin was
restored as a memorial and furnished
as it was when he lived there.
*Operated by Mr. and Mrs. P.A. Rust,
owners. Open daily 8–8*

## BOICOURT

### MARIAS DES CYGNES MASSACRE MEMORIAL PARK
**five miles northeast of U.S. Route 69**
This park memorializes the massacre
of five "free-staters" men by a band of
proslavery adherents in 1858. Later
that year the land was purchased by
Charles C. Hadsall, who gave John
Brown rights to build a "fort" there;
Brown's log fort was subsequently

stripped by souvenir hunters. After the Civil War Hadsall built a small stone house adjoining the site of Brown's fort; it is now a museum. *Operated by Kans. State Historical Soc. Open Mon.–Fri. 9–12, 2–5, Sun. 1:30–5; closed national holidays*

## COLBY

### SOD TOWN PRAIRIE HISTORICAL MUSEUM
**U.S. Route 24**
Reproductions of sod houses built by pioneers during the settlement of the treeless Plains. Furnished with pieces from the 1870–1930 period. Indian artifacts and indigenous plant and animal life are also displayed. *Operated by Sons and Daughters of the Soddies. Open May–Oct: evgs. 7–9*

## COUNCIL GROVE

### ■ COUNCIL GROVE HISTORIC DISTRICT
An important stop on the historic Santa Fe Trail; here caravans of traders organized to protect themselves from hostile Indians along the route. Named for an 1825 treaty between the U.S. and Osage nation, the town boasts a number of 19th-century landmarks, including the Old Kew Mission, built 1850–51.

## DODGE CITY

### HOME OF STONE, 1879–80
**112 E Vine St**
Two-story house with a raised basement built of hand-hewn natural stone with wooden truss by John Mueller, an early bootmaker. Sold in 1890 to Adam Schmidt, local blacksmith, whose descendants owned the house until 1960. Furnished with pieces of the Mueller and Schmidt families *Operated by Ford Co. Historical Soc. Open June–Labor Day: daily 1–8 and by appointment*

## ELLIS

### WALTER CHRYSLER HOME, before 1880
Boyhood home of inventor and automobile manufacturer Walter Chrysler.

Restored as it was when he lived there in the 1880s and 1890s *Operated by Ellis Chamber of Commerce. Open May–Aug: daily 9–5*

## ELLSWORTH

### HODGDEN HOUSE, about 1872
**104 W South Main St**
Early Kansas house built of natural sandstone found locally. Restored as a museum in 1962; exhibits include period furniture and pioneer artifacts *Operated by Ellsworth Co. Historical Soc. Open Tues.–Sat. 10–5, Sun. 1–5; closed Thanksgiving, Christmas, and New Year's Day*

## HILLSBORO

### PIONEER ADOBE HOUSE AND MUSEUM, 1885
**D and Ash Streets**
Typical adobe house built by Peter Loewen, an early settler; museum features exhibits of local history *Operated by City of Hillsboro. Open Mar.–Oct: Mon.–Sat. 9–5, Sun., holidays 2–5*

## IOLA VICINITY

### FUNSTON MEMORIAL HOME, 1859
**U.S. Route 169**
One-and-a-half-story frame farmhouse; boyhood home of Gen. Frederick Funston, hero of the Spanish-American War and the Philippine insurrection of 1899–1902 *Operated by Kans. State Historical Soc. Open Mon.–Sat. 10–5, Sun. 1:30–5*

## MANHATTAN

### ISAAC T. GOODNOW HOME, 1857–69
**2301 Claflin Rd**
Two-story native limestone and frame house added onto a stone cabin by Isaac Goodnow, who purchased the property in 1857. Goodnow, known as the father of the Kansas common school, was the state's first full-term superintendent of public instruction and was a co-founder of what is now Kansas State University. *Operated by Kans. State Historical Soc. Hours to be determined*

## RILEY COUNTY PIONEER CABIN
**Manhattan City Park**
Reconstructed pioneer cabin depicts life on the Plains; furnished with household utensils and farm equipment from the period 1854–1900, when the county was settled
*Operated by Riley Co. Historical Soc. Open Sun. 1–5*

## MEDICINE LODGE
### CARRY NATION HOME, before 1880s
**211 W Fowler Ave**
One-story stone house was the home of Carry Nation, militant prohibitionist, from the late 1880s until the early 20th century. Maintained as a museum
*Operated by Women's Christian Temperance Union. Open evgs. 6–10*

### MEDICINE LODGE STOCKADE
**U.S. Routes 160 and 281**
Reconstruction of the original stockade built on this site in 1874. A two-story cottonwood log house built in 1877 and shown with typical pioneer furnishings has been moved here. Also on display are an 1886 jail and other artifacts of the "Old West."
*Private. Open Apr.–Sept: daily 8:30–6. Oct.–Dec: Sat., Sun. 8:30–6; closed Christmas*

## MUNCIE
### MOSES GRINTER HOUSE, 1857
**1420 S 78 St**
Large two-story house of hand-molded brick; the oldest house standing in the county and one of the oldest in the state. Built by Moses Grinter, who operated the only ferry across the Kansas River; Grinter came here in 1831 and was thus the first permanent white settler in the Wyandotte County area.
*Operated by Kans. State Historical Soc. Hours to be determined*

## NEWTON
### ■ BERNHARD WARKENTIN HOME, 1886–87
**211 E First St**
Home of pioneer miller Bernhard

Warkentin, leader of the Russian Mennonites of German origin. Warkentin influenced many of his former countrymen to settle on the Plains and was instrumental in introducing hard winter wheat to Kansas, which was the beginning of the state's leading industry.
*Operated by Preservation of Kans. Landmarks. Open June–Aug: daily 1:30–4:30. Sept.–May: Sat., Sun. 1:30–4:30*

*Bernhard Warkentin Home*

## NORTH NEWTON
### PIONEER LOG CABIN, 1875
**Kauffman Museum**
Typical log cabin with a thatched roof and mud chinking; built by Russian Mennonite settlers. Shown with homemade furnishings of the pioneer era. On the grounds of the Kauffman Museum, which displays Indian and pioneer artifacts and a fine collection of stuffed birds and animals
*Operated by Bithel College. Open Mon.–Fri. 9–5, Sat. 9–12, Sun. 1–5*

## OBERLIN
### SOD HOUSE
**South Penn Avenue**
Replica of a sod house, the typical pioneer dwelling on the treeless Plains. Shown with authentic furnishings, including fancy curtains cut from newspaper. The house is on the grounds of the Last Indian Raid in Kansas Museum, which displays relics of Indian history.
*Operated by Decatur Co. Historical Soc. Open Apr.–Dec: Mon.–Sat. 9–5, Sun. 1:30–5*

## OSAWATOMIE
### JOHN BROWN LOG CABIN, 1855
**John Brown Memorial Park**
Log cabin built by the Rev. Charles

Adair, brother-in-law of John Brown; served as Brown's home when he was in Kansas. Once a station on the Underground Railroad
*Operated by Kans. State Historical Soc. Open Mon.–Sat. 9–12, 2–5, Sun. 1:30–5; closed national holidays*

## SCOTT CITY VICINITY
### HERBERT L. STEELE HOUSE, about 1894
**Lake Scott State Park**
Home of homesteaders Herbert and Eliza Steele, who first built a "dugout," which became the first floor of the house when the four-room upper story of sandstone was added. Occupied by them until 1930 and now part of 1,280-acre park; period furnishings, including some Steele family pieces
*Operated by Kans. State Park and Resources Authority. Open by appointment*

## TOPEKA
### CEDAR CREST (GOVERNOR'S MANSION), 1928
Norman-style chateau of native stone, brick, and stucco designed by architect William D. Wight for publisher Frank MacLennan. Bequeathed to the state by Mrs. MacLennan in 1955 for use as the governor's residence; after a great political battle and much re-

modeling, occupied by the governor's family in 1962
*Operated by State of Kans. Open Mon.–Fri. afternoons by appointment*

## WICHITA
### HISTORIC WICHITA COW TOWN, 1870s
**1717 Sim Park Dr**
A restoration of some of Wichita's earliest buildings, including the *Munger House*, a two-story log home, built in 1869–70 as the town's first permanent dwelling. Furnishings are from the period. Among the other restored buildings are a church, the original train depot, a jail used when Wyatt Earp was marshal, and a one-story log schoolhouse topped by a sod roof.
*Operated by Historic Wichita Cow Town. Open Mar. 20–Nov: Tues.–Sun. 9–5*

### LOG CABIN, 1870
**Friends University**
A plain homesteader log cabin shown with simple furnishings typical of the early pioneers. Adjacent to the Fellow-Reeve Museum, which features farm equipment, covered wagons, and other items of local history
*Operated by Fellow-Reeve Museum. Open Mon.–Fri. 2–4*

## BARBOURVILLE
### DR. THOMAS WALKER STATE PARK
**Kentucky Route 459**
Replica of the one-room log cabin built in 1750 by Dr. Thomas Walker and his surveying party, who explored this part of the country for the Loyal Land Company of London 20 years before Daniel Boone passed this way
*Operated by Ky. Dept. of Parks. Open daily 9–5*

## BARDSTOWN
### MY OLD KENTUCKY HOME (FEDERAL HILL), 1795
**My Old Kentucky Home State Park, U.S. Route 150**
Immortalized through Stephen Collins

Foster's song, which was inspired when he visited his cousins, the Rowans, in 1852. The stately home was built on a thriving plantation by Judge John Rowan, a U.S. senator and member of Kentucky's court of appeals. Four generations of Rowans lived in the house through the years until 1922. Period furnishings
*Operated by Ky. Dept. of Parks. Open Mar.–Nov: daily 9–5. Dec.–Feb: Tues.–Sun. 9–5*

### "WICKLAND" (HOME OF THREE GOVERNORS), 1813
**U.S. Route 62**
Two-and-a-half-story brick Georgian mansion built by Charles A. Wickliffe

from designs by the architects John Marshall Brown and John Rogers. Charles A. Wickliffe, Kentucky's chief executive (1839–40), was the first governor to reside here. The second was his son Robert Charles Wickliffe, governor of Louisiana (1856–60), and the third was Charles A. Wickliffe's grandson, John Cripps Wickliffe Beckham, governor of Kentucky from 1900 to 1907. Especially noteworthy are the fine doorways, large fanlights, hand-carved woodwork, carved mantels showing the Adam influence, and fine period furnishings
*Operated by Mr. and Mrs. Robert S. Trigg, owners. Open daily 8:30–6; closed Thanksgiving and Christmas*

## CARROLLTON

**BUTLER MANSION, early 19th century**
**Gen. Butler State Park**
This two-and-a-half-story brick structure in Georgian colonial style was originally the home of Thomas L. Butler, eldest son of Percival Butler and aide to Gen. Jackson at the Battle of New Orleans.
*Operated by Ky. Dept. of Parks. Open May–Oct: daily 9–5*

## CRAB ORCHARD VICINITY

**WILLIAM WHITLEY HOUSE, between 1787 and 1794**
**off U.S. Route 150, between Stanford and Crab Orchard**
Built by Col. William Whitley, famous Kentucky pioneer leader and Indian fighter, this was one of the first brick houses built west of the Alleghenies. It served as a fort and as a stop for travelers on the Wilderness Road. William Whitley's initials were set in slightly darker bricks on the front façade of the house, and his wife, Esther's, initials were set in the back. The house was a gathering place for such frontier leaders as George Rogers Clark, Daniel Boone, and Isaac Shelby, Kentucky's first governor. Restored and furnished with early Kentucky pieces
*Operated by Ky. Dept. of Parks. Open Sept.–May: Tues.–Sun. 9–5. June–Aug: daily 9–5*

## DANVILLE

■ **DR. EPHRAIM McDOWELL HOUSE AND APOTHECARY SHOP, about 1800**
**125-27 S Second St**
Home of the famous pioneer surgeon who on Christmas Day, 1809, performed the first recorded abdominal operation to successfully remove an ovarian tumor. Dr. McDowell was the foremost surgeon west of the Allegheny Mountains. The apothecary shop was the first drugstore west of the Alleghenies, the back room serving as the doctor's office and the front to prepare the medicines. The home is restored and furnished with period furnishings, and the shop exhibits a collection of 18th- and early 19th-century medicine bottles, delft drug jars, a leech jar, and mortars, pestles, and balances.
*Operated by Ky. Medical Assn. Open Mon.–Sat. 10–4:30, Sun. 2–5*

## FRANKFORT

**THE GOVERNOR'S MANSION, completed 1914**
Elegant mansion overlooking the Kentucky River. Styled after the classic architecture of the French Renaissance, the exterior resembles the *Petit Trianon*, Marie Antoinette's villa. The mansion is faced with Bowling Green limestone and has eight Ionic columns supporting the front portico. The interiors include paneled walls, some covered with brocade, parquet floors, and crystal chandeliers. Furnishings represent the span of styles from early American to Victorian.
*Operated by Commonwealth of Ky. Open Tues., Thurs. 9–11:30, unless in use for official functions*

*Governor's Mansion*

# HARRODSBURG

## MANSION MUSEUM, 1836
**Old Fort Harrod State Park**
This two-story brick house built by Maj. James Taylor serves now as a museum, with antique furnishings and Kentucky memorabilia.
*Operated by Old Fort Harrod State Park. Open daily 9–5*

## LIBERTY HALL, about 1796
**218 Wilkinson St**
Stately Georgian-style residence of John Brown, one of Kentucky's first two U.S. senators, and his wife, Margaretta Mason Brown, of New York City. The Browns entertained many notables of the age here. Portraits, heirlooms, and period furnishings are of interest.
*Operated by Soc. of Colonial Dames. Open Tues.–Sat. 10–5, Sun. 2–5*

## OLD GOVERNOR'S MANSION, 1797
**420 High St**
This fine Georgian mansion was the official residence of 33 Kentucky governors between 1798 and 1914. Such notables as Louis Philippe of France, the Marquis de Lafayette, and Henry Clay and several U.S. Presidents have visited here. Restored, it is the official residence of the state's lieutenant governors. The first floor is maintained as a public shrine. Furnishings are of the Georgian and Federal periods.
*Operated by Commonwealth of Ky. Open Mon.–Fri. 10–4 and by appointment*

## ORLANDO BROWN HOUSE, about 1835
**202 Wilkinson St**
Colonial-style house designed by architect Gideon Shyrock. The house was a gift from Sen. John Brown to his son, Orlando. Now a house museum with period furnishings
*Operated by Soc. of Colonial Dames. Open Tues.–Sat. 10–5, Sun. 2–5*

# HODGENVILLE

## ■ ABRAHAM LINCOLN BIRTHPLACE, about 1808
**U.S. Route 31 and Kentucky Route 61**
The birthplace site comprises 116 acres of land and contains the memorial building designed by John Russell Pope and built between 1909 and 1911 of Connecticut pink granite and Tennessee marble. About 100 acres of this land were part of the original Thomas Lincoln farm. Within the memorial building is the traditional Lincoln log cabin birthplace.
*Operated by National Park Service. Open daily 9–5; closed Christmas*

# LEXINGTON

## ■ ASHLAND, 1857
**Route 25**
Italianate mansion reconstructed by Maj. Thomas Lewinski on the site of the 1805 home of Henry Clay and following the plan of the original house. Henry Clay lived at Ashland from 1811 until his death in 1852. The interiors are predominantly Victorian, with Clay family furniture throughout. Now a house museum
*Operated by Henry Clay Memorial Foundation. Open Sept.–May: Tues.–Sat. 9:30–4:30, Sun. 1:30–4:30. June–Aug: Mon.–Sat. 9:30–4:30, Sun. 1:30–4:30*

*Ashland*

## HOPEMONT (HUNT-MORGAN HOUSE), about 1814
**201 N Mill St**
Fine Georgian house built by Lexington's most prominent citizen, John Wesley Hunt. The house was later the home of the builder's grandson, Gen. John Hunt Morgan, Confederate cavalry commander who led the Morgan Raiders. Thomas Hunt Morgan, Kentucky's only Nobel Prize winner, was born here. The house is operated as a museum representing the days when Lexington was known as the "Athens of the West."

Operated by The Blue Grass Trust for Historic Preservation. Open Tues.–Sat. 10–4, Sun. 2–5

## LEXINGTON VICINITY

### WAVELAND, 1847
**Higbee Mill Pike**

One of Kentucky's most distinguished Greek Revival mansions, Waveland was built for Joseph Bryan, Sr., grand-nephew of Daniel Boone, who originally surveyed the acreage on which the structure stands. Meticulously restored, the rooms have been furnished with antiques representing the styles of the mid-19th century. Other interesting features at Waveland are the country store, the blacksmith shop, the icehouse, the herb and flower garden, and the orchard.

*Operated by University of Ky. Open Tues.–Sat. 9–4, Sun. 1–4:30; closed university holidays*

## LOUISVILLE

### FARMINGTON, 1810
**3033 Bardstown Rd**

Brick house built by John Speed on a tract of land granted his father, Capt. James Speed, by Patrick Henry, governor of Virginia. Thomas Jefferson, it is said, drew the plans for the house. Joshua Speed, a son of the builder, was a lifelong friend of Abraham Lincoln, and his brother James was Attorney General in Lincoln's administration. Lincoln paid a visit here in 1841. The house is furnished with American and English antiques made prior to 1820. An early 19th-century garden and a working blacksmith shop may be seen.

*Operated by Historic Homes Foundation. Open Tues.–Sat. 10–4:30, Sun. 1:30–4:30*

### LOCUST GROVE, about 1790
**561 Blankenbaker Lane**

An excellent example of frontier Georgian architecture, this house was built by Maj. William Croghan and his wife, Lucy Clark Croghan. Located on 55 acres, the house has been restored and furnished with period pieces, some of which were made by Kentucky cabinetmakers. Locust Grove was the home of Lucy Clark Croghan's brother, the pioneer hero George Rogers Clark. Among the notables who visited here

were Aaron Burr, Meriwether Lewis and William Clark, President Zachary Taylor, and President James Monroe. The grounds and various outbuildings have also been restored.

*Operated by Historic Homes Foundation. Open Tues.–Sat. 10–4:30, Sun. 1:30–4:30*

*Locust Grove*

## PARIS

### DUNCAN TAVERN, 1788
### ANNE DUNCAN HOUSE, about 1801
**Public Square, 323 High St**

Duncan Tavern, an imposing 20-room, three-story limestone house, was built by Maj. Joseph Duncan and served as an inn, dwelling, and birthplace of the six Duncan children. Maj. Duncan died about 1800, and his young widow was forced to lease out the inn. She then built a home of log construction and clapboard siding (now faced with stone) flush against the tavern wall. Both the tavern and the house have been restored and furnished with period pieces. One of the finest historical and genealogical libraries in Kentucky is housed at Duncan Tavern.

*Operated by Daughters of the American Revolution. Open daily 10–5; closed holidays*

## SHAKERTOWN

### PLEASANT HILL, early 19th century
**off U.S. Route 68**

Community founded by The United

Soc. of Believers in Christ's Second Appearing, commonly called Shakers. The community at Pleasant Hill lasted about 100 years. The village of about 20 buildings has been restored with with Shaker-style furnishings.
*Operated by Shakertown. Open Mon.– Sat. 9–6, Sun., holidays 10–6*

## WASHINGTON

### ALBERT SIDNEY JOHNSTON BIRTHPLACE, about 1795
Frame clapboard house in the center of town, the birthplace of Albert Sidney Johnston, Confederate general in charge of the army in the West in 1861. Gen Johnston was killed at the Battle of Shiloh in 1862.
*Operated by Albert Sidney Johnston Birthplace. Open daily 9–5*

### ■ WASHINGTON HISTORIC DISTRICT
A charming village, Washington was once the second-largest town in Kentucky. It was situated at the crest of a hill that was so long and difficult to climb that a day was sometimes required to bring heavily laden wagons to the top. Once on the crest, travelers usually spent the night or at least stopped for a while. There are several fine homes of the early and mid-19th century still standing.

## ARABI

### ■ JUDGE RENE BEAUREGARD HOUSE, about 1833
**Chalmette National Historical Park**
Located on the site of the Battle of New Orleans, this Louisiana-style plantation house with Doric columns and double galleries was built by Alexander Baron, owner of the Chalmette Plantation, for his mother-in-law. Many years later Rene Beauregard, son of the famous Confederate general, bought the house. It is now the visitors' center and administration building of the park, with exhibits relating to the War of 1812.
*Operated by National Park Service. Open daily 8–5; closed Christmas and Mardi gras*

## BATON ROUGE

### MAGNOLIA MOUND PLANTATION HOUSE, 1780s
**2161 Nicholson Dr**
This large plantation house, originally a four-room house covered with shingles, was built of mud walls between pillars of hand-hewn cypress by John Joyce, an early Louisiana settler. Facing the Mississippi and built on a mound in a grove of magnolias and live oaks, the house is being restored and furnished with appropriate pieces.
*Operated by Foundation for Historical La. and The Baton Rouge Parks and Recreation Comm. Hours to be determined*

## BURNSIDE

### HOUMAS HOUSE, 1840
**River Road, Louisiana Route 44**
Lovely, large ante-bellum Greek Revival mansion built by John Smith Pres-

*Beauregard House*

LOUISIANA

ton; a four-room dwelling at the rear dates from the late 18th century. In 1857 the plantation, named for a local tribe of Indians, was sold to John Burnside, who developed it into the nation's leading sugar producer. Carefully restored by Dr. George B. Crozat after 1940, it is shown with antique furnishings; the grounds have lovely period gardens.
*Operated by the heirs of Dr. George B. Crozat. Open daily 10–4*

## CLOUTIERVILLE

### BAYOU FOLK MUSEUM, early 1800s
**Louisiana Route 1**
Early Louisiana-type "raised cottage" constructed of cypress, heart pine, and slave-made brick; the house is thought to have been built by Alexis Cloutier, the town's founder. In the 1880s the home of Kate Chopin, who later wrote *Bayou Folk*, a collection of stories about the Cane River country. Now a museum of local history with period furnishings of the poorer people depicted in Mrs. Chopin's stories.
*Operated by Bayou Folk Museum. Open Mar.–Nov: Sat., Sun. 2–6, and by appointment*

*Bayou Folk Museum*

## COLUMBIA

### SYNOPE, before 1860
**ten miles north of Columbia, on U.S. Route 165**
Creole "raised cottage" plantation house features four fireplaces and 12-foot ceilings. Part of a 1,500-acre plantation, the house is surrounded by a five-acre landscaped garden.
*Private. Open daily 10–5*

## CROWLEY VICINITY

### BLUE ROSE MUSEUM, about 1860
**five miles southwest of Crowley**
Acadian cottage built of cypress and bricks, with walls of mud and moss. Moved here from Youngsville, it now houses a collection of furniture, china, cut glass, and silver.
*Operated by Blue Rose Museum. Open Mar.–Dec: Tues.–Sat. 9–12, 2–5, Sun. 3–5*

## FRANKLIN

### OAKLAWN MANOR, 1827
**Irish Bend, off U.S. Route 90**
Original plantation house built here by Alexander Porter was destroyed by fire during a 1926 restoration, but a replica was built immediately from photographs. Large classical revival mansion of brick and stone, with six Doric columns and wrought-iron-decorated balconies on the façade. Interiors feature the bed Henry Clay slept in during his frequent visits here and a 19th-century bathtub cut from a single block of marble.
*Private. Open daily 8–6*

## JACKSON

### ASPHODEL, 1820–35
**Louisiana Route 68, off U.S. Route 61**
A 14-room Greek Revival house built by Benjamin Kendrick was the center of a onetime thriving plantation. The mansion—still used as a private residence—is now the headquarters of a "village" of guesthouses.
*Operated by Robert E. and Nootsie Couhig, owners. Open by appointment*

## JEANERETTE

### ALBANIA PLANTATION HOUSE, 1837–42
**U.S. Route 90**
Large frame house with six square wooden columns across the front and three dormer windows along the gable roof. Built by Charles Grevemberg, a French Royalist refugee, the house

features a beautiful unsupported spiral staircase. On display is a lovely collection of dolls.
*Private. Open Mon.–Sat. 9–5, Sun. 1–5*

## LAFAYETTE

### LAFAYETTE MUSEUM, before 1836
**1122 Lafayette St**
Home of Alexander Mouton, the ninth governor of Louisiana and the first elected by the Democratic party. The first floor of the three-story frame house and the separate kitchen, now a cottage, were built by his father, an early Acadian settler. Now a museum featuring antiques and heirlooms of local families
*Operated by Lafayette Museum Assn. Open Tues.–Sat. 9–12, 2–5, Sun. 3–5*

## MEEKER

### LOYD'S HALL, 1816
**U.S. Route 71**
Stately brick house built early in the 19th century; recently restored by the present owners
*Private. Open daily 9–5; closed Tues.*

## MONROE

### COLONIAL DAMES MUSEUM HOUSE, about 1839
**520 S Grand St**
Small one-story building, known locally as "The Little Red Brick House," now a museum featuring exhibits of dolls, jewelry, lace, and other items of local interest
*Operated by Soc. of Colonial Dames. Open by appointment*

## NAPOLEONVILLE

### MADEWOOD, 1840–48
**Highway 308**
Stately Greek Revival ante-bellum plantation house built of stucco over brick by Col. Thomas Pugh; all the wood used in the mansion came from the builder's 3,000-acre plantation. After Louisiana's surrender at the close of the Civil War, the Union commandant stationed troops around Madewood, thereby saving it from looting and destruction. Completely restored and furnished in 1964 by the present owners

*Operated by Mr. and Mrs. Harold K. Marshall, owners. Open daily 10–5*

## NATCHITOCHES

### HISTORIC TOUR
The first white settlement in Louisiana, this city was founded as an outpost in 1714 by Louis Juchereau de St. Denis and a party of 30 Frenchmen and Indian guides. Many houses reflecting the city's Spanish and French heritage are still in existence as private homes, and many are open during the historic tour held the second weekend of October. For information contact Assn. of Natchitoches Women for the Preservation of Historic Natchitoches.

### BEAU FORT, 1830
**Cane River Road**
Early plantation house built by slave labor, with walls of adobe mixed with deer hair. After falling into disrepair the house was carefully restored and furnished with period pieces by the present owner.
*Operated by Mrs. C. Vernon Cloutier, owner. Open by appointment*

### LAUREATE HOUSE, between 1843 and 1860
**225 Poete St**
One-and-a-half-story brick house with brick columns across the façade and a fanlight over the door. Believed to have been built by architects Trizzini and Soldini. Restored by the present owner in 1950
*Operated by Mrs. Ruby Dunkleman, owner. Open by appointment*

### LEMEE HOUSE, 1830
**308 Jefferson St**
One-and-a-half-story brick house covered with plaster built by Swiss-Italian architects Trizzini and Soldini. The house has 18-inch-thick walls, is topped by a cradle roof, typical of 18th-century Italian houses, and has a cellar, a very unusual feature for homes in this area. Completely restored in 1950 and furnished with period pieces
*Operated by Assn. for Natchitoches Women for the Preservation of Historic Natchitoches. Open daily 2–4*

### OAKLAND PLANTATION, 1818
**River Road**
This "raised cottage" plantation house of hand-hewn cypress and adobe walls

of mud, hair, and Spanish moss was built by Jean Pierre Emanuel Prudhomme, whose descendants still live here. A ten-foot-wide gallery surrounds the house, and an avenue of live oaks, planted in 1823, leads up to it. Shown with the family furnishings and a museum collection of early medical equipment and hand tools
*Private. Open by appointment*

**PRUDHOMME-ROUQUIER, about 1803**
**436 Jefferson St**
Two-and-a-half-story adobe house with wide columns, broad galleries, and dormer windows. Built on land granted by the Spanish to François Rouquier, whose daughter married Jean Baptiste Prudhomme
*Private. Open by appointment*

**ROCQUE HOUSE, 1790**
**on the Cane River**
One of the few unaltered French colonial dwellings left in Louisiana, built of hand-hewn cypress beams and uprights, with a mixture of mud and Spanish moss used as a filler. This one-story dwelling with a large overhanging hipped roof features a period kitchen and displays of Natchitoches artifacts.
*Operated by Museum Contents. Open May–Aug: daily 9–1. Sept.–Oct: Sat., Sun. 9–1*

**TANTE HUPPE HOUSE, about 1827**
**424 Jefferson St**
Two-story house of hand-hewn cypress and brick covered with plaster; looks deceptively small but contains 18 rooms with nine fireplaces and 11 outside doors (all the ground-floor rooms have exterior doors). Never altered architecturally but restored by the present owners and furnished with antiques, all from Natchitoches Parish
*Operated by Mr. and Mrs. R. B. De-Blieux, owners. Open by appointment*

**WELLS HOME, about 1776**
**607 Williams Ave**
One of the oldest homes in northwest Louisiana; built of hand-hewn cypress and adobe mixed with deer hide. Restored and furnished with antique pieces, including a music box made for Jerome Bonaparte
*Private. Open by appointment*

## NEWELLTON VICINITY

**WINTER QUARTERS, before 1860**
**three miles southwest of Newellton on Louisiana Route 604**
Originally a three-room hunting cottage built on one of the last land grants given by the Spanish in Louisiana. Expanded to a 19-room mansion with a gallery and five square columns across the front; the house was taken over by Grant's troops during the Civil War.
*Private. Open daily 9–5*

## NEW IBERIA

**DULCITO, 1788**
**off U.S. Route 90**
Typical of Spanish architectural styles, this frame house is built on high pillars and has long galleries. During the Civil War it was used as a hospital.
*Private. Open by appointment*

**JUSTINE, 1822**
**Louisiana Route 96**
This quaint cottage, originally built in Centerville, was shipped by barge on Bayou Teche to its present location.
*Private. Open Wed.–Sun. 10:30–5*

**THE SHADOWS-ON-THE-TECHE, 1831–34**
**217 E Main St**
Stately classical revival town house of pink-colored brick built by planter David Weeks on the banks of the Bayou Teche. Outside stairway leads from the first- to the second-floor gallery; interiors feature fine woodwork and plaster detail. During the Civil War Gen. Nathaniel P. Banks made his Union headquarters here. Shown with the furnishings of five generations
*Operated by National Trust. Open daily 9–4:30; closed Christmas*

*Shadows-on-the-Teche*

# NEW ORLEANS

## SPRING FIESTA

Founded by the French in 1718, New Orleans is one of the most exciting cities in the nation. For two weeks, beginning on the first Friday after Easter, tours are held of the many fascinating districts in and around the city. Included are the houses of the Vieux Carré, the Garden District homes, and the plantations along River Road and the bayous. For information contact the New Orleans Spring Fiesta.

## CASA HOVE, 1720s
### 723 Toulouse St

One of the oldest buildings in Louisiana, this two-story house with a charming second-floor balcony was once the home of the Spanish grandee Don Geronimo Hinard. Now occupied by a business firm; furnished with 18th-century antiques
*Operated by Hové Parfumeur. Open daily 10–5*

## ■ JACKSON SQUARE (*PLACE D'ARMES*)
### bounded by Decateur, St. Peter, St. Ann, and Chartres Streets

Once the center of New Orleans, now a public park, where on Dec. 20, 1803, the U.S. flag was raised for the first time in the Louisiana Territory. Lining the square are many historic buildings, including the Cabildo, built in 1795 as the seat of the Spanish administration; now houses the Louisiana State Museum

## PONTALBA APARTMENTS, 1849–50
### flanking Jackson Square on St. Peter and St. Ann Streets

These handsome red brick apartment houses were built by Baroness de Pontalba from designs by James Gallier, Sr. The baroness's initials, A.P., are incorporated into the cast-iron railings along the second- and third-floor galleries. At 523 St. Ann Street is the *1850 House*, a complete apartment furnished in the style of the period. At 532 St. Peter Street the Soc. of Colonial Dames has its headquarters; two rooms, furnished with French Empire and Directoire pieces, are open by appointment.
*1850 House—Operated by La. State Museum. Open Tues.–Sun. 9–5*

## ■ VIEUX CARRE HISTORIC DISTRICT

The French Quarter, an 85-block area that was the original city laid out on a gridiron plan in 1718. The buildings in the Quarter represent many architectural styles of the 18th and 19th centuries, ranging from those of the French and Spanish colonial periods to those of the post-Civil War era.

*French Quarter street*

# NEW ROADS VICINITY

## ■ PARLANGE, about 1750
### U.S. Route 93, Louisiana Routes 1 and 78

French colonial one-and-a-half-story "raised cottage" of cypress set over a brick basement, topped by a steeply pitched hipped roof with dormer windows; a wide gallery wraps around the house. Built by Marquis Vincent de Ternant and owned ever since by his descendants; restored in 1918 after years of neglect. Shown with the furnishings collected by the family
*Operated by Mrs. Walter Parlange and Mr. and Mrs. Walter Parlange, Jr., owners. Open daily 9–5*

# RESERVE

## SAN FRANCISCO PLANTATION HOUSE, before 1860
### Route 44, River Road

Unusual "Steamboat Gothic" house with raised basement and ornate trim.

Set on eight acres and furnished with 18th-century antiques, including frescoes by Dominique Canova
*Private. Open daily 9–5*

San Francisco

## ST. FRANCISVILLE

**OAKLEY PLANTATION, about 1799**
**U.S. Route 61, Audubon Memorial State Park**
Two-story frame house over a raised brick basement with balustrades on the lower gallery and permanent shutters on the upper. John James Audubon spent four months on the plantation and worked as a tutor to the owner's daughter. Set in a 100-acre park, furnished with period pieces and some original Audubon prints
*Operated by La. State Park and Recreation Comm. Open—House: Mon.– Sat. 9–4:30, Sun. 1–4:30. Park: Mon.– Sat. 9–7, Sun. 1–7*

**ROSEDOWN, 1835**
**U.S. Route 61**
Elegant two-story frame plantation house with one-story wings of cement-covered brick; six Doric columns support the lower gallery along the façade, and an identical set above supports the gabled roof. Furnishings include beautiful European and American antiques collected by the builder of the house, David Turnbull, and his descendants. Ten acres of magnificent gardens, including many rare plants and shrubs, surround the house.
*Private. Open Mar.–Nov: daily 9–5. Dec.–Feb: daily 10–4; closed Christmas Eve and Christmas*

## ST. FRANCISVILLE VICINITY

**CATALPA, early 1800s**
**Louisiana Route 61**
Cottage set in a 30-acre garden show-ing almost every variety of plant and tree native to Louisiana. The house, which is approached along an oak-lined double-horseshoe drive, is still owned by the family that built it and is shown with antique furnishings.
*Private. Open Feb.–Nov: daily 9–5*

**THE COTTAGE, 1795**
**U.S. Highway 61**
"Raised cottage" was begun in 1795; many additions were made until 1859, when the house was finally completed. After the Battle of New Orleans, Andrew Jackson stayed here. The house and 15 plantation outbuildings are shown with furnishings from the period 1795–1815; accommodations are available for overnight guests.
*Operated by Mr. and Mrs. J.E. Brown and Mr. and Mrs. R.H. Weller, owners. Open daily 9–5; closed Christmas*

**THE MYRTLES, before 1860**
**U.S. Route 61**
Ante-bellum house with lovely iron grillwork along its long veranda. Set in a grove of moss-hung oak and shown with interesting interiors, including French chandeliers
*Private. Open daily 9–5*

## ST. MARTINVILLE

**ACADIAN HOUSE MUSEUM, about 1765**
**Longfellow-Evangeline State Park**
Two-story house with wide gallery; the lower floor is made of hand-shaped, sun-dried brick, and the upper of a mixture of mud and green moss plastered on the interior and boarded on the exterior. Originally the home of Pelletier de la Houssaye, an early French commandant at Poste des Attakapas, later St. Martinville. Furnished as a typical Acadian home; located in a large park commemorating the early Acadian settlers
*Operated by La. State Park and Recreation Comm. Open Mon.–Sat. 8:30– 4:30, Sun. 12:30–4:30*

## SHREVEPORT VICINITY

**LANDS END, 1847**
**17 miles north of Shreveport on Red Bluff Road**
Two-and-a-half-story Greek Revival

mansion built by a Confederate congressman, planter, and lawyer. Still owned by his descendants and shown with many of the original furnishings
*Private. Open by appointment*

## THIBODAUX
**EDWARD DOUGLASS WHITE COTTAGE, about 1830**
**Edward Douglass White State Park**
One-and-a-half-story frame "raised cottage" over a brick basement, the birthplace of Edward Douglass White, Chief Justice of the U.S. Supreme Court from 1910 to 1921. Set in a six-acre park and shown with furnishings from the period 1830–90
*Operated by La. State Park and Recreation Comm. Open Tues.–Sat. 9–5, Sun. 1–5*

## VACHERIE
**OAK ALLEY MANSION, about 1830**
**State Highway 18**
Magnificent ante-bellum plantation house famous for its colonnade of 28 Doric columns and the avenue of live

oaks that leads from the house to the Mississippi River
*Private. Open daily 9–5*

## WASHINGTON
**ARLINGTON, 1829**
**Louisiana Route 103**
This large three-story red brick house was built by Maj. Amos Webb. Among its features is an interesting cellar.
*Private. Open daily 10–5*

## WESTWEGO
**MAGNOLIA LANE PLANTATION, 1784**
**River Road, Louisiana Route 18**
"Raised cottage" plantation house originally built on the Old Spanish Trail, then the only wagon road to the West from New Orleans. It was here— on what was known as the Fortier Plantation until 1867—that the first strawberries in the South were raised. Shown furnished with outbuildings, including the original slave cabins
*Operated by Magnolia Lane Plantation. Open by appointment*

LOUISIANA

## AUGUSTA
■ **JAMES G. BLAINE HOUSE [EXECUTIVE MANSION], about 1830**
**Capitol and State Streets**
Frame, two-story classical revival-style home of the Speaker of the House of Representatives (1869–75), Presidential candidate (1884), and Secretary of State (1889–92). Given to the state in 1919 to serve as governor's residence; period furnishings, painting collection, James G. Blaine study
*Operated by State of Maine. Open Mon.–Fri. 2–4*

## BANGOR
**GRAND ARMY OF THE REPUBLIC HOUSE, about 1834**
**159 Union St**
Fine old house with front porch supported by Ionic columns built by

Thomas Hill, pioneer lumberman, and soon after purchased by Samuel Dale, mayor of Bangor during the Civil War years. Now shared by the historical society and the Sons of Union Veterans of the Civil War as a memorial; vast collection of Grand Army material
*Operated by Bangor Historical Soc. Open July–Aug. 22: Tues.–Sat. 10–4 and by appointment*

**SYMPHONY HOUSE, 1833; 1890s**
**166 Union St**
Red brick mansion in modified English Renaissance style designed by architect Richard Upjohn for Isaac Farrar, a Bangor lumber baron. In the 1890s the house was remodeled in late Victorian style: a mansard roof, classic portico, and several bay windows were added. Handsome interiors with mahogany paneling, fine embossed wallpaper, and stained-glass window on stair landing. Houses the

MAINE

Northern Conservatory of Music
*Operated by Bangor Symphony Orchestra. Open during conservatory hours*

## BATH

### HAROLD M. SEWALL HOUSE (BATH MARINE MUSEUM), 1844; 1910
**963 Washington St**
Two-story Greek Revival house, with balustraded roof and entrance portico, now used as a maritime museum celebrating Bath's long shipbuilding history. Some period furnishings and paintings also. The 1910 addition contains a Federal interior from another old Bath house.
*Operated by Marine Research Soc. of Bath. Open May 30–Oct. 15: daily 10–5*

## BLUE HILL

### ■ PARSON FISHER HOUSE, 1814
**Main Street**
Designed and partly built by Jonathan Fisher, called from Dedham, Massachusetts, to be first minister in town. He made the paint from yellow ocher and constructed almost all the furnishings. Paintings, books, and furnishings
*Operated by Jonathan Fisher Memorial. Open July 5–Sept. 15: Tues., Fri. 2–5*

## BOOTHBAY HARBOR

### NICHOLAS-KNIGHT COREY HOUSE, 1784
The house museum of the regional historical society. The town, a picturesque old seaport, is a popular resort for artists and sport fishermen and is famed for yachting.
*Operated by Boothbay Region Historical Soc. Open Mon.–Sat. 1–5*

## BRUNSWICK

### ■ HARRIET BEECHER STOWE HOUSE, 1804
**63 Federal St**
White frame house with high-pitched roof where Harriet Beecher Stowe wrote her indictment of slavery, *Uncle Tom's Cabin*. Now open as an inn. Mrs. Stowe's study is intact and furnished with original items. .
*Private. Open daily*

## CALAIS

### JOSEPHINE MOORE HOUSE, late 18th century
**241 Main St**
One-story frame house, the oldest house in Calais, now used as house museum of the historical society. Over the years it was the home of the first three doctors to practice in town. Miss Moore, a direct descendant of Dr. John Holmes, deeded the property to the society. Early furnishings, maps, pictures
*Operated by St. Croix Historical Soc. Open July–Aug: daily 1–5*

## CAMDEN

### ■ OLD CONWAY HOUSE, about 1768
**Conway Road and U.S. Route 1**
Typical 18th-century farmhouse authentically restored with period furnishings, a blacksmith shop, and barn housing collection of carriages, sleighs, and farm implements
*Operated by Camden Historical Soc. Open July–Labor Day: Tues.–Sun. 1–5*

## COLUMBIA FALLS

### ■ RUGGLES HOUSE, 1818
**Main Street**
Built by Judge Thomas Ruggles, a wealthy lumber dealer, after a design by Aaron Sherman of Massachusetts. Notable for the delicate detail of its exterior trim, its flying staircase, and the unusually fine interior woodwork — such as rope beading on the cornices of the fireplaces — executed by an English artisan. Period furnishings
*Operated by Ruggles House Soc. Open June–Sept: Mon.–Sat. 8:30–4:30, Sun. 10–4*

## DAMARISCOTTA

### ■ CHAPMAN-HALL HOUSE, 1754
**Main and Church Streets**
Built by Nathaniel Chapman, Jr., housewright, this is a typical village farmhouse of the 18th century with interesting wainscoting and paneling. Authentic furnishings, craft tools, historical reference material, and herb garden
*Operated by Chapman-Hall House Preservation Soc. Open June–Sept. Tues.–Sun. 1–5*

## DEER ISLE

### SALOME SELLERS HOUSE, 1830
**Town Center**

An old house now used as a museum of early home furnishings and marine relics; collection of ships' papers, charts, records, and pictures of sailing vessels and steamboats of the area on display
*Operated by Deer Isle-Stonington Historical Soc. Open July 6–Sept. 15: Wed., Sat., Sun. 2–5*

## ELLSWORTH

### ■ COL. JOHN BLACK MANSION, 1802
**West Main Street**

Two-story brick mansion in modified Georgian style built by Col. John Black, land agent, and inhabited by three generations of the Black family. Elegant interiors with gracefully curving spiral staircase, period furnishings, and art objects; carriage house on grounds with old sleighs and carriages
*Operated by Hancock Co. Historical Soc. Open June–Oct. 15: Mon.–Sat. 10–5*

*Black Mansion*

### STANWOOD HOMESTEAD, 1850
**Route 3**

Cape Cod-style frame house set on granite blocks over the small cellar of a previous Stanwood homestead. Built by sea captain Roswell Leland Stanwood and home of his sister Cordelia (1865–1958), a pioneer ornithologist, nature photographer, and author. The homestead, with its original family furnishings, is set in a 40-acre woodland sanctuary called "Birdsacre."
*Operated by Stanwood Wildlife Foundation. Open June 15–Labor Day: 10–4 and by appointment*

## FARMINGTON

### ■ NORDICA HOMESTEAD, about 1810

One-and-a-half-story cottage, birthplace and home of Lillian (Norton) Nordica (1859–1914), great American opera singer. Stage costumes, jewelry, and other memorabilia of her career, as well as family furnishings
*Operated by Nordica Memorial Assn. Open June–Labor Day: Tues.–Sun. 10–12, 1–5*

## GORHAM

### BAXTER HOUSE, about 1800
**South Street**

Birthplace of the Hon. James Phinney Baxter, former mayor of Portland, and home of his son Percival P. Baxter, governor of Maine (1921–24). Early American furnishings, historical records, and local items of interest
*Operated by Town of Gorham. Open July–Aug: Wed., Sat 2–5*

## KENNEBUNK

### WEDDING CAKE HOUSE
**State Highway 35**

One of the country's most fanciful houses, an extraordinary relic of the scroll-saw era. The two-story brick house with central doorway and Palladian window above was built sometime before the elaborate wooden gingerbread trim was added. The slim wooden pinnacles on the roof, Gothic tracery over windows, and crenelated canopy over the doorway give the effect of an old-fashioned lacy valentine. This is a private residence and may be viewed from the exterior only.

*Wedding Cake House*

## KITTERY POINT

### ■ LADY PEPPERRELL HOUSE, 1760
**Route 103**

Fine late Georgian frame mansion, with hip roof and Ionic pilasters two stories high, built by the widow of Sir William Pepperrell—hero at siege of Louisbourg, Nova Scotia, 1745, and first native American created a baronet by the crown. Gracing the front door are a pair of carved dolphins—symbolic of the sea, upon which the Pepperrell fortune was built. Here Lady Mary lived in considerable state enjoying her title and fortune. Beautifully furnished rooms with great fireplaces and fine woodwork
*Operated by Soc. for the Preservation of New England Antiquities. Open June 15–Sept. 15: Tues.–Sat. 11–4*

## LIVERMORE

### ■ THE NORLANDS, 1867
**Norlands Street**

Two-story frame mansion built on site of earlier homestead by famed local family. Israel Washburn, storekeeper and farmer, and his wife, Martha Benjamin, had seven sons, every one of whom achieved national prominence in the service of their country. Empire and Victorian family furnishings; also a library, school, and church
*Operated by Israel Washburn Estate. Open by appointment*

## MACHIAS

### BURNHAM TAVERN, 1770
**High and Free Streets**

Plain, two-story gambrel-roofed structure built by Joe Burnham. Here the townspeople gathered during the Revolution to discuss their moves against the British, including the exciting capture of the *Margaretta*. The original sign still hangs over the door: "Drink for the thirsty, food for the hungry, lodging for the weary, and good keeping for horses."
*Operated by Daughters of the American Revolution. Open June–Aug: Tues., Wed. 2–5 and by appointment*

## POLAND SPRING VICINITY

### ■ SHAKER VILLAGE, 1793

One of the last remaining Shaker communities in the country; originally established in 1793 to adhere to the tenets of the faith as set forth by Mother Ann Lee, founder of the first Shaker colony in the U.S. In 1931 the remaining members of the Alfred, Maine, colony joined this group, which engages in farming and small industries. The village tour includes the old Shaker Meeting-House (1794), the four-story Stone Building, once a community house, and the museum, featuring furniture and craft and agricultural exhibits.
*Operated by Shaker Community. Open summer for tours*

## PORTLAND

### ■ McLELLAN-WINGATE-SWEAT MANSION, 1800
**111 High St**

Fine Federal mansion with semicircular porch built by Hugh McLellan according to plans of Boston architect Alexander Parris. At one time the home of Gen. Joshua Wingate; left to the Portland Soc. of Art by Mrs. L.D.M. Sweat on condition that its late Victorian furnishings be kept intact
*Operated by Portland Soc. of Art. Open Tues.–Sat. 10–5, Sun. 2–5*

### ■ MORSE-LIBBY HOUSE [VICTORIA MANSION], 1859
**109 Danforth St**

Victorian mansion in the Italian villa style designed by prominent architect Henry Austin for Ruggles S. Morse. With its central tower, irregular roof line, and pedimented windows, it is

*Victoria Mansion*

considered to be one of the finest examples of Italianate architecture in the country. Ornate interiors, with flying staircase, carved woodwork, and excellent Victorian furnishings
*Operated by Victoria Soc. of Maine Women. Open June–Sept. 15: Mon.–Sat. 10:30–4:30*

■ **SPRING STREET HISTORIC DISTRICT, 19th century**
The several examples of notable architecture from the Federal through the Victorian periods reflect Portland's progress and growth in the 19th century as a center for shipbuilding and later as a steamboat and rail center.

■ **TATE HOUSE, 1755**
**1270 Westbrook St**
Home of George Tate, mast agent for the British navy, in the style of a London town house; said to be Portland's oldest dwelling. George Tate, Jr., left this home for the sea, spent 50 years in the service of the Russian navy, and became a first admiral. Interiors feature unusual wood paneling said to have been brought from England. Restored with period furnishings
*Operated by Soc. of Colonial Dames. Open July–Sept. 15: Tues.–Sat. 11–5, Sun. 1:30–5*

■ **WADSWORTH-LONGFELLOW HOUSE, 1785; 1815**
**487 Congress St**
Dignified old brick house built by Gen. Peleg Wadsworth, grandfather of the famous poet, who lived here until he entered Bowdoin College at the age of 14. Set behind a high iron fence, the house's only ornamentation is a Doric portico forming the front entrance; the third story and hip roof were added after a fire in 1815. Family furnishings used by the two families, documents, manuscripts, and other memorabilia
*Operated by Maine Historical Soc. Open June 15–Sept. 15: Mon.–Sat. 9:30–4:30*

## ROCKLAND

**FARNSWORTH HOMESTEAD, 1840**
**19 Elm St**
Greek Revival home of the Farnsworth

family, with Victorian-style furnishings. Now used to exhibit some of the collection of the art museum
*Operated by William A. Farnsworth Library and Art Museum. Open June 15–Sept. 15: Tues.–Sat. 10–4, Sun. 1–4*

## SEARSPORT

**PENOBSCOT MARINE MUSEUM**
The museum's collections are housed in four buildings—the Old Town Hall and three houses: *Capt. Merithew House* (1816), a fine two-story Federal dwelling with collections of charts, navigational instruments, paintings, pressed glass; *Fowler-True-Ross House* (1825), which offers many other fine paintings and models; *Nickels-Colcord-Duncan House* (about 1880), Victorian-style structure with research library and rooms for special exhibits.
*Operated by Penobscot Marine Museum. Open June–Sept: Mon.–Sat. 9–5, Sun. 1–5*

## SKOWHEGAN

**HISTORY HOUSE, 18th century**
**Elm Street**
An 18th-century homestead on the Kennebec River turned into a museum to reflect the town's history as well as the region of the upper Kennebec. Period furnishings, books, china, etc.
*Operated by History House Assn. Open June 15–Sept. 15: Tues.–Sat. 1–5*

## SOUTH BERWICK

**HAMILTON HOUSE, about 1785**
**Route 236**
Built by Col. Jonathan Hamilton, an affluent West India merchant, high above the Salmon Falls River in a garden setting overlooking his wharves. The mansion has handsome architectural details—such as rose-and-scroll pediments over the dormer windows—and 18th-century-style furnishings. Sarah Orne Jewett made this house the setting of *The Tory Lover.*
*Operated by Soc. for the Preservation of New England Antiquities. Open June–Sept: Wed.–Sat. 1–5*

**JEWETT MEMORIAL, 1774**
**101 Portland St**
Two-and-a-half-story frame house with

Doric portico built by Capt. Theodore Jewett; birthplace in 1849 of his granddaughter, novelist Sarah Orne Jewett. Graceful center staircase, fine paneling and early wallpapers, family furnishings. Many of Miss Jewett's novels were written here, and her bedroom-study has been preserved as she arranged it.
*Operated by Soc. for the Preservation of New England Antiquities. Open June–Sept: Wed.–Sat. 1–5*

## SOUTH CASCO

### ■ NATHANIEL HAWTHORNE BOYHOOD HOME, 1812
**Raymond Cape Road**
Two-and-a-half-story frame house erected by Richard Manning for his sister, the mother of the famous author, who lived here in seclusion after her husband's death. From the age of seven Nathaniel lived here, and he spent his vacations from Bowdoin College at his boyhood home. Now used as a community center, with few furnishings
*Operated by Board of Trustees. Open June–Aug: Sun. 1–5 and by appointment*

## SOUTH WINDHAM

### PARSON SMITH HOMESTEAD, 1764
**89 River Rd**
Substantial farmhouse built by Rev. Peter T. Smith on the site of Old Province Fort, a stockade against Indian attacks. Two large chimneys provide for a fireplace in every room, the kitchen one being ten feet wide.
*Operated by Soc. for the Preservation of New England Antiquities. Open June–Sept: Tues., Thurs., Sun. 1–5, and by appointment*

## STANDISH

### DANIEL MARRETT HOUSE, 1789
**Route 25**
Large, two-and-a-half-story house that became the home of Rev. Marrett on his appointment to the parish. During the War of 1812 the coin from Portland banks was stored in the basement for safekeeping. Early furnishings with family portraits; fine group of connected outbuildings

*Operated by Soc. for the Preservation of New England Antiquities. Open June–Sept: Tues., Thurs., Sun. 1–5, and by appointment*

## THOMASTON

### ■ MONTPELIER, 1793
**High Street**
Replica of the original mansion of Gen. Henry Knox, first U.S. Secretary of War. Imposing two-story structure with elliptical central façade and balustrade on roof. Antique furniture from original house and personal possessions of the general
*Operated by Knox Memorial Assn. Open daily 10–5*

## WISCASSET

### NICKELS-SORTWELL HOUSE, 1807
**Main and Federal Streets**
Large three-story Federal mansion famed for its imposing façade with a story-high entrance portico, Corinthian pilasters, and second-story Palladian window. Appealing family furnishings
*Operated by Soc. for the Preservation of New England Antiquities. Open June–Sept: Tues.–Sat. 11–5, Sun. 2–5*

*Nickels-Sortwell House*

## YORK

### ELIZABETH PERKINS HOUSE, 1686; 1732
**South Side Road**
Old frame colonial house; the central part is the original small cottage and its

chimney, the front part was built by Joseph Holt in 1732. Original white oak beams, stenciled drawing room, period furnishings, Simon Willard tall case clock, and portraits. Summer residence of the Perkins family, whose last descendant, Miss Elizabeth Perkins, founded the York preservation society
*Operated by Soc. for the Preservation of Historic Landmarks in York Co. Open May 30–Labor Day: Mon.– Sat. 9:30–5, Sun. 1:30–5*

### EMERSON-WILCOX HOUSE, about 1740
**York Street**
Typical New England country home with trim fence which was enlarged over the years as the needs of the family changed. Historical associations

with local York families; period furnishings. The house has been a tavern and post office as well as a residence. *Operated by Old Gaol Museum Committee. Open May 28–Sept: Mon.– Sat. 9:30–5, Sun. 1:30–5*

### JEFFERDS' TAVERN, about 1750
**Lindsay Road**
Frame saltbox building built by Capt. Samuel Jefferds to serve stagecoach travelers on the run between York and Kennebunk. Moved from the nearby town of Wells and reconstructed in York with original chimney and old paneling. Interesting taproom, kitchen, scenic wall paintings
*Operated by Soc. for the Preservation of Historic Landmarks in York Co. Open May 30–Labor Day: Mon.– Sat. 9:30–5, Sun. 1:30–5*

# ANNAPOLIS

### ■ ANNAPOLIS HISTORIC DISTRICT
Annapolis is one of America's first planned cities. It was the capital of the colony and, subsequently, the state. The boundaries of the historic district approximate those of the original town plan of 1695. Many outstanding mid-18th-century mansions survive, some designed by noted architect William Buckland. In addition to the homes listed below, others may be visited in an open-house tour in mid-October.

### ■ CHASE-LLOYD HOUSE, 1769
**22 Maryland Ave**
Three-story Georgian mansion designed by William Buckland for Samuel Chase, a signer of the Declaration of Independence. This is considered one of Buckland's best works. Francis Scott Key and Mary Tayloe Lloyd were married here in 1802. Fine interior woodwork and furnishings. Now serves as home for elderly ladies
*Operated by Board of Trustees. Open Mon., Tues., Thurs., Sat. 10–12, 2–4*

### GOVERNMENT HOUSE, 1868
**College Avenue and Bladen Street**
Originally built in the Victorian style

during the administration of Thomas Swann (1865–69), the mansion was converted in 1935 to colonial lines, in keeping with adjacent buildings and the overall pattern of Annapolis. It has been the residence of Maryland's governors since its construction. Its 54 rooms are furnished with antiques, some original to the house. Paintings by such noted artists as Rembrandt Peale, Hogarth, and Sully on view
*Operated by State of Md. Open Labor Day–June 15: Tues., Thurs. 10–3:30 by appointment*

### ■ HAMMOND-HARWOOD HOUSE, 1774
**19 Maryland Ave**
Two-story Georgian mansion built for Matthais Hammond, a man of wealth and education who was deeply involved in the public affairs of his day. The house was designed by William Buckland and is considered to be his masterpiece. Buckland is believed to have executed the fine woodwork carving of the interiors as well. Furnishings are of the 18th century, many pieces original to the house, some made by such well-known cabinetmakers as John Shaw of Annapolis.

*Operated by Hammond-Harwood House Assn. Open Mar.–Oct: Mon.–Sat. 10–5, Sun. 2–5. Nov.–Feb: Mon.–Sat. 10–4, Sun. 1–4; closed Christmas*

Hammond-Harwood House

## QUYNN-BREWER HOUSE, 1734
**26 West St**
Restored house now serving as offices and bank. Furnishings are of the Queen Anne style.
*Operated by Capitol City Federal Savings and Loan Assn. Open Mon.–Fri. 9–4*

## ST. JOHN'S COLLEGE
**St. John's College Campus**
There are several historic buildings on the campus, and although most are not open on a regular basis, arrangements may be made to see them by contacting the college. Two houses are open, however. *Charles Carroll The Barrister House*, 1722–23, King George Street—two-story 18th-century mansion, the birthplace of the barrister. The structure was moved to this location in 1955 and restored; it now houses the offices of admissions of St. John's College. *Open daily 9–5. McDowell Hall*, 1744; 1789—originally planned to be the home of colonial governor Thomas Bladen. After much wrangling between Bladen and the legislature over building costs construction ceased, and the unfinished house, by then dubbed "Bladen's Folly," fell to ruin. The house was finally completed in 1789 and donated to the college. Restored, it now houses classrooms and offices of the college staff.
*Open by appointment*

# BALTIMORE

## CARROLL MANSION, about 1812
**Front and Lombard Streets**
Christopher Deshon built this fine town house, and according to John H. B. Latrobe, Benjamin H. Latrobe's son, it was the finest house in Baltimore in its day. Charles Carroll of Carrollton, the only signer of the Declaration of Independence to include his address on the document, lived here the last ten years of his life. As the sole survivor of the signers, he received a stream of visitors at the house. It is now a museum, furnished in the styles popular 1810–45.
*Operated by City of Baltimore and the Peale Museum. Open Wed.–Sat. 10:30–4:30, Sun. 1–4*

Carroll Mansion

## EDGAR ALLAN POE HOUSE, 1830
**203 N Amity St**
Small house, restored and furnished with period pieces, the residence of Poe from 1832 to 1835, when he was courting his 13-year-old cousin, Virginia Clemm, who became his wife. He wrote his first short stories here.
*Operated by Edgar Allan Poe Soc. Open Wed., Sat. 1–4*

## EVERGREEN, about 1850; 1885
**4545 N Charles St**
Classical revival-style mansion on 36 acres of beautifully wooded grounds built by a family named Broadbent,

prominent merchants and brokers. An archway and north wing were added by T. Harrison Garrett, and in the 1920s his son John Work Garrett (U.S. ambassador to Italy, 1929–33) enlarged and magnificently decorated the house. It is now a museum, with a collection of about 8,300 rare books, modern paintings by artists such as Dufy, Bonnard, Picasso, Vuillard, and others, Oriental art objects, blue and white Chinese export porcelain, a Victorian room, a garden room with Dutch furniture of the 18th century, and a theater decorated by Léon Bakst, an eminent designer of the *ballet russe*. *Operated by Evergreen House Foundation. Open Mon.–Fri. 2–5*

■ **FEDERAL HILL HISTORIC DISTRICT**
Consisting of Federal Hill Park and the houses on the streets facing and sloping away from the park to the west and south, Federal Hill commands a magnificent view of the city of Baltimore, which surrounds the hill. Several hundred early dwellings remain from the 18th and mid-19th centuries.

■ **FELLS POINT HISTORIC DISTRICT**
Laid out as a town in 1763 by Edward Fell and incorporated, into Baltimore Town in 1773, Fells Point contains many two-and-a-half-story houses which were the homes of artisans involved in port activities, such as ships' carpenters and sailmakers, and seamen. There are also some more elaborate three-and-a-half-story homes of the shipyard owners, merchants, and sea captains.

**MARYLAND HISTORICAL SOC. (ENOCH PRATT HOME), 1847**
**201 W Monument St**
Residence of Enoch Pratt, philanthropist. This structure, with a new addition, now houses the society's collection of books, paintings, manuscripts, and artifacts of American history. It is being redecorated in the 1820–40 style with fine furniture, paintings, and so

forth. The original manuscript of "The Star-Spangled Banner," by Francis Scott Key, may be seen here.
*Operated by Md. Historical Soc. Open Tues.–Sat. 11–4, Sun. 1–4*

**MOTHER SETON HOUSE, about 1800**
**600 N Paca St**
Mrs. Elizabeth Seton conducted a Roman Catholic girls' school here in 1808, a year before she took her vows as a nun. Mother Seton founded the American Sisters of Charity and was beatified in 1963. Open as a furnished house museum; a stained-glass window of Mother Seton may be seen.
*Operated by Mother Seton's House in Baltimore. Open Tues., Thurs., Sat., Sun. 1–3*

■ **MOUNT CLARE, 1754**
**Carroll Park**
The city's only remaining pre-Revolutionary mansion, this distinguished Georgian plantation house was the summer home of Charles Carroll the Barrister, distant cousin of Charles Carroll of Carrollton, signer of the Declaration of Independence. Many original furnishings recall the elegance of the 18th century, and portraits of the Carrolls by Charles Willson Peale hang in the drawing room. Except for the wings adjoining, which are a later addition, the house is much as Charles Carroll left it.
*Operated by Soc. of Colonial Dames. Open Apr.–Oct: Tues.–Sat. 11–4:30, Sun. 2–4:30. Nov.–Mar: Tues.–Sat. 11–4, Sun. 2–4*

■ **STAR-SPANGLED BANNER FLAG HOUSE, 1793**
**844 E Pratt St**
Built only 150 feet from the water's edge, this salmon-colored brick house is the birthplace of Mary Young Pickersgill, the maker of the Fort McHenry battle flag that inspired Francis Scott Key when he wrote the battle hymn in 1814 that became the national anthem in 1931. Authentic 1812 period furnishings and possessions of Mary Pickersgill exhibited, as well as a replica of the flag and the battle hymn in Key's handwriting

*Operated by Star-Spangled Banner Flag House Assn. Open Tues.–Sat. 10–4, Sun. 2–4:30*

*Star-Spangled Banner Flag House*

## BURKITTSVILLE VICINITY

**GATHLAND STATE PARK**
**off Maryland Routes 17 and 67**
Once the estate of George Alfred Townsend, one of the most important American journalists of the Civil War and Reconstruction eras. Townsend lived here between 1885 and 1906, writing, entertaining, and assembling nine buildings and a monumental arch on 100 acres he called Gapland. A number of the buildings still stand, and the remains of some of the others may be seen.
*Operated by Md. Dept. of Forests and Parks. Open Apr.–Oct: daily, daylight–dark. Museum: Sat., Sun., holidays, 10–dark*

## CAMBRIDGE

**MEREDITH HOUSE, about 1760**
**Maryland Avenue**
Three-story brick Georgian house, with a wooden wing on one side, built by the Meredith family, prominent in the affairs of the area at that time. Furnished with items of the period and memorabilia of the five Maryland governors from Dorchester County. An adjacent building exhibits old farm implements. Also of interest are a smokehouse and a library of early Maryland history.
*Operated by Dorchester Co. Historical Soc. Open by appointment*

## CHESTERTOWN
■ **CHESTERTOWN HISTORIC DISTRICT, 18th century**
A major port from about 1730 to 1790, shipping tobacco and wheat to all parts of the world. Many fine Georgian town houses were built by the merchants and planters during this period, and about 50 of these structures have survived the ravages of time.

## CUMBERLAND

**HISTORY HOUSE, after 1866**
**218 Washington St**
Originally a 16-room Victorian-style house, with beautiful fireplaces, built by Josiah Gordon. A second-floor bedroom shows initials of the Gordons cut into a windowpane. Now a house museum containing a collection of toys, military and transportation items, and a library of genealogical data
*Operated by Allegany Co. Historical Soc. Open. Apr.–Oct: Sun. 1:30–4:30 and by appointment*

## EASTON

**HISTORICAL SOC. OF TALBOT COUNTY, 1795–1802**
**29 S Washington St**
Four-story brick town house with Federal furnishings, models of 18th- and 19th-century sailing vessels, colonial artifacts, woodworking tools, and kitchen utensils. Restored as the headquarters of the historical society
*Operated by Historical Soc. of Talbot Co. Open Tues.–Fri. 10–4*

## FREDERICK

**BARBARA FRITCHIE HOME**
**156 W Patrick St**
Reconstruction of the home of the heroine of Whittier's Civil War poem "Barbara Frietchie." Relics and furniture of hers and her times exhibited.
*Operated by Barbara Fritchie Home. Open Mar.–Nov: daily 9–5*

**ROGER BROOKE TANEY HOME, 1799**
**121 Bantz St**
Restored home of the Chief Justice of the Supreme Court who handed down the Dred Scott decision. Justice Taney

also administered the oath of office to Abraham Lincoln. The house is now a memorial and museum with furnishings of the Taney family and Francis Scott Key, Taney's brother-in-law.
*Operated by Francis Scott Key Memorial Foundation. Open June–Oct: daily 10–4. Rest of the year: by appointment*

## GLEN ECHO

■ **CLARA BARTON HOUSE, 1891**
**5801 Oxford Rd**
Residence of the founder of the American Red Cross from 1890 until her death in 1912. Miss Barton was fond of Mississippi River steamboats and had the house built on the steamboat plan with Gothic-style interiors. Original furnishings; gardens as Miss Barton designed them
*Operated by Friends of Clara Barton. Open Tues.–Sat. 1–5; closed holidays*

## HAGERSTOWN

**JONATHAN HAGER HOUSE, 1739–40**
**on Memorial Boulevard, near Walnut Street**
Early fieldstone house, said to be the first in the area, built by the founder of Hagerstown, Maryland. The house was built over two springs to assure a protected water supply. Hager engaged in the fur trade, and it is evident that the house was also used as a combined fur post and storehouse. An adjacent building exhibits Hager memorabilia and artifacts found during restoration of the house in 1953.

*Jonathan Hager House*

*Operated by Washington Co. Historical Soc. Open Apr.–Oct: Tues.–Sat. 10–5, Sun. 1–5. Nov.–Mar: by appointment*

**MILLER HOUSE, 1823–24**
**135 W Washington St**
Town house with a typical Latrobe-type spiral stairway to the third floor. The drawing rooms are furnished in the Empire style, and 12 other rooms contain exhibits of clocks, Victorian antiques, early quilts, and paintings. In addition, the house serves as headquarters and library of the Washington County Historical Soc.
*Operated by Washington Co. Historical Soc. Open summer: Sun. 2–5*

## HOLLYWOOD

**SOTTERLEY MANSION, about 1730**
**Route 245, three miles from Hollywood**
Long low plantation house built on land originally granted by Lord Baltimore. It takes its name from the English ancestral home of the Plater and Satterlee families. Four generations of Platers lived here from 1730 to 1822, one of whom was George Plater, governor of Maryland in 1791–92. Unusually fine interiors; Chinese Chippendale stairway; shell cupboards flanking the drawing room fireplace; period furnishings
*Operated by Sotterley Mansion Foundation. Open June–Sept: daily 11–6 and by appointment*

## LAUREL

■ **MONTPELIER, 1740–51; 1770–71**
**Laurel-Bowie Road, Route 197**
Georgian brick plantation house built by Thomas Snowden and later enlarged by his son Maj. Thomas Snowden. It was here that George Washington stopped in 1787 on his way to and from the Constitutional Convention. The central section is a superior example of the early period, and the wings and connecting links, which were added about 20 years later, make of the whole an excellent example of a late Georgian five-part composition. Hand-carved interior woodwork; furnishings of late 18th century

Operated by Md. National Capital Park and Planning Comm. Open by appointment

*Montpelier*

## LEONARDTOWN

**TUDOR HALL, mid-18th century**
**two blocks east of courthouse**
Rectangular stuccoed brick building built by Abraham Barnes, who directed that his 300 slaves be freed upon his death providing they assumed his family name. Barnes is now one of the most common surnames of the black families in St. Marys County. Now houses the county library
*Operated by St. Marys Co. Historical Soc. Open Mon.–Sat. 9–5, Mon., Thurs. evgs. 5–9*

## PIKESVILLE VICINITY

**GREY ROCK, about 1700; 1890**
**Reisterstown Road**
Large gray stone house, the birthplace of John Eager Howard, a general of distinction in the Revolutionary War. Howard was governor of the state, 1788–91, and a U.S. senator, 1796–1803.
*Operated by the Trinitarian Order of the Roman Catholic Church. Hours to be determined*

## PRINCESS ANNE

**TEACKLE MANSION, 1801**
**Mansion Street**
Built by Littleton Dennis Teackle, an associate of Jefferson, Madison, and Monroe, this mansion is reminiscent of a Scottish manor house. Great pains were taken in its construction to achieve perfect symmetrical balance throughout the house. The hall and drawing room on the first floor are particularly interesting for their elaborate plasterwork ceilings and mirrored windows. Restoration in progress

Operated by Olde Princess Anne Days. Open Sun. 2–4 and by appointment

## RISON

**GEN. SMALLWOOD'S RETREAT, 1760**
**Gen. Smallwood State Park, U.S. Route 224**
Restored two-story brick country residence of the Revolutionary general from 1760 until his death in 1792. The brick was brought from England. About one-third of the original house is incorporated into the present structure. Now a museum with furnishings, some of which belonged to Smallwood's family, spanning the years 1658–1800
*Operated by Md. Dept. of Forests and Parks. Open Mar.–Memorial Day and Labor Day–Nov: Sat., Sun., holidays 10–6. Memorial Day–Labor Day: daily 10–6; closed Dec.–Feb.*

## ROCKVILLE

**BEALL-DAWSON MANSION, 1815**
**103 W Montgomery Ave**
Large Georgian mansion built of solid brick by Upton Beall, gentleman farmer and member of a prominent Maryland family. Upton Beall's daughter Margaret inherited the house and lived here for many years with her cousin Amelia Somerville, who married John Lawrence Dawson. Dawson descendants occupied the house until 1946. The house and grounds have been restored, and furnishings, many of local origin, are of the early 1900s.
*Operated by Montgomery Co. Historical Soc. Open Tues.–Sat. 12–4*

## ST. MARYS CITY

■ **ST. MARYS CITY HISTORIC DISTRICT**
Founded in 1634, this is probably the only surviving major 17th-century town in the U.S. remaining so unaltered. It has never been overbuilt or seriously intruded upon. The undisturbed foundations of about 60 17th-century structures provide an interesting archaeological site for studying building techniques and architecture of that period.

## TOWSON

■ **HAMPTON MANSION, 1783–90**
**535 Hampton Lane**
Late Georgian structure, one of the largest houses of its time, built by Charles Ridgely, a member of the Maryland legislative assembly. It is built of stone and stuccoed, with its two-and-a-half-story main section balanced by one-story wings. Restored formal gardens, outbuildings, slave quarters, and overseer's house. Original furnishings and portraits
*Operated by National Park Service and Soc. for the Preservation of Md. Antiquities. Open Tues.–Sat. 11–5, Sun., holidays 1–5; closed Labor Day, Christmas, and New Year's Day*

## UNION MILLS

**SHRIVER HOMESTEAD, 1797; 1820; 1865**
**Route 140**
A 23-room clapboard house of a Z-shape, which was originally a double house connected by a porch and passage. Each house had an upper and a lower room. Built by two brothers, Andrew and David Shriver, the homestead and mill, which they also built, began as outposts of early expansion into western Maryland. From that time to the present, the house has always been occupied by members of the same family. Over the years it has served as a stagecoach station, post office, store, and magistrate's court.
*Operated by Union Mills Homestead Foundation. Open May–Oct: Mon.–Sat. 10–5, Sun. 1–5*

## WESTMINSTER

**SHELLMAN HOUSE, about 1807**
**206 E Main St**
Three-storied late Georgian-style brick house built for David Shriver, one of the early pioneers of Carroll County. The house was built by Jacob Sherman, Shriver's father-in-law. Alexander Graham Bell visited here about 1886. The house is restored and furnished with antiques ranging from 1807 through the Victorian period. Excellent doll collection and artifacts and pictorial history of the first country-wide rural free delivery service are exhibited.
*Operated by Historical Soc. of Carroll Co. Open Mon.–Sat. 2–5*

## AMESBURY

■ **JOHN GREENLEAF WHITTIER HOME, 1836**
**86 Friend St**
Ten-room frame home of the poet from 1836 to his death in 1892. Whittier family furnishings including his desk and manuscripts on exhibit
*Operated by Whittier Home Assn. Open Tues.–Sat. 10–5*

**MACY-COLBY HOUSE, 1654**
**Main Street**
The 17th-century saltbox-type home of Thomas Macy and Anthony Colby. In 1655 Macy was exiled for sheltering Quakers during a rainstorm, an incident related in John Greenleaf Whittier's poem "The Exile." Furnished as a typical pioneer home
*Operated by Bartlett Cemetery Assn. Open July–Aug: Wed. 2–4*

**MARY BAKER EDDY HISTORICAL HOUSE, early 18th century**
**227 Main St**
Early 18th-century home of Squire Lowell Bagley; lived in by the founder of Christian Science from 1868 to 1870 when she wrote *The Science of Man* See also Lynn, Stoughton, Swampscott
*Operated by Longyear Foundation. Open May–Oct: Tues.–Sun. 2–5; closed holidays*

## AMHERST

**NEHEMIAH STRONG HOUSE, 1744**
**67 Amity St**
Gambrel-roofed frame dwelling built by local craftsmen of hand-hewn timber and hand-wrought hardware. The oldest house in town; period furnishings and items of historical interest
*Operated by Amherst Historical Soc. Open July–Labor Day: Mon.–Fri. 2–5*

## ANDOVER

### AMERICA HOUSE, before 1832
**147 Main St**

A 19th-century house of little architectural but great historical interest. For here in 1832 Samuel F. Smith, a 24-year-old student at Andover Theological Seminary, wrote the patriotic hymn "America." The verses were first publicly sung at a Sunday school in Boston in 1832 and rapidly spread.
*Operated by Phillips Academy. Open by appointment*

### DEACON AMOS BLANCHARD HOUSE, 1819
**97 Main St**

Lovely three-story Federal house Deacon Blanchard built in the center of his farm. Existing account books show total cost of land, house, and barn: $4,100. All original interior woodwork intact; period furnishings and objects of local historical interest
*Operated by Andover Historical Soc. Open Mon., Wed., Fri. 2–4*

## ARLINGTON

### JASON RUSSELL HOUSE, about 1680
**7 Jason St**

Frame dwelling of Russell family and descendants until 1890. Site of massacre of Jason Russell and 11 other Minutemen who took cover there on April 19, 1775, date of the fateful Battle of Lexington and Concord. Furnishings and memorabilia of Revolutionary period, including British bullet holes
*Operated by Arlington Historical Soc. Open April–Nov: weekdays, 2–5*

## BARNSTABLE

### WILLIAM STURGIS HOUSE, 1644
**Main Street**

House originally built for Rev. John Lothrop in 1644. Probably a half house of two stories. His descendant William Sturgis, a wealthy sea captain in the China trade, grew up here and later willed the house and his book collection to the inhabitants of Barnstable. Now open as a public library with Cape Cod genealogy, history, and the sea as specialties
*Operated by Trustees of the Sturgis Library. Open library hours*

*John Balch House*

## BEVERLY

### JOHN BALCH HOUSE, 1636
**448 Cabot St**

A medieval frame dwelling built by John Balch in 1636 on part of the original land grant given the "Old Planters." Occupied by the Balch family until 1914, it is the oldest wooden frame house in the U.S. with a record. Early implements of home industries
*Operated by Beverly Historical Soc. Open June 15–Sept. 15: Mon.–Sat. 10–4*

### JOHN CABOT HOUSE, 1781
**117 Cabot St**

Stately 18th-century home built by John Cabot. Now headquarters of the local historical society with two research libraries and a museum with many items of historical interest
*Operated by Beverly Historical Soc. Open July–Aug: Mon.–Sat. 10–4. Sept.–June: Mon., Wed., Fri., Sat. 10–4*

### REV. JOHN HALE HOUSE, 1694
**39 Hale St**

Beautiful old home of John Hale, first minister of Beverly and great-grandfather of the Revolutionary patriot Nathan Hale. Mistress Hale, exemplary wife of the minister, was accused during the last days of the witchcraft hysteria; her case was dismissed and the trials were soon after abandoned. Period family furnishings
*Operated by Beverly Historical Soc. Open June 15–Sept. 15: Tues.–Sat. 10–4*

## BILLERICA

### CLARA E. SEXTON MEMORIAL HOUSE, about 1729
**36 Concord Rd**

House with conventional early plan:

two main rooms upstairs and down, with smaller rear rooms on both levels, central chimney. Façade features pedimented doorway; small doctor's office and bay window added in 19th century. Period furnishings
*Operated by Billerica Historical Soc. Open June–Labor Day: Sun. 2–5 and by appointment*

## BOSTON

■ **BEACON HILL HISTORIC DISTRICT, 18th and 19th centuries**
Residential district of many distinguished American personages in the late 18th and 19th centuries. Also significant for a number of fine Federal and Greek Revival homes, some designed by Charles Bulfinch

**BEACON HILL MANSIONS [WOMEN'S CITY CLUB OF BOSTON], 1818**
**39–40 Beacon St**
Twin Federal town houses designed in Charles Bulfinch's office by Alexander Parris with curved walls and doors, original French wallpapers, and fine Federal furnishings
*Operated by Women's City Club of Boston. Open Wed. 10–4; closed holidays*

**FENWAY COURT [ISABELLA STEWART GARDNER MUSEUM], 1903**
**280 The Fenway**
An Italian-style palace built by Mrs.

*Fenway Court*

Isabella Stewart Gardner with lovely central courtyard celebrated for changing flower displays. Now established as a museum for the owner's extensive art collection and furnishings
*Operated by Isabella Stewart Gardner Museum. Open Tues., Thurs., Sat. 10–4, Sun. 2–5; closed Aug. and national holidays*

**GIBSON HOUSE, 1859**
**137 Beacon St**
Brownstone-and-brick Victorian residence built by Mrs. John Gardiner Gibson. Excellent example of Back Bay décor of 1890s; endowed by Charles Hammond Gibson as Victorian museum
*Operated by Gibson House. Open Tues.–Sun. 2–5; closed holidays*

**HARRISON GRAY OTIS HOUSE, 1796**
**141 Cambridge St**
First of three houses designed by Charles Bulfinch for the U.S. senator and mayor of Boston. Sophisticated example of Federal style with Palladian window, exquisite Adamesque ornamentation, and period furnishings. Now operated as a museum and headquarters for the Society for the Preservation of New England Antiquities
*Operated by Society for the Preservation of New England Antiquities. Open Mon.–Fri. 10–4; closed holidays*

■ **HEADQUARTER'S HOUSE, 1807–8**
**55 Beacon St**
Early Federal house built by merchant prince James Smith Colburn and designed by influential architect Asher Benjamin, whose pattern books spread the post-colonial style throughout New England. Owned by Samuel Ward, the father of Julia Ward Howe, from 1819 to 1833 and by William H. Prescott, the historian, from 1845 to 1859. Period furnishings
*Operated by Soc. of Colonial Dames. Open by appointment*

■ **MOSES PIERCE-HICHBORN HOUSE, 1680–1710**
**29 North Square**
A 17th-century brick town house built by Moses Pierce, typical of pre-Georgian brick dwellings erected to replace

the wooden structures destroyed in the fire of 1676. Antique furnishings of 17th and 18th centuries
*Operated by Moses Pierce-Hichborn House. Open May 15–Oct. 15: Tues.–Sun. 10–4; closed holidays*

**NICHOLS HOUSE, about 1810**
**55 Mount Vernon St**
Four-story Federal brick house designed by Charles Bulfinch. Contains antique furnishings and art works of Miss Rose Standish Nichols, who left her home as a museum
*Operated by Nichols House Museum. Open Wed., Sat. 1–5; closed holidays*

■ **PAUL REVERE HOUSE, about 1677**
**19 North Square**
Frame dwelling with overhang restored to original 17th-century exterior; the only survivor of Boston's first half century; interiors restored and furnished in style of period the famous patriot and silversmith lived here, 1770–1800
*Operated by Paul Revere Memorial Assn. Open Mon.–Sat. 9–3:45; closed holidays*

*Paul Revere House*

**BOXFORD**

**HOLYOKE-FRENCH HOUSE, 1760**
**Elm Street**
Symmetrical mid-18th-century house with twin chimneys and gambrel roof. Originally served as rectory for the First Congregational Church; now a period museum
*Operated by Boxford Historical Soc. Open Memorial Day–Columbus Day: Sat., Sun. noon to dusk*

**BRAINTREE**

**GEN. SYLVANUS THAYER BIRTHPLACE, 1720**
**786 Washington St**
Frame house built by Nathaniel Thayer in 1720; the birthplace of the "Father of the U.S. Military Academy." Restored as a town museum
*Operated by Braintree Historical Soc. Open Apr.–Oct: Tues., Fri., Sun. 1:30–4, Thurs., Sat. 10:30–4. Nov.–Mar: Tues., Sat. 1:30–4*

**BROOKLINE**

**EDWARD DEVOTION HOUSE, about 1740**
**347 Harvard St**
18th-century dwelling now maintained as house museum with period furnishings and portraits. One of few extant houses passed by Paul Revere on his famous ride
*Operated by Brookline Historical Soc. Open Wed. 2–4 and by appointment*

■ **JOHN F. KENNEDY BIRTHPLACE, about 1908**
**83 Beals St**
Modest frame house, birthplace of our 35th President, who was born here in 1917. Maintained as a house museum
*Operated by National Park Service. Open daily 10–5, Sun. 1–5*

**CAMBRIDGE**

**COOPER-FROST-AUSTIN HOUSE, 1657; 1720**
**21 Linnaean St**
East half built by Deacon John Cooper in 1657 and is the oldest building still standing in Cambridge; west half was probably added around 1720. Later Frost and Austin owners were Cooper descendants. Steeply pitched roof and pilastered chimney retain 17th-century flavor. Much of original interior detail has been preserved, shown with period furnishings. A Massachusetts Historic Landmark
*Operated by Soc. for the Preservation of New England Antiquities. Open June–Oct: Mon., Thurs. 2–5, Tues. 7–9. Nov–May: Mon. 7–9, Thurs. 2–5*

**LEE-NICHOLS HOUSE, about 1660**
**159 Brattle St**
Frame dwelling with stone west end

begun in 17th century but mainly built after 1758. Occupied at time of Revolution by Joseph Lee, a Tory so esteemed that his property was not confiscated
*Operated by Cambridge Historical Soc. Open Thurs. 3–5 and by appointment*

■ VASSALL-CRAIGIE-
LONGFELLOW HOUSE, 1759
**105 Brattle St**
Fine Georgian two-story frame house built by Tory Maj. John Vassall in 1759; headquarters of Gen. George Washington during siege of Boston; enlarged by Henry Wadsworth Longfellow from 1837 to 1882; here he wrote his best-known works. Furnished as Longfellow left it
*Operated by Longfellow Memorial Trust. Open weekdays 10–5, weekends 1–5*

## CENTERVILLE

MARY LINCOLN HOUSE, about 1840
**513 Main St**
Charming old Cape Cod house once belonging to Clark Lincoln, who willed it to his daughter Mary Ellen; Mr. Lincoln's tinsmith shop is still next door. Recently restored with a new wing added to house collection of local historical society; period furnishings
*Operated by Centerville Historical Soc. Open end of June–Labor Day: Sun., Thurs. 2–4:30*

## CHATHAM

OLD ATWOOD HOUSE, 1752
**Stage Harbor Road**
An 18th-century house with gambrel roof and central chimney; interiors have fine paneling and old hardware. Home of novelist Joseph C. Lincoln (1870–1944), especially known for his Cape Cod stories. Period furnishings
*Operated by Chatham Historical Soc. Open June 15–Sept 15: Wed., Fri. 2–5*

## CHELMSFORD

"OLD CHELMSFORD" GARRISON HOUSE, about 1690
**Garrison Road**
One of the 19 original garrison houses built for protection against Indians.

A saltbox type with great fieldstone central chimney, huge fireplace, chamfered summer beam, gunstock posts, and wide paneling. First owner Lt. Thomas Adams was related to President John Adams. Carefully restored with early period furnishings
*Operated by "Old Chelmsford" Garrison House Assn. Open June–Oct: Sun. 2–5 and by appointment*

## CHELSEA

GOV. BELLINGHAM-CARY HOUSE, 1659
**34 Parker St**
Hip-roof frame house originally built by Gov. Bellingham as a hunting lodge in 1659. Enlarged in early 18th century and again by Samuel Cary in 1791–92, it is the oldest house extant in Suffolk County. In it Gen. Washington quartered troops besieging Boston. Period furnishings
*Operated by Gov. Bellingham-Cary House Assn. Open Thurs. 2–5 and by appointment*

## COHASSET VILLAGE

COHASSET HISTORIC HOUSE, about 1804
**Elm Street**
A frame New England village house built by David Nichols against a ledge so that the first floor is half the depth of the second. Capt. John Wilson purchased it in 1810 and used the first floor as a ship chandlery for some years. Now a house museum completely furnished in style of early 19th century
*Operated by Cohasset Historical Soc. Open June 21–Labor Day: Tues.-Sat. 1:30–4:30*

## CONCORD

ANTIQUARIAN HOUSE
**Lexington Road**
A museum with 14 authentic New England period rooms from 1685 to 1870 showing furniture and decorative arts from the locality. Includes Ralph Waldo Emerson's study and its contents, Henry David Thoreau room, Revolutionary relics, and diorama of fight at North Bridge
*Operated by Concord Antiquarian Soc. Open Mon.-Sat. 10–4:30, Sun. 2–4:30*

■ **OLD MANSE, 1769**
**Monument Street**
Clapboard house with gambrel roof and two pedimented doorways built by Rev. William Emerson, whose family watched the battle at North Bridge in 1775 from an upper window. His philosopher grandson, Ralph Waldo Emerson, spent much of his boyhood here. Nathaniel Hawthorne and his wife lived here from 1842 to 1846 and gave the house its name; he described it in *Mosses from an Old Manse*. The Ripley family lived in it before and after this time. Furnished with objects associated with its famous residents. A Massachusetts Historic Landmark
*Operated by The Trustees of Reservations. Open June–Oct 15: weekdays 10–4:30, Sun. 1–4:30. Apr.–May, Nov: Sat., Sun., holidays 1–4:30*

■ **ORCHARD HOUSE, 1650; 1730**
**399 Lexington Rd**
Formerly two old houses joined and remodeled by the Alcott family, who lived here 1858–68. Here Louisa May Alcott wrote the first part of *Little Women;* she called the house "Apple Slump" after the orchard on the grounds. Interiors, furnishings, paintings, and books associated with Alcott family on exhibit
*Operated by Louisa May Alcott Memorial Assn. Open Apr.–Nov: Mon.–Sat. 10–5, Sun. 2–6*

■ **RALPH WALDO EMERSON HOUSE, 1828**
**Cambridge Turnpike**
Frame dwelling occupied by Emerson from 1835 until his death in 1882. Victorian furnishings, hangings, and portraits of Emerson's day, except for replica of his study and library. Emerson's library of classics and first editions has been transferred to the Concord Antiquarian Soc.
*Operated by Emerson House Assn. Open Apr.–Dec: Tues.–Sat. 10–11:30, 1:30–5:30, Sun 2:30–5:30*

## CUMMINGTON

■ **WILLIAM CULLEN BRYANT HOMESTEAD, about 1799; 1856**
**Route 112**
White clapboard house with two wings; new lower floor added in 1856. Child-hood home and later summer residence of William Cullen Bryant. Here he wrote two of his best-known poems. A historic house museum with the poet's furnishings and memorabilia
*Operated by The Trustees of Reservations. Open June 15–Sept: Tues.–Sun. 10–5*

## DANVERS

■ **DERBY SUMMERHOUSE, 1792–93**
**Glen Magna Estate**
Federal garden house with Adam-style decoration originally built for wealthy merchant Elias Haskett Derby's summer residence at Peabody. Designed by Salem craftsman-architect Samuel McIntire, the roof has typical McIntire urns at each corner and life-sized wooden carvings of a milkmaid and a farmer by John and Simeon Skillen of Boston.
*Operated by Danvers Historical Soc. Open daily 10–4*

*Derby Summerhouse*

**GLEN MAGNA MANSION HOUSE, 17th century; 1890s**
**Glen Magna Estate**
Handsome, white-pillared mansion whose oldest section stood on the site from before 1692. The inland farm

property was owned by the Ingersoll family throughout the 18th century and was purchased by Capt. Joseph Peabody of Salem in 1814 to protect his family and goods from the British attacks on the seacoast. The modest two-story clapboard house was in continuous family summer occupancy for 144 years. When descendant Mrs. William Crowninshield Endicott acquired the property in the 1890s she retained Boston architect Herbert Browne to transform it from a farmhouse to a stylish country mansion. Thus the mansion while retaining Federalist elements reflects architecturally the 1890s and first quarter of the 20th century. The beautiful grounds, to which Samuel McIntire's Derby Summerhouse was moved in 1901, were laid out by America's pioneer landscape architect Frederick Law Olmstead. The Essex Institute of Salem has lent some of the fine furnishings on display.
*Operated by Danvers Historical Soc. Open daily 10–4*

### JEREMIAH PAGE HOUSE, 1754
**11 Page St**
Attractive mid-18th-century dwelling with gambrel roof and dormer windows built by Jeremiah Page, a colonel in the Revolutionary War. Scene of amusing incident just prior to the Revolution: his rebellious wife responded to his edict that no British-taxed tea be served under his roof by holding a tea party on the roof. Period furnishings
*Operated by Danvers Historical Soc. Open July–Aug: Wed. 2–4 and by appointment*

### JUDGE SAMUEL HOLTEN HOUSE, about 1670
**171 Holten St**
Dwelling with steeply pitched roof and central chimney and ells; home of Revolutionary patriot Judge Holten. Maintained as a memorial with collections of glass and china
*Operated by Daughters of the American Revolution. Open June–Sept: by appointment*

### REBECCA NURSE HOUSE, 1678
**149 Pine St**
Frame medieval dwelling of 17th cen-

tury with steeply pitched roof built by Francis Nurse. His wife Rebecca was a victim of the witchcraft hysteria and was hanged in 1692 stoutly protesting her innocence. Restored in 20th century and partially furnished in period of Pilgrim century
*Operated by Soc. for the Preservation of New England Antiquities. Open July–Sept: Tues., Thurs., Sun. 1–5*

## DANVERSPORT

### SAMUEL FOWLER HOUSE, 1810
**166 High St**
Fine brick Federal mansion built in 1810. Exhibited with original woodwork and scenic wallpapers by Jean Zuber of France. Well furnished with antiques
*Operated by Soc. for the Preservation of New England Antiquities. Open June–Sept: Tues., Thurs., Sun. 1–5*

## DEDHAM

### ■ FAIRBANKS HOUSE, 1636
**511 East St**
A medieval-style dwelling built by Jonathan Fayerbanke in 1636, and added to in 1648 and 1654, considered to be the oldest wood-frame structure in the United States. Eight generations of the same family lived here, and it is now maintained as a house museum by the Fairbanks. All the furnishings and objects within make an intimate commentary on three centuries of American home life. A Massachusetts Historic Landmark
*Operated by Fairbanks Family Assn. Open May–Nov: Tues.–Sun. 9–12, 1–5*

*Fairbanks House*

## DEERFIELD

### FRARY HOUSE, 1685
**Main Street**
A 17th-century saltbox built by Samson Frary and reputed to have withstood the Indian raids. The Barnard Tavern added in 1765 contains a fine colonial ballroom.
*Operated by Pocumtuck Valley Memorial Assn. Open May–Nov: Tues.-Sat. 9–12, 1:15–5, Sun. 2–5*

### JOHN SHELDON INDIAN HOUSE, 1698
**Main Street**
Reproduction of the house that was the focal point of the 1704 massacre. The original door with a tomahawk still embedded in it is in Memorial Hall.
*Operated by Indian House Memorial. Open May–Nov: Mon.-Sat. 9:30–12, 1–5, Sun. 1:30–5; closed Tues.*

### OLD DEERFIELD VILLAGE, 18th and 19th centuries
**Route 5**
Ten buildings from 1717 (*Wells-Thorn House*) to 1824 (*Wright House*) depicting various modes of life from the early 18th-century pioneer to the later wealthy landowner. Excellent period furnishings
*Operated by Heritage Foundation. Open May 15–Oct: Mon.-Sat. 9:30–12, 1–4:30, Sun. 1:30–4:30*

*Ashley House*

### ■ OLD DEERFIELD VILLAGE HISTORIC DISTRICT
Laid out in 1666, by the beginning of the 18th century Deerfield was the outpost of New England's northwestern frontier. In 1675 and 1704 the town rebuilt itself after devastating French and Indian raids. Today many of the 18th-century buildings remain and much of the village has been restored.

## DENNIS

### JOSIAH DENNIS MANSE, 1736
**Nobscussett Road and Whig Street**
Two-story, shingled saltbox built for the Rev. Josiah Dennis for whom the town was named. Features wide-board floors, five enormous central fireplaces, hand-hewn beams, and gunstock corner posts. In the process of being furnished with gifts of antiques
*Operated by Town of Dennis. Open July–Aug: Wed.-Fri. 2–5*

## DORCHESTER

### BLAKE HOUSE, about 1648
**Edward Everett Square**
Two-and-a-half-story shingled cottage, built by James Blake, with steeply pitched roof and diamond-shaped casements. Hand-hewn beams and old hardware in interior
*Operated by Dorchester Historical Soc. Open by appointment*

### PIERCE HOUSE, about 1650
**24 Oakton Ave**
Unique 17th-century house originally built about 1650 and added to once before the end of the 1600s and then again in the 1760s. Descended in the Pierce family until mid-20th century and reflects ten generations of uninterrupted occupancy by the same family; sparse furnishings
*Operated by Soc. for the Preservation of New England Antiquities. Open June–Sept: Tues., Thurs., Sat. 1–5*

### ROGER CLAP HOUSE, 1633; 1761
**23 Willow Court**
Early 17th-century house built by Roger Clap, commander of the fort at Castle Island. Enlarged in 1761 and used to quarter American soldiers during Revolution
*Operated by Dorchester Historical Soc. Open by appointment*

## DOVER

### BENJAMIN CARYL HOUSE, 1777
**Dedham Street**
Built for the first minister of Dover,

a simple colonial dwelling with central chimney in original condition. Completely furnished in keeping with the period of the house
*Operated by Dover Historical Soc. Open Sat. 1–5*

## DUXBURY

### JOHN ALDEN HOUSE, 1653
**105 Alden St**
A 17th-century dwelling built by Jonathan Alden, third son of Pilgrims John and Priscilla Alden, who also lived here. Period furnishings
*Operated by Alden Kindred of America. Open June 20–Labor Day: daily 9–5*

## EAST BRIDGEWATER

### DR. ORR HOUSE, 1749
### 1791 HOUSE
**The Old Common**
Two old houses, part of a museum complex including an art gallery, church, and nature walks. The Dr. Hector Orr house recalls the busy life of an early Massachusetts doctor; much of the original paneling and hardware is preserved. The 1791 house was originally owned by the Alden family and, like many New England homes, expanded over the years.
*Operated by Standish Museums. Open Mon.–Sat. 10–5, Sun. 1–5*

*Dr. Orr House*

## EAST WEYMOUTH

### ABIGAIL ADAMS BIRTHPLACE, 1685
**North and Norton Streets**
Built in 1685 by the Rev. Samuel Lowry, only a portion of the original dwelling remains where Abigail Smith Adams, daughter of a Weymouth clergyman, was born. Period furnishings
*Operated by Abigail Adams Historical Soc. Open July–Aug: Tues.–Fri. 1–4*

## EDGARTOWN

### THOMAS COOKE HOUSE, 1765
**Cooke Street**
Squire Thomas Cooke, collector of customs and justice of the peace, had his two-and-a-half-story shingled house, with central doorway and chimney, built by ship carpenters in 1765. Distinctive features are the slanted beams, the floors and paneling; furnishings are authentic pieces gathered from other homes on Martha's Vineyard. Choice scrimshaw collection
*Operated by Dukes Co. Historical Soc. Open June–Sept: Tues.–Sat. 10–4:30, Sun. 2–4:30. Oct–May: Tues., Wed. 1–4, Sat. 10–12, 1–4*

## FALL RIVER

### FALL RIVER HISTORICAL SOC., 1843
**451 Rock St**
Granite mansion built by an affluent mill owner during the period of Fall River's greatest prosperity; used as a station of the Underground Railway. Moved to present location in 1870 and now used as a house museum with 16 rooms filled with objects mostly of local interest
*Operated by Fall River Historical Soc. Open Tues.–Fri. 9–4:30, Sat. 9–12; closed holidays*

### JULIA WOOD HOUSE, 1790
### CONANT HOUSE, about 1794
**55 Palmer Ave**
Two 18th-century frame colonial houses separated by a boxwood garden on landscaped grounds containing a gazebo and barn. The Wood House, topped by a widow's walk, was built by Dr. Francis Wicks, early crusader for smallpox inoculation. Both houses are museums, with period furnishings and other historical society exhibits, such as the whaling collection.

# MASSACHUSETTS

Operated by Falmouth Historical Soc.
Open June 15–Sept. 15: daily 1–5

*Saconesset Homestead*

## SACONESSET HOMESTEAD, 1678
**Route 28A**

A "Ship's Bottom Roof House," the largest of the few remaining colonial bowed-roof houses. Built in 1678, it has remained in the hands of the Bowerman and Gifford families for nearly 300 years. All their accumulated possessions represent a unique collection of Americana. The grounds have early farm implements and livestock.
*Operated by Saconesset Homestead Museum. Open May 20–Oct. 29: daily 10–6*

## GLOUCESTER

### "BEAUPORT"
**Eastern Point Boulevard**

An extraordinary house with different rooms built to represent various architectural styles and periods starting from the colonial era. Material for these rooms was brought from all parts of Massachusetts and assembled under one roof; each is completely furnished in its period.
*Operated by Soc. for the Preservation of New England Antiquities. Open June–Sept: guided tours at 2:30, 3:30, 4:30; closed weekends and holidays*

### CAPT. ELIAS DAVID HOUSE, 1804
**27 Pleasant St**

Federal-style house built in 1804 for one of Gloucester's merchant traders, Capt. Davis. Period furnishings, children's rooms, basket collection, costumes, ships' models
*Operated by Cape Ann Historical Assn. Open Tues.–Sat. 11–4; closed holidays*

■ **FITZ HUGH LANE HOUSE, 1849–50**
**harbor side of Rogers Street**

A three-story Gothic Revival house, of hand-cut stone blocks with massive granite jambs and lintels on the numerous windows and seven steeply pitched gables, built by famous marine painter Fitz Hugh Lane. Inside four Gothic vaults cover the chambers of the upper floors. A Massachusetts Historic Landmark
*Operated by Gloucester Housing Authority. Under restoration*

### SARGENT - MURRAY - GILMAN - HOUGH HOUSE, 1768
**49 Middle St**

Georgian house with gambrel roof, dentil cornice, and quoined corners. Sometime after 1788 it was the home of the Rev. John Murray, "Father of American Universalism." Carved and paneled interiors, antique furniture
*Operated by Sargent-Murray-Gilman-Hough House. Open June 24–Sept. 15: Mon.–Fri. 11–5*

## GROTON

### GOV. BOUTWELL HOUSE, 1851
**Main Street**

Frame mansion of the Victorian period. Home of George Sewall Boutwell, an organizer of the Republican party, governor of Massachusetts, and Secretary of Treasury under President Grant. Period furnishings
*Operated by Groton Historical Soc. Open June–Oct: Sat. 3–5*

## HADLEY

### PORTER - PHELPS - HUNTINGTON HOUSE ("FORTY ACRES"), 1752; 1770–99
**128 River Drive**

Standing in a beautiful grove and surrounded by a split-rail fence, a mid-18th-century gambrel-roofed structure with additions made from 1770 to 1799 by Charles Phelps and unchanged since then. For many years the summer home of Frederic Dan Huntington (1819–1904), first Episcopal bishop of the diocese of Central New York. Period furnishings and family papers from 1697
*Operated by Porter-Phelps-Huntington Foundation. Open May–Oct. 15: daily 1–5*

# HANCOCK

■ **HANCOCK SHAKER VILLAGE,**
**late 18th century**
Third oldest of Shaker communities
exemplifying leader Mother Ann Lee's
injunction to "put your hands to work
and your hearts to God." On over
a thousand acres, the architecture of 18
Shaker buildings is that of functional
simplicity as characterized by family
houses and the unique round stone
barn. New England and New York
Shaker furnishings of simple beauty
exhibited in 65 rooms. A Massachusetts Historic Landmark
*Operated by Shaker Community.*
*Open June–Oct. 15: daily 9:30–5*

*Hancock Shaker Village*

## HANOVER CENTER

**SAMUEL STETSON HOUSE, about**
**1694**
**514 Hanover St**
A shingled two-and-a-half-story frame
dwelling built about 1694 as a one-
room house, it was enlarged before
1716 by "Drummer" Samuel Stetson
to its present size. Now restored with
original wide-plank floors, a broad collection of colonial and Indian relics
*Operated by Soc. for the Preservation*
*of New England Antiquities. Open*
*June–Oct: Tues., Thurs. 1–5*

## HARVARD

**FRUITLANDS MUSEUMS**
**Prospect Hill Road**
An "open-air" museum complex with
four buildings, including the early-

18th-century farmhouse where Bron-
son Alcott and other Transcendentalist
leaders attempted in 1843 to found a
new social order. Also on the grounds:
Harvard Shaker Soc. building, erected
1794; an Indian museum; and an art
gallery of New England primitives and
Hudson River landscapes. A Massachusetts Historic Landmark
*Operated by Fruitlands Museums.*
*Open June–Sept: Tues.–Fri. 1–5;*
*open holidays*

## HAVERHILL

**JOHN GREENLEAF WHITTIER**
**BIRTHPLACE, 1688**
**305 Whittier Rd**
Built by Thomas Whittier in 1688, a
fine example of an early New England
farmhouse. Birthplace of the gentle
Quaker poet and scene of his popular
"Snow-bound." Restored with the
original family furnishings
*Operated by John Greenleaf Whittier*
*Homestead. Open Tues.–Sat. 9–5,*
*Sun. 1–5*

**JOHN WARD HOUSE, before 1645**
**"THE BUTTONWOODS," 1814**
**240 Water St**
The first frame house in Haverhill was
built for the town's first minister, the
Rev. John Ward, sometime before
1645. It has been restored and furnished in 17th-century style. Adjacent
and high above the Merrimack River
is the clapboard brick-ended "Buttonwoods," built in 1814, furnished with
18th- and 19th-century period styles,
and housing the society's collections.
*Operated by Haverhill Historical Soc.*
*Open June–Sept: Tues.–Sat. 2–5. Oct–*
*May: Tues., Thurs., Sat. 2–5*

## HINGHAM

**"THE OLD ORDINARY," about**
**1650**
**19 Lincoln St**
A 17th-century structure with two
additions made in the next century.
Now operated as a house museum with
period furnishings, restored taproom,
collection of hand tools, and changing
craft exhibits
*Operated by Hingham Historical Soc.*
*Open June–Sept. 15: Tues.–Sat. 11:30–*
*4:30*

## SAMUEL LINCOLN HOUSE, about 1741
**182 North St**

An 18th-century wooden house, two-and-a-half stories with gambrel roof, built about 1741 with later addition. Standing on part of the original Lincoln family grant, it has two rooms open as a Lincoln Memorial.
*Operated by Soc. for the Preservation of New England Antiquities. Open by appointment*

## HOLYOKE

### WISTARIAHURST, about 1848; 1913
**238 Cabot St**

Victorian mansion of William Skinner, founder of Skinner Silk & Satin Mills, moved from its original site in Williamsburg in 1874. English-style interiors, parquetry floors, marble fireplaces, Tiffany-glass windows, interesting wallpapers, period rooms, and museum collections. The Skinner collection of old musical instruments is now at Yale University.
*Operated by Holyoke Museum. Open Mon.–Sat. 1–5, Sun. 2–5*

## IPSWICH

### EMERSON-HOWARD HOUSE, about 1648; 1709
**41 Turkey Shore Rd**

A 17th-century house with second-story overhang, steep roof, and large central chimney. Built over two periods; now partially restored
*Operated by Soc. for the Preservation of New England Antiquities. Open June–Oct: Tues., Thurs., Sun. 1–5*

### JOHN HEARD HOUSE, 1795
**40 S Main St**

Federal house, built by John Heard and occupied by his descendants until 1936, with Palladian window over entrance and Chippendale-style staircase in wide central hall. Period furnishings with emphasis on many Oriental treasures brought back during the China trade. Formal garden in the courtyard
*Operated by Ipswich Historical Soc. Open Apr.–Nov: Tues.–Sat. 10–5, Sun. 1–5*

### ■ JOHN WHIPPLE HOUSE, 1640
**53 S Main St**

Charming medieval house with steep-pitched roof and casement windows built by John Fawn in 1640. By 1642 Elder John Whipple lived here and his descendants occupied the house for 200 years, adding the east half in 1670 and the lean-to after 1700. Unusually fine architectural details in interior and rare furnishings of 17th and 18th centuries; 17th-century herb garden. One of the earliest restorations, dating from 1898
*Operated by Ipswich Historical Soc. Open Apr.–Nov: Tues.–Sat. 10–5, Sun. 1–5*

*John Whipple House*

### LAKEMAN-JOHNSON HOUSE, about 1850
**16 East St**

Built in the second quarter of the 19th century, a good example of the simple home of a typical New England sea captain with period furnishings
*Operated by Soc. for the Preservation of New England Antiquities. Open June–Oct: Tues., Thurs., Sun. 1–5*

## JAMAICA PLAIN

### LORING-GREENOUGH HOUSE, 1760; 1811
**12 South St**

Frame house built in 1760 by Commodore Joshua Loring, an officer in the royal navy, and embellished by Charles Bulfinch in 1811. A Massachusetts Historic Landmark with period furnishings, collections of calling-card cases, snuff boxes, beaded bags, and dolls
*Operated by Jamaica Plain Tuesday Club. Open by appointment*

# KINGSTON

## MAJ. JOHN BRADFORD HOUSE, 1674
**Landing Road**
Weather-beaten old frame house with unstained shingles and diamond-shaped window panes retaining medieval appearance. Huge fireplace with Dutch oven; period furnishings
*Operated by Bradford House. Open July–Labor Day: daily 10–5*

# LEXINGTON

## HANCOCK-CLARKE HOUSE, 1698; 1734
**35 Hancock St**
A frame dwelling of hand-hewn oak originally built as a parsonage for Rev. John Hancock in 1698; his son Thomas added the front section in 1734. At the outbreak of the Revolution it was the home of Rev. Jonas Clarke, whose guests, Samuel Adams and John Hancock, were awakened by Paul Revere on the night of April 18, 1775. Period furnishings and Revolutionary relics. Two taverns, Buckman (1690) and Munroe (1695), connected with the events of that fateful April 19th are included in a local tour with this house.
*Operated by Lexington Historical Soc. Open Apr. 19–Oct. 31: Mon.–Sat. 10–5, Sun. 1–5*

# LONGMEADOW

## COLTON HOUSE, 1734
**787 Longmeadow St**
Frame house characteristic of Connecticut River Valley. According to town legend, one of the family, Jabez Colton, recorded unusually complete local genealogical data by carrying a book and inkhorn wherever he went.
*Operated by Soc. for the Preservation of New England Antiquities. Open June–Oct: Tues., Thurs., Sat. 1–5*

## STORRS HOUSE, 1786
**697 Longmeadow St**
Built by Richard Salter Storrs, second pastor of the First Church of Christ, and lived in by three generations of the Storrs family. Moved and redecorated about 1930; period furnishings
*Operated by Longmeadow Historical Soc. Open June–Sept: Fri., Sat. afternoons*

# LOWELL

## WHISTLER HOUSE, 1823
**243 Worthen St**
A 19th-century house standing directly on the sidewalk; birthplace of the famous American painter and etcher James Abbott McNeill Whistler (1834–1903), who went to Paris in 1855 and never returned to the U.S. Displayed in the nearby Parker Art Gallery are etchings by Whistler as well as works of contemporary artists in changing exhibits.
*Operated by Parker Art Gallery. Open Tues.–Sun: 1–5:30*

# LYNN

## HYDE-MILLS HOUSE, 1838
**125 Green St**
White frame Greek Revival "double" house built and occupied by two leading carpenters and builders of the time, Messrs. Hyde and Mills. Interiors have been changed to house the collection of the local historical society, but the character of the original house has been preserved. Period furnishings, museum collections, an 18th-century shoemaker's shop
*Operated by Lynn Historical Soc. Open Mon.–Fri. 10–12, 1–4*

## MARY BAKER EDDY RESIDENCE, 19th century
**12 Broad St**
One of residences of Mary Baker Eddy, founder of Christian Science. Now open as a Christian Science reading room with many of the original furnishings. See also Amesbury, Stoughton, Swampscott
*Operated by The First Church of Christ, Scientist, Boston. Open Mar.–Nov: Mon.–Sat. 10–5. Dec.–Feb: Mon.–Sat. 10–3:30*

# MANCHESTER

## TRASK HOUSE, 1814
**12 Union St**
Early 19th-century house with later additions now serving as headquarters of the local historical society. Period furnishings made in Manchester and other items of local interest
*Operated by Manchester Historical Soc. Open July–Aug: Wed. 2–5*

## MANSFIELD

### FISHER-RICHARDSON HOUSE, 1704; 1800
### 354 Willow St

Originally a little frame half house built by Ebenezer Hall, the west half was added in 1800 and doubled the size of the house. The house was sold to Rev. Ebenezer White in 1760 and was lived in by his descendants until the 20th century when it was deeded to the town of Mansfield as a historical landmark. Restored with period furnishings and examples of early American industries
*Operated by Mansfield Historical Soc. Open June 15–Sept. 15: Sat., Sun. 2–5*

## MARBLEHEAD

### ■ JEREMIAH LEE HOUSE, 1768
### 161 Washington St

An excellent example of New England Georgian architecture with rusticated wooden façade, Ionic entrance portico, and cupola on hip roof; exemplifies the wealth and position of the 18th-century merchant. Fine interior paneling, richly decorated main stairway, hand-painted wallpaper, period furnishings
*Operated by Marblehead Historical Soc. Open Mon.–Sat. 9:30–4*

*Jeremiah Lee House*

### KING HOOPER MANSION, 1728; 1745
### 8 Hooper St

Three-story mansion, with a wooden façade simulating stone, built by merchant Robert Hooper, called "King" after his great wealth and royal manner of life. He added the Georgian front rooms in 1745. Changing art exhibits of local and well-known artists
*Operated by Marblehead Arts Assn. Open Tues.–Sun. 1:30–5*

## MARSHFIELD

### HISTORIC WINSLOW HOUSE, 1699; about 1756
### Webster and Carswell Streets

Built in 1699 by the Hon. Isaac Winslow, this large hip-roofed house with quoin trim was remodeled about 1756. Shown with period furnishings. Daniel Webster's law office is on the grounds.
*Operated by Historic Winslow House. Open July–Labor Day: daily 10–5; closed Tues.*

## MEDFIELD

### "THE PEAK HOUSE," 1680
### Route 109

Named for its extraordinarily high-peaked roof, this small 17th-century dwelling with leaded casements is the oldest in Medfield. According to legend, townsman Seth Clark received indemnity from the colonial government for his first home burnt by the Indians during King Philip's War in 1676; he then built this house on the site. However it is more authentically attributed to Benjamin Clark. Restored
*Operated by Medfield Historical Soc. Open July–Aug: Sun. 2–5*

*Peak House*

# MEDFORD

■ **ISAAC ROYALL HOUSE,**
**mid-18th century**
**15 George St**
The brick nucleus of this house was built in the 17th century on Gov. John Winthrop's Ten Hills Farm. In 1732 wealthy merchant Col. Isaac Royall acquired the property and enlarged it to a Georgian-style mansion covering up the existing brickwork with wood. His son, Isaac, Jr., inherited the estate in the 1740s, doubled the depth of the house, and refinished the interior. Very fine paneling, wood carving, and period furnishings
*Operated by Royall House Assn. Open May–Oct. 15: daily 2–5; closed Mon., Fri.*

*Isaac Royall House*

■ **PETER TUFTS HOUSE, 1678**
**350 Riverside Ave**
Probably the oldest New England brick 17th-century structure, only 11 of which are known to have been built, with gambrel roof and walls 18 inches thick. Although the house was restored in the 1890s, the elaborately molded oak summer beams and girts and early staircase are authentic and superb examples.
*Operated by Soc. for the Preservation of New England Antiquities. Open June–Oct: Tues.–Thurs. 1–5*

# MELROSE

**PHINEAS UPHAM HOUSE, 1703**
**255 Upham St**
Early 18th-century house, with 13-inch oak beams and massive fireplaces, dedicated to James Bailey Upham, author of the original Pledge of Allegiance to the Flag. Also with period furnishings
*Operated by Upham House. Open by appointment*

# MIDDLEBORO

**MIDDLEBOROUGH HISTORICAL MUSEUM, about 1820**
**Jackson Street**
Two houses dating about 1820 with historical memorabilia; costume room, children's room, country store, an 18th-century law office, blacksmith shop with authentic tools, and old carriage shed
*Operated by Middleborough Historical Museum. Open July–Aug: Wed., Fri., Sun. 1–5. June, Sept: Sun. 1–5*

# MIDDLETON

**CAPT. ANDREW FULLER HOUSE, 1750**
**47 King St**
Built by Capt. Fuller, a soldier during the French and Indian wars whose two sons fought in the Revolution. A mid-18th-century house with center entrance, eight rooms, paneled interiors; furnished with antiques throughout and houses the museum of the Middleton Historical Society
*Privately owned. Open by appointment*

# MILTON

■ **CAPT. ROBERT BENNET FORBES HOUSE, 1833**
**215 Adams St**
Greek Revival country mansion built according to Boston architect Isaiah Rogers' plans by a merchant sea captain who became head of the China-trade firm Russell and Co. Now a museum of the Boston China trade with Chinese, Empire, and Victorian family furnishings characteristic of Boston in that era
*Operated by Capt. Robert Bennet Forbes House. Open May–Oct: Wed., Sat. 2–5*

## NANTUCKET

### 1800 HOUSE
**Mill Street**
Home, typical of the first part of the 19th century, of the high sheriff of the county of Nantucket. Furnishings appropriate to the early days of whaling *Operated by Nantucket Historical Assn. Open June 10–Sept. 14: Mon.–Fri. 10–5*

### HADWEN HOUSE-SATLER MEMORIAL, 1845
**96 Main St**
Considered by some the most beautiful on Nantucket, this fine neoclassic dwelling was built by William Hadwen, a silversmith turned whale-oil merchant. Hadwen married Eunice Starbuck, daughter of Jason Starbuck who built three brick houses for his sons on the opposite side of Main Street. Empire and Victorian furniture *Operated by Nantucket Historical Assn. Open June 10–Oct. 13: daily 10–5*

*Hadwen House*

### ■ JETHRO COFFIN HOUSE, 1686
**Sunset Hill**
The "Oldest House" on the island was built as a wedding gift for Jethro Coffin and Mary Gardner in 1686. It is a restored example of a 17th-century frame New England saltbox with a long rear roof slope; the inverted

horseshoe in raised brick on the huge central chimney was to discourage witches from entering.
*Operated by Nantucket Historical Assn. Open June 10–Sept. 14: daily 10–5*

### MARIA MITCHELL BIRTHPLACE, 1790
**1 Vestal St**
Vassar College's first professor of astronomy, Maria Mitchell, was born here in 1818. Built by Hezekiah Swain in 1790, the house has a roof walk, a long mahogany door latch, Quaker furnishings, and a small observatory.
*Operated by Nantucket Maria Mitchell Assn. Open June 15–Sept. 15: Mon.–Fri. 10–12, 2–5, Sat. 10–12*

### ■ NANTUCKET HISTORIC DISTRICT, about 1700–1874
**Nantucket Island**
Nantucket was the birthplace of the American whaling industry and for a period of over 150 years maintained its supremacy. Numerous fine houses associated with this era are to be found on Main Street, between Centre Street and Monument Square.

## NEW BEDFORD

### ■ NEW BEDFORD HISTORIC DISTRICT, 18th and 19th centuries
In the 1760s New Bedford began whaling and in 80 years became America's major whaling port. The commerce and wealth produced by this industry are evident in a number of buildings still standing from this era.

## NEWBURY

### SHORT HOUSE, about 1732
**39 High Rd**
An early wooden house with brick gable ends built about 1732. It has a fine carved doorway and interior paneling and period furnishings.
*Operated by Soc. for the Preservation of New England Antiquities. Open June–Sept: Tues., Thurs., Sat. 1–5*

## SWETT-ILSLEY HOUSE, about 1670
**4 and 6 High Rd**
A 17th-century frame dwelling originally built as a one-room, two-story house sometime around 1670 with additions made at a later date. Features a huge fireplace and early woodwork *Operated by Soc. for the Preservation of New England Antiquities. Open by appointment*

## TRISTRAM COFFIN HOUSE, about 1651
**16 High Rd**
The original ell was built about 1651 by selectman and representative to the General Court Tristram Coffin. The eight generations of the family that followed made additions but did not basically change the house. Coffin family furnishings. A Massachusetts Historic Landmark
*Operated by Soc. for the Preservation of New England Antiquities. Open June 15–Sept. 15: Mon., Wed., Fri. 2–5*

## NEWBURYPORT

### CUSHING HOUSE, 1808
**98 High St**
Federal three-story brick house with notable cornice built by Caleb Cushing, distinguished statesman. This fine survival on a street known for the beauty of its Federal architecture recalls the days of Newburyport's maritime supremacy. Period furnishings with silver, toy, and marine collections; 18th-century garden
*Operated by Historical Soc. of Ould Newbury. Open Tues.–Sat. 10–4, Sun. 2–5*

## NEWTON

### JACKSON HOMESTEAD, 1809
**527 Washington St**
Typical early 19th-century homestead with clapboard front, brick ends, and four end chimneys. Period furnishings, old maps and documents, colonial kitchen and fireplace; special changing exhibits, lectures, and "learn by doing" classes on colonial crafts
*Operated by Town of Newton. Open Sept.–June: Mon.–Fri. 2–4. July, Aug: Wed. 2–4; open house every third Sun. afternoon*

## NORTHAMPTON

### CORNET JOSEPH PARSONS HOUSE, 1658
**58 Bridge St**
Small two-and-a-half-story clapboard dwelling with central chimney and small ells (probably added at a later date) typical of the architecture of the 17th century; period furnishings
*Operated by Northampton Historical Soc. Open Wed., Fri., Sat. 2–4:30*

### ISAAC DAMON HOUSE, 1814
**46 Bridge St**
Federal-style home built by the famous New England architect and bridgebuilder for his own use. Damon had come to Northampton in 1811 from the studio of Asher Benjamin to build the First Church; this marked the beginning of his architectural career. Period furnishings include Damon's family furniture, architectural implements, and personal memorabilia.
*Operated by Northampton Historical Soc. Open Summer: Wed., Fri., Sun. 1–4:30 and by appointment*

## NORTH ANDOVER

### PARSON BARNARD HOUSE, about 1715
**179 Osgood St**
Early 18th-century house built by Rev. Thomas Barnard; considered one of the best examples in New England of the transition period in architecture between 1700 and 1725. The rooms have been restored to the periods of the four major owners with furnishings based on their actual inventories. A Massachusetts Historic Landmark
*Operated by North Andover Historical Soc. Open May–Oct: Fri., Sat. 1–5*

### STEVENS-COOLIDGE PLACE, about 1800
**Andover Street**
Built in the opening years of the 19th century, the "Home Place" is a good example of the early Federal style; the ell was added some 30 years later. Set in some 89 acres of woods, fields, lawns, and gardens; period furnishings, china, and glass
*Operated by Stevens-Coolidge Trustees of Reservations. Open May 15– Oct. 12: Tues.–Sun. 2–5:30*

MASSACHUSETTS

## NORTH ATTLEBORO
### WOODCOCK GARRISON HOUSE, 1669
**362 N Washington St**
Built by John Woodcock, an Indian fighter of some repute, to serve as a tavern and hostel. In its earliest days it also served as a link in the chain of garrisons stretching from Boston to Rhode Island. Period furnishings and special exhibits
*Operated by North Attleboro Historical Soc. Open Sept.–June: third Sun. each month and by appointment*

## NORTH OXFORD
### CLARA BARTON BIRTHPLACE, 1805
**Clara Barton Road**
Built by Stephen Barton in 1805, this early 19th-century dwelling was the birthplace in 1821 of the founder of the American Red Cross. Clara Barton started as a successful school-teacher, and from the Civil War on through the rest of her long life she worked to relieve the suffering of others. The house has period furnishings and memorabilia of the Bartons and the Red Cross.
*Operated by Clara Barton Birthplace. Open Tues.–Sat. 10–12, 1–4, Sun. 1–4*

## NORTH SWANSEA
### MARTIN HOUSE, 1728
**22 Stoney Hill Road**
A small mid-18th-century New England farmhouse with gambrel roof on 38 acres of woodland. Lived in by the Martin family for about 200 years. Period furnishings, china, silver, clocks, needlework, portraits, and a fine collection of pewter
*Operated by Soc. of Colonial Dames. Open May 15–Oct: daily 10–6*

## NORWELL
### JACOBS FARMHOUSE, 1726
**Main Street and Jacobs Lane**
Farmhouse built in the early 18th century with additions made at a later date. There is an extensive collection of early fire apparatus (1760–1900) in the barns.
*Operated by Soc. for the Preservation of New England Antiquities. Open*

*June–Sept: Mon., Tues., Fri. 2–5, and by appointment*

## NORWOOD
### DAY HOUSE, about 1815
**93 Day St**
A stuccoed brick house with exposed timbers in the English manner; now used as headquarters for the local historical society. Period furnishings, costumes, and genealogical records
*Operated by Norwood Historical Soc. Open by appointment*

## OSTERVILLE
### CAPT. JONATHAN PARKER HOUSE, about 1795
**Parker and West Bay Roads**
This house, once belonging to sea captain Parker, has been added to over the past 150 years so that only two of the original rooms remain. It is now a house museum with representative rooms of different periods and antiques brought back by sea-faring residents.
*Operated by Osterville Historical Soc. Open July–Aug: Thurs., Sun. 3–5*

## PITTSFIELD
### GOODRICH HOUSE, 1792; 1813
**823 North St**
Late 18th-century house built by Caleb Goodrich with an addition made in 1813. Period furnishings, objects of local historical interest, children's room with books, toys, and clothes
*Operated by Berkshire County Historical Soc. Open May 1–Oct. 15: Tues.–Sat. 10–4, Sun. 1–4*

## PLYMOUTH
### ANTIQUARIAN HOUSE, 1809
**126 Water St**
Early 19th-century house completely furnished in Federal style. Children's playroom with dolls and toys, 19th-century costumes, kitchen with utensils, china, and old cookbooks
*Operated by Plymouth Antiquarian Soc. Open June 15–Sept. 15: daily 10–5*

### HARLOW-HOLMES HOUSE, 1649
**8 Winter St**
Built by William Harlow about 1649,

this old house has been little changed over the centuries. The original plan with old stairway, the chambers on lower floor and above, and great central chimney has been preserved. Family furnishings and historical records
*Operated by Cora Holmes, owner. Open daily 10–5*

## HARLOW OLD FORT HOUSE, 1677
**119 Sandwich St**
A Pilgrim house with a low gambrel roof of the last quarter of the 17th century built by William Harlow of timber taken from the Old Fort on Burial Hill. Early furniture, tools, and utensils. Demonstrations with audience participation of household crafts—candle dipping, wool and flax spinning, weaving, yarn dyeing, etc.
*Operated by Plymouth Antiquarian Soc. Open May–Sept: daily 10–5*

## JABEZ HOWLAND HOUSE, 1667
**33 Sandwich St**
Built by Jacob Mitchell in 1667, this is the only house still standing in Plymouth where an original Pilgrim—John Howland, servant of Gov. Carver, father of Jabez, and founder of Howland family—actually lived. One half was built in the 17th and the other in the 18th century. Restored in 20th century with period furnishings
*Operated by Pilgrim John Howland Soc. Open May 15–Oct. 15: daily 9:30–5*

## PLIMOTH PLANTATION, 1627
**Route 3A**
Full-scale re-creation of the original Pilgrim colony as it was in 1627 with a

*Plimoth Plantation*

replica of the fort-meetinghouse, houses and gardens, and Indian camp-site beside. Midway between Plymouth Rock and *Mayflower II* are replicas of *First House* and *1627 House* showing the earliest permanent type of house and an improved version from a few years later. Demonstrations of 17th-century crafts at the village
*Operated by Plimoth Plantation. Open Apr.–Dec: daily 9–5. July–Aug: daily 9–7*

## RICHARD SPARROW HOUSE, 1636–40
**42 Summer St**
Restored medieval-type dwelling framed with red-oak timbers, diamond-shaped casements, and a "hall" which preserves the 17th-century atmosphere. Decorative arts of the period on display. Demonstrations and classes in pottery making given by Plymouth Pottery Guild
*Private. Open June–Oct: Mon.–Sat. 10–5*

## SPOONER HOUSE, 1747
**27 North St**
Built in the middle of the 18th century, this house was occupied by the Spooner family for 200 years. Shown with their heirlooms and furnishings dating from the 18th to 20th century
*Operated by Plymouth Antiquarian Soc. Open June 15–Sept. 15: daily 10–5*

## WINSLOW HOUSE [MAYFLOWER SOCIETY], 1754
**4 Winslow St**
Mid-18th-century house built by Edward Winslow, great-grandson of Pilgrim Gov. Edward Winslow. Restored in 1890 with period rooms and furnishings of the 18th and 19th centuries. Now the national headquarters of the society of Mayflower descendants
*Operated by General Society of Mayflower Descendants. Open May 30–Sept. 15: daily 10–5*

## QUINCY

■ **ADAMS NATIONAL HISTORIC SITE, 1731**
**135 Adams St**
Georgian clapboard home with five chimneys and brick end; commemorates four generations of the dis-

tinguished Adams family who lived here from 1788 to 1927: John Adams, second President of U.S. (1797–1801); his son John Quincy, sixth President (1825–29); his son Charles Francis, minister to Court of St. James (1861–68); Charles Francis' son Henry, a historian. Extensive gardens and stable, a stone library, family furnishings and memorabilia
*Operated by National Park Service. Open Apr. 19–Nov. 10: daily 9–5*

*Adams National Historic Site*

## COL. JOSIAH QUINCY HOUSE, 1770
### 20 Muirhead St

Once the countryseat, with block quoins and pillared portico, of Col. Josiah Quincy, prominent merchant and patriot. His son, Josiah, Jr., was a noted orator and patriot and his grandson, Josiah III, was mayor of Boston, congressman, and president of Harvard. Fine period furnishings
*Operated by Soc. for the Preservation of New England Antiquities. Open May–Oct. 15: Tues., Thurs., Fri. 1–5*

## ■ JOHN ADAMS BIRTHPLACE, 1681
### 133 Franklin St

Saltbox house with later lean-to, birthplace of the second President of the U.S. in 1735. John Adams lived here until his marriage to Abigail Smith in 1764, at which time he moved into an adjacent house left to him by his father. Period furnishings
*Operated by Quincy Historical Soc. Open Apr. 19–Sept. 30: Tues.–Sun. 10–5*

## ■ JOHN QUINCY ADAMS BIRTHPLACE, 1663
### 141 Franklin St

Birthplace of the sixth President of the U.S. in 1767. His father, John Adams, used the kitchen as his law office until the family moved in 1783. Originally two upper and two lower chambers with later lean-to; period furnishings
*Operated by Quincy Historical Soc. Open Apr. 19–Sept: Tues.–Sun. 10–5*

## ■ QUINCY HOMESTEAD, 1706
### 34 Butler Rd

Spacious, hip-roofed early 18th-century mansion, ancestral home of a family who has played a great part in the history of Massachusetts. Birthplace and childhood home of the spirited Dorothy Quincy who married the patriot John Hancock. Furnished according to records made by Miss Quincy in 1822. A Massachusetts Historic Landmark
*Operated by Soc. of Colonial Dames. Open Apr. 19–Oct: Tues.–Sun. 10–5*

# READING

## PARKER TAVERN, 1694
### 103 Washington St

Old saltbox built in last decade of the 17th century; example of farmhouse showing changing fashions over the years. During the War of 1812 captured British officers were "housed" here. Objects of local historical interest, re-creation of flower and herb garden
*Operated by Reading Antiquarian Soc. Open May–Nov: Sun. 2–5 and by appointment*

# ROCKPORT

## OLD CASTLE, 1678; 1792
### Old Castle Lane

Saltbox house with a lean-to added in 1792 and shingled sides; set back in a tree-shaded yard. Early American furniture and utensils, granite quarry artifacts, objects of local interest
*Operated by Pigeon Cove Village Improvement Soc. Open July–Aug: Sat., Sun. 2–5*

## SEWALL-SCRIPTURE HOUSE, 1832
### 40 King St

Built in 1832, this house now serves

as a museum with period furnishings, a marine room, a Victorian room, a children's room, a library, and objects of local interest.
*Operated by Sandy Bay Historical Soc. and Museum. Open July–Aug: daily 2–5*

# ROWLEY

## CHAPLIN-CLARK-WILLIAMS HOUSE, about 1671
**109 Haverhill St**
The oldest house in Rowley; unrestored but still picturesque with its second-story overhang and sloping roof
*Operated by Soc. for the Preservation of New England Antiquities. Open by appointment only*

## PLATTS-BRADSTREET HOUSE, 1677
**Main Street**
Overlooking a small village green, a two-and-a-half-story frame 17th-century house with English gardens. Owned by the Platts family until 1771 and then by the Bradstreet family until 1906. Period furnishings; also a shoemaker's shop and old barn
*Operated by Rowley Historical Soc. Open Aug: Thurs. 2–5 and by appointment*

# SALEM

## CHESTNUT STREET AREA, 19th century
Architecturally, Chestnut Street has

*Chestnut Street*

been called one of the finest in America. The majority of the houses, some by Samuel McIntire, were completed by 1830 and are fine examples of the Federal style with beautiful exterior details of porches, columns, and Palladian windows. The affluent merchants and shipowners, congressmen, diplomats, and literary men that came from these Chestnut Street houses made the name of Salem famous. A Massachusetts Historic Landmark

## CROWNINSHIELD-BENTLEY HOUSE, 1727
**126 Essex St**
Built by John Crowninshield in 1727 with later 18th-century additions, this house was lived in by four generations of the Crowninshield shipping family; the Rev. William Bentley, whose famous diary described Salem life, boarded there from 1791 to 1819. It presents under one roof the main architectural styles of the 18th century with appropriate furnishings based on documentary evidence.
*Operated by Essex Institute. Open June–Oct. 15: Tues.–Sat. 10–4, Sun. 2–4:30*

## GEDNEY HOUSE, 1655
**21 High St**
A 17th-century frame house with two additions made about 1800 and about 1900. Recently all finish trim has been removed to permit study of the original structure of 1655.
*Operated by Soc. for the Preservation of New England Antiquities. Open June–Sept: Tues., Thurs., Sat. 1–5*

## HOUSE OF THE SEVEN GABLES (TURNER HOUSE), 1668
**54 Turner St**
Built in 1668 by sea captain John Turner and made famous by Nathaniel Hawthorne's novel; even though the original two-room structure has been added to over the years, it still retains its medieval character with peaked gables, huge chimneys, and overhang. Antiques, paintings, china, and secret stairway on exhibit. In the garden are two other 17th-century houses—the *Retire Beckett House* (1655) and the *Hathaway House* (1682)—and the 18th-century *Hawthorne House* (1750), birthplace of the novelist in 1804, moved here from its original site.

*Operated by House of the Seven Gables Settlement Assn. Open after Labor Day–June 1: daily 10–5. July–Labor Day: daily 9:30–7:30*

*House of the Seven Gables*

### ■ JOHN WARD HOUSE, 1684
**132 Essex St**
Standing on the grounds of the Essex Institute, this house is a good example of the organic growth of the 17th-century frame dwelling. John Ward originally built only the western portion consisting of the parlor and chamber above; at a later date he added the eastern half; prior to 1732 the last addition, the rear lean-to, was added. Period furnishings
*Operated by Essex Institute. Open June–Oct. 15: Tues.–Sat. 10–12:30, 2–4*

### ■ PEIRCE-NICHOLS HOUSE, 1782; 1801
**80 Federal St**
The first important example of Samuel McIntire's work is the late Georgian-style house with early Federal elements he designed for shipping mer-

*Peirce-Nichols House*

chant Jerathmiel Peirce in 1782. The exterior clapboard frame structure has a hip roof with balustraded parapet, a central Doric pedimented porch, and fluted Doric pilasters at the corners. The interior contains a fully realized contrast in McIntire's earlier and later styles. While the original west parlor is elaborately paneled in Georgian style, in 1801 Peirce ordered McIntire to remodel the east parlor with the refined Adamesque details of the Federal style in honor of his daughter Sally's wedding to George Nichols. The original furnishings are on exhibit. *Operated by Essex Institute. Open Tues.–Sat. 2–5*

### PICKERING MANSION, 1651; 1841
**18 Broad St**
The home of ten generations of the Pickering family; birthplace of soldier-statesman Col. Timothy Pickering, Secretary of State under Presidents Washington and Adams. The medieval core of the house has been hidden under later alterations, and the exterior finish was added in the remodeling of 1841. Period furnishings, portraits, and documents
*Operated by The Pickering Foundation. Open by appointment*

### PINGREE HOUSE, 1804
**128 Essex St**
The brick Federal house Samuel McIntire built for sea captain John Gardner in 1804 has been called his finest work. The restrained exterior with semicircular portico supported by slender Corinthian pillars is matched by the refined elegance of the Adamesque interiors. The carved woodwork shows McIntire's superb repertoire of baskets of fruit, sheaves of wheat, horns of plenty, plus the delicate roping and pearling in relief. Some of the furnishings have been attributed to McIntire.
*Operated by Essex Institute. Open June–Sept: Tues.–Sat. 10–12:30, 2–4:30, Sun. 2–4:30*

### PIONEER VILLAGE (SALEM WILLOWS), 1630
**Clifton Avenue**
Replica of the wilderness village of Salem built by the city in 1930. The oldest house in Salem, the *Ruck House*, is part of the group that also includes

the *Governor Fayre House*, thatched and weather-boarded houses, wigwams, and dugouts.
*Operated by Town of Salem. Open June–Labor Day: daily 9:30–6:30. Labor Day–Oct: daily 10–5*

## ROPES MANSION, 1719
**318 Essex St**
Stately gambrel-roofed building outlined by a railing on upper slope of roof and enclosed by graceful wooden fence with carved posts. Judge Nathaniel Ropes and his descendants for four generations owned and occupied the house. It still has its original furnishings and a rare collection of china and glass; there are also formal gardens.
*Operated by Ropes Memorial. Open May–Oct: Mon.–Sat. 10–4:30; closed holidays*

## ■ SALEM MARITIME NATIONAL HISTORIC SITE, 18th and 19th centuries
**Derby Street**
A group of buildings recalling Salem's great shipping days and the romance of the swift clipper ships: the Derby wharf begun by Capt. Richard Derby after 1762, central wharf built 1791–92 by Simon Forrester, the Custom House (1819) where Nathaniel Hawthorne worked, the Rum Shop (1800), and two famous houses. The *Derby Mansion*, built by Capt. Richard Derby in 1761 as a wedding present for his son, is a fine symmetrical Georgian brick house with paired chimneys and pedimented doorway, paneled interiors, 18th-century furnishings, china, and paintings. Next door is the Federal-style *Hawkes House*, designed about 1780 by Samuel McIntire for Elias Haskett Derby and remodeled by Benjamin Hawkes in 1801.
*Operated by National Park Service. Open daily 8:30–5; closed Thanksgiving, Christmas, and New Year's Day*

## THE WITCH HOUSE, 1642
**310½ Essex St**
Restored example of 17th-century frame dwelling with peaked gables, second-story overhang, and leaded casements. Home of Judge Jonathan Corwin, one of the judges of the witchcraft court, and site of some preliminary witchcraft examinations; period furnishings
*Operated by Town of Salem. Open May–Labor Day: daily 10–6. After Labor Day–Oct: daily 10–4*

## SANDWICH
### HOXIE HOUSE AND DEXTER'S GRIST MILL, about 1637
**Sandwich Historical Center**
Saltbox house built, according to local legend, in 1637–the same year the town was settled by "ten men from Saugus"–and thus called the oldest house on Cape Cod. Restored to 1680–90 period with such authentic features as gunstock posts, chamfered beams, wide floorboards; fine period furnishings on loan from Boston Museum of Fine Arts. Restored, working 17th-century gristmill on grounds
*Operated by Town of Sandwich. Open June 16–Sept: Mon.–Sat. 10–5, Sun. 1–5*

Hoxie House

## SAUGUS
### ■ IRONMASTER'S HOUSE, 1636
**Saugus Iron Works National Historic Site**
Built by Timothy Dexter in 1636, one of the original owners of the ironworks. Fine example of 17th-century frame dwelling with peaked gables, overhang ornamented with carved pendants, and batten doors. Restored on grounds of completely reconstructed ironworks; period furnishings
*Operated by National Park Service. Open May 15–Oct. 15: Tues.–Sun. 9–4*

# MASSACHUSETTS

*Ironmaster's House*

■ "SCOTCH"-BOARDMAN
HOUSE, about 1686
17 Howard St

A 17th-century house of exceptional architectural interest with much of the original framework and interior detail intact, including sheathing, early staircase, and sponge painting. Built by William Boardman about 1686 and home of six generations of Boardmans, it has long been associated with the Scots taken prisoner by Oliver Cromwell at the Battle of Dunbar and sent to Saugus to work at the nearby ironworks. Unfurnished to facilitate architectural study. A Massachusetts Historic Landmark
*Operated by Soc. for the Preservation of New England Antiquities. Open June–Aug: Tues., Wed., Thurs. 11–5*

*"Scotch"-Boardman House*

## SCITUATE

### CUDWORTH HOUSE, 1797
First Parish Road

Built at the close of the 18th century around a chimney dating back to 1646, this two-and-a-half-story structure now houses the collection of the local historical society, including period furniture, china, glass, portraits, etc.
*Operated by Scituate Historical Soc. Open June 15–Sept. 15: Wed.–Sat. 2–5*

## SHEFFIELD

### COL. JOHN ASHLEY HOUSE, 1735
foot of Cooper Hill

Oldest complete house extant in Berkshire County. Paneled interiors and period furnishings
*Operated by Ashley House. Open June–Oct. 15: Wed.–Sun. 1–5*

## SHREWSBURY

### ARTEMAS WARD HOUSE, 1728; 1785
786 Main St

Unusual 18th-century shingled "double house" with two front entrances and two red brick chimneys. The home of Revolutionary general Artemas Ward, first commander in chief of Massachusetts troops; largely unaltered and contains the Ward family furnishings
*Operated by Harvard University. Open May–Oct: afternoons and by appointment*

## SOUTH DENNIS

### JERICHO HOUSE, 1801
Old Main Street and Trotting Park Road

Built for Theophilus Baker in 1801, a small, sturdy, story-and-a-half Cape Cod cottage with hand-hewn pine beams pegged with oak pins. Completely restored with antique furnishings and an old barn museum
*Operated by Town of Dennis Jericho Committee. Open July–Aug: Wed.–Fri. 2–5*

## SPRINGFIELD

### LINDEN HALL (ALEXANDER HOUSE), 1811
284 State St

Fine urban Federal-style mansion the design of which is attributed to Asher

Benjamin. At one time it was the home of the 19th-century portrait painter Chester Harding.
*Operated by Soc. for the Preservation of New England Antiquities. Open by appointment only*

## STOCKBRIDGE

### ■ CHESTERWOOD, 1900–1901
**two miles west of Stockbridge**
The home, studio, and garden of Daniel Chester French, the famous sculptor who gave America two of its best-known and most-cherished statues: the "Minute Man" in Concord and the seated figure in the Lincoln Memorial in Washington, D.C. A barn sculpture gallery houses his statuary and memorabilia, and there are nature trails through the gardens and woods. A Massachusetts Historic Landmark
*Operated by National Trust. Open June 15–Labor Day: daily 10–6. After Labor Day–Oct. 15: Sat.–Sun. 10–6*

### MERWIN HOUSE ("TRANQUILITY"), about 1825
**39 Main St**
A simple late Federal brick house standing on the main street of the village. Remodeled and furnished in the late 19th century by a local family; reflects late 19th-century cultural interests and foreign travel. The furnishings remain almost exactly as reconstructed in the Edwardian era.
*Operated by Soc. for the Preservation of New England Antiquities. Open June–Oct: Tues.–Sat. 10–2, 2–5*

### ■ MISSION HOUSE, 1739
**Main Street**
Built in 1739 by Rev. John Sergeant, first missionary to the Housatonic Indians, who was succeeded by Jonathan Edwards, this house represents the architecture of the Massachusetts frontier. The sole embellishment on the plain clapboard exterior is the Connecticut Valley door with carved framework; the interior is paneled in natural pine. Period furnishings and crewelwork; gardens. A Massachusetts Historic Landmark
*Operated by The Trustees of Reservations. Open Apr.–Nov: Mon.–Sat. 10–5:30, Sun., holidays 2–5:30*

### NAUMKEAG GARDENS, about 1885
**Prospect Street**
The Victorian summer home of Joseph H. Choate, ambassador to the Court of St. James (1899–1905). Designed by the famous architect Stanford White, the house has fine collections of furniture, china, paintings, engravings, and books. Formal gardens
*Operated by The Trustees of Reservations. Open summer: Tues.–Sun. 10–5:30*

## STOUGHTON

### MARY BAKER EDDY HISTORICAL HOUSE, 19th century
**133 Central St**
Home of Sally Wentworth where the founder of Christian Science lived from 1868 to 1870. See also Amesbury, Lynn, Swampscott
*Operated by Longyear Foundation. Open May–Oct: Tues.–Sun. 2–5; closed holidays*

## STURBRIDGE

### OLD STURBRIDGE VILLAGE, 1790–1840
A complete New England country town re-created with homes, shops, mills, school, meetinghouse, and general store to illustrate American rural life between 1790 and 1840, the years before the Industrial Revolution. The more than 35 buildings are authentic and have been moved here, including a covered bridge, from all parts of New England. Includes 15 craft demonstrations and 10 collection exhibits
*Operated by Old Sturbridge Village. Open summer: daily 9:30–5:30. Winter: Mon.–Fri. 10–4, Sat.–Sun. 9:30–4:30*

*Old Sturbridge Village*

MASSACHUSETTS

## SUDBURY

### LONGFELLOW'S WAYSIDE INN, about 1686
**Old Boston Post Road**
America's oldest inn was built about 1686 by Samuel Howe and originally called the Howe Tavern. Its present name was taken from Longfellow's *Tales of a Wayside Inn*. Restored by the Ford Foundation after a fire in 1955, a two-story north wing was added and authentic period furnishings placed in the old barroom, kitchen, and early American bedrooms
*Operated by Trustees of Wayside Inn. Open daily 9–6; closed Christmas*

## SWAMPSCOTT

### JOHN HUMPHREY HOUSE, 1634
**99 Paradise Rd**
A 17th-century dwelling with second-story overhang built by John Humphrey, a wealthy English lawyer who later became a magistrate of the Bay Colony and member of the first Board of Overseers of Harvard. Some period furnishings and local historical records
*Operated by Swampscott Historical Soc. Open daily 10–5*

### MARY BAKER EDDY HISTORICAL HOUSE, 19th century
**23 Paradise Rd**
Home of Mrs. Eddy in 1866 where she was healed after reading Matthew 9:2 and discovered Christian Science. See also Amesbury, Lynn, Stoughton
*Operated by Longyear Foundation. Open May 15–Oct. 15: Mon.–Sat. 10–5, Sun. 2–5. Oct. 16–May 14: Mon.–Fri. 10–3; closed holidays*

## TEMPLETON

### NARRAGANSETT HISTORICAL SOC., 1810
**Templeton Common**
Lovely two-story Federal house built of English brick by trader John W. Stiles and housing a country store for many years. Restored as a house museum using the old timbers and wood; period furnishings and re-creation of the old store
*Operated by Narragansett Historical Soc. Open July–Sept: Sat. 2–5. July–Aug: first Sun. afternoon*

## TOPSFIELD

### ■ PARSON CAPEN HOUSE, 1683
**1 Howlett St**
Built for Parson Joseph Capen on a hill site, one of the finest surviving 17th-century frame dwellings in U.S., with overhang, central chimney, and high-pitched roof. Restored early 20th century; fine 17th- and 18th-century furnishings
*Operated by Topsfield Historical Soc. Open June 15–Sept. 15: Tues.–Sat. 10–4:30, Sun. 1–4:30*

*Parson Capen House*

## TOWNSEND HARBOR

### CONANT HOUSE, about 1720
**South Street**
An early 18th-century house later enlarged for use as a tavern. It features fine woodwork, including a hinged partition between parlors and an early stenciled dado.
*Operated by Soc. for the Preservation of New England Antiquities. Open July–Oct: Mon., Wed., Fri. 2–4*

## TYRINGHAM

### GINGERBREAD HOUSE, about 1860; 1930s
**Tyringham Road**
A 19th-century farmhouse converted into a sculpture studio in the 1930s by Henry Hudson Kitson. The contoured roof designed to represent the rolling Berkshire hills, actually a gigantic sculpture, is supported by three rock pillars and grottoes. The house, now open as a museum and art gallery, is part of a two-acre complex with lovely gardens.
*Operated by Tyringham Art Galleries. Open May–Nov: daily 10–5*

*Gingerbread House*

## WAKEFIELD

### COL. JAMES HARTSHORNE HOUSE, 1681; 1742
**41 Church St**
A 17th-century frame dwelling with several 18th-century additions and twin entrances. Restored and furnished with authentic colonial pieces
*Operated by Hartshorne House. Open Oct.–July: Tues., Sun. 1–5 and by appointment*

## WALTHAM

### GORE PLACE, about 1805
**52 Gore St**
Country estate of Gov. Christopher Gore, a 20-room brick mansion considered one of the finest examples of Federal architecture in the country. The main building has two long low wings with a projecting elliptical salon as its focal point. Contains magnificent period furnishings, many of them original

*Operated by Gore Place Soc. Open Apr. 15–Nov. 15: Tues.–Sat. 10–5, Sun. 2–5*

### LYMAN HOUSE (THE VALE), 1793
**Lyman Street**
Federal mansion built from plans by Samuel McIntire, one of his most ambitious works and sole survivor of those country houses he is known to have designed. Many fine rooms, including ballroom and bow parlor with two authentic pieces McIntire designed for this room. McIntire stable, outstanding old greenhouses, gardens, and landscaped grounds
*Operated by Soc. for the Preservation of New England Antiquities. Open June–Oct: Wed.–Sat. 11–5*

## WATERTOWN

### ABRAHAM BROWNE HOUSE, about 1698
**563 Main St**
A weather-beaten old 17th-century frame dwelling with two important exhibits: one of few existing original three-part casement window frames, and the actual appearance of a 17th-century parlor with crewel bed hangings from the ceiling and other period furnishings
*Operated by Soc. for the Preservation of New England Antiquities. Open May–Oct: Mon.–Fri. 2–5. Nov.–Apr: Tues.–Fri. 2–5*

### MARSHALL FOWLE HOUSE, before 1775
**28 Marshall St**
A large, rectangular clapboard building associated with the American Revolution. Here the poet and historian Mercy Warren entertained Gen. Wash-

*Gore Place*

ington; the council of the Provincial Congress met here in 1775; and it was claimed Mercy's husband Gen. Warren spent his last night before the Battle of Bunker Hill at the Fowle House. *Operated by Historical Soc. of Watertown. Open by appointment*

## WENHAM

### CLAFLIN-RICHARDS HOUSE, about 1664
**Town Center**
A restored 17th-century dwelling with huge serpentine braces, said to be the only ones in New England. Distinctive interior treatment with period furnishings; collections of costumes, quilts, needlework, fans, and utensils *Operated by Wenham Historical Assn. Open Mon.–Fri. 1–4*

## WESTON

### JOSIAH SMITH TAVERN (JONES HOUSE), about 1756
**358 Boston Post Rd**
Built about 1756 with later additions; now houses objects and records of local historical interest. Period rooms with furniture, clothing, and muskets *Operated by Soc. for the Preservation of New England Antiquities. Open Wed. 2–4 and by appointment*

## WEST SPRINGFIELD

### OLD DAY HOUSE, 1754
**70 Park St**
Brick saltbox, two stories with lean-to at rear, built by Josiah Day in 1754 and now a historical museum. Enormous fireplaces, period furnishings, some original to the house *Operated by Ramapogue Historical Soc. Open Wed.–Sun. 1–5*

### STORROWTON VILLAGE, 1767–1834
**Eastern States Exposition Grounds**
A restored New England village showing early American life with authentic old buildings dismantled and reassembled here. Includes *Gilbert Homestead* (1794), *Phillips House* (1767), and *Potter House* (1777); period furnishings
*Operated by Storrowton Village. Open May 30–July 3: Sat.–Sun. 1–5. July 4–Labor Day: Tues.–Sun. 1–5*

## WINTHROP

### DEANE WINTHROP HOUSE, 1637
**40 Shirley St**
Two-story frame dwelling with pitched roof and central chimney built by Capt. William Pierce, a skipper of the *Mayflower*. Purchased by Deane Winthrop in 1647, it contains Winthrop family relics, objects of local interest, and period furnishings
*Operated by Winthrop Improvement and Historical Assn. Open Tues., Wed., Fri., 2–5*

## WOBURN

### RUMFORD HOUSE, 1714
**90 Elm St**
Built in 1714, this modest frame dwelling was the birthplace of Benjamin Thompson, a noted expatriate scientist who was created a count of the Holy Roman Empire (Count Rumford). Period furnishings, models of his early experiments, and a copy of the Gainsborough portrait of the count
*Operated by Rumford Historical Assn. Open daily 2–5*

## YARMOUTHPORT

### CAPT. BANGS HALLET HOUSE, 1740; 1840
**Strawberry Lane**
An early Cape Cod house added to in 1840 by sea captain Bangs Hallet for his wife Anna and children. The new elements were in the Greek Revival style and the large, airy rooms proclaim a family of substance. Fine period furnishings and children's room with toy collection and dolls
*Operated by Historical Soc. of Old Yarmouth. Open Mon.–Sat. 2–5*

### COL. JOHN THACHER HOUSE, about 1680
### WINSLOW CROCKER HOUSE, about 1780,
**King's Highway and Thacher Lane**
Two old houses built about a century apart next door to each other provide interesting comparison between styles of architecture in early America. Interesting woodwork in Crocker house; both with period furnishings
*Operated by Soc. for the Preservation of New England Antiquities. Open June 15–Sept: Mon.–Sat. 10–12, 2–5*

# ADRIAN

## GOV. CROSWELL HOUSE, about 1840
### 228 N Broad St

Red brick structure with a one-story wing that exactly duplicates the main façade. This was the home of Charles M. Croswell, governor of Michigan between 1877 and 1881. Now restored, the house serves as a museum.
*Operated by Daughters of the American Revolution. Open by appointment*

# ALPENA VICINITY

## THE OLD LIGHTHOUSE, 1840
### off U.S. Route 23

Second lighthouse built on the shores of the Great Lakes. Restored, the keeper's home is furnished with antiques and marine artifacts. Offers a unique view of the surrounding area
*Private. Open June–Aug: daily 9–7*

# AU TRAIN

## PAULSON HOUSE HISTORICAL PIONEER HOME MUSEUM, 1883
### U.S. Forest Road 2278

Log house built of cedar. Restored, with period furniture and household equipment exhibited
*Operated by Avery Color Studios. Open summer: 8–8. Fall: 8:30–7:30*

# BIG RAPIDS

## MECOSTA COUNTY MUSEUM, late 19th century
### Stewart and Elm Streets

Victorian structure built by the Phelps family, pioneers in the lumbering industry of the region. Now a museum with Victorian furnishings
*Operated by Mecosta Co. Historical Soc. Open Fri. 1–9*

# CONCORD

## ■ MANN HOUSE, 1880s
### 205 Hanover St

Typical middle-class Victorian house built by Daniel Sears Mann, an industrious farmer. Interiors contain elaborate furnishings, marble fireplaces, and a gallery of tintypes and photographs of the Mann family and friends. A collection of farm implements and household utensils and the family cutter and buggy are on display.

*Operated by Mich. Historical Comm. Open Tues.–Fri. 10–5, Sat., Sun. 1–5*

*Mann House*

# CONSTANTINE

## JOHN S. BARRY HOUSE, 1835–36
### 280 N Washington St

Colonial-style house built by John S. Barry, prominent merchant and the third governor of Michigan. Now a museum furnished with antiques
*Operated by Gov. Barry Historical Soc. Open summer: Sun 2–5*

# DEARBORN

## ■ COMMANDANT'S QUARTERS, 1833,
## McFADDEN-ROSS HOUSE, 1839
### 915 Brady St

The Dearborn Historical Museum consists of: Commandant's Quarters, the oldest and most historic building in the city, built as the home of the officer in charge of the old Detroit Arsenal. Constructed of handmade local red brick, massive wood beams, and a slate roof. Restored, containing period rooms with furnishings and an exhibition room with changing displays. McFadden Ross House, originally built as the powder magazine of the Detroit Arsenal, was purchased in 1883, after the closing of the arsenal, and converted into a farmhouse. Now a house museum, with domestic exhibits and furnishings of the period 1890 and later

*Operated by City of Dearborn and the Dearborn Historical Comm. Open Tues.–Fri. 10:30–5:30, Sat. 9–5, Sun. 2–5; closed Sun. Dec.–Feb.*

*Commandant's Quarters*

■ **GREENFIELD VILLAGE, 1920s**
**Village Road and Oakwood Boulevard**
Collective historical site, with many houses and buildings brought by Henry Ford from various parts of the country to form a village museum covering over 200 acres. Houses range from one-room log cabins to elaborate dwellings. Included among more than 100 buildings are structures associated with William Holmes McGuffey, Noah Webster, Robert Frost, Thomas Edison, Abraham Lincoln, and others. Also of interest here is the Henry Ford Museum, which spreads over 14 acres and is filled with a vast collection of American art and artifacts relating to the growth and development of the country. The façade of the museum resembles three famous buildings: Independence Hall, Congress Hall, and old City Hall of Philadelphia.
*Operated by Greenfield Village and Henry Ford Museum. Open June 15–Labor Day: daily 9–5:30. After Labor Day–June 14: daily 9–6:30; closed some holidays*

## DETROIT

**INDIAN VILLAGE HISTORIC DISTRICT**
In the early 19th century the property was known as Abraham Cook Farms, but in 1894 the area was subdivided and named Indian Village. Here there are 347 homes of varied styles in various stages of restoration.

**LITTLE HARRY'S, 1863**
**2681 E Jefferson Ave**
Alexandre Chene, a prominent French landholder and merchant, erected this building on land that had been granted by Louis XIV in 1707. Now operated as a restaurant
*Operated by Mr. Diamond T. Phillips, owner. Open daily 9–9*

## DETROIT VICINITY

**RUSSELL A. ALGER HOUSE, 1910**
**Grosse Pointe Farms**
Italian Renaissance-style mansion situated on a hill overlooking Lake St. Clair. Now the Grosse Pointe War Memorial. Furnishings include some belonging to the Alger family.
*Operated by Grosse Pointe War Memorial Assn. Open Mon.–Sat. 9–9, Sun. 12–5*

## FRANKLIN

■ **VILLAGE OF FRANKLIN HISTORIC DISTRICT**
Typical farming community settled in the 1830s. Remaining are many original structures representing a variety of styles from Greek Revival to Gothic Revival to late Victorian.

## GRAND RAPIDS

■ **ABRAM W. PIKE HOUSE [GRAND RAPIDS ART MUSEUM], 1845**
**230 E Fulton St**
Classical revival-style house built by Abram W. Pike, a prosperous businessman and active public servant. The front pillars are of particular interest, supposedly having been hauled from Port Sheldon (now submerged beneath Lake Michigan), where they once graced a lake-front hotel. Now a museum, with collections of prints and German expressionist paintings
*Operated by Grand Rapids Art Museum. Open Sept.–May: Mon.–Sat. 9–5, Sun. 2–5. June–Aug: Tues.–Sat. 9–5, Sun. 2–5; closed holidays*

## HARBOR BEACH

**FRANK MURPHY BIRTHPLACE, before 1890**
**142 S Huron St**
Birthplace of Frank Murphy, governor

of Michigan, 1936–38, and associate justice of the U.S. Supreme Court, 1940–49. A one-story wing of the house was used by Justice Murphy's father as a law office. Operated as a museum, with papers, photographs, and furniture belonging to Justice Murphy exhibited
*Operated by Mr. Harold L. Richards for the Huron Co. Historical Soc. and local U.A.W.U. Open July–Sept: Fri–Sun. 1–5*

## JACKSON

### ELLA SHARP MUSEUM, 1840s
**3225 Fourth St and Harton Rd**
Restored house with reproductions of Victorian period rooms. Displays pertaining to early history of Jackson County as well as exhibits of fine art, science, and industry
*Operated by City of Jackson. Open Tues.–Sat. 10–5, Sun. 12–5*

## MACKINAC ISLAND

### BIDDLE HOUSE, before 1800
**Market Street**
Probably the oldest surviving residential house on the island, purchased by Edward Biddle, a prominent citizen, in the 1820s and lived in by his descendants until the 1920s. Restored, with furnishings of the period 1820
*Operated by Mackinac Island State Park Comm. Open June 15–Labor Day: daily 10–5*

*Biddle House*

### FORT MACKINAC, 1780
**Huron Road**
The central historical feature on the island, this fort was built by Capt. Patrick Sinclair because he believed the earlier post, Fort Michilimackinac, to be too vulnerable to enemy attack. The following are a few of the buildings of interest at the fort: Barracks

Museum, a two-story wooden structure built in the 1850s; a wooden hospital building built about 1828; the officers' quarters, one of the original buildings constructed in the 1780s and the oldest surviving building in Michigan; and a guardhouse of 1828.
*Operated by Mackinac Island State Park Comm. Open June–Sept: daily 9–6*

*Fort Mackinac*

### INDIAN DORMITORY, 1838
**Huron Street**
Dormitory built as a result of a clause in the Treaty of Washington to house Indians who came to Mackinac Island on business with the U.S. Now restored to its original appearance, with exhibits, period furnishings, Indian museum, and an 1840 kitchen
*Operated by Mackinac Island State Park Comm. Open June 15–Labor Day: daily 10–5*

### STUART HOUSE, early 19th century
**Market Street**
This house was one of several built for employees of the American Fur Company, owned by John Jacob Astor. Now a museum containing documents and exhibits relating to the fur trade
*Operated by City of Mackinac Island. Open June–Sept: daily 9–6*

## MACKINAW CITY

### FORT MICHILIMACKINAC, 1715
Reconstruction of the early fort built by the French and subsequently occupied by British troops after France surrendered her North American empire to the English. Among the buildings to be visited are the *French Trader's House,* the *Commanding Officer's House,* the *British Trader's House,* and the Church of Ste. Anne.
*Operated by Mackinac Island State*

Park Comm. Open June 15–Labor Day: daily 10–6

Fort Michilimackinac

## MANISTIQUE

SCHOOLCRAFT POST HOUSE MUSEUM, late 19th century
104 S Cedar St
Victorian house with period rooms located in resort on Lake Michigan
*Operated by Schoolcraft Co. Historical Soc. Open summer: Mon.–Sat. 2–5*

## MARQUETTE

JOHN BURT HOUSE, about 1858
220 Craig St
One of the first buildings in Marquette, this little stone house was built by John Burt, an inventor and pioneer surveyor. Restored, with furnishings
*Operated by Marquette Co. Historical Soc. Museum. Open July–Aug: daily 10–5*

## MARSHALL

■ HONOLULU HOUSE, 1860
107 N Kalamazoo St
Italianate house built by Abner Pratt, U.S. consul to the Sandwich (Hawaiian) Islands. The house comingles tropical and Victorian architecture.
*Operated by Marshall Historical Soc. Open Mon.–Fri. 2–5, Sat., Sun. 1–7*

## MONROE

SAWYER MANSION, 1872
320 E Front St
Large Italianate house. Period rooms, collection of Gen. George Custer mementos, and pioneer-era exhibits
*Operated by Monroe Co. Historical Soc. Open Tues.–Sat. 1–5*

## MUSKEGON

■ HACKLEY HOUSE, 1888–89
484 W Webster Ave
The Muskegon Chapter of the Red Cross has its offices in this large and ornate Victorian mansion. Built by Charles H. Hackley, an important figure in the town's late 19th-century lumber boom. The interiors boast many fireplaces, much stained glass, and beautiful wood carving.
*Operated by Red Cross. Open by appointment*

## PONTIAC

■ GOV. MOSES WISNER HOUSE (PINE GROVE), 1844; 1848
405 Oakland Ave
Two-story brick Greek Revival house built as the residence of Moses Wisner, 13th governor of the state, and his wife, Angeolina. The house has been restored and refurnished with many original items.
*Operated by Oakland Co. Pioneer and Historical Soc. Open summer: Tues.–Sat. 1–4 and by appointment*

Pine Grove

## PORT SANILAC

LOOP-HARRISON MUSEUM AND DAIRY SHRINE, 1872
228 S Ridge Rd
Victorian mansion built by Dr. Joseph Miller Loop, an early pioneer in this area. Now a museum with a collection of paintings, navigational instruments, Rogers statuary, antique firearms, and Victorian furnishings
*Operated by Sanilac Co. Historical*

*Soc. Open Memorial Day–Labor Day: Tues.–Sat. 1–5*

## ROMEO

### ■ ROMEO HISTORIC DISTRICT

Originally an Indian village and trading point for French settlers, Romeo was established by 60 New Englanders who came here in 1827. Nine years later 30 frame houses showing the strong influence of New England architecture had been erected.

## SAGINAW

### SAGINAW HISTORICAL MUSEUM, 1868
**1105 S Jefferson St**
Double brick home built for Henry Passalt, a soap manufacturer. Period furniture, lumbering industry exhibits, and an old schoolroom may be seen.
*Operated by Saginaw Historical Soc. Open Sun., Tues., Thurs. 1:30–4:30*

## SAULT STE. MARIE

### BARAGA HOUSE, 1860s
**305 E Portage Ave**
Small frame house, the residence of Bishop Baraga, first bishop of this diocese. The house contains items made or used by the bishop.
*Operated by St. Mary's Church. Open June–Sept: daily 9–5*

### ■ JOHN JOHNSTON HOUSE, 1815–22
**415 Park Place**
One-and-a-half-story log house covered with clapboard built by John Johnston, a famous fur trader and explorer. It was for several years the residence of Henry Schoolcraft, Johnston's son-in-law, and is now furnished and operated as a museum.
*Operated by Chippewa Co. Historical Soc. Open Mon.–Fri. 11–5*

## SOUTH HAVEN

### LIBERTY HYDE BAILEY BIRTHPLACE, about 1855; 1870
**903 Bailey Ave**
Frame house, home of the botanist Liberty Hyde Bailey for 24 years. Now maintained as a memorial to the famous scientist, with several exhibition rooms
*Operated by City of South Haven. Open Tues., Fri. 2–4:30, and by appointment*

## STOCKBRIDGE

### WATERLOO FARM MUSEUM, about 1840
**9998 Waterloo-Munith Rd**
Brick-and-stone farmhouse with frame addition, restored as a museum. Ten furnished rooms of the era 1850–1900. Farm implements on display as well as examples of pioneer craftsmanship
*Operated by Waterloo Area Historical Soc. Open June–Labor Day: Tues.–Sat. 1–4*

## BLUE EARTH

### WAKEFIELD HOUSE, 1880
**405 E Sixth St**
Two-story brick house of onetime lieutenant governor J.B. Wakefield. Now a museum, with period furnishings
*Operated by Faribault Co. Historical Soc. Open Tues.–Sun. 11–5*

## BRAINERD

### LUMBERTOWN, U.S.A., 1870s
**off U.S. Route 371 on County Road 7**
Re-creation of a typical lumber town with reconstructed and restored struc-

tures, including the *Pioneer House*, a two-story house of hand-hewn, square-cut logs built in 1873 and furnished with appropriate pieces. Also featured are a cobbler's shop, livery stable, photographer's and print shop.
*Operated by Lumbertown, U.S.A. Open Memorial Day–Sept. 15: daily 10:30–5*

## BROWNS VALLEY

### SAM BROWN LOG HOUSE, about 1863
**Sam Brown Memorial Park**
Two-story log house built by Joseph R.

Brown, who came to Minnesota in 1819 as a young drummer boy. Named for his son Samuel Jerome, who in 1866 rode 120 miles through a storm to warn the settlers of a Sioux attack.
*Operated by Traverse Co. Historical Soc. Open Memorial Day–Sept. 14: daily 1–9*

## ELK RIVER

### ■ OLIVER H. KELLEY FARM, 1860s
**U.S. Route 10**
An 11-room frame house built by Oliver H. Kelley, founder of the National Grange, which had its headquarters here from 1868 to 1870. The frame home, now restored as a typical post-Civil War farmhouse, replaced the original log cabin Kelley had built.
*Operated by Minn. Historical Soc. Open May–Sept: daily 10–4. Oct: Sat., Sun. 10–4*

## FARIBAULT

### ■ ALEXANDER FARIBAULT HOUSE, 1853
**12 NE First Ave**
This house was built by fur trader Alexander Faribault, who in 1826 founded a trading post here from which the town grew. Restored and now historical society headquarters
*Operated by Rice Co. Historical Soc. Open daily 1–5*

## HASTINGS

### ■ WILLIAM G. LE DUC HOUSE, about 1863
**Highway 61**
Gothic Revival stone mansion modeled after a house pictured in Andrew Jackson Downing's *Cottage Residences;* built during the Civil War for Gen. Le Duc, pioneer agriculturist and railroad promoter, who served as U.S. commissioner of agriculture, 1877–81
*Operated by Minn. Historical Soc. Open Mon.–Fri. 9–5*

## LITTLE FALLS

### CHARLES A. LINDBERGH, SR., HOUSE, 1907
**Charles A. Lindbergh Memorial Park**
Large frame house set over a raised basement; the home of Charles A. Lindbergh, Sr., pioneer lawyer and progressive congressman. His famous son spent his boyhood years in this house, which is set in a large public park. Restored and furnished with memorabilia of both Lindberghs
*Operated by Minn. Historical Soc. Open June–Aug: daily 10–6. May, Sept: daily 10–4*

## MANKATO

### HUBBARD HOUSE, 1871
**606 S Broad St**
Large 18-room Victorian house with mansard roof; contains three fireplaces taken from southern plantations burned during the Civil War, Tiffany lamps, and the original bathroom fixtures, with flush toilets. Since 1938 the county museum, with some furniture and many exhibits of historical items. A completely restored and furnished 1873 log cabin is on display in the basement.
*Operated by Blue Earth Co. Historical Soc. Open Tues.–Sun. 1–5*

*Hubbard House*

## MENDOTA

### FARIBAULT HOUSE, 1836–37
Two-story house of locally quarried yellow limestone built by pioneer fur trader Jean Baptiste Faribault. This house was one of several Faribault built; the others were destroyed by flooding of the Minnesota River. Restored and shown with some of the Faribault family furnishings and a fine collection of Indian relics
*Operated by Daughters of the American Revolution. Open May–Oct: Mon.–Sat. 10–5, Sun. 1–6. June 15–Aug: closed Mon.*

# ■ MENDOTA HISTORIC DISTRICT

This trading post village — its name is derived from the Sioux word meaning "meeting of the waters" — is located at the confluence of the Minnesota and Mississippi rivers. The first permanent white settlement in the state, Mendota boasts several dwellings from the 1830s, when the village was the center of the Red River of the North fur trade.

## SIBLEY HOUSE, 1835

Limestone house, the oldest stone dwelling still standing in the state, built as a home and office by Henry Hastings Sibley. Elected the state's first governor in 1858, Sibley had come to Minnesota as a factor for the American Fur Company in 1834. House was restored in 1910 and is shown with period furnishings, some belonging to the Sibley family. Also on the property is a brick house, now known as the *Sibley Tea House*, built in 1854 by Sibley's private secretary.
*Operated by Daughters of the American Revolution. Open May–Oct: Mon.–Sat. 10–5, Sun. 1–6. June 15– Aug: closed Mon.*

# MINNEAPOLIS

## THE AMERICAN SWEDISH INSTITUTE, completed 1907
**2600 Park Ave**
Swan J. Turnblad, publisher of the nation's largest Swedish-American newspaper, built this 33-room castle of Indiana limestone and lived here for less than a decade. Lavish interiors highlighted by plaster ceiling sculpture and magnificent wood carvings; the Great Hall, paneled in African mahogany, is considered the finest installation of its kind in North America. In 1929 Turnblad donated his castle for the creation of a cultural institute. Among the various exhibits are Swedish pioneer items and antiques.
*Operated by The American Swedish Institute. Open Tues.–Sun. 2–5, tours by appointment*

# MONTEVIDEO

## CHIPPEWA CITY PIONEER VILLAGE, 1870s, 1880s
**junction of Highways 7 and 59**
A typical pioneer village with wooden

sidewalks centered around a village square. Among the buildings is a farmhouse built of hand-hewn logs interlocking at the corners or held together with wooden pins where necessary; built prior to 1870 and appropriately furnished. Also featured is a fur company and trading post, a blacksmith's shop, and a rooming house.
*Operated by Chippewa Co. Historical Soc. Open May 17–Sept: Thurs.–Sun. 1:30–5:30*

## OLOF SWENSSON FARMSTEAD, 1901
**five miles south of Highway 7 on County Road 6**
Large brick-faced house built by pioneer farmer Olof Swensson, who with his daughter gathered and cut the stones for the foundation. The 22-room house has 52 doors and 59 windows; in a large room on the second floor Swensson, a lay preacher, conducted services. Shown with family furnishings, some handmade
*Operated by Chippewa Co. Historical Soc. Open May 17–Sept: Sun. 1:30– 5:30 and by appointment*

# MOORHEAD

## SOLOMON G. COMSTOCK HOUSE, 1883
**Eighth Street and Fifth Avenue, South**
An 11-room, two-story frame house designed by Minneapolis architects Kees and Finch for Solomon G. Comstock, who came to Minnesota from Maine and was instrumental in developing the railroad system in the Red River Valley. Comstock later served in the state legislature and in the U.S. Congress and donated land for what is now Moorhead State College.
*Operated by Minn. Historical Soc. Open June–Oct: Tues.–Fri. 10–4, Sat., Sun. 1–4*

# ROCHESTER

## MAYOWOOD, 1910–11
This 38-room home of poured concrete was built by Dr. Charles H. Mayo and was later the home of his son Dr. Charles W. Mayo. Originally set on 3,000 acres, the house and ten acres were donated to the county by Dr. C.W. Mayo in 1965. Furnishings belonged to the family and include many

fine European and American antiques. Tours leave from the historical society headquarters; no private cars are admitted to Mayowood.
*Operated by Olmsted Co. Historical Soc. Open May–Oct: Wed., Thurs., Sat., tours at 1, 3, Sun., tours at 2, 4*

*Mayowood*

## ST. PAUL

### ■ ALEXANDER RAMSEY HOUSE, 1868–72
**265 S Exchange St**
This 16-room, native limestone house with mansard roof is one of the best remaining examples of late Victorian architecture in Minnesota. Built by Alexander Ramsey, who served as first territorial governor, second state governor, U.S. senator, and Secretary of War under Rutherford B. Hayes. Called the "mansion house" and occupied by the family until 1964; the interiors feature 15-foot ceilings, arched doorways, and hand-carved walnut woodwork. Most of the original furnishings remain.
*Operated by Minn. Historical Soc. Open Tues.–Fri. 10–4, Sat., Sun. 1–4*

### ■ BURBANK-LIVINGSTON-GRIGGS HOUSE, 1862–65
**432 Summit Ave**
Lavish limestone mansion designed by architect Otis Wheelock for James Burbank. Later owned by Crawford Livingston, whose daughter Mary Livingston Griggs added a wing in the 1920s and in the 1930s imported ten complete period rooms of European antiques. Included are an English Jacobean room, an 18th-century Venetian dining room, and Louis XV and Louis XVI bedroom suites. Of the original interiors only the main entrance, stairs, and upper hall remain.
*Operated by Minn. Historical Soc. Open Tues.–Fri. 10–4, Sat., Sun. 1–4*

### GIBBS FARM MUSEUM, 1854; 1867
**2097 Larpenteur Ave, W**
Originally a one-room frame house built in 1854 by homesteaders Herman and Jane De Bow Gibbs. In 1867 the cabin became part of a larger, two-story frame house with a wide front gallery; another addition was made in the 1870s. Restored as the home of a prosperous farmer, with appropriate furnishings. The reconstructed barn houses an agricultural pioneer museum with displays of various tools and machinery; a one-room schoolhouse, 1878, is also on the grounds.
*Operated by Ramsey Co. Historical Soc. Open June–Aug: Tues.–Fri. 10–5, Sun. 2–5. May, Sept.–Oct: Tues.–Fri., Sun. 2–5. Dec. 15–Mar. 15: Sun. 2–5*

## SAUK CENTRE

### ■ SINCLAIR LEWIS BOYHOOD HOME, about 1882
**812 Sinclair Lewis Ave**
Two-story frame house, with gingerbread trim on gables and porch, where famed author Sinclair Lewis lived until the age of 18; *Main Street* is partially based on his recollections of his home town. Lewis refused the Pulitzer Prize in 1926 but four years later became the first American to be awarded the Nobel Prize for literature.

*Sinclair Lewis Boyhood Home*

Furnished with Victorian pieces, some belonging to the Lewis family
*Operated by Sinclair Lewis Foundation. Open Memorial Day–Labor Day: Mon.–Sat. 10–4, Sun. 1–5*

## TAYLORS FALLS

### FOLSOM HOUSE, 1855
**Government Road**
Frame house reflecting the New England heritage of the builder, William Henry Carman Folsom; built of pine lumber taken from the property. Folsom, a pioneer lumberman, came to Minnesota from Maine and later served as a member of the state legislature. Furnished with period pieces
*Operated by Minn. Historical Soc. Open June–Oct: Thurs., Fri. 10–4, Sat., Sun. 1–4*

## WILLMAR

### ENDRESON LOG CABIN, 1870
Log cabin of hand-hewn oak taken from the surrounding woods. Built by Lars Endreson, a Norwegian who migrated to Minnesota around the time of the Civil War.
*Operated by Kandiyohi Co. Historical Soc. Open daily 9–5*

## WINDOM

### MONSON LOG CABIN, 1869
**Island Park**
Pioneer log cabin built by Mons O. Monson and Thomas Chester on the line between their respective homestead claims, thereby satisfying the law that a dwelling stand on a claim. After being awarded their homestead rights, the cabin was moved onto Monson's land; the sod roof was replaced with one of shingles, and a chimney was built.
*Operated by Cottonwood Co. Historical Soc. Open by appointment*

## WINONA VICINITY

### WILLARD BUNNELL HOUSE, early 1850s
**Highways 14 and 61**
Quaint three-story wooden house with unpainted batten-and-board exterior and unusual gingerbread trim on the eaves and windows. Built by Willard Bunnell on land given to him as a token of friendship by Wapasha, chief of the Dakotas. Period furnishings
*Operated by Winona Co. Historical Soc. Open June–Sept. 15: Mon.–Sat. 11–5, Sun., holidays 11–6*

## BILOXI VICINITY

### BEAUVOIR, 1852
**Route 90, between Biloxi and Gulfport**
Beautiful one-and-a-half-story house set high over a raised basement, with a wide veranda on three sides and a hipped roof; the last home of Confederate President Jefferson Davis. Set on 70 acres, the house and cottages have been restored and are maintained as a southern shrine. The house and cottage where Davis wrote *The Rise and Fall of the Confederate Government* are shown as they were when he lived here.
*Operated by Sons of Confederate Veterans. Open daily 8:30–5*

## CARROLLTON

### CEDAR HILL, before 1834
Simple clapboard house with Greek Revival details; originally a six-room cottage greatly enlarged in a 1940s renovation matching the old style. Furnished with antiques
*Private. Open by appointment*

### COTTAGE HOME, 1840
**Lexington Street**
Frame house with broad front veranda

*Beauvoir*

and a later rear addition; once served as the Episcopal rectory. Furnishings include some antiques.
*Private. Open by appointment*

## JOHNSTON HOME, before 1834; about 1855

Two-story Victorian house, with second floor added during a remodeling of the house shortly before the Civil War. Furnishings are mainly Victorian, with some pieces handmade by the pioneer ancestors of the owners.
*Private. Open by appointment*

## OLD METHODIST PARSONAGE, before 1858

Nine-room cottage with four porches and enclosed dogtrot. In continuous use as the Methodist parsonage from the time of its construction until 1948. Now a private residence with period furnishings and family heirlooms
*Private. Open by appointment*

## COLUMBUS

### COLUMBUS PILGRIMAGE

During the annual Pilgrimage in the first week in April many of the loveliest homes in Columbus are open to the public. In addition to all the homes listed below, two of the houses on the tour are the *Pratt Thomas Home*, a "raised cottage" built in 1833, with an unusual horseshoe-shaped stairway, and *Shadowlawn*, built by slave labor in 1861 and combining the Greek and Gothic Revival styles. For further information contact the Columbus Pilgrimage Assn.

*Shadowlawn*

## AMZI LOVE HOUSE, 1848
### 305 Seventh St, S
Rambling cottage combining Gothic and Greek Revival styles; built by Amzi Love for his bride and still owned by his descendants. Several outbuildings, including the privy and dairy, remain; the kitchen has been moved alongside and attached to the house. Noteworthy are the jib doors under the front windows and the walnut handrail and S-shaped newel post. Many of the original furnishings
*Private. Open by appointment with the Chamber of Commerce*

## CAMELLIA PLACE, 1840s
### 416 Seventh St, N
Elegant brick mansion built by local architect J.S. Lull as his residence. Interior woodwork stripped in 1870s and replaced with dark-stained mahogany; a spiral mahogany staircase rises, unsupported, to the second floor. Furnished with late Victorian pieces. Many camellias on lovely grounds
*Private. Open by appointment with the Chamber of Commerce*

## ERROLTON, 1848
### 216 Third Ave, S
Basically Greek Revival in style, with Gothic and Tudor elements; built of fine wood shipped here by steamboat from Mobile, Alabama. Front and rear entrances feature red and blue Bohemian glass sidelights. Completely restored after having been divided into apartments; shown with early Victorian and Empire furniture
*Private. Open by appointment with the Chamber of Commerce*

## FRANKLIN SQUARE, 1835; 1870
### 423 Third Ave, N
Graceful mansion house with sunken gardens; set off by two pairs of twin pillars flanking the entrance and a wing added in 1870. Built and still owned by the Franklin-Pratt families. Restored 1918–20 and shown with the early Victorian and Empire pieces
*Private. Open by appointment with the Chamber of Commerce*

## HICKORY STICKS, about 1820
### 1206 Seventh St, N
Originally a two-storied log house that was enclosed by an ante-bellum home early in the 19th century; the logs are still visible in one of the original rooms. Furnished with Mississippi antiques from the 1830s

*Private. Open by appointment with the Chamber of Commerce*

## STEPHEN D. LEE HOME, 1844
**300 Seventh St, N**
Large brick house combining Georgian and Greek Revival styles; built by Maj. Thomas Blewett and inherited by his granddaughter, the wife of Stephen D. Lee, the Confederate general who later became the first president of what is now Mississippi State University. Partially furnished; some rooms are used as a museum of local history
*Operated by Stephen D. Lee Foundation. Open by appointment with the Chamber of Commerce*

## TEMPLE HEIGHTS, 1839–43
**515 Ninth St, N**
Four-story Greek Revival frame house with 14 Doric columns on three sides. Each of the four columns of the south façade was carved from a single tree trunk; the remaining ten columns were added in 1854. The house is being restored with period pieces.
*Private. Open by appointment with the Chamber of Commerce*

*Temple Heights*

## THEMERLAINE, 1844
**510 Seventh St, N**
Large home combining Gothic details with lacy filigree wood carving; second story features small balconies. The two-story house has a full raised basement, which may have been used as servants' quarters or a cooking area, an unusual feature for its day. Since 1960 a nurses' home; furnished with Victorian pieces
*Private. Open by appointment with the Chamber of Commerce*

## TWELVE GABLES, 1838
**220 Third St, S**
Small wooden cottage with some Greek Revival details; the boards of the façade are cut to resemble ashlar, a style made popular in Mount Vernon. Used as a hospital during the Civil War and the scene of the planning of the first Decoration Day in 1866. Restored; Victorian furnishings
*Private. Open by appointment with the Chamber of Commerce*

## WHITE ARCHES, 1857
**122 Seventh Ave, S**
Beautiful large house combining antebellum style with Gothic Revival elements; unusual floor plan in that a cross hall meets the central hall directly in the middle of the house on each floor. Venetian glass windows over each entrance. Partially restored with some of the original furnishings
*Private. Open by appointment with the Chamber of Commerce*

## WISTERIA PLACE, 1854
**524 Eighth St, N**
Typical ante-bellum Greek Revival mansion, with six columns across the front and Bohemian glass sidelights framing the door; built by state senator William R. Cannon. Except for modernization of the kitchen and bathrooms the mansion has remained largely unchanged. Furnished with fine period pieces
*Private. Open by appointment with the Chamber of Commerce*

## COLUMBUS VICINITY
### WAVERLY, 1852
**Highway 50**
Unusual frame mansion, with each room 22 by 25 feet, featuring a four-story octagonal central hall that rises 65 feet to an octagonal cupola exactly the size of the hall below. Designed so that heat would rise to the cupola and go out the long windows in order that the house might be ventilated in summer. During the Civil War the house served as a refuge for girls from New Orleans and Memphis. Restored and furnished with period antiques; original mirrors and chandeliers remain
*Private. Open daily 8–6*

## GAUTIER
### THE OLD PLACE, 1860
**U.S. Route 90, east of Biloxi**
Fernando Gautier's plantation house,

with hipped roof supported by columns on four sides resulting in wide verandas around the house; built of yellow pine and cypress from the Pascagoula swamp and oyster-shell mortar. Restored by the Gautier family, who still own the property. Interiors feature the original kitchen fireplace, the punka over the dining room table, and the Aubusson rugs.
*Private. Open Mon.–Sat. 9–5, Sun. 12–5, evgs. by appointment*

## HOLLY SPRINGS

### HOLLY SPRINGS PILGRIMAGE
Since 1938 Holly Springs has sponsored a Pilgrimage tour of some of its lovely Old South mansions. Held during the last weekend in April, the tour includes *Herndon*, built in 1839, and the city's oldest two-story brick house, *Cedarhurst*, a charming French Gothic-style house with ornate trim built in 1857, as well as the houses listed below. Further information can be obtained from the Holly Springs Garden Club.

*Cedarhurst*

### MONTROSE, 1858
Stately classical revival brick mansion built by Alfred Brooks as a wedding present for his daughter. Some interior features are a spiral stairway with a niche for statuary, parquet floors, and ceilings with rosettes. A wide brick walkway, bordered with boxwoods, leads to the mansion.
*Operated by Holly Springs Garden Club. Open by appointment*

### MOSSWOOD, before 1860
One-and-a-half-story clapboard house reflecting both the Greek Revival and late Georgian architectural styles. Built by Adrian N. Mayer, who migrated to Mississippi from Georgia in the 1830s. Recently restored
*Private. Open by appointment*

### WALTER PLACE, late 1850s
**331 W Chulahoma Ave**
Large Greek Revival brick mansion dominated by two battlemented octagonal towers flanking a portico supported by four Corinthian columns. Built by Col. Harvey W. Walter and used by Gen. and Mrs. Grant in 1862. Birthplace of noted Shanghai surgeon Dr. Anne Walter Fearn; the house is still owned by descendants of Col. Walter
*Private. Open by appointment*

## JACKSON

### ■ GOVERNOR'S MANSION, completed 1842; 1908
**316 E Capital St**
Graceful mansion with Greek Revival details designed by architect William Nicholas; rear wing added in 1908. Occupied by every Mississippi governor since its completion, it is one of the oldest houses built by a state to be a governor's official residence. During the Civil War Gen. William T. Sherman made his headquarters here, thereby assuring the mansion's survival despite destruction of the city.
*Operated by State of Mississippi. Open Mon.–Fri. by appointment*

*Governor's Mansion*

## THE OAKS, 1846
### 823 N Jefferson St

Greek Revival frame cottage built for James H. Boyd, an early settler of Jackson and three-term mayor of the city. Occupied by his descendants until 1960. During the Civil War the house was used as officers' quarters by the Union army; it is one of the few ante-bellum buildings left in the city. Shown with period furnishings and an old-fashioned garden
*Operated by Soc. of Colonial Dames. Open daily 10–5*

## JACKSON VICINITY

### SUB ROSA PLANTATION HOME, before 1860
### U.S. Route 49, seven miles north of Jackson

Ante-bellum plantation house, one of the few left unscathed after the War Between the States. Furnished with fine antiques
*Private. Open by appointment*

## MERIDIAN

### MERREHOPE, 1857; 1867; 1903
### 905 31 Ave

Begun as a two-room house and subsequently enlarged to the present 26-room mansion highlighted by nine Ionic columns, this is one of four homes left standing after Gen. Sherman's troops burned Meridian in 1864. Now being restored and furnished
*Operated by Meridian Restorations Foundation. Open Mar.–Dec. 15: Tues.–Sat. 10–12, 2–4:30, Sun. 2–4:30*

## NATCHEZ

### NATCHEZ PILGRIMAGE

Most of the beautiful ante-bellum mansions in Natchez, a city founded by the French in 1716, are still private residences but are open to the public once a year during the annual Pilgrimage. This house tour is usually held for four weeks beginning in early March. Among the many mansions on the tour are *Gloucester,* a classical revival mansion begun prior to 1803 and once the home of the first governor of the Mississippi Territory; *Elgin Plantation,* begun in 1780 and completed in 1840; and *Elms Court,* 1810, featuring lacy grillwork across its double galleries. Many of the Natchez homes listed below have special hours during Pilgrimage to conform to the preset schedule. For further information contact The Natchez Pilgrimage.

*Elms Court*

### CHEROKEE, 1794–1810
### North Wall and High Streets

One of the earliest of the city's large homes, with a beautiful classical entrance, interesting cross hall, and graceful winding stairway. Furnished with fine ante-bellum antiques
*Operated by Mr. and Mrs. Charles Byrne, owners. Open Mon.–Sat. 9–3; closed holidays*

### CHOCTAW, 1836
### North Wall and High Streets

Stately Greek Revival mansion with a massive portico and pillars topped by Ionic capitals. Designed by architect James Hardie and for many years the home of Alvarez Fisk, a benefactor of the city's first free white schools
*Operated by the American Legion. Open by appointment*

### CONNELLY'S TAVERN ON ELLICOTT'S HILL, before 1795
### Jefferson and Canal Streets

Two-story frame house with narrow double galleries; a notable example of Spanish provincial architecture. The brick-floored tap room and second-story bedrooms are furnished with fine-quality period pieces. In defiance of the Spanish rulers the U.S. flag was first raised here in 1797.
*Operated by Natchez Garden Club. Open daily 9–5*

### D'EVEREUX, 1840
### Highway 61

Stately Greek Revival ante-bellum mansion with six columns supporting the roof. Henry Clay was a frequent guest here.

Operated by Mr. and Mrs. T.B. Buckles, owners. Open Mon.–Sat. 9–5; closed holidays

## DIXIE, 1828
### 211 S Wall St

Typical classical town house with a rear dependency that was built in 1795. Interior boasts fine woodwork and moldings and is highlighted by walnut and cherry floors. Restored and furnished with fine period antiques
Operated by Mr. and Mrs. T.L. Ketchings, owners. Open daily 9–5

## EVANSVIEW (BONTURA), 1790–1830
### 107 S Broadway

Two-story brick house in the Creole style overlooking the Mississippi River, with beautiful lacy ironwork across the front galleries. L-shaped house was built in three separate sections and boasts a courtyard garden. Formerly called Bontura, it is now named for the Hugh Evans family, who restored and furnished the house with period antiques.
Operated by Soc. of Colonial Dames. Open by appointment

## GREEN LEAVES, before 1812
### Washington and South Rankin Streets

Greek Revival brick-and-frame house sits in the shade of a gigantic live oak beneath which the Natchez Indians are believed to have held their powwows. The 14-room house is occupied by descendants of the family who acquired it in 1849.
Operated by the M.R. Beltzhoover family. Open Mon., Wed., Thurs., Sat. 9–1

## HAWTHORNE, 1814
### Lower Woodville Road

Beautiful white one-and-a-half-story frame house with a gambrel roof, square columns, and a covered porch. This typical southern planter's house is still a private residence.
Operated by Mr. and Mrs. Hyde Jenkins, owners. Open Mon.–Sat. 9–2; closed holidays

## HOPE FARM, 1774–89
### Auburn Road and Homo Chitto Street

The rear of this house was built while the city was under British rule; the front wing was added by Carlos de Grandpe, then Spanish governor. The house features long galleries facing onto an exquisite garden; shown with family furnishings and other antiques
Operated by Mr. and Mrs. Balfour Miller, owners. Open Mon.–Sat. 9–4; closed holidays

## LANSDOWNE, 1853
### off Pine Ridge Road

Classical revival house, with a widow's walk and three tall chimneys, built by George M. Marshall and still owned by his descendants. Shown with the original furnishings, including a large collection of antique silver
Operated by Mr. and Mrs. George M. Marshall and Mrs. Singleton Gardner, owners. Open daily 9–5; closed Thanksgiving, Christmas Eve, and Christmas

## MELROSE, 1845
### Melrose Avenue

Excellent example of a stately classical revival southern mansion; the house, gardens, and furnishings have remained unchanged since ante-bellum days. Audubon's famous landscape of Natchez hangs in the house, which is still a private residence.
Operated by Mrs. G.M.D. Kelly, owner. Open by appointment

## ■ MOUNT LOCUST, 1779
### Natchez Trace Parkway

Frontier house and farmstead was used as an inn by travelers on the Natchez Trace, a road following an old Indian trail for 500 miles from Nashville, Tennessee, to Natchez.
Operated by National Park Service. Open Mar., June–Aug: daily 9–5 and by appointment

## ROSALIE, about 1820
### 100 Orleans St

Stately mansion combining Georgian and classical revival styles; built on the site of Fort Rosalie, a French bastion that was the scene of an Indian massacre in 1729. Mansion served as Union headquarters in 1863, and later Gen. Grant stayed here. Now a state shrine furnished with period pieces
Operated by Daughters of the American Revolution. Open daily 9–5; closed Thanksgiving, Christmas Eve, and Christmas

## STANTON HALL, 1851–58
### 401 High St

Exquisite Greek Revival southern

mansion occupying a full city block; built by Frederick Stanton, who made a special trip to Europe to buy furnishings for his new home. Parlors are separated by folding doors which open to form a 70-foot ballroom. Restored with lovely gardens and a carriage house restaurant
*Operated by Pilgrimage Garden Club. Open daily 9–5*

### THE ELMS, 1782
**South Pine Street**
Unusual three-story house believed to have been built by Spanish governor Don Pedro Piernas. The house features low ceilings, narrow windows, and wide galleries on two sides; set in an old-fashioned garden
*Operated by Mrs. Joseph P. Kellogg, owner. Open daily 9–2; closed Thanksgiving and Christmas*

## NATCHEZ VICINITY

### ■ LONGWOOD (NUTT'S FOLLY), about 1860
The largest and most ornate octagonal house in the country, with five stories topped by a glass-enclosed "Moorish" tower; built for Dr. Haller Nutt by architect Samuel Sloan. Outbreak of the Civil War prevented the completion of the house; only the ground floor with its rotunda and eight huge rooms has been fully furnished.
*Private. Open daily 9–5*

*Nutt's Folly*

## OXFORD

### CEDAR OAKS, late 1850s
**Murry Street**
Stately Greek Revival frame house

built by William Turner and saved during the Civil War by his sister. Moved to this site in 1963 to save it from being razed; shown with antique furnishings
*Operated by Federated Clubwomen. Open by appointment*

## SANDY HOOK

### JOHN FORD HOME, about 1800
**Mississippi Highway 35**
Three-story house with a raised basement built by the Rev. S. John Ford. Originally surrounded by a stockade and known as Ford's Fort, it is built of bricks made on the premises and wood found there. Shown with appropriate furnishings
*Operated by Marion Co. Historical Soc. Open Mon.–Wed., Fri., Sat. 10–5, Sun. 1–5*

## VICKSBURG

### CANDON HEARTH, 1840s
**2530 Confederate Ave**
"Crackerbox" farmhouse with two brick and weatherboard wings sits on the site of the Confederate troop line on the Vicksburg battlefield and bears many scars from the siege. Built by William Newman, who was killed by a Yankee cannonball. Still occupied and preserved by his descendants; shown with the family furnishings
*Operated by Mrs. C.M. Dearing, owner. Open daily 8–dusk*

### CEDAR GROVE, 1840, 1858
**2200 Oak St**
Beautiful ante-bellum house with four white Doric pillars; built by slave labor for John Alexander Klein, local financier. During the siege of Vicksburg the house was struck by Union forces; a cannonball is still embedded in one of the parlor walls. Furnished with period pieces, many belonging to the Klein family
*Operated by Vicksburg Theatre Guild. Open Feb.–Nov: Mon.–Sat. 9–4:30, Sun. 1:30–5*

### McRAVEN, 1797; 1836; 1849
**Harrison and Gates Eastern Streets**
Rear brick section of this house was built when the city was a small settlement called Walnut Hills; the middle section reflects the Creole style, while

the final section is built in the Greek Revival style. The front hall still bears shell marks left from the siege of Vicksburg. Period furnishings
*Operated by Mr. and Mrs. O.E. Bradway, Jr. Open Mon.–Sat. 9–4:30, Sun. 2–4:30*

## WOODVILLE

### ROSEMOUNT, about 1812
The boyhood home of Jefferson Davis, President of the Confederacy; plantation established here by his father, Samuel Davis. One-and-a-half-story cottage with raised basement has front and rear verandas and a small Palladian window. The house, outbuildings, and gardens are being restored.
*Private. Restoration in progress*

McRaven

## ARROW ROCK

### ■ GEORGE CALEB BINGHAM HOME, about 1837
**First and High Streets**
Two-room brick cottage with paneled doors and a carved walnut mantel; built by noted painter George Caleb Bingham, who intermittently lived here from 1837 to 1845. Bingham made sketches for many of his famous genre paintings of river boatmen here.
*Operated by Mo. State Park Board. Open Tues.–Sun. 12–7*

### MATTHEW HALL HOME, 1847
**Main Street**
Two-room brick house with raised basement, paneled doors, and wideboard pine floors. Built by the village doctor Matthew Wilson Hall, one of the original settlers and a state representative from 1860 to 1862
*Operated by Mo. State Park Board. Open Tues.–Sun. 12–7*

## BRANSON

### OLD MATT'S CABIN, 1884
**State Highway 76, Shepherd of the Hills Farm**
Log cabin with a rock chimney and

fireplace, the homestead of the J.K. Ross family, principal characters in Harold Bell Wright's novel *The Shepherd of the Hills.* The cabin still contains its original furnishings; a nearby museum displays Indian relics and Ozark handicrafts.
*Private. Open Apr.–Oct: daily 8–6*

## BUNCETON

### RAVENSWOOD, about 1880
**State Highway 5**
Built by Charles E. Leonard, this red brick 30-room Victorian house with white columns and a Gothic tower stands on a 1,930-acre farm established in 1825. The original house, also built by the Leonard family, was destroyed during the Civil War; the present one is still occupied by the family and has 18 fireplaces and authentic furnishings.
*Operated by Charles W. Leonard. Open Apr.–Nov: daily 9–6*

## CAPE GIRARDEAU

### GLENN HOUSE AND CARRIAGE HOUSE, 1880
**725 S Spanish St**
Architect Edwin Branch Dean, an

early settler, designed this large Victorian home with a carriage house in the rear. Restoration is in progress on the main house; the carriage house, a brick building with an asbestos shingle roof, has been restored.
*Operated by Historical Assn. of Greater Cape Girardeau. Hours to be determined*

## CARTHAGE

### RANKIN-KENDRICK HOME, 1849–54
**U.S. Routes 66 and 71**
Two-story brick house with two cherry wood mantels and wide-board oak floors; a wooden frame addition in the rear is a reconstruction of one built in 1908 to replace the original slave quarters and kitchen. Now a museum with antique furnishings and Civil War memorabilia
*Operated by Mr. and Mrs. Jack Janey, owners. Open Mon.–Sat. 10–3*

## CRESTWOOD

### THOMAS JOHN SAPPINGTON HOME, 1808–9
**1015 S Sappington Rd**
One of the few remaining examples of Federal architecture in the St. Louis area, a small two-and-a-half-story brick house built by an early Missouri pioneer. Restored in 1961; shown with early 19th-century pieces
*Operated by City of Crestwood. Open Tues.–Fri. 10–4, Sat., Sun. 12–4; closed national holidays*

*Thomas Sappington House*

## DEFIANCE

### ■ DANIEL BOONE HOME, 1803–10
**Highway 7**
Two-story L-shaped house of native limestone built by Daniel Boone and his son Nathan. Interiors feature walnut doors, handmade locks, and fireplace mantels carved by the legendary frontiersman, who died here in 1820. Furnished with appropriate pieces
*Operated by Shelband Corp. Open daily 8:30–dusk*

## FLORIDA

### ■ MARK TWAIN BIRTHPLACE MEMORIAL SHRINE, before 1835
**Mark Twain State Park**
Two-room frame cottage where Samuel L. Clemens was born Nov. 30, 1835; now enclosed within a modern museum building. Included among the many exhibits are several first editions and the original manuscript of the English edition of *Tom Sawyer*. Located in 1,192-acre state park
*Operated by Mo. State Park Board. Open Tues.–Sun. 10–5*

*Mark Twain Birthplace*

## FLORISSANT

### TAILLE DE NOYER, 1790; 1820
**1892 S Florissant Rd**
The original portion of this 23-room frame house was a log cabin believed to have been built by a French fur trader. The larger main house was added by John Mullanphy, an early St. Louis millionaire, who purchased the property about 1798; a much later addition was made in 1920. Now the historical society museum
*Operated by Florissant Valley Historical Soc. Open Tues.–Fri. 1–4, Sat., Sun. 12–5*

## FROHNA

### SAXON LUTHERAN MEMORIAL, late 1820s
off Missouri Highway 61

Two-room, one-and-a-half-story log cabin with a massive double center fireplace; additions were made in 1842, 1870, and 1913. Restored and shown with some of the original furnishings *Operated by Concordia Historical Institute. Open daily 9–5*

## HANNIBAL

### "BECKY THATCHER" HOME, 1840
211 Hill St

Two-story frame house where Mark Twain's childhood playmate Laura Hawkins grew up. It is said that Becky Thatcher, a character in *Tom Sawyer* and *Huckleberry Finn*, was modeled after the author's young friend. Two rooms are furnished; the rest of the house is a bookshop.
*Private. Open Sept.–May: daily 8–5; June–Aug: daily 8–8*

### ■ MARK TWAIN BOYHOOD HOME, 1844
206 Hill St

Unpretentious two-story frame house built by John Clemens, Mark Twain's father. This house, restored to the period of the author's boyhood, provided the setting for *Tom Sawyer* and *Huckleberry Finn*. A vast collection of Twain memorabilia is displayed here and in the museum next door.

*Mark Twain Boyhood Home*

*Operated by Mark Twain Home Board. Open June–Aug: daily 7:30–6. Sept.–May: daily 8–5; closed Thanksgiving, Christmas, and New Year's Day*

### ROCKCLIFFE MANSION, 1898–1900
1000 Bird St

Elaborate, eclectic Victorian mansion with Corinthian columns, mansard roof, and gingerbread trim. The 30-room house built by John J. Cruikshank features such modern innovations as electricity, cedar-lined closets, walk-in closets with brass thermostats, and pocket sliding doors. Both house and gardens have been restored and appropriately furnished.
*Private. Open Apr., May, Oct: Sat., Sun. 1–5. Memorial Day–Sept: daily 9:30–5:30*

## HERMANN

### CARL P. STREHLY HOME, about 1845
131 W Second St

Brick one-and-a-half-story section of this house was built by Edward Muehl, who brought a printing press here and published *Licht Freund*, a German-language abolitionist monthly newspaper. The three-story addition was built before the Civil War by Muehl's brother-in-law Carl Strehly, an expert in the dyeing and block printing of cloth.
*Private. Open by appointment*

### G. HENRY GENTNER HOME, about 1850
108 Market St

Built by one of the original party sent from Philadelphia to settle the town, a two-story brick house, with a formal 18th-century façade and projecting center portion topped by a pedimented gable. A rear balcony overlooks a period garden and carriage house.
*Operated by Brush and Palette Club. Open Apr.–Oct: first Sun. of each month*

## INDEPENDENCE

### ■ MARSHAL'S HOUSE AND JAIL, 1859
217 N Main St

Federal-style house of handmade brick served as a home for county marshals

and their families. Directly behind is the two-story limestone jail where William Quantrill and Frank James were held prisoner. The 12-cell jail has two-foot-thick walls and hand-wrought iron bars and doors; the house is furnished in the style of the 1870s.
*Operated by Jackson Co. Historical Soc. Open June–Aug: Mon.–Sat. 9–5, Sun. 1–5. Sept.–May: Tues.–Sat. 10–4, Sun. 1–5*

## JEFFERSON CITY

### ■ GOV. B. GRATZ BROWN HOME, 1871
**109 Madison St**
Tall, narrow four-story brick house with a mansard roof, once part of a row of houses. Built by Missouri's 12th governor, B. Gratz Brown, who lived here while the new executive mansion was being built across the street. Restored and shown with period furnishings; also on display are paintings by George Caleb Bingham and the inaugural gowns worn by wives of Missouri's governors.
*Operated by Cole Co. Historical Soc. Open Tues.–Sat. 1–5*

## KANSAS CITY

### ■ WORNALL HOUSE, 1858
**146 W 61 St**
Two-story L-shaped brick house is one of the earliest Greek Revival buildings in this area. Built by Kentuckian John B. Wornall, farmer and prominent local citizen. When Wornall refused to give proof of his loyalty to the Union, his property was confiscated. The house subsequently served as headquarters and a hospital for both Union and Confederate forces; presently being restored
*Operated by Jackson Co. Historical Soc. Open by appointment*

## KANSAS CITY VICINITY

**MISSOURI TOWN, 1855**
A collection of authentic log houses, taverns, stables, and shops built between 1820 and 1860 has been moved here to form this "pioneer town," typical of mid-19th-century Missouri. The buildings are shown with appropriate furnishings.

*Operated by Jackson Co. Park Dept. Open daily 9–5; closed Thanksgiving, Christmas, and New Year's Day*

## KEYTESVILLE

### ■ HILL HOMESTEAD, 1832
**100 W North St**
Original portion of this two-story frame house built by William Reading, who was killed by Union soldiers as he ran out the back door. Georgian-style wing added in 1866, and octagonal tower added after 1872. Continuously in use as a private residence; shown with the original furnishings
*Operated by Mr. and Mrs. Marksberry, owners. Open May 15–Sept: by appointment*

## LACLEDE

### ■ GEN. JOHN J. PERSHING BOYHOOD HOME, about 1857
Two-and-a-half-story clapboard house with ornate moldings where Pershing lived as a boy from 1866 through 1882. Restored and shown with period furniture and the general's papers and belongings
*Operated by Mo. State Park Board. Open Tues.–Sat. 10–4, Sun. 12–5*

*Gen. John J. Pershing Boyhood Home*

## LAMAR

### ■ HARRY S. TRUMAN BIRTHPLACE, about 1881
**1009 Truman Ave**
Two-story, six-room frame house purchased by John A. Truman in 1882; his son Harry S. Truman was born here on May 8, 1884. The family lived in the house until the future President was 11 months old.

**MISSOURI**

Operated by Mo. State Park Board. Open Tues.–Sat. 10–4, Sun. 12–6

## LEXINGTON

### ■ COL. OLIVER ANDERSON HOME, 1853
**Battle of Lexington State Park**
Greek Revival L-shaped brick mansion was at the center of a Civil War battle. The one-story portico features cast-iron Corinthian capitals on the four columns; windowsills and lintels are also of iron. During the war the house was used as a Union hospital; battle scars can still be seen, and trenches are visible on the surrounding grounds. Operated by Mo. State Park Board. Open Tues.–Sun. 10–4

*Col. Oliver Anderson Home*

## LOUISIANA

### JAMES STARK CABIN, about 1830
**U.S. Route 54**
Two-room log cabin built by Stark some two and one-half miles from here on the site of a nursery he had opened in 1816. The present nursery is one of the largest and probably the oldest in the nation. The cabin has been restored and furnished. Operated by Stark Brothers Nursery. Open by appointment

## MANSFIELD

### ■ ROCKY RIDGE FARM, 1895–1912
**Business Route 60**
Begun as a one-room cabin about 1895 and subsequently added to until 1912; the white frame house has an irregular plan. Laura Ingalls Wilder lived here while writing many children's books. Private. Open Apr.–Oct. 15 daily 9–5. Oct. 16–Mar. by appointment

*Laura Ingalls Wilder Home*

## MEXICO

### JOHN P. CLARK HOME (ROSS HOUSE), 1850s
**435 S Western St**
Square 10-room frame house in the classical revival style featuring a two-story portico with fanciful scrollwork trim and a captain's walk. Built by John Clark, prominent local citizen, who entertained Gen. Grant here during the Civil War. Home of banker James Ross from 1874 to 1920; now a museum with period furnishings Operated by Audrain Co. Historical Soc. Open Mar.–Nov: Tues.–Sun. 2–5. Dec.–Feb: Tues.–Sat. 2–5; closed national holidays

## ROCHEPORT

### GROSSMAN-BARTH HOME, about 1855
Small frame cottage, typical of many 19th-century Missouri country houses. The house features a low-pitched tin roof, oak siding, walnut windowsills, and six-over-six paned windows. Built and owned by early German immigrants; restored and furnished Operated by Mrs. J.C. Caldwell, owner. Open Sun. 2–5

### KEISER-DIMMITT-RUSSELL GREEN HOME, before 1852
Two-story red brick house built in a rectangular shape; the 13-inch-thick walls are topped by a red tin roof.

156

Shown with appropriate furnishings
*Private. Open Sun. 2–5*

## ST. CHARLES

■ **ST. CHARLES HISTORIC DISTRICT**
Founded in 1769 as "Les Petites Cotes," St. Charles was the first permanent white settlement on the Missouri River. In 1821 the city became the capital of the newly admitted state of Missouri; the three buildings where the state government first sat can still be seen.

## STE. GENEVIEVE

**AMOUREAUX HOUSE, about 1770**
**St. Mary's Road**
Fine Creole-style house with hipped roof, one of the oldest houses of its kind still in existence. Furnished with antiques of the area and a collection of silver, china, glass, and old dolls
*Operated by Mr. and Mrs. Norbert Donze, owners. Open Mar.–Nov: daily 9–5*

**BEAUVAIS HOUSE, 1770s**
**Main and Merchant Streets**
Built in the original French settlement on the Mississippi River and moved to the new town before 1790, this house of cedar and walnut beams filled between with stone and lime mortar, has been greatly altered over the years. Restored and furnished; a brick smokehouse built in the early 1800s remains
*Operated by Mr. and Mrs. Norbert Donze, owners. Open daily 9–5*

**GREEN TREE, 1790**
**St. Mary's Road**
Built as a residence by Nicholas Janis, this house soon became an inn when the number of travelers in the area greatly increased. Constructed in the *maison de poteaux sur sole* style (house of posts set on a sill supported by a stone foundation); restored and shown with 18th-century furnishings
*Operated by Mrs. Fred Foley, owner. Open daily 9–5*

■ **LOUIS BOLDUC HOME, 1770s**
**Main and South Gabouri Streets**
Early French colonial house with walls constructed of oak timbers set upright into a stone foundation; the spaces between the uprights are filled with clay and straw. Steeply pitched hipped roof forms a gallery around the house. Furnished with authentic pieces, many French-Canadian and some belonging to wealthy merchant Louis Bolduc, who owned the house
*Operated by Soc. of Colonial Dames. Open Apr.–Oct: daily 10–4*

*Louis Bolduc Home*

**MAMMY SHAW HOUSE, about 1790**
**Merchant and Second Streets**
One-and-a-half-story frame house built by an early physician. Large double interior doors and other fixtures come from an early Mississippi River steamboat. Adjacent to the house is an Indian trading post built about the same time. Partially used as an art gallery, the house has period furnishings.
*Operated by Matthew Ziegler, owner. Open Feb.–Nov: daily 10–5*

■ **STE. GENEVIEVE HISTORIC DISTRICT**
The first permanent white settlement in Missouri, Ste. Genevieve was founded in 1735 on the west bank of the Mississippi River but had to be abandoned in 1796 because of flooding. The present town, three miles north, retains some of the atmosphere of the early fur-trading, mining, and military post. A number of late 18th-century structures remain.

## ST. JOSEPH

**WYETH-TOOTLE HOME, 1879**
**11 and Charles Streets**
A 43-room Gothic-style sandstone

mansion dominated by a battlemented octagonal tower. Built by pioneer saddlery and hardware merchant William M. Wyeth and purchased by banker Milton Tootle in 1882. Now the St. Joseph Museum, with exhibits of Indian relics and Civil War artifacts
*Operated by St. Joseph Museum. Open May–Sept. 15: Mon.–Sat. 9–5, Sun. 2–5. Sept. 16–Apr: Tues.–Sat. 1–5, Sun., holidays 2–5*

## ST. JOSEPH VICINITY

### JESSE JAMES HOME, 1879
**U.S. Routes 59, 71, and 169**
Frame cottage where Bob Ford shot Jesse James for a $10,000 reward; at the time James was living here with his family posing as the mild-mannered "Mr. Howard." Furnished with Jesse James memorabilia
*Private. Open Thurs.–Tues. 9–5:30*

*Jesse James Home*

## ST. LOUIS

### CHATILLON-DE MENIL HOUSE, 1848; after 1856
**3352 S 13 St**
Fine example of Greek Revival architecture; original portion of the present 15-room, two-and-a-half-story house was built by fur trader Henri Chatillon. Dr. Alexander Nicholas De Menil bought the house in 1856 and added the fine two-story portico with four Ionic columns and a second-story balcony with a cast-iron railing.
*Operated by Chatillon-De Menil House Foundation. Open Tues.–Sun. 10–4*

### EUGENE FIELD HOME, 1845
**634 Broadway**
Charming three-story red brick town house, once connected to 11 other houses called Walsh's Row; surrounded by a walled formal garden. Author Eugene Field was born here in 1850; his artifacts and belongings are displayed.
*Operated by St. Louis Board of Education and Landmarks Assn. of St. Louis. Open Tues.–Sun. 10–5; closed first Tues. of each month*

### GEN. DANIEL BISSELL HOME, about 1819
**10225 Bellefontaine Rd**
Original stone house was very much enlarged to a two-story brick dwelling in 1819; minor additions were made in the 1880s. Gen. Bissell, who served in the Revolution and the War of 1812, came here to live after his retirement in 1821. His family owned the house until 1961, when it was restored; furnishings are from the period 1812–50.
*Operated by St. Louis Co. Dept. of Parks and Recreation. Open Wed.–Sat. 8–5, Sun. 1–5*

### GRANT'S FARM
**10501 Gravois Rd**
Included in the 281-acre tract is land farmed by Ulysses S. Grant from about 1854 to 1860; the frame cabin where he lived has been restored. The farm was acquired by August A. Busch, Sr., and now features a collection of vehicles, a miniature zoo, a game preserve, and the famous stable of Clydesdales. Reservations are required
*Operated by Anheuser-Busch. Open Apr.–Oct: Tues.–Sat., tours 9–3*

### JOHN HALL-ROBERT CAMPBELL HOUSE, 1851
**1508 Locust St**
Three-story brick town house with interesting bay windows; surrounded by an ornate iron fence. Irish-born fur trader and merchant Robert Campbell purchased the house in 1854 and once entertained President and Mrs. Grant here. Campbell's son lived here until his death in 1938; the house and period furnishings are intact and offer an accurate picture of the early life of the city.
*Operated by Campbell House Foundation. Open Tues.–Sat. 10–4, Sun. 12–5*

## SHAW'S GARDEN, 1849
**2315 Tower Grove Ave**
Henry Shaw, merchant and botanist, built his country home here and in 1860 opened this botanical garden, today one of the largest in the world. *Tower Grove*, his Italian Renaissance home designed by architect George Barnett, is a 17-room stucco-over-brick mansion dominated by a tall square tower; it has been restored and furnished with period pieces. Shaw's town house, also designed in the Italian Renaissance style by Barnett, was moved here and is now the administration building and botanical library. Linnean House, the only greenhouse remaining from Shaw's lifetime, is also open and in use.
*Operated by Mo. Botanical Garden. Open May–Oct: Mon.–Sat. 9–6, Sun. 9–7. Nov.–Apr: Mon.–Sat. 9–5, Sun. 9–7*

## VIENNA

### OLD FELKER HOUSE, 1855
Log house of two rooms connected by a bridgeway; now part of a museum. Shown with pioneer furnishings and items of local historical interest
*Operated by Historical Soc. of Maries Co. Open Mar.–Oct: daily 8–5*

## WEBSTER GROVES

### ■ HAWKEN HOUSE, 1857
**Southwest Webster Park, Rock Hill Road**
Two-story brick house built in the Federal style by Christopher Hawken, whose father designed and manufactured the Hawken rifle – the gun that "won the West." Moved to this park and restored
*Operated by Webster Groves Historical Soc. Hours to be determined*

## BUTTE
### ■ BUTTE HISTORIC DISTRICT, 1876
The first copper boom began when the railroad was laid through Butte in 1881. Mining of this mineral has continued to the present. The largest copper-mining region in the world, with less than five square miles beneath the city yielding more than two billion dollars' worth of ore since 1864

### ■ COPPER KING MANSION, 1884–88
**219 W Granite St**
Built by William Andrews Clark, one of Butte's copper magnates and a U.S. senator (1901–7), this fine mansion is considered by some to be one of the best examples of Victorian architecture in the U.S. It is a three-story brick structure, with 27 rooms, beautiful wood paneling, frescoed ceilings, stained- and etched-glass windows, and antique furnishings. The house remained in the Clark family until 1934, after which it was used as a Roman Catholic convent. It is now a private home.
*Operated by Mr. and Mrs. Robert Smith, owners. Open daily 9–6*

*Copper King Mansion*

### DILLON VICINITY
### ■ BANNACK HISTORIC DISTRICT
**off Montana Route 278**
Montana's oldest town and first territorial capital as well as the site of Montana's first gold discovery. Abandoned since 1938, most buildings are of frame and log construction, typical of a frontier boom town.

### GREAT FALLS
### ■ CHARLES M. RUSSELL HOUSE AND STUDIO, about 1900
**12 Street and Fourth Avenue, N**
The home (not open to the public) and

log cabin studio commemorating the life of the famous cowboy artist with his personal memorabilia on exhibit. Nearby is the C.M. Russell Gallery, which contains a permanent collection of his watercolors, models, illustrated notes, and letters.
*Operated by Josephine Trigg-C.M. Russell Foundation. Open Tues.–Sat. 10–5, Sun. 1–5*

## HELENA

### ■ GOVERNOR'S OLD MANSION, 1884–85
**304 N Ewing St**
Stately three-story house of brick and terra cotta built by William A. Chessman, president of the Consolidated Water Company and owner of placer claims and valuable water rights at the Last Chance Gulch gold strikes. The house was purchased in 1913 as the official residence of Montana's governors, and it served as such until 1959, when a new mansion was built. Efforts are being made to save this fine old building and restore it, with furnishings, to its original elegance. *Operated by City of Helena. Open by appointment*

*Governor's Old Mansion*

### LAST CHANCE GULCH RESTORATION, 1864–80
**212 S Park Ave**
Re-creation of Montana's gold rush days, with buildings and furnishings of the period
*Operated by Last Chance Gulch Res-*

*toration Assn. Open June 15–Labor Day: daily 9–5*

*Kluge House*

## VIRGINIA CITY

### ■ VIRGINIA CITY HISTORIC DISTRICT, 1863
**Wallace Street**
Re-creation of the boom town that developed after the gold strike at Alder Gulch, one of the greatest strikes in the West. Between 1865 and 1875 Virginia City was the territorial capital of Montana. Many reconstructed buildings of brick, log, and stone
*Operated by Virginia City Trading Co. Open May 15–Sept: daily 8–8*

## WHITE SULPHUR SPRINGS

### STONE CASTLE, 1890–92
**310 Second Ave, NE**
Victorian castlelike structure constructed of granite blocks by B. R. Sherman, rancher, miner, and businessman. The castle has been refurbished and furnished with many original and historic pieces of furniture and antiques.
*Operated by Meagher Co. Historical Assn. Open May 15–Oct. 15: daily 9–9*

*Stone Castle*

## BANCROFT

■ **JOHN G. NEIHARDT STUDY,**
**about 1898**
**Washington and Grove Streets**
Small frame house where the "Prairie
Poet Laureate" wrote the major part
of his *Cycle of the West*. Many of his
literary works were completed during
his 21 years in Bancroft. The study
has been restored and furnished exactly as it was during his occupancy;
outside is a symbolic prayer garden.
*Operated by John G. Neihardt Founda-*
*tion. Open May 15–Sept. 15: Sun. 2–5*
*and by appointment*

## BEATRICE VICINITY

■ **PALMER-EPARD CABIN, 1867**
**Homestead National Monument**
This two-story 14- by 16-foot cabin,
built of logs with a minimum of bricks
and lumber, was the home of Mr. and
Mrs. G.W. Palmer and their ten children. Moved here from a nearby site,
this typical dwelling of the homestead
period displays pioneer furnishings of
the late 1860s. The monument stands
on the site of Daniel Freeman's original homestead, one of the first of
millions of land claims made under
the Homestead Act of 1862.
*Operated by National Park Service.*
*Open daily 8–4:30*

## BELLEVUE

■ **LOG CABIN, 1835**
**1805 Hancock St**
Log cabin dating from preterritorial
days is believed to be the oldest in
the state. Moved from its original site
for preservation and provided with
typical pioneer furnishings of the
1850s and 1860s
*Operated by Sarpy Co. Historical Soc.*
*Open summer: daily 1–5. Winter: Sat.,*
*Sun. 1–5*

## BROKEN BOW VICINITY

■ **ISADORE HAUMONT'S SOD**
**HOUSE, 1883–84**
**Rural Route 3**
Reputed to be the only two-story sod
house ever built and the only early-
day soddy still standing. Built by
pioneer Isadore Haumont in 1883, it
has never been restored and is in poor

condition. According to the descendant now living there, 1971 may be the
last year for this historic house.
*Operated by Henry Haumont. Open*
*by appointment*

*Isadore Haumont's Sod House*

## BROWNVILLE

■ **BROWNVILLE HISTORIC**
**DISTRICT, 1860s**
Once an important trading center on
the Missouri River; several old residences and buildings are being restored and rebuilt to commemorate
this era.

**CARSON HOUSE, 1860; 1880**
**Main Street**
The original one-story brick house
was built for the town's founder, Richard Brown, who added a frame wing
the next year. About 1880 John L.
Carson, leading financier, added a
frame second story and a handsome
carriage house. Now maintained as a
house museum with furnishings of the
Civil War period
*Operated by Brownville Historical*
*Soc. Open June–Aug: daily 2–5*

## CHADRON

**JAMES BORDEAUX TRADING**
**POST [MUSEUM OF THE FUR**
**TRADE], mid-19th century**
**U.S. Highway 20**
Indian trading post, reconstructed of
hewn pine logs on the original foundations, combines living quarters, trade
room, and detached storehouse of
James Bordeaux, who operated here
from 1850 to 1872. The living quarters
are furnished with period pieces, the
store shelves are stocked with trade
goods; other exhibits include furs,
trapping equipment, guns, and a garden of nearly extinct Indian crops.
*Operated by Museum Assn. of the*
*American Frontier. Open June–Labor*
*Day: 8–6. Rest of year: by appoint-*
*ment*

NEBRASKA

## CRAWFORD VICINITY

■ **FORT ROBINSON, 1874**
**U.S. Highway 20**
An important post established in the 1870s that together with the nearby Red Cloud Agency influenced the course of Indian-white relations on the northern Plains during the days of resistance to the advancing frontier. The old post headquarters is now a state museum devoted to this colorful period. A typical officers' quarters of the 1890s, with furnishings, is on view.
*Operated by Nebr. State Historical Soc. Open Apr.–Nov. 15: Mon.–Sat. 8–5, Sun. 1–5*

*Fairview*

## GRAND ISLAND

**STUHR MUSEUM VILLAGE**
**junction of U.S. Highways 34 and 281**
A reconstructed prairie community on a 267-acre tract showing pioneer buildings moved here from their original locations. The main museum building was designed by prominent architect Edward Durell Stone. Among the restored residences are: *Milisen House* (1878–80), a two-story frame dwelling – with wrought-iron railing on the roof and stained-glass windows and front door – built by Charles and Anna Milisen; *Fonda House* (about 1887), a frame cottage built by W.H. Hooper and birthplace of actor Henry Fonda. Period furnishings
*Operated by Stuhr Museum of the Prairie Pioneer. Open Memorial Day– Labor Day: Mon.–Sat. 9–7, Sun. 1–7*

## LINCOLN

■ **FAIRVIEW, 1901–2**
**4900 Sumner St**
Unusual mansion of mixed style, home from 1902 to 1917 of "The Commoner," William Jennings Bryan – orator, statesman, writer, and political leader. One of the show places of Lincoln, it was elegantly furnished with the carved furniture of the period and Oriental items acquired on a round-the-world trip. The first floor has been restored as a historical museum with many of the family pieces.
*Operated by Nebr. State Historical Soc., Junior League of Lincoln, and Bryan Memorial Hospital. Open May– Sept: Thurs., Sat., Sun. 1–4*

■ **THOMAS P. KENNARD HOUSE (NEBRASKA STATEHOOD MEMORIAL), 1869**
**1627 H St**
Fine Italianate masonry mansion, topped by a cupola, designed by architect John Keyes Winchell for Thomas P. Kennard, one of the three commissioners who selected Lincoln as the state capital. Of the three similar mansions the commissioners built to express their confidence in the future of the raw prairie capital, this is the only one remaining and the oldest house within the original city plot. In 1965 the legislature designated it as the official Nebraska Statehood Memorial; it has been restored and furnished to approximate its 1870s appearance.
*Operated by Nebr. State Historical Soc. Open Tues.–Sat. 9 -4, Sun. 2–5*

*Thomas P. Kennard House*

# McCOOK

**■ SEN. GEORGE W. NORRIS HOME, before 1899**
**706 Norris Ave**
Home of Sen. Norris (1861–1944), the "Gentle Knight of Progressive Ideals," who served 40 years in the Congress of the U.S. championing the rights of the common man. His legislation (e.g., the Tennessee Valley Authority Act, 1933) empowered the Federal government to assume major responsibility in furthering national well-being. Now a museum with the family furnishings
*Operated by Nebr. State Historical Soc. Open June–Aug: Tues.–Sat. 9–7, Sun. 2–7*

# MINDEN

**HAROLD WARP PIONEER VILLAGE**
**U.S. Routes 6 and 34 and Nebraska Route 10**
A pioneer village with 22 buildings on 20 acres covering the period 1830 to the present. The *Elm Creek Fort* (1869) is a two-story log building, with authentic furnishings, moved from Webster County, Nebraska, where it served as a dwelling and a community fort against Indian attack. There is also a fully furnished replica of a prairie sod house. Other exhibits include a pony express station and a barn, a firehouse, store, school, livery stable, et cetera.
*Operated by Harold Warp Pioneer Village. Open daily 8–sundown*

# NEBRASKA CITY

**■ J. STERLING MORTON HOMESTEAD, about 1855; 1902**
**Arbor Lodge State Historical Park**
Stately colonial revival-style 52-room mansion, which assumed its present appearance after its final enlargement in 1902; the home of J.S. Morton, pioneer Nebraska journalist, territorial secretary, and conservation leader. Morton was Secretary of Agriculture under President Grover Cleveland and is remembered as the founder of Arbor Day. The mansion is furnished with antiques and relics of Nebraska's pioneer days. To the south is an Italianate terraced garden landscaped by Frederick Law Olmsted about 1903.
*Operated by Nebr. State Game and Parks Comm. Open June 15–Sept. 14: daily 10–12, 1–5:30. Apr. 15–June 14 and Sept. 15–Oct. 31: daily 1–5:30*

# NORTH PLATTE

**BUFFALO BILL CODY HOME, 1886**
**Scouts Rest Ranch State Park**
Frame Victorian mansion built by the famous "Buffalo Bill" on his 4,000-acre ranch during the affluent days of his Wild West show. Some interesting features of the design are the cone-shaped lightning rods on the central tower, stained-glass windows, and gunstock-eave supports. Wallpaper, designed by the frontiersman, depicts scenes from his life and show. Original Victorian furnishings; the house, barn, and outbuildings are maintained as a state historical park.
*Operated by Nebr. State Game and Parks Comm. Open Memorial Day–Labor Day: daily 8–9. Winter: by appointment*

# RED CLOUD

**■ WILLA CATHER CHILDHOOD HOME, 1878**
**Third and Cedar Streets**
The house is best described by Miss Cather in her *Song of the Lark:* "They turned into another street and saw before them lighted windows: a low story-and-a-half house, with a wing built on at the right and a kitchen addition at the back, everything a little on the slant—roofs, windows, and doors. . . . She saw everything clearly in the red light from the isinglass sides of the hard-coal burner—the nickel trimmings on the stove itself, the pictures on the wall . . . the flowers on the Brussels carpet . . . the upright piano." Cather family furnishings of the 1880s
*Operated by Willa Cather Pioneer Memorial. Open by appointment*

*Willa Cather Childhood Home*

**NEVADA**

## CARSON CITY

### BLISS MANSION, 1879
**710 W Robinson St**
Victorian house built by Duane Bliss on an old Indian campground. Bliss was in the lumber business, and only the finest wood went into the construction of his mansion.
*Operated by Mr. and Mrs. Fred Raymond, owners. Open summer: daily 10–5. Winter: by appointment*

### GOVERNOR'S MANSION, 1908–9
**600 Mountain St**
Classical revival–style mansion designed by the architect George A. Ferris. Throughout the 16-room structure are historical and rare furnishings. A rare Duncan Phyfe dining set graces the luncheon room, and a 1760 grandfather's clock still keeps accurate time near the governor's study. This has been the residence of Nevada's governors since 1910.
*Operated by State of Nev. Open Wed. 1–5*

*Governor's Mansion*

## CARSON CITY VICINITY

### BOWERS MANSION, 1860s
**U.S. Route 395, between Reno and Carson City**
Palatial mansion built by Eilley Orrum Bowers and her husband Sandy, early millionaires of the Comstock Lode. The house cost $407,000 to build and was furnished with objects they collected on a grand tour of Europe. Restored, the mansion serves as a museum and as a reminder of the grand scale on which life was lived during this era.
*Operated by Washoe Co. Dept. of Parks and Recreation. Open May 15–Sept: daily 11–4:30*

## VIRGINIA CITY

### THE CASTLE, 1863–68
Victorian mansion built after a castle in Normandy by Robert N. Graves, a superintendent of the Empire Mine. Superintendents of the silver mines were indispensable and earned fantastic salaries. Robert Graves is said to have received $800,000 a year for his services. Interiors are as they were when the house was built, even to the original white paint on the woodwork. Many of the furnishings were brought from Europe, traveling around the Horn to San Francisco and Sacramento and on to Virginia City by mule and ox teams. Private residence
*Operated by the McGuirk family, owners. Open May–Oct: daily 10–6*

*The Castle*

### MACKAY MANSION, 1860
**129 D St**
Red brick building, one of the oldest in Virginia City, and one of the few that escaped the fire that destroyed most of the city in 1875. Built for the Gould and Curry Mining Company, of which George Hearst, father of William Randolph, was half owner. After 1875 the house became the residence of John W. Mackay, the richest man of the Comstock Lode. It became the headquarters of the four silver kings, Mackay, James G. Fair, James L. Flood, and William S. O'Brien, when they mined the strike known as the "Big Bonanza." Well maintained, original furnishings

164

*Operated by Mr. and Mrs. Howard Kiehlbauch. Open May 28–Oct: daily 8–6*

## SAVAGE MINE OFFICE AND MANSION, 1862
**146 D St**
Early Victorian mansion built as the residence and office of the superintendent of the Savage Mining Company. Gen. Grant and his family stayed here several days in 1879, and according to newspaper accounts of the day, the town turned itself upside down to welcome the great man. The house has been restored over the last eight years by Mr. and Mrs. Harwood and is open as a museum.
*Operated by Mr. and Mrs. Gerald Harwood. Open daily 11–6*

## ■ VIRGINIA CITY HISTORIC DISTRICT, 1860
With the fabulous gold and silver strike in 1859, Virginia City became the West's mining metropolis. The Comstock Lode was one of the richest deposits of those precious minerals ever discovered, and the prosperity of Virginia City was unequaled. Much of the city has been restored to its 1870 appearance.

## CANDIA HILL

### FITTS MUSEUM, late 1700s
**Town Center**
Two-story house with low hip roof and two slender chimneys now housing museum founded by Rev. James H. Fitts and J. Lane Fitts in 1885. Relics of Seneca Indians and early settlers
*Operated by Fitts Museum. Open July–Aug: daily 2–5*

## CANTERBURY

### SHAKER VILLAGE, 1792–early 1800s
**off Route 106**
Religious community (started in 1792 by Elder Clough) founded on such tenets of the Shaker faith as celibacy, belief in visions, and communal ownership of property. Compact group of white frame buildings surrounding the main dwelling and a museum of Shaker furniture, inventions, and handicrafts
*Operated by Shaker Village Museum. Open June–Oct. 12: Tues.–Sat. 9:30–11, 1–4*

## CENTER SANDWICH

### SANDWICH HISTORICAL SOC., about 1850
**State Highways 109 and 113**
House museum of local historical society, with household articles and furnishings and replica of old country store and post office

*Operated by Sandwich Historical Soc. Open July–Aug: Mon., Wed., Sat. 2–5*

## CONCORD

### ■ FRANKLIN PIERCE HOUSE, 1854–57
**52 S Main St**
Victorian mansion in the French style, with mansard-type roof, built by Willard Williams for the 14th President of the U.S., who lived in it from his retirement in 1857 until his death in 1869. Period furnishings of the 1850s; Pierce's original bedroom in the Renaissance Revival style
*Operated by Muriel and John Gravelle. Open by appointment*

*Franklin Pierce House*

## CRAWFORD NOTCH

**BEMIS MUSEUM, 1860**
U.S. Route 302
First country estate in the White Mountains; built with 26 rooms in the style of an English Gothic manor house. Contains 18th-century New Hampshire pioneer furnishings and 19th-century Boston antiques
*Operated by Florence Morey. Open June 15–Sept: daily 10–4:30*

## DOVER

**DAMM GARRISON, 1675**
**HALE HOUSE, 1813**
**WOODMAN HOUSE, 1818**
182–192 Central Ave
Two large Federal-style brick houses and a small log cabin joined into a single architectural unit by a latticed colonnade. Built by John Williams, the founder of the cotton industry in Dover, the 1813 house was for many years the home of John Parker Hale, U.S. senator. The log cabin, moved here from its original site, was built by William Damm and his son for protection against Indian attacks. The buildings now house a historical and scientific museum.
*Operated by Annie E. Woodman Institute. Open Tues.–Sun. 2–5; closed holidays*

**THE LAFAYETTE HOUSE, 1805**
5 Hale St
Three-story Federal house built by William Hale, who entertained the Marquis de Lafayette and President James Monroe here in 1825. Fine architectural detail in interiors; now used as a parish house
*Operated by St. Thomas' Episcopal Church. Open daily*

## EXETER

**GILMAN-GARRISON HOUSE, about 1650; 1772**
12 Water St
The main part of this rambling "wooden castle" was built by John Gilman to thwart Indian attacks; with second-story overhang, hand-hewn logs, portcullis door. Brig. Gen. Peter Gilman added the front wing in 1772 and often entertained New Hampshire's second royal governor, John

Wentworth, in the elaborately carved and paneled rooms. Daniel Webster boarded here while a student at Phillips Exeter Academy in 1796. Furnishings of both periods
*Operated by Soc. for the Preservation of New England Antiquities. Open June–Sept: Thurs., Sat. 2–4:30*

**LADD-GILMAN HOUSE, 1721**
Water and Governor Streets
Two-story house, with pitched roof pierced by dormer windows, built by Nathaniel Ladd; the original brick was covered over by wood and later expanded into the present rambling structure. In the 1750s the distinguished Gilman family acquired the house, and it thus became the home of several famous men, including Nicholas Gilman, a signer of the Constitution. Furnishings of the Revolutionary period
*Operated by Soc. of the Cincinnati. Open Apr. 15–Oct. 15: Thurs. 2–4*

## FRANKLIN

**DANIEL WEBSTER BIRTHPLACE, about 1780**
off Route 127
Restored frame house where Daniel Webster — orator, congressman, and twice Secretary of State—was born in 1782 and spent his boyhood. Memorabilia relating to Webster and furnishings of the period
*Operated by State of N.H. Div. of Parks. Open June–Labor Day: daily 9–6. After Labor Day–Oct. 15: Sat., Sun. 9–6*

## HENNIKER

**OCEAN-BORN MARY HOUSE, about 1750**
Bear Hill Road
Georgian-style house built by James Wallace with interesting legend about the builder's wife, who was born on the high seas en route to America. The ship was boarded by pirates who named the baby "Mary" and gave her silk for her wedding gown. Years later, when she married, she wore the pirates' silk, a piece of which is carefully preserved in this house the young couple built. Antique furnishings
*Private. Open May–Oct: daily 10–5*

# HILLSBORO VICINITY

## ■ FRANKLIN PIERCE HOMESTEAD, 1804
### New Hampshire Route 31

Two-story frame Federal house with hipped roof built by Benjamin Pierce, governor of New Hampshire in 1827 and 1829 and father of the 14th President. Home of Franklin Pierce from his infancy (1804) until his marriage in 1834. This fine country house has an unusual ballroom, the original scenic wallpaper, and period furnishings. *Operated by N.H. Div. of Parks. Open June–Labor Day: daily with guide service. After Labor Day–Oct. 15: Sat., Sun.*

*Franklin Pierce Homestead*

# KEENE

## WYMAN TAVERN, 1762
### 339 Main St

Two-story frame house, with large central chimney and columns at the entrance, built by Capt. Isaac Wyman, veteran of the Indian Wars. The first meeting of the trustees of Dartmouth College was held here in 1770, and on April 22, 1775, Capt. Wyman led 29 Minutemen to Lexington from the

*Wyman Tavern*

front yard of his tavern. Original woodwork in interiors, period furnishings *Operated by Historical Soc. of Cheshire Co. Open May–Oct: two afternoons a week and by appointment*

# MANCHESTER

## JOHN STARK HOUSE, about 1737
### 2000 Elm St

Story-and-a-half Cape Cod house, with central chimney and a wing, built by Archibald Stark, father of Gen. John Stark of Revolutionary War fame. It was the boyhood home of the future general, who also lived there during his early married life. Restored in 1969 with period furnishings *Operated by Daughters of the American Revolution. Open May 15–Oct: Wed., Sun., holidays 1:30–4:30*

# NEWINGTON

## THE OLD PARSONAGE, 1699

Severely plain two-story frame house, with a long, sloping rear roof and a huge central chimney, built by Richard Pomeroy, first church sexton. Period furnishings *Operated by Newington Historical Soc. Open July–Aug: Sun. 2–4*

# NEW IPSWICH

## BARRETT HOUSE (FOREST HALL), 1800
### Main Street

Impressive three - story clapboard country mansion in the Federal style with a ballroom featured on the top floor. Furnished with fine furniture and family portraits. Carriage sheds on the extensive grounds include a special exhibition of equipment for spinning and weaving. *Operated by Soc. for the Preservation of New England Antiquities. Open June–Oct: Tues.–Sat. 11–5*

# NORTH GROTON

## MARY BAKER EDDY HISTORICAL HOUSE, 18th century

Standing beside a rushing stream is the comfortable mountain home of the founder of Christian Science. From 1855 to 1860, when she was Mrs. Daniel Patterson, Mary Baker Eddy

lived here. See also Rumney Village
*Operated by Longyear Foundation.
Open May 30–Oct: Sun. 2–5 and by
appointment; closed national holidays*

## ORFORD

### ORFORD MUSEUM HOUSE, 1799
**Route 10**
The museum house was once the
home of artist Henry Cheever Pratt,
born in Orford in 1803. Furnished authentically as a home in the 18th-cen-
tury manner; three Pratt paintings on
exhibit. Also a museum barn
*Operated by Orford Museum. Open
Tues.–Sun. 11–5*

## PETERBOROUGH

### ■ MacDOWELL COLONY, 1907
**west of U.S. Route 202**
In 1896 composer Edward MacDowell
bought an old 60-acre farm and built a
log cabin studio deep in the woods;
here he composed some of his most
famous works. In 1907 a colony was
founded as a retreat and workshop for
writers, painters, and composers.
Today the colony covers over 400
acres with 27 artistically built studios
and other buildings.
*Operated by MacDowell Colony.
Open Mon.–Sat. 1–5*

## PLAINFIELD VICINITY

### ■ SAINT-GAUDENS NATIONAL
### HISTORIC SITE, about 1800
**off New Hampshire Route 12A**
The home, studio, and gardens of Augustus Saint-Gaudens, eminent American sculptor (1848–1907). The large
two-story brick house with stepped
gable ends was once a country tavern;
Saint-Gaudens acquired it in 1885,
had it remodeled, named it *Aspet*, and
lived here with his family until his
death. He attracted many students to
his studio who later became famous.
Collection of his works
*Operated by National Park Service.
Open June–Oct. 15: daily 10–6*

## PORTSMOUTH

### GOV. JOHN LANGDON MANSION
### MEMORIAL, 1784
**143 Pleasant St**
Elaborately decorated frame mansion

with portico and captain's walk built
by John Langdon, first pro tempore
president of the U.S. Senate, who noti-
fied George Washington of his election as President. Entertained here in
1789, Washington wrote warm praise
of house and host. Noted scenic wallpaper and carved fire frame in parlor;
furnished in style of period and situated in extensive gardens
*Operated by Soc. for the Preservation
of New England Antiquities. Open
June–Oct: Tues.–Sat. 10–5*

### JOHN PAUL JONES HOUSE, 1758
**43 Middle St**
Dignified frame gambrel-roofed dwelling built by sea captain Gregory Pur-
cell, whose widow conducted a "gen-
teel boarding house" after his death in
1776 to support her family of seven
children. Among her lodgers was
John Paul Jones, the dashing captain
who had come to Portsmouth to super-
vise the outfitting of the *America*.
Period furnishings plus valuable collections of portraits, china, silver
*Operated by Portsmouth Historical
Soc. Open May–Sept: Mon.–Sat. 10–
5. July–Aug: Sun. 2–5*

### ■ MACPHEADRIS-WARNER
### HOUSE, 1716
**150 Daniel St**
Fine example of early Georgian brick
urban dwelling built by Capt. Archibald Macpheadris, wealthy Scottish
fur trader, whose daughter married
Col. Jonathan Warner of His Maj-
esty's Council. The two stories are

*MacPheadris-Warner House*

topped by a dormered gambrel roof with balustrade and have large sash windows evenly disposed on the façade. The central doorway is framed with fluted Corinthian pilasters and capped with an arched pediment. The interior has remarkable Indian murals on the staircase walls, fine paneling, and a number of exquisite furniture pieces and portraits.
*Operated by Warner House Assn. Open May 15–Oct 15: Mon.–Sat. 10–5, Sun. 2–5*

■ **MOFFATT-LADD HOUSE, 1763**
**154 Market St**
Late Georgian frame mansion, overlooking the wharves of the Piscataqua River, built by Capt. John Moffat as a wedding gift for his son Samuel and later the home of Gen. William Whipple, a signer of the Declaration of Independence. The three-story clapboard house, with quoined corners and hipped roof topped by a balustraded captain's walk, offers insight into the life of the wealthy mercantile class at the end of the 18th century; adjoining is the shipping office and counting-house. Beautiful interiors handsomely paneled and fine furnishings
*Operated by Soc of Colonial Dames. Open May 15–Oct. 15: Mon.–Sat. 10–5, Sun. 2–5*

■ **RICHARD JACKSON HOUSE, about 1664**
**Northwest Street**
Frame saltbox of medieval design built by shipbuilder Richard Jackson and lived in by his descendants for 250 years. Believed to be the oldest house standing in New Hampshire; the original central portion has a sharply sloping gable roof nearly reaching the ground in the rear. Two frame end wings were added about 1764; the exterior clapboards are unpainted and weather-stained. Simply furnished in keeping with the period
*Operated by Soc. for the Preservation of New England Antiquities. Open June–Sept: Tues.–Sat. 1–5*

**STRAWBERY BANKE RESTORATION PROJECT**
**entrance on Hancock Street**
In 1630 the first permanent settlement was made on the Piscataqua River and

named for the wild strawberries found growing along the riverbanks. Blessed with an excellent harbor and fine timber around the bay, the town prospered as a seaport and was renamed Portsmouth in 1653. Shipbuilding and other mercantile interests made the town flourish during the 18th and early 19th centuries. In 1960 a private, nonprofit corporation undertook an admirable restoration project on a ten-acre site, with 30 buildings showing a variety of early American architecture ranging from the *Joseph Sherburne House*, 1660, through many examples of 18th-century Georgian houses to the restored Federal-style *Gov. Goodwin Mansion*, 1811. In addition, there are stores, taverns, and craft exhibits.
*Operated by Strawbery Banke. Open May 18–Oct: Mon.–Sat. 10–5, Sun. 12–5. Aug. 5–Sept. 3: Wed., Thurs. evgs. until 8*

*Governor Goodwin Mansion*

**THOMAS BAILEY ALDRICH MEMORIAL, 1790**
**386 Court St**
Two-and-a-half-story frame home of the grandfather of poet, writer, editor, Thomas Bailey Aldrich and the setting of the author's best work, *The Story of a Bad Boy*, 1870. The interior is an authentic picture of early Victorian times with furniture and decorations of that period. A brick museum at the rear contains collections of first editions, autographs, and letters.
*Operated by Thomas Bailey Aldrich Memorial Assn. Open June–Sept: Mon.–Sat. 1–5*

■ **WENTWORTH-COOLIDGE MANSION, 1695; 1730; 1750**
**foot of Little Harbor Road**
Significant 42-room frame house re-

flecting three periods of New England architecture: typical two-story saltbox farmhouse had a wing added in 1730 and another in 1750 at right angles, thus giving the house its H shape. The mansion served as official residence and provincial seat for the first royal governor of the province of New Hampshire, Benning Wentworth, 1741–66, at the time when Portsmouth aristocracy was at its height of wealth and fashion. Restored by last owner, J. Templeton Coolidge, to preserve the colonial phases; governor's council chamber with paneled walls and carved mantel on first floor
*Operated by State of N.H. Div. of Parks. Open May 30–Oct. 12: daily 10–5*

■ **WENTWORTH-GARDNER HOUSE, 1760**
**140 Mechanic St**
Called "one of the most nearly perfect examples of Georgian architecture in America," this two-and-a-half-story frame house was built by ships' carpenters for Madam Mark Wentworth as a present for her son Thomas. The large, pine-wood clapboards of the façade are rusticated to imitate cut stone; the corners are emphasized by large quoins, and the lower windows

by pediments. The gilded pineapple in the pediment of the doorway symbolizes hospitality. Fine carved and paneled interiors, scenic wallpaper, and Dutch-tiled fireplaces
*Operated by Wentworth-Gardner and Tobias Lear Houses Assn. Open May–Oct: Tues.–Sun. 1–5*

## RUMNEY VILLAGE

**MARY BAKER EDDY HISTORICAL HOUSE, 18th century**
One of the homes—from 1860 to 1862—of the founder of Christian Science. Here she received one of her early proofs of spiritual healing. See also North Groton
*Operated by Longyear Foundation. Open May 30–Oct: Tues.–Sat. 10–5, Sun. 2–5; closed national holidays*

## WOLFEBORO

**CLARK HOUSE, 1778**
**South Main Street**
Restored 18th-century dwelling now serving as a house museum with early American furnishings; five fireplaces
*Operated by Wolfeboro Historical Soc. Open July–Aug: Mon.–Sat. 10–12, 2–4:30*

## ALLAIRE

**DESERTED VILLAGE AT ALLAIRE, 19th century**
**Allaire State Park, Route 524**
Site of a 19th-century bog-iron producing community which at its height had 500 employees living on the property in 60 brick buildings.
*Operated by N.J. Dept. of Environmental Protection. Open May–Aug: Mon.–Sat. 10–5, Sun. 12–5. Sept.–Apr: Tues.–Sat. 10–5, Sun. 12–5; closed Thanksgiving, Christmas, and New Year's Day*

## BORDENTOWN

**GILDER HOUSE, 1740s**
**Crosswicks and Union Streets**
Two-and-a-half-story frame house; fa-

mous as the home of the Gilders—four brothers and a sister—a distinguished literary, artistic, and scientific family of the 1880s. Period furnishings
*Operated by City of Bordentown. Open daily 9–6*

## BURLINGTON

**JAMES FENIMORE COOPER HOUSE, about 1780**
**457 High St**
Famous author was born here in 1789; now historical society headquarters and museum. Displays include a portion of the manuscript of Cooper's *The Spy,* many Revolutionary and Civil War relics, and household articles.
*Operated by Burlington Co. Historical Soc. Open Sun. 3–5*

## JAMES LAWRENCE HOUSE, 1742
### 459 High St
Stucco-covered brick house with alterations and additions made in the early 1800s; birthplace in 1781 of Capt. James Lawrence, naval hero of the War of 1812, who gained immortality with his cry of "Don't give up the ship!" During the Revolutionary War Lawrence's father, John, was the town's Tory mayor.
*Operated by N.J. Dept. of Environmental Protection. Open Tues.–Sat. 10–12, 1–5, Sun. 2–5; closed Thanksgiving, Christmas, and New Year's Day*

## CALDWELL

### GROVER CLEVELAND BIRTHPLACE, 1832
### 207 Bloomfield Ave
Two-and-a-half-story frame house was the original parsonage of the Caldwell Presbyterian Church. In 1834 Richard Cleveland was chosen pastor; his son, Stephen Grover (the Stephen was dropped later in life) was born here on March 8, 1837. Now a museum furnished with many of Cleveland's personal belongings
*Operated by N.J. Dept. of Environmental Protection. Open Tues.–Sat. 10–12, 1–5, Sun. 2–5; closed Thanksgiving, Christmas, and New Year's Day*

*Grover Cleveland Birthplace*

## CAMDEN

### POMONA HALL, 1726
### Euclid Avenue and Park Boulevard
Georgian mansion of Flemish-bond brick and white trim, with well-preserved interior, built by Joseph Cooper, Jr. Now museum and library of the historical society; colonial bedroom, early American kitchen, and Indian relics on display.
*Operated by Camden Co. Historical Soc. Open Tues.–Fri., Sun. 12:30–4:30*

## ■ WALT WHITMAN HOUSE, 1848
### 330 Mickle St
Simple, gray frame house; Walt Whitman's home from 1884 until his death in 1892. Furnishings include many of the great poet's personal mementos, including some of his furniture, clothing, and books.
*Operated by N.J. Dept. of Environmental Protection. Open Tues.–Sat. 10–12, 1–5, Sun. 2–5; closed Thanksgiving, Christmas, New Year's Day*

*Walt Whitman House*

## CAPE MAY

### VICTORIAN VILLAGE MUSEUM, 1870s
### Washington and Ocean Streets
Late 19th-century house is a showcase for a collection of Victorian memorabilia, including furniture. Behind the house is a small, early 19th-century house that can be seen by appointment.
*Operated by Cape May City. Open summer: daily 10–12, 1–5*

## CRANBURY

### CRANBURY MUSEUM, about 1870
### 15 S Main St
White clapboard farmhouse; restored as a museum in 1970. Furnishings include some pre-Revolutionary pieces,

local items, and Indian relics.
*Operated by Cranbury Historical and Preservation Soc. Open Tues., Fri: 2–5*

## TRUXTUN HOUSE, before 1778
### 107 N Main St
Pre-Revolutionary house with heavy doors, hand-wrought hardware, and wide floorboards. Purchased in 1804 by Com. Thomas Truxtun and believed to have been Washington's headquarters prior to the Battle of Monmouth. Restored and furnished by the present owners
*Operated by Mr. and Mrs. S. Beneze. Open by appointment*

## ELIZABETH

### BELCHER-OGDEN MANSION, about 1700; after 1800
#### 1046 E Jersey St
East half of brick house built by John Ogden, Jr., one of the founders of Elizabeth; west wing with classical revival porch added a century later. Ogden family lived here until 1751 when the royal governor, Jonathan Belcher, took it over. Col. Aaron Ogden, a descendant of the original builder and Revolutionary hero, bought the house in 1797; he became governor in 1812. Restored and partially furnished with period pieces from an inventory left by Governor Belcher.
*Operated by Elizabethtown Historical Foundation. Open Wed. 10–12 and by appointment*

### BONNELL HOUSE, about 1682
#### 1045 E Jersey St
Two-story clapboard house believed to be the oldest in the city; built by Nathaniel Bonnell on six acres of land allotted to him in the 1660s. Furnished with period pieces
*Operated by Sons of the American Revolution. Open by appointment*

### BOXWOOD HALL, about 1755
#### 1073 E Jersey St
Two-story shingle house, with classical details in the New England tradition. Home of Elias Boudinot, president of Congress under the Articles of Confederation and a signer of the peace treaty with England. Furnished with colonial and Federal pieces
*Operated by N.J. Dept. of Environmental Protection. Open Tues.–Sat.*

*10–12, 1–5, Sun. 2–5; closed Thanksgiving, Christmas, and New Year's Day*

*Boxwood Hall*

## FLEMINGTON

### DORIC HOUSE, 1846
#### 114 Main St
Four Doric columns dominate this classical revival house built by architect Mahlon Fisher as his home. When restoration is completed the house will be furnished with period pieces and will feature special exhibits of music and medicine.
*Operated by Hunterdon Co. Historical Soc. Under restoration*

### FLEMING CASTLE, 1756
#### 5 Bonnell St
Small, two-story, white plaster house built as an inn and a home by Samuel Fleming, the town's founder. Called a castle because of its grandeur in comparison with the log cabins then in the area. Restored in 1928; furnished with period antiques
*Operated by Daughters of the American Revolution. Open Sat., Sun. by appointment*

## FREEHOLD

### CLINTON'S HEADQUARTERS HANKINSON MANSION, between 1690 and 1709
#### 150 W Main St
Pre-Revolutionary house with some of the original shingles still on it; fine interior paneling. Occupied by Sir Henry Clinton, the British commander, prior to the Battle of Monmouth
*Operated by Monmouth Co. Historical Assn. Restoration in progress*

## GREENWICH

### GIBBON HOUSE, 1730
**Ye Great Street**
Two-and-a-half-story red brick house with beautiful interior woodwork built by Nicholas Gibbon, maritime merchant, whose ships carried most of the colonial trade to this port. Restored and furnished with period pieces
*Operated by Cumberland Co. Historical Soc. Open Apr.–Oct: Sat., Sun. 2–5*

## HADDONFIELD

### GREENFIELD HALL, 1747; 1841
**343 King's Highway East**
Three-story brick mansion with balustraded roof built by John Gill IV, a descendant of one of the town's early settlers; wing addition built in 1841. Historical society headquarters featuring a research library; furnished with period pieces
*Operated by Historical Soc. of Haddonfield. Open Sept.–June: Tues., Thurs. 2–4:30, and by appointment*

## HAMMONTON

### BATSTO VILLAGE, begun 1766
**County Road 542**
Restored village was a thriving bog-iron producing community from 1766 until 1846; when a glass-blowing industry developed but failed, the village became a ghost town. Among the restored buildings are the *Iron-master's Mansion,* a 36-room house begun in 1786 and altered to its present Victorian style about 1880; several stark frame workers' cottages indicative of early 19th-century working conditions; barns, mills, and shops. The mansion and a worker's cottage are furnished with period pieces.
*Operated by N.J. Dept. of Environmental Protection. Open May 30–Labor Day: daily 10–6. Sept.–May: daily 11–5*

## HANCOCKS BRIDGE

### CEDAR PLANK HOUSE, about 1640
Tiny house built of cedar from nearby swamps; excellent example of Swedish pioneer construction with hand-hewn planks dovetailed at the corners. Furnished with colonial relics
*Operated by N.J. Dept. of Environmental Protection. Open Tues.–Sat. 10–12, 1–5, Sun. 2–5; closed Thanksgiving, Christmas, and New Year's Day*

### HANCOCK HOUSE, 1734
Unusual example of glazed brickwork; two-and-a-half-story house has 19 zigzag lines of red and blue glazed brick on the west exterior wall and Flemish bond on the façade. Built by Judge William Hancock, who received ten bayonet wounds in a massacre that occurred here during the Revolution. Furnished with colonial pieces
*Operated by N.J. Dept. of Environmental Protection. Open Tues.–Sat. 10–12, 1–5, Sun. 2–5; closed Thanksgiving, Christmas, and New Year's Day*

*Hancock House*

## HOLMDEL

### HENDRICKSON HOUSE, about 1715
**Longstreet Road**
A fourteen-room early Dutch clapboard house with kitchen wing; original interior woodwork throughout the house. Owned by the Hendrickson family until 1873; shown with appropriate antiques
*Operated by Monmouth Co. Historical Assn. Open May–Oct: Tues., Fri. 1–5*

## HOPEWELL

### HOPEWELL MUSEUM, 1887
**28 E Broad St**
Three-story brownstone with mansard

roof and wide veranda; since 1924 a museum of local history. Among the exhibits are colonial and Victorian furniture, costumes from many eras, Indian relics, and antique guns.
*Operated by Hopewell Museum. Open Mon., Wed., Sat. 2–5*

## LIVINGSTON

### FORCE HOUSE, about 1745
**South Livingston Avenue**
Pre-Revolutionary frame farmhouse, with later additions built by Deacon Thomas Force, farmer and sawmill operator. Restored and furnished with period pieces. Adjacent to the homestead is the *Condit-Williams Cook House*, an unusual structure that over the years served as a dwelling, kitchen, and slaughterhouse.
*Operated by Livingston Historical Soc. Open Apr.–June, Sept.–Oct: second and fourth Sun. 2–4. July 4: 2–4*

## MIDDLETOWN

### MARLPIT HALL, about 1684
**137 King's Highway**
Long Dutch-style, one-and-a-half-story house with bull's-eye glass used in the top panels of the divided door. Interiors contain beautiful panelings and overmantels and a rare type of Dutch *kas*, or cupboard; furnished with fine colonial pieces.
*Operated by Monmouth Co. Historical Assn. Open Tues., Thurs., Sat. 11–5, Sun. 2–5; closed Jan. and holidays*

*Marlpit Hall*

## MILLVILLE

### DAVID WOOD MANSION, 1804
**Columbia Avenue**
A 20-room mansion, one of the oldest in the town, built by ironmaster David

C. Wood; the house is noted for its decorative iron pillars. Three rooms are headquarters of the historical society; these are furnished with articles of local history.
*Operated by Millville Historical Soc. Open by appointment*

## MONTCLAIR

### ISRAEL CRANE HOUSE, 1796
**110 Orange Rd**
Two-and-a-half-story Federal mansion remodeled about 1840 in Greek Revival style with full third floor added; built by Israel Crane, known for his many business successes as "King" Crane. The Crane family lived in the house until 1912, when the Y.M.C.A. purchased it; in 1965 the historical society bought the house to save it. Furnishings date from the 18th and 19th centuries.
*Operated by Montclair Historical Soc. Open Sun. 2–5*

## MORRISTOWN

### ■ FORD MANSION, 1774
**230 Morris Ave**
Stately Georgian mansion with arched doorway and Palladian window above; built by Col. Jacob Ford, Jr., and used by George Washington as his headquarters during the winters of 1777–78 and 1779–80, when the army was encamped at nearby Jockey Hollow. In 1873 the mansion and a newly built wing were converted into a museum of Washington and Revolutionary War relics; the house is furnished with period antiques.
*Operated by National Park Service. Open daily 10–5; closed Thanksgiving, Christmas, and New Year's Day*

### MACCULLOCH HALL, 1810
**45 Macculloch Ave**
Manor house built by George Perot Macculloch, promotor of the now defunct Morris Canal (1831), which linked the Delaware River and Newark Bay. Restored as a museum, with fine period furnishings
*Private. Open Mon.–Fri. 10–5*

### SCHUYLER-HAMILTON HOUSE, 1760
**5 Olyplant Place**
White clapboard colonial house owned

during the Revolution by surgeon Jabez Campbell. Famous as the scene of the courtship of Alexander Hamilton and Elizabeth Schuyler in the winter of 1779–80. Restored in 1923 and furnished with period antiques
*Operated by Daughters of the American Revolution. Open Tues., Sun. 2–5*

■ **WICK HOUSE, about 1750**
**Jockey Hollow**
Weathered-shingle farmhouse, now located in the Jockey Hollow national forest preserve; headquarters of Maj. Gen. Arthur St. Clair when the Continental Army was encamped here in the winter of 1779–80. Built by Henry Wick, it was restored in 1935 and furnished with 18th-century country pieces.
*Operated by National Park Service. Open Feb.–Nov: daily 1–5; closed Thanksgiving*

## MOUNT HOLLY

### JOHN WOOLMAN MEMORIAL, 1783
**99 Branch St**
Two-story red brick house built by celebrated Quaker abolitionist John Woolman as a home for his daughter. Now a Quaker center with an 18th-century garden and period furnishings, including one of his chairs and other Woolman memorabilia. Overnight accommodations available
*Operated by John Woolman Assn. Open daily 9–4*

## NEW BRUNSWICK

### BUCCLEUCH MANSION, 1739
**Buccleuch Park**
Georgian mansion of brick and clapboard built by Lt. Col. Anthony White for his bride, the daughter of the provincial governor, Lewis Morris. The house was lived in until 1911 and is shown with period furnishings.
*Operated by Daughters of the American Revolution. Open June–Oct: Sat., Sun. 3–5*

### JOYCE KILMER BIRTHPLACE, before 1886
**17 Joyce Kilmer Ave**
Simple frame house where Joyce Kilmer was born in 1886. The house contains memorabilia related to the poet's literary career; now headquar-

ters of the American Legion post
*Operated by Joyce Kilmer Post of the American Legion. Open daily 1–6*

## PATERSON

### LAMBERT CASTLE, 1892
**Garret Mountain Reservation**
Huge, brownstone mansion with towers and turrets modeled after Warwick Castle in England; built by silk manufacturer Catholina Lambert to house his vast art collection. Interiors feature gold-leaf ceilings, hand-stenciled walls, and carved oak woodwork. Part of the castle is now a museum of the county historical society.
*Operated by Passaic Co. Park Comm. Open Wed.–Fri. 1–4:45, Sat., Sun., 11–4:45*

*Lambert Castle*

## PLAINFIELD

### DRAKE HOUSE, 1746; 1860s
**602 W Front St**
White clapboard house, extensively altered in 1860s, built by patriot and clergyman Nathaniel Drake; served as Washington's headquarters on June 26, 1777. Now a museum featuring Queen Anne and Empire furnishings and other historical exhibits
*Operated by Historical Soc. of Plainfield and North Plainfield. Open Mon., Wed., Sat., 2–5*

## PRINCETON

### BAINBRIDGE HOUSE, 1766
**158 Nassau St**
Small frame house built by Job Stockton; in 1774 William Bainbridge, commander of the U.S.S. *Constitution*, was born here. Restored and refurnished with period pieces; changing exhibits of the historical society museum on display

Operated by Historical Soc. of Princeton. Open Mon.–Fri. 10–3, Sat. 1–3, Sun. 2–4

## RAMSEY

### OLD STONE HOUSE, about 1745
### 536 Island Rd
Colonial, fieldstone house with gambrel roof; partially restored. Kitchen, bedroom, and parlor are furnished with 18th-century pieces.
*Operated by Ramsey Historical Assn. Open Sun. 2–4:30 and by appointment*

## RINGWOOD

### ■ RINGWOOD MANOR, about 1810
### Ringwood State Park
Ringwood was long associated with some of America's most famous ironmasters. Martin Ryerson built a Federal house here following the destruction of the original 1765 manor; subsequent owners Peter Cooper and Abram S. Hewitt expanded the house to 78 rooms. Set in a 579-acre park featuring formal gardens, the mansion is shown with some of the Ryerson and Hewitt furnishings.
*Operated by N.J. Dept. of Environmental Protection. Open May–Oct: daily 10–4:30, holidays 10–5*

*Ringwood Manor*

## RIVER EDGE

### VON STEUBEN HOUSE, 1739
### Main Street
Dutch colonial stone house built by the Zabriskie family. Because of their Tory sympathies, the property was confiscated by the state in 1783 and given to Gen Von Steuben; he in turn sold it back to the Zabriskies. In 1780 Washington briefly had his headquar-

ters here. Furnished with colonial pieces; museum of county history
*Operated by N.J. Dept. of Environmental Protection. Open Tues.–Sat. 10–12, 1–5, Sun. 2–5; closed Thanksgiving, Christmas, and New Year's Day*

## ROCKY HILL

### ROCKINGHAM, about 1730
### Route 518
White, clapboard farmhouse with unusual second-story balcony served as Washington's headquarters from August to November, 1783, while Congress met in Princeton and deliberated the final peace treaty with England. Washington entertained Thomas Paine and others here and prepared his farewell address to the army. Furnishings include some used by Washington
*Operated by N.J. Dept. of Environmental Protection. Open Tues.–Sat. 10–12, 1–5, Sun. 2–5; closed Thanksgiving, Christmas, and New Year's Day*

## SALEM

### ALEXANDER GRANT HOUSE, 1721
### 79-83 Market St
Colonial house of red brick with blue salt-glaze headers built in three sections; occupied as a home until willed to the historical society in 1929. In 1957 the adjoining house, called the Rumsey Wing, was purchased and restored. Fine period furnishings
*Operated by Salem Co. Historical Soc. Open Sept.–June: Tues.–Fri. 1–3*

## SMITHVILLE

### HISTORIC TOWNE OF SMITHVILLE
### Route 9, 12 miles north of Atlantic City
About a dozen buildings earmarked for demolition have been moved to this "village" centered around the restored and operating inn built in 1787. Included in the "village" are a gristmill, a chapel, a cobbler's shop, and a home.
*Operated by Fred and Ethel Noyes. Open daily 10:30–10*

## SOMERS POINT

### SOMERS MANSION, 1720–26
### Shore Road and Mays Landing
Wooden, colonial house built by

Quaker Richard Somers, whose father gained title to the land in 1695; oldest surviving structure in the county. Owned by descendants until 1937, when the house was deeded to the historical society; now a museum of the Atlantic County Historical Soc. *Operated by N.J. Dept. of Environmental Protection. Open Tues.–Sat. 10–12, 1–5, Sun. 2–5; closed Thanksgiving, Christmas, and New Year's Day*

## SOMERVILLE

### OLD DUTCH PARSONAGE, 1751
**65 Washington Place**
Brick house built as a parsonage for Rev. John Frelinghuysen, founder of America's first Dutch Reformed Theological Seminary, which eventually grew into Rutgers University. Moved from its original site on the Raritan River; some Dutch furnishings
*Operated by N.J. Dept. of Environmental Protection. Open Tues.–Sat. 10–12, 1–5, Sun. 2–5; closed Thanksgiving, Christmas, and New Year's Day*

### WALLACE HOUSE, 1778
**38 Washington Place**
White clapboard house with small kitchen wing served as residence for Gen. and Mrs. Washington from Dec., 1778, to June, 1779. The house, which Washington rented for $10,000, is furnished with Revolutionary War relics, including his campaign chest.
*Operated by N.J. Dept. of Environmental Protection. Open Tues.–Sat. 10–12, 1–5, Sun. 2–5; closed Thanksgiving, Christmas, and New Year's Day*

*Wallace House*

## SPRINGFIELD

### CANNON BALL HOUSE, about 1750
**126 Morris Ave**
Homestead of Abraham Hutchings;

house takes its name from a cannonball embedded in the west wall during a Revolutionary War battle fought here. Now a museum of Revolutionary and early American artifacts; the cannonball is among the items on display. *Operated by Springfield Historical Soc. Open Sept.–June: Sun. 2–4 and by appointment; closed Easter, Christmas, and New Year's Day*

## STANHOPE

### WATERLOO VILLAGE RESTORATION, mid-18th century
Village first developed around a short-lived blast furnace and refinery founded here in the 1760s; the area expanded with the completion of the Morris Canal in 1838. Restored to the mid-18th-century period, the village features houses, shops, a gristmill, church, and inn.
*Private. Open Apr.–June, Sept.–Nov: Mon.–Fri. by appointment, Sat., Sun. 11–6. July–Aug: Tues.–Sun. 11–6*

## TRENTON

### ISAAC WATSON HOUSE, 1708
**151 Westcott St.**
Five-room fieldstone house built by Isaac Watson and shown with 18th-century furnishings. The house is located in a seven-acre park.
*Operated by Daughters of the American Revolution. Open Mon.–Fri. 10–4, weekends by appointment*

### ■ WILLIAM TRENT HOUSE, 1719
**539 S Warren St**
Early Georgian red brick house considered to be the oldest in the city; built by New Jersey's first chief justice, after whom Trenton was named. The house served as official residence of the first royal governor and a number of state governors. Restored in 1936 and furnished with period pieces
*Operated by Trent House Assn. Open Mon.–Sat. 10–4, Sun. 1–4; closed Thanksgiving, Christmas, and New Year's Day*

## WAYNE

### DEY MANSION, about 1740
**199 Totowa Road**
Georgian manor house, with strong Dutch influence seen in steep gambrel

roof and combination of various building materials; built by carpenter Dirck Dey for his son Col. Theunis Dey. George Washington had his headquarters here in 1780; he returned later that year to escape a kidnaping plot. Restored with a garden and furnished with 18th-century pieces
*Operated by Passaic Co. Park Comm. Open Tues., Wed., Fri. 1–5, Sat., Sun. 10–5*

*Dey Mansion*

### VAN RIPER-HOPPER HOUSE, 1787
**533 Berdan Ave**
One-and-a-half-story, long, typical New Jersey Dutch-style farmhouse of native fieldstone with gable roof and six fireplaces; built by Uriah Richard Van Riper and owned by his descendants in the Hopper family. Now a museum with antiques
*Operated by Township of Wayne. Open Tues., Fri., Sat., Sun., 1–5*

## WEST ORANGE

### ◼ EDISON NATIONAL HISTORIC SITE, 1880–87
**Main Street and Lakeside Avenue**
In 1886 Thomas Edison purchased Glenmont, a 23-room Victorian house built in 1880; the following year he built the laboratory where he worked until his death in 1931. Included in the historic site are laboratories built later and an archive and museum housing some of the inventor's original models and experiments. The house is furnished as it was when Edison lived there; he and his second wife are buried on the 13½-acre estate.
*Operated by National Park Service. Open – House – Mon.–Sat. 10–4. Laboratory – daily 9:30–4:30; closed Thanksgiving, Christmas, and New Year's Day*

*Edison National Historic Site*

## WOODBURY

### CANDOR HALL (LADD'S CASTLE), 1688
**1337 Lafayette St**
Two-story, Dutch colonial brick house, greatly altered over the years, built by John Ladd, surveyor, who plotted Philadelphia. Because as a court officer he had to marry couples outside the Quaker faith, he was expelled from the Woodbury meeting.
*Private. Open by appointment*

### HUNTER-LAWRENCE HOUSE, 1765; 1871
**58 N Broad St**
Colonial house of native brick owned by Rev. Andrew Hunter, a participant in the · 1774 Greenwich Tea Party. Later owned by John Lawrence, whose brother James, naval hero of the War of 1812, lived here with him while attending Woodbury Academy. In 1871 a new owner added a mansard roof and altered the interiors. Now a historical museum with items of local interest and library
*Operated by Gloucester Co. Historical Soc. Open Wed. 1–4, Fri. 7–9:30, and by appointment*

### WHITALL HOUSE, 1748
**100 Hessian Ave, National Park**
Main section of brick house built by James and Ann Whitall, in whose orchard Fort Mercer was built; the older stone kitchen wing was probably built in the early 1700s. Here, on October 22, 1777, a band of patriots held back 2,000 Hessian soldiers; the 20-acre battlefield is now a public park with a picnic area, maintained by the county.
*Operated by Gloucester Co. Board of Freeholders. Open Sat., Sun. 2–4*

## ACOMA

■ **ACOMA PUEBLO**
**New Mexico Highway 23**
Said to be the oldest continuously occupied settlement in the U.S., Acoma was well established when Coronado reached New Mexico in 1540. Because of their location on a high mesa, the Indians were successful in resisting the Spaniards until the Franciscans finally established the San Esteban Rey Mission in 1629. It remains among the least altered in the state. Only a few families live here today, but the tribe reassembles for periodic festivals.

## AZTEC VICINITY

■ **AZTEC RUINS NATIONAL MONUMENT, 1100–1300**
**Route 1**
Built by the Pueblo Indians, this large pre-Columbian community was mistakenly called "Aztec" by early pioneer settlers. By the early 1100s Indians in the scattered farm villages along the Animas River had congregated in large multistoried masonry structures facing plazas, an architectural style borrowed from their Chaco Canyon neighbors. In the mid-1100s Aztec was abandoned and its people moved to the Mesa Verde area in southwestern Colorado, from which they returned about 1225. At Aztec they reused the east and west pueblos, built a row of rooms across the open end of the plaza, and added rooms around the Great Kiva. During the long drought of 1276–99 the village was abandoned permanently.
*Operated by National Park Service. Open summer: daily 7–6:30. Winter: daily 8–5*

## BLOOMFIELD

■ **CHACO CANYON NATIONAL MONUMENT, 650–1250**
**Star Route**
A major center of the Pueblo Indian culture reaching its peak between A.D. 1000 and 1100, Chaco Canyon contains 12 large ruins and more than 400 smaller ones in an area about eight miles long and two miles wide. The Pueblo culture developed flat-roofed houses of mud, rock, and poles constructed above ground in clusters of rectangular rooms, the walls of which were built of masonry by the mid-900s. The largest of these was Pueblo Bonito, four or five stories high, in a floor plan exceeding three acres, able to house about 1,000 people in its 800 rooms. Great Kivas, circular and semisubterranean, were the focus of religious life; Casa Rinconada, 64 feet in diameter, with masonry walls, is the most impressive. Most of the great apartment houses were vacated by the 1200s.
*Operated by National Park Service. Open summer: daily 7–9. Winter: daily 8–5*

*Pueblo Bonito interior*

## CHICO SPRINGS

**DORSEY MANSION, 1878–79; 1884**
A 36-room mansion, consisting of two distinct but connected elements – the older L-shaped log section and the sandstone Italian villa section with an octagonal tower. Stephen W. Dorsey, U.S. senator from Arkansas (1873–76), built the mansion to serve as headquarters for his large-scale working ranch; but after his financial reversal in 1893 both ranch and mansion were sold at a foreclosure sale. The present owners are working at the laborious task of restoration.
*Private. Open daily 10–4*

NEW MEXICO

## LAS CRUCES VICINITY
### ■ MESILLA PLAZA, 1848
Mesilla retains the flavor of a Mexican village and is built around the plaza, with a church at one end and adobe buildings on the other three sides. On July 4, 1854, the American flag was raised over the Mesilla Plaza confirming the Gadsden Purchase treaty, by which the U.S. acquired the southern route to California from the Rio Grande Valley.

## LAS TRAMPAS
### ■ LAS TRAMPAS HISTORIC DISTRICT, 1751
A Spanish-American agricultural village that preserves its 18th-century appearance and culture. The center of village communal life is the church of San Jose de Garcia de Las Trampas (1780), an important example of Spanish colonial architecture. Typical Spanish colonial adobe houses still may be found around the plaza along the edges of the valley floor.

## LINCOLN
### ■ LINCOLN HISTORIC DISTRICT, 1870s and 1880s
Much of Lincoln—considered one of the best-preserved frontier cow towns—remains little changed since 1878. One of the most famous feuds of the cattle frontier, the Lincoln County War of 1878, was played out here, reputedly involving such famous figures as Gen. Lew Wallace, John Chisum, and Billy the Kid. The adobe headquarters of the rival factions are still standing.

## LOS ALAMOS VICINITY
### ■ BANDELIER NATIONAL MONUMENT, about 1200–1550
A wilderness area of more than 46 square miles accessible by more than 60 miles of trails, the scene of one of the later flowerings of Pueblo culture. In Frijoles Canyon the cliff ruins, or talus (rock debris) villages, extend along the base of the northern wall of the canyon for approximately two miles. These masonry houses, one to three stories high, were irregularly terraced and had many cave rooms gouged out of the solid cliff. Also ruins of large pueblos, such as Tyuonyi—once three stories high with about 400 rooms—may be viewed. The large pueblos were occupied until 1550. *Operated by National Park Service. Open June–Aug: daily 8–7:30. Sept.–May: daily 8–5*

## MOUNTAINAIR VICINITY
### ■ GRAN QUIVIRA NATIONAL MONUMENT, 900–1672
New Mexico Route 10
The ruins of the Indian *Pueblo de los Humanas* and two Franciscan churches are preserved in this 611-acre monument. Located on a high ridge in central New Mexico, individual family dwellings by the 1300s had given way to community houses of grayish-blue limestone. In the 17th century the village was the scene of Spanish missionary activity, but severe drought and increasing Apache raids brought about the abandonment of the pueblo sometime between 1672 and 1675. *Operated by National Park Service. Open summer: daily 8–6. Winter: daily 8–5*

## PECOS VICINITY
### ■ PECOS NATIONAL MONUMENT, about 1300
U.S. Alternate Route 84–85
About A.D. 1300 the Pueblo Indians in the Pecos Valley began moving into compact one- or two-story pueblos. By 1450 they were living in a multistoried (up to five stories), quadrangular pueblo built around a central plaza on a rocky ridge with up to 600 rooms used for living quarters and storage and at least 22 kivas—subterranean ceremonial chambers. They were visited by Coronado's party in 1540, and in the 1620s the Franciscans established a mission there with a church and convent, which were destroyed during the rebellion of 1680; a new church was built about 1707. In the 18th century the Pecos Pueblo declined as a result of disease and warfare with the Comanches, and in 1838 it was abandoned by the last 17 survivors. Today a restored kiva and the ruins of the two major pueblos, the convent, and church may be seen.

Operated by National Park Service. Open summer: daily 8–8. Winter: daily 8–5

## SANTA FE

### ■ BARRIO DE ANALCO HISTORIC DISTRICT, 1620

One of the oldest settled areas in the country of European inception, the district is still an active working-class neighborhood of Spanish colonial heritage. It is characterized by the adobe construction indigenous to the Southwest and first used by the Indians of the area in their cliffside dwellings (flat pueblo roof with tamped earth and poles [vigas]). The Spanish introduced adobe bricks, an interior patio, and porch. This merging of Indian and Spanish styles produced the architecture still seen today in the Barrio.

### HEWETT HOUSE, about 1865
### 116 Lincoln Ave

One of the two remaining examples of the houses that formed a part of the U.S. Army's Fort Marcy officers' quarters. About 1917 Hewett House was remodeled to reflect pueblo architectural style. Since then it has been the headquarters of the School of American Research, housing its offices and anthropological exhibits.
Operated by School of American Research. Open Mon.–Fri. 8–12, 1–5

### ■ PALACE OF THE GOVERNORS, about 1610
### Santa Fe Plaza

Probably the oldest dwelling built by white men in the U.S., the historic low adobe building was designed by Don Pedro de Peralta and his officers

when he established Santa Fe as the capital of the vast Spanish empire in the Southwest. The palace is the prototype of the southwestern architectural form – Indian and Spanish designs are combined in the adobe-brick building with roof supported by huge vigas, or beams. It served as the residence for 30 Spanish governors until 1846, when Santa Fe came under the sway of the U.S. government. Thereafter 24 territorial and state governors occupied it in succession until 1900, when its official use was abandoned. It now houses a museum devoted to the 350 years of New Mexico's history. Operated by Museum of N. Mex. Open Mon.–Sat. 9–5, Sun., holidays 2–5; closed Thanksgiving, Christmas, and New Year's Day

### ■ RANDALL DAVEY HOUSE, 1847
### Upper Canyon Road

Two-story stone-and-adobe building originally built as a sawmill by the U.S. Army to provide lumber for Fort Marcy. By 1852 it was in private hands, and it has since been owned by several well-known people. The late artist Randall Davey bought it in 1920 and converted it into a gracious home and studio where he lived and worked for more than 40 years.
Operated by Mrs. E.G. Cullum, owner. Open Tues., Fri. 2–4

### ■ SANTA FE PLAZA, about 1610

Historically the city's commercial and social center, the plaza was the terminus of the famous Santa Fe Trail. Two landmarks associated with the site are the Palace of the Governors (1610) and the nearby San Miguel

Palace of the Governors

Mission (about 1640). Gen. Stephen Watts Kearny raised the American flag at the palace in 1846 to establish U.S. rule in New Mexico.

## SILVER CITY VICINITY

### ■ GILA CLIFF DWELLINGS NATIONAL MONUMENT, 1272–84
**West Fork of Gila River**
The term "cliff dweller" refers to Pueblo people who built their homes in natural caves; but the Pueblos also built in the open, and there are examples of both types of settlements at the monument: The Gila Conglomerate—found in five of the caves high in the southeast-facing cliff of a side canyon—includes a total of 35 rooms with walls of stone from the formation exposed in the cliff. The TJ Ruin, a pueblo near the visitors' center, was once composed of square houses built above ground of masonry or adobe. The earliest ruin at the site is a pit house dating from about A.D. 100 to 400. By about 1400 the Indians had abandoned these homes and fields.
*Operated by National Park Service. Open summer: daily 8:30–7. Winter: daily 9–5*

## TAOS

### ■ ERNEST L. BLUMENSCHEIN HOUSE, 18th century
**Ledoux Street**
The 11-room adobe home, dating from Spanish times, of the co-founder of the Taos Art Colony. Members of the colony, started in 1898 and led by Ernest Blumenschein and Bert Phillips, inspired the modern art movement in the Southwest, and their exhibitions made Taos the most important art center west of the Mississippi.
*Operated by Kit Carson Memorial Foundation. Open by appointment*

### ■ KIT CARSON HOUSE, 1825
**Old Kit Carson Road**
Old adobe house, with walls 30 inches thick and viga ceilings, bought in 1843 by the famous trader, trapper, and scout Kit Carson for his beautiful bride Josefa Jaramillo. It served as the permanent home for their large family for 25 years and as a gathering place for the famous men of the period visiting Taos. Now a house museum with Carson family rooms as well as Indian, Spanish, and Catholic Church exhibits. Beautiful patio with beehive oven and restored well house
*Operated by Kit Carson Memorial Foundation. Open winter: 8–5. Spring and fall: 8–6. Summer 7:30–7:30; closed Thanksgiving, Christmas, and New Year's Day*

### ■ TAOS PUEBLO
**three miles north of Taos**
Still lived in today, the two terraced communal dwellings—the highest pueblo buildings in the Southwest, five stories high—were known to Spanish explorers as early as 1540. The pueblo commemorates Indian resistance to Spanish rule during the uprisings of the 17th century. The mission of San Geronimo, built near Taos Pueblo, though twice destroyed and rebuilt prior to the revolt of 1680, continued until 1847, when it was bombarded by the Americans under Col. Sterling Price during the Taos Rebellion.

*Taos Pueblo*

## ALBANY

### GEN. TEN BROECK MANSION, 1797–98
**9 Ten Broeck Place**
Federal-style brick mansion with prominent chimneys and balustraded roof, built by Abraham Ten Broeck, a hero of the Battle of Saratoga, member of the first New York State constitutional convention, and mayor of Albany. The house was in use as a private residence until 1948, when it was given to the historical society; furnished with fine Federal pieces
*Operated by Albany Co. Historical Assn. Open daily 3–4*

### HISTORIC CHERRY HILL, 1768
**South Pearl Street**
Colonial, yellow clapboard house with gambrel roof built by Col. Philip Van Rensselaer; alterations and a wing added later. Occupied by the family until 1963 and furnished with their possessions covering many periods
*Operated by Board of Trustees. Open Tues.–Sat. 10–4, Sun. 1–4; closed Thanksgiving, Christmas, and New Year's Day*

### ■ SCHUYLER MANSION (THE PASTURES), 1761–62
**Clinton and Schuyler Streets**
An elegant Georgian brick mansion built by Gen. Philip Schuyler; the scene of Gen. Burgoyne's imprisonment, following his defeat at Saratoga, and the wedding, in 1780, of Elizabeth Schuyler and Alexander Hamilton. The 1950 restoration includes very fine Revolutionary period antiques and much of the original Schuyler furnishings. See also Schuylerville
*Operated by N.Y.S. Historic Trust. Open Tues.–Sat. 9–5, Sun. 12–5*

*Schuyler Mansion*

## ALBION

### TOUSLEY-CHURCH HOUSE, 1840s
**249 N Main St**
Greek Revival brick house with 1850s addition; hand-carved woodwork, original fireplaces, and unusual column-supported stairway. Restored in 1929 as a museum and meeting hall
*Operated by Daughters of the American Revolution. Open by appointment*

## ALEXANDRIA BAY

### BOLDT CASTLE, begun 1897
**Heart Island**
Turreted castle begun by George C. Boldt as a gift for his wife and abandoned when she died in 1902. On one of the Thousand Islands in the St. Lawrence River; ferries and tour boats stop at the 100-room castle complex
*Operated by Edward John Noble Foundation. Open May 15–Oct. 15: daily 10–7*

## AMSTERDAM

### GUY PARK MANOR, 1773; 1858
**366 W Main St**
Stone Georgian-style manor built by Sir William Johnson in 1766 as a wedding present for his daughter Mary and her husband, Guy Johnson. The house was destroyed by fire in 1773 and immediately rebuilt; the wings were added in 1858. Although the interiors have been greatly altered over the years, the restoration furnishings are 18th-century. Sir Guy succeeded his father-in-law as superintendent of Indian affairs, and his house, like the other two Johnson holdings (see Fort Johnson and Johnstown), was used for Indian council meetings.
*Operated by N.Y.S. Historic Trust. Open Tues.–Sat. 9–5, Sun. 12–5*

## AUBURN

### CASE MANSION, 1836
**203 Genesee St**
Greek Revival house built by John Seymour with four Ionic columns and pediment above; later the home of Theodore Willard Case and the first studio of Case Fox Movietone News and 20th Century pictures. Case and the others who perfected talking pictures had their offices here.

*Operated by Cayuga Museum of History and Art. Open Tues.–Fri. 1–5, Sat. 9–12, 1–5, Sun. 2–5*

## HARRIET TUBMAN HOUSE, before 1850
**180 South St**

Home of Harriet Tubman, who escaped from slavery in 1849 and helped free more than 300 Negroes through her Underground Railway. In 1908 the small house became a home for indigent Negroes; it is now a shrine to Miss Tubman, "the Moses of her people."

*Operated by AME Zion Church. Open by appointment*

## MILLARD FILLMORE MEMORIAL CABIN, 1791
**Washington Street**

Log cabin with rafters secured with wooden pegs built about the same time as and similar to the one in which Millard Fillmore was born; the actual birthplace of the 13th President burned down in 1852. The present structure was moved from its original site and dedicated in 1965; furnishings are based on an authentic report of the Fillmore cabin.

*Operated by Cayuga Museum of History and Art. Open Apr.–Nov: Tues.–Fri. 1–5, Sat. 9–12, 1–5, Sun. 2–5*

## OWASCO STOCKADED INDIAN VILLAGE
**Emerson Park, Route 38A**

Reconstructed Indian village based on archaeological and historical research. Noteworthy features include two long houses, one furnished, an herb and vegetable garden, and seminars in Indian crafts. This is believed to be one of the earliest farming communities in the country.

*Operated by Cayuga Museum of History and Art. Open June–Sept: Mon.–Fri., Sun. 1–5, Sat. 9–5*

## ■ SEWARD HOUSE, 1816
**33 South St**

Home of William H. Seward, governor of New York, U.S. senator, Secretary of State during the Civil War, and a founder of the Republican party. The house was built by Elijah Miller, Seward's father-in-law, and occupied by the family until the death of Seward's grandson in 1951. The 13 rooms open to the public contain

family furniture from colonial through Victorian eras; on display are many of Seward's mementos, including letters from President Lincoln and items connected with the purchase of Alaska, known as Seward's Folly.

*Operated by Foundation Historical Assn. Open Mar.–Dec: Mon.–Sat. 1–5; closed national holidays*

*Seward House*

## BEACON

### MADAM BRETT HOMESTEAD, 1709
**50 Van Nydeck Ave**

One-and-a-half-story frame Dutch homestead with original scalloped shingles and sloping dormer windows; wing and kitchen added later. Built by Roger and Catharyna Brett and maintained by Madam Brett for many years after her husband's death. The house remained in the family until 1955; furnished with period pieces

*Operated by Daughters of the American Revolution. Open Apr. 15–Nov. 15: Mon.–Fri. 1–4, Sat., Sun. by appointment*

## BELMONT

### CHARLES SMITH WHITNEY MANSION [THE AMERICANA MANSE], 1870
**39 South St**

Brick Italianate mansion, with gingerbread trimming and a ten-foot stained-glass window, built by local rags-to-riches hero. In process of restoration as a museum and furnished with Victorian pieces including an 1870 rosewood concert grand piano

*Operated by Ruth L. Czankus. Open May–Oct: Tues.–Sun. 10–5*

## BETHPAGE, L.I.

### OLD BETHPAGE VILLAGE RESTORATION
**Round Swamp Road**
Reconstruction of a pre-Civil War village of Long Island houses, shops, churches, and inns, some dating from the 18th century. Several buildings are open to the public, others are being restored. The village grows yearly. *Operated by Nassau Co. Dept. of Public Works. Open May–Oct: daily 10–5. Nov.–Apr: daily 9–4; closed Christmas and New Year's Day*

## BRIDGEHAMPTON, L.I.

### CORWITH HOMESTEAD, about 1775; 1833
**Montauk Highway**
Early home of William Corwith, with many later alterations, including the addition of a church as a wing in 1833. Museum with colonial, Empire, and Victorian furnishings, and changing summer exhibits *Operated by Bridgehampton Historical Soc. Open July–Sept: Mon., Wed., Fri.–Sun. 1:30–5*

### SAYRELANDS, 1734
**Montauk Highway**
Built by D. Halsey of white oak and purchased by whaling captain Uriah Sayre in 1832. Noteworthy features include original freehand decorated walls, fine Duncan Phyfe furnishings, and an extensive clock collection. The house is still occupied by a descendant of Captain Sayre. *Operated by Soc. for the Preservation of Long Island Antiquities. Open May–Sept: Fri.–Mon. 2–5*

*Sayrelands*

## BUFFALO

■ **WILCOX HOUSE, about 1838; mid 1890s**
**641 Delaware Ave**
Begun as officers' quarters attached to an army barracks. Greek Revival mansion became a residence in 1845 when the post was abandoned. In the 1880s Ansley Wilcox acquired the house and commissioned architect George Cary to add the rear portion, doubling the original size. The house was made famous in 1901 when Vice President Theodore Roosevelt took the Presidential oath there following the assassination of William McKinley. Restoration in progress *Operated by National Park Service. Open by appointment*

## CANANDAIGUA

### GRANGER HOMESTEAD, 1814–16
Federal-style mansion built by Gideon Granger, postmaster general under Presidents Jefferson and Madison and later New York State senator; north wing added by his son Francis before 1868. In 1876 the mansion was converted into a ladies' seminary; it was reoccupied as a home by the Granger family from 1906 to 1930. Restoration was begun in 1946 and continues; furnishings are mainly Federal period and Regency original house pieces. *Operated by Granger Homestead Soc. Open Tues.–Sun. 10:30–5:30; closed Thanksgiving, Christmas, New Year's Day, and Easter*

## CASTILE

### HENRY CUMMING HOUSE [CASTILE HISTORICAL HOUSE], 1865
**17 E Park Rd**
Victorian house built by Henry Cumming, a Civil War veteran, became headquarters of the historical society in 1956. It is primarily a research center of local history with exhibits of costumes, farm equipment, Civil War memorabilia, and many other items. *Operated by Castile Historical Soc. Open daily by appointment*

### MARY JEMISON LOG CABIN, about 1800
**Letchworth State Park**
Log cabin built by the "white woman

of the Genesee," Mary Jemison, who was captured by Indians as a child and elected to stay with them when offered her freedom. Married first to a Delaware chief and then to a Seneca chief, she built this cabin for her daughter. *Operated by Genesee State Park Comm. Open May 15–Oct: daily 10–10*

## CENTERPORT

### EAGLE'S NEST (VANDERBILT MUSEUM), 1929–30
**Little Neck Road**
This 24-room Spanish-Moroccan-style mansion was built by William K. Vanderbilt, Jr. A two-story building in the same style houses the vast collections amassed by Vanderbilt from 1928–44. *Operated by Vanderbilt Museum Comm. of Suffolk Co. Open May–Oct: Tues.–Sat. 10–4, Sun., holidays 12–5*

## COHOES

### VAN SCHAICK MANSION, 1735
**Van Schaick Island**
Two-story, brick manor house with gambrel roof built by Anthony Van Schaick; served as General Gates's headquarters during the Battle of Saratoga, 1777. Located on an island in the Hudson River opposite Cohoes *Private. Open Sat., Sun. by appointment*

## CONSTABLEVILLE

### CONSTABLE HALL, 1810–19
Limestone mansion, modeled after an ancestral home in Ireland, was built by William Constable, Jr.; it was passed down to the eldest son of six generations and remained in the family until 1948 when it was restored. The period furnishings, many original to the house, include a complete set of Napoleon's china, initialed N.B., a sewing table owned by Marie Antoinette, a Duncan Phyfe mahogany wine cooler, and Chippendale four-poster. *Operated by Constable Hall Assn. Open June–Oct: Tues.–Sat. 10–5, Sun. 1–5*

## CONSTITUTION ISLAND

### WARNER HOUSE, about 1800 and 1836
Henry Warner bought this island in

the Hudson River opposite West Point in 1836 and added a wing to the cottage already there. His daughters, Anna and Susan, popular Victorian authors, lived there and took an active part in the life of West Point. In 1908 the island was presented as a gift to the government and became part of the United States Military Academy Reservation. Furnished and maintained as a memorial to the sisters *Operated by Constitution Island Assn. Open May–Sept: by appointment*

## COOPERSTOWN

### LIPPITT HOMESTEAD, FARMER'S MUSEUM, AND VILLAGE CROSSROADS, late 1790s
Modified saltbox farmhouse originally stood six miles south in Hinman Hollow and was built by Joseph Lippitt, a Rhode Island pioneer. Since 1952 it has been part of a re-created 19th-century village adjoining The Farmer's Museum. Lippitt Homestead is fully operated year round as a 19th-century farm. Furnishings in the house, as in the other buildings throughout the village, are from the period between the Revolution and the Civil War. The New York State Historical Assn. also operates *Fenimore House*, with collections of folk and fine art, and The Carriage and Harness Museum. *Operated by N.Y.S. Historical Assn. Open May–Oct: daily 9–6. Nov.–Apr: Tues.–Sat. 9–5, Sun. 1–5*

## CORTLAND

### SUGGETT HOUSE, about 1868
**25 Homer Ave**
Large Victorian frame house built by John Suggett. Now historical society headquarters and a museum featuring furniture and items of local interest *Operated by Cortland Co. Historical Soc. Open Mon., Wed., Fri. 1–5, and by appointment*

## COXSACKIE

### ■ BRONCK HOUSE MUSEUM, 1663; 1685
**Route 9W**
Complex of buildings highlighted by the 1663 stone house, with 1685 addition, built by Pieter Bronck, son of

Jonas Bronck after whom the Bronx is named. Other buildings include a 1738 Dutch-style brick house, an 1820s miniature house, and a 13-sided "Freedom Barn" built about 1800 to celebrate independence. The houses are restored to the Federal period with fine furnishings and artifacts belonging to the Bronck family, who lived here until 1939.
*Operated by Greene Co. Historical Soc. Open May 15–Sept: Tues.–Sat. 10–5, Sun. 1–6*

*Bronck House*

## CROTON-ON-HUDSON

■ **VAN CORTLANDT MANOR, 1749**
**off Route 9**
Stone, frame, and brick manor house and gardens of the Van Cortlandt family estate that once included 86,000 acres. The original stone structure first occupied in the 17th century remained in the family, with later additions of a second story and porch, until 1945. Carefully restored with appropriate furnishings recalling Dutch traditions. The restoration includes a Ferry House and a reconstructed Ferry-House Kitchen building that once serviced the crossing of the Croton River.
*Operated by Sleepy Hollow Restorations. Open Apr.–Nov. 15: daily 10–5. Nov. 16–Mar: Mon.–Fri. 12–4, Sat., Sun. 10–5; closed Thanksgiving, Christmas, and New Year's Day*

## CUTCHOGUE, L.I.

■ **THE OLD HOUSE, 1649**
**E Main St**
A 17th-century frame house with central chimney and lean-to addition built by John Budd in Southold, Long

Island; he had it moved to its present site in 1660 as a wedding present for his daughter. Restored in 1949 with period furnishings
*Operated by Independent Congregational Church Soc. Open July–Labor Day: daily 2–5, June, Sept: Sat., Sun. 2–5*

## DELHI

**FRISBEE HOUSE, 1804**
**Route 10**
Judge Gideon Frisbee built this graceful two-story Federal house along the Delaware on the site of an earlier log cabin where the first county court met in 1797. Restored in 1965, the clapboard house, accented by long narrow windows, is furnished with 18th-century pieces, all donated by local families. Also on the 66 acres are a schoolhouse, gunsmith shop, and tollgate house moved here from other towns in the vicinity.
*Operated by The Delaware Co. Historical Assn. Open May 30–Labor Day: Sat., Sun., national holidays 2–5, and by appointment*

## DRESDEN

**INGERSOLL MEMORIAL HOUSE, before 1833**
**Route 14**
Birthplace of Robert G. Ingersoll, Civil War officer and lawyer who gained fame for his agnostic beliefs and writings. Furnished with some of his possessions; still owned by his family
*Private. Open June–Sept: by appointment*

## EAST HAMPTON, L.I.

**"HOME, SWEET HOME," 1660**
**14 James Lane**
Built by Robert Dayton, this saltbox

*"Home, Sweet Home"*

has been immortalized as John Howard Payne's birthplace and his boyhood "Home, Sweet Home." Since 1927 the house has been maintained as a shrine to Payne with exhibits of his belongings. Furnished with antiques of town families from 1660 to 1852, the year of Payne's death *Operated by Village of East Hampton. Open Oct.-May: daily 10-4. June-Sept: daily 10-5; closed Tues.*

## MULFORD HOUSE, about 1670
**James Lane**

Early, weathered-shingle saltbox of 11 rooms and five fireplaces. Owned by the Mulford family until 1948; now historical museum with period furnishings and Hemerocallis garden *Operated by East Hampton Historical Soc. Open June-Sept. 15: Mon.-Sat. 1-4, Sun. 2-4*

## EAST SETAUKET, L.I.

### SHERWOOD-JAYNE HOUSE, 1730; 1790
**Old Post Road**

Saltbox with unusual wall paintings built by the family of William Jayne, an early Long Island settler; east end of house added 1790. Long-time summer home of Howard Sherwood, founder of Soc. for the Preservation of Long Island Antiquities, who added to and altered the house. Furnished with his antiques collection *Operated by Soc. for the Preservation of Long Island Antiquities. Open May-Oct. 18: daily 1-5; closed Tues.*

*Sherwood-Jayne House*

## ELMIRA

### MARK TWAIN STUDY, 1872
**Elmira College Campus**

"Cozy nest" was built as a surprise gift for Mark Twain by his sister-in-law on an isolated hilltop on her farm. Used as a summer retreat; here Twain wrote portions of *Tom Sawyer, Huckleberry Finn*, and many other books. In 1952, to protect the small study from vandals, it was moved to the campus. *Operated by Elmira College. Open daily 8-5*

## FISHKILL

### HENDRICK KIP HOUSE, 1753
**Old Glenham Road**

A Dutch stone farmhouse built by the son of the original patentee of Kipsbergen, although one or two rooms may be from an earlier 1720 house that had occupied this site. During the early days of the Revolution, the house was headquarters of Baron von Steuben, the outstanding Prussian officer who aided the Americans. *Private. Open by appointment*

## FORT EDWARD

### OLD FORT HOUSE, 1773
**27 Broadway**

Simple frame house with gambrel roof and two chimneys was built by Patrick Smyth and is the oldest frame building still standing in Washington County. In 1943 the house was restored and additions were removed. Furnished with colonial and Federal pieces and fine displays of locally made pottery *Operated by Fort Edward Historical Assn. Open July-Aug: daily 1-5*

## FORT JOHNSON

### OLD FORT JOHNSON, 1749
**Route 5**

Beautiful gray, stone manor was the first of three houses built by Sir William Johnson, superintendent of Indian affairs and general of the royal militia. Originally called Mount Johnson, the name was changed during the French and Indian wars when the house was fortified with a palisade. In 1777 it was confiscated by the Americans, and the lead roof was stripped to be used for bullets. Some of the original furniture is still in the house, along with other pieces from the 1749 to 1763 period, the years Sir William lived there. Also on the grounds are a miller's house and store built about

1745 and the original outdoor privy, paneled inside. See also Amsterdam and Johnstown
*Operated by Montgomery Co. Historical Soc. Open May–June, Sept.–Oct: daily 1–5. July–Aug: Tues.–Sat. 10–5, Sun., Mon. 1–5*

# GARRISON-ON-HUDSON

## BOSCOBEL, 1805
### Route 9D
Built for States Morris Dyckman in style of the eminent Scottish architect Robert Adam, this elegant 20-room mansion was originally in Westchester Co. Dyckman family occupied it until 1923 when it was sold to the county. After World War II the house became Federal property, was declared surplus and sold to a house wrecker for $35. Retrieved by huge private grants, disassembled into small pieces for storage, the house was reconstructed on present site overlooking the Hudson and opened in 1961. Furnished with period pieces, including 300 books from Dyckman's library
*Operated by Boscobel Restoration. Open Mar.–Oct: daily 9:30–5; closed Tues. Nov.–Dec: daily 9:30–4; closed Tues.*

## DICK'S CASTLE, 1908–11
### Route 9D
What was to have been a Roman-Moorish castle built in concrete and copied from the Alhambra. Mrs. Evans R. Dick began the castle but had to abandon it, after spending three million dollars, when her husband suffered financial reverses. The walls and courtyards were partially destroyed by vandalism before Anton Chmela, an Austrian engineer, purchased the property in 1944. He and his family live in the castle and are in the process of completing it. It will house a museum of American industry.
*Operated by Anton J. Chmela and family. Open daily 10–6*

# GENEVA

## PROUTY-CHEW MUSEUM, 1825
### 543 S Main St
Federal house with various additions and modifications from the Civil War era. Restored in 1960, the house reflects both styles; the kitchen is of the

Federal period and many of the furnishings are Empire. Now headquarters of historical society and a museum of local history
*Operated by Geneva Historical Soc. Open Tues.–Sat. 1:30–4:30*

## ROSE HILL, 1839
### Route 96A
Greek Revival mansion built by retired New York City merchant William K. Strong on land purchased from the Rose family. Acquired in 1850 by Robert Swan, who converted the estate into an award-winning farm. Restored and furnished with Empire pieces
*Operated by Geneva Historical Soc. Open May–Oct: Mon.–Sat. 10–4, Sun. 1–4*

# GERMANTOWN

## CLERMONT, 1782
### Clermont State Park
Large Georgian mansion in the Catskill Mountains overlooking the Hudson River; built on part of the original manorial grant to Robert Livingston in 1673. The first mansion on the estate was built in 1730 and was burned by the British in 1777. Robert Fulton named his steamboat for the estate, then occupied by his benefactor, Chancellor Robert Livingston. Furnishings of the 18th and 19th centuries
*Operated by Taconic State Park Comm. Open summer: daily 9–5*

# HUDSON

## ■ FRONT STREET–PARADE HILL–LOWER WARREN STREET HISTORIC DISTRICT
Built on a slope overlooking the Hudson River, Hudson was not settled permanently until 1783 when a number of New Englanders, mainly Nantucket Quakers, arrived there. Most of the early houses reflect this New England influence.

## OLANA, 1870–72
### east of Rip Van Winkle Bridge, off Route 9G
Home of noted landscape artist and leader of the famous "Hudson River School of Painting" Frederick E. Church. Stone-and-brick Moorish dwelling and bell tower, with painted arches, balconies, and colored tiles

reflecting the unusual Eastern theme throughout. Church's extensive collection of antiques and mementos from his wide travels are displayed along with his own paintings. The 327-acre estate offers spectacular views of the Hudson River.

*Operated by N.Y.S. Historic Trust. Open May–Oct: daily 9–5*

*Olana*

## HUNTINGTON, L.I.

### CONKLIN HOUSE, about 1750
**2 High St**
Saltbox farmhouse with two-story addition built by David Conklin, whose forebears established a Massachusetts glass factory in 1639. The 1911 restoration combines colonial, Empire, and Victorian furnishings and is maintained as a museum and library of local history.

*Operated by Huntington Historical Soc. Open Tues.–Fri. 12–5, Sun. 2–5*

### POWELL HOUSE, about 1663; 1668
**434 Park Ave**
Thomas Powell, influential town officeholder, built a three-room house, the oldest in Huntington, and enlarged it in 1668. Subsequent owners include engineer John Jervis, born in the house in 1794, and Hilda G. Taylor, portrait painter, who lived here from 1943 to 1967.

*Operated by Huntington Historical Soc. Open Wed., Thurs. 1–4:30*

## HUNTINGTON STATION, L.I.

### WALT WHITMAN HOUSE, about 1810
**246 Walt Whitman Rd**
Walt Whitman was born in 1819 in this simple, two-story farmhouse built by his father. The first floor is sparsely furnished as it was in the poet's boyhood; the second floor houses a large collection of Whitman manuscripts and paintings and sculptures of the poet.

*Operated by N.Y.S. Historic Trust. Open daily 10–4*

## HURLEY

■ **HURLEY HISTORIC DISTRICT**
Founded in 1661 as Nieuw Dorp by Dutch and Huguenot families, Hurley retains original Dutch flavor and is billed as "America's colonial stone house community." Especially noteworthy are ten houses on the main street that are still privately owned, some by descendants of the original builders. *Jan Van Deusen House,* 1725, can be seen by appointment.

## HYDE PARK

■ **FRANKLIN D. ROOSEVELT HOME, about 1826**
**Route 9**
Birthplace and home of the 32nd President. His father bought a simple frame house in 1867 and by 1916 had changed it into this 50-room stone-and-stucco mansion. In 1939 F.D.R. built a library-office which now is a museum of his artifacts and library of his Presidential papers. The house is kept as it was during F.D.R.'s lifetime; he and Mrs. Roosevelt are buried

*Franklin D. Roosevelt Home*

in the Rose Garden.
*Operated by National Park Service.
Open daily 9–5*

■ **VANDERBILT MANSION, 1896–98**
**Route 9**
Frederick Vanderbilt's three-story Italian Renaissance mansion of 54 rooms and 20 baths, designed by McKim, Mead and White as an autumn and spring residence. Lavish furnishings include antiques, works of art, and an extensive tapestry collection. The 211-acre estate was in use until Vanderbilt's death in 1938.
*Operated by National Park Service.
Open daily 9–5*

## IRONVILLE – CROWN POINT

**PENFIELD HOMESTEAD, 1828**
Simple, Federal-style house occupied by three generations of the Penfield family and shown with their furnishings. House museum also contains a replica of an early electromagnet used in the Penfield ironworks and other items of local history.
*Operated by Penfield Foundation.
Open May 15–Oct. 15: Tues., Thurs., Sat. 1–5*

## JOHNSTOWN

■ **JOHNSON HALL, 1763**
**139 Hall Ave**
Sir William Johnson, superintendent of Indian affairs and hero of the French and Indian wars, designed this Georgian-style clapboard house, which also served as meeting place for Iroquois councils. Two flanking stone blockhouses, unique in the state, were built for protection in 1763 but never used; the eastern one was destroyed by fire and rebuilt in 1968. Some of the period furnishings in the restored house, the second built by Sir William, belonged to the Johnson family. See also Amsterdam and Fort Johnson
*Operated by N.Y.S. Historic Trust
Open Tues.–Sat. 9–5, Sun. 12–5*

## KATONAH

**JOHN JAY HOMESTEAD, about 1800**
**Route 22**
John Jay, first chief justice of the Supreme Court, diplomat, and governor of New York, lived in this two-story wooden house after he retired from public life. It is built on land purchased from the Indians by Jay's grandfather and remained in his family until 1958. Except for a wing, added in 1922 to house a fine art collection, the homestead remains much as it was when Jay lived there.
*Operated by N.Y.S. Historic Trust.
Open daily 9–5*

## KINDERHOOK

**HOUSE OF HISTORY, 1810**
**16 Broad St**
Two-story, Federal brick house with marble arches, built by architect Barnabas Waterman for James Vanderpoll, assemblyman and later judge of the state supreme court. Restored with Federal furnishings
*Operated by Columbia Co. Historical Assn. Open May 30–Sept. 15: Tues–Sat. 10:30–4:30, Sun. 1:30–4:30*

■ **VAN ALEN HOUSE, 1737**
**Route 9H**
One of the few remaining early Dutch farmhouses that have not been added to or severely altered over the years. Tradition tells that Washington Irving used a Van Alen daughter as a model for his character Katrina Van Tassel and that the house was the scene of the famous party in "The Legend of Sleepy Hollow." In 1964 the house was near total ruin; but the Van Alen family donated it with 30 acres for restoration; furnished with Dutch colonial pieces
*Operated by Columbia County Historical Assn. Open May 30–Sept. 15: Tues.–Sat. 10:30–4:30, Sun. 1:30–4:30*

## KINGSTON

**BEVIER HOUSE, early 1700s**
**Route 209**
Dutch colonial stone house with later additions and modifications. Furnished with period pieces, including an early Dutch kitchen; headquarters of local historical society
*Operated by Ulster Co. Historical Soc. Open June 15–Sept. 15: daily 10–4:30*

## CHAPTER HOUSE, 1696
**Crown and Green Streets**
An unknown French Huguenot settler built this stone house. John Tappan, local printer, owned the house in the late 1700s and published a newspaper, the *Ulster Plebian*, here. Restored in 1907 and furnished with pieces representative of Huguenot society from 1750s to 1830s
*Operated by Daughters of the American Revolution. Open by appointment*

## ■ CLINTON AVENUE HISTORIC DISTRICT
Three centuries of architecture and history can be seen along this street, including the old stockade area built to protect the first settlement in 1658, the Academy Green where Peter Stuyvesant signed a treaty with the Indians, and the historic Senate House described below.

## SENATE HOUSE, 1676
**312 Fair St**
Limestone-and-brick house built by Col. Wessel Ten Broeck and owned by a descendant when the first publicly elected New York State Senate met in a room there, Sept. 10, 1777. Burned by British, but rebuilt and used as a private residence by Ten Broeck family until purchased by New York State in 1888. Senate Chamber furnished as it was in 1777; kitchen stocked with colonial utensils; attic houses extensive antique doll collection; adjacent museum built in 1927 contains paintings by John Vanderlyn
*Operated by N.Y.S. Historic Trust. Open Mon.–Sat. 9–5, Sun. 1–5*

## LAKE PLACID

### JOHN BROWN FARM, 1855
**Route 73**
Clapboard farmhouse built for abolitionist John Brown by his son-in-law on 244 acres purchased from Gerrit Smith, founder of a farming colony for free Negroes. Brown was buried at the farm on Dec. 8, 1859, six days after his execution for the unsuccessful raid at Harpers Ferry, Virginia. The farm was restored in 1958; some furnishings belonged to the Brown family.
*Operated by N.Y.S. Historic Trust. Open Mon.–Sat. 9–5, Sun. 1–5*

## LAWRENCE, L.I.

### ROCK HALL, 1767
**199 Broadway**
Fine example of Georgian architecture; has been owned by two families only. It was built for wealthy West Indian planter Josiah Martin, whose heirs renovated the first-floor drawing room for a family wedding in 1806. Thomas H. Hewlett bought the house in 1824; extensive repairs were made then and in 1881. In 1948 the house was deeded to the town of Hempstead and restored. The first two floors are furnished with Federal period pieces; the third floor houses exhibits of Indian relics, antique toys, and Civil War memorabilia.
*Operated by Soc. for the Preservation of Long Island Antiquities. Open Apr.–Nov: daily 10–5, Sun. 12–5; closed Tues.*

## LE ROY

### LE ROY HOUSE, 1817
**22 E Main St**
Two-story brick house begun by Judge Egbert Hubbard, relative and land agent for Herman Le Roy (for whom the town was named), as his residence and land office; additions built from 1819 to 1823 by descendant Jacob Le Roy. Since 1941 headquarters and museum of historical society
*Operated by Le Roy Historical Soc. Open July–Aug: Sun. 2–5, and by appointment*

## LITTLE FALLS

### GEN. HERKIMER HOUSE, 1764
**Town of Danube**
Two-story brick home of Revolutionary War hero Gen. Nicholas Herkimer;

*Gen. Herkimer House*

now situated in a 135-acre park over-looking the Mohawk River. This German Palatinate family was influential in pioneering the development of upper New York State. Colonial furnishings include some Chippendale pieces owned by the general.
*Operated by N.Y.S. Historic Trust. Open Mon.-Sat. 9-5, Sun. 1-5*

## LOCKPORT

### COL. BOND HOUSE, 1824-25
**143 Ontario St**
Classical revival brick house with kitchen wing built by New Hampshire land speculator Col. William Moulton Bond. Restored and furnished with Empire pieces
*Operated by Niagara Co. Historical Soc. Open by appointment*

### OUTWATER-SCOTT HOUSE, 1860
**215 Niagara St**
Two-story red brick house built by Dr. Samuel Outwater; furnished with period pieces. Now headquarters of the historical society with exhibits of Indian relics, pioneer artifacts, and other items of local history. Adjacent to the house is the 1835 law office of Washington Hunt, governor of New York from 1851 to 1853.
*Operated by Niagara Co. Historical Soc. Open Tues.-Fri. 10-5, Sat., Sun. 1-5*

## LYONS

### WAYNE COUNTY HISTORICAL SOC. MUSEUM, 1854
**21 Butternut St**
Built as a residence for the sheriff, with an adjacent office and 24 stone jail cells. In use until 1961, the house, jail, and a barn are part of a museum of local history.
*Operated by Wayne Co. Historical Soc. Open Mon.-Fri. 2-4; closed national holidays*

## MONROE

### OLD MUSEUM VILLAGE OF SMITH'S CLOVE
**Route 17**
Founded by Roscoe W. Smith in 1950 as a setting for his vast collection of early Americana; now 36 buildings, some original, others reconstructed, showing life in a 19th-century rural community. Exhibits emphasize tools and machinery with demonstrations of such trades as spinning and weaving.
*Operated by Old Museum Village of Smith's Clove. Open Apr. 15-June 14: daily 10-5. June 15-Oct: daily 10-6*

## MOUNT McGREGOR

### GRANT'S COTTAGE, before 1885
Gen. Ulysses S. Grant came to this frame cottage at the summit of Mt. McGregor in the Adirondacks in June, 1885, hoping that the air would help his throat condition and allow him to complete his memoirs; he died on July 23, exactly one week after he finished. The furnishings and a few of the ex-President's personal belongings are shown as they were that summer.
*Operated by N.Y.S. Historic Trust. Open Tues.-Sat. 9-5, Sun. 12-5*

## NEWBURGH

### CRAWFORD HOUSE, 1829-31
**189 Montgomery St**
Home of David Crawford, merchant and War of 1812 captain. 40-foot Ionic columns, Palladian windows, and second-floor balconies give house southern quality. Interiors have black marble fireplaces and unusual dolphin newel post of solid mahogany; furnished with period pieces
*Operated by The Historical Soc. of Newburgh Bay and the Highlands. Open Tues., Wed., Thurs. 2-4*

### ■ WASHINGTON'S HEAD-QUARTERS (JONATHAN HAS-BROUCK HOUSE), 1750
**Liberty and Washington Streets**
Fieldstone farmhouse with sharply pitched roof of hand-riven shingles served as Washington's headquarters

*Washington's Headquarters*

from Apr. 1, 1782, to end of the war. Here he refused to proclaim himself king and established the "Order of the Purple Heart." In 1850 this house became first historic site to be preserved by a state; furnished with period furnishings from local families *Operated by N.Y.S. Historic Trust. Open daily 9–5, Sun. 1–5*

## NEW PALTZ

### ■ HUGUENOT STREET HISTORIC DISTRICT

Rare grouping of five stone dwellings on what is said to be "oldest street in America with its original houses." Restored to the period of 1678 to 1720 when the core of each was built. *Jean Hasbrouck House*, with museum of New Paltz history, is only one open to the public year round. *Operated by The Huguenot Historical Soc. Open May 15–Oct. 15: Tues.– Sun. 10–4*

*Jean Hasbrouck House*

## NEW ROCHELLE

### THOMAS PAINE COTTAGE, about 1800
#### Paine and North Avenues

Two-story frame house with shingle exterior and stone foundation; home of Thomas Paine, author of *Common Sense*. Congress gave Paine a confiscated Loyalist farm after the Revolution. The nearby Paine Memorial Building was built in 1925 and contains many of his personal effects. The historical society is in the cottage. *Operated by Huguenot and Historical Assn. of New Rochelle. Open Tues.– Sun. 2–5*

## NEW YORK CITY, BRONX

### BARTOW-PELL MANSION, about 1842
#### Pelham Bay Park and Shore Road

Greek Revival stone mansion built for Richard Bartow, a descendant of the Pell family, Lords of the Manor of Pelham, on the site of a 1675 house destroyed during the Revolution and another house built in 1790. The present mansion, restored in 1914, is furnished with period pieces. The extensive grounds were landscaped by the International Garden Club. *Operated by International Garden Club. Open Tues., Fri., Sun. 1–5*

### POE COTTAGE, about 1812
#### Poe Park at Grand Concourse and Kingsbridge Road

Edgar Allan Poe moved to this tiny one-and-a-half-story frame farmhouse in 1846, hoping that the country air would improve his wife's health, but she died of tuberculosis the first winter. Many early editions of Poe's works and some of his mementos are now in the cottage. *Operated by N.Y.C. Dept. of Parks. Open Tues.–Sat. 10–1, 2–5, Sun. 1–5*

### VALENTINE-VARIAN HOUSE, 1758
#### East 208 Street and Bainbridge Avenue

Country farmhouse built of fieldstone by Isaac Valentine was captured by the Hessians in 1776 and used as their headquarters. The house later became the home of Isaac Varian, mayor of New York City from 1839 to 1841. It was moved to the present location in 1965 and is now the Museum of Bronx History. *Operated by Bronx Co. Historical Soc. Open Sun. 1–5*

### ■ VAN CORTLANDT MANSION, 1748
#### Van Cortlandt Park at 242 Street and Broadway

This Georgian manor house is a rare example of grand-scale colonial architecture in New York City. Two-and-a-half-story fieldstone mansion has unusual carved masks over the brick-trimmed windows on the façade. Built by Frederick Van Cortlandt, it was given to the city by his heirs in 1889 and contains fine furnishings and china. The once prosperous farm is

now a large public park.
*Operated by Soc. of Colonial Dames.*
*Open Tues.–Sat. 10–5, Sun. 2–5*

*Van Cortlandt Mansion*

## WAVE HILL HOUSE, 1820–30
### 675 W 252 St
A 20-acre estate overlooking the Hudson River, with center section in the Federal style and wings added in 19th and 20th centuries. Conservationist George Perkins owned the house from 1903 to 1932, and at other times it has been the residence of Mark Twain, Theodore Roosevelt, and Arturo Toscanini. It is now owned by a foundation devoted to arts and sciences; only gardens are open.
*Operated by Wave Hill. Open Thurs.– Sun. 10–4*

## NEW YORK CITY, BROOKLYN
### ■ BROOKLYN HEIGHTS HISTORIC DISTRICT
Across the East River from Manhattan, area first developed as a residential community in the early 19th century with many excellent buildings by outstanding architects. In 1950s many houses were restored, and the neighborhood today retains much of the look and charm of pre-Civil War days.

### COBBLE HILL HISTORIC DISTRICT
Residential area south of Brooklyn Heights, but never as elegant. Its development began in 1830s and continued for about a century with many styles of 19th-century architecture represented. Renamed Cobble Hill in 1959 in an effort to revitalize the area; many houses are being restored.

## LEFFERTS HOMESTEAD, between 1777 and 1783
### in Prospect Park
Country farmhouse built by Peter Lefferts on site of a 17th-century family homestead destroyed during the Battle of Flatbush in 1776. The attractive entrance with Federal door attributed to Pierre L'Enfant was a later addition. Moved to the present location in 1918; period furnishings
*Operated by N.Y.C. Dept. of Parks. Open Nov.–May: Wed., Fri., Sat., Sun. 1–5*

## NEW YORK CITY, MANHATTAN
### ABIGAIL ADAMS SMITH HOUSE, 1799
### 421 E 61 St
Plain, two-story, ashlar stone building which was originally the stable and only completed building on estate of John Adams' son-in-law, Col. William Smith, who supposedly gambled the property away. Restored in 1924 as the clubhouse of the Colonial Dames
*Operated by Colonial Dames of America. Open Mon.–Fri. 10–4*

### ■ DYCKMAN HOUSE, 1783
### 204 Street and Broadway
Only remaining 18th-century farmhouse in Manhattan; it was built by William Dyckman on site of a 1784 house destroyed in the Revolution. "Flemish colonial" style with gambrel roof, covered porches, brick-and-fieldstone lower walls, and typical garden. Family furnishings
*Operated by N.Y.C. Dept. of Parks. Open Tues.–Sun. 11–5*

### FRAUNCES TAVERN, 1719; 1907
### 54 Pearl St
Originally built as a residence for Etienne de Lancey and converted to a tavern by Samuel Fraunces in 1763. Gen. Washington delivered his famous farewell address to his officers here in 1783. The building was completely rebuilt in 1907 and is now a restaurant and museum of the Revolution.
*Operated by Sons of the Revolution. Open Mon.–Fri. 10–4*

### FRICK RESIDENCE, 1914
### 1 E 70 St
Renaissance Revival mansion built by

Carrère and Hastings for steel magnate Henry Clay Frick. Renovated by John Russell Pope in 1935 as a museum for Frick's extensive art collection
*Operated by The Frick Collection. Open Tues.–Sat. 10–6, Sun. 1–6*

## GRAMERCY PARK HISTORIC DISTRICT

First developed in 1831 by Samuel B. Ruggles, this is an early example of town planning. The gate-enclosed park is reserved for residents of surrounding houses. The area has many fine 19th-century town houses and still retains much of its original charm.

## GREENWICH VILLAGE HISTORIC DISTRICT

65 blocks with numerous Georgian, Federal, Greek Revival, and later Victorian-style houses; most still private residences; some commercial establishments

## ■ HAMILTON GRANGE, 1801–2
### 287 Convent Ave

Built by John McComb, Jr., for Alexander Hamilton, who lived here until his death in 1804. Gracious Federal-style country house was moved from its original site about 1889 and abandoned. The house is now in the process of being restored; some rooms have been refurnished.
*Operated by National Park Service. Open daily 9–4:30*

## HENDERSON PLACE HISTORIC DISTRICT
### off East 86 Street between York and East End Avenues

One block of 24 tiny town houses built in 1880s by Lamb & Rich in Queen Anne style. Intended for people "of modest means"; these are still private residences.

## HENRY VILLARD HOUSES, 1882–85
### 50 and 51 Streets on Madison Avenue

Outstanding complex of Italian Renaissance-style brownstone mansions designed after a 16th-century palace in a U-shape around a central courtyard. Architects McKim, Mead and White built the major part of the "House of Mansions" for financier Henry Villard; two side sections were added in 1886 and 1909. Part of the complex is now headquarters for the Roman Catholic

Archdiocese of New York; these offices open Mon.–Fri. 9–5, Sat. 9–1

## ■ MORRIS-JUMEL MANSION, 1765; 1810
### 160 Street and Edgecomb Avenue

Summer home of Loyalist Roger Morris and Washington's headquarters during the Battle of Harlem Heights in 1776. Stephen Jumel saved the house from ruin when he bought it in 1810 and had it restored in the Federal style then popular. In 1903, and again in 1945, the house was renovated as a museum; period furnishings
*Operated by N.Y.C. Dept. of Parks. Open Tues.–Sun. 11–4:30*

*Morris-Jumel Mansion*

## ST. MARK'S HISTORIC DISTRICT
### 11 and Stuyvesant Streets between Second and Third Avenues

This land was once Peter Stuyvesant's farm. The area contains some of Manhattan's oldest Federal houses (*Stuyvesant-Fish House*, 1803–4) and is best known for St. Mark's-in-the-Bouwerie (1799 Georgian-style church), built on the site of Stuyvesant's garden chapel. Stuyvesant is buried beneath the church.

## ST. NICHOLAS HISTORIC DISTRICT
### 138 and 139 Streets between Seventh and Eighth Avenues

One of the finest examples of 19th-century urban development, this complex is made up of four rows of houses (158 individual buildings) commissioned in 1891 by builder David H. King, Jr., and designed by New York City's leading architectural firms, including McKim, Mead and White. The buildings have small front yards, rear entryways enclosed by wrought-iron fences, and have been popularly dubbed Striver's Row.

## SAMUEL TILDEN HOUSE [NATIONAL ARTS CLUB], 1874
**15 Gramercy Park, S**
Built by Calvert Vaux for Samuel Tilden the year of his election as New York's governor. Because of the violent political climate growing out of the 1876 Presidential election, Tilden built steel doors behind the windows and an escape tunnel to the street. *Operated by National Arts Club. Open for special exhibits*

## ■ SEABURY TREDWELL HOUSE (OLD MERCHANT'S HOUSE), 1832
**29 E 4 St**
Representative of the transition between the Federal and Greek Revival styles, this house was built as one of a row of fashionable town houses. It was owned and occupied by the Tredwell family from 1835 to 1933 and has been preserved intact with the family furnishings *Operated by Historic Landmarks Soc. Open Tues.–Sun. 2, 3, 4; closed Aug.*

## SNIFFEN COURT HISTORIC DISTRICT
**36 Street between Lexington and Third Avenues**
Romanesque Revival carriage houses on a mews built from about 1850 to 1860; converted to town houses in 1920s and still private residences

## ■ THEODORE ROOSEVELT BIRTHPLACE, 1848
**28 E 20 St**
In 1858 T.R. was born in the house that originally stood here. This exact replica was built by architect Theodate Pope in 1922. Five rooms have been restored with their original furniture; a museum contains T.R. memorabilia. *Operated by National Park Service. Open Mon.–Fri. 9–4:30*

## TREADWELL FARMS HISTORIC DISTRICT
**61 and 62 Streets between Second and Third Avenues**
District comprises houses built between 1868 and 1876 on Adam Tredwell's farm. First owners of plots signed a covenant in 1868 specifying height, width, and construction of buildings, and those businesses deemed undesirable. Houses still retain a uniformity; most are three or four stories and in the style of Second French Empire, although façades of many have been altered.

## TURTLE BAY HISTORIC DISTRICT
**226–247 E 49 St**
Two rows of ten back-to-back houses built in 1860s. Assembled by Mrs. Walton Martin and remodeled by Clarence Davis, 1919 to 1920; they are connected by a path and garden.

## NEW YORK CITY, QUEENS

### BOWNE HOUSE, 1661
**37–01 Bowne St**
Home of John Bowne, a Quaker who was jailed by Peter Stuyvesant for refusing to renounce his religion. His subsequent trial and acquittal helped to establish the principle of religious freedom. Nine generations of the Bowne family occupied this two-story frame house, which is now maintained as a shrine; some original furnishings *Operated by Bowne House Historical Soc. Open Tues., Sat., Sun. 2:30–4:15*

*Bowne House*

### KING MANSION, 1730
**150 Street and Jamaica Avenue**
The home after 1805 of Rufus King, delegate to the Constitutional Convention, U.S. senator, and minister to Great Britain, and his son John Alsop King, governor of New York from 1857 to 1859. The original house was expanded in 1750s and again, after King purchased it, in 1806. The 17-room mansion remained in the King family until 1896. It is now a museum. *Operated by King Manor Assn. Open Mon., Wed. 1:30–4; closed August*

## NEW YORK CITY, STATEN ISLAND

### BILLIOU STILLWELL-PERINE HOUSE, 1662
**1476 Richmond Rd**

The only remaining house on Staten Island built during New Netherland period. The oldest section, the stone house with steeply pitched roof and huge fireplace, was built in 1662 by Pierre Billiou, a French Walloon settler. The center section was added by Thomas Stillwell in the 1670s; other additions built by the Perine family in 1760, 1790, and 1830.
*Operated by Staten Island Historical Soc. Open Apr.–Oct: Sat., Sun. 2–5*

### ■ CONFERENCE HOUSE (BILLOPP HOUSE), 1680
**Hylan Boulevard**

Built by Capt. Christopher Billopp, this imposing manor house was the scene of an abortive peace conference to end the Revolution. Held on Sept. 11, 1776, the conference included Benjamin Franklin, John Adams, Edward Rutledge, and Lord Richard Howe, Admiral of the British fleet. The two-and-a-half-story stone house, built between 1680 and 1688, was restored with colonial furnishings in 1929 and is now a museum.
*Operated by Conference House Assn. Open Apr.–Oct: Tues.–Sun. 10–5. Nov.–Mar: Tues.–Sun. 10–4*

### GARIBALDI AND MEUCCI MEMORIAL MUSEUM, about 1845
**420 Tompkins Ave**

One-and-a-half-story clapboard house was the home of Giuseppe Garibaldi, Italian patriot, and Antonio Meucci, supposed inventor of the telephone, from 1851 to 1853. First dedicated as a memorial in 1907 and rededicated in 1956 as a museum with Garibaldi's artifacts and models of Meucci's first telephones
*Operated by Sons of Italy in America. Open Tues.–Fri. 10–5, Sat., Sun. 1–5*

### RICHMONDTOWN RESTORATION
**south end of Richmond Road**

Originally called Coccleston by the Dutch, Richmondtown was the county seat until 1898 when Staten Island was incorporated into New York City. Restoration began in 1939 with the ■ *Voorlezer's House*, built before 1695

and believed to be the oldest extant schoolhouse in U.S. When completed, restoration will include 36 buildings (some moved from other sites on Staten Island) and will show the evolution of an American village since the 17th century. Included is a museum housed in the 1848 "Old County Clerk's and Surrogate's Office."
*Operated by Staten Island Historical Soc. Museum open Tues.–Sat. 10–5, Sun. 2–5*

## NORTH TARRYTOWN

### ■ PHILIPSBURG MANOR ("UPPER MILLS"), 1680s; 1720
**Route 9**

Built by Frederick Philipse, once Peter Stuyvesant's carpenter and, 20 years later, owner of 90,000-acre estate, for which "Upper Mills," with its stone house, dam, and gristmill, served as the northern headquarters. Original house doubled in size by Frederick Philipse II in 1720. The present restoration shows the manor house and outbuildings as they were 1720–50.
*Operated by Sleepy Hollow Restorations. Open Apr.–Nov. 15: daily 10–5. Nov. 16–Mar: Mon.–Fri. 12–4, Sat., Sun. 10–5; closed Thanksgiving, Christmas, and New Year's Day*

*Philipsburg Manor*

## NORTH WHITE PLAINS

### MILLER HOUSE [WASHINGTON'S HEADQUARTERS], about 1730
**Virginia Road**

Small frame farmhouse with a wide

porch built by Elijah Miller and used by Washington during the Battle of White Plains, 1776. Most of the furnishings are original to the house and were used by Washington.
*Operated by Daughters of the American Revolution and Westchester Co. Open Feb. 22–Nov: Wed.–Fri. 10–4, Sat., Sun. 1–4, Tues. by appointment*

## OGDENSBURG

### FREDERIC REMINGTON ART MEMORIAL MUSEUM, 1809–10
**303 Washington St**
Built by the Parish family and since 1923 a memorial museum to Remington, who grew up in Ogdensburg. On display are his studio collection of paintings and bronzes, his library, and other personal effects. The museum also houses other fine antique collections, as well as period furnishings of the original owners.
*Operated by City of Ogdensburg. Open June–Sept: Mon.–Sat. 10–5, Sun. 1–5. Oct.–May: Mon.–Sat. 10–5*

## OLD WESTBURY, L.I.

### OLD WESTBURY GARDENS, 1906
**Westbury Road**
Designed by London architect George Crawley for sportsman-financier John S. Phipps in the style of an 18th-century English manor, with several formal gardens, lakes, pools, and terraces providing spectacular views of the 70-acre estate. Additions built 1911 and 1924. Beautifully furnished, as it was during Phipps's occupancy
*Operated by Old Westbury Gardens. Open May–Oct: Wed.–Sun. 10–5*

## ORIENT, L.I.

### ORANGE WEBB HOUSE, about 1740
**Village Lane**
Constant Booth built this house as an inn near the town of Greenport and later sold it to Orange Webb. In 1810 new owners used 40 oxen to move the house a mile away. When the house was slated for demolition in 1955, Mr. and Mrs. Latham purchased it and had it moved five miles away by barge to its present site. Antique furnishings
*Operated by Mr. and Mrs. George Latham. Open July–Sept: Tues., Thurs., Sat., Sun. 2–5*

### VILLAGE HOUSE, about 1790
**Village Lane**
Built as an inn, this two-story building became a home in the 19th century. The restoration is now part of a four-building museum complex and is furnished in the Victorian style. Exhibits include Indian artifacts, colonial toys, and period costumes.
*Operated by Oysterponds Historical Soc. Open July–Sept: Tues., Thurs., Sat., Sun. 2–5*

## OYSTER BAY

### RAYNHAM HALL, 1738; 1851
**20 W Main St**
Built by Samuel Townsend, whose son Robert, known as Culper, Jr., played a large part in uncovering the Benedict Arnold-Major André conspiracy when this house was British headquarters on Long Island. A Victorian wing was added by Samuel's grandson in 1851. Furnishings combine 18th-century and Victorian pieces, including the bed Major André slept in. Colonial garden added during 1953 restoration
*Operated by Town of Oyster Bay. Open daily 10–12, 1–5, Sun. 1–5; closed Tues.*

### ■ SAGAMORE HILL, 1884–85
**Cove Neck Road**
Designed by Lamb & Rich for Theodore Roosevelt, this frame-and-brick, 22-room informal Victorian mansion served as the summer White House from 1901 to 1909. The North Room, added in 1905, houses T.R.'s vast collection of hunting trophies and other memorabilia. Furnishings throughout are the original family pieces.
*Operated by National Park Service. Open daily 9–5; closed Christmas, New Year's Day*

*Sagamore Hill*

## PALMYRA

### JOSEPH SMITH HOUSE, 1822–23
**Stafford Road**
Frame, clapboard farmhouse; the boy-hood home of Joseph Smith, founder of the Mormon Church. Here Smith had the miraculous vision that led to the publishing of the *Book of Mormon* in 1830 and the establishment of the Church. Furnished with period pieces *Operated by Church of Jesus Christ of Latter-day Saints. Open daily 8–6*

## PENN YAN

### OLIVER MANSION, 1852
**200 Main St**
Two-story, pre-Civil War brick house occupied by three generations of the Oliver family, all practicing physicians. Now a historical society museum shown with furniture, costumes, Indian artifacts, and other exhibits *Operated by Yates Co. Genealogical and Historical Soc. Open Sept.–June: Thurs. 2–4. July, Aug: Tues., Thurs.2–4*

## PLATTSBURGH

### KENT-DE LORD HOUSE, 1797
**17 Cumberland Ave**
Two-story house with end chimneys and pedimented entrance portico; purchased and remodeled by French refugee Henry De Lord in 1810. Briefly occupied by British forces during the War of 1812. House museum with De Lord family collections *Operated by William H. Miner Foundation and Trustees. Open Mon.–Sat., tours at 10, 2, 4; closed Dec. 20–Jan. 20*

## PORT CHESTER

### BUSH HOMESTEAD, about 1750
**479 King St, John Lyon Park**
Georgian home of sea captain Abraham Bush; from 1777 to 1778 headquarters of Gen. Israel Putnam. Furnishings include the general's bed and desk. *Operated by Port Chester Park Comm. Open Thurs. 1:30–4:30*

## POUGHKEEPSIE

### CLINTON HOUSE, about 1765
**549 Main St**
Modeled after the manor houses of the wealthy, a two-story, central-hall, fieldstone home believed to have been built for Richard Everett and his father, Clear Everett. The house was associated with Gov. George Clinton during the years that Poughkeepsie served as the state capital. Furnished with a mingling of Dutch and English styles *Operated by N.Y.S. Historic Trust. Open daily 9–5*

### GLEBE HOUSE, 1767
**635 Main St**
One-and-a-half-story brick house built by the local Episcopal congregations for their first permanent minister, John Beardsley. Occupied by American officers during the Revolution and sold by the Church in 1792; remained in private hands until 1929. Restored with furnishings from the time of the first Dutch settlement to 1825 *Operated by Dutchess Co. Historical Soc. and the Junior League of Poughkeepsie. Open Mon., Tues., Thurs., Fri. 1–5*

## PURCHASE

### OPHIR HALL [REID HALL], about 1864
**Manhattanville College**
Frontier-bred Ben Holladay built his 84-room, six-story, granite palace with Norman Gothic chapel and coach house on a 900-acre estate; by 1876 he had lost his money and his palace. In 1887 it was sold to *New York Tribune* publisher Whitelaw Reid, but while the house was being modernized the following year it caught fire and burned down. Reid had the mansion rebuilt and in 1912 added a Jacobean library wing designed by McKim, Mead and White. Lush interiors include medieval stained-glass windows, marble fireplaces, sterling-silver and crystal fixtures, and allegorical

*Ophir Hall*

ceiling paintings. Since 1949 it has served as the administration building. *Operated by Manhattanville College. Open daily 9–4*

## RED HOOK

### MAIZEFIELD, 1797
**75 W Market St**
Federal-style home of David Van Ness, Revolutionary War captain, general of the state militia, and Presidential elector. Before 1900 a third floor and south wing were added, but the house retains its Federal lines. Furnishings range from 1700s to 1900s *Private. Open by written request*

## REMSEN

### STEUBEN MEMORIAL, about 1794
**Starr Hill Road**
This cabin is a replica of one constructed for Revolutionary War hero Baron von Steuben. Granted 16,000 acres of land for his services, Steuben died before his plans for clearing and farming the land were complete; his grave is marked by a simple monument. The replica cabin was built during the 1930s and contains some of Steuben's personal belongings. *Operated by N.Y.S. Historic Trust. Open Apr. 15–Oct. 15: Mon.–Sat. 9–5, Sun. 1–5; closed Easter*

## RENSSELAER

### ■ FORT CRAILO, about 1704
**Riverside Avenue**
Built by Hendrick Van Rensselaer on the site of a 1642 house, this fine brick manor house with red tile roof was once the center of the 800,000-acre Van Rensselaer estate. The outer walls

*Fort Crailo*

of the main building are 21 inches thick and have holes through which rifles could have been shot during an attack. Furnishings include period antiques; many Dutch, English, and family heirlooms
*Operated by N.Y.S. Historic Trust. Open Tues.–Sat. 9–5, Sun. 12–5*

## ROCHESTER

### CAMPBELL-WHITTLESEY HOUSE, 1835–36
**123 S Fitzhugh St**
Fine Greek Revival mansion, with four two-story Ionic columns, built during the heyday of Erie Canal for Benjamin Campbell, merchant and miller. Interior details reflect influence of Minard Lafever, who may have drawn plans for the house. Bought by Frederick Whittlesey in 1852 and kept in his family until 1937. Restored and furnished in Empire style with some fine stenciled pieces
*Operated by The Landmark Soc. of Western N.Y. Open Tues.–Sat. 10–5, Sun. 2–5*

### ELY HOUSE, 1837
**11 Livingston Park**
When flour milling was one of Rochester's leading industries, architect Hugh Hastings designed this stately Greek Revival mansion for wealthy miller Hervey Ely. Since 1920 it has been headquarters of the local Daughters of the American Revolution chapter; Revolutionary War relics *Operated by Irondequoit Daughters of the American Revolution. Open by appointment*

### ■ GEORGE EASTMAN HOUSE, 1905; 1919
**900 East Ave**
A two-story concrete residence designed by a local architect largely from photographs of other houses Eastman admired. Bequeathed in 1932 to University of Rochester, it was opened as a photographic museum in 1949 while still retaining the original Eastman furnishings. In 1954, on the centennial of his birth, the house where Eastman was born, a Greek Revival house built about 1830, was moved to the grounds from Waterville, New York.
*Operated by University of Rochester. Open daily 10–5*

## STONE-TOLAN HOUSE, begun 1789
**2370 East Ave**
This clapboard house, begun the year of Washington's election as President, is the oldest surviving dwelling in Monroe County. Built by Orringh Stone, a Massachusetts pioneer, the house served for many years as a tavern and inn. The Tolan family acquired the house in 1860; now under restoration
*Operated by The Landmark Soc. of Western N.Y. Open by appointment*

## ■ SUSAN B. ANTHONY HOUSE, about 1850
**17 Madison St**
Two-story brick home of the noted suffrage leader for the last 40 years of her life. Now maintained as a museum displaying much of Miss Anthony's furniture and artifacts, as well as the mementos of other suffragettes
*Operated by Susan B. Anthony Memorial. Open daily 11–4, Sun. 1–5; closed Wed.*

## WOODSIDE, 1838–40
**485 East Ave**
Built by architect Alfred Mason Badger in Greek Revival style for Silas O. Smith, who in 1813 built the first store in "Rochesterville." Brick mansion topped by a cupola with grille-covered frieze windows on third floor. Interior, dominated by spiral staircase rising into cupola, has remained largely unaltered. The most notable change is an 1890s smoking room paneled in wood and leather and decorated with art nouveau animals. Maintained as a museum with exhibits of furniture, weapons, costumes, etc.
*Operated by Rochester Historical Soc. Open Mon.–Fri. 10–4:30*

*Woodside*

## ROSLYN, L.I.

### VALENTINE HOUSE, about 1800
**1 Paper Mill Rd**
Original-shingle Federal house, with large Civil War-era addition, was owned by the Valentine family from 1801 to 1911. Ground floor rooms are open to the public and are furnished with pieces made in New York State during the years from 1770 to 1825. Upper floors serve as the Village Hall.
*Operated by Village of Roslyn. Open Mon.–Fri. 9–4, Sat., Sun. by appointment*

## ROXBURY

### ■ WOODCHUCK LODGE, early 1860s
John Burroughs' summer home for the last ten years of his life was built in the early 1860s on the Burroughs Homestead by his brother Curtis. It was remodeled for the naturalist writer in 1910 and was where he chose to be buried. Memorial Field, with his grave, was declared a New York State Historic Site in 1966. The Lodge, still occupied by a family member, contains the original John Burroughs furnishings plus other family heirlooms.
*Private. Open by appointment*

## RYE

### THE SQUARE HOUSE, about 1700
**Purchase Street and Boston Post Road**
Two-story house with hand-split shingles and wooden-peg beams was an inn on the Boston Post Road from 1760 to 1830; Washington, John Adams, and Lafayette were among the guests. For many years a home, and from 1905 to 1965 the village town hall. Restored and furnished with 18th-century pieces
*Operated by Rye Historical Soc. Open Mon.–Fri., Sun. 2:30–4:30*

## SACKETS HARBOR

### PICKERING-BEACH HOUSE, 1817
**503 W Main St**
Built by a local shipbuilder and later owned by Allen C. Beach, lieutenant governor of New York. House contains Pickering's original furniture.
*Operated by The Civic Improvement League of Sackets Harbor. Open summer: daily 10–5*

## SAG HARBOR, L.I.

### BENJAMIN HUNTTING HOUSE, 1845
**Main Street**
Wooden Greek Revival mansion designed by Minard Lafever for Benjamin Huntting, wealthy whale-boat owner. Since 1936 the whaling museum has occupied the first floor of the house. Museum exhibits include a fine collection of scrimshaw, harpoons, lamps, and an authentic whaler.
*Operated by Suffolk Co. Whaling Museum. Open May 15–Sept: Mon.–Sat. 10–5, Sun. 2–5*

## SAINT JOHNSVILLE

### FORT KLOCK RESTORATION, 1750
**Route 5**
Story-and-a-half, native limestone house built by Palatine immigrant Johannes Klock; fortification added during the Revolution by his son Col. Jacob Klock. Other buildings in the restoration include an Indian trading post and a wood house. Homestead furnished with colonial antiques
*Operated by Tryon Co. Muzzle Loaders and Fort Klock Historic Restoration. Open June–Sept: daily 9–5*

## SARANAC LAKE

### STEVENSON COTTAGE, before 1887
**Stevenson Lane**
Robert Louis Stevenson spent the winter of 1887 to 1888 in this simple clapboard cottage prior to his national speaking tour. He wrote a number of essays during the six-month stay, including *Christmas Sermon* and *The Lantern Bearers;* cottage is maintained as a literary shrine.
*Operated by Village of Saranac Lake. Open June: Tues.–Sun. 9–12, 1–5. July, Aug: daily 9–12, 1–6*

## SAYVILLE, L.I.

### EDWARDS HOMESTEAD, about 1785
**Edwards Street and Collins Avenue**
Built one block away by Matthew Edwards on land owned by his father, John, one of the original settlers of the area. Moved to its present site by Matthew's son, the house contains Edwards family memorabilia and their furnishings, as well as those of other local families.
*Operated by Sayville Historical Soc. Open June–Sept: Wed., Sat. 2–5*

## SCARSDALE

### WAYSIDE COTTAGE, before 1729
**1039 Post Rd**
Small frame house with many early 18th-century architectural features; operated as an inn by the Varian family from 1761 to 1835. Saber cuts in the walls still remain from Revolutionary War fighting. Donated to the village in 1919 and used as headquarters by various women's organizations. Restoration begun in 1953; furnished with 18th-century pieces
*Operated by Junior League of Scarsdale. Open by appointment*

## SCHAGHTICOKE

### KNICKERBOCKER MANSION, before 1770
Brick, Georgian farmhouse stands at confluence of a river and creek in sparsely settled rural district. Begun in early 1700s, the mansion was completed in 1770 by Johannes Knickerbocker II, who fought in the battle at nearby Saratoga. Washington Irving was a frequent visitor to the house and is said to have written part of his *Knickerbocker History* here. Property remained in the Knickerbocker family for 239 years; family furnishings from those years on display
*Operated by Knickerbocker Historical Soc. Open May–Sept: daily 2–5. Oct.–Apr: by appointment*

## SCHENECTADY

### SCHENECTADY COUNTY HISTORICAL SOC. MUSEUM, about 1900
**32 Washington Ave**
Built in the 18th-century Georgian style, this two-and-a-half-story frame house was the former home of Jones Mumford Jackson. In 1920 it was acquired by the General Electric Co. as a women's club. Since 1958 it has served as the historical society's headquarters.
*Operated by Schenectady Co. Historical Soc. Open Mon.–Sat. 12:30–5:30, Sun. 1–5*

## SCHUYLERVILLE

### ■ GEN. PHILIP SCHUYLER HOUSE, 1777

Two-story frame house, with kitchen wing added later, was built by Gen. Philip Schuyler, November 1777, to replace "the handsome country house" retreating British had burned following their defeat at Saratoga that October. The 900-acre estate, used by the Schuylers mainly as a summer home (see Schuyler Mansion, Albany), was a farming and milling center; the first flax-spinning mill in the colonies was opened there in 1767. The general's grandson was forced to sell the house in 1839; it was transferred with 25 acres to the National Park Service in 1950. Period furnishings
*Operated by National Park Service and Old Saratoga Historical Assn. Open June 15–Labor Day: daily 10–5. Sept.–Oct: Sat., Sun. 10–5*

## SENECA FALLS

### BECKER HOUSE, 1823; 1850s; 1875
**55 Cayuga St**
Three-story Italianate villa, completed in 1875, was begun as a one-room frame dwelling in 1823 and converted into a two-story Federal-style brick house in the 1850s. This 22-room historical museum features cherry and oak interior woodwork and various exhibits, including toys, games, and fire engines.
*Operated by Seneca Falls Historical Soc. Open Mar.–Nov: Mon., Tues., Thurs., Fri. 1–4*

## SETAUKET, L.I.

### THOMPSON HOUSE, about 1700
**North Country Road**
Main part of this saltbox was built in

*Thompson House*

early 18th century, kitchen wing added later. Restoration is furnished with period pieces and items belonging to Thompson family, who occupied the house for 178 years. Pleasant colonial herb garden open in summer
*Operated by Soc. for the Preservation of Long Island Antiquities. Open May–Oct. 18: daily 1–5; closed Tues.*

## SHIRLEY, L.I.

### MANOR OF ST. GEORGE, before 1825
**Smith's Point**
Manorial estate of Col. William Tangier Smith granted by royal patent in 1693. The date of the oldest part of the house is unknown, the newer section was built in 1825. During the Revolution the manor was taken by the British, who built a fort there. The property remained in the Smith family until 1954 when the last descendant died. Now maintained as a 127-acre park and museum with unusual collection of family papers on display
*Operated by Estate of Eugenie A. T. Smith; George C. and Hugh S. Furman, trustees. Open May 15–Nov. 15: Tues.–Sun. 9–5*

## SMITHTOWN, L.I.

### CALEB SMITH HOUSE, about 1819
**Route 25A**
Early 19th-century farmhouse. Recently restored, with furnishings and artifacts relating to Smithtown; headquarters of the local historical society
*Operated by Smithtown Historical Soc. Open June–Oct. 15: Thurs., Sun. 2–5*

## SOUTHAMPTON, L.I.

### CAPTAIN ROGERS HOMESTEAD, 1843
**17 Meeting House Lane**
This old homestead, distinctive for the winding staircase leading to the widow's walk, now houses the Southampton Historical Museum with displays of Shinnecock and Montauk Indian relics and other antique collections. Also on the grounds are a one-room school, country store, and barns.
*Operated by Southampton Colonial Soc. Open June 12–Sept. 12: Tues.–Sat. 11–4:30, Sun. 1–4:30*

## THOMAS HALSEY HOUSE, 1648
**South Main Street**
A 17th-century saltbox, considered to be the oldest English-built frame house in New York State. Restored under the direction of Henry Francis duPont, with furnishings from the 17th and 18th centuries and surrounding herb gardens
*Operated by Southampton Colonial Soc. Open June 12–Sept. 12: Tues.–Sat. 11–4:30, Sun. 1–4:30*

## SOUTHOLD, L.I.

### SOUTHOLD HISTORICAL SOC. MUSEUM
**Main Street**
Four buildings – a barn, tool house, buttery, and house – make up this museum. "Turn of the Century House," built between 1899 and 1900, is furnished with Victorian pieces.
*Operated by Southold Historical Soc. Open June 15–Sept. 15: Tues., Thurs., Sun. 2–5*

## STAATSBURG

### OGDEN MILLS MUSEUM AND STATE PARK, 1832; 1895
The core of this 65-room mansion was built in 1832 by New York governor Morgan Lewis. In 1895 Stanford White remodeled the house for Lewis' great-granddaughter and her husband Ogden Mills. The house with its fine furnishings and extensive art collection and the 200-acre estate were deeded to the state by the family.
*Operated by Taconic State Park Comm. Open Apr. 15–Nov. 15: daily 10:30–4. Nov. 16–Apr. 14: Sat., Sun., national holidays 10:30–4; closed Dec. 15–Jan. 1*

## ■ STILLWATER

### JOHN NEILSON HOUSE, 1775
**Saratoga National Historic Park**
During the Battle of Saratoga in 1777, John Neilson's farmhouse served as headquarters for Gen. Enoch Poor and Gen. Benedict Arnold. The restored frame house, furnished with period antiques, is the only original building left from the time of battle. The Freeman Farm log cabin, scene of the heaviest fighting, is a reconstruction.

*Operated by National Park Service. Open summer: daily 9–5*

## TAPPAN

### ■ DE WINT HOUSE [WASHINGTON SHRINE], 1700
**20 Livingston St**
Early Dutch colonial stone-and-brick house with steeply pitched roof and very low ceilings, built by Daniel De Clark and sold to West Indian planter John De Wint in 1746. At various times during the Revolution, Washington had his headquarters in this house; here in 1780 he ordered the trial of spy Major André and in 1783 entertained Sir Guy Carleton, the defeated British commander. Furnished with appropriate pieces
*Operated by Grand Lodge of Masons. Open daily 10–4; closed Thanksgiving*

## TARRYTOWN

### ■ LYNDHURST, 1838; 1864
**635 S Broadway**
Outstanding example of Gothic Revival architecture, overlooking the Hudson River, designed by the celebrated 19th-century architect Alexander Jackson Davis for Gen. William Paulding and his son Philip. Built of marble and enlarged in the same style and with the same stone in 1864 for a new owner, George Merritt. Bought and partially refurnished in 1880 by the financier Jay Gould. Bequeathed in 1961 to the National Trust by Gould's daughter Anna, Duchess of Talleyrand-Périgord. House contains furnishings of the successive owners, including some furniture designed by Davis, and Gould's art collection.
*Operated by National Trust. Open daily 10–5; closed Christmas*

*Lyndhurst*

## ■ SUNNYSIDE, 1835–47
**off Route 9**

Washington Irving's "snuggery" on the Hudson, his home from 1835 to his death in 1859. Transformed by him from the original 17th-century farmhouse to a fairy-talelike Gothic Revival cottage with Dutch stepped gables topped by wrought-iron weather vanes and "Pagoda," a three-story tower of rooms. Beautifully restored with Irving memorabilia, including part of his vast library
*Operated by Sleepy Hollow Restorations. Open Apr.–Nov. 15: daily 10–5. Nov. 16–Mar: Mon.–Fri. 12–4, Sat., Sun. 10–5; closed Thanksgiving, Christmas, New Year's Day*

*Sunnyside*

## TROY

## ■ FIFTH AVENUE-FULTON STREET HISTORIC DISTRICT

Two blocks on the eastern edge of business district of Troy, which first became industrialized during the War of 1812 when one of the nation's largest arsenals was opened. In the 1820s many iron foundries began operating, and by the 1950s the city was a prominent industrial center.

## HART-CLUETT MANSION, 1827
**59 Second St**

Built by William Howard as a wedding present for his daughter and Troy industrialist Richard Hart and purchased by the Cluett family in 1892. The 28-room mansion is of neoclassical design; carriage house and gardens have been preserved intact. Furnishings are 19th-century antiques, many original to the house.

*Operated by Rensselaer County Historical Soc. Open Tues.–Sat. 10–4*

## UTICA
### FOUNTAIN ELMS, 1852
**318 Genesee St**

Built in the Italianate style from designs by Albany architect William L. Woolett, this villa was a wedding present to James and Elizabeth Williams from the bride's father, Alfred Munson. It was restored by the Institute in 1960 with fine furnishings in the Empire and Rococo Revival styles. Open as a museum, it is also the home of the Oneida Historical Soc. The Institute's fine art collection is displayed in a nearby museum designed by Philip Johnson in 1960.
*Operated by Munson-Williams-Proctor Inst. Open Mon.–Sat. 10–5, Sun. 1–5*

## VAILS GATE
### KNOX HEADQUARTERS, 1754
**Route 94**

Main section of colonial fieldstone house was built for John Ellison for about $150. Many American military leaders were housed here during Revolution, but it was most often headquarters of Gen. Henry Knox, chief of Continental Artillery and, later, first Secretary of War. Authentic furnishings and historic artifacts document Revolutionary era.
*Operated by N.Y.S. Historic Trust. Open daily 9–5, Sun. 1–5*

## WADING RIVER, L.I.
### WADING RIVER HISTORICAL SOC., about 1810
**North Country Road**

Early 19th-century frame farmhouse with a fully "dressed" attic; now local historical society headquarters. Varied antique collection, including costumes, crafts, and paintings
*Operated by Wading River Historical Soc. Open summer: Tues.–Sat. 10–4*

## WALDEN
### JAMES T. WALDEN HOUSE, about 1761
**North Montgomery Street**

Central chimney, six-room colonial stone house has the original hardware and Adam knocker on the double

Dutch front door and boasts three fireplaces on the first floor. The house was purchased by manufacturer James Treadwell Walden, for whom the village is named, in 1813. Completely restored and furnished with 18th-century and Empire pieces
*Operated by Historical Soc. of Walden and Wallkill Valley. Open by appointment*

## WARSAW

### GATES HOUSE, 1824
**15 Perry Ave**
Two-story frame house was built by a local carriage maker and purchased in 1843 by Seth M. Gates, abolitionist congressman who is said to have used his home as a "station" on the Underground Railroad. Renovated and repaired in 1930s, the house is now a museum of local history; furnishings from the Civil War era
*Operated by Warsaw Historical Soc. Open by appointment*

## WARWICK

### 1810 HOUSE
**80 Main St**
Small story-and-a-half frame house with herb garden in back. Furnishings from Queen Anne to Duncan Phyfe period, with examples of work of local cabinetmakers; collection of 19th-century guns and sports equipment
*Operated by Warwick Historical Soc. Open by appointment*

### OLD SHINGLE HOUSE, 1764
**Forester Avenue**
Well-preserved, 18th-century saltbox built by Daniel Burt. A small collection of Revolutionary War relics is shown.
*Operated by Warwick Historical Soc. Open May–Oct: Tues., Sat. 2–5*

## WATERFORD

### HUGH WHITE HOUSE, 1830
**2 Museum Lane**
A 24-room house, representative of the transition between the Federal and Greek Revival styles, built by architect Joshua Clark for Hugh White, whose brother was a principal engineer for the Erie Canal. Now a museum with changing exhibits; Empire

and Victorian furnishings
*Operated by Waterford Historical Museum and Cultural Center. Open Sat., Sun. 2–4*

## WATERLOO

### MEMORIAL DAY MUSEUM, 1850s
A 20-room Victorian mansion reputed to be the birthplace of Memorial Day in 1866. Some rooms furnished with mid-19th-century pieces, others being restored. Displays relate to the first Memorial Day and the Civil War.
*Operated by Waterloo Library and Historical Soc. Open Memorial Day–Sept: Tues.–Fri. 2–5*

## WATERTOWN

### EDWIN PADDOCK HOUSE, 1874
**228 Washington St**
Queen-Anne-style mansion stands on the site of two previous dwellings. The first, built about 1803, is the frame house now to the northwest of the mansion; it is still occupied and is believed to be the oldest frame dwelling in Watertown. A Georgian limestone mansion next occupied the site, but it was razed to make way for the present structure, which was willed to the county historical society in 1922. It now serves as a museum with exhibits of Indian culture and early Americana.
*Operated by Jefferson Co. Historical Soc. Open Tues.–Fri. 12–5, Sat. 10–5*

## WATKINS GLEN

### JOHN IRELAND MANOR HOUSE [YORKERS' YANKEE VILLAGE], 1833
**Old Irelandville**
Greek Revival manor house of merchant landowner John Ireland; now part of preservation Yorkers' Yankee Village, restored under guidance of Dr. and Mrs. Larry Freeman. Furnished with period antiques and displays of 19th-century Americana
*Operated by American Life Foundation. Open June–Aug: Tues.–Sun. 10–4*

## WEST BAY SHORE, L.I.

### SAGTIKOS MANOR, 1692; 1890s
**Route 27**
The oldest part of this house was built

by Stephanus Van Cortlandt with wings added in 1890s. The house has belonged to the Thompson family since 1758, when Jonathan Thompson bought it as a wedding gift for his son. Famous guests included Sir Henry Clinton, commander of British forces during the Revolution, and George Washington, who slept here during a 1790 Presidential tour.
*Operated by Sagtikos Manor Historical Soc. Open May 15–Oct: Wed., Sat., Sun. 1–4*

## WEST PARK

### ■ SLABSIDES, 1895–96

John Burroughs, naturalist writer, built this small cabin of bark-covered slabs as a rustic retreat. Burroughs himself helped clear the land and construct the tiny cottage and its furniture. President Theodore Roosevelt was among the many famous guests to visit the cabin, which has been left exactly as it was when the conservationist lived there.
*Operated by John Burroughs Memorial Assn. Open by appointment*

## YONKERS

### ■ PHILIPSE MANOR, about 1682; 1740s
**Warburton Avenue and Dock Street**
Center of vast holdings of Frederick Philipse (see Philipsburg Manor in North Tarrytown), who built this two-story manor house. His grandson Frederick II added the brick wing in the 1740s creating an elegant balance between Dutch and English architectural tastes. In 1860 the manor became the Yonkers Village Hall; Mrs. Eva Smith Cochran purchased the property in 1911 and had the house restored. The Cochran collection of early American portraits is displayed.
*Operated by N.Y.S. Historic Trust. Open daily 9–5*

## ALAMANCE

### ■ ALLEN HOUSE, about 1782
**Alamance Battleground**
Typical frontier log dwelling with shed porch and rear addition built by John Allen on land granted his father by the Earl of Granville. Moved from its original site; period furnishings
*Operated by N.C. Dept. of Archives and History. Open Tues.–Sat. 9–5, Sun. 1–5*

## ASHEVILLE

### ■ BILTMORE HOUSE, 1890–95
**U.S. Route 25**
Designed by Richard Morris Hunt for George Vanderbilt, this imposing mansion, reminiscent of French palatial chateaux, was built by artisans and craftsmen from all over the world. Now a museum of art, with collections of paintings, prints, sculpture, tapestries, carpets, and furniture; gardens designed by landscape architect Frederick Law Olmsted

*Operated by Mr. William A. V. Cecil. Open Feb.–Dec. 15: daily 9–5; closed Thanksgiving*

*Biltmore*

**THOMAS WOLFE MEMORIAL, late 1800s**
**48 Spruce St**
Boarding house in which the famous novelist lived as a child, the "Dixie-

land" of his *Look Homeward, Angel.*
Many of Wolfe's characters were based
on persons who stayed at the house.
Furnished as he knew it as a boy
*Operated by City of Asheville Park
and Recreation Dept. Open May–Oct:
Mon.–Sat. 10–12:30, 2–6, Sun. 2–6*

## BATH

### ■ BATH HISTORIC DISTRICT
The town of Bath, now a state historic
site, was settled around 1690. Once the
capital of the colony and home of five
governors, it is the oldest town in the
state. The parish of St. Thomas Episcopal Church, oldest standing church in
North Carolina and one of the oldest
in the U.S., was formed here in 1701.
*Operated by N.C. Dept. of Archives
and History. Open Tues.–Sat. 10–5,
Sun. 2–5; closed Thanksgiving and
Christmas*

### ■ BONNER HOUSE, about 1825
**North Carolina Route 92**
Fine old frame house belonging to the
Joseph Bonner family from 1830 until
late 1940s. Restored from 1958 to 1962;
furnishings of the period
*See Bath Historic District for hours*

### GLEBE HOUSE, about 1830
**corner of Main and Craven Streets**
Two-story frame dwelling, the home of
John F. Tomkins, founder of the state
fair and publisher of *Farmers' Journal;*
now used as a community library
*See Bath Historic District for hours*

### ■ PALMER-MARSH HOUSE, 1744
**North Carolina Route 92**
Early Georgian frame house noted for
its particularly large double chim-
neys. The home of Robert Palmer in
the 18th century, it was purchased by
Rhode Island sea captain Jonathan
Marsh in 1802. Period paneling and
furnishings; restored
*See Bath Historic District for hours*

## BEAUFORT

### JOSEPH BELL HOUSE, late 18th
**century**
**Turner Street**
Town house in the West Indian style,
with double front porches, typical of

Beaufort domestic architecture; built
by Joseph Bell, prominent plantation
owner, legislator, and sheriff. Restored, period furnishings
*Operated by Beaufort Historical Assn.
Open Tues.–Sun. 1–4:30*

## BLOWING ROCK

### FLAT TOP MANOR, 1900
**Moses H. Cone Memorial Park**
Mansion built by Moses H. Cone, the
"Denim King," on his nearly 4,000-
acre estate, the center of a lavish social
life until he died in 1908. The house
now serves as headquarters of the
Parkway Craft Center, which has
demonstrations and sells handmade
items of mountain craftsmen.
*Operated by Southern Highland
Handicraft Guild. Open May–Oct:
daily 10–5:30*

## CARTHAGE

### ■ PHILIP ALSTON HOUSE
### (HOUSE-IN-THE-HORSESHOE),
**about 1770**
**8–10 miles north of Carthage**
Imposing two-story frame house, its
style similar to that found on the
coastal lowlands. Scene of a battle
between the Whigs and Tories in
1781. It was the cotton plantation of
Gov. Benjamin Williams after 1798.
Interiors notable; excellent woodwork; carved mantel and cornices in
the "great room"
*Operated by Moore County Historical
Soc. Open daily by appointment*

*House-in-the-Horseshoe*

## CHARLOTTE

### ■ HEZEKIAH ALEXANDER HOUSE, 1774
**3420 Shamrock Drive**
Stone house, with two-foot-thick walls, built by one of the drafters and signers of the Mecklenburg Declaration of Independence in 1774. Hezekiah Alexander was a prime agitator for independence and, as a member of the Provincial Congress of North Carolina, helped to draft the first constitution of the state. A project is in effect to restore and furnish the house—and outbuildings—and make of it a public museum. *Operated by Hezekiah Alexander Foundation. Restoration in progress*

*Hezekiah Alexander House*

## CRESWELL

### ■ SOMERSET PLACE (JOSIAH COLLINS PLANTATION), about 1829
**Pettigrew State Park**
Built by Josiah Collins, III, an Englishman, this ante-bellum coastal plantation house is constructed of hand-hewn cypress. The interiors include woodwork and trim in the early Greek Revival style and fine period furnishings. State historic site
*Operated by N.C. Dept. of Conservation and Development. Open daily 9–5*

## DURHAM

### ■ BENNETT PLACE, between 1840 and 1865
**west of Durham**
Reconstructed farmhouse and kitchen, site of Gen. Joseph E. Johnston's surrender April 26, 1865, of remaining Confederate troops to Gen. W. T. Sherman, bringing an end to the Civil War
*Operated by N.C. Dept. of Archives and History. Open June–Aug: Tues.-Sat. 9–5, Sun. 1–5. Sept.–May: Sat. 9–5, Sun. 1–5*

### ■ WASHINGTON DUKE HOMESTEAD, 1852
**Duke Homestead Road**
Ancestral home of the Duke family, long associated with the tobacco industry, and site of their first factory. Furnishings include numerous family pictures and some original as well as donated items typical of the period from 1852 to 1874.
*Operated by Duke University Dept. of Operations. Open Apr.–Oct: Sun. 2:30–5:30 and by appointment*

## EDENTON

### BARKER HOUSE, about 1782
**South Broad Street**
Home of Thomas Barker, London agent for the colony. Mrs. Barker is said to have presided over the "Edenton Tea Party" in 1774, an act believed to be the earliest known instance of political activity by women in the colonies. Moved from its original site in 1952, the house is a museum and visitors' center for historic Edenton.
*Operated by Barker House Assn. Open Tues.–Sat. 10–4:30, Sun. 2–5; closed holidays*

### ■ CUPOLA HOUSE, about 1725; 1756–58
**408 S Broad St**
Unique Jacobean-style house in the South, with a bold second-story overhang supported by hewn brackets such as those found in medieval European and New England architecture. The octagonal cupola, an established feature in New England, was a recent import to the South. The drawing room and library interiors were completed by Francis Corbin in 1758, the date appearing on the gable finial. Collection of early local furniture, portraits, and china, as well as an archive of local documents
*Operated by Cupola House Library and Museum. Open Sat. 10–4:30, Sun. 2–5; closed holidays*

■ **IREDELL HOUSE, about 1760; 1821**
**East Church Street**
White-painted frame house, home of jurist James Iredell and later his son, James Iredell, Jr., governor of North Carolina from 1827 to 1828. Old iron collection; it has been provided with period furnishings.
*Operated by Daughters of the American Revolution. Open Tues.–Sat. 10–4:30, Sun. 2–5; closed holidays*

## FAYETTEVILLE

**HERITAGE SQUARE**
**225 Dick St**
A restoration project involving three structures of historical interest: *Sanford House*, about 1800: Georgian-style building with hand-carved rope trim. Interior ornamented with fine mantels, doorways, and moldings. *Baker-Haigh-Nimocks House*, about 1804: Called "the house with the spiral stair." It is a tradition that the staircase was built by New England sailors who wintered here. In any case, it is a good example of upper Cape Fear architecture. The entrance is crowned by a fan-lighted door, and the interior cornices and wainscoting are of interest. *Oval Ballroom*, about 1830: Unusual room of octagonal shape built by John Holliday for his daughter's wedding. The room features well-proportioned pilasters and elaborate plaster cornices.
*Operated by Fayetteville Woman's Club. Open by appointment*

## FREMONT

■ **CHARLES B. AYCOCK BIRTHPLACE, 1840**
**U.S. Route 117**
Weatherboard frame house, birthplace of North Carolina's "educational governor," who launched a crusade in 1902 to improve the state's educational facilities. An average of one schoolhouse a day was built over the following ten years. Now a state historic site which includes dwelling, farm buildings, restored 1870 school, and a visitors' center museum
*Operated by N.C. Dept. of Archives and History. Open Mon.–Fri. 8:30–5, Sat. 1–5, Sun. 2–5*

## GRANITE QUARRY

**MICHAEL BRAUN HOUSE (OLD STONE HOUSE), 1758–66**
**off U.S. Route 52**
Considered one of the finest examples of German architecture in the South, this austere stone house (3,000 tons of local stone was used in its construction) was built by Braun, a Rhinelander who migrated first to Philadelphia and then to Rowan County, North Carolina. A wooden kitchen with a massive fireplace is attached to the main building. Saved from being razed, the house has been restored, and the interiors are in the process of being furnished.
*Operated by Rowan Museum. Open Sat., Sun. 2–5*

## GREENSBORO

**BLANDWOOD (JOHN M. MOREHEAD HOUSE), 1825; 1840**
**411 W Washington St**
Early "Tuscan Villa," designed by Alexander J. Davis for John M. Morehead, progressive governor of North Carolina. Gen. Beauregard and his staff rested here in 1865 before joining Gen. Lee in Virginia. The house is being restored and furnished.
*Operated by John Motley Morehead Memorial Commission and Greensboro Preservation Soc. Open by appointment while under restoration*

*Blandwood*

**FRANCIS McNAIRY HOUSE, 1762**
**130 Summit Ave**
Log house, with a separate frame kitchen, restored to the period from 1762 to 1862. Used as a hospital after Battle of Guilford Courthouse in 1781. Andrew Jackson's residence for a short time while a young lawyer. Furnishings from Virginia, Pennsylvania, and North Carolina

Operated by Greensboro Historical Museum. Open Sat. 10–5, Sun. 2–5; closed New Year's Day, Easter, Thanksgiving, and Christmas

## HALIFAX

### CONSTITUTION HOUSE, about 1770
**U.S. Route 301**
Small, unassuming clapboard house in which the first constitution for the state was drafted by a nine-man committee appointed by the provincial congress in 1776. Restored and moved from its original location in 1920, with period furnishings, it is now a part of Halifax historic site.
*Operated by Historic Halifax Restoration Assn. Open Mon.–Fri. 8:30–5, Sat. 1–5, Sun. 2–5*

### ■ HALIFAX HISTORIC DISTRICT
Halifax, an early borough town, was settled about 1723. It was named in 1757 for the second Earl of Halifax, president of the British Board of Trade, which then administered colonial affairs. The state's first constitutional convention was held here.

### OWEN'S HOUSE, about 1760
**U.S. Route 301**
Restored and furnished pre-Revolutionary frame house with gabled ends and a gambrel roof pierced by shed dormer windows; once the home of George W. Owen, prominent merchant
*Operated by Historic Halifax Restoration Assn. Open Mon.–Fri. 8:30–5, Sat. 1–5, Sun. 2–5*

## HIGH POINT

### JOHN HALEY HOUSE, 1786
**1805 E Lexington Ave**
Quaker house built on a land grant from Richard Caswell, first governor of North Carolina. Interior restored to its original three-room plan and furnished with Piedmont, North Carolina, pieces of the period from 1780 to 1820
*Operated by High Point Historical Soc. Open Tues.–Sat. 10–4:30, Sun. 1–4:30*

## HILLSBOROUGH

### MOOREFIELDS, 1795
**Orange County, Route 2**
Country colonial-style house was the summer residence of U.S. Supreme Court Associate Justice Alfred Moore. Furnished with family heirlooms
*Operated by Edward T. Draper-Savage. Open by appointment*

## KERNERSVILLE

### KORNER'S FOLLY, 1878–80; 1900
**South Main Street**
Victorian mansion built by Jule Gilmer Korner, Sr. The house contains 22 rooms and 20 fireplaces, with no two rooms and no two doors in any room being the same size. The ceilings range in height from under six feet to 25 feet. Victorian furnishings
*Operated by Korner's Folly. Open Sun. 1–5 and by appointment*

*Korner's Folly*

## MARION

### ■ CARSON HOUSE, about 1810
**Highway 70, in Pleasant Gardens Community**
Built by Col. John Carson, Irish immigrant and pioneer, of walnut logs covered with white clapboard. It is restored, with space given for exhibits of memorabilia of the Carson family and appropriate furniture of early residents of the area.
*Operated by Carson Home Restoration and McDowell Co. Historical Soc. Open May: Sun. 2–5. June–Oct: Sat., Sun. 2–5, and by appointment*

## MURFREESBORO

### HISTORIC MURFREESBORO
Murfreesboro is located on the Meherrin River and has many old homes

dating from the late 18th and 19th centuries. A project is under way to restore as many of these old houses as possible, and several should be open in the near future. Contact the Murfreesboro Historical Assn.

## NEW BERN

### ATTMORE-OLIVER HOUSE, about 1791
**513 Broad St**
Built by Samuel Chapman, a lieutenant under Gen. Washington during the Revolutionary War, who became a leading merchant and clerk of the superior court of Craven County. The house combines 18th-century features with those of the early 19th, when the house was considerably enlarged and altered. Restored to the latter period and furnished with fine antiques
*Operated by New Bern Historical Soc. Open Tues.–Sun. 2:30–5*

### ■ JOHN WRIGHT STANLY HOUSE, 1780s
**307 George St**
Carefully restored frame house, attributed to the architect John Hawks. The style is more characteristic of Hudson River mansions than those of the Carolinas, with a roof topped by a balustrade of sheaf of wheat design that was copied from samples found in the attic. President Washington visited the house during his southern tour in 1791. The interiors are considered to be the finest of the period in the state, furnished with excellent American and some English antiques of the late 18th century. Part of the Tryon Palace complex
*Operated by Tryon Palace Commission. See opposite for hours*

### JONES-LIPMAN HOUSE, about 1808–9
**Pollock and Eden Streets**
Small frame structure, a Federal prison at one time; Emeline Pigott, Confederate spy, was imprisoned here during the Civil War. Restored and furnished with Victorian antiques by the Tryon Palace Commission, it is now used as a guesthouse and meeting place for the commission.
*Operated by Tryon Palace Commission. Open on special occasions*

### ■ STEVENSON HOUSE, about 1805
**611 Pollock St**
Outstanding example of early 19th-century architecture, a stately building in coastal Carolina style, topped by a widow's walk. Restored and furnished with fine Federal and Empire antiques; hand-carved woodwork. Part of the Tryon Palace complex

### TRYON PALACE, 1767–70; burned 1798
**George Street**
Elegantly furnished reconstruction of the magnificent colonial mansion designed for Gov. William Tryon by John Hawks, first English architect to remain in America. The first provincial congress met here in 1774, the first constitutional general assembly in 1777, and the first constitutional governor of North Carolina, Richard Caswell, was inaugurated here. Served as the statehouse and residence of the governor until the capital was moved to Raleigh in 1794
*Operated by Tryon Palace Commission. Complex open Tues.–Sat. 9–3, Sun. 1:30–4; closed New Year's Day, Thanksgiving, and Dec. 24–26*

*Tryon Palace*

## NEWTON GROVE

### ■ HARPER HOUSE, before 1865
**Bentonville Battlefield**

Two-story frame house around which the Battle of Bentonville was fought in 1865. It served as a hospital for both armies during the war. Restored, with the upper floor as bedrooms and the lower as the hospital may have appeared
*Operated by N.C. Dept. of Archives and History. Open Mon.–Fri. 9–5, Sat., Sun. 1–5*

## PINEVILLE

### JAMES K. POLK BIRTHPLACE
**U.S. Route 521**

Reconstructed two-room log cabin furnished in the period prior to 1806. Polk, eleventh President of U.S., was born in 1795 in the original structure.
*Operated by N.C. Dept. of Archives and History. Open Mon.–Fri. 9–5, Sat., Sun. 1–5*

## RALEIGH

### ANDREW JOHNSON BIRTHPLACE, about 1800
**Pullen Park**

Tiny, gambrel-roof frame house, birthplace of the 17th President of the U.S. Moved from its original site in 1937, it has been restored and furnished with period furniture and utensils.
*Operated by City of Raleigh. Open Sun.–Fri. 2–5; closed Thanksgiving and Christmas*

### ■ THE GOVERNOR'S MANSION, 1885–91
**200 N Blount St**

Designed by Gustavus A. Bauer with numerous gables, patterned roof, paneled chimneys, and lathe-turned

*Governor's Mansion*

porches, the mansion is considered one of the state's best examples of Victorian architecture. Convict labor was used to complete the construction. Extensively restored and redecorated in 1949; furnishings are of historic significance to the state
*Private. Open by appointment*

### ■ JOEL LANE HOUSE, about 1760
**729 W Hargett St**

This is the oldest house in the capital city, built by its earliest settler, who donated the land upon which the city is located. Extensively remodeled and refurnished in the style of its period
*Operated by Wake County Soc. of Colonial Dames of America. Open Mon.–Fri. 9–5*

## SALISBURY

### MAXWELL CHAMBERS HOUSE [ROWAN MUSEUM], 1819
**114 S Jackson St**

Built by Judge James Martin and later purchased by Chambers. Fine example of domestic architecture of the period in this region; many features reflect the classical trend of early 19th-century design. Several rooms have Federal-style furnishings; collection of relics of county's past
*Operated by Rowan Museum. Open June–Sept: Wed., Sat. 2–5, Sun. 2–5. Oct.–May: Tues.–Sat. 2–5, Sun. 2–4*

## SANFORD

### RAILROAD HOUSE, about 1872
**Hawkins Ave and Carthage St**

Quaint gingerbread building, believed to be the oldest house in Sanford, the home of the town's first mayor and first depot agent. Restored, with period furnishings and exhibits; steam locomotive and tender on grounds
*Operated by Railroad House Historical Assn. Open Mon.–Fri. 9–5, Sat. 9–12*

## SOUTHERN PINES

### SHAW HOUSE, before 1850

Typical house of Civil War or pre-Civil War period, probably the oldest house in Southern Pines. Built by a member of the prominent Shaw family
*Operated by Moore County Historical Soc. Open Feb.–Apr: daily 10–4*

## SOUTHPORT VICINITY

### ■ BRUNSWICK HISTORIC DISTRICT

Brunswick was founded about 1725 by settlers from South Carolina. Before the Revolution it was an important port as well as a center of political activity.

## TARBORO

### THE PENDER MUSEUM
**Phillip and St. Andrews Streets**

The museum is housed in a small, restored farmhouse built about 1810 and recently moved from its original location to its present site on the Blount property. A project is under way to restore the *Thomas Blount House,* also on the property, creating a typical plantation with its main house, dependencies, and garden.
*Operated by Edgecombe County Historical Soc. Open Sun. 2–5*

## VAUGHAN VICINITY

### ■ "BUCK SPRING" (NATHANIEL MACON HOUSE), 18th century
**off Highway 158**

Plantation complex operated from 1783 by Nathaniel Macon, a Jeffersonian figure of importance in the political development of the state and country during the late 18th and early 19th centuries. The present house is a single-space structure above a field-stone cellar.
*Operated by Warren County Historical Soc. Restoration in progress*

## WADESBORO

### BOGGAN-HAMMOND HOUSE, about 1783; 1839
**210 Wade St**

Small frame house built by Capt. Patrick Boggan, a Revolutionary War leader and donor of the land for the town of Wadesboro. It was a wedding gift for one of Boggan's seven daughters, Eleanor, when she married William Hammond. During restoration the later addition, built by Alexander Little, was separated from the small 18th-century structure. Both are furnished with period antiques, some belonging to the Boggan family.
*Operated by Anson County Historical Soc. Open Sun. and Wed. 3–5*

## WAGRAM

### JOHN CHARLES McNEILL HOUSE, probably 1850s
**Old Wire Road, 2 miles southeast of Wagram**

Restored farmhouse, birthplace of the poet McNeill. Furniture of the family, portrait of McNeill, and mementos exhibited
*Operated by Richmond Temperance and Literary Commission. Open Sun. 3:30–5:30 and by appointment; closed Jan. and Feb.*

## WEAVERVILLE

### VANCE BIRTHPLACE, 1795
**Route 1, Reems Creek Road**

Pine log house, 1830 birthplace of Zebulon Baird Vance, three-term governor of North Carolina. Considered a show place in its day, it was three times larger than the average cabin. It is now a state historic site, restored with period furnishings and memorabilia of Vance's life displayed.
*Operated by N.C. Dept. of Archives and History. Open Tues.–Sat. 9–5, Sun. 1–5*

*Vance Birthplace*

## WHITE OAK

### HARMONY HALL (COL. JAMES RICHARDSON HOUSE), before 1768

Simple, stately home of Col. Richardson, built on a 12,000-acre tract of land acquired, in part, by a grant from King George III. Exterior restored; interiors (under restoration) include wide pine paneling, chair rails, and Adam-style mantels.
*Operated by Bladen County Historical Soc. Open by appointment*

# NORTH CAROLINA

## WILMINGTON

### BURGWIN-WRIGHT HOUSE (CORNWALLIS HOUSE), 1771
**224 Market St**
Fine framed Georgian mansion with a large Palladian doorway, built by John Burgwin, treasurer of the Carolina colony. Lord Cornwallis, the British general, used the house as headquarters during the Revolution, keeping his prisoners in the dungeon below the massive stone foundation walls (which were originally the walls of the old jail). Judge Joshua Grainger Wright purchased the house from Burgwin in 1799. Now a museum of colonial furnishings; 18th-century gardens
*Operated by Colonial Dames of America. Open Mon.–Fri. 9–4*

### LATIMER HOUSE, 1852
**126 S Third St**
Actually a double house, with main living area in the front and servants' quarters in the rear, this excellent example of classic revival architecture was designed by R. B. Wood. It was the residence of Zebulon Latimer for many years. Period furnishings
*Operated by Cape Fear Historical Soc. Open by appointment*

### WILMINGTON HISTORIC AREA
Incorporated in 1739 and strategically located at the junction of two branches of Cape Fear River, the city prospered and at times was the largest port in the world for naval stores during the 18th and 19th centuries. The old residential part of the city has been designated a historic area by the city, and it includes many fine dwellings and public buildings dating from before the Revolution through the Victorian period.

## WINDSOR

### ■ HOPE PLANTATION, about 1800
**N.C. Route 308**
Birthplace of David Stone, governor of N. C. from 1808 to 1810. Considered one of the most impressive colonial buildings in the state. The paneled drawing room and library on the second floor are especially noteworthy.
*Operated by Historic Hope Foundation. Restoration in progress*

## WINSTON-SALEM

### JOHN VOGLER HOUSE, 1819
**700 S Main St**
Home and shop of Vogler, silversmith and clockmaker. Now restored and furnished with many original 19th-century furnishings made by local craftsmen. Part of Old Salem tour
*See Old Salem Historic District*

### ■ OLD SALEM HISTORIC DISTRICT
Well-preserved town founded in 1766 by immigrant Moravians from Bethlehem, Pennsylvania. Many original structures remain; seven are open to the public. Restoration includes homes, shops, taverns, and church. Also noteworthy is the Museum of Early Southern Decorative Arts.
*Operated by Old Salem. Tours: Mon.–Sat. 9:30–4:30, Sun. 1:30–4:30; closed Christmas*

*Old Salem houses*

### REYNOLDA HOUSE, completed 1917
**Reynolda Road**
Conceived as a self-sustaining model community by Mr. and Mrs. R.J. Reynolds, of the R.J. Reynolds Tobacco Co., the estate was, in effect, a 1,000-acre village and farm. The main house was designed by Charles B. Keen of Philadelphia. Furnishings eclectic; fine antiques added in 1935 when house was remodeled. Collection of American art, ranging in time from 1755 to present and including works by such famous artists as Copley, Stuart, Church, Eakins, and Wyeth, as well as first complete collection of Doughty Birds in a public institution. Gardens noted for weeping cherry trees that bloom in spring

*Operated by Reynolda House. Open Tues.–Sat. 9:30–4:30, Sun. 1:30–4:30; closed Jan.*

■ **SINGLE BROTHERS' HOUSE, 1768–69; 1786**
**600 S Main St**
Excellent example of German traditional half-timber-and-brick construction. Property of Moravian Church since first built. This exceptional restoration is part of the Old Salem tour. *See Old Salem Historic District*

## YADKINVILLE

**RICHMOND, about 1848**
**North Carolina Route 67**
Two-story brick residence of Richmond M. Pearson, chief justice of the North Carolina supreme court from 1858 to 1878. It was here he conducted his famous law school, which trained many of the state's lawyers and justices in the late 19th century. Restoration *Operated by Yadkin Co. Historical Soc. Hours to be determined*

*Single Brothers' House*

## ABERCROMBIE

**FORT ABERCROMBIE STATE HISTORIC PARK, 1858**
**off U.S. Highway 81**
Army post on the Red River of the North established by Lt. Col. John J. Abercrombie in 1858 to protect the northwestern frontier. It played a dramatic role during the Sioux uprising in Minnesota in 1862. An original guardhouse, three reconstructed blockhouses, and a pioneer-military museum may be visited.
*Operated by N. Dak. Park Service. Open June–Aug: daily 9–9. May, Sept.–Oct: daily 9–5*

## EPPING

**BUFFALO TRAILS MUSEUM**
A museum exhibiting such examples of the region's history as the interior of a homesteader's shack and a diorama of an Assiniboin Indian village *Operated by Buffalo Trails Museum. Open June–Aug: Mon.–Sat. 9–5, Sun. 1:30–5:30*

## FARGO

**THE FORSBERG HOUSE, 1905**
**815 Third Ave, S**
Victorian home of early Fargo pioneer Anna Marie Bergan (born in Norway) and her three children after the death of her Swedish husband, Peter Gustav Forsberg. Family members still live in the house, which they have made into a museum as a memorial to their parents. Four floors of rooms show a variety of American interiors – with furnishings dating from 1700 to 1850 – including a Victorian parlor, an early

217

kitchen, and a children's playroom. *Private. Open by appointment*

## JAMESTOWN VICINITY

### PIONEER VILLAGE
off U.S. Highway 281

A pioneer village re-creating homesteading days in the Dakota Territory in the 1880s, when the coming of the railroad opened the way for settlers. It features a log cabin, school, church, and a Northern Pacific railroad depot. *Operated by Pioneer Village. Open June–Labor Day: daily 8–8*

## MANDAN

### FORT ABRAHAM LINCOLN STATE PARK
Route 2, on Lewis and Clark Trail

At the confluence of the Missouri and Heart rivers is a 750-acre state park with sites of historic interest: Fort McKeen and Fort Abraham Lincoln, where Lt. Col. George Custer was stationed when he led his troops to destruction in the 1876 battle of the Little Big Horn. The Fort McKeen blockhouses and Mandan Indian lodge dwellings have been reconstructed on an ancient village site. There is also an Indian and military museum. *Operated by N. Dak. Park Service. Open May–Oct: daily 9–5*

## MEDORA

### CHATEAU DE MORES, 1883
U.S. Highway 10 and Interstate 94

Sprawling 26-room frame chateau built by Antoine de Vallombrosa, Marquis de Mores, who established the town of Medora (named for his wife) to be the center of his operations. He planned a giant meat-packing empire, and to this end he purchased cattle, built a packing plant and cold-storage facilities from Montana to Chicago, ran a stage line between Medora and the Black Hills; he even built a Catholic church for his wife. But the venture had only a short three-year life span because range-fed beef would not sell back East as well as corn-fed beef. A park, the packing plant ruins, and the chateau, with its French period furnishings, are a state historic site. *Operated by State Historical Soc. of N. Dak. Open daily 8–5*

### ■ MALTESE CROSS RANCH CABIN, 1883
Theodore Roosevelt National Memorial Park

Theodore Roosevelt first came to the Dakotas in 1883 to hunt big game; he became interested in ranching and purchased the Maltese Cross Ranch, seven miles south of Medora. The next year he established his Elkhorn Ranch, some 35 miles north, which he operated until 1887. His ranching experiences in this area made him aware of the necessity for conserving our natural resources. Roosevelt's first cabin from the Maltese Cross Ranch may be visited at the park's headquarters, just inside the Medora entrance. *Operated by National Park Service. Open summer: 8–8. Winter: 8–5*

*Maltese Cross Cabin*

### VON HOFFMAN HOUSE [MEDORA DOLL HOUSE], 1884

Six-room brick house originally built by the French nobleman Marquis de Mores for his in-laws Baron and Mrs. Von Hoffman. Later lived in by the poet laureate of North Dakota, James Foley, and afterwards a museum pertaining to early life in the western part of the Dakota Territory. Now displays antique and modern dolls from all over the world *Operated by Gold Seal Co. Open May–Sept: daily 9–8*

## WASHBURN

### JOSEPH HENRY TAYLOR CABIN, about 1869
U.S. Highway 83

Small unfurnished one-room log cabin built by Civil War veteran Joseph H. Taylor, who became a trader, trapper, author, and editor. Brought to Washburn and restored for the town's 50th anniversary, it is located in a city park and may be viewed from the exterior. *Operated by Washburn Park Board*

# AKRON

## JOHN BROWN HOME MUSEUM, before 1844
**514 Diagonal Rd**
Remodeled frame building, home of the abolitionist who was executed here for his raid at Harpers Ferry, West Virginia. Now a house museum
*Operated by Summit Co. Historical Soc. Open Tues.–Sun. 1–5*

## PERKINS MANSION, 1835–37
**550 Copley Rd**
Greek Revival-style stone mansion, the home of the son of Col. Simon Perkins, the city's founder and entrepreneur. Now serves as a museum
*Operated by Summit Co. Historical Soc. Open Tues.–Sun. 1–5; closed holidays*

## STAN HYWET HALL, 1911–15
**714 N Portage Path**
A 65-room Tudor revival mansion — with extensive hand-carved woodwork of oak, walnut, sandalwood, and chestnut — built by Frank A. Seiberling, founder of The Goodyear Tire & Rubber Company and Seiberling Tire and Rubber Company. Furnishings date from the 14th to the 20th century and include some designed especially for the building.
*Operated by Stan Hywet Hall Foundation. Open Tues.–Sat. 10–4:15, Sun. 1–5*

*Stan Hywet Hall*

# BATH

## JONATHAN HALE HOMESTEAD, 1825
**Oak Hill Road**
Federal-style brick house built by Jonathan Hale on land he purchased in 1810 and owned by the Hale family until the 1950s; many of the original furnishings of the home have been preserved. Construction of a Western Reserve village is under way near the Hale homestead. Original structures built in the Reserve have been moved to the area and restored. On display at present are a saltbox (1830) from Richfield, Ohio, and a Greek Revival house (1840) from Bath as well as a law office, log cabin, and a school.
*Operated by Western Reserve Historical Soc. Open May–Oct: Tues.–Sat. 10–5, Sun. 1–5*

# BRECKSVILLE

## SQUIRE RICH HOUSE, 1840–45
**9367 Brecksville Rd**
Western Reserve Federal-style farmhouse. Restored, with period furnishings and a collection of farm tools
*Operated by Brecksville Historical Soc. Open Sun. 2–5 and by appointment*

# BURTON

## PIONEER VILLAGE, mid-19th century
**14653 E Park St**
Restoration and reconstruction of a pioneer village of the Western Reserve with buildings moved here from their original sites. The *Eleazer Hickox House* (1838) is a museum with records and relics of the period displayed. The *Boughton House* (1834), built by George Boughton, is restored and furnished with typical Western Reserve period pieces. The *Law House* (1817), an example of New England architecture, built by expert craftsman Merritt Nettleton, is being restored and furnished with antiques. Also on the property are a church (1846), a barn (1856), a one-room country schoolhouse (1872), and a blacksmith shop, of about 130 years old.
*Operated by Geauga Co. Historical Soc. Open May–Oct: Tues.–Sat. 10–5, Sun. 1–5*

# CAMP DENNISON

## CHRISTIAN WALDSCHMIDT HOUSE, 1804
**7567 Glendale Milford Rd**
Pennsylvania Dutch-style stone house built by Christian Waldschmidt, who with several companions crossed the Alleghenies from Pennsylvania to found the town of New Germany.

During the period of the Civil War, New Germany became a training and induction center for Union troops and was renamed Camp Dennison. The house has been restored as a museum. *Operated by Daughters of the American Revolution. Open June–Aug: Tues.–Sun. 1–5. Apr.–May, Sept.–Oct: Sun. 1–5. Nov.–Mar: by appointment*

## CARROLLTON

### McCOOK HOUSE STATE MEMORIAL, about 1837
**Public Square**
Federal-style brick residence of Maj. Daniel McCook, whose family—including his nine sons, five nephews, and himself—became known as the "Fighting McCooks" as a result of their distinguished participation in the armed services prior to and during the Civil War. Interior partially furnished with period pieces
*Operated by Ohio Historical Soc. Open June–Sept: Wed.–Sun., holidays 10–5*

## CHILLICOTHE

### ADENA (THOMAS WORTHINGTON ESTATE), 1806–7
**Allen Avenue Extended**
One of Ohio's most important early houses, built by Thomas Worthington, sixth governor of the state. Benjamin Latrobe was the architect for this well-designed and excellently furnished home. Thomas Jefferson was also consulted by Worthington about his plans.
*Operated by Ohio Historical Soc. Open Apr.–Oct: Tues.–Sun. 9:30–4:30*

### SEN. ALLEN G. THURMAN HOUSE, 1838
**45 W Fifth St**
Home of A.G. Thurman, congressman, chief justice of Ohio's supreme court, and U.S. senator (1867–79); now operated as a museum, with collections of prehistoric artifacts, household furnishings, 19th- and 20th-century toys and costumes, and many items and books relating to regional history
*Operated by Ross Co. Historical Soc. Open Thurs.–Tues. 1–5; closed two weeks in Dec.*

## CINCINNATI

### JOHN HAUCK HOUSE, about 1870
**812 Dayton St**
Two-storied Renaissance revival town house with a brick front stuccoed to resemble a sandstone ashlar. Built by John Hauck, a prominent German brewer. Period furnishings
*Operated by Miami Purchase Assn. Open Thurs. 10–4*

### KEMPER LOG HOUSE, 1804
**985 Laurel Ave**
Log house built by the Rev. James Kemper, who with his family moved from Virginia to Kentucky and on to Cincinnati. Here the Kempers raised their large family of 15 boys and girls, all of whom reached maturity. The house was dismantled and moved to this location from Kemper Lane in 1913 and contains many of the family possessions and items in common use during its early period.
*Operated by Soc. of Colonial Dames Open May–Sept: daily 10–5*

### TAFT MUSEUM (SINTON-TAFT HOUSE), 1820
**316 Pike St**
Built by Martin Baum, an early citizen of Cincinnati, this is one of the finest classical revival houses in the Midwest. It was subsequently the home of Nicholas Longworth, Daniel Sinton, and Mr. and Mrs. Charles Phelps Taft. Now serves as a public museum, with paintings by such masters as Rembrandt, Turner, Goya, Gainsborough, and Corot. One of the most representative collections of Duncan Phyfe furniture may be seen here.
*Operated by Cincinnati Institute of Fine Arts. Open Mon.–Sat. 10–5, Sun., holidays 2–5; closed Thanksgiving and Christmas*

*Taft Museum*

# COSHOCTON

## ROSCOE VILLAGE
**RESTORATION, mid-19th century**
**334 Whitewoman St**
Two historic buildings relating to the 1800s canal period. The large red brick building was owned by John Burns and Joseph K. Johnson, prominent local businessmen. The smaller white building served as the office of Dr. Maro Johnson, Roscoe's leading physician. Both with period furnishings
*Operated by Montgomery Foundation. Open June–Aug: daily 11–6*

# DAYTON

## ■ DUNBAR HOUSE STATE MEMORIAL, about 1890
**219 N Summit St**
Two-story brick house in which Paul Laurence Dunbar, the first American Negro to attain eminence in the field of literature and poet laureate of his people, lived the last three years of his life. Maintained as a memorial, with its original furnishings and Dunbar's personal belongings
*Operated by Ohio Historical Soc. Open June–Sept: Wed.–Sun. 10–5*

*Dunbar House*

## RUBICON, 1816
**1815 Brown St**
Federal- or post-colonial-style farmhouse built by Col. Robert Patterson, proprietor of Lexington, Kentucky, and one of the original owners of the site of Cincinnati. He was one of Dayton's earliest settlers and purchased a 700-acre tract of land south of that city. Restored and furnished with period pieces, the house is now a cultural, civic, and educational center.
*Operated by City of Dayton. Open by appointment*

# FREMONT

## ■ RUTHERFORD B. HAYES STATE MEMORIAL (SPIEGEL GROVE), 1859–63; 1880; 1889
**1337 Hayes Ave**
Beautiful wooded estate of Rutherford B. Hayes, 19th President of the U.S. On the grounds are the Hayes home (which may be toured if arranged in advance in writing), his tomb, and the Hayes Library and Museum. In the museum are exhibits of the life and work of President Hayes and his wife and of America in his time.
*Operated by Ohio Historical Soc. Open Mon.–Sat. 9–5, Sun., holidays 1:30–5*

# GALLIPOLIS

## OUR HOUSE STATE MEMORIAL, 1819
**434 First Ave**
Red brick Federal-style structure built by Henry Cushing as a tavern. The Cushings were a prominent family in early Gallipolis, and their house was the center of the community's social life for many years. Restored and furnished as a house museum
*Operated by Ohio Historical Soc. Open Apr.–Oct: Tues.–Sun. 9:30–5*

# GENEVA-ON-THE-LAKE

## GREGORY MEMORIAL HOUSE, 1823–26
**Putnam and Grandview Drives**
First frame house on the lake shore, built by the family of Solomon Fitch. Now a museum with period rooms
*Operated by Ashtabula Co. Historical Soc. Open May 15–Nov: Thurs.–Sun. 1–5*

# GEORGETOWN

## ULYSSES S. GRANT BOYHOOD HOME, 1822–23; 1828
**219 E Grant Ave**
Two-story brick house built by Jesse

Root Grant, Ulysses S. Grant's father. The family lived here from 1823, when Ulysses was about 11 months old, until 1847. Grant was the first of eight Ohioans to become President. *Operated by Judge and Mrs. George T. Campbell, owners. Open daily 9–4 by appointment*

## GREENVILLE

### GARST HOUSE, 1852
205 N Broadway
Two-story red brick house built by George Coover as an inn for travelers when the Dayton and Miami railroad ran through Darke County. The Garst family owned the house from 1861 until 1946. Now a historical museum, with period furnishings, Indian relics, handicrafts of early Darke County pioneers, and mementos of Annie Oakley and Frank Butler, who are buried in Greenville
*Operated by Darke Co. Historical Soc. Open Sun., Tues., Fri. 1–5*

## HUDSON

### BALDWIN-BABCOCK HOUSE, about 1833
49 E Main St
Birthplace of Caroline Baldwin Babcock, founder of the Hudson Library and Historical Soc. in 1910. This simple Greek Revival house is thought to have been built by the carpenters who built the Western Reserve College buildings. Restored in 1925, with an early Victorian parlor
*Operated by Hudson Library and Historical Soc. Open Mon., Tues., Thurs.–Sat. 10–5*

### DAVID HUDSON HOUSE, 1806
318 N Main St
Built in the manner of an 18th-century Connecticut farmhouse by David Hudson, who arrived in 1799 with a party of settlers to establish the town of Hudson, the first settlement in Summit County. Private residence
*Operated by Western Reserve Academy. Open by appointment*

## LAKEWOOD

### OLDEST STONE HOUSE, 1838
14710 Lake Ave
Ashlar residence, typical of the pioneer dwellings of this area that replaced the earlier log cabins. The house was moved from Detroit Road to its present site and restored and furnished with authentic artifacts of pioneer settlers.
*Operated by Lakewood Historical Soc. Open Feb.–Nov: Wed., Sun. 2–5*

## LANCASTER

### MUMAUGH HOUSE, 1805; 1824
162 E Main St
Restored brick residence in which the first Roman Catholic services were held in Lancaster in 1817. Partially furnished with antiques
*Operated by City of Lancaster. Open by appointment*

### ■ SHERMAN HOUSE STATE MEMORIAL, 1811; 1816
137 E Main St
Small frame house in which William Tecumseh and John Sherman and their nine brothers and sisters were born. The house, with its later brick front section, is preserved as a memorial to the two famous Sherman brothers; furnishings range from 1811 through the Victorian period.
*Operated by Ohio Historical Soc. Open spring–fall: Tues.–Sun. 9:30–5*

## LEBANON

### GLENDOWER, after 1836
U.S. Route 42
Palatial Greek Revival-style mansion (the first of five erected here in a row) built by John Milton Williams, successful county prosecutor and later a member of the Ohio legislature. Furnished with personal and household items of pioneer families, portraits,

*Glendower*

and gowns belonging to Ohio governors' wives and daughters
*Operated by Ohio Historical Soc. Open Apr.–Oct: Tues.–Sun. 9:30–5*

## LIMA

**MacDONELL HOUSE, 1890**
**632 W Market St**
Victorian mansion, one of the few remaining in Lima, built by Frank Banta, a candy factory owner; added to shortly thereafter by John VanDyke, head of the Standard Oil Company plant in town. Furnishings of the late 1800s
*Operated by Allen Co. Historical Soc. Open Tues.–Sun. 1:30–5; closed legal holidays*

## LISBON

**OLD STONE HOUSE, 1805**
**100 E Washington St**
The oldest house in Lisbon, formerly New Lisbon, used as a tavern and stagecoach stop on the road from Georgetown, Pennsylvania, to New Lisbon and points westward. It has served as a courtroom, bank, church, and private residence. Now a historical museum with furniture and household items from the area
*Operated by Lisbon Historical Soc. Open June–Aug: Tues.–Sat. 1–4. Sept–Oct. 15: Sun. 1–4*

## LOUDONVILLE

**LOG CABIN, 1828**
**Central Park**
Partially restored cabin moved to this location in 1964 and exhibited with pioneer relics, furniture, and utensils
*Operated by Mohican Historical Soc. Open Memorial Day–Labor Day: Fri.–Sun. 1–5*

## MANSFIELD

**KINGWOOD HALL, 1926**
**900 Park Ave, W**
French provincial mansion built on a 47-acre estate by Charles Kelley King, chairman of the board of the Ohio Brass Company. Now an educational institution and cultural center, with special emphasis on gardening, nature study, and related subjects. The house

contains most of its original furnishings. Magnificent formal gardens
*Operated by Kingwood Center and Gardens. Open–Gardens, Greenhouse, and Nature Area–daily 8–sundown. House–Easter–Oct: Tues.–Sat. 8–5; closed holidays*

■ **OAK HILL COTTAGE (SHANE'S CASTLE), 1847**
**310 Springmill St**
Gothic Revival house – distinguished by pointed-arch windows and steep pointed gables – exemplifies a type of architecture that was rare in the Midwest during the first half of the 19th century. Restored in the Victorian style
*Operated by Richland Co. Historical Soc. Open by appointment*

## MARIETTA

**RUFUS PUTNAM HOUSE, before 1788**
**Campus Martius Museum, Washington and Second Streets**
This house, the oldest fortified residence in Ohio, was built by Rufus Putnam, who led a group of settlers into Marietta, the oldest surviving settlement in the state. The house is enclosed in a wing of the modern museum building. Other exhibits in the museum include portraits, furniture, china, silver, glass, and pewter, as well as textiles; a section is devoted to mementos of the Ohio River steam era.
*Operated by Ohio Historical Soc. Open Mon.–Sat. 9–5, Sun. 1–5*

## MARION

■ **WARREN G. HARDING HOUSE, 1890–91**
**380 Mount Vernon Ave**
Late 19th-century house built by Warren G. Harding and Florence Kling DeWolfe during the period of their engagement. This was the Harding home from the day of their marriage here in 1891 until they left for the White House in 1921. The house has been restored and is operated as a memorial museum, with authentic period furnishings.
*Operated by Harding Memorial Assn. Open summer: Mon.–Sat. 10–5, Sun. 1–6. Winter: Tues.–Sun. 1–5*

## MASSILLON

### FIVE OAKS, 1892-93
### 210 Fourth St

Palatial 30-room stone mansion, castlelike in appearance – designed by Cleveland architect Charles F. Schweinfurth for Mr. J. Walter McClymonds, successful businessman – with ornately carved woodwork throughout. All the light fixtures, chandeliers and lamps, as well as a large stained-glass window, were designed by the famous jewelry and glass designer Louis Comfort Tiffany.
*Operated by Massillon Woman's Club. Open July–Aug: Fri., Sun. 1–4, and by appointment*

### JAMES DUNCAN HOUSE
### [MASSILLON MUSEUM], 1835
### 212 Lincoln Way, E

Home of the founder of Massillon; now operated as a museum, with historical, scientific, and art exhibits
*Operated by Massillon Museum and Public Library. Open Mon.–Fri. 10–5, Thurs. evg. 7–9, Sun. 2–5; closed last three weeks of Sept.*

## MAUMEE

### ■ WOLCOTT HOUSE
### MUSEUM, 1827
### 1031 River Rd

Large clapboard house with a two-story veranda built by James Wolcott, a Lucas County judge and mayor of Maumee. (Mrs. Wolcott was the granddaughter of the famous Miami Indian chief Little Turtle.) Restored as a museum of local history with interiors and furnishings of the period
*Operated by Maumee Valley Historical Soc. Open Mon.–Fri. 1–4*

## MENTOR

### ■ JAMES A. GARFIELD HOME
### (LAWNFIELD), 1831; 1876; 1886
### 8095 Mentor Ave

Rambling Victorian mansion from which James A. Garfield ran his Presidential campaign in 1880. The first two floors of the house have been restored and furnished with Garfield family possessions. A wing was added in 1886, after the President's assassination (1881), to include an outstanding art nouveau memorial library.

*Operated by Western Reserve Historical Soc. and Lake Co. Historical Soc. Open May–Oct: Tues.–Sat. 9–5, Sun., holidays 1–5*

Lawnfield

## MILAN

### DR. LEHMAN GALPIN HOUSE, 1846
### 10 Edison Dr

Handsome brick house built by Dr. Lehman Galpin, who assisted at the birth of Thomas A. Edison. The main living room is furnished with antiques and serves as a memorial to the late Ohio supreme court judge Roy H. Williams and his wife. Other rooms contain a gun and doll collection, and an addition to the house contains American pattern and art glass.
*Operated by Milan Historical Museum. Open Apr.–May, Sept.–Oct: daily 1–5. June–Aug: daily 10–5*

### ■ THOMAS ALVA EDISON
### BIRTHPLACE, 1842
### 9 Edison Dr

Federal-style cottage in which the inventor was born in 1847. The Edisons moved to Michigan in 1853 and the house was sold. In 1894, however, Mrs. Marion Edison Page bought the house back, and Thomas A. Edison became the owner in 1906.
*Operated by Edison Birthplace Assn. Open Feb. 11–Mar: Fri., Sat. 9–5, Sun. 1–5. Apr.–Nov: Tues.–Sat. 9–5, Sun. 1–5. Rest of year: by appointment*

## NEWARK

### SHERWOOD-DAVIDSON HOUSE, 1820
### Sixth and West Main Streets

Federal-style frame house now a mu-

seum, with period furnishings
*Operated by Licking Co. Historical Soc. Open Tues.–Sun. 9–5*

## NEW CONCORD

### WILLIAM R. HARPER HOUSE, before 1856
**U.S. Route 40**
Two-story log cabin birthplace of William R. Harper, first president of the University of Chicago. Partially furnished with 19th-century pieces
*Operated by Harper House. Open by appointment*

## NEW PHILADELPHIA

### SCHOENBRUNN VILLAGE STATE MEMORIAL, 1772
Reconstructed Moravian Indian settlement originally established in 1772 by David Zeisberger, a Moravian missionary, and his following of 28 Christian Indians. They were joined a few months later by missionaries John Heckewelder and John Ettwein leading 200 converts. The village was abandoned in 1777 and excavated in the 1920s.
*Operated by Ohio Historical Soc. Open Apr.–Oct: 9–dark. Nov.–Mar: daily 9–5*

## NORWALK

### PRESTON-WICKHAM HOUSE, 1835
**4 Case Ave**
White frame house of two and a half stories built by Samuel Preston, local newspaper editor, as a wedding gift for his daughter, Lucy. The house serves as a museum, with natural history exhibits and a collection of antique guns, pioneer farm and household implements, costumes, etc.
*Operated by Firelands Historical Soc. Open May–June, Sept.–Oct: Tues.– Sun. 12–6. July–Aug: Mon.–Sat. 9–6. Apr., Nov: Sat., Sun. 12–6*

## OXFORD

### PIONEER FARM AND HOUSE MUSEUM, 1830s
**Doty Road**
Small brick house, built by Joseph Morris, was purchased by Samuel Doty in 1844, and the Doty family lived here until 1890. Purchased by the state in 1950 and renovated, it is shown with pioneer furnishings.
*Operated by Oxford Museum Assn. Open May–Nov: Sat., Sun. 1:30–5*

### ■ WILLIAM H. McGUFFEY HOUSE, about 1833
**Spring and Oak Streets**
Two-story brick house built by William Holmes McGuffey, where he wrote his now-famous readers. Now a depository of McGuffey readers, spellers, and primers as well as of thousands of children's textbooks published before 1900. The house also contains his memorabilia and furnishings.
*Operated by Miami University. Open Tues., Sun. 2–4:30, Sat. 9–11, 2–4:30; closed Christmas recess and Aug.*

*William H. McGuffey Home*

## PIQUA

### JOHN JOHNSTON HOUSE, 1811
**Ohio Route 66**
Restored brick home and two-story springhouse of Indian agent and canal promoter John Johnston
*Operated by Ohio Historical Soc. Open Tues.–Sun. 9:30–5*

## POINT PLEASANT

### ULYSSES S. GRANT BIRTHPLACE, 1817
**U.S. Route 52 and Ohio Route 232**
Small frame house in which the 18th President of the U.S. was born in 1822. Restored and open as a museum
*Operated by Ohio Historical Soc. Open Apr.–Oct: Tues.–Sun. 9:30–5*

*Ulysses S. Grant Birthplace*

## RAVENNA

### CHARLOTTE STRICKLAND HOUSE, 1829
**337 Main St**
Originally built as a tavern by the Carter family, of which Miss Strickland was a descendant. Now the historical society's headquarters, with 19th- and 20th-century relics
*Operated by Portage Co. Historical Soc. Open Tues., Thurs. 2–4, Sun. 2–5*

## RIPLEY

### RANKIN HOUSE STATE MEMORIAL, 1828
**Liberty Hill**
Small brick house, home of the Rev. John Rankin, one of the first and most active "conductors" of the Underground Railroad. The house has been restored and furnished with period pieces, some Rankin family pieces.
*Operated by Ohio Historical Soc. Open Apr.–Oct: Tues.–Sat. 9:30–5*

## SPRINGFIELD

### PENNSYLVANIA HOUSE, about 1839
**1311 W Main St**
Three-story brick structure which served as home, inn, and tavern for travelers on the National Road and the Dayton-Springfield Pike
*Operated by Daughters of the American Revolution. Open first Sun. of each month 1–4 and by appointment*

## UNIONVILLE VICINITY

### SHANDY HALL, 1815
**Ohio Route 84**
Frame structure with 17 rooms—one

of the oldest houses in the Western Reserve—built by Col. Robert Harper, son of Connecticut-born pioneer Col. Alexander Harper. Carefully restored, with lavishly finished interiors, including French scenic wallpaper and furnishings original to the house
*Operated by Western Reserve Historical Soc. Open May–Oct: Tues.–Sat. 10–5, Sun. 2–6*

## WARREN

### FREDERICK KINSMAN HOUSE, 1832; 1846; 1860
**Mahoning Avenue**
Greek Revival structure built by the master builder Isaac Ladd for Frederick Kinsman, a prominent Warren citizen and personal friend of James A. Garfield. Interior abounds with black walnut woodwork—including the staircase—arched doorways, and white marble mantels.
*Operated by Trumbull Co. Heritage Assn. and City of Warren. Restoration in progress*

### JOHN STARK EDWARDS HOUSE, 1807
**309 South St, SE**
Frame home of John Stark Edwards, grandson of the great early New England preacher Jonathan Edwards. Restored, with furnishings from the Edwards and Iddings (a later occupant) families. A library includes county histories and atlases as well as old Warren newspapers.
*Operated by Trumbull Co. Historical Soc. Open Tues., Thurs., Sun. 2–4, and by appointment*

## WATERVILLE

### ■ COLUMBIAN HOUSE, 1818; 1828
**River and Farnsworth Roads**
One of the finest Federal-style structures in northwestern Ohio, this three-story, 23-room building was the home, trading post, post office, and inn of John Pray. Now a restaurant
*Operated by Mrs. Ethel Arnold, owner. Open Mon.–Sat.*

## WELLSVILLE

### HENRY ATEN MANSION, 1811
**1607 Buckeye Ave**
Historic house operated as a museum,

with Indian artifacts, railroad memorabilia, Civil War items, and relics relating to early transportation on the Ohio River
*Operated by Wellsville Historical Soc. Open Memorial Day–Labor Day: Tues.–Sun. 12–5*

## WESTERVILLE

### HANBY HOUSE, before 1853
**160 W Main St**
Frame house in which Benjamin R. Hanby, clergyman and composer of "Darling Nelly Gray," lived during his young adult life. Moved from its original site and shown with many pieces of furniture and personal items of the Hanby family
*Operated by Ohio Historical Soc. Open June–Sept. 15: Sat., Sun., holidays 10–5*

## WEST LIBERTY

### PIATT CASTLES
**Ohio Route 245**
*Castle Piatt Mac-A-Cheek* (1864) was built of hand-chiseled limestone by Gen. Abram Saunders Piatt in the style of a Norman French chateau. Finely carved interior woodwork, paneling, and tapestries; original furniture —many pieces American and French antiques. *Mac-O-Chee Castle* (1879), also limestone, was built by the general's brother, Col. Donn Piatt, in the

*Mac-O-Chee Castle*

style of a Flemish castle. The ceilings and walls were frescoed by Oliver Frey, of Menton, France; some of the walls are paneled. Furnishings are mainly European antiques.
*Operated by William M. Piatt, J.J. Piatt, and Frances M. Piatt, owners. Open – Castle Piatt Mac-A-Cheek – Jan.–Mar., Nov.–Dec: daily 9:30–5. Both –Apr.–Oct: daily 9:30–5:30*

## WILMINGTON

### ROMBACH PLACE, 1835
**149 E Locust St**
This house now serves as a museum, with furniture and art objects of the period 1620–1820.
*Operated by Clinton Co. Historical Soc. Open May–Oct: Thurs., Sun. 1–5; closed national holidays*

## WOOSTER

### GEN. REASIN BEALL HOME, 1815–17
**546 E Bowman St**
Classical revival-style brick structure, the home of Gen. Reasin Beall. Collections include original Beall and other 19th-century furnishings as well as town and county historical records. On the grounds are a Civil War-era log house, with pioneer mementos, and a reconstructed one-room schoolhouse.
*Operated by Wayne Co. Historical Soc. Open Tues.–Sun. 2–4:30; closed holidays*

## WORTHINGTON

### ORANGE JOHNSON HOUSE, 1816
**956 High St**
Red brick Federal-style house built by Orange Johnson, a comb vender who later became a successful road builder and banker. The house is under restoration, and furnishings are being collected. An extensive doll collection is on display.
*Operated by Worthington Historical Soc. Open Sun. 2–5*

## XENIA

### WARREN K. MOOREHEAD HOUSE, about 1865
**Detroit and West Church Streets**
Restored boyhood home of W.K. Moorehead, prominent archaeologist of the late Victorian period and author

of *The Stone Age in North America.*
Nearby are the *Galloway Cabin* (1789),
with antique furnishings, and an old
barn, with farm implements exhibited.
*Operated by Greene Co. Historical
Soc. Open by appointment*

## ZANESVILLE

### BAILEY HOUSE [ART INSTITUTE OF ZANESVILLE], 1893
**Maple and Adair Streets**
Three-story stone building with ornamented gables. Now a museum, with
a permanent art collection and exhibits
*Operated by Art Institute of Zanes-
ville. Open Mon.–Thurs., Sat. 10–5,*

*Sun. 2–5, Mon., Thurs. evgs. 7:30–10;
closed July–Aug. and national holidays*

## ZOAR

### ■ ZOAR HISTORIC DISTRICT, 1817
Village founded by German Separatists
from Württemberg, Germany. The
group thrived between 1817 and 1853
under the leadership of Joseph Bäume-
ler, whose house has been restored
and is maintained as a museum. A
number of early buildings survive.
*Operated by Ohio Historical Soc.
Open May–Sept: Tues.–Sun. 9:30–5*

## ANADARKO

### INDIAN CITY, U.S.A.
**State Highway 8**
Typical villages of seven Indian tribes,
with representative structures depicting Indian life, have been built on this
160-acre tract. Dwellings include a
Navajo hogan, an Apache wickiup,
a typical Kiowa winter camp tepee, a
Caddo "wattle-and-daub" house, a
Pawnee earth house, a Pueblo adobe,
and a Wichita grass house. Indian
crafts are also displayed, especially
during the annual exposition usually
held the third week in August.
*Operated by Indian City, U.S.A. Open
May–Oct: daily 9–6. Nov.–Apr: daily
9–5*

*Wichita Grass House*

## CACHE

### ■ QUANAH PARKER'S STAR HOUSE, 1884
**Eagle Park, Wichita Mountains High-
way**
Two-story, 12-room house built by
Quanah Parker, the last chief of the
Comanches. Moved to this site as part
of the Frontier Collection of historic
buildings. Restored and shown with
period furnishings, some original to
the house
*Operated by Eagle Park. Open Me-
morial Day–Labor Day: daily 9–5.
Rest of year: Sat., Sun. 9–6*

## CLEO SPRINGS VICINITY

### ■ HOMESTEADER'S SOD HOUSE, 1894
**State Highway 8, six miles north of
Cleo Springs**
The only original homesteader sod
house remaining in Oklahoma, built
by Marshall McCully, who came here
during the great land run of 1893. The
walls of the sod house are about 36
inches thick and are plastered with a
mixture of alkali and water; the dirt
floor was replaced with a wooden one
in 1895. Occupied as a home until
1909 and used as a storage house by
McCully until his death in 1963. Restored and shown with furnishings
typical of 1907, the year Oklahoma became a state

*Operated by Okla. Historical Soc. Open Tues.–Fri. 9–5, Sat., Sun. 2–5*

## HEAVENER

### PETER CONSER HOUSE, 1894
Two-story frame house built by Peter Conser, prominent citizen of the Choctaw nation and a leader of his district. Shown with furnishings typical of the area at the turn of the century
*Operated by Okla. Historical Soc. Open Tues.–Fri. 9–5, Sat., Sun. 2–5*

## KINGFISHER

### SEAY MANSION, 1892
**11 and Overstreet**
Colonial revival red brick house was the home of the second governor of the Oklahoma Territory, Abraham Jefferson Seay. Restored in 1966, it is shown with furnishings of the period, some original to the house.
*Operated by Okla. Industrial Development and Park Dept. Open daily 9–5*

## LINDSAY

### ERIN SPRINGS HOUSE, 1879–80
Three-story ranch house built by Frank Murray, an Irish rancher who settled in the territory of the Chickasaw nation and married a Choctaw woman. Restored and furnished with appropriate pieces
*Operated by Okla. Historical Soc. Open Tues.–Sat. 9–5, Sun. 2–5*

## MUSKOGEE

### GRANT FOREMAN HOME, 1898
**1419 W Okmulgee St**
Home of Grant and Carolyn Thomas Foreman, noted historians and authors of many books on the Five Civilized Tribes of Oklahoma. The house was built by Mrs. Foreman's father, Judge John Robert Thomas. Occupied by Mrs. Foreman until her death at 95 in 1967; with the family furnishings
*Operated by Okla. Historical Soc. Open Tues.–Fri. 9–5, Sat., Sun. 2–5*

## OOLOGAH VICINITY

### ■ WILL ROGERS BIRTHPLACE, 1875
**Will Rogers State Park**
Two-story, five-room white clapboard house; the original section is built of logs, with a rear frame portion added later. Here Will Rogers was born on Nov. 4, 1879. Recently moved to the present site and restored with period furnishings. At the Will Rogers Memorial in nearby Claremore the late humorist's personal possessions are displayed; his tomb is in the garden.
*Operated by Okla. Industrial Development and Park Dept. Open Wed.–Sun. 1–5*

*Will Rogers Birthplace*

## PAWNEE

### PAWNEE BILL MUSEUM AND MANSION, 1910
**Blue Hawk Peak, Highway 64**
Rambling brick mansion built by Gordon W. Lillie, frontiersman and scout, who became known as Pawnee Bill—leader of the Wild West Circus. The 14-room mansion is maintained and furnished as it was while Lillie and his wife lived there. Also on the grounds is a log cabin built by Lillie as his first home on the land.
*Operated by Okla. Industrial Development and Park Dept. Open May–Oct: daily 9–7. Nov.–Apr: daily 9–5*

## PONCA CITY

### PONCA CITY INDIAN MUSEUM, 1916
**1000 E Grand Ave**
Once the home of E.W. Marland, oil magnate and tenth governor of the state. Now a museum, with a fine collection of Indian arts and costumes
*Operated by Ponca City Indian Museum. Open Mon., Wed.–Sat. 10–5, Sun., holidays 1–5; closed Christmas and New Year's Day*

## SALLISAW

### ■ SEQUOYAH'S HOME, 1829
**State Highway 101**
One-room log cabin built by Sequoyah,

inventor of the Cherokee alphabet. After experimenting for nearly 12 years, Sequoyah developed his alphabet of 84 characters, from which any Cherokee word could be written. The cabin is housed in a protective stone building and is maintained as a shrine.
*Operated by Okla. Historical Soc. Open Tues.–Fri. 9–5, Sat., Sun. 2–5*

## TAHLEQUAH

■ **MURRELL HOME, 1844**
**one mile east of U.S. Route 82**
Stately home of George Murrell, prominent merchant and leader of the Chief John Ross faction of the Cherokee nation. Considered one of the finest ante-bellum houses in the state; shown with many of the furnishings Murrell had imported from France.
*Operated by Okla. Industrial Development and Park Dept. Open May–Oct: daily 9–7. Nov.–Apr: daily 9–5*

**TSA-LA-GI**
Reconstructed Cherokee village, with typical dwellings, reflects daily life as it was before the coming of the white man. Staffed completely by Cherokees, the village offers displays of such handicrafts as pottery, basket weaving, and blowgun manufacture, as well as demonstrations of ancient dances and rituals. The village is part of a planned cultural center that will include the national museum and archives of the Cherokee nation.
*Operated by Cherokee National Historic Soc. Open May–Sept. 15: Tues.–Sun. 10–5*

## WANETTE

**LOG CABIN MUSEUM, 1894**
Pioneer log cabin with walls measuring 18 by 14 feet is now a museum. On display are pioneer artifacts and other items of historical interest.
*Operated by Henry L. Neal, owner. Open by appointment*

## YALE

**JIM THORPE BUNGALOW, 1916**
Jim Thorpe's family occupied this bungalow in the 1920s. It is the only known home of the famed American Indian athlete. To be furnished when restoration is completed
*Operated by Okla. Historical Soc. Hours to be determined*

## ASTORIA

**OLD FLAVEL MANSION, 1883–84**
**441 Eighth St**
Luxurious Victorian mansion built by the shipping magnate and mariner Capt. George Flavel. Designed by a San Francisco architect, this large structure reflects the lavish taste of the era. It was continuously resided in by Flavel descendants until 1933.
*Operated by Clatsop Co. Historical Soc. Open May–Sept: Tues.–Sun. 10–5. Oct.–Apr: Tues.–Sun. 12–5; closed Thanksgiving, Christmas, and New Year's Day*

## AURORA

**OX BARN MUSEUM, about 1860**
**KRAUS HOUSE, about 1864**
**Second and Liberty Streets**
The so-called Ox Barn was built as a change station on the stage line between Portland and Sacramento; this building now serves as a museum, with furniture and artifacts of Aurora Colony. The Kraus House was moved to this location recently, has been restored, and serves as a house museum of the early colony. Many original furnishings of the Kraus family are on display.
*Operated by Aurora Historical Soc. Open Wed.–Sat. 2–4:30, Sun. 2–5*

## AURORA VICINITY

**ROBERT NEWELL HOUSE, 1852**
**Champoeg Memorial State Park**
Rural farmhouse—one of the few buildings to survive the flood of 1861—of Robert Newell, a former Rocky Mountains trapper. Newell became an agent of the Nez Perce in 1867 and

accompanied the Indian chiefs to Washington, D.C., a year later in their quest for the "White Man's Bible." House is now a museum, with a collection of inaugural gowns of governors' wives
*Operated by Daughters of the American Revolution. Open Feb.–Oct: Tues.–Sun. 8–8*

*Robert Newell House*

## BROWNSVILLE

### MOYER HOUSE, 1881
**204 Main St**
Italian villa-style house built by J.M. Moyer, an early Brownsville businessman. His wife was the daughter of Hugh Brown, for whom the town was named. Now restored, with furniture of the period
*Operated by Linn Co. Historical Soc. Open Tues.–Sat. 2–4*

*Moyer House*

## CANYON CITY

### JOAQUIN MILLER CABIN, 1864
**Highway 395**
Located on the grounds of the Grant County historical museum is this restored cabin of the poet, who had a

multifarious career before publishing his *Songs of the Sierras* (1871). The museum itself has a gold display.
*Operated by Grant Co. Museum and Historical Soc. Open Apr.–Oct: Tues.–Sat. 9–5, Sun. 1–5. June–Aug: daily 9–5*

## COLUMBIA CITY

### DR. CHARLES GREEN CAPLES HOUSE, 1871–72
Frame home of the noted pioneer physician now operated as a museum, with period artifacts, costumes, and furniture. Several outbuildings have been reconstructed and are also open.
*Operated by Daughters of the American Revolution. Open Tues.–Sun. 1–5*

## JACKSONVILLE

### BEEKMAN HOME, 1890
**California and Seventh Streets**
Late 19th-century house built by Cornelius C. Beekman, Oregon's first successful banker. The house is furnished in the style of the period and operated as a museum. The Beekman bank building has been restored and is also open to the public.
*Operated by University of Oreg., Jackson Co., and the Siskiyou Pioneer Sites Foundation. Open summer: daily 10–4*

### ■ JACKSONVILLE HISTORIC DISTRICT, 1852–84
Jacksonville was founded after a gold strike was made nearby; the town became the principal distribution, financial, and trading center of southern Oregon. Numerous commercial and residential buildings remain, basically unaltered, making Jacksonville an important example of a mid-19th-century inland town. Architectural styles are mainly Greek Revival, Gothic Revival, and Italian villa.

### McCULLY HOUSE, 1861
**Fifth and California Streets**
Two-story frame house built by John Wilmer McCully, the earliest known physician in Jackson County. Dr. McCully stayed in Jacksonville ten years, leaving in 1862 for the gold fields of Idaho and Montana. The house now serves as a museum, with Victorian furnishings and a collection of antique dolls.

*Operated by Mrs. Leona Stone Salver, owner. Open July–Aug: daily 10–5. June, Sept: daily 12–5. Rest of year: by appointment*

McCully House

## KERBY

### KERBYVILLE MUSEUM, 1878
**Oregon Route 199**
Two-story wooden building erected by Frank Stith for William Naucke, an early Kerbyville merchant. Restored, the home is furnished with pioneer possessions of county families.
*Operated by Josephine Co. Open May–Oct: daily 10–5*

## MILWAUKIE

### FAILING RESIDENCE, before 1858
**2515 Lake Rd**
Victorian house believed to have been barged from downtown Portland to Milwaukie before 1893. Restored and shown with Victorian furnishings
*Operated by Mrs. Curtis Holt, owner. Open Sat. 10–3 and by appointment*

## NEWBERG

### MINTHORN HOUSE (HERBERT HOOVER BOYHOOD HOME), 1881
**115 S River St**
Boyhood home of Herbert Hoover. Dr. Henry Minthorn was the first superintendent of the Friends Pacific Academy, a Quaker school, which Hoover attended for several years. The Minthorn's were Herbert Hoover's foster parents, taking him to live with them after the death of their only son in 1883. The house is now operated as a house museum, with many relics and souvenirs of President Hoover, including some original furnishings from his boyhood days in this house.
*Operated by Herbert Hoover Foundation. Open winter: Tues.–Sun. 10–12, 2–4. Summer: Tues.–Sun. 2–5*

## OREGON CITY

### AINSWORTH HOUSE, 1851
**19195 S Leland Rd**
Greek Revival house built by John Commigers, a pioneer steamboat captain and banking magnate. This is the only early example of Greek Revival architecture on a grand scale in the Northwest. Furnishings of the period and sea chests from the U.S.S. *Constitution* and *Old Ironsides*
*Operated by Mrs. Albert H. Powers, owner. Open Fri.–Mon. 9–5*

### BARCLAY HOUSE, 1850
**719 Center St, McLoughlin Park**
Built by Dr. Forbes Barclay, a prominent civic leader and former surgeon at Fort Vancouver. The house was moved to this site near the McLoughlin House in 1936. Dr. Barclay and Dr. John McLoughlin, agent for the Hudson's Bay Company, were close friends. The house contains Oriental and West Coast antiques, artifacts, and historical documents.
*Operated by Glen Dougherty, owner. Open daily 10–5:30*

### McCARVER HOUSE (LOCUST FARM), 1850–52; 1900
**554 Warner Parrott Rd**
The first prefabricated house in Oregon; the lumber was brought around the Horn from Maine to San Francisco and was shipped with Gen. Morton Matthew McCarver when he returned to Oregon City from California. The general had platted Sacramento for John Sutter and was a delegate to the first California constitutional convention in Monterey in 1849. McCarver House is now a private residence.
*Operated by Mrs. Albert H. Powers, owner. Open by appointment*

### ■ McLOUGHLIN HOUSE, 1845–46
**McLoughlin Park**
Pioneer dwelling—one of the two remaining in the region—of Dr. John McLoughlin, chief factor of the Hudson's Bay Company and founder of Oregon City. From 1824 to 1846 Dr. McLoughlin controlled the Oregon

Country, which once encompassed most of British Columbia, Oregon, Washington, Idaho, and parts of Montana and Wyoming; his aid to settlers in the area won him enduring acclaim. Furnishings of the period
*Operated by McLoughlin Memorial Assn., Municipality of Oregon City, and National Park Service. Open summer: Tues.–Sun. 10–5. Winter: Tues.–Sun. 10–4*

*McLoughlin House*

### MERTIE STEVENS HOME, 1908
**603 Sixth St**
Built by H.C. Stevens—Mertie Stevens' father—an astute businessman and station agent for the East Side Railroad. The house incorporated many modern conveniences, such as a furnace with radiators in each room. Miss Mertie Stevens inherited her father's business acumen and left a fortune to be used in scholarships.
*Operated by Clackamas Co. Historical Soc. Open by appointment*

## PORTLAND

### BYBEE-HOWELL HOUSE, 1856
**Howell Park Road, Sauvie Island**
Oldest standing residence on the island and the first one in the state to have its interiors plastered, this Greek Revival house was built by James F. and Julia Ann Bybee. The Bybees lived here a short time before they sold it to their neighbors, the Howells, who owned the house until 1961.
*Operated by Oregon Historical Soc. Open May–Oct: daily 11–5*

### CAPT. JOHN ANDREW BROWN HOUSE, about 1898
**NW 19 Avenue and NW Hoyt Street**
Victorian house built by J.A. Brown, a pioneer sea and river boat captain originally from New England. He developed the port of Portland and founded a noted local stevedoring firm (which was purchased in 1908 by Henry Rothschild after Brown's death). The house is partially restored and serves as a community center.
*Operated by Capt. Brown House Assn. Hours to be determined*

### MacKENZIE HOUSE, 1890s
**615 NW 20 Ave**
Three-story gabled stone mansion built by Dr. K.A.J. MacKenzie, leading physician of the area, founder of the University of Oregon Medical School, and owner of the Oregon Railway and Navigation Company. Called "Scotch Baronial," the house was designed by the architects Whidden and Lewis, who incorporated many Richardsonian features on the exterior. William Temple House, an Episcopalian-sponsored nondenominational counseling and rehabilitation agency, is now raising funds for its preservation.
*Operated by William Temple House. Open daily 10–4*

### PITTOCK MANSION, 1909–14
**NW Pittock Drive, Pittock Acres Park**
Built by Henry L. Pittock, founder and publisher of the *Daily Oregonian* newspaper in Portland, this magnificent example of French Renaissance architecture stands nearly 1,000 feet above the city. Now a house museum
*Operated by City of Portland. Open Wed., Thurs., Sat., Sun by appointment*

## PRINEVILLE

### PRINEVILLE HISTORICAL MUSEUM, 1880
**Pioneer Park**
A museum, with objects of pioneering days in Prineville and Crook County, is located in this old log cabin.
*Operated by Prineville Historical Museum. Open June–Sept: Tues.–Sun. 12–5*

## ROSEBURG

### JOSEPH LANE HOUSE, 1853–54
**554 SE Douglas Ave**
Two-story southern-style frame house, home of Joseph Lane, the first territorial governor of Oregon, a U.S. sen-

ator, and onetime candidate for Vice President of the U.S. The house has been restored and furnished as a pioneer museum.
*Operated by Douglas Co. Historical Soc. Open Sat., Sun. 1–5, and by appointment*

## SALEM

### BUSH HOUSE, 1877
### 600 Mission St, SE
Located in Bush Pasture, an 80-acre city park planted with rare trees and shrubs, is the home of Asahel Bush, pioneer banker and newspaper publisher. The house is now a museum furnished with objects of the period. Nearby is Bush Barn, an art center, which features exhibitions by Northwest artists.
*Operated by Salem Art Assn. Open— Bush House—June–Aug: Tues.-Sat. 12–5, Sun. 2–5. Sept.-May: Tues.-Sun. 2–5. Bush Barn—Tues.-Fri. 9:30–5, Sat., Sun. 1–5*

## SALEM VICINITY

### JASON LEE'S HOME, 1841
### METHODIST PARSONAGE, 1841

### Thomas Kay Historical Park
Two buildings which survive from the Methodist mission established by Rev. Jason Lee on the Willamette River in 1834. The Jason Lee house is a two-story structure, rectangular in shape, with lath and plaster walls and lap siding. The mission parsonage was built for Gustavus Hines, Director of the Mission Indian Manual Labor Training School. This structure has been moved from its original site to the historical park. Both houses are undergoing restoration.
*Operated by Mission Mill Museum Corp. Hours to be determined*

## THE DALLES

### SURGEON'S QUARTERS, 1856
### 1500 Garrison St
Gothic Revival-style cottage, the last remaining structure of historic Fort Dalles. Now a museum with period rooms
*Operated by Wasco Co.-Dalles City Museum Comm. Open May–Sept: Wed.-Mon. 9–5. Oct.-Apr: Wed.-Fri., Sun. 1–5, Sat. 10–5*

## ALLENTOWN

### TROUT HALL, 1770
### 414 Walnut St
The city's first mansion, a Georgian limestone house, was built by James Allen, son of the city's founder, as a hunting and fishing lodge. Later known as Livingston Manor and subsequently the first home of Muhlenberg College, the house is now the library and museum of the Lehigh County Historical Soc., with colonial furnishings and Indian artifacts.
*Operated by Lehigh Co. Historical Soc. Open Tues.-Sat. 2–4; closed national holidays*

## ALTOONA

### ELIAS BAKER MANSION, 1840s
### 3500 Baker Blvd
Fine, two-and-a-half-story Greek Re-

vival house built by ironmaster Elias Baker, who brought some of the carved furniture for his house from Belgium. Now a museum and library with displays relating to Portage Railroad, Pa. Canal, and other aspects of local history; library contains a collection of newspapers and manuscripts.
*Operated by Blair Co. Historical Soc. Open June–Oct: Sat. 1:30–4:30*

## AMBRIDGE

### ■ OLD ECONOMY, after 1825
### 14 and Church Streets
Third and final home of the Harmony Soc., a pietist community led by "Father" George Rapp. Founded in 1805, the society moved to a 3,000-acre tract in Economy in 1825. The present village is the center of the town with numerous shops, the Feast Hall, wine

cellar, a typical dwelling, and Rapp's *Great House* restored as they were before the society dissolved in 1905. *Operated by Pa. Historical and Museum Comm. Open May–Oct: Tues.–Sat. 8:30–5, Sun. 1–5. Nov.–Apr: Tues.–Sat. 9–4:30, Sun. 1–4:30*

*Old Economy street*

## AUDUBON: LOWER PROVIDENCE TOWNSHIP

### MILL GROVE, 1762
**Audubon Wildlife Sanctuary**
Ivy-covered stone farmhouse purchased in 1789 by Capt. Jean Audubon, father of the renowned naturalist John James Audubon, who lived here and managed the estate from 1804 to 1806. This 130-acre wildlife sanctuary has six miles of hiking trails for public use. House furnished with early 19th-century pieces; attic restored as a studio and taxidermy room
*Operated by Commissioners of Montgomery Co. Open Tues.–Sun. 10–5; closed Thanksgiving, Christmas, and New Year's Day*

## BAUMSTOWN

### DANIEL BOONE HOMESTEAD, before 1750
Daniel Boone was born in 1734 in a log cabin that stood on this site. It is believed that his father built part of the present two-story stone house before the family moved to North Carolina in 1750. Completely restored and furnished, the house and outbuildings depict rural life in 18th-

century Pennsylvania. The homestead also serves as a state-run sanctuary for deer, quail, and other game and has good public fishing areas.
*Operated by Pa. Historical and Museum Comm. Open May–Oct: Tues.–Sat. 8:30–5, Sun. 1–5. Nov.–Apr: Tues.–Sat. 9–4:30, Sun. 1–4:30*

## BETHLEHEM

### HISTORIC BETHLEHEM
Bethlehem was founded in the 1740s by Moravians, a religious sect forced to flee their native Germany. Today many of the community's original buildings remain, some restored and open to the public, others not. Among those open are the *Single Brethren's House*, 1748; the *Piston's House*, 1744; the *Gemein House*, 1741, oldest existing structure in the city. For further information contact *Historic Bethlehem, Main and Church Streets. Open Mon.–Fri. 9–5*

## BOALSBURG

### BOAL MANSION, 1789
**Route 322**
Captain David Boal began this mansion, which was enlarged in 1798 and added to subsequently. It contains fine woodwork and American and European furnishings. Most outstanding is the *Columbus Family Chapel*, brought to the grounds in 1919 from Spain, which belonged to Christopher Columbus' descendants and contains many 17th-century objects, including the altar, doors, and drapes. Also on the grounds is a museum with items of local history.
*Operated by Columbus Chapel-Boalsburg Estate Soc. Open May–Oct: daily 10–6*

## BROOMALL, MARPLE TOWNSHIP

### THOMAS MASSEY HOUSE, 1696, 1730, 1840–60
**Lawrence and Springhouse Roads**
Quaker farmhouse, earliest section built of brick and added to an already existing log cabin by former indentured servant Thomas Massey. Two-story stone section replaced the log cabin in 1730, and other additions were built in 1840 and 1860. House

remained in the Massey family until 1924. The entire house will be furnished when restoration is completed. *Operated by Township of Marple, Broomall, Pa. Open May–Oct. 15: Sun. 2–5 and by appointment*

## BROWNSVILLE

**NEMACOLIN CASTLE, begun 1789**
**Front Street**
A 22-room stone "castle" complete with octagonal tower and battlements built on the remnants of Old Fort Burd; many additions were made on the house throughout the 19th century. Jacob Bowman, trading-post operator and community leader, began the castle, which his heirs owned until 1957; shown with family furnishings. *Operated by Brownsville Historical Soc. Open Apr. 15–May: Sat., Sun. 1–5. May 30–Sept. 15: Tues.–Sun. 1–5. Sept. 16–Nov. 15: Sat., Sun. 1–5*

## CATASAUQUA

**GEORGE TAYLOR MANSION, 1768**
Ironmaster and signer of the Declaration of Independence George Taylor built his summer home on the Lehigh River; the rich and extensive interior paneling are unusual for this area. Restored and furnished with period pieces and surrounded by an 18th-century garden *Operated by Lehigh Co. Historical Soc. Open Apr.–Oct: Wed. 1–3, Sun. 2–4*

## CHADDS FORD

**BARNES-BRINTON HOUSE,**
**before 1776**
**U.S. Route 1**
Brick house with shake roof served as a roadside inn about the time of the Revolution. Later converted to a residence, it is the subject of Andrew Wyeth's painting "Tenant Farmer." To be furnished with period pieces *Operated by Chadds Ford Historical Soc. Open by appointment*

■ **BRANDYWINE BATTLEFIELD**
Reconstructed Georgian stone house used by Gen. Washington as headquarters during the Battle of Brandywine, Sept. 11, 1777. Also on site is Lafayette's headquarters–the restored home of Quaker Gideon Gilpin. The

earliest part of the house is of hand-split, red oak clapboards, with stone section added in 1745. Several other restored and furnished buildings are in the park. *Operated by Brandywine Battlefield Park Comm. Open May 30–Labor Day: daily 10–5. Sept.–May: Sat, Sun. 11–4*

**JOHN CHAD HOUSE, before 1725**
**Route 100**
Simple, stone colonial house with oak beams, built by John Chad, who operated the first ferry across the Brandywine Creek in 1737. The house served as an inn for several years before 1760; during the Battle of Brandywine Chad's widow lived here, and during the restoration damage from the battle was discovered. Furnishings date from the 18th century. *Operated by Chadds Ford Historical Soc. Open by appointment*

## COATESVILLE

**HIBERNIA, early 19th century**
**Hibernia Park**
Large, brick mansion built in the classical style; added to and greatly altered by Col. Franklin Swayne after he purchased the property in 1894. The mansion and 700 acres were purchased by the county in 1963 for a public park. *Operated by Chester Co. Park and Recreation Board. Open–House–May 30–Oct: Wed., Sat., Sun., holidays 1–4, and by appointment*

## DANVILLE

**MONTGOMERY HOUSE, 1792**
**1 Bloom Street**
Georgian house of gray stone with a slate roof built by pioneer settler Gen. William Montgomery, whose son Daniel later laid out and founded the town named for him. Now historical society headquarters and a museum *Operated by Montour Co. Historical Soc. Open Wed. 1:30–4:30*

■ **DILWORTHTOWN**
**THE BRINTON HOUSE, 1704**
**Route 202**
Two-and-a-half-story house with chimneys at either end of the steep gable roof was built of stone from a local

quarry by William Brinton, the younger. Restored in 1954, the house had 22-inch-thick walls, walnut window and door frames, and leaded glass in its 27 windows. Furnishings are based on inventories taken after the deaths of Brinton and his wife; a Conestoga wagon and other early vehicles are housed in the barn.
*Operated by Chester Co. Historical Soc. Open May–Oct. 31: Tues., Thurs., Sat. 1–4; closed national holidays*

## DOUGLASSVILLE

### MOUNS JONES HOUSE, 1716
Two-and-a-half-story red stone and shale farmhouse built by Swedish pioneers Mouns and Ingabor Jones, who settled in this area in 1701. Mouns Jones acted as a scrivener and interpreter between the Delaware Indians and the provincial government of Pennsylvania.
*Operated by Historic Preservation Trust of Berks Co. Hours to be determined*

## DOYLESTOWN

### FONTHILL, 1908–10
**East Court Street**
Large chateaulike mansion of concrete and stone built by Dr. Henry C. Mercer, archaeologist and manufacturer of pottery and tile. Multilevel house is topped by a red tile roof; each room is decorated with colored tiles. Shown with Dr. Mercer's furnishings; his pottery works is open as a museum.
*Private. Open—House—by appointment*

*Fonthill*

## EASTON

### GEORGE TAYLOR HOME, 1757
**Ferry and H Streets**
Georgian fieldstone house is the oldest residence still standing in Easton. Built by William Parsons, pioneer surveyor, who founded the city in 1752, it later became the home of George Taylor, member of the Continental Congress and signer of the Declaration of Independence.
*Operated by Daughters of the American Revolution. Open by appointment*

### JACOB MIXWELL HOUSE, 1833
**101 S Fourth St**
This 19th-century brick house with two dormer windows jutting out of the slate roof is now a museum and library of local history. Among the displays are Indian arrowheads and early costumes.
*Operated by Northampton Co. Historical Soc. Open Sat. 2–5*

## EGYPT

### TROXELL-STECKEL HOUSE, 1755
Stone homestead of Peter Troxell built in the medieval German tradition with pent roof and large fireplaces. Peter Steckel bought the house before the Revolution, and it remained in his family until 1904.
*Operated by Lehigh Co. Historical Soc. Open by appointment*

## ELVERSON

### ■ HOPEWELL VILLAGE NATIONAL HISTORIC SITE
Restored ironmaking community of

*Ironmaster's House, Hopewell*

the early 19th century; feature attractions are the cold-blast, charcoal-burning iron furnace and the adjoining Cast House. Also on the grounds are the stone home of the ironmaster (or furnace owner), with four of the 15 rooms restored to the mid-19th century, and a typical worker's home of the same period furnished with appropriate pieces.
*Operated by National Park Service. Open Nov.–Feb: daily 8–5. Mar.–Oct: daily 9–6; closed Christmas and New Year's Day*

## EMMAUS

### SHELTER HOUSE, 1734
**South Fourth Street Extension**
Six-room, two-story log house with addition built in 1741. Original interiors and period furnishings
*Operated by The Shelter House Soc. Open by appointment*

## EPHRATA

### ■ EPHRATA CLOISTER, begun 1735
One of the earliest religious and secular communal societies, founded by Johann Conrad Beissel. Community constructed Beissel's log house and some of the stone buildings between 1735 and 1749, based on the style of their native Rhineland. Among the surviving buildings are Beissel's house, married couples' living quarters, sisters' house, chapel, and the Academy, built in 1837.
*Operated by Pa. Historical and Museum Comm. Open May–Oct: Tues.–Sat. 8:30–5, Sun. 1–5. Nov.–Apr: Tues.–Sat. 9–4:30, Sun. 1–4:30*

## ERIE

### COMMODORE PERRY MEMORIAL HOUSE AND DICKSON TAVERN, 1809
**201 French St**
Early tavern built by John Teel served as headquarters for Oliver Hazard Perry during the Battle of Lake Erie in September, 1813. The walls of the tavern are crisscrossed with secret passageways used to hide runaway slaves. Restored and furnished with early 19th-century pieces
*Operated by Perry Memorial House Comm. Open June–Sept. 15: daily 1–4. Sept. 16–May: Sat., Sun. 1–4*

## ERWINNA

### JOHN J. STOVER HOUSE, about 1810
**Pennsylvania Route 32, River Road**
Brick house, with additions built in 1840 and 1860, showing the architectural transition from the Federal to the Victorian styles. Owned by the family that built the nearby Stover-Myer Mill in 1800. In use for over a century and restored in 1970, the mill is also open to the public.
*Operated by Bucks County, Dept. of Parks and Recreation. Open Apr.–Oct: Sat., Sun. 2–5*

## FALLSINGTON

### BURGES-LIPPINCOTT HOUSE, 1780
**Meetinghouse Square**
Charming two-and-a-half-story house built by Samuel Burges, who purchased his land from William Penn;

*Ephrata Cloister*

noteworthy for the carved, fine mantel and doorway and unusual wall-bannister. Penn worshiped in this town which today boasts 25 pre-Revolutionary houses, some still occupied as residences. The Burges-Lippincott House and Stage Coach Tavern are furnished and open to the public; other houses are being restored.
*Operated by Historic Fallsington. Open Mar. 15–Nov. 15: Wed.–Sun. 1–5*

## FORT WASHINGTON

### HOPE LODGE, 1723
**Bethlehem Pike**
One of the earliest and finest Georgian manor houses in Pennsylvania and believed to have been built after plans by Sir Christopher Wren. The elegant, two-and-a-half-story mansion of brick and stucco was saved from destruction in 1922 and restored with period furnishings, Delft tile fireplaces, original molded wainscotings, and Pennsylvania-style kitchen. James Watmough, owner of the house from 1784 to 1812, named it after his guardian, Henry Hope, from whose family the Hope Diamond takes its name.
*Operated by Pa. Historical and Museum Comm. Open May–Oct: Tues.–Sat. 8:30–5, Sun. 1–5. Nov.–Apr: Tues.–Sat. 9–4:30, Sun. 1–4:30*

## GETTYSBURG

### DOBBIN HOUSE, 1776
**87–89 Steinwehr Ave**
Two-and-a-half-story stone house built by Rev. Alexander Dobbin and used by him as a school; during the Battle of Gettysburg the house was converted into a hospital. Used as a private residence into the 20th century, the house is now a museum featuring Civil War memorabilia and a diorama of the battlefield with over 3,000 figures.
*Operated by J.P. Adamik. Open Easter–Labor Day: daily 9–9. Sept.–Nov. 15: daily 12–9*

### ■ GETTYSBURG NATIONAL MILITARY PARK
More than 3,000 acres make up the park which includes the national cemetery dedicated by President Lincoln and the 1863 battlefield. One-and-a-half-story log farmhouse that served as headquarters for Gen. Meade, commander of the Union army, has been restored to its wartime appearance.
*Operated by National Park Service. Open June 18–Labor Day: daily 9–8:30. Sept.–Oct: daily 9–6. Nov.–June 17: daily 9–5*

### JENNIE WADE HOUSE, before 1863
**Baltimore Street**
On the third day of the Battle of Gettysburg, Jennie Wade was killed by a stray bullet while she was kneading dough. There are many nicks in the walls and holes in the door of the red brick house, originally built as the home of the McClellan family; now a museum with Civil War memorabilia
*Private. Open Mar. 15–May: daily 9–5. June–Aug: daily 9–9. Sept.–Nov: daily 9–5*

### WILLS HOUSE [LINCOLN ROOM MUSEUM], 1849
**Lincoln Square**
In the second-floor bedroom of David Wills's house, Abraham Lincoln completed his Gettysburg Address the night before he delivered the speech. The room was restored in 1956 and appears as it did when Lincoln spent the night there.
*Operated by Le Roy E. Smith. Open spring and fall: daily 9–5. Summer: daily 9–9*

## GOSHEN

### ■ ROBERT FULTON BIRTHPLACE, about 1765
**U.S. Route 222**
The famed inventor and builder of the first successful American steamboat was born in a small stone house on this

*Robert Fulton Birthplace*

site in 1765. Destroyed by fire in 1822, the existing house was rebuilt from the ruins and is today a memorial. *Operated by Pa. Historical and Museum Comm. Open May–Oct: Tues.– Sat. 8:30–5, Sun. 1–5. Nov.–Apr: Tues.–Sat. 9–4:30, Sun. 1–4:30*

## HARRISBURG

**FORT HUNTER MUSEUM, about 1789**
**5300 N Front St**
A stockaded blockhouse was built on this site in 1756 during the French and Indian War; used as a supply base, it was soon abandoned and in ruins by 1763. The present gray stone building, built in 1789 with a larger 1814 wing addition, houses the museum's collection, including colonial household articles and dolls.
*Operated by Fort Hunter Foundation. Open May 5–Oct. 15: Tues.–Sun. 8–5*

**JOHN HARRIS MANSION, 1764–66**
**219 S Front St**
Georgian gray stone mansion built by the city's founder and considered to be the oldest building in Harrisburg. Interiors of the two-and-a-half-story building have undergone many alterations and bear little resemblance to Harris' original home. From 1863 to 1889 Sen. Simon Cameron lived here and made the house the center of Pennsylvania political and social life. Furnished with period pieces and historical displays
*Operated by Historical Soc. of Dauphin Co. Open Mon.–Fri. 1–4:30, Sat. 1–4*

**MACLAY MANSION, 1791**
**401 N Front St**
Home of William Maclay, Pennsylvania senator to the first Congress, famous for his journal of the government's early years. A leader of Jefferson's Democratic-Republican party, Maclay was an outspoken critic of Washington and Hamilton.
*Operated by Pa. Bar Assn. Open by appointment*

## HAVERTOWN

**LAWRENCE CABIN MUSEUM,**
**early 1700s**
**Karakung Drive**
One-room log house with a loft built

early in the 18th century. The cabin is furnished with pieces typical of those found in 17th- and 18th-century Pennsylvania homes.
*Operated by Haverford Township Historical Soc. Open May–Nov: Sun. 1–5 and by appointment*

## HORSHAM

■ **GRAEME PARK, 1722**
**County Line Road**
Charming two-and-a-half-story fieldstone house, highlighted by fine interior woodwork; built as a malt house by Sir William Keith, governor of the province from 1717 to 1726. Dr. Thomas Graeme acquired the property and converted it to a residence when he married Sir William's step-daughter in 1737.
*Operated by Pa. Historical and Museum Comm. Open Tues.–Sat., holidays 8:30–5, Sun. 12–5*

*Graeme Park*

## INDIANA

**CROYLANDS, 1813**
A 13-room Victorian house; the home of Harry White, Civil War general and later a judge of Indiana County. Sparsely furnished with some of the White family furnishings
*Operated by Historical and Genealogical Soc. of Indiana Co. Open by appointment*

**PIONEER LOG HOUSE, about 1840**
**South Sixth and Wayne Avenues**
Two-story log house with kitchen; moved from its original site and reconstructed in 1961. Furnished
*Operated by Historical and Genealogical Soc. of Indiana Co. Open May 15–Labor Day: Sat., Sun. 2–5*

## JIM THORPE

### ASA PACKER MANSION, 1859–62
**Packer Hill**
Italian Renaissance-style mansion built by Asa Packer, millionaire railroad magnate and founder of Lehigh University. The 19-room mansion was occupied until 1913, when Packer's eldest daughter died. Opened in 1953, the mansion retains Packer's original, opulent Victorian furnishings.
*Operated by Jim Thorpe Lions Club. Open May–Oct: Tues.–Sun. 11–5*

## LANCASTER

### THE AMISH HOMESTEAD, about 1750
**Route 462**
Old Amish house located on a 71-acre farm. Horses and mules are raised to work the farm, which was established in 1744.
*Operated by the Amish Homestead. Open daily 9–5*

### HANS HERR HOUSE, 1719
**Willow Street**
One of the earliest examples of Swiss-German architecture in America and the oldest surviving structure used as a meetinghouse by Mennonites; built as a home by Hans Herr, who emigrated to Pennsylvania in 1710. Under restoration; when completed the house will contain period furnishings
*Operated by Lancaster Mennonite Conference Historical Soc. Open by appointment during restoration*

### ROCK FORD, 1793
**South Duke Street**
Revolutionary War commander and member of the Continental Congress Gen. Edward Hand built this simple brick mansion overlooking the Conestoga River. The four-story, center-hall house retains the original panelings, window glass, doors, cupboards, shutters, and floors. Long-lost house inventory served as a guide to restoration and refurnishing; numerous outbuildings are being reconstructed.
*Operated by the Rock Ford Foundation. Open Mon.–Sat. 10–5, Sun. 12–5*

■ **WHEATLAND, 1828**
**Marietta Avenue**
James Buchanan bought this two-and-a-half-story brick mansion in 1848 while he was Secretary of State. He returned to Wheatland after his term as President and lived here until his death in 1868. Built for a local banker, the 17-room house is kept as it was during the Buchanan years, with his furniture, china, and memorabilia.
*Operated by James Buchanan Foundation for the Preservation of Wheatland. Open Mon.–Sat. 9–5, Sun. 10–5*

*Wheatland*

## LANDIS VALLEY

### PENNSYLVANIA FARM MUSEUM
**Route 222**
Museum village reminiscent of 19th-century rural life among the Pennsylvania Dutch. Built around the Victorian farmhouse and Americana collection of Henry and George Landis, the village also features a tavern, two barns, wagon shed, other farmhouses, and two log houses. Seminars and demonstrations of handicrafts held during the year
*Operated by Pa. Historical and Museum Comm. Open May–Oct: Mon.–Sat. 8:30–5, Sun. 1–5. Nov.–Apr: Mon.–Sat. 9:40–4:30, Sun. 12–4:30*

## LITITZ

### JOHANNES MUELLER HOUSE, 1792
**137–139 E Main St**
Log-and-stone house of typical German-American design built by the community dyer, a member of a sect of Christian Socialists. Restored in 1965, it is furnished with period pieces and local artifacts. Lining the street are other 18th-century buildings, most still in use, including the bakery where the first commercial pretzels were made.
*Operated by Lititz Historical Foun-*

*dation. Open May 30–Labor Day: Tues.–Sat. 10–4 and by appointment*

## MEADVILLE

### BALDWIN-REYNOLDS HOUSE, 1843
**Terrace Street**
Home of congressman and Supreme Court justice Henry Baldwin, built along the Venango Trail. In 1847 William Reynolds, nephew of Mrs. Baldwin, acquired the Greek Revival house, which remained in his family until 1963. Extensively altered over the years, it is now furnished and open as a museum with exhibits of local history.
*Operated by Crawford Co. Historical Soc. Open May 30–Labor Day: Wed., Sat., Sun. 2–5, including July 4*

## MERCER

### MAGOFFIN HOUSE, 1821; 1825–26
**119 S Pitt St**
One room of this two-story frame house was built in 1821; the remaining 11 rooms were added between 1825 and 1826. Now a museum with exhibits of Indian relics, pioneer furniture, and clothing
*Operated by Mercer Co. Historical Soc. Open Tues.–Sat. 1–4:30, Fri. evgs. 7–9; closed holidays*

## NAZARETH

### GREY HOUSE, 1740
**East Center Street**
One-story log-and-limestone house is the oldest Moravian building in the country. A boys' school was opened here in 1743.
*Operated by Moravian Historical Soc. Under restoration*

### WHITEFIELD HOUSE, 1740–55
**210 E Center St**
Three-story colonial house of native limestone, with hand-hewn timbers and slate-covered gambrel roof, begun by Moravian pioneers for Rev. George Whitefield, English-born evangelist. The house was not completed until 1755 because of a dispute between the reverend and the Moravians. Completely renovated in 1871, it now houses the historical society museum.
*Operated by Moravian Historical Soc. Open by appointment*

## NEW GENEVA

■ **FRIENDSHIP HILL, 1789; 1823**
**Route 166**
Albert Gallatin, Swiss-born congressman and Secretary of the Treasury under Jefferson and Madison, purchased this estate in 1788. The following year the brick portion of the mansion was built, and in 1823 the stone addition was completed. When Gallatin retired to New York City in 1832 he sold the estate, which today retains the original furnishings.
*Operated by Friendship Hill Assn. Open May–Oct: daily 10–6*

## NEW HOPE

### PARRY MANSION, 1780s
**Main Street**
Two-and-a-half-story gray stone house, with kitchen wing, built by Benjamin Parry, owner of the New Hope Mills, after which the town was named. When restoration is complete the house will feature furnishings from 1775 to 1900, showing the evolution of middle-class taste in interior design.
*Operated by New Hope Historical Soc. Under restoration*

## NORTHUMBERLAND

■ **JOSEPH PRIESTLEY HOUSE, 1794**
Joseph Priestley, the discoverer of oxygen, built this house following his emigration from England. A two-and-a-half-story frame house with kitchen wing on one side and a laboratory on the other, it looks much as it did during Priestley's lifetime. Restored, with a small museum of his personal effects
*Operated by Pa. Historical and Mu-*

*Joseph Priestley House*

*seum Comm. Open May–Oct: Tues.–Sat. 8:30–5, Sun. 1–5. Nov.–Apr: Tues.–Sat. 9–4:30, Sun. 1–4:30*

## NORWOOD

### MORTON MORTONSON HOUSE, about 1750
**East Winona Avenue, Norwood Municipal Park**
Unusual brick farmhouse features a combination gambrel and gable roof. The interior, which will be furnished when restoration is completed, boasts the original paneling and hardware.
*Operated by Norwood Fourth of July Assn. Hours to be determined*

## OLEY

### DE TURK HOUSE, 1767
One-and-a-half-story stone cabin built by John and Deborah De Turk; John was the son of one of the earliest Huguenot settlers in the Oley Valley. A Moravian synod was held here in 1742 in an attempt to unite the various German Protestant sects.
*Operated by Historic Preservation Trust of Berks Co. Restoration in progress*

## PHILADELPHIA

### BETSY ROSS HOUSE, before 1720
**239 Arch St**
In this two-and-a-half-story brick house Betsy Ross supposedly fashioned the first American flag. Restored in 1937, it is furnished with colonial pieces and maintained as a shrine.
*Operated by City of Philadelphia. Open daily 9:30–5:15*

### ■ BISHOP WHITE HOUSE, 1786
**309 Walnut St**
Built while the Rev. White was in London for his consecration as Episcopal Bishop of Philadelphia, the house has eight levels from the ice well in the root cellar to the loft above the fourth floor. Bishop White served as chaplain of the Continental Congress and later of the Senate when Philadelphia was the nation's capital. Restored as part of Independence National Historical Park and furnished with period pieces
*Operated by National Park Service. Open June–Oct: Tues.–Sun., tours at 11, 1, 2, 3. Nov.–May: Tues.–Fri., tours at 11, 1, 2*

### CEDAR GROVE, about 1745
**Fairmount Park**
Stone mansion with gambrel roof and interesting covered porch was expanded from a three-room cottage first in 1756 and later by Isaac Wistar Morris in the 1790s. It was moved to the park from its original site in 1927. Lydia Thompson Morris refurnished it with pieces acquired by the family in the years they owned the house.
*Operated by Philadelphia Museum of Art. Open daily 10–5; closed national holidays*

### ■ EDGAR ALLAN POE HOUSE, about 1800
**530 N Seventh St**
Small cottage was Poe's home from 1842 to 1844. Restored in 1927 as a library and museum with exhibits of manuscripts, including "The Raven" and "The Gold Bug," and memorabilia of Poe and other contemporaneous authors
*Operated by Richard Gimbel Foundation for Literary Research. Open Mon.–Fri. 10–5, Sat., Sun. 2–5*

### ■ ELFRETH'S ALLEY HISTORIC DISTRICT
Two- and three-story houses built in the 17th and 18th centuries line this six-foot-wide street in the heart of Philadelphia. The façades of the houses are flush with the street, which has remained as it was in colonial days.

### HILL-PHYSICK-KEITH HOUSE, 1786; 1815
**321 S Fourth St**
Federal house with four-story section built by the Hill family. Dr. Philip Syng Physick, the "Father of American Surgery," bought the house in 1815 and added a three-story wing. The house was occupied by Dr. Physick's descendants until 1941; restored and furnished with fine Federal pieces.
*Operated by Philadelphia Soc. for the Preservation of Landmarks. Open Tues.–Sun. 10–4; closed holidays*

### ■ JOHN BARTRAM HOUSE AND GARDENS, 1731
**54 Street and Eastwick Avenue**
Two-and-a-half-story Georgian stone

house built by John Bartram, America's first native botanist. Bartram collected and cultivated rare, exotic plants in the gardens surrounding the house. Furnished with period pieces *Operated by Fairmount Park Comm. Open daily 8–4*

### LEMON HILL, before 1770
**Fairmount Park**
Elegant, late Georgian mansion was owned by Robert Morris, financier of the Revolution, until 1799, when financial ruin sent him to debtors' prison. Henry Pratt, whose work with lemon trees gave the 300-acre estate its name, lived here until his death in 1838; the city then purchased the property for a public park, the nucleus of today's Fairmount Park. Among the noteworthy features of the house are three dramatic elliptical rooms, one above the other, and the delicate interior detail. In 1926 Fiske Kimball restored and refurnished the mansion with fine period pieces.
*Operated by Colonial Dames of America. Open winter: Thurs. 11–3. Summer: Thurs. 11–4, Sun. 1–4*

*Lemon Hill*

### LETITIA STREET HOUSE, 1711–13
**Fairmount Park**
Small brick house built between 1711 and 1713 for Quaker merchant and itinerant preacher Thomas Chalkley. In 1883 the house was moved to Fairmount Park when it was mistakenly believed to have been one of William Penn's residences. Restored in 1932 and furnished with pieces representing Philadelphia's early mercantile society
*Operated by Philadelphia Museum of Art. Open daily 10–5; closed national holidays*

### MAN FULL OF TROUBLE MUSEUM, 1759
**127 S Second St**
Two adjoining brick half-gambrel buildings, a tavern and the *Benjamin Paschall House,* were used as an inn until the late 19th century. They were saved from demolition and restored with colonial furnishings as a museum of decorative arts.
*Operated by Knauer Foundation. Open Apr.–Nov: Tues.–Sun. 1–4. Dec.–Mar: Sat., Sun. 1–4*

### ■ MOUNT PLEASANT, 1762
**Fairmount Park**
Considered to be the finest example of a colonial country house in the North, built by Scottish sea captain and privateer John Macpherson and at one time the property of Benedict Arnold. The stuccoed brick mansion with grand Palladian window and hipped roof, balustraded deck and two quadruple chimneys, is furnished with outstanding examples of Chippendale furniture made in Philadelphia from 1760 to 1785.
*Operated by Philadelphia Museum of Art. Open daily 10–5; closed national holidays*

*Mount Pleasant*

### ■ REYNOLDS-MORRIS MANSION, 1787
**225 S Eighth St**
A fine example of a Georgian Philadelphia row town house, built by John Reynolds of red brick laid in Flemish bond. In 1817 Luke Wistar Morris bought the house, which now stands alone without the adjoining 18th-century houses. The mansion and

gardens are now used as a guesthouse of the firm of N.W. Ayer & Son.
*Private. Open by appointment*

## SAMUEL POWEL HOUSE, 1765
**244 S Third St**
Fine, three-story Georgian town house of red brick built for Samuel Powel, mayor of Philadelphia before and after the Revolution. George Washington, Lafayette, and other notables of the era were entertained here by Powel. Exceptional interior paneling and wood carving
*Operated by Philadelphia Soc. for the Preservation of Landmarks. Open Mon.–Fri. 10–5*

## STRAWBERRY MANSION, 1798; about 1830
**Fairmount Park**
Somerton, the original house on this site, was burned by the British during the Revolution. The central portion of the present mansion was rebuilt in the Federal style and named "Summerville." Joseph Hemphill added the Greek Revival wings in the 1830s; his son, renowned as a cultivator of strawberries, gave the house its present name. Restored to its former elegance in 1930, it is furnished with period antiques.
*Operated by The Committee of 1926. Open Tues.–Sun. 11–5*

*Strawberry Mansion*

## SWEETBRIAR, 1797
**Fairmount Park**
Congressman Samuel Breck built this gracious Federal mansion as the first year-round residence on the Schuylkill River. It was acquired by Fairmount Park in 1868 and restored with Federal furnishings in 1927.
*Operated by Modern Club of Philadelphia. Open Mon.–Sat. 10–5; closed national holidays*

## ■ TODD HOUSE, 1777
**Walnut and Fourth Streets**
Jonathan Dilworth, a local carpenter, built this three-story brick row house with two-story kitchen wing, but apparently he never lived here. In 1791 it was sold to John Todd and his wife Dolley. Todd died in 1793, and the following year Dolley married James Madison. The house remained in the Todd family until 1818; after a succession of owners it was acquired by the government in 1950 as part of Independence National Historical Park.
*Operated by National Park Service. Open June–Oct: Tues.–Sat. 10–3, Sun 1–4. Nov.–May: Tues.–Sat. 11–3, Sun. 1–4*

## ■ WOODFORD, before 1742; 1756
**Fairmount Park**
In 1756 Judge William Coleman bought a one-story brick house and added a second story and wing to create this interesting Georgian mansion. Noteworthy features include the projecting cornice between the stories that runs around three sides of the house and the fine drawing room. Authentically restored in 1929 and furnished with the Naomi Wood collection of 18th-century furniture
*Operated by Estate of Naomi Wood, deceased; Martin P. Snyder, trustee. Open Tues.–Sun. 1–5; closed Aug. and national holidays*

## PHILADELPHIA (GERMANTOWN)

### BAYNTON HOUSE, 1802
**5208 Germantown Ave**
Brick house with heavy stone entrance steps and a slate roof is now the historical society's library. Although some alterations have been made for library purposes, the interiors have been largely preserved.
*Operated by Germantown Historical Soc. Open Wed. 1–5*

### ■ DESHLER-MORRIS HOUSE, 1772
**5442 Germantown Ave**
For brief periods in 1793 and 1794 George Washington used this house as his Presidential residence when an outbreak of yellow fever forced the government out of Philadelphia, then the national capital. The two-and-a-

half-story house with 24 paned windows was built by David Deshler; it was owned by Col. Isaac Franks when Washington occupied it and later sold to Samuel Morris, in whose family it remained until it was acquired for inclusion in Independence National Historical Park.
*Operated by National Park Service. Open Tues.–Sun. 1–4*

*Deshler-Morris House*

### ■ GERMANTOWN HISTORIC DISTRICT

Settled in 1683 by Netherlanders fleeing religious persecution, Germantown retains its distinctive character today. Approximately 50 18th- and 19-century buildings — taverns, homes, churches, and a school — are preserved in the district.

### GRUMBLETHORPE, 1744
**5267 Germantown Ave**

Two-and-a-half-story stone house built by John Wister was the first summer home to be built in Germantown. Much of Sarah Wister's famous *Journal of Life in Philadelphia* is set in the house. Furnished with period pieces
*Operated by Philadelphia Soc. for the Preservation of Landmarks. Open Tues.–Fri. 2–5*

### HACKER HOUSE, about 1772
**5214 Germantown Ave**

Core of this two-and-a-half-story, gray stone building was built by William Forbes with later additions made at various times. Restored in 1927 the house is now the historical society's main museum featuring colonial and

Revolutionary period antiques.
*Operated by Germantown Historical Soc. Open Tues., Thurs., Sat. 1–5; closed Sat. in Aug.*

### HOWELL HOUSE, 1770
**5218 Germantown Ave**

Stone house with large extension added later is used by the historical society as an adjunct to the larger museum in the Hacker House. Displays include samplers and toys.
*Operated by Germantown Historical Soc. Open Tues., Thurs., Sat. 1–5; closed Sat. in Aug.*

### LOUDOUN, 1801; 1830
**4650 Germantown Ave**

East section of three-story house built by Berry & Ardis for Thomas Armat and his son when a yellow fever epidemic forced them to leave Philadelphia; portico added in 1830, changing the house to the present Greek Revival style. Occupied by descendants of Thomas Armat until 1939; the furnishings include many 18th-century family heirlooms.
*Operated by Fairmount Park Comm. and Friends of Loudoun. Open Tues., Thurs. 1–4, and by appointment*

### ■ STENTON, 1723–30
**18 and Courtland Streets**

Three-story brick Georgian mansion was designed and built by James Logan, William Penn's secretary and attorney and later chief justice of Pennsylvania. The deep closets found in the principal rooms are most unusual in a house of this period. Both Gen. Washington and Sir William Howe used Stenton as headquarters during the Revolution. The mansion was occupied until 1900 by six generations of the Logan family and has

*Stenton*

remained largely unaltered; furnishings are 18th-century antiques.
*Operated by National Soc. of Colonial Dames. Open Tues.–Sat. 1–5*

**UPSALA, 1798–1801**
**6430 Germantown Ave**
Fine Federal mansion, one of Philadelphia's most lovely homes. Interior woodwork includes carved mantelpieces and stairways and paneled wainscoting. Restoration began in 1944; furnished with pieces from the period of 1725 to 1830
*Operated by Upsala Foundation. Open Tues., Fri. 1–4*

**VERNON MANSION, 1770; 1803**
**Vernon Park**
Late 18th-century country farmhouse with large fireplaces is now the rear portion of the present house. Federal-style front section with detailed interior woodwork added in 1803
*Operated by Germantown Community Council. Open Mon.–Fri. 9–5*

## PITTSBURGH

**FORT PITT BLOCKHOUSE, 1764**
**Point Park**
Built as a redoubt outside the walls of Fort Pitt by Col. Henry Bouquet following the seizure of the fort in Pontiac's War of 1763 and believed to be the oldest building in Pittsburgh. Converted to a residence by Isaac Craig in 1784 after an addition was put on, it remained a home until donated to the Daughters of the American Revolution in 1894.
*Operated by Pa. Historical and Museum Comm. Open Mon.–Sat. 9:30–4:30, Sun. 2–4:30*

**NEAL LOG HOUSE, about 1787**
**Schenley Park**
One-room log house with loft, large fieldstone chimney, and double fireplace. Built by Robert Neal, it is the oldest log house in the city; completely restored and furnished with appropriate 18th-century pieces
*Operated by Pittsburgh History and Landmarks Foundation. Open summer: daily 1–5 and by appointment*

## POTTSTOWN

**POTTSGROVE MANSION, begun in 1752**
Elegant Georgian mansion built by John Potts, ironmaster and founder of Pottstown. Famous for its large central hallway, beautiful overmantels, corner cupboards, and cushioned window seats. After many years as a hotel, the house was purchased by Pott's descendants, who presented it to the state. Restored with fine colonial furnishings, primarily Philadelphia Chippendale, and an 18th-century flower and herb garden; the house was reopened on its 200th anniversary.
*Operated by Pa. Historical and Museum Comm. Open May–Oct: Tues.–Sat. 8:30–5, Sun. 1–5. Nov.–Apr: Tues.–Sat. 9–4:30, Sun. 1–4:30*

## PROSPECT PARK

**MORTON HOMESTEAD, about 1650**
**Route 420, Darby Creek**
Original log portion of this typical Swedish-Finnish pioneer cabin was built by Morton Mortonson in the mid-17th century and is probably the oldest surviving structure in the state. Morton's son built a second log cabin in 1698; the two were connected with a stone section in 1806. Morton's great-grandson, John Morton, signer of the Declaration of Independence, was born here in 1724.
*Operated by Pa. Historical and Museum Comm. Open May–Oct: Tues.–Sat. 8:30–5, Sun. 1–5. Nov.–Apr: Tues.–Sat. 9–4:30, Sun. 1–4:30*

*Morton Homestead*

## ROSEMONT

**ASHBRIDGE HOUSE, 1769**
**Montgomery Avenue and Aeredale Road**
Colonial house of stone with three dormer windows; furnished with

antiques. Historical society museum featuring objects of local history
*Operated by Lower Merion Historical Soc. Open by appointment*

## SMICKSBURG

### JOHN B. McCORMICK HOUSE, 1817
**Rural Free Delivery #1**
Two-and-a-half-story stone house built by Judge Lewis, a prominent local citizen; sold upon his death to John Stewart, great-grandfather of actor Jimmy Stewart. Home in retirement of John B. McCormick, inventor of the Holyoke turbine. Various industrial engines and turbines are exhibited.
*Private. Open May 30–Oct. 15: daily 10–5*

## STRASBURG

### THE AMISH VILLAGE, 1840
**Route 896**
Furnished Amish house built in 1840 is part of a reconstructed village featuring a smokehouse, blacksmith shop, and waterwheel.
*Operated by The Amish Village. Open spring and fall: daily 8:30–5. Winter: Sat., Sun. 8:30–5. Summer: daily 8:30–8*

## STROUDSBURG

### STROUD MANSION, 1795
**Ninth and Main Streets**
Three-and-a-half-story stucco-covered stone house built for Daniel Stroud by his father, the founder of the town. The historical society has a library and museum in the house featuring over a century of newspapers and exhibits of Indian artifacts, furniture, and household items.
*Operated by Monroe Co. Historical Soc. Open Tues. 1–4*

## SUNBURY

### HUNTER MANSION, 1852
**1150 N Front St**
Attractive two-and-a-half-story brick house; now a museum for the scale replica of Fort Augusta, a log fortification built in 1756 to protect the frontier. When the fort was abandoned after the Revolution, Col. Samuel Hunter, the last commander, remained

and lived in the commandant's quarters; these burned in 1852, and his grandson erected the present structure.
*Operated by Pa. Historical and Museum Comm. Open May–Oct: Tues.–Sat. 8:30–5, Sun. 1–5. Nov.–Apr: Tues.–Sat. 9–4:30, Sun. 1–4:30*

## TULLYTOWN

### ■ PENNSBURY MANOR, begun 1680s
Built on the foundation of the original, this is a complete re-creation of William Penn's manor on the Delaware River, where he lived from 1700 to 1701. Based on letters to the overseer of construction and inventories of his furnishings, the manor reconstruction was completed in 1939. The 17th-century furnishings are the largest collection in Pennsylvania; also on the estate are seven outbuildings and extensive gardens.
*Operated by Pa. Historical and Museum Comm. Open May–Oct: Tues.–Sat. 8:30–5, Sun. 1–5. Nov.–Apr: Tues.–Sat. 9–4:30, Sun. 1–4:30*

*Pennsbury Manor*

## UPLAND

### CALEB PUSEY HOUSE, 1683
**Race Street**
Red brick and whitewashed stone house built by Richard Townsend for Caleb Pusey, manager (in partnership with William Penn) of the colony's first gristmill. Believed to be the oldest English-built house remaining intact in Pennsylvania
*Operated by Friends of the Caleb Pusey House. Open Tues.–Sun. 1–5*

## VALLEY FORGE

■ **WASHINGTON HEAD-QUARTERS, before 1768**
Valley Forge State Park
Simple stone building, built by Isaac Potts, was Gen. Washington's headquarters from December, 1777, to June, 1778. Other buildings in the park include Gen. Varnum's headquarters, the bakehouse, a reconstructed soldiers' hut, and headquarters of Baron von Steuben, who drilled and trained the Continental Army here. *Operated by Valley Forge State Park Comm. Open daily 9–5*

## WASHINGTON

**DAVID BRADFORD HOUSE, 1788**
173 Main St
Stone house, one of the first in the town, built by David Bradford, prominent lawyer and businessman. Bradford was forced to flee Pennsylvania after acting as leader of the Whisky Rebellion of 1794, a protest against the high Federal excise taxes on grain. The house, with its rich interior featuring a mahogany staircase, was restored to its 18th-century design and furnished with period pieces. *Operated by Pa. Historical and Museum Comm. Open May–Oct: Tues.–Sat. 8:30–5, Sun. 1–5. Nov.–Apr: Tues.–Sat. 9–4:30, Sun. 1–4:30*

**LeMOYNE HOUSE, 1812**
49 E Marden St
Two-story Greek Revival house of gray stone built by Dr. Francis LeMoyne, professor at Washington College and leading abolitionist. Now a museum featuring Indian artifacts, Oriental objects, and items of local history; furnishings throughout the house are the original LeMoyne family pieces. *Operated by Washington Co. Historical Soc. Open Mon.–Fri. 1–5*

## WASHINGTON CROSSING

■ **WASHINGTON CROSSING STATE PARK**
Scene of Washington's famed crossing of the Delaware River on Christmas night, 1776. The *Thompson-Neely "House of Decision,"* requisitioned as headquarters for Gen. Stirling and Lt.

James Monroe, is furnished with period pieces. Among the other sites in the park are The Ferry Inn, a wildflower preserve, and the renowned painting "Washington Crossing the Delaware" in the Memorial Building. *Operated by Washington Crossing Park Comm. Open – Thompson-Neely House – Mon.–Sat. 10–5, Sun. 1–5. Memorial Building – daily 9–5*

## WATERFORD

**JUDSON HOUSE, 1820**
31 High St
Amos Judson, local merchant, built his Greek Revival house on the site of Fort Le Boeuf, a French outpost built in 1753 and burned in 1758 – later rebuilt by the British and again destroyed by fire in 1763. The Judson House today contains a small museum and a model of the French fort. Across the street are the ruins of an American fort built in 1796 to protect the frontier. *Operated by Pa. Historical and Museum Comm. Open May–Oct: Tues.–Sat. 8:30–5, Sun. 1–5. Nov.–Apr: Tues.–Sat. 9–4:30, Sun. 1–4:30*

## WAYNE

**FINLEY HOUSE, 1789; 1889**
113 W Beechtree Lane
Two-story house of cement-covered stone was completely renovated when the Victorian wing was added; none of the 18th-century features have been retained. Furnished with period pieces and the library and museum collection of the historical society *Operated by Radnor Historical Soc. Open Tues. 2–5 and by appointment*

## WEST CHESTER

**DAVID TOWNSEND HOUSE, 1790s; 1830**
225 N Matlack St
Original small farmhouse was converted into a brick town house in 1830. David Townsend, local banker and botanist, added the kitchen wing with a porch in 1849 and directed the landscaping of the house. Donated to the society in 1951, it is furnished with Federal, Empire, and Victorian pieces; many of the shrubs and trees date from Townsend's residence.

PENNSYLVANIA

Operated by Chester Co. Historical
Soc. Open May–Oct. 31: Tues., Thurs.,
Sat. 1–4; closed national holidays

## WEST OVERTON
### ABRAHAM OVERHOLT HOUSE, 1838
Three-and-a-half-story red brick house,
with two-story wooden porch and
white woodwork, built by distiller
Abraham Overholt. Furnished with
19th-century pieces in various styles
*Operated by Westmoreland-Fayette
Historical Soc. Open May 15–Oct. 15:
Sat., Sun. 2–5*

### FRICK BIRTHPLACE, before 1849
Henry Clay Frick was born in this
stone springhouse with a slate roof in
December, 1849. His parents lived
here while their house was being
completed.
*Operated by Westmoreland-Fayette
Historical Soc. Open May 15–Oct. 15:
Sat., Sun. 2–5*

## WOMELSDORF
### ■ CONRAD WEISER HOUSE, 1729; 1751
U.S. Route 422
Small stone house with sloping roof,
set in a park, built by Conrad Weiser,
German immigrant, pioneer, and 18th-
century "ambassador" of peace to the
Iroquois nation. This one-room house
with sleeping quarters above was expanded in 1751 and is now a museum
with period furnishings. The more
elaborate stone house, built in 1824,
is used by the park's caretaker. Weiser,
his wife, and several children are
buried nearby.
*Operated by Pa. Historical and Mu-
seum Comm. Open May–Oct: Tues.–
Sat. 8:30–5, Sun. 1–5. Nov.–Apr:
Tues.–Sat. 9–4:30, Sun. 1–4:30*

Conrad Weiser House

## WYOMING
### SWETLAND HOUSE, 1797
885 Wyoming Ave
Originally a rectangular one-room
"settler's cottage," with sleeping loft
above, built by Luke Swetland; rooms
were added in front of the cottage over
a period of years and the entire house
was "modernized" about 1850. Furnishings in the house reflect changing
tastes from 1797 to 1864.
*Operated by Wyoming Historical and
Geological Soc. Open June–Sept:
Tues.–Sun. 1–5*

## YORK
### BONHAM HOUSE, about 1870
152 E Market St
Three-story Victorian brick town house
with bay window reflects life of a local
family around the turn of the century.
Furnishings represent various 19th-
century periods; china, silver, and
glassware are displayed.
*Operated by Historical Soc. of York
Co. Open Mon.–Sat. 10–4, Sun. 1–5*

### GEN. GATES HOUSE, 1751
West Market Street and Pershing
Avenue
Two-story stone house occupied by
Gen. Horatio Gates in 1777 when the
Continental Congress met in York.
Here Gates advanced a plan to oust
Washington and make himself com-
mander of the Continental Army, but
Lafayette squelched the scheme. Ad-
joining the house is the Golden Plough
Tavern, built about 1740 in the medi-
eval half-timber style popular with
18th-century German settlers.
*Operated by Historical Soc. of York
Co. Open May–Oct: Mon.–Sat. 10–5,
Sun. 1–5. Nov.–Apr: Mon.–Sat. 10–4,
Sun. 1–4*

### LOG HOUSE, 1812
West Market Street and Pershing
Avenue
Two-story log house representative of
dwellings in colonial York. Rediscov-
ered and restored in 1960; furnished
with pieces typical of those belonging
to early German settlers
*Operated by Historical Soc. of York
Co. Open May–Oct: Mon.–Sat. 10–5,
Sun. 1–5. Nov.–Apr: Mon.–Sat. 10–4,
Sun. 1–4*

## BRISTOL

### HERRESHOFF HOUSE, about 1800
**142 Hope St**
Boyhood home after 1856 of the Herreshoff brothers, Nathanael Greene and John Brown, designers and builders of successful America's Cup defender yachts. Outstanding 18th-century furniture and decorations
*Operated by Mr. Norman Herreshoff, owner. Open July–Aug: Sat., Sun. 2–5. Labor Day weekend: 2–5*

## COVENTRY

### GEN. NATHANAEL GREENE HOMESTEAD, 1774
**Route 117**
Neat frame home divided by a wide hall, with four rooms on each floor, built for his new bride by Gen. Greene, who became second in command to Gen. Washington. They lived here until 1783 when the house was purchased by Jacob Greene, his brother; the house remained in the hands of Greene descendants until 1899. Exhibits connected with the Revolutionary War and the Greene family
*Operated by Nathanael Greene Homestead Assn. Open Mar.–Nov: Wed., Sat., Sun. 2–5*

### PAINE HOUSE, 1668
**1 Station St**
An old saltbox built in the 17th century; used as a tavern for 80 years by the Holden family. The 22 rooms were restored in 1952 as a house museum with furnishings as near as possible to the original.
*Operated by Western R.I. Civic Historical Soc. Open May: Sun., Tues. 1–5. June–Aug: Tues. 1–5 and by appointment*

## CRANSTON

### GOV. SPRAGUE MANSION, 1790; 1864
**1351 Cranston St**
Two-and-a-half-story house with Doric portico adjoining the earlier home of the politically and financially prominent Sprague family. The second William Sprague was a Civil War governor (1860–63) and U.S. senator (1863–75). Carrington collection of Oriental art on display, also a carriage house with sleighs

*Operated by Cranston Historical Soc. Open May 17–Sept. 13: Tues., Sun. 2–4*

*Gov. Sprague Mansion*

### JOY HOMESTEAD, 1770
**156 Scituate Ave**
A gambrel-roofed farmhouse built by Job Joy typical of homes owned by prosperous farm families of the 18th and 19th centuries. The Joys increased their land holdings for three generations and created an early industrial center about their home known as Joystown. Restored with period furnishings and craft demonstrations
*Operated by Cranston Historical Soc. Open May: Sun. 1–5*

## EAST GREENWICH

### GEN. JAMES MITCHELL VARNUM HOUSE, 1773
**57 Pierce St**
Handsome two-story frame mansion, home of distinguished Revolutionary officer James Mitchell Varnum, who later became judge for the Northwest Territory. The interior paneling is so fine that the northeast parlor was copied by architect Stanford White for one of the buildings at the Jamestown Exposition. Period furnishings, adjacent carriage house, garden
*Operated by Gen. Varnum Assn. Open June: Sun. 3–5. July–Sept: Wed., Sun. 3–5*

## JOHNSTON

### CLEMENCE-IRONS HOUSE, about 1680
**38 George Waterman Rd**
Stone-end house of one story with loft and rear lean-to built by carpenter Thomas Clemence after Indians burned the original house in 1676, leaving only the great main stone chimney standing. Home of five gen-

erations of the Irons family; finely restored
*Operated by Soc. for the Preservation of New England Antiquities. Open June–Oct: Tues.–Thurs. 1–5*

## LINCOLN

### ■ ELEAZER ARNOLD HOUSE, 1687
**499 Great Rd**
In this fine example of the characteristic Rhode Island stone-end house (with enormous pilaster-top stone chimney), Arnold once kept a tavern. Various lean-tos and a two-story frame section with a separate chimney at the east end have been added. Period furnishings
*Operated by Soc. for the Preservation of New England Antiquities. Open June 15–Oct. 15: Tues.–Sat. 12–5*

*Eleazer Arnold House*

## LITTLE COMPTON

### WILBOR HOUSE, 1685–90; 1740; 1850
**West Road**
Frame dwelling with clapboard front and shingled side in the Wilbor family for eight generations, thus typical of a New England family homestead which grew over the centuries. Restored with original details intact: exposed corner posts, great summer beam, feather-edge boards, etc.; furnished with local antiques of the different periods of the house
*Operated by Little Compton Historical Soc. Open June–Sept: Tues.–Sun. 2–5*

## MIDDLETOWN

### ■ WHITEHALL, 1729
**Berkeley Avenue**
Frame hipped-roof home of the Irish philosopher and Anglican dean George Berkeley for the three years he spent in Newport (1729–31) while en route to Bermuda to establish a college which never materialized. He gave great impetus to the cultural development of the colonies—he had America's first professional artist, John Smibert, in his entourage, and he founded the Philosophical Soc. of Newport.
*Operated by Soc. of Colonial Dames. Open July–Labor Day: daily 10–5*

## NEWPORT

### ABRAHAM RODRIGUES RIVERA HOUSE, 1740
**Washington Square**
Three-story gambrel-roofed house where in July of 1763 Rev. James Manning formulated the original plans to establish Rhode Island College, which in 1804 became Brown University. Now houses a bank
*Operated by Newport National Bank. Open daily during banking hours*

### BELCOURT CASTLE, 1894
**Bellevue Avenue**
Louis XIII-style 52-room mansion designed by architects Richard Morris Hunt and John Russell Pope for Oliver H. P. Belmont. Contains famous collection of antique treasures from 32 countries, including armor, wood carvings, and stained glass. Visitors can see the making of stained glass; costumed guides
*Operated by Belcourt Castle. Open May: Sat., Sun. 10–5. June–Sept: daily 10–6. Oct–Nov. 11: Sat., Sun. 10–5*

### THE BREAKERS, 1895
**Ochre Point Road**
Designed by Richard Morris Hunt for Cornelius Vanderbilt, this mansion is the most magnificent of all Newport summer residences. Resembling the northern Italian palaces of Genoa and Turin, all the ornamentation and furnishings of the 70 rooms were designed as an integral part of the overall plan. The first floor—with the formal rooms for entertaining—and part of the

*Hunter House*

*Chateau-Sur-Mer*

*Marble House*

second – with all the original furnishings – are open to visitors. The "Cottage," a Victorian children's playhouse, is located on the beautiful grounds, while the carriage house–stables are at Coggeshall–Bateman avenues.
*Operated by Preservation Soc. of Newport Co. Open Apr. 15–May: Sat., Sun. 10–5. June–Nov. 15: daily 10–5 and July–Sept 15: Fri. until 9*

### ■ CHATEAU-SUR-MER, 1852; 1872
**Bellevue Avenue**
Lavish granite Victorian mansion built for William S. Wetmore, who made his fortune in the China trade. In 1872 his son George Peabody Wetmore, governor and U.S. senator, commissioned Richard Morris Hunt to add an Eastlake library, a French ballroom, and an Italian dining room. Hunt also added a mansard roof and increased the number of towers, windows, and rooms. Elaborately carved and inlaid interiors and stained-glass window by John La Farge. Landscaped grounds
*Operated by Preservation Soc. of Newport Co. Open June 14–Nov. 15: daily 10–5*

### ■ EDWARD KING HOUSE, 1845–47
**Aquidneck Park, Spring Street**
Red brick mansion in the Italian villa style designed by Richard Upjohn for Edward King, who had made his fortune in the China trade. This is one of the two oldest "summer cottages" in Newport. From 1915 to 1969 it served as the people's library, and it is now a center for senior citizens.
*Operated by Senior Citizens' Center. Open daily*

### THE ELMS, 1901
**Bellevue Avenue**
Beautiful French chateau, modeled after the 18th-century *Chateau d'Asnieres* near Paris, designed by Horace Trumbauer for Edward J. Berwind, Philadelphia coal magnate. Completely furnished with outstanding museum pieces. Extensive grounds with statuary, fountains, terraced stables, and sunken French gardens
*Operated by Preservation Soc. of Newport Co. Open Apr. 15–May: Sat., Sun. 10–5. June–Nov. 15: daily 10–5 and July–Sept. 15: Sat. until 10*

**RHODE ISLAND**

253

## HUNTER HOUSE, 1748
**54 Washington St**
Early New England Georgian house with a balustraded gambrel roof constructed for Deputy Gov. Jonathan Nichols, Jr. Severe exterior except for the broken pediment with carved pineapple over central doorway; fine interior paneling and wainscoting; special exhibition of Newport's famous Townsend-Goddard furniture, silverware, and portraits of the period
*Operated by Preservation Soc. of Newport Co. Open June–Sept: daily 10–5. Oct.–May: by appointment*

## J.N.A. GRISWOLD HOUSE, 1862–63
**76 Bellevue Ave**
Designed by Richard Morris Hunt in the stick style, this wooden house may be considered one of his best works in free design. Some of the features are a stickwork porte-cochere, gable-roofed pavilions, a central octagonal hall, and a sense of open interior space expanded by piazzas. Now houses the collection of the Art Assn. of Newport and is open for exhibits
*Operated by Art Assn. of Newport. Open Mon.–Sat. 10–5, Sun., holidays 2–5*

## MARBLE HOUSE, 1889–92
**Bellevue Avenue**
Designed by Richard Morris Hunt for William K. Vanderbilt, based on the *Grand Trianon* and *Petit Trianon* at Versailles, this is one of the most sumptuous of Newport's "cottages." Lavish use of marble and gilding throughout; the Gothic Room contrasts markedly with the 17th- and 18th-century French styles which characterize the house. The "Gold Room" (ballroom) is the most elaborate, completely furnished with the original pieces. The lacquered Chinese tea house on Cliff Walk was added in 1913.
*Operated by Preservation Soc. of Newport Co. Open Apr. 15–May: Sat., Sun. 10–5. June–Nov. 15: daily 10–5 and July–Sept. 15: Fri. until 9*

## MAWDSLEY-GARDNER-WATSON-PITMAN HOUSE, about 1700
**Spring and John Streets**
Fine two-story house with hipped roof built by Capt. John Mawdsley, an 18th-century merchant and priva-

teersman noted for his hospitality. Caleb Gardner purchased the house in 1795. Only two rooms are open.
*Operated by Soc. for the Preservation of New England Antiquities. Open by appointment with Mrs. Lillian Feller*

## NEWPORT HISTORIC DISTRICT
Newport was one of the colonies' major ports, and the numerous Georgian structures still standing present a virtual history of mid-18th-century architecture. The Georgian public buildings rank among the most advanced in style because of the work of Richard Munday, master carpenter, and Peter Harrison, distinguished colonial architect. There are also the mansions of wealthy merchants as well as the rows of small 18th-century dwellings and shops.

## SWANHURST, 1851
**Bellevue Avenue and Webster Street**
Summer "cottage" in the Italianate manner built by Alexander MacGregor, Scottish stonemason and builder, for Judge Swan. Projecting piazzas of this stucco-over-masonry structure are trimmed with wooden latticework. The ground floor has some French and Victorian furnishings.
*Operated by Art Assn. of Newport. Open by appointment*

## VERNON HOUSE, late 1750s
**46 Clarke St**
Late Georgian frame house built by Metcalf Bowler, who became chief justice of the Rhode Island supreme court, and purchased in 1773 by William Vernon, who served as president of the Eastern Navy Board during the Revolution. Count de Rochambeau, commander of French force aiding Americans during the Revolutionary War, used the house as headquarters during the Newport occupation by the French. Noted for its fine interior trim and stairway, it also has some curious 18th-century Chinese-style wall murals found under some paneling.
*Operated by Mr. and Mrs. Peter Manganini, owners. Open by appointment*

## WANTON-LYMAN-HAZARD HOUSE, late 17th century
**17 Broadway**
Two-and-a-half-story frame house, the

oldest in Newport, with rear lean-to combining architectural elements of the 17th and 18th centuries: the steeply pitched roof and huge pilastered central chimney being medieval while the elaboration of structural detail (pedimented doorway supported by pilasters and a heavy cornice) reflects the changes which developed into the Georgian style. The house was occupied by several governors of Rhode Island and was damaged during the 1765 Stamp Act riots. Period furnishings
*Operated by Newport Historical Soc. Open July–Labor Day: daily 10–5*

*Wanton-Lyman-Hazard House*

## NORTH KINGSTOWN

### ■ GILBERT STUART BIRTHPLACE, 1751
**Gilbert Stuart Road**
Barnlike, two-story frame house with gambrel roof where America's great portrait painter was born in 1755. Gilbert Stuart's father was a Scottish snuff grinder, and the site includes the snuff mill still in operation with its water wheel. House restored with period furnishings
*Operated by Gilbert Stuart Assn. Open daily 11–5; closed Fri.*

### SILAS CASEY FARM, about 1750
**Route 1A**
Typical New England farmhouse and complex of farm buildings in lovely rural setting
*Operated by Soc. for the Preservation of New England Antiquities. Open June–Oct: Tues., Thurs., Sun. 1–5; closed holidays*

*Silas Casey Farmhouse*

### SMITH'S CASTLE, 1678
**U.S. Route 1**
Believed to be the only house still standing where the founder of the state, Roger Williams, visited and preached. Built on the site and with the timbers of an earlier house burned during King Philip's War. In the 18th century the influential Updike family, typical of the Narragansett planters, lived here. Period furnishings and 18th-century garden
*Operated by Cocumscussoc Assn. Open Mar. 15–Dec. 15: Mon.–Wed., Fri., Sat. 10–5, Sun. 2–5*

## PAWTUCKET

### DAGGETT HOUSE, 1685
**Slater Park**
Two-and-a-half-story frame house built by John Daggett to replace an earlier structure burned during King Philip's War; the one-story addition and enclosed entry were constructed later. Restored and furnished with antiques and historical relics, including articles used by Samuel Slater, builder of the first cotton mill in America.
*Operated by Daughters of the American Revolution. Open June–Sept. 15: Sun. 2–5 and by appointment*

## PROVIDENCE

### ADM. ESEK HOPKINS HOUSE, about 1750
**97 Admiral St**
Gambrel-roofed frame home of Esek Hopkins, the first commander in chief of the Continental Navy and brother of Stephen Hopkins, signer of the

Declaration of Independence. Partially furnished
*Operated by City of Providence. Open afternoons by appointment*

## BETSY WILLIAMS COTTAGE, 1773
**Roger Williams Park**
Small gambrel-roofed house last owned by Betsy Williams, descendant of Roger Williams and donor of the first hundred acres of land to establish the park in honor of her famous ancestor. Colonial furniture and items of historic interest
*Operated by Providence Dept. of Parks. Open Mon.–Wed., Fri. 10–5, Sun., holidays 12–5*

## ■ GOV. STEPHEN HOPKINS HOUSE, 1707; 1742
**Benefit and Hopkins Streets**
Moderate-sized colonial dwelling with doorway framed by pilasters and a pediment; home of Stephen Hopkins, a signer of the Declaration of Independence and for ten years governor of the state. George Washington visited here twice; the bed in which he slept is one of many well-preserved relics.
*Operated by Soc. of Colonial Dames. Open Wed., Sat. 1–4, and by appointment*

## ■ JOHN BROWN HOUSE, 1786–88
**52 Power St**
Splendid Georgian brick mansion de-

*John Brown House*

signed by Joseph Brown, based on English architectural pattern books, for his brother John, a prosperous Providence merchant. The facade has a central, pedimented pavilion and a balustraded Doric portico. John Quincy Adams described the house as "the most magnificent and elegant private mansion that I have ever seen on this continent." Now open as a historic museum with fine examples of Rhode Island furniture, paintings, ceramics, silver, textiles, and items relating to the history of the people and the state of Rhode Island.
*Operated by R.I. Historical Soc. Open Tues.–Fri. 11–4, Sat., Sun. 2–4; closed holidays*

## SOUTH KINGSTOWN

### FAYERWEATHER HOUSE, about 1820
**Route 138**
One-and-a-half-story shingled frame home of the village blacksmith George Fayerweather, a Negro whose descendants lived here and continued working the smithy. Recently restored; free weekly craft demonstrations during summer
*Operated by Fayerweather Craft Guild. Open Tues.–Sat. 11–4*

## WARWICK

### LISLE HOUSE MUSEUM, 18th century
**4365 Post Rd**
An 18th-century house containing diverse collections gathered by the late Mr. and Mrs. Arthur B. Lisle during their world travels. It features Italian objects from the 16th to the 18th centuries and also some choice Oriental pieces.
*Operated by R.I. School of Design. Open Mon.–Fri. 10–4:30; closed holidays*

### WATSON HOUSE, about 1790
**University of Rhode Island Campus**
The original farmhouse on the Oliver Watson farm and the oldest structure on the university campus. Now restored and refurnished in the period style
*Operated by University of R.I. Open Mon.–Fri. 9–12, 1–4, weekends by appointment*

# BEAUFORT

## ■ BEAUFORT HISTORIC DISTRICT

Located on Port Royal Island, Beaufort is the second-oldest town in the state, dating from 1710. Because of its inaccessibility until the advent of good roads, the town remains much as it was in appearance over 150 years ago. Many handsome old houses remain with their high basements and spacious verandas.

### HOLMES-HALL HOUSE, about 1840
### Bay and Charles Streets

Spacious house built by William or George Elliott; confiscated and used as a troop hospital during the Civil War; bought by George Holmes after the war and later inherited by L.A. Hall. Interior features include rococo plasterwork by Italian craftsmen. Reproductions and antique furnishings
*Operated by Bank of Beaufort Historic Foundation. Open Tues.–Sat. 11–3, Sun. 2–4; closed national holidays*

### JOHN MARKS VERDIER HOUSE (LAFAYETTE BUILDING), 1795–1800

Fine Adam-style residence built by one of the town's leading merchants and shipowners. The Marquis de Lafayette was entertained here during his grand tour of the South in 1825. Presently being restored and furnished; Verdier family silver displayed
*Operated by Historic Beaufort Foundation. Open Mon.–Fri. 10–4*

# CHARLESTON

## ■ CHARLESTON HISTORIC DISTRICT
### bounded by Broad, Bay, Logan, East Battery, and South Battery Streets and by Cumberland, State, Chalmers, and Meeting Streets

In the spring of 1970 Charleston celebrated its 300th anniversary. It is one of the oldest and most historic cities in the country and retains an 18th-century charm and atmosphere. Rice and indigo before the Revolution and cotton afterward were the bases of Charleston's great wealth, which is reflected in the magnificent Georgian and Federal mansions built in this section.

## ■ HEYWARD-WASHINGTON HOUSE, about 1770
### 87 Church St

Excellent and little-altered example of a three-story brick Georgian town house, the home of Thomas Heyward, Jr., a signer of the Declaration of Independence. President Washington stayed here while in Charleston in 1791. Restored, with 18th-century furnishings of local origin
*Operated by The Charleston Museum. Open Sat. 10–5, Sun. 2–5*

### JOSEPH MANIGAULT HOUSE, between about 1790 and 1803
### 350 Meeting St

Notable house of the Adam period, designed by Gabriel Manigault, one of Charleston's earliest native-born architects, for his brother Joseph. Gabriel had lived in London several years and returned to Charleston with an understated version of the Adam style that was to predominate in the city for a quarter of a century. Fine collection of Louis XV and XVI and Charleston-made furniture, English porcelains, and Waterford glass
*Operated by The Charleston Museum. Open Tues.–Sun. 10–5; closed national holidays*

## ■ NATHANIEL RUSSELL HOUSE, before 1809
### 51 Meeting St

An extremely fine example of Adam-

*Nathaniel Russell House*

style architecture, built with the then-great sum of $80,000 by Russell, a transplanted Rhode Islander and long one of the city's principal merchants. Interiors include a free-flying spiral staircase, oval drawing rooms, and excellent period furnishings, many from the Charleston area.
*Operated by Historic Charleston Foundation. Open Mon.–Sat. 10–1, 2–5, Sun. 2–5*

■ **THOMAS ROSE HOUSE,**
**about 1735**
**59 Church St**
Handsome early Georgian town house with exceptionally fine original wood paneling throughout. Elegantly furnished with 18th-century English antiques; minor restoration made 1928 *Operated by Church Street Historic Foundation. Open by appointment*

## CLEMSON

■ **FORT HILL (JOHN C. CALHOUN HOUSE) 1802; 1825**
**Clemson University Campus**
A 14-room ante-bellum frame mansion, the residence from 1825 to 1850 of John C. Calhoun, Vice President of the U.S., Secretary of War, and champion of states' rights. He greatly enlarged the house, which contains many of its original furnishings. Calhoun's estate was willed to the state of South Carolina by his son-in-law for establishment of the school which is now Clemson University.
*Operated by United Daughters of the Confederacy and Clemson University. Open Tues.–Sat. 10–12, 1–5, Sun. 2–6*

**HANOVER HOUSE, 1714–16**
**Clemson University**
Luxurious home built by Paul de St. Julien, member of a wealthy and prominent French Huguenot family. The house was named for England's King George I (Elector of Hanover when he ascended the throne), who befriended the Huguenots. The house was saved from destruction in the 1940s and painstakingly dismantled, removed, and reconstructed at its present location. The interiors have 17th- and 18th-century furnishings.
*Operated by Colonial Dames and Clemson University. Open Tues.–Sat. 8–12, 1–5, Sun. 2–6*

## COKESBURY VICINITY

■ **OLD COKESBURY HISTORIC DISTRICT**
**Route 246**
Cokesbury, dating from 1824, was a Methodist community of which the college and schools were the center. At Cokesbury today is the largest group of ante-bellum structures remaining in Greenwood Co. The 116-year-old building which began as the Masonic female college and is now known as Cokesbury College is being restored and may be visited.

## COLUMBIA

**AINSLEY HALL MANSION [ROBERT MILLS HISTORIC HOUSE AND PARK], 1820s**
**Henderson Street**
Meticulously restored classical revival mansion designed by Robert Mills, the first architect for the Federal government, for Ainsley Hall and his wife Sarah. The Halls never resided in the house, however, and Mills himself is most intimately associated with the structure. Rooms have been furnished in the classical style, and the house serves as a monument to Robert Mills and a museum of American taste in the 1820s.
*Operated by Historic Columbia Foundation. Open Tues.–Sat. 10–1, 2–4, Sun. 2–5*

**GOVERNOR'S MANSION, 1856**
**800 Richland St**
Originally built to be used as the officers' quarters of a state-operated military school, this white stucco house was designated as the executive residence in 1868. It has been used as such continuously since 1879. The furnishings, which have been secured by a committee formed in 1965, include many used by former governors and are 19th-century authentic pieces as well as reproductions.
*Operated by State of S.C. Open Mon.–Fri. 9:30–3 by appointment*

■ **HAMPTON-PRESTON HOUSE,**
**about 1818–20**
**1615 Blanding St**
Originally a red brick Federal structure, this house was considerably

altered in the 1830s and 1850s. The exterior was stuccoed and scored, and a "piazza" was built across the entire front of the house. It has been restored as it may have appeared about 1840 and furnished with Hampton family furnishings.
*Operated by State of S.C. Open Mon.–Sat. 10–6, Sun. 1–6*

■ **THE LACE HOUSE, 1854**
**803 Richland St**
Located directly opposite the Governor's Mansion is this double-porched classical-style mansion. It is obviously named for its lavish ironwork on the porch supports, railings, fence, and grills. The architecture of the house reflects the New Orleans influence of its French architect. To be made part of the Governor's Mansion complex after restoration and used by the governor for entertaining. It will, however, also be open to visitors.
*Operated by Governor's Mansion and Lace House Comm. Restoration in progress*

**WOODROW WILSON'S BOYHOOD HOME, about 1870**
**1705 Hampton St**
Victorian house built by President Wilson's father, the family's home from 1872 to 1875. Typical of the period, with bay windows, arched doorways, and iron mantels painted to look like marble. Collection of furniture includes some that belonged to the Wilsons.
*Operated by Historic Columbia Foundation. Open Tues.–Sat. 10–1, 2–4, Sun. 2–5*

**EDGEFIELD**

**MAGNOLIA DALE (ALFRED J. NORRIS HOUSE), before 1830**
**320 Norris St**
Believed to have been built by Erasmus Youngblood, grandson of Arthur Simkins, founder of Edgefield; sold to Samuel Brooks in 1830. Alfred J. Norris purchased the property from Brooks in 1873 and altered and enlarged the dwelling to the style typical of that period. Now restored with furnishings of the Empire period; serves as a museum of early Edgefield history
*Operated by Edgefield Co. Historical Soc. Open by appointment*

**OAKLEY PARK (RED SHIRT SHRINE), 1835**
**intersection of U.S. Route 25 and South Carolina Route 23**
Built for Daniel Byrd of Virginia, it became the home of Gen. Martin Witherspoon Gary, who in 1876 organized the Red Shirts, which succeeded in electing Gen. Wade Hampton as governor and restoring a native white government in the state. In later years this was the home of Gov. John Gary Evans, nephew of Gen. Gary. Now a house museum with furniture of the Confederate period
*Operated by United Daughters of the Confederacy. Open Tues.–Fri. 9:30–11:30, 2–4:30*

*Oakley Park*

**GEORGETOWN**

**HOPSEWEE PLANTATION, about 1740**
**Highway 17, south of Georgetown**
Typical clapboard low-country rice plantation house, the birthplace of Thomas Lynch, Jr., signer of the Declaration of Independence. Thomas Lynch, Sr., was also supposed to sign the document, but he died en route to Philadelphia. The house is now the residence of the Maynard family.
*Operated by Mrs. James T. Maynard. Open Tues.–Fri. 10–5 and by appointment*

**PYATT-DOYLE HOUSE, about 1790**
**630 Highmarket St**
Carolina low-country-style four-story town house constructed of handmade bricks of clay and oyster shell. Restored, handsome interiors with fine English and American furnishings from the Queen Anne to early Victorian periods.

*Operated by Mr. and Mrs. Arthur Hazard Doyle. Open Mon.–Fri. 9–2, 4–6; closed holidays*

## WICKLOW HALL, about 1850
### Cat Island Road

Restored plantation house built by slave carpenters for the father of Rawlins Lowndes, a captain in the Confederate army and aide to Gen. Wade Hampton. Lowndes inherited the house by 1860 and used it in the winter to be near his rice fields. Though a disastrous fire in 1966 destroyed much of an outstanding collection of 17th- through 19th-century furnishings, that part remaining is of excellent quality and interest.

*Operated by Mr. and Mrs. M.T. Paris. Open May–Sept: Mon.–Sat. 10–7. Oct.–Apr: Mon.–Sat. 10–5*

## KINGSTREE

### ■ THORNTREE HOUSE (WITHERSPOON HOUSE), 1749
#### Fluitt-Nelson Memorial Park

Restored plantation house of beaded clapboard, the oldest residence known in the Pee Dee area. The original owners, the Witherspoons, were a prominent 18th-century family. Pine interiors, furniture, and accessories of 1759 to 1826 period

*Operated by Williamsburg Co. Historical Soc. Restoration in progress*

## MOUNT PLEASANT

### BOONE HALL PLANTATION, 1750; 1935
#### off Route 17

Named for Major John Boone, who was among the first settlers of the colony and who acquired the land in 1676 from the Lords Proprietors of England. Mr. Thomas Stone, a retired Canadian diplomat, purchased the plantation in 1935 and constructed a large, handsome building, retaining as much of the old as possible. Boone Hall is the mansion seen in the film "Gone With the Wind." Gardens of camelias and azaleas flank the mansion, and an avenue of oaks one-half mile long leads to it.

*Operated by Mr. and Mrs. Harris M. McRae. Open Mon.–Sat. 9–5, Sun. 1–6; closed Thanksgiving and Christmas*

## PENDLETON

### ASHTABULA, about 1828
#### Route 88

Plantation home (described in 1834 as "a new style house and improvements") typical of those built in this area in the early 19th century. Enlarged about 1855, it is a two-story "mansion house" with columned one-story porches. Ashtabula was the residence of several prominent individu-

*Boone Hall*

als, including the niece of Arthur Middleton, a signer of the Declaration of Independence. The interiors feature high-ceilinged rooms, simple mantels and woodwork, and a wide staircase. 19th-century furnishings *Operated by Foundation for Historic Restoration in Pendleton Area. Open Apr.–Oct: Sun. 2–5 and by appointment*

■ **PENDLETON HISTORIC DISTRICT**
Named for Judge Henry Pendleton of Culpeper, Virginia, when it was founded in 1790. Pendleton was the center of business, culture, and government in the northwestern part of the state for many years. It was noted for its fine cabinet and carriage makers, and it has been said that wealthy Charlestonians preferred Pendleton carriages to those made in Europe.

## SPARTANBURG VICINITY
■ **WALNUT GROVE PLANTATION MANOR HOUSE, 1765**
Route 1
Built on land granted to Charles Moore by King George III in 1763, this simple Georgian-type structure was the home of Margaret Catherine "Kate" Moore, who acted as scout for Gen. Daniel Morgan during the Revolution. Now restored and furnished to represent life before 1830
*Operated by Spartanburg Co. Historical Assn. and Spartanburg Junior League. Open Mar.–Nov: Tues.–Sat. 11–5, Sun. 2–5. Dec.–Feb: Sun. 2–5; closed holidays*

## UNION
■ **ROSE HILL (GIST MANSION), about 1828**
Rose Hill State Park, Route 2
Built overlooking a grove of hickory and oak trees, this three-story brick plantation house was the home of secessionist Gov. William H. Gist. After 1860 the brick was covered with stucco and two-story porches were added to the front and back. The house has been restored and furnished with pre-Civil War and Gist family pieces.
*Operated by S. C. Dept. of Parks. Open Tues.–Sun. 9–sundown*

## BLUNT
**MENTOR GRAHAM HOUSE (LINCOLN PRAIRIE SHRINE), 1880s**
The prairie home of the village schoolmaster from New Salem, Illinois, who tutored Abraham Lincoln in writing and diction and who is generally credited with teaching the President his succinct style of speaking and writing. The house has been restored and furnished in styles of the 1880s through the efforts of the members of the state historical society.
*Operated by S. Dak. State Historical Soc. Open daily 9–5*

## CUSTER
**LOG CABIN MUSEUM, 1875**
Main Street, Way City Park
One of the oldest log cabins in the Black Hills, built by soldiers sent to clear settlers from Indian lands. Now operated as a museum with historical and natural history exhibits
*Operated by Log Cabin Museum. Open daily 8–8*

## CUSTER VICINITY
**JOSEPH HUMPHREUS HOUSE, 1890**
Twelve Mile Ranch
Sturdy two-story log ranch house built by cattleman Joseph Humphreus near the old stage trail between Custer and Cheyenne, Wyoming. While still run as a cattle ranch by the Humphreus family, it has become a center of scientific and cultural activities relating to the Black Hills. The old house has an extensive library and a sizable collection of art objects and antiques. Guest cabins available
*Operated by the Humphreus family, owners. Open by appointment*

# DEADWOOD

## ■ DEADWOOD HISTORIC DISTRICT, 1876

The last rich strike of precious metals was in the Black Hills region. The great Homestake gold claim in 1874 was made in Lead, South Dakota, and Deadwood owes its importance to its proximity to Lead. Soon after the gold strike Deadwood attracted such notorious people as Deadwood Dick, Calamity Jane, and Wild Bill Hickok. Many of the original buildings remain to give an authentic mining town atmosphere.

*Town of Deadwood*

## DEADWOOD VICINITY

### HOME OF DEADWOOD DICK, 1890s

**Sunrise Mountain**

The colorful frontiersman Richard W. Clarke was the supposed prototype of the dime-novel hero "Deadwood Dick." Born in England in 1845, he came to America as a young man, went prospecting for gold in the Black Hills, and remained there the rest of his life. After serving as a stagecoach driver, Indian scout, and deputy U.S. marshal, he retired to the solitude of his mountain cabin to escape the fame the novels had brought to him.

*Operated by Town of Deadwood. Open by appointment*

## FAULKTON

### HON. JOHN H. PICKLER HOME, early 1900s

**Pickler Park**

Home of Maj. Pickler, prominent

attorney and congressman; the 17-room rambling house features a tower which had a lantern to guide night travelers across the prairies. The handsomely appointed interiors, once the scene of many parties with such prominent visitors as Theodore Roosevelt, Grover Cleveland, and Susan B. Anthony are now being restored and will be open to the public within the next two years.

*Operated by S. Dak. State Historical Soc. Restoration in progress*

## HERMOSA

### BADGER CLARK MEMORIAL, 1920s

**Custer State Park**

Native stone-and-lumber cabin near Legion Lake where the poet laureate of South Dakota lived alone and worked for nearly 30 years. Badger Clark's works, including cowboy lyrics, verse, and a novel, were published from 1915 to 1935. The interiors are as he left them, with his clothing and personal memorabilia and furnishings on display.

*Operated by S. Dak. Game, Fish, and Parks Comm. Open daily 8–5*

## MADISON

### PRAIRIE VILLAGE

**Highways 34 and 81**

A 140-acre authentic pioneer village with 17 restored buildings moved here from the surrounding area; ten more will be located here in the near future. Among the dwellings are: *Thormodsgaard Log House* (1872), a two-story hand-hewn log house, with some original furnishings, built near Canton by four brothers; *Smith Ranch House* (1881), one of the first permanent residences in Lake County and typical of the region at that time, built by the Civil War veteran Capt. H.P. Smith and containing the Smith family furnishings; *Jacobs Sod House,* a copy of the sod house occupied by the Jacobs family during the years the area was being homesteaded. In August a steam threshing jamboree is held at the village.

*Operated by Prairie Historical Soc. Open Memorial Day–Labor Day: daily 8–8*

# RAPID CITY VICINITY

## LOG CABIN, 1878
**Rockerville Gold Town**
The log cabin is the only original building remaining of Old Rockerville, one of the first placer mining camps in the area. After the miners moved on the town died; but it has now been rebuilt as a tourist attraction.
*Operated by Rockerville Gold Town. Open late May–Sept: daily 7–9*

# SIOUX FALLS

## SEN. RICHARD F. PETTIGREW HOUSE, 1875
**131 N Duluth Ave**
Victorian home of the first senator from the state of South Dakota. R.F. Pettigrew, born in Vermont in 1848, was influential in the settlement of Sioux Falls and the beginning of its industries. The exterior of the house is of Sioux Falls granite and polished and unpolished petrified wood. The senator donated his home, library, and museum collections to the city at the time of his death in 1926. While the Pettigrew Museum of Natural Arts and History is open daily, the house, with its Victorian furnishings, serves as the residence of the curator and is not generally open to the public. However, anyone deeply interested may apply to the curator for admittance.
*Operated by City of Sioux Falls. Open weekdays by appointment*

# STURGIS VICINITY

## FREEMAN SMALLEY HOUSE ("CASTLE ON THE PRAIRIE"), about 1910
Built by prosperous rancher Freeman Smalley, this huge Gothic-style castle is about 40 feet square, with towers and turrets constructed of sandstone and with the upper portion finished in shingles. Interiors feature oval dining room, carved woodwork, and a beautiful broad stairway.
*Private. Open by appointment*

# VERMILLION

## AUSTIN-WHITTEMORE HOUSE, 1882
**108 Austin St**
Two-story brick Victorian house, with a cupola on the roof and scroll-sawn Gothic brackets as ornamentation, built by Horace A. Austin—surveyor who laid out the town of Vermillion and later served in the state legislature. Presented to the historical society for use as a house museum by Mrs. Pansy Austin Whittemore
*Operated by Clay Co. Historical Soc. Restoration in progress*

# WATERTOWN

## ARTHUR C. MELLETTE HOUSE, about 1883
**421 Fifth Ave, NW**
Two-story Victorian brick mansion—with a three-story tower and wide cornices ornamented with fanciful eave brackets—built for Arthur C. Mellette, who in 1889 became the first governor of the state of South Dakota. Now a house museum restored and furnished in the style of the 1880s, with some original pieces of the Mellette family
*Operated by Mellette Memorial Assn. Open May–Oct: Tues.–Sun. 2–5*

*Arthur C. Mellette House*

## OLIVE CHATEAU, about 1883
**Highway 81**
Late Victorian mansion with fanciful towers and turrets built by prominent Watertown banker and real estate promoter H.D. Walrath. The present owners moved the house to its new location, completely restored it, and opened it to the public in 1967. Antique furnishings
*Operated by Mr. and Mrs. William J. Wensing, owners. Open by appointment*

## BOLIVAR

### THE LITTLE COURTHOUSE, 1824; 1849
**East Market Street**

Originally a two-story courthouse; at mid-century Dr. Thomas E. Moore incorporated the log structure into his new residence. The house has been enlarged and altered over the years. Restoration in progress

*Operated by Assn. for the Preservation of Tenn. Antiquities. Hours to be determined*

## CHATTANOOGA

### CRAVENS HOUSE, 1856
**Cravens Terrace**

The oldest surviving structure on Lookout Mountain, a white clapboard house built by Robert Cravens, pioneer ironmaster and early industrialist. The house served as a Confederate field hospital during the Civil War and as headquarters for Gen. E.C. Walthall. After the "Battle above the Clouds" (1863), Union generals Whitaker and Hooker took over the house as their headquarters. Restored and furnished in the period prior to the Civil War

*Operated by Assn. for the Preservation of Tenn. Antiquities. Open Mar.–Nov: Tues.–Sat. 9–5, Sun. 1–5*

*Cravens House*

## COLUMBIA

### ■ JAMES K. POLK HOUSE, 1816
**301 W Seventh St**

Federal-style brick house built by Samuel Polk, father of President James K. Polk, who spent his early manhood here. Antique furnishings, some of which were used by the Polks while they were in the White House

*Operated by Polk Memorial Assn. and Polk Memorial Auxiliary of Columbia. Open Mon.–Sat. 9–5, Sun. 1–5; closed Christmas*

## FRANKLIN VICINITY

### ■ CARTER HOUSE, 1830
**1140 Columbia Ave**

Brick house built by Fountain Branch Carter, a sixth-generation member of the well-known Carter family of Virginia. In 1864 the Battle of Franklin raged around this house while the Carter family took refuge in the basement. Restored and furnished, the house still shows its scars from the battle.

*Operated by State of Tenn. Open Mon.–Sat. 9–4:30, Sun. 2–4:30*

*Carter House*

## GALLATIN

### ■ CRAGFONT, 1798–1802
**Tennessee Route 25**

Gray limestone mansion built in the form of a "T," with the stem forming the back wing. The main section is Georgian in feeling, and the wing includes first- and second-floor Spanish galleries extending the full length on each side. The interior was finished by artisans brought from Baltimore, Maryland, by Gen. James Winchester, who, with Judge John Overton and Andrew Jackson founded Memphis in 1819 on the site of U.S. Fort Adams, built on the bluff in 1797.

*Operated by Assn. for the Preservation of Tenn. Antiquities. Open Apr. 15–Oct: Tues.–Sat. 10–5, Sun. 1–6*

## GREENEVILLE

■ **ANDREW JOHNSON NATIONAL HISTORIC SITE, about 1850**
**Depot and College Streets**
Modest brick house, home of Andrew Johnson from 1851 to 1875, situated on a 17-acre site dedicated to the 17th President of the U.S. Restored and furnished with period pieces. Also at the site are Johnson's tailor shop (1830) and his grave.
*Operated by National Park Service. Open daily 9–5; closed Christmas*

*Andrew Johnson National Historic Site*

## HOHENWALD VICINITY

**LOG CABIN**
**Meriwether Lewis Park**
Rustic log cabin, representative of early frontier houses of Tennessee, serves as a museum, with exhibits of the life of Meriwether Lewis.
*Operated by State of Tenn. Open daily 8–5*

## JACKSON

**CASEY JONES HOME AND RAILROAD MUSEUM, 1880**
**211 W Chester St**
Home occupied by "Casey" Jones at the time of his fatal crash in 1900. Now a museum containing personal items of the Jones family
*Operated by City of Jackson. Open Mon.–Sat. 9–5, Sun. 1–5; closed Thanksgiving, Christmas, and New Year's Day*

## JOHNSON CITY

■ **TIPTON-HAYNES HOUSE, about 1782; 1838**
**Tennessee Route 23**
Farmhouse built by Col. John Tipton and enlarged by Landon Carter Haynes. Restored to 1838 period when Haynes, "silver-tongued orator of the South," lived here. His adjacent law office, the first in Johnson City, has been called a perfect example of Greek Revival architecture and has also been restored. Outbuildings, including a double-crib barn, stillhouse, smokehouse, springhouse, and pigpen, have been rebuilt.
*Operated by Tipton-Haynes Living Historical Farm. Open daily 10–6*

## JONESBORO

■ **JONESBORO HISTORIC DISTRICT, 1779**
Jonesboro is the oldest town in Tennessee. The state of Franklin was organized here in 1784 with John Sevier as its first and only governor. From the beginning this was a planned community, and the owner of each lot was required to build "one brick, stone, or well-framed house" of specified dimensions. Andrew Jackson began his law practice in Jonesboro in 1788.

## KNOXVILLE

**BLEAK HOUSE [CONFEDERATE MEMORIAL HALL] 1858**
**3148 Kingston Pike, SW**
A 15-room, ante-bellum mansion named for the novel by Charles Dickens. It was used as the headquarters of Gen. James Longstreet during the siege of Knoxville in 1863. Drawn on a wall in the tower are three crude portraits labeled "men who were shot up here." Period furnishings
*Operated by United Daughters of the Confederacy. Open by appointment*

**DULIN HOUSE [DULIN GALLERY OF ART], 1915**
**3100 Kingston Pike**
Exceptionally fine example of early 20th-century revival of the classical tradition in architecture, designed by John Russell Pope for H.L. Dulin, Esq. The building now serves as a gallery of art, with changing exhibitions, an educational program for students, Thorne miniature rooms, and a rental and sales gallery.
*Operated by Dulin Gallery of Art. Open Tues.–Sun. 1–5, Thurs. evg. 7:30–9:30*

■ **WILLIAM BLOUNT MANSION, 1792**
**200 West Hill Ave**
Two-story frame house built by William Blount—governor of the territory south of the Ohio River and a delegate to the Federal Constitutional Convention. Tennessee became a state in 1796 largely as a result of the efforts of William Blount. The house and governor's office behind it have been restored and furnished.
*Operated by Blount Mansion Assn. Open Nov.–Apr: Tues.–Sat. 9–5. May–Oct: Tues.–Sat. 9–5, Sun. 2–5*

## KNOXVILLE VICINITY

■ **RAMSEY HOUSE, 1795–97**
**Thorngrove Pike**
Rough-hewn version of the Georgian style, using bluestone and pink marble. The English architect Thomas Hope was brought from Charleston, South Carolina, to produce this simple but stately structure for Francis A. Ramsey, pioneer surveyor of Knoxville. Restored and furnished in the period of 1797–1820
*Operated by Assn. for the Preservation of Tenn. Antiquities. Open Apr.–Oct: Sat., Sun. 1–5*

## MEMPHIS

**MEMPHIS COTTON CARNIVAL**
Each May Memphis holds a Cotton Carnival incorporating a tour of many of the city's finest private homes and gardens. Contact the Chamber of Commerce for further information.

■ **BEALE STREET HISTORIC DISTRICT, early 1900s**
Noted in song and story as the center of Negro life in Memphis and as the birthplace of the "blues." On Beale Street, W.C. Handy composed and first played "The Memphis Blues" (1909), "St. Louis Blues" (1914), and others.

**JAMES LEE HOUSE, 1843; 1853; 1873**
**NOLAND FONTAINE HOUSE, 1870**
**680–690 Adams Ave**
The James Lee House was built in three sections over an extended period of time. William Harsson erected the oldest, square section at the rear of the structure. Mr. Charles Wesley Goyer, Harsson's son-in-law, enlarged the house considerably and added the ornate front with its tower. In 1890 James Lee, Jr., founder of the famous Lee Line, a fleet of palatial passenger steamers on the Mississippi River, acquired the house. The Noland Fontaine House is a French Victorian mansion designed by the architects M.H. Baldwin and E.C. Jones for wealthy banker and industrialist Amos Woodruff. In 1883 the house was sold to Fontaine, a prominent cotton factor, whose family lived in it until 1929. This house has been restored and furnished with many Woodruff and Fontaine family items.
*Operated by Assn. for the Preservation of Tenn. Antiquities. James Lee House —under restoration, hours to be determined. Open—Noland Fontaine House—daily 1–4; closed July 4, Labor Day, and Christmas Eve and Day*

**MAGEVNEY HOME, 1831**
**198 Adams Ave**
Pioneer home of an early Memphis schoolmaster; furnished with antiques
*Operated by Memphis Park Comm. Open Tues.–Sat. 10–4, Sun. 1–4; closed Thanksgiving, Christmas, and New Year's Day*

**PILLOW-McINTYRE HOUSE, about 1852**
**707 Adams Ave**
Greek Revival-style mansion, home of Gideon Johnson Pillow, active in both the Mexican-American and Civil wars. The house was purchased by Peter McIntire, a successful merchant, in 1890. The structure now serves as an antique shop.
*Operated by Lary-Vanlandingham. Open Mon.–Fri. 10–4*

## MORRISTOWN

**CROCKETT-TAVERN MUSEUM**
**U.S. Route 11E**
Reproduction of the John Crockett Tavern, a log cabin with two open fireplaces, pioneer furnishings, and a collection of items pertaining to the Crocketts
*Operated by Assn. for the Preservation of Tenn. Antiquities. Open Mon.–Sat. 9–5, Sun. 2–5*

## MURFREESBORO

■ **OAKLANDS, 1798; 1820; 1850**
**North Maney Avenue**
Constructed between the early 1800s and mid-1850s, Oaklands reflects a succession of styles with the addition of the Romanesque revival veranda and rococo revival detail to a basically neoclassic form. The house, originally consisting of four rooms, was built by Dr. James Maney and remained in the Maney family 86 years. It is now a 14-room mansion, restored, with antique furnishings.
*Operated by Oakland Assn. Open Apr.–Oct: daily 10–4:30. Nov.–Mar: by appointment*

## NASHVILLE

■ **BELLE MEADE, 1853**
**5025 Harding Rd**
Classical revival-style mansion attributed to William Strickland, renowned American architect and designer of the state capitol. It was the home of Gen. William Giles Harding, built on the site of an earlier house destroyed by fire in 1852. On the property may also be seen the carriage house and stable, smokehouse, gardener's house, mausoleum of the Harding family, Tudor-Gothic-style stone dairy house, and the log cabin in which the builder was born in 1808.
*Operated by Assn. for the Preservation of Tenn. Antiquities. Open Apr.–Nov: Mon.–Sat. 9–5, Sun. 1–5. Dec.–Mar: Mon.–Sat. 10–4:30, Sun. 1–4:30*

**BELMONT, 1850**
**1900 Belmont Blvd**
Mansion built in the manner of an Italian Renaissance villa by Col. J.A.S. Acklen and his wife Adelicia after their 19-month honeymoon in Europe. William Strickland, building the state capitol at Nashville, was consulted about the design of this mansion. Strickland lived in Nashville the last nine years of his life and exerted great influence on Tennessee architecture during this period. This structure now forms the nucleus of Belmont College.
*Operated by Belmont College. Open by appointment*

**GOVERNOR'S MANSION (FARHILLS), 1927**
**Curtiswood Lane**
Georgian-style brick mansion designed by the architectural firm of Hart, Freeland, and Roberts for Mr. and Mrs. Ridley Wills. The estate and house were purchased in 1949 to be used as the governor's official residence. Georgian furnishings
*Operated by State of Tenn. Open Tues., Thurs. 2–4*

■ **TRAVELLERS' REST, 1793**
**Radnor Yards, Farrell Parkway**
Two-story clapboard house built by Judge John Overton, the first lawyer in Nashville. When Andrew Jackson settled in Nashville he and Overton became close friends, which they remained throughout their lives. Overton is said to have been the wealthiest man in the state prior to the Civil War.
*Operated by Soc. of Colonial Dames. Open Mon.–Sat. 8:30–5, Sun. 1–5*

## NASHVILLE VICINITY

■ **ANDREW JACKSON HOUSE (THE HERMITAGE), 1818–19; 1831; 1834**
**U.S. Route 70N**
Classical revival-style mansion, the home of Andrew Jackson from 1818 until his death in 1845. The mansion was partially burned in 1834, when Jackson was serving his second term as President, and rebuilt in 1835. Original furniture and nearly all the known personal effects of President and Mrs. Jackson are in this house. The garden, planted by Rachel Jackson, is as she originally planned it.
*Operated by Ladies' Hermitage Assn. Open daily 9–5*

*The Hermitage*

■ **TULIP GROVE, 1836**
**U.S. Route 70N**
Set in a grove of tulip trees is the classical revival-style mansion built by President Andrew Jackson for his nephew and namesake, Andrew Jackson Donelson. Original furnishings
*Operated by Ladies' Hermitage Assn. Open daily 9–5*

## PINEY FLATS VICINITY

■ **COBB-MASSENGILL HOUSE, 1770**
**Rutherford County Route 11E**
Nine-room, two-and-a-half-story house, one of the oldest in Tennessee, built by William Cobb. William Blount, governor of the territory, spent the winter here as a guest of Cobb; thus it became the first capitol of the territory. Displayed are 18th-century furnishings and articles and manuscripts of interest.
*Operated by State of Tenn. and Rocky Mount Historical Soc. Open Apr.–Oct: Mon.–Sat. 10–5, Sun. 2–6*

## RUGBY

**KINGSTON LISLE, 1884**
Queen Anne-style cottage built for Thomas Hughes, the British author of *Tom Brown's School Days*, who founded Rugby as a colony for younger sons of English aristocracy. Furnished with original colony pieces
*Operated by Rugby Restoration Assn. Open June–Sept: Tues.–Sat. 10–5, Sun. 2–5*

## RUTHERFORD

**DAVID CROCKETT CABIN**
**Highway 45**
Log cabin, a duplicate of the one in which Davy Crockett left his family when he went to Texas after being denied re-election to Congress in 1835
*Operated by David Crockett Memorial Assn. of Gibson Co. Open May 15–Sept: Mon.–Sat. 9–5*

## SMYRNA

■ **SAM DAVIS HOME, 1810**
**Tennessee Route 102**
Two-story home of the heroic Confederate scout who when captured by Federal troops in 1863 refused to reveal the name of his informant even on pain of death. The house has period furnishings, some original; nearby are an early 19th-century garden and the graves of the Davis family.
*Operated by Sam Davis Memorial Assn. Open Apr.–Oct: Mon.–Sat. 9–5, Sun. 1–5. Nov.–Mar: Mon.–Sat. 10–4, Sun. 1–4*

## ARLINGTON

**SIX FLAGS OVER TEXAS**
**between Dallas and Fort Worth at State Highway 360**
This 145-acre park includes original buildings moved here from other parts of the state as well as many replicas. Historical items depict Texas' history under six regimes.
*Operated by Six Flags Over Texas. Open Apr. 15–May, after Labor Day–Nov: Sat., Sun. 10–10. June–Labor Day: daily 10–10*

## AUSTIN

■ **BREMOND BLOCK HISTORIC DISTRICT**
One entire block of six houses built from about 1870 to about 1890 representing various types of architectural styles. All were once owned by the Bremond and Robinson families, who made for their children a fenced-off playground of the alley running down the center of the block. Most of the houses are still private residences.

■ **CARRINGTON HOUSE, 1850s**
**1511 Colorado St**
Two-story limestone house, with walls 20 inches thick, built by merchant and land speculator L. Davis Carrington.
*Operated by Tex. State Historical Survey Comm. Restoration in progress*

■ **FRENCH LEGATION, 1841**
**802 San Marcos St**
This provincial French cottage, con-

sidered the oldest home in Austin, was built by the French government for their representative to the Republic of Texas. Built of hand-hewn lumber with French imported doors, locks, and hinges, it has been restored and furnished with period pieces, some original to the house.
*Operated by Daughters of the Republic of Tex. Open Tues.–Sun. 1–5*

■ **GOVERNOR'S MANSION, 1855**
**11 and Colorado Streets**
Stately white brick two-story Greek Revival mansion with upper and lower galleries designed and built by Abner Cook at a cost of $14,500. The first-floor state rooms and second-floor Sam Houston Room, with Gov. Houston's massive four-poster bed and Stephen Austin's desk, are open to visitors.
*Operated by State of Tex., Board of Control. Open Mon.–Fri. 10–12*

■ **LITTLEFIELD HOUSE, 1894**
**24 Street and Whitis Avenue**
Victorian house of red brick with sandstone trim was built by Maj. George W. Littlefield, cattleman and banker. The 17-room house features a mansard roof pierced with turrets, spires, and dormer windows and a two-story veranda flanked by columns of blue granite trimmed with white limestone.
*Operated by University of Tex. Hours to be determined*

■ **NEILL-COCHRAN MUSEUM HOUSE, about 1853**
**2310 San Gabriel St**
Called a "perfect example of the Texas version of the Greek Architecture revival in the South" and built of hand-hewn native limestone by master builder Abner Cook. The front floor-to-ceiling windows feature the original blue glass; the interior hand-hewn woodwork is put together with square pegs. Shown with fine Texas colonial and French antiques
*Operated by Soc. of Colonial Dames. Open Tues. 10–12, Sat., Sun. 3–5*

**NORTH-EVANS MANSION, 1874**
**708 San Antonio Ave**
Two-story late Victorian limestone mansion with a French flavor. A 40-foot drop in the rear terminates in a garden. Furnished with period pieces
*Operated by Austin Women's Club. Open Mon.–Fri. 9–4*

**O. HENRY MUSEUM, 1886**
**409 E Fifth St**
One-story frame cottage with jigsaw trim where O. Henry (William Sydney Porter) lived from 1893 to 1894; shown with period furnishings and O. Henry memorabilia
*Operated by City of Austin Recreation Dept. Open Mon., Wed.–Sat. 10–12, 2–5, Sun. 2–5; closed national holidays*

**SWEDISH PIONEER CABIN, about 1840**
**Zelker Park, 2220 Barton Springs Rd**
Typical Swedish, hand-hewn cedar log cabin built on the Colorado River by one of Texas' earliest Swedish pioneers. Occupied until after the Civil War and moved in 1964 to its present location, a large botanical park. Furnished with pioneer household items
*Operated by Austin Area Garden Center, Texas Swedish Pioneers Assn., and Austin Parks and Recreation Dept. Open daily 10–4*

## BASTROP

**WILBARGER HOUSE, 1842**
**1403 Main St**
Two-story frame house with upper and lower porches built by the Wilbarger family on land settled by Joseph Pugh Wilbarger, who is remembered for having survived a scalping by local Indians. The house is still occupied by Wilbarger descendants and is shown with family furnishings.
*Operated by Mrs. Ivor Wilbarger Young, owner. Open by appointment*

## BIGFOOT

**BIGFOOT WALLACE MUSEUM**
**Main Street**
Two-room log cabin and an old six-room school building house a collection of Texas memorabilia. Many items pertain to famous frontiersman William Alexander "Bigfoot" Wallace, hero of the Mexican War.
*Operated by Bigfoot Wallace Ex-Students Assn. Open daily 9–5*

## BROWNSVILLE

**STILLMAN HOUSE MUSEUM, about 1850**
**1305 E Washington St**
One-story house with end chimneys

and four heavy columns built by Charles Stillman, founder of Brownsville, for his wife, Elizabeth. Now a museum, with furnishings belonging to the Stillmans and other items of local history
*Operated by Brownsville Historical Assn. Open Mon.–Fri. 10–12, 2–5, Sun. 3–5*

## BURNET

### FORT CROGHAN, 1850–55
**State Highway 29**
Two pioneer log cabins—one of cedar and one of oak—have been moved to this restoration of a fort built in 1848 as protection for settlers against Indian raids. Other buildings include a blacksmith shop and powder house. The cabins have appropriate furnishings.
*Operated by Burnet Co. Historical Soc. Open Memorial Day–Labor Day: Wed.–Sat. 11–5, Sun. 1–5*

## CALVERT

### ■ HAMMOND HOUSE, about 1879
**bounded by Burnet, Elm, China, and Hanna Streets**
Two-story Gothic Revival building of dark red brick built but never used as the county courthouse; for nine years this town served as the county seat. In 1885 banker Robert A. Brown converted this building and the adjacent jail into a home. From 1909 until 1966 the house was owned by the Hammond family, who presented it to the historical society as a museum.
*Operated by Robertson Co. Historical Soc. Restoration in progress*

## CASTROVILLE

### CARLE STORE AND RESIDENCE, about 1850
**Angelo and Madrid Streets**
Two-story home and store built in French-Alsatian provincial style. The limestone and cypress building features a second-floor balcony swing on wrought-iron brackets.
*Operated by Mr. and Mrs. J. Lawton Stone, owners. Open by appointment*

### ■ CASTROVILLE HISTORIC DISTRICT
Founded by Count Henri de Castro in

1844, this town still bears the stamp of its early Alsatian settlers. Having survived the initial difficulties of establishing a community, Castroville grew but never lost the appearance of a Rhineland village.

### LANDMARK INN, 1846; about 1856
**U.S. Route 90 and Florence Street**
Originally a home built by early settlers, this limestone building was converted into an inn and post office when a second story was added about 1856. The Alsatian-style building features along the rear a gallery with a carved wooden railing, which the rooms open onto; still used as an inn. Display rooms feature European and locally made settlers' furniture and other items of local history.
*Operated by Ruth C. Lawler, owner. Open Mon.–Sat. 9–11:30, 1–5:30*

## CHIRENO

### HALFWAY HOUSE, 1830s
**State Highway 21**
Two-story frame house built by James B. Johnson; because it stood halfway between Nacogdoches and San Augustine on the Camino Real, it soon developed into a stagecoach inn. Built by slave labor, it features huge stone fireplaces at either end of the house and a covered porch; shown with some antique furnishings
*Operated by Dixie Branch. Open daily 9–5*

## CLEBURNE

### LITTLE OLD HOUSE, 1868
**409 N Buffalo St**
Originally a white frame house with two rooms on each side of a central hall; the dining room and keeping room were added later. The house and grounds have recently been restored and are shown with period furnishings.
*Operated by Heritage Hall of Cleburne and Garden Club. Open by appointment*

## CORPUS CHRISTI

### CENTENNIAL HOUSE, 1848–49
**411 N Broadway**
Classical revival house is believed to have been the first two-story house in the city and the first to have had a base-

ment. Built by Capt. Forbes Britton, it served as a Confederate hospital during the Civil War and as local Federal headquarters during Reconstruction. Restored and shown with ante-bellum furnishings
*Operated by Corpus Christi Area Heritage Soc. Open Wed., Sun. 3–5, and by appointment; closed holidays*

## CORSICANA

### PIONEER VILLAGE
**900 W Park Ave**
Seven pioneer log buildings constructed in the county from 1838 to 1865 have been moved here, including an Indian trading post, slave cabin, settler's house, and blacksmith shop. All are furnished and restored.
*Operated by Navarro Co. Historical Soc. Open daily 9–5*

## CROSBYTON

### CROSBY COUNTY PIONEER MEMORIAL MUSEUM
**101 W Main St, U.S. Route 82**
This replica of the county's first home — a rock house built by early settler Hank Smith — is a museum of Indian artifacts and pioneer relics. Also featured are a reconstructed half dugout furnished as a pioneer dwelling and a barn filled with agricultural tools.
*Operated by Crosby Co. Historical Assn. Open Tues.–Sat. 9–12, 2–5, Sun. 2–5; closed national holidays*

## DALLAS

### JOHN NEELY BRYAN CABIN, 1843
**Main and Market Streets**
This cabin of cedar chinked with clay is a reconstruction of the one built by John Neely Bryan, the founder of Dallas. Moved many times, it is now being rebuilt at the present location. The bed, fastened to the wall with pegs, belonged to Bryan.
*Operated by Dallas Co. Hours to be determined*

### MILLERMORE MANSION, 1855
**1400 S Envoy St**
Two-story L-shaped house, with four 47-foot Greek columns, built by prospector William Miller. The house originally stood on Miller's land, from which his slaves cut down cedars and

oaks for its construction; the chimneys and hearths are of native stone. Shown with the family furnishings
*Operated by Dallas Co. Heritage Soc. Open Tues.–Fri., tours at 10:30, 1:30, first and third Sun. of each month, tours at 1:30, 4:30*

## DECATUR

### OLD STONE PRISON, about 1859
**103 E Pecan St**
Native stone house built by prison labor; the sheriff occupied the original three rooms, and the basement was used as a jail. A dumb-waiter in the house was used to send meals down to the prisoners in the dungeon. Occupied as a private residence until 1967; now a museum furnished as a turn-of-the-century home
*Operated by Wise Co. Historical Soc. Open by appointment*

## DENISON

### EISENHOWER BIRTHPLACE STATE PARK, about 1880
**Lamar and Day Streets**
Two-story frame house where Dwight D. Eisenhower was born on Oct. 14, 1890. Restored to its appearance at the time of his birth, with such personal family furnishings as a quilt made by Ike's mother
*Operated by Tex. Parks and Wildlife Dept. Open June–Labor Day: daily 8–6. After Labor Day–May: daily 10–5*

## FAIRFIELD

### MOODY-BRADLEY HOUSE, before 1860
**Coleman Street, off Bateman Road**
This Greek Revival ante-bellum house is furnished with antiques, some original to the house. Also on display is a fine collection of china dolls.
*Operated by History Club. Open June–Sept: Sun. 1–5*

## FORT DAVIS

### TRUEHART [NEILL MUSEUM], 1899
**seven blocks west of courthouse**
Large turn-of-the-century house furnished with period pieces. Now a museum, with an extensive collection of antique toys made in Texas and

antique and contemporary dolls
*Operated by Teda Neill, owner. Open June–Aug: daily 9–5 and by appointment*

## FORT WORTH

### LOG CABIN VILLAGE, about 1850s
**2121 Colonial Pkwy**
Seven log cabins—the earliest one built in 1832—depict pioneer life in the mid-19th century. All are restored with appropriate furnishings.
*Operated by City of Fort Worth Parks and Recreation Dept. Open Mon.–Fri. 8–4:30, Sat. 9–5, Sun. 1–5*

## FREDERICKSBURG

### ■ FREDERICKSBURG HISTORIC DISTRICT
Founded by a party of German settlers in 1846, this town was named for Frederick the Great of Prussia. Many of the original stone houses remain, as well as "Sunday Houses"—dwellings built by farmers and ranchers who lived too far from town to be able to go to church and return home in one day. Small and inexpensively built, they enabled rural dwellers to be in town weekly without imposing on friends or relatives.

### KAMMLAH HOUSE (PIONEER MUSEUM AND COUNTRY STORE), about 1850
**309 W Main St**
Heinrich Kammlah built these two buildings—one as a residence, the other as a store—soon after German immigrants founded a settlement here. The house has many European features, including a deep stone cellar, an outdoor oven, and an enclosed courtyard. Now a historical museum
*Operated by Gillespie Co. Historical Soc. Open June–Aug: daily 10–5. Sept.–May: Sat., Sun. 1–5, and by appointment*

## GALVESTON

### ■ BISHOP'S PALACE, 1886
**1402 Broadway**
Ornate, eclectic Victorian mansion designed by architect Nicholas J. Clayton for Galveston attorney Walter Gresham; the four-story stone man-

sion was named one of the 100 outstanding buildings in the U.S. by the American Institute of Architects. Among the notable features are the ornate hand-carved main stairway, circular stained-glass windows, and a fireplace of Mexican silver, onyx, and satinwood. Since 1923 the house has served as the residence of the bishop of the Galveston-Houston diocese.
*Operated by Newman Center of the University of Tex. Medical Branch. Open Memorial Day–Labor Day: daily 10–5; closed Tues. Rest of year: daily 1–5; closed Tues.*

*Bishop's Palace*

### SAMUEL MAY WILLIAMS HOUSE, 1837–40
**3601 Avenue P**
One-story house of northern white pine with a brick kitchen built by Samuel May Williams, land agent for Stephen Austin's colony. It is now a museum featuring many items of local history.
*Operated by Galveston Historical Foundation. Open June–Sept: daily 1–5*

### ■ THE STRAND HISTORIC DISTRICT
This district was once the central part and leading commercial area of Galveston. Located on the eastern half of Galveston Island, the city is now guarded from the floods, which nearly wrecked it many times, by a ten-mile sea wall. A roadway atop the sea wall provides a scenic view of the Texas mainland two miles away.

# GREENVILLE

### ENDE-GAILLARD HOUSE, 1859
Graham Park

Frame house of pine and cypress on an oak base is the oldest in the town; built by Fred Ende, a German immigrant who played a prominent role in the development of the frontier village. Occupied until 1957 by Ende's descendants, who returned most of the original furnishings to the house
*Operated by Hunt Co. Historical Soc. Open June–Sept: Sun. 2–5 and by appointment*

# HENDERSON

### HOWARD-DICKINSON HOUSE, 1855
**South Main Street**

Two-story house was the first brick home in the county; built by the Howard brothers, who made these bricks of mud, although they later developed a patented method of producing brick by machine. A frame wing was added by a later owner after 1905. Restored and furnished with period pieces
*Operated by Rusk Co. Heritage Assn. Open May–Aug: Tues.–Sun. 1–5. Sept.–Dec., Mar.–Apr: Sat., Sun. 1–5, and by appointment*

### M. KANGERGA HOUSE, 1901
**North High Street and Webster Walk**

Designed by the Nashville architectural firm of George F. Barker & Co., this fine turn-of-the-century house was built by Croatian Michael Kangerga, who with his younger brother operated a successful mercantile and financial institution here. Now a center for the fine arts with changing exhibits
*Operated by Rusk Co. Heritage Assn. Open during exhibits and by appointment*

# HOUSTON

### KELLUM-NOBLE HOUSE, 1847
**Sam Houston Park, 1100 Bagby St**

Large two-story brick house encircled by double galleries; built by Nathaniel Kellum, who operated a brick kiln, and believed to be the oldest brick house in Houston. During the 1850s Mrs. Z.M. Noble conducted one of the city's first private schools in the house; occupied by the Noble family until

1898, when the city purchased it; now restored with period furnishings
*Operated by Harris Co. Heritage Soc. Open Mon.–Fri. 10–4, Sat. 11–3, Sun. 2–5*

*Kellum-Noble House*

### NICHOLS-RICE-CHERRY HOUSE, about 1850
**Sam Houston Park, 1100 Bagby St**

Charming two-story Greek Revival house with four pillars supporting the gallery and an identical set above supporting the roof. Once owned by philanthropist William Marsh Rice, it was moved to the park and restored in 1963; now shown with period furnishings.
*Operated by Harris Co. Heritage Soc. Open Mon.–Fri. 10–4, Sat. 11–3, Sun. 2–5*

*Nichols-Rice-Cherry House*

### OLD PLACE, between 1823 and 1825
**Sam Houston Park, 1100 Bagby St**

This one-room cabin is believed to be the oldest house in Harris County. It was originally located on Clear Creek on an Austin colony "labor" of land granted to John R. Williams in 1824. Moved to Sam Houston Park in 1971; restored and furnished
*Operated by Harris Co. Heritage Soc.*

Open Mon.–Fri. 10–4, Sat. 11–3, Sun. 2–5

## PILLOT HOUSE, 1868
Sam Houston Park, 1100 Bagby St
Small Victorian house with four floor-to-ceiling windows across the façade and a hipped roof with twin chimneys. Occupied by the Pillot family until 1964 and believed to have been built with the first inside kitchen in Houston. Moved to the park, restored, and appropriately furnished
*Operated by Harris Co. Heritage Soc. Open Mon.–Fri. 10–4, Sat. 11–3, Sun. 2–5*

*Pillot House*

## SAN FELIPE COTTAGE, about 1840
Sam Houston Park, 1100 Bagby St
This typical east Texas cottage with three dormer windows piercing the pitched roof is one of Houston's oldest surviving buildings. Originally situated on the old San Felipe stage route, it was moved to the park, restored, and furnished with period pieces.
*Operated by Harris Co. Heritage Soc. Open Mon.–Fri. 10–4, Sat. 11–3, Sun. 2–5*

## HUNTSVILLE

### SAM HOUSTON SHRINE
U.S. Route 75
On this 15-acre site is Sam Houston's *Wigwam*, the home he built in 1847 from a one-room pioneer cabin. The six-room frame house contains many Houston family effects. Also here is the *Steamboat House*, where Houston died in 1863. Built in 1858, it resembles a Mississippi river boat and is furnished with period pieces. Other

buildings in the complex are his log law office and a memorial museum. *Operated by the State of Tex. Open daily 9–5; closed Thanksgiving and Christmas*

## JEFFERSON

### ANNUAL HISTORICAL PILGRIMAGE
For a few days each April a number of Jefferson's lovely ante-bellum homes are open to the public. Among the houses on the tour are the *W.P. Schulter Home*, a two-story frame house built in 1852, and *Guarding Oak*, 1859, dominated by a huge oak tree on the front lawn. For further information contact the Pilgrimage Commission.

### ■ THE OLD MANSE, begun 1839
411 East Delta St
Considered "the most distinctive small house in East Texas," this unusual one-story frame Greek Revival house with two four-columned porticoes was built by Gen. James H. Rogers, an officer under Sam Houston. From 1903 to 1957, when it was restored, it was a Presbyterian manse.
*Operated by Jessie Allen Wise Garden Club. Open by appointment*

## JOHNSON CITY

### ■ LYNDON B. JOHNSON BOYHOOD HOME, 1896
Ninth Street and Avenue G
Small, one-story white frame house where Lyndon Johnson lived from about 1914 to 1924. Here he made his first speech in his first political campaign for national office in 1936. Shown with Johnson family furnishings and memorabilia
*Operated by National Park Service. Open daily 9–5; closed Christmas*

## LA GRANGE

### NATHANIEL W. FAISON HOME, 1840s
822 S Jefferson St
Early Victorian frame house with an 1855 addition. After 1866 the home of Nathaniel W. Faison, who took part in Capt. Nicholas Dawson's ill-fated battle against Mexico in 1842. Restored and shown with the furnishings of the Faison family, who owned the

house until 1960
*Operated by La Grange Garden Club.*
*Open Apr.–Sept: Thurs.–Sun. 1–5.*
*Oct.–Mar: by appointment*

*Nathaniel W. Faison Home*

## LEVERETT'S CHAPEL

**LEVERETT HOUSE, begun 1840**
**junction of Routes 135 and 42**
Large plantation house built around and incorporating the original log house begun in 1840. M.B. Leverett, an early planter and Confederate sympathizer, operated the plantation here. Still occupied by his descendants
*Operated by Mr. and Mrs. Donald Leverett, owners. Open by appointment*

## LIVINGSTON VICINITY

**LIVING INDIAN VILLAGE**
**Alabama-Coushatta Indian Reservation, U.S. Route 190**
This typical village depicts Indian life in 1805; here tribal members demonstrate cooking, pottery, beadwork, and other crafts. Part of a large complex, which includes camping grounds, historical tours, and a historical museum
*Operated by Alabama-Coushatta Indian Museum. Open June–Aug: Mon.–Sat. 12:30–5, Sun. 1:30–5. Sept.–May: Sun. 1:30–5*

## McCAMEY

**ADRIAN HOUSE, 1914**
**U.S. Route 67**
Frame western bungalow furnished with period pieces is part of the Mendoza Trail Museum. On display are Indian artifacts, settlers' mementos, and exhibits of the ranching and oil industries.
*Operated by City of McCamey and Upton Co. Open Tues.–Sat. 1:30–5*

## MARLIN

**HIGHLANDS MANSION,**
**1890–1900**
**Highway 7**
Two-and-a-half-story house of cypress with a wide porch on three sides features gold-leaf-ornamented ceilings, leaded stained-glass windows, and rich oak paneling. Restored and furnished with period pieces
*Operated by Mr. and Mrs. Thomas A. Michalsky. Open Mon.–Sat. 10–4, Sun. 1–4*

## MT. ENTERPRISE

**ROSS HOUSE, 1845**
**U.S. Highway 84**
Fine example of an early Texas house, with "side rooms" at each end of the front porch. Built by Dr. William McDonald Ross, pioneer doctor, surveyor, sheriff of Rusk County, and member of the Texas legislature. Never vacant and still owned by the Ross family; some of the furnishings are original to the house
*Private. Open by appointment*

## NACOGDOCHES

**HOYA MEMORIAL LIBRARY AND MUSEUM, about 1828**
**211 S La Nana St**
L-shaped clapboard house with massive chimneys built by Texas patriot Adolphus Sterne, who served as alcalde of the town when it was under Mexican rule and later aided in the Texas war for independence. Sterne served in the Republic of Texas congress and was later a member of the state legislature. The house now has displays of early Texas memorabilia.
*Operated by Hoya Memorial Library and Museum. Open Mon.–Sat. 2–5*

## NEW BRAUNFELS

■ **FERDINAND LINDHEIMER HOUSE, 1852**
**491 Comal St**
Fine example of German *fachwerk* (half-timber construction) as adapted

to Texas cedar and limestone. Built by Ferdinand Lindheimer, internationally known botanist and German political refugee. In this house for 20 years he published *The Zeitung*, the community's German-language newspaper. Fully restored and shown with period furnishings
*Operated by New Braunfels Conservation Soc. Open May–Sept: daily 2–5. Oct.–Apr: Sat., Sun. 2–5*

*Ferdinand Lindheimer House*

## PALESTINE

### HOWARD HOUSE, about 1853
**1011 N Perry St**
This frame house is the oldest in town. Restored and shown with furniture, clothing, and other local items
*Operated by Anderson Co. Historical Survey Comm. Open Sat., Sun. 1–6*

### WATFORD HALL, about 1890
**107 S Sycamore St**
Two-story frame Victorian house with gingerbread trim sits behind an iron fence. Restored with period furnishings
*Operated by Carl Avera, owner. Open Sat., Sun. 1–9*

## PANHANDLE

### SQUARE HOUSE MUSEUM, 1880s
**Elsie and Fifth Streets**
This small stick-style Victorian cottage

is the oldest house in the city. Built as a ranch house by the Francklyn Land and Cattle Company and first occupied as a home in 1887. With the addition of a modern wing, the house, which is 24 feet square, was converted into a historical museum of the Panhandle region. Also featured is a restored and furnished pioneer dugout house.
*Operated by Carson Co. Historical Survey Comm. and Directors of the Square House Museum. Open June–Aug: daily 10–12, 1:30–5:50. Sept.–May: Sat., Sun. 1:30–5:30*

## ROUND ROCK

### EL MILAGRO MUSEUM, 1854–59
**U.S. Route 79**
Stone house built before the Civil War was restored in 1950. It is shown with the American and Oriental antique collection of the four generations who have lived here.
*Private. Open by appointment*

## ROUND TOP

### ■ WINEDALE STAGECOACH INN, 1834–48
**four miles east of Round Top**
This eight-room frame house of Texas cedar was probably begun in 1834. It reached its present proportions about 1848, when Sam Lewis bought the property and began to operate it as a "Stopping Place" as well as a home for his family. Restored and shown with decorative ceiling and wall painting and typical German-American furnishings. Also on the site are a number of restored log outbuildings.
*Operated by University of Tex. System, Winedale Inn Properties. Open June–Oct: daily 10–6. Nov.–May: daily 9–5*

## SALADO

### COL. STERLING C. ROBERTSON HOUSE, 1852
**Chisholm Trail**
Two-story house, with the living section of cypress and the service section (now attached) of native limestone, is one of the few remaining complete plantation units in Texas. Six generations—all named Sterling Clack Robertson—have lived on this still operating ranch, which has the original

cabins, stables, and burial grounds. *Operated by Mrs. Sterling C. Robertson, owner. Open by appointment*

## SAN ANTONIO

### CELSO NAVARRO HOUSE, 1835
**Witte Memorial Museum Grounds, 3801 Broadway**
This house of hand-cut limestone covered with plaster is typical of the Texas revolutionary period. Moved to the museum in the 1940s, it houses a large collection of dolls from 80 different countries.
*Operated by Witte Memorial Museum. Open Tues.–Sat. 10–5, Sun. 10–6*

### JOSE ANTONIO NAVARRO HOUSES, 1850
**228–232 S Laredo St**
A complex of three limestone buildings used as a town house and office by Texas patriot José Antonio Navarro, who fought against the Spanish for Mexican freedom and who later signed the Texas Declaration of Independence; he and his uncle, Francisco Ruiz, were the only native Texans to sign the document. Furnished with antiques of Louisiana, Texas, and Mexico
*Operated by San Antonio Conservation Soc. Open Tues.–Sun. 10–4*

### LA VILLITA
**Villita Street between South Presa and South Alamo Streets**
By 1722 "Little Village" was an established settlement of adobe houses of Spanish soldiers and their Indian wives; it became fashionable after 1819 when high ground there spared the district from a flood that devastated most of San Antonio. In the 20th century the area began to deteriorate, but a restoration project started in 1939 returned La Villita to its antique charm. Many of the adobe houses are now art galleries and handicraft shops.
*Operated by City of San Antonio. Open daily 8–6*

### O. HENRY HOUSE, about 1850
**600 Lone Star Blvd**
Two-story stone house built at a cost of $96 and rented by O. Henry in 1895. On display are first editions of *Rolling Stone*, a humorous weekly that he edited while living in Texas.
*Operated by Lone Star Brewery. Open daily 10–6*

### ■ SPANISH GOVERNOR'S PALACE, 1749
**105 Military Plaza**
Ten-room town house of adobe covered with plaster built as the residence of the Spanish governors. The only remaining aristocratic 18th-century Spanish house in Texas, the palace features massive doors—hand-carved with floral and symbolic designs—and a keystone above with the Hapsburg coat of arms and building date. Completely restored and furnished with period pieces
*Operated by City of San Antonio. Open Mon.–Sat. 9–5, Sun. 10–5*

### STEVES HOMESTEAD, 1876
**509 King William St**
Large Victorian house with a mansard roof built by Edward Steves in the old German residential section on the banks of the San Antonio River. Set in a grove of pecan trees, the house is furnished with fine period antiques, including an ornate Belter table. Formal gardens surround the house; the River House, built as a natatorium with its own artesian well, remains.
*Operated by San Antonio Conservation Soc. Open daily 10–12, 2–4*

### TWOHIG HOUSE, 1841
**Witte Memorial Museum, 3801 Broadway**
Imposing, two-story house of hand-cut limestone built by prosperous merchant John Twohig at a time when few of the town's buildings were over one story. Moved to the museum grounds in 1941 and shown with period furnishings, some original to the house. The original outdoor fireplace can also be seen.
*Operated by Witte Memorial Museum. Open Tues.–Sat. 10–5, Sun. 10–6*

### YTURRI-EDMUNDS HOME AND MILL, about 1729
**257 Yellowstone St**
This very early house made of soft stone and a mill which predates it have been restored and furnished with period pieces.
*Operated by San Antonio Conservation Soc. Open Tues. 9–5*

## SAN AUGUSTINE

### HISTORIC HOUSE TOUR
During the first weekend of June a

number of historic homes are open to view in San Augustine, a city that developed around the *Mission Nuestra Señora de los Dolores de los Ais,* established here by the Spanish in 1717. Among the early 19th-century buildings on the tour are the home of Stephen W. Blount, signer of the Texas Declaration of Independence, and the *Columbus Cartwright Home,* both built in 1839.

## CULLEN HOME, 1839
**205 S Congress St**
Massive Doric columns support the porch of this Greek Revival house built by Ezekiel Cullen, an early settler. Donated as a community house and museum by his grandson in 1953, it is shown with period furnishings and a collection of paintings by S. Seymour Thomas, a town native.
*Operated by Daughters of the Republic of Texas. Open by appointment*

## WILLIAM GARRETT PLANTATION, 1861–64
**two miles west of San Augustine**
Large house of Texas pine built by slave labor for plantation owner William Garrett. Two-story house features large windows and six fireplaces. Restored in 1943 and shown with period antiques, it is still in use as a family home.
*Operated by Mr. and Mrs. Cornell T. Dorsey and Mr. and Mrs. S. Parker Dorsey, owners. Open by appointment*

## SAN MARCOS
### TEXANA VILLAGE
**Aquarena Springs**
This village is made up of restored and reconstructed buildings, including the town's oldest residence, the *Dr. Eli Merriman Home,* a log cabin built about 1845 and shown with period antiques. Also featured is a reproduction of the family log cabin of Gen. Edward Burleson, frontiersman, soldier, and vice president of the Republic of Texas. Among the other buildings are a gristmill, jail, and blacksmith shop.
*Operated by Aquarena Springs. Open Memorial Day–Labor Day: daily 8–9:30. Rest of year: daily 8:30–6*

## SAN SABA
### SAN SABA COUNTY HISTORICAL MUSEUM
**Mill Pond Park**
Two log cabins of hand-hewn elm, which once served as stables, now house historical items depicting ranch, farm, and western life.
*Operated by San Saba Co. Historical Soc. Open Apr.–Aug: Sun. 3:30–5:30. Sept.–Mar: by appointment*

## SEGUIN
### ■ SEBASTOPOL, 1850s
**704 W Court St**
Unusual T-shaped ante-bellum house with a striking squared-off top. The roof was designed to catch a pool of rain water, which would cool the house in hot weather. Built by Col. Joshua Young and named for the famous Crimean War battle
*Private. Open by appointment*

## STEPHENVILLE
### STEPHENVILLE HISTORICAL HOUSE MUSEUM, about 1869
**525 E Washington St**
Victorian stone house surrounded by a five-acre park is furnished with pieces from the period between the close of the Civil War and World War I. Also on display are maps, pictures, and other items of local history.
*Operated by Stephenville Study Club. Open daily 2–5*

## STONEWALL
### ■ LYNDON B. JOHNSON BIRTHPLACE, before 1908
**Park Road 49 on the L.B.J. Ranch**
Reconstructed five-room house with a dogtrot where Sam and Rebekah Baines Johnson lived when their oldest child, Lyndon, was born, August 27, 1908. Furnished with belongings of L.B.J.'s parents and grandparents
*Operated by National Park Service. Open daily 9–5; closed Christmas*

## TYLER
### GOODMAN MUSEUM, begun about 1859
**624 N Broadway**
Stately classical revival frame house

begun as a four-room cottage and greatly enlarged by later owners Dr. Samuel Goodman and his son Dr. W.J. Goodman. The house features a two-story columned semicircular portico and covered side porches. Now a museum with antique furnishings
*Operated by Smith Co. Historical Soc. Open daily 1–5; closed Christmas*

## UVALDE

### GARNER MEMORIAL MUSEUM, 1920
333 N Park St

Former home of John Nance Garner, who served as Vice President during the first two administrations of Franklin Delano Roosevelt. On display, along with other memorabilia, is the Garner collection of gavels — which range in size from a half-inch gavel to one over two feet long.
*Operated by City of Uvalde. Open daily 9–12, 1–5; closed holidays*

## VICTORIA

### W.J. McNAMARA HOME, about 1870
502 N Liberty St

Large frame Victorian house built by hide and cattle dealer W.J. McNamara and owned by his family until 1959. Restored as a museum and shown with furnishings and other items of local history. Art exhibits changed monthly
*Operated by McNamara-O'Connor Historical and Fine Arts Museum Assn. Open Wed. 10–12, Sun. 3–5*

## WACO

### EARLE-HARRISON HOUSE, 1858
1901 N Fifth St

Nine fluted Doric columns dominate this Greek Revival mansion built by Dr. Baylis Wood Earle and for many years the home of Gen. Tom Harrison. The windows are tall enough to serve as doors, and each room opens onto the upper or lower gallery. After decades of neglect the house was restored.
*Operated by G.H. Pape Foundation. Open Sat., Sun. 2–5, and by appointment*

### EARLE-NAPIER-KINNARD MUSEUM, 1860–68
814 S Fourth St

Begun as a small brick house by John

Baylis Earle, manufacturer of uniforms for Confederate troops, this two-story classical revival mansion of pink Waco brick was completed by a later owner, Capt. John Napier. Restored and furnished with period pieces
*Operated by Historic Waco Foundation. Open Sat., Sun. 2–5, and by appointment*

### EAST TERRACE, about 1872
100 Mill St

Large Italianate villa, the home of John Wesley Mann — pioneer industrialist, businessman, and banker — who manufactured the rose pink brick of which it is built. Restored and furnished as a fine Victorian home
*Operated by Historic Waco Foundation. Open Sat., Sun. 2–5, and by appointment*

*East Terrace*

### ■ FORT HOUSE MUSEUM, about 1868
503 S Fourth St

Greek Revival mansion built in an L-shape to provide cross ventilation in each room. The pink brick mansion features two fluted columns with a balcony between; the back of the house has a two-storied porch. Of the original outbuildings, only the bathhouse remains. Restored and shown with appropriate furnishings
*Operated by Historic Waco Foundation. Open Sat., Sun. 2–5, and by appointment*

### NELL PAPE GARDEN CENTER, about 1879
1705 N Fifth St

Stately classical revival red brick mansion with four fluted columns supporting the portico; the south side features a one-story porch, also supported by fluted columns. The grounds are graced with live oak trees and an enclosed garden.
*Operated by Waco Council of Garden Clubs. Open Sat., Sun. 2–5, and by appointment*

### SIMS LOG CABIN, 1859
**1020 Sleepy Hollow**
This 18- by 18-foot log cabin has been restored to its original appearance. It is shown with settlers' tools and furnishings and Indian artifacts.
*Private. Open by appointment*

## WASHINGTON

### ANSON JONES HOME, 1844
**Washington-on-the-Brazos State Park**
Simple, story-and-a-half clapboard house built by Dr. Anson Jones, the last president of the Republic of Texas. Named "Barrington" for the Massachusetts town where he was born, the house was built on Jones's 300-acre plantation during his presidential campaign. Nearby stands a blacksmith shop, a replica of the building in which the Texas Declaration of Independence was signed.
*Operated by The Barrington Soc. Open Wed.–Sun. 10–5*

## WEST COLUMBIA

### VARNER-HOGG PLANTATION, 1835
**Varner-Hogg State Historic Park**
Martin Varner received this land as one of the original 300 land grants in Stephen Austin's first colony; he built a small log cabin which was replaced with a two-story brick house by Columbus Patton in 1835. After years of use as a sugar plantation, the property was bought in 1901 by James Hogg, onetime Texas governor; his children did a vast remodeling job on the house in 1920, adding the six columns and new kitchen. Now part of a 65-acre park, the house features furnishings from the period 1835–50.
*Operated by Tex. Parks and Wildlife Dept. Open Tues., Thurs.–Sun. 10–12, 1–5*

*Varner-Hogg Plantation*

## WIMBERLY

### PIONEER TOWN
**7-A Ranch Resort**
A re-creation of an Old West Texas town with original buildings and some reproductions. Highlighted is the *Schlameus House,* two log cabins connected by a dogtrot, built in 1854 by Adolph Schlameus, who migrated to New Braunfels from Germany and operated the first school in the area. Shown with period furnishings; other buildings include a general store and a house made entirely from soda water bottles.
*Operated by Pioneer Town. Open Memorial Day–Labor Day: 8 A.M.–10 P.M. Rest of year: 8–dusk*

## WOODVILLE

### HERITAGE GARDEN VILLAGE, before 1900
**U.S. Route 190**
A pioneer village of 27 historical buildings furnished with authentic pieces, all of which may be handled. Highlighted is the *Tolar Cabin,* built of board and batten with a cypress shake roof by pioneer Robert Tolar in 1866. Except for the hand-blown glass windows, all the materials for the house came from Tolar's land. Occupied until 1960 and never restored; many of the furnishings are original to the house
*Operated by Clyde E. Gray. Open daily 9–dusk; closed Thanksgiving and Christmas*

## FAIRFIELD

### JOHN CARSON HOUSE, about 1858
Main Street
Two-story adobe house with a gallery across the front and a gable roof; built by John Carson and used as a stagecoach inn. Gen. Albert S. Johnston lived here while commander of adjacent Camp Floyd, the largest army encampment in the U.S. in the 1850s. Now a museum, pioneer furnishings *Operated by Utah State Park and Recreation Comm. Open Apr.–Nov: daily 10–6*

## ST. GEORGE

### BRIGHAM YOUNG WINTER HOME, before 1873
Dixie State Park, U.S. Route 91
Because of the warm climate, Brigham Young spent his last winters here; a two-story north wing was added to an existing structure in 1873. Built of adobe brick and ponderosa pine on a lava rock foundation, the house has been restored and furnished with period pieces.
*Operated by Utah State Park and Recreation Comm. Open June–Aug: daily 8–7. Sept.–May: daily 9–5*

## SALT LAKE CITY

### ■ BEEHIVE HOUSE, 1854
75 E South Temple St
Greek Revival home of pioneer Brigham Young, governor of the Mormon state of Deseret and the Territory of Utah; designed by architect Truman O. Angell. The name is taken from a beehive-shaped cupola, the beehive being the symbol of Mormon industry. After serving as the official residence of later presidents of the Mormon Church, the house was restored to its original appearance; furnished with period pieces, some belonging to Brigham Young
*Operated by Church of Jesus Christ of Latter-day Saints. Open Mon.–Sat. 9:30–4:30*

### FOREST FARM HOME, 1861–63
732 Ashton Ave
Two-story house on a stone foundation built on the plan of a double cross. Brigham Young founded an experimental farm here and imported vegetables, fruit trees, and animal stock to determine the best crops for Utah; 25 acres of mulberry trees were planted, and a cocoonery was established. The farm has disappeared; the house has been restored and furnished.
*Operated by Church of Jesus Christ of Latter-day Saints. Open June–Aug: Mon.–Sat. 9:30–4:30. Sept.–May: Mon.–Sat. 1–4:30*

### KEITH-BROWN MANSION, 1900
529 E South Temple St
Three-story, 16-room classical revival mansion with a copper tile roof built for silver millionaire David Keith. A later owner, Ezra Thompson, added the massive front doors of wrought iron and glass. The interior features carved cherry wood, octagonal-shaped entry hall that rises 13 feet, Tiffany lamps, and beautiful leaded-glass windows. Now the offices of a land development corporation.
*Operated by Terracor Corp. Open Mon.–Fri. 8–5*

### LESTER F. WIRE HOUSE, 1887
668 S Third St, E
In this Dutch colonial-style house Lester Farnsworth Wire invented the traffic light in 1912. Now a museum with displays of traffic signals and other items of local history. Some of Wire's personal belongings – including some of the original furniture. *Operated by Wire Memorial Museum and Historical Assn. Open by appointment*

*Beehive House*

## PIONEER VILLAGE MUSEUM, 1847–1900
**2998 Connor St**
A complex of 25 buildings dating from the period of Utah's settlement makes up this village. Included are a pony express station, Mormon meeting-house, general store, and train station, with a narrow-gauge engine and car. All are furnished with appropriate period pieces.
*Operated by National Soc. of the Sons of Utah Pioneers. Open Apr.–Oct: Mon.–Sat. 9–5, Sun. 1–5*

## ■ THOMAS KEARNS MANSION, 1900–1902
**603 E South Temple St**
Lavish stone mansion, dominated by three round towers, built by silver magnate and U.S. senator Thomas Kearns. Among the 32 original rooms are an all-marble kitchen, six all-marble bathrooms, a bowling alley, ballroom, and billiard room; the beautiful floating staircase is of French oak. In 1937 Mrs. Kearns donated her house for use as the governor's mansion; since 1957 it has been a museum and historical society headquarters. Shown with most of the Kearns' furnishings
*Operated by Utah State Historical Soc. Open Mon.–Fri. 9–5, Sat. 9–1*

## SANTA CLARA

### JACOB HAMBLIN HOME, 1862
**Dixie State Park, U.S. Route 91**
Two-story house of rough-hewn natural sandstone, with a roof of hand-split cedar shingles, built by Jacob Hamblin, pioneer Mormon scout and missionary to the Hopi and Navajo Indians. Restored to its original appearance and shown with handmade pine furniture of the pioneer period
*Operated by Utah State Park and Recreation Comm. Open June–Aug: daily 8–7. Sept.–May: daily 9–5*

## VERNAL

### LITTLE ROCK HOUSE, 1887
**178 S Fifth St, W**
Built of hand-quarried native rock, this house was the first Mormon tithing office. Moved to the present location and restored in 1961, it is shown with pioneer furnishings.
*Operated by Daughters of Utah Pioneers. Open May 31–Sept. 3: daily 9–5*

## ADDISON

### GEN. JOHN STRONG MANSION, 1795
**Chimney Point**
Fine brick Federal mansion, with Palladian window above entrance portico, built by early Vermont pioneer and Revolutionary soldier John Strong. Interesting interiors, wide hall with arch, great kitchen fireplace, furnished in period
*Operated by Daughters of the American Revolution. Open July–Aug: daily 10–5*

## BARNET

### GOODWILLIE HOUSE, 1790–91
One-and-a-half-story frame home of Rev. David Goodwillie, first pastor of Barnet Center Presbyterian Church, who built it for his bride. Interiors with original large beams, gunstock corner posts, wide floorboards; furnished with antiques contributed by members of local historical society
*Operated by Barnet Historical Soc. Open May 15–Oct. 15: by appointment*

## BRANDON

### STEPHEN DOUGLAS HOUSE, early 1800s
White frame birthplace in 1813 of Stephen A. Douglas, famed as the "Little Giant" of national politics. He worked as a cabinetmaker in Middlebury then began to study law before moving to Illinois in 1833. There his political career reached its height in his famous debates with Abraham Lincoln in 1858. Antique furnishings include the Douglas cradle.
*Operated by Daughters of the American Revolution. Open by appointment*

## BROOKFIELD
### MARVIN NEWTON HOUSE, 1835
**Brookfield Center**
Two-and-a-half-story clapboard village home with nine rooms, most containing soapstone fireplaces. Now a house museum with period furnishings, kitchen equipment, needlework, costumes, and old hand tools
*Operated by Historical Soc. of Brookfield. Open July–Aug: Sun. 3–5*

## BROWNINGTON
### OLD STONE HOUSE, 1836
**Brownington Village**
Ruggedly severe granite house built almost single-handedly by Rev. Alexander Twilight, headmaster of Orleans County Grammar School, to serve as a dormitory. When the school closed after the Civil War, the Old Stone House became the property of Mrs. Twilight. Now a house museum with 18th- and 19th-century furniture
*Operated by Orleans Co. Historical Soc. Open May 15–Oct 15: daily 9–5*

*Old Stone House*

## CALAIS
### KENT TAVERN MUSEUM, about 1832
**Kent's Corner**
Originally built as a tavern but later the residence of Abdiel Kent after his marriage in 1846. Presented to the Vermont Historical Soc. in 1944 by Atwater Kent. Period rooms and antique furnishings
*Operated by Vt. Historical Soc. Open July–Aug: Wed.–Sun. 2–5*

## FERRISBURG
### ROBINSON HOMESTEAD ("ROKEBY"), 1789
Ancestral home of an abolitionist Quaker family whose most famous son was Rowland E. Robinson – 19th-century folk and nature writer. The house was a station on the Underground Railroad during the Civil War period. Family heirlooms on display
*Operated by Rowland E. Robinson Memorial Assn. Open June–Sept: daily 10–5*

## GRAND ISLE
### HYDE LOG CABIN, 1783
**U.S. Route 2**
Built by Jedediah Hyde, Jr., Revolutionary soldier, of hand-hewn white cedar logs 14 inches wide, on an island in Lake Champlain
*Operated by Grand Isle Co. Historical Soc. Open July–Labor Day: daily 10–5*

## MIDDLEBURY
### ■ EMMA WILLARD HOUSE, 1809
**Middlebury College Campus**
Two-story brick house with long front porch supported by columns; home of Emma Willard, pioneer in the movement for female education in the U.S.
*Operated by Middlebury College. Open as admissions office*

### SEYMOUR HOUSE [COMMUNITY HOUSE], 1816
**Main Street**
Horatio Seymour, U.S. senator from 1821 to 1833, built this brick Federal-style house set off by the white wooden balustrade on roof, curved hood over doorway, and picket fence. Interiors feature Adamesque hand-turned woodwork and ten hand-carved

*Seymour House*

mantels; period furnishings
*Operated by Board of Trustees of Community House. Open Tues.–Sun. 9–5*

## SHELDON MUSEUM, 1829
**1 Park St**
Built by Eben Judd and Lebbeus Harris, a three-story brick house braced with massive hand-hewn beams and a front porch supported by six columns. Now the oldest New England village museum (dating from 1882), it depicts life in a typical community of the 19th century.
*Operated by Sheldon Museum. Open June–Oct. 15: Mon.–Sat. 10–5. Oct. 16–May: Tues., Thurs. 1–5; closed national holidays*

## MORRISVILLE

### NOYES HOUSE, 1820
**Main Street**
Two-story Federal-style brick mansion restored to serve as historical museum. Period furnishings, antique wallpapers, glass, china, Toby mug collection, costumes, clocks, et cetera
*Operated by Morristown Historical Museum. Open May–Oct: daily 2–5*

## NORTH BENNINGTON

### GOV. McCULLOUGH MANSION, 1865
**Park and West Streets**
White frame Victorian mansion, laden with gingerbread trim, built by Trenor W. Park—a Bennington citizen who made his fortune in the California gold rush. Park's son-in-law, John G. McCullough, served as governor of Vermont from 1902 to 1904. The mansion is furnished in Victorian *décor* and serves the community's cultural and educational needs.

*Gov. McCullough Mansion*

*Operated by McCullough-Park Foundation. Open May 30–Oct. 12: Sat., Sun. 1–5*

## NORTH FAIRFIELD

### PRESIDENT CHESTER A. ARTHUR BIRTHPLACE
**off Route 36**
Replica of the small one-story clapboard dwelling in which the 21st President of the U.S. was born on October 5, 1830. It was built in 1954 by the state, with an old photograph as documentation. Furnishings of the 1830 period
*Operated by State of Vt., Div. of Historic Sites. Open Memorial Day–Labor Day: Tues.–Sun. 10–5. After Labor Day–Oct. 15: weekends only*

## PLYMOUTH

### ■ CALVIN COOLIDGE HOMESTEAD, about 1850
Simple, story-and-a-half white house with barn and shed connected, boyhood home of Calvin Coolidge. Here on the early morning of August 3, 1923, he was sworn in as 30th President of the U.S. by his own father, a Vermont notary public, Col. John Coolidge. Exact interiors and furnishings that were there that historic morn
*Operated by State of Vt., Div. of Historic Sites. Open Memorial Day–Oct. 15: daily 9–6*

### WILDER HOUSE, about 1820
**Route 100A**
Commodious old house next door to the Coolidge Homestead; birthplace and home of President Coolidge's mother, Josephine Victoria Moor, until she married Col. John Coolidge. Now serves as hospitality center where visitors may enjoy home-cooked Vermont food and obtain travel information
*Operated by State of Vt., Div. of Historic Sites. Open Memorial Day–Oct. 15: daily 9–6*

## PROCTOR

### WILSON'S CASTLE, 1867
**West Proctor Road**
A 32-room castle built in the heart of the Green Mountains in a blend of European styles, complete with arches,

turrets, and parapets. The façade is set with English brick, slate, marble, and copper; the interiors are richly paneled and feature 84 stained-glass windows. The furnishings include Far Eastern and European antiques as well as American Victorian pieces. Extensive grounds with aviary; guides costumed as Swiss guards

*Operated by Helen and Col. Herbert Wilson, owners. Open May 15–Oct. 15: daily 8–6*

## SHELBURNE

### SHELBURNE MUSEUM
**Shelburne Road**
On a 45-acre tract stands an outdoor museum complex of 35 buildings showing early American life over a span of three centuries. Eight original homes from other parts of New England and New York have been dismantled and reassembled on the museum site; these include the *Stencil House,* a small frame house of 1790, noted for the stenciling on the walls; the *Salmon Dutton Homestead,* a saltbox of 1783; the *Vermont House,* of stone and elegantly furnished in Queen Anne style as a sea captain's home of the 1790s; a Shaker building and the Stagecoach Inn. Besides houses, there are shops, craft exhibits, art collections, et cetera.

*Operated by Shelburne Museum. Open May 25–Oct. 20: daily 9–5*

## STRAFFORD

### ■ JUSTIN SMITH MORRILL HOMESTEAD, 1848–51
**south of the Common**
Charming Gothic Revival cottage designed and built by J. S. Morrill, con-

*Justin Smith Morrill Homestead*

gressman (12 years) and senator (32 years) famous for his legislation establishing the land-grant colleges. The plan of the cottage is similar to the designs of Andrew Jackson Downing's Italianate villas. The architectural trim is a fanciful Victorian adaptation of the repertoire of Gothic details. Furnished in mid-19th-century style

*Operated by State of Vt., Div. of Historic Sites. Open Memorial Day–Labor Day: Tues.–Sat. 9–12, 1–4:30*

## WESTON

### FARRAR-MANSUR HOUSE, 1797
**on the Common**
Built by Capt. Oliver Farrar as an inn, tavern, and home for his family, the plain unornamented white frame exterior is relieved by the charm of the interior: formal council room with fine woodwork, barroom, ballroom, and best bedchamber. Restored with period furnishings

*Operated by Town of Weston. Open May 30–Oct. 12: Tues.–Sun. 1–5*

## WINDSOR

### OLD CONSTITUTION HOUSE, about 1760
**U.S. Route 5**
Originally a tavern operated by Elijah West, it is now called the "Birthplace of Vermont." On July 2, 1777, a group of delegates from the New Hampshire grants met here to discuss and draw up the constitution for an independent state that was adopted on July 8. Vermont became a republic until 1791, when it was admitted to the Union as the 14th state.

*Operated by State of Vt., Div. of Historic Sites. Open Memorial Day–Oct. 15: daily 9–6*

## WOODSTOCK

### DANA HOUSE, 1807
**26 Elm St**
A fine early 19th-century house in an unspoiled rural Vermont village. Restored as a historic house museum, with nine period rooms and portraits of early Woodstock residents

*Operated by Woodstock Historical Soc. Open May 25–Oct. 25: Mon.–Sat. 10–12, 2–5, 7–9, Sun. 2–5:30*

## ABINGDON

### ■ ABINGDON HISTORIC DISTRICT

Called Wolf Hills at the time of its settlement between 1765 and 1770, the village was established as Abingdon in 1778. Old houses, mainly brick, line Main Street.

## ALDIE

### ■ ALDIE HISTORIC DISTRICT

Tiny early 19th-century community named for the home of Charles Fenton Mercer, member of the Virginia House of Delegates, brigadier general in the War of 1812, and a member of Congress. Aldie Mill, one of the state's best-preserved mills, the original miller's house, and Mercer's home are of interest.

## ALEXANDRIA

### ■ ALEXANDRIA HISTORIC DISTRICT

Consisting of almost 100 blocks in the heart of the original town, with numerous mid-18th- to 19th-century houses. George Washington was the assistant of county surveyor, John West, Jr., in 1749 and as such helped lay out the plan of the town.

*Prince Street*

### ■ CARLYLE HOUSE, 1752; early 19th century
### 121 N Fairfax St

Georgian mansion built by John Carlyle, a Scottish merchant who emigrated to America in 1740. He was commissary of the Virginia forces when, in 1755, Gen. Braddock, Com. Keppell, and the governors of five colonies met here to plan a campaign against the French and Indians. George Washington, a colonel, received his commission as an aide on Braddock's staff at this meeting. Now a house museum with an extensive collection of early American furniture *Operated by Mr. Lloyd Diehl Schaeffer. Open daily 10–5; closed Christmas*

### ■ GADSBY'S TAVERN, 1752; 1792 Royal and Cameron Streets

Two-story brick structure with large Federal-style addition; a coffee house originally and later the tavern in which George Washington recruited volunteers in 1754 and made his headquarters during the French and Indian wars. The ballroom paneling is now installed in the American Wing of the Metropolitan Museum of Art in New York. The interiors have been restored and represent one of the more elaborate 18th-century hostelries in the country.
*Operated by the American Legion. Open May–Oct: daily 10–5*

*Gadsby's Tavern*

### ROBERT E. LEE BOYHOOD HOME, about 1795
### 607 Oronoco St

Two-and-one-half-story Georgian mansion built by John Potts, who sold

the property to William Fitzhugh. Both men were business associates of George Washington, and it was here that Washington's adopted grandson married Fitzhugh's daughter in 1831. Robert E. Lee spent part of his childhood here, and it is now a house museum and memorial to him. Interiors reflect the influence of the Adam style; period furnishings
*Operated by Stonewall Jackson Memorial. Open daily 9–5*

*Robert E. Lee Boyhood Home*

## VOWELL-SMITH HOUSE, about 1840
**510 Wolfe St**
Victorian house, the surviving twin of two identical houses built by Mr. Vowell for his daughters. Rich interiors; black and white marble fireplaces with white marble mantels decorated with fruit-laden vines and overflowing fruit baskets; fourteen-foot ceilings with typical plaster ornamentation
*Operated by Mrs. Zerelda C. McConnell. Open by appointment*

## ALEXANDRIA VICINITY
■ **GUNSTON HALL, 1755–58**
**Route 95 from Washington, D.C. (Lorton exit)**
Built by George Mason, author of the Virginia constitution and Declaration of Rights and a leading Revolutionary. Mason was fortunate in having the services of William Buckland, a skilled draftsman from Oxford who was indentured to Mason and who later became

a noted colonial architect. The interiors were executed by him and are particularly distinctive. His ideas were fresh and up-to-date, and of the two principal rooms, one is Chinese Chippendale in design and the other Palladian. Restored in 1920, Gunston Hall is now a historic house museum.
*Operated by Soc. of Colonial Dames. Open daily 9:30–5; closed Christmas*

*Gunston Hall*

## APPOMATTOX VICINITY
■ **APPOMATTOX COURT HOUSE NATIONAL HISTORIC SITE**
**Virginia Route 24**
Restoration of village to 1865 appearance, including reconstruction of various buildings. One such building is the *Wilmer McLean House*, originally built about 1848. It was in this house that Robert E. Lee surrendered his army to Ulysses S. Grant on April 9, 1865.
*Operated by National Park Service. Open June–Labor Day: daily 8–6. Labor Day–May: Mon.–Fri. 9–5, Sat., Sun. 9–5:30; closed national holidays*

## ARLINGTON
■ **CUSTIS-LEE MANSION (ARLINGTON HOUSE), 1802–17**
**Arlington National Cemetery**
Greek Revival-style mansion built by George Washington Parke Custis, grandson of Martha Washington. His daughter, Mary Ann Custis, inherited the house, and it was here she and her husband, Robert E. Lee, spent most

VIRGINIA

287

of their married life. The interior of the mansion is more of the Federal style than Greek Revival and contrasts markedly with the sturdy white-columned portico. Furnishings include some from Mount Vernon and personal effects of George Washington. Restored, now a house museum
*Operated by National Park Service. Open April–Sept: daily 9:30–6. Oct.–Mar: daily 9:30–4:30*

Custis-Lee Mansion

## ASHLAND VICINITY

■ **SCOTCHTOWN, about 1719**
**Virginia Route 685**
Large, simple frame house built by Charles Chiswell. Patrick Henry owned the house from 1771 to 1777, the period in which he made his mark on American history. It was later the childhood home of Dolley Payne Madison. The house has been restored and is now a house museum.
*Operated by Assn. for the Preservation of Va. Antiquities. Open Apr.–Oct: Wed., Fri., Sat. 10–5, Sun. 2–5, and by appointment*

## BLACKSBURG VICINITY

■ **SMITHFIELD PLANTATION, 1772**
**on Route 314, one-quarter mile east of Route 460**
Built by Col. William Preston, this L-shaped frame plantation house is one of the earliest surviving in the remote western section of the state. It was the home of three Virginia governors. Now restored, it is a house museum with several rooms of the colonial and Federal periods.
*Operated by Assn. for the Preservation*

*of Va. Antiquities. Open Apr. 15–Nov. 15: Wed., Sat., Sun. 1–5, and by appointment*

## BRANDON VICINITY

■ **BRANDON, about 1765–70**
**at Burrowsville**
Uncertainly attributed to Thomas Jefferson, the five-part plan of this house is quite similar to a plate in Robert Morris' *Select Architecture*, 1755. The main house is linked to two earlier houses, which form the wings for the central portion.
*Operated by Mrs. Robert W. Daniel. Open—Gardens only—daily 9–5:30*

Brandon

## BROOKNEAL

**RED HILL SHRINE (LAST HOME OF PATRICK HENRY)**
**off Route 40, five miles east of Brookneal**
Reconstruction of the house in which the fiery patriot who declared "Give me liberty, or give me death," spent his retirement days. Interiors furnished with many original pieces and some Henry family possessions. Besides the main house, the cook's cabin, smokehouse, stables, and law office may be seen, as well as the graveyard in which Patrick Henry is buried with his wife and several of their children.
*Operated by Patrick Henry Memorial Foundation. Open Apr.–Oct: daily 9–5. Nov.–Mar: daily 9–5; closed Christmas*

## CHANTILLY

**SULLY PLANTATION, 1794**
**Sully Road, Route 28 at Dulles Airport**
Plantation home built by Richard Bland Lee for his bride, Liza Collins of Philadelphia. Richard Lee was the

younger brother of "Light-Horse Harry" Lee and uncle of Gen. Robert E. Lee. The house was saved from destruction by an act of Congress in 1959 after the land had been condemned for Dulles Airport. Some original furnishings
*Operated by Fairfax Co. Park Authority. Open daily 9–5; closed Christmas*

## CHARLES CITY

**BELLE AIR, about 1670; late 18th century; 1880**
**one-quarter mile east of Charles City on Route 5**
Originally a small 17th-century house with a clipped-gable roof, this structure has been enlarged and remodeled over the years and very little of the earlier exterior remains. The interior does retain some of its 17th-century features, such as pine framing and staircase. In 1950 a detached kitchen, built in 1880, was connected to the house.
*Operated by Mr. and Mrs. Walter O. Major. Open Mon.–Sat. 9–5, Sun. by appointment*

## CHARLES CITY VICINITY

■ **SHERWOOD FOREST (JOHN TYLER HOUSE), about 1780; 1842–62**
**east of Charles City on Route 5**
Retirement home of John Tyler, tenth President of the U.S., during the last 20 years of his life. He purchased the estate in 1842 and remodeled the colonial structure that was on it, adding a colonnade to connect the main house with the kitchen and laundry and a wing to serve as an office and a ballroom. Now a house museum
*Private. Open by appointment*

## CHARLOTTESVILLE

**ASH LAWN, 1796–98**
**Virginia Route 53**
Simple, frame two-story structure, with a one-story L at the rear, built by James Monroe near his friend Thomas Jefferson's home. While Monroe was minister to France he wrote to Jefferson about the house, which was to "cost not more than three or four thousand dollars." Monroe used Ash Lawn as his refuge until 1820, when

he moved to Oak Hill near Leesburg. Restored, furnished with many of Monroe's belongings
*Operated by John W. Johns. Open daily 7–7*

■ **FARMINGTON, 1802; 1850s**
**Route 250**
George Divers inherited his estate about 1785 and from 1802 to 1803 engaged Thomas Jefferson to draw plans for enlarging and remodeling a house on the property. Jefferson's displeasure with the quality of workmanship by the builders and then the death of Divers stopped the work. Bernard Peyton completed the building in the 1850s and added the central section. The building has been enlarged and modernized, though remaining Jeffersonian in appearance, and now serves as a country clubhouse and hotel.
*Operated by Farmington Country Club. Open daily 7:30–10*

## CHARLOTTESVILLE VICINITY

■ **MONTICELLO (THOMAS JEFFERSON PLANTATION), 1770–89**
**Virginia Route 53**
Well-known classical revival-style mansion, designed by Thomas Jeffer-

*Monticello*

289

son, which served as his home for more than half a century. Jefferson incorporated into the house his personal expression of the Græco-Roman designs of Palladio, and it is generally agreed that his careful, symmetrical arrangement, the drawing room with octagonal bay, and an emphasized white portico had a far-reaching influence on the development of Early Republican or Federal-style architecture. The house is filled with gadgets and clever devices, which Jefferson loved, and some he invented, such as dumbwaiters, disappearing beds, unusual lighting and ventilating arrangements, and a duplicating machine.

*Operated by Thomas Jefferson Memorial Foundation. Open daily 8–5*

## CLARKSVILLE

■ **PRESTWOULD, 1794–95**
**three miles north on Route 15**
Mansion built of native limestone for Sir Peyton Skipwith, son of Sir William Skipwith. Sir William won the land in a three-day card game with William Byrd III. Wade Hampton, of South Carolina, said of the mansion in 1800, "Upon the whole except about New York or up the North River I have never seen anything so handsome." The building now houses the Roanoke River Museum, the Roanoke River Chapter of the Archaeological Soc. of Virginia, and the Roanoke River Art Assn.

*Operated by Assn. for the Preservation of Va. Antiquities. Open June–Aug: Wed., Sun. 2–5*

*Prestwould*

## COLONIAL HEIGHTS

**VIOLET BANK, early 19th century**
**Arlington Avenue**
Headquarters of Gen. Robert E. Lee

from June 8 until about November 1, 1864. Now operated as a Confederate museum. On the grounds is the Cucumber Tree, a species of magnolia said to have been brought from the valley of Virginia in 1718.

*Operated by Colonial Heights Federated Woman's Club. Open June–October: daily 10–4*

## DANVILLE

■ **SUTHERLIN HOUSE**
**[DANVILLE PUBLIC LIBRARY],**
**about 1868**
**Main Street**
Ante-bellum mansion in which Jefferson Davis and his cabinet held their last meeting. It was the home of Maj. W. T. Sutherlin at that time. Serving now as the Danville Public Library, there are plans to restore the house and open it as a museum of Civil War memorabilia.

*Operated by City of Danville. Open Mon.–Sat. 9–9*

## FALMOUTH

■ **FALMOUTH HISTORIC DISTRICT**
Founded in 1727, Falmouth was a rich and lively port for the tobacco and flour trade. Significant 18th- and 19th-century structures survive.

## FINCASTLE

■ **FINCASTLE HISTORIC DISTRICT**
Notable example of a typical 19th-century town. Fincastle was one of the last outposts for pioneers moving west through the valley of Virginia.

## FREDERICKSBURG

■ **JAMES MONROE MUSEUM AND MEMORIAL LIBRARY, 1758**
**908 Charles St**
Restored building in which James Monroe began his law practice in 1786. Some of the Louis XVI furniture bought while the Monroes were in France in 1794 and used during their years at the White House is exhibited. Of particular interest is the desk on which the Monroe Doctrine was signed. Adjoining the law office is a library of letters and documents re-

lating to James Monroe, the Monroe Doctrine, and diplomatic relations with Latin America at that time.
*Operated by Pres. James Monroe Foundation. Open daily 9–5; closed Christmas*

■ **KENMORE, about 1752**
**1201 Washington Ave**
Two-story brick house built by Fielding Lewis, brother-in-law of George Washington. The exterior of the house is plain, of early Georgian style, but the interior is extraordinarily rich, with rococo and Adamesque plasterwork decoration of ceilings and overmantels on the first floor. The library plasterwork design has been traced to a plate in Batty Langley's *City and Country Builders' Treasury*, 1740, which indicates the influence of English architectural design books on American architecture.
*Operated by Kenmore Assn. Open Mar.–Nov. 15: daily 9–5. Nov. 16–Apr: daily 9–4:30; closed Christmas and New Year's Day*

Kenmore

**MARY BALL WASHINGTON HOUSE, before 1772**
**1200 Charles St**
George Washington's mother spent her last 17 years in this story-and-a-half cottage, to which was added a two-story wing before she moved in. Authentic 18th-century furnishings, some of which belonged to Mrs. Washington. Restored, including an 18th-century garden
*Operated by Assn. for the Preservation of Va. Antiquities. Open daily 9–5*

■ **RISING SUN TAVERN (CHARLES WASHINGTON HOME), about 1760**
**1306 Caroline St**
One-and-a-half-story frame house built by George Washington's brother Charles. This was a popular meeting place for early colonial leaders who gathered to protest the tyranny of England; the Masonic Lodge held regular meetings here after 1813. It has been restored and refurnished with late 18th-century pieces and is operated as a historic shrine.
*Operated by Assn. for the Preservation of Va. Antiquities. Open Mar.–Nov. 15: daily 9–5. Nov. 16–Feb: daily 9–4:30*

## FREDERICKSBURG VICINITY

■ **GEORGE WASHINGTON BIRTHPLACE NATIONAL MONUMENT**
Reconstructed story-and-a-half brick structure representing the house in which Washington was born on February 22, 1732. Old furnishings and some relics exhibited
*Operated by National Park Service. Open daily 8–5; closed Christmas and New Year's Day*

■ **HOUSE WHERE STONEWALL JACKSON DIED, 1828**
**Fredericksburg and Spotsylvania National Military Park**
Restored house in which Gen. Jackson died following the fall at Chancellorsville in 1863. The bed in which he died is exhibited as well as other furnishings of the period.
*Operated by National Park Service. Open summer: daily 9–5. Winter: closed Wed., Thurs.*

■ **MARMION, about 1725 and 1770–80**
**off Route 609**
The simplicity of the exterior of this frame house, with its clipped gables and massive end chimneys, belies the elegance of its interior. The marbleized parlor woodwork and paneling, which were probably executed between 1770 and 1780, were taken from the house and used in a reconstruction of the room in the Metropolitan Museum of Art in New York; however, the rest of the interior is

VIRGINIA

291

virtually unchanged.
*Operated by Mr. Jay G. Powell. Open by appointment*

## HARDY

### ■ BURROUGHS PLANTATION (BOOKER T. WASHINGTON NATIONAL MONUMENT)
**Virginia Route 122**
Small plantation where Booker T. Washington spent many years in slavery. One of the cabins has been reconstructed from an old photograph; the interior follows Washington's description of the "kitchen cabin" in which he was born and raised. A visitors' center contains exhibits on Washington's life, and a winding trail for sightseeing through the old plantation.
*Operated by National Park Service. Open Apr.–May: and Labor Day–Oct: Mon.–Fri. 8–4:30, Sat., Sun. 9:30–6. June–Labor Day: Mon.–Fri. 8–6, Sat., Sun. 9:30–6. Nov.–Mar: daily 8–4:30; closed Christmas*

## HOPEWELL VICINITY

### ■ SHIRLEY, about 1740; 1769 and 1831
**25 miles east of Richmond on Route 5**
One of the most complete 18th-century estates surviving in the state. A square, three-story tidewater mansion with a double-hipped roof topped by a single pineapple finial, double porticoes believed constructed front and back about 1831, and plain gabled dormers on all four sides. Ann Hill

*Shirley*

Carter was married to "Light-Horse Harry" Lee here in 1793. The asymmetrical interior includes a number of completely paneled rooms, a "hanging staircase" in the large hall, and deep cornices, mantels, and overmantels. Broken pediments, each different, surmount the doors connecting the hall and reception rooms. The house is still operated as a plantation by the descendants of the original Carter builders.
*Operated by Mr. and Mrs. Charles Hill Carter, Jr. Open daily 9–5; closed Christmas*

## JAMESTOWN

### ■ JAMESTOWN NATIONAL HISTORIC SITE, 1607
**Jamestown Island**
First permanent English settlement in America. No remains of the settlement exist above ground except the ruins of the Old Church Tower built in 1647. Current archaeological excavations have uncovered foundations of houses, however, as well as remains of streets and artifacts of the early settlement.
*Operated by Jamestown Foundation. Open Mar. 16–June: daily 9–5. July–Sept. 5: daily 9–5:30. Sept. 6–Nov. 1: 9–5. Nov. 2–Mar. 15: daily 9–4:30*

## JAMESTOWN VICINITY

**ROLFE–WARREN HOUSE, about 1652**
**Route 31 between Surry and Scotland Wharf**
One-and-a-half-story brick house built by Thomas Warren on land given to John Rolfe by Chief Powhatan in 1614. The structure was restored in 1935. Furnishings are of the 17th and 18th centuries.
*Operated by Assn. for the Preservation of Va. Antiquities. Open April–Oct: daily 9–5*

## LEESBURG

### ■ LEESBURG HISTORIC DISTRICT
Leesburg, one of the best-preserved towns in the state, was established in 1758, and many structures dating from the late 18th century through the early 19th century are still extant.

## LEESBURG VICINITY

■ **OATLANDS, 1800–1803; 1827**
**U.S. Route 15, six miles south of Leesburg**
Large mansion built by George Carter, great-grandson of Robert "King" Carter, and designed with the staircases enclosed within semioctagonal projections on each end of the main structure. A tall portico with Corinthian columns designed by Henry Farnham in New York was added to the central portion in 1827. A porch was added to the rear of the house in 1910, and the gardens were enlarged.
*Operated by National Trust. Open April–Oct: daily 10–5*

## LEXINGTON

### STONEWALL JACKSON'S HOME, 1800
**8 Washington St**
Restored home of "Stonewall" Jackson, the only home he ever owned. The building served as a hospital until 1954; it is now a museum with Jackson family memorabilia and furniture exhibited.
*Operated by Stonewall Jackson Memorial. Open summer: 8:30–4:30. Winter: 9–4*

## LYNCHBURG

### MILLER-CLAYTOR HOUSE, about 1790
**Riverside Park**
Charming two-and-a-half-story frame house built in what became the center of town by John Miller, one of Lynchburg's earliest settlers. Many individuals occupied the house over the years, including the prominent Ann Ursula Byrd, widow of Francis Otway Byrd of Westover. Dismantled and moved to its present location, the house has been restored and furnished with antiques.
*Operated by Lynchburg Historical Soc. and Lynchburg Junior League. Open by appointment*

## MIDDLETOWN

■ **BELLE GROVE, about 1794**
**Cedar Creek Battlefield**
Classical revival-style mansion attributed to Thomas Jefferson. The house

was built for Maj. Isaac Hite, Jr., and his first wife, Eleanor Conway Madison, sister of James Madison. It was here that James and Dolley Madison spent part of their honeymoon and that 70 years later Gen. Philip Sheridan had his headquarters during the Battle of Cedar Creek. Interiors distinguished by fine woodwork in the Georgian and Federal styles
*Operated by National Trust. Open Apr.–Oct: Mon.–Sat. 10–4, Sun. 1–5; closed Nov.–Mar.*

## MOUNT VERNON

■ **MOUNT VERNON, 1743, completed 1787**
**George Washington Memorial Parkway, seven miles south of Alexandria**
Plantation home of George Washington, which was started by his half-brother, Lawrence Washington. Later additions (made by the "Father of His Country" after he acquired the property in 1752) transformed the original story-and-a-half structure into the two-story Georgian mansion so familiar to most Americans today. Contains furnishings and memorabilia associated with the Washington family; tomb of George and Martha Washington on the estate
*Operated by Mount Vernon Ladies' Assn. of the Union. Open daily 9–5*

*Mount Vernon*

■ **WOODLAWN PLANTATION, about 1800**
**junction of U.S. Route 1 and Virginia Route 232**
Georgian-style brick mansion designed by Dr. William Thornton, first architect of the Capitol. It was built for Lawrence Lewis, George Washington's favorite nephew, who was married to Eleanor (Nelly) Custis,

Martha Washington's granddaughter. The land was a wedding present to the couple from George Washington, and he chose the site for their house.
*Operated by National Trust. Open daily 9:30–4:30; closed Christmas*

## NEW MARKET

### BUSHONG HOUSE, 1830s; 1850
New Market Battlefield Park
Restored frame farmhouse around which the Battle of New Market was fought May 15, 1864. The house was then used as a field hospital for the wounded of both sides. Two rooms of the building are furnished with mid-19th-century pieces, and the house now serves as a visitors' center.
*Operated by Va. Military Institute. Open daily 9–5*

*Bushong House*

## NORFOLK

### HERMITAGE FOUNDATION MUSEUM, 1906–46
North Shore Road
Romantic Tudor-style house erected by Mrs. William Sloane and continuously altered over a long period of time. It is now a museum of Chinese and Indian art.
*Operated by Hermitage Foundation. Open Apr.–Labor Day: daily 1–5. Winter: daily 12–5*

### ■ MOSES MYERS HOUSE, 1791–92; 1797
Bank and Freemason Streets
Late 18th-century Georgian-style town house, one of the few surviving in tidewater Virginia, built by Moses Myers, a merchant of Dutch-Jewish ancestry who moved here from New York. His descendants owned and lived in the house until the 1930s. The interiors are of the finest in the Adam style in the country, with elaborate plaster decoration, probably executed at the later date when the dining room and rooms above it were added. The molds for this plasterwork are in the collection of the Metropolitan Museum of Art in New York. Much of the original furniture, American and English, survives in the house as well as portraits of members of the Myers family by Gilbert Stuart and Thomas Sully.
*Operated by Norfolk Museum of Arts and Sciences. Open Apr.–Labor Day: Mon.–Sat. 10–5, Sun. 11–6. Winter: Mon.–Sat. 12–5, Sun. 1–5*

## NORFOLK VICINITY–VIRGINIA BEACH

### ■ ADAM THOROUGHGOOD HOUSE, about 1636–40; 1742–45
Pleasure House Road
One of the oldest residences in existence in the state, a brick structure built by Adam Thoroughgood, who came to Virginia in 1621 as an inden-

*Adam Thoroughgood House*

tured servant. Later Thoroughgood became a member of the House of Burgesses as well as a prosperous landowner. The house underwent some alterations over the years and has recently been restored to its 17th-century appearance.
*Operated by Norfolk Museum of Arts and Sciences. Open Mon.–Sat. 10–5, Sun. 11–6*

## ONANCOCK

■ **KERR PLACE, about 1799**
**Market Street**
Large, red brick, Federal mansion built by John Shepard Kerr from Scotland. Building is being restored and is the headquarters of the Eastern Shore of Virginia Historical Soc. Rich interior woodwork
*Operated by Eastern Shore of Va. Historical Soc. Open by appointment*

## PETERSBURG

**CENTRE HILL MANSION, completed 1823**
**400 E Washington St**
One of the city's oldest and most historic residences, originally situated in a beautifully planted and enclosed park of more than eight acres. The mansion was built by Robert Bolling, member of a well-known Virginia family. The interior had hand-carved woodwork and lavish cornices. It is now a museum, with a collection of Civil War relics and exhibits depicting early Petersburg history.
*Operated by Petersburg Battlefield Museum Corp. and the City of Petersburg. Open Tues.–Sat. 10–1, 2–5; Sun. 2–5; closed national holidays*

## PORT ROYAL

■ **PORT ROYAL HISTORIC DISTRICT**
Established 1744, Port Royal retains its early atmosphere even though it has not been restored or had special protection. It is one of the few towns in the Caroline Co. area that is contained within its original boundaries.

## PORTSMOUTH

**HILL HOUSE, about 1810**
**221 North St**
Early 19th-century town house with

English basement. This was the residence of the Hill family until recent years, when the town house was given to the Portsmouth Historical Assn. Interiors and furnishings collected by the Hill family represent many periods.
*Operated by Portsmouth Historical Assn. Open Tues.–Sun. 2–5*

■ **PORTSMOUTH OLDE TOWNE HISTORIC DISTRICT, late 18th and early 19th centuries**
The town was established in 1752 by Col. William Crawford. Along its streets are occasional survivals of 18th-century buildings with their gambrel roofs. Contrasting with these are the 19th-century houses with high English basements and imaginative use of decorative ironwork.

## POWHATAN

■ **POWHATAN COURT HOUSE DISTRICT**
**Route 13**
The village of Powhatan has existed since the courthouse, a small stuccoed brick structure with Roman Doric recessed portico, was built after 1777. Because Powhatan Co. was created during the Revolution, its name honors Chief Powhatan of the tidewater Indian confederacy rather than a representative of the English crown.

## RICHMOND .

**BRANCH HOUSE, 1916**
**2501 Monument Ave**
Built by John Kerr Branch as a setting for his collection of decorative arts. This elaborate town house was designed by John Russell Pope in the Tudor style; although three-storied, it has 11 levels, all supported by fireproof concrete.
*Operated by United Givers Fund of Richmond. Open by appointment*

■ **BROCKENBROUGH HOUSE (WHITE HOUSE OF THE CONFEDERACY), 1816–18; about 1852**
**1201 E Clay St**
Originally a two-story house built for Dr. John Brockenbrough; a third story was added about mid-century which somewhat interferes with its original

neoclassic proportions designed by Robert Mills. The house served as the executive mansion of Jefferson Davis between 1861 and 1865 and has been a museum of Civil War relics since 1896.
*Operated by Confederate Museum. Open Sat. 9–5, Sun. 2–5*

## ELLEN GLASGOW HOUSE (BRANCH-DAVENPORT HOUSE), 1841
**1 West Main St**
Greek Revival-style mansion built by David M. Branch, a tobacconist. Isaac Davenport purchased the house in 1846, and his family lived here until 1887. Ellen Glasgow's father acquired the mansion when she was 13 years old, and it was here she wrote her stories of Richmond life. Restored, some original furnishings survive
*Operated by Assn. for the Preservation of Va. Antiquities and the University Center of Va. Open Mon.–Fri. 8:30–4:30*

## ■ GOVERNOR'S MANSION, 1811–12
**Capital Square**
This mansion, designed by Alexander Parris, was built on the site of an earlier small frame house. That house and the present one have been the residence of the governor since the capital moved to Richmond in 1779. Although the mansion has been remodeled many times, the original early Federal character of the exterior of the house has in general been retained. Badly damaged by fire in 1926, very little of the original interior remains.
*Operated by Commonwealth of Va. Open by appointment*

## ■ HANCOCK-WIRT-CASKIE HOUSE, 1808–9
**2 N Fifth St**
Built by Michael Hancock, this was one of several octagonal houses in Richmond and is the only surviving example in the city today. The house was once the home of William Wirt, a member of counsel for the prosecution of Aaron Burr and Attorney General under James Monroe and John Quincy Adams. It is now successfully adapted for office use.
*Operated by Assn. for the Preservation*

*of Virginia Antiquities. Open office hours and by appointment*

## ■ JOHN MARSHALL HOUSE, 1788–91; 1810
**818 E Marshall St**
Fine late Georgian brick house, the oldest brick house surviving in Richmond, built by John Marshall, first Chief Justice of the U.S. Supreme Court. It was the home of Marshall for 45 years; in 1810 a small wing was added. Now a house museum with a valuable collection of Marshall papers and furnishings
*Operated by Assn. for the Preservation of Va. Antiquities. Open Mon.–Sat. 10–5, Sun. 2–5*

## LEWIS GINTER HOUSE, 1888
**901 W Franklin St**
Victorian mansion, the home of Maj. Lewis E. Ginter, who was the founder of the American Tobacco Co. Maj. Ginter was a very wealthy man, and at the age of 67 he retired from the business world to lead the life of a gentleman of leisure. The mansion now houses the administrative offices of Virginia Commonwealth University, some of which are furnished in keeping with the Victorian period. It also is noted for its exceptionally fine woodwork.
*Operated by Va. Commonwealth University. Open Mon.–Sat. 8–4:30*

## ■ MONUMENT AVENUE HISTORIC DISTRICT, 1906
**west from Lombardy Street**
A tree-shaded avenue, 130 feet wide, with a central section of grass and trees dotted by statues of distinguished Virginians. Lined with handsome residences, it is one of the most fashionable streets in the city.

## NORMAN STEWART HOUSE (ROBERT E. LEE HOUSE), 1844
**707 E Franklin St**
The only surviving example of a residential dwelling in this neighborhood, this simple, well-proportioned Greek Revival-style house was rented by Lee's family in the last years of the war, and Lee lived here for a short time after Appomattox. Furnished with period pieces
*Operated by Confederate Memorial Literary Soc. Open Mon.–Fri. 10–4*

## OLD STONE HOUSE [EDGAR ALLAN POE MUSEUM], about 1686
**1914-16 E Main St**
This is apparently the oldest surviving structure in Richmond. It is a two-story pioneer house furnished in the period of 1736, when it was registered by William Byrd. Some of Poe's possessions are on exhibit in the house. This building and three others (one of which is an old carriage house) are maintained as a museum of memorabilia of the famous poet.
*Operated by Edgar Allan Poe Foundation. Open May–Oct: Tues.–Sat. 10–4:30, Sun., Mon. 1:30–4:30. Nov.–Apr: Tues.–Sat. 10–4, Sun., Mon. 1:30–4*

## ■ ST. JOHN'S CHURCH HISTORIC DISTRICT, about 1800–1850
Declared a historic zone in 1958, this area has been restored and preserved without the aid of public funds. Carrington Square, a block west of St. John's Church, was selected as the pilot restoration block of the area and was named for the Carrington family, several members of which built homes there. Some notable houses, though not a complete list of those of interest in the area, are: *Turner House* (1803), 2520 E Franklin St; *Hilary Baker House* (1810), 2302 E Grace St; *Ann Carrington House* (1810), Broad St; *Morris Cottages* (1830–35), 25th and Grace Streets; *Hardgrove House* (1849), 2300 E Grace St; and *Harwood and Estes Houses* (1869), 2308-10 E Grace St. *Hardgrove House*, with its Greek Revival portico, is particularly interesting.

## ■ WICKHAM-VALENTINE HOUSE, 1812; 1850s
**BRANSFORD-CECIL MEMORIAL HOUSE, 1840**
**GRAY-VALENTINE HOUSES, 1869 or 1870**
**1007-15 E Clay St**
These houses comprise the Valentine Museum, a repository for Richmond and Virginia history. The *Wickham-Valentine House* was built by John Wickham, chief defense counsel for Aaron Burr. A main feature of the interior is the cantilevered and spiral stairway. Modernized in the 1850s in the Victorian taste; restored in 1930 leaving the parlor in the Victorian style. Furnishings of the Federal period. The *Bransford-Cecil Memorial House* is a Greek Revival-style town house moved to its present site to serve as an annex to the museum. Considerably altered, very few original interior architectural features remain. *Gray-Valentine Houses*, a Victorian row house of three dwellings, built by James G. Brooks. Typical of the period are the cornice and bracketed pediments over the doors and windows.
*Operated by Valentine Museum. Open Mon.–Sat. 10–5, Sun. 2:30–5; closed Thanksgiving, Christmas, and New Year's Day*

## WILTON, 1750–53
**South Wilton Road**
William Randolph III built this Georgian-style mansion on the north bank of the James River six miles below Richmond. The exterior has some of the finest domestic brickwork in the state, and the interiors are completely paneled, floor to ceiling, in each room. The house was rescued from many years of neglect in 1933, moved to its present site, and restored and furnished in the style of the period.
*Operated by Soc. of Colonial Dames. Open Mon.–Sat. 10–5, Sun. 3–5; closed Sun. July 1–Labor day*

## RICHMOND VICINITY
**BERKELEY, 1726; about 1790**
**Route 5, between Williamsburg and Richmond**
Two-storied, red brick mansion, the

*Berkeley*

birthplace of Benjamin Harrison, a signer of the Declaration of Independence, and of William Henry Harrison, ninth President of the U.S., as well as the ancestral home of Benjamin Harrison, the 23rd President of the U.S. Berkeley was plundered by Benedict Arnold in 1781, and the estate, called Harrison's Landing, was for a time a base and camping ground of the Federal army during the Civil War. About 1790 the original paneling was removed by Benjamin Harrison, the signer, and a simpler one installed.
*Operated by Mr. Malcolm Jamieson. Open daily 8:30–5*

■ **WESTOVER, about 1730**
**28 miles east of Richmond on Route 5**
Built by William Byrd II, this red brick Georgian mansion is one of the earliest houses built on a grand scale in Virginia. It suffered from two fires in its first 15 years, and most of the interior trim was probably installed after 1749. Two dependencies flanking the main house were connected by passages about 1900 to 1905, and the east dependency, which had been burned during the Civil War, was restored. The gardens and grounds only are open to the public.
*Private. Open daily 9–5*

*Westover*

## STAUNTON

■ **WOODROW WILSON BIRTHPLACE, 1846**
**24 N Coalter St**
Greek Revival-style house in which

the 28th President of the U.S. was born in 1856. The house was built as the manse of the First Presbyterian Church, of which Wilson's father was pastor. A house museum, with Wilson memorabilia and family furniture displayed
*Operated by Woodrow Wilson Birthplace Foundation. Open Mon.–Sat. 9–5; closed Dec.–Feb.*

## STAUNTON VICINITY

■ **McCORMICK FARM AND WORKSHOP**
**Route 606 at Walnut Grove**
Restored homestead and outbuildings of Cyrus Hall McCormick, who perfected the mechanical grain reaper here in 1831. One of the original binders may be seen in the workshop.
*Operated by Va. Polytechnic Institute. Open summer: 8:30–5*

## STRATFORD

■ **STRATFORD (THOMAS LEE PLANTATION), 1725–30**
**40 miles east of Fredericksburg on Route 3, left on Route 214 two miles**
Stratford exemplified the pinnacle of colonial cultural, social, and plantation life. The house was built by Thomas Lee, a native Virginian appointed by England as governor of Virginia. It is considered one of the most important houses in the Commonwealth and, for its early date, an exceptional architectural accomplishment. A massive and severe H-shaped brick structure, it is the birthplace of Robert E. Lee, son of "Light-Horse Harry" Lee and Ann Hill Carter. When "Light-Horse Harry" owned the house he undertook major remodeling of the interior and removed or replaced the exterior stairs. Most of the interior was

*Stratford*

restored, with the exception of Lee's birth room, an adjoining bedroom, corridors, and parlor, which were left in their 1800 state. Now a house museum
*Operated by Robert E. Lee Memorial Foundation. Open daily 9–4:30; closed Christmas*

## WATERFORD

### ■ WATERFORD HISTORIC DISTRICT, 18th and 19th centuries
Established by Quakers from Pennsylvania about 1730, Waterford is the oldest settlement in the county. It grew in three separate stages, 1750, 1800, and 1812, and each section of the expanded town is rich with the architectural examples of typical buildings of its period; an excellent and rare example of 18th- and 19th-century town preserved in its rural setting. A project for restoration is planned.
*Operated by Waterford Foundation*

## WAYNESBORO

### ■ SWANNANOA, 1912
**Route 610 at junction of Route 250 and Skyline Drive**
Florentine villa built by Major James Dooley of Richmond for his wife, who is immortalized in a massive Tiffany stained-glass window in the mansion. Georgia marble was used on the exterior, and Italian marbles, oak paneling, and stretched damask in the interior. Elaborate terraced and balustraded gardens
*Operated by University of Science and Philosophy. Open summer: daily 8–6. Winter: daily 9–5*

## WILLIAMSBURG

### ■ COLONIAL WILLIAMSBURG (WILLIAMSBURG HISTORIC DISTRICT), 18th century
Now a show place of historic restoration and reconstruction, Williamsburg was originally settled as Middle Plantation as early as 1633. It was the capital of Virginia from 1699 to 1779, when the capital was moved to Richmond. The city began to decline at this time and, except for brief revivals, never recovered from its loss. Restoration was begun in 1926, and the following are especially noteworthy

houses among the almost 450 buildings on 130 acres:
*Brush-Everard House,* 1717–19; later additions, Palace Green. Typical, small frame house with two later wings resulting in a U-shaped plan
*Governor's Palace,* about 1706–20; 1751, Palace Green. Reconstruction of the residence for royal governors. Interior is notable for its fine woodwork and furnishings. Formal garden
*John Blair House:* 18th century, Duke of Gloucester St. Restored house with early-type hipped dormers and original stone steps imported from England. Small, formal herb garden
*Ludwell-Paradise House,* about 1737, Duke of Gloucester St. An early Georgian residence built by Philip Ludwell II as a town house, this was the first house to be restored by Colonial Williamsburg.
*Peyton Randolph House,* about 1715 and 1750, Nicholson St. Originally two houses, joined by a center section about 1750. The west wing and center section are original; the east wing is a reconstruction. Paneling in the west wing is considered to be the finest in Williamsburg.
*St. George Tucker House,* about 1714; 1788–95, Nicholson St. Originally a story-and-a-half house facing Palace Green, it was enlarged to two stories and moved to face Nicholson St.
*Semple House,* about 1780, Francis St. Design of this early Federal-style house is attributed to Thomas Jefferson.
*Wythe House,* 1752, Palace Green. Rectangular brick mansion, most impressive of the private houses in Williamsburg. Probably designed by Col. Richard Taliaferro. The house was Washington's headquarters before the Siege of Yorktown and Rochambeau's afterward.
*Operated by Colonial Williamsburg. Open summer: daily 9–9. Spring and fall: daily 9–5. Winter: daily 10–5; closed Christmas*

## WILLIAMSBURG VICINITY

### ■ CARTER'S GROVE, 1750–53
**Route 60, six miles southeast of Williamsburg**
Fine Georgian mansion built for Carter Burwell by David Minitree, a

master craftsman. This house was once the center of a distinctive social life and has been described as "the most beautiful house in America." The pitch of the roof was raised in 1927–28, and dormers were installed, giving the exterior an appearance of earlier houses. The main house and its flanking dependencies were also linked at this time. The interior woodwork is exceptional, particularly in the central hall with its great arch and stairway.
*Operated by Colonial Williamsburg. Open Mar.–Thanksgiving: daily 10–5*

### HOLLINGSWORTH HOUSE (ABRAMS DELIGHT), 1754
**610 Tennyson Ave**
Built by early Quaker settlers, this limestone structure shows the Pennsylvania influence. Restored, with period furnishings
*Operated by Winchester-Frederick Co. Historical Soc. Open Mon.–Sat. 9–5, Sun. 2–5*

### ■ STONEWALL JACKSON'S HEADQUARTERS, before 1861
**415 N Braddock St**
Gothic Revival-style brick house that Gen. Jackson occupied during the winter of 1861 to 1862. Large collection of Jackson relics, including many of his personal possessions, and Civil War memorabilia exhibited
*Operated by Stonewall Jackson Memorial. Open daily 9–5*

## YORKTOWN

### ■ COLONIAL NATIONAL HISTORICAL PARK
The park includes Yorktown, Yorktown Battlefield, and Jamestown Island. Yorktown was established in 1691 and is the site of the surrender of Lord Cornwallis in 1781, ending the American Revolution. Of the houses open to visitors, the *Moore House,* built earlier in the 18th century, is where the articles of capitulation of the British army were drafted. The house is furnished with 18th-century period pieces and Moore family articles.
*Operated by National Park Service. Open – Visitors' center – summer: 8–6. Winter: 8:30–5. Moore House – summer only: daily 9–5*

*Carter's Grove*

## BELLINGHAM

### PICKETT HOUSE, 1856
**910 Bancroft St**
Frame home of Capt. George E. Pickett when he was assigned to Fort Bellingham to protect settlers from Indian attack. He gained lasting fame as the Confederate general who led the charge against Cemetery Ridge during the Battle of Gettysburg. Furnishings of the 1860s period
*Operated by Daughters of the Pioneers of Wash. Open second Fri. of each month and by appointment*

## BOTHELL

### W.A. HANNAN HOUSE, 1893
**10222 Main St**
Two-story pioneer residence built by William Hannan, merchant and town postmaster, for his bride, Mima Campbell. Now restored as a house museum, with historical items relating to the early-day Bothell area and turn-of-the-century furnishings
*Operated by Bothell Historical Soc. Open Sat., Sun. 1-4*

## CASHMERE

### WILLIS CAREY PIONEER VILLAGE
**East Sunset Highway**
Restoration of a typical western community made up of original buildings moved here from their original sites all over Chelan County. It includes a log mission, an assay office and gold mine, blacksmith shop, store, school, barbershop, and two original log cabins built by homesteaders — *Richardson Cabin* (1888) and *Horan Cabin* (1872).
*Operated by Chelan Co. Historical Soc. Open Apr.–Oct: Mon.–Sat. 10–5, Sun. 1–5*

## CHEHALIS VICINITY

### JOHN R. JACKSON HOUSE (JACKSON COURTHOUSE), 1844
**Mary's Corner, U.S. Highway 12**
Built by John R. Jackson of vertical split cedar with puncheon floors, the first pioneer home constructed north of the Columbia River. The U.S. district court convened here for the first time in November of 1850. Many of the original furnishings are on display from Mother's Day to October 15th.
*Operated by Wash. State Parks and Recreation Comm. Open by appointment*

*John R. Jackson House*

## CHINOOK

### ■ COMMANDING OFFICER'S HOUSE, 1902
**Fort Columbia State Park**
This post, built to guard the mouth of the Columbia River, is a registered historic landmark. The commander's frame house is typical of western military post architecture of the 1900 period. Now a house museum with period furnishings
*Operated by Daughters of the American Revolution. Open June–Labor Day: daily 10–5*

## ELLENSBURG VICINITY

### OLMSTEAD PLACE, 1875
**Squaw Creek Trail Road**
Farm homesteaded by a descendant of a founder of Hartford, Connecticut, Samuel Bedient Olmstead, and a good example of pioneer agriculture in the state. An original log cabin of 1875, the granary, wagon shed, and barns

*Olmstead Log Cabin*

still remain. The family house of 1908 is currently occupied by the original settler's granddaughters, who deeded the 218-acre Olmstead Place to the state for a heritage site.
*Operated by Wash. State Parks and Recreation Comm. Open by appointment*

## KELSO

### COWLITZ COUNTY MUSEUM
**Court House Annex**
The museum commemorates the pioneer past of this historic county where the original settlers gathered more than a century ago to petition for division of Oregon Territory to create the Washington Territory. The *Ben Beighle Cabin* (1880s), built ten miles east of Castle Rock by a homesteading pioneer, was dismantled and reassembled within the museum piece by piece. The furnishings are authentic relics of the homestead period of the 19th century in the Northwest.
*Operated by Cowlitz Co. Historical Museum. Open Tues.–Sat. 10:30–4:30, Sun. 2–5*

## OLYMPIA

### C.J. LORD MANSION, 1923
**214 W 22 St**
Handsome stucco Spanish Renaissance-style mansion with tile roof designed by architect Joseph Wohleb. The 32 rooms are now used as a museum with exhibits pertaining to the history of the Northwest.
*Operated by State Capitol Historical Assn. Open Tues.–Sat. 10–5, Sun. 1–5; closed Thanksgiving, Christmas, and New Year's Day*

## PORT GAMBLE

### ■ PORT GAMBLE HISTORIC DISTRIC, 1853
One of the earliest and most important lumber-producing centers on the Pacific Coast, Port Gamble remains an active sawmill town today. The still-standing Greek Revival cottages, New England boxlike houses, and Victorian houses exemplify the mid-19th-century company-owned town. The sawmill and docks were rebuilt in 1926 to complete the 19th-century atmosphere.

## PORT TOWNSEND

### ■ FRANCIS WILCOX JAMES HOUSE, 1889
**Washington and Harrison Streets**
Three-story Victorian shingled house, with a commanding view of the harbor — the residence of one of the town's earlier capitalists. Features are five chimneys, beautiful inlaid parquet floors, and wild cherry woodwork. Now being restored as a Victorian inn
*Operated by Mr. and Mrs. W. A. Eaton, owners. Restoration in progress*

### HOLLY MANOR (SAUNDERS HOME), 1889
**Sims Way**
Victorian show place with a third-story ballroom built by J.C. Saunders, banker and part-time collector of customs in Port Townsend. Now operated as a house museum, with a large collection of antiques of all periods from around the world
*Operated by Holly Manor. Open daily 9–6*

### ■ MANRESA HALL (EISENBEIS CASTLE), 1892
**Sheridan Street**
Built by Prussian Charles Eisenbeis as a home, this impressive three-story brick-and-stone structure with its towers and turrets suggests a Rhine castle. Owned by the Jesuits from 1925 to 1968 and now operated as an inn, with a public dining room
*Operated by Mr. and Mrs. Joshua North, owners. Open daily*

*Manresa Hall*

## ROTHSCHILD HOUSE, 1868
**Jefferson and Taylor Streets**
An eight-room frame house with column-supported front porch built by the merchant D.C.H. Rothschild and his wife, Dorette. Restored and furnished with very little change in architecture or decoration; also a flower and herb garden maintained as they were
*Operated by Wash. State Parks and Recreation Comm. Open June: Wed.– Sun. 12:30–4:30. July–Labor Day: daily 10–4:30*

*Rothschild House*

## ■ STARRETT HOUSE, about 1885
**744 Clay St**
Four-level Victorian carpenter Gothic house built by lumberman George Starrett on brick foundation, with many gables, turrets, and gingerbread trim. Having been used as an apartment house, it is now being restored to a one-family house with period furnishings by the present owners, who have uncovered original four season frescoes on the tower ceiling.
*Operated by George Nichols family. Open daily 10–4 and by appointment*

## PUYALLUP

### EZRA MEEKER MANSION, about 1890
**321 E Pioneer St**
The 17-room Victorian mansion, with carved wooden porch railings and a widow's walk outlined by iron fretwork, built by the pioneer founder of Puyallup. Meeker became nationally known for his efforts to mark the his-

toric Oregon Trail with two trips by ox team and one by "aeroplane" at the age of 95. Ornately carved interiors, stained-glass windows, elaborate tile fireplaces, and period furnishings
*Operated by Ezra Meeker Historical Soc. Open summer: Wed.–Sun. 12–6. Rest of year: Sun. 12–6*

*Ezra Meeker Mansion*

## SEATTLE

### ELIZA FERRY LEARY HOME [DIOCESAN HOUSE], 1901–5
**1551 Tenth Ave, E**
Stone mansion built by John and Eliza Leary, active civic and church leaders, served as a center for social and civic meetings. During World War I it was given to the American Red Cross, and in 1948 it became headquarters of the Episcopal diocese. The vaulted baronial hall was carved by six Belgian artisans over a span of four years.
*Operated by Diocese of Olympia. Open Mon.–Fri. 9–5*

*Diocesan House*

## ■ PIONEER SQUARE-SKID ROW HISTORIC DISTRICT
**First Avenue at James Street**
The heart of old Seattle, settled in the

mid-19th century, is now marked by a 60-foot totem pole. The site's fine natural harbor combined with the expanse of virgin timberland made an ideal setting for the first industry, a sawmill. The mill cut timber for export, and the road down which the logs were rolled to it gave birth to the expression "skid row."

## SPOKANE

### GRACE CAMPBELL HOUSE, 1898
**W 2316 First Ave**
Turn-of-the-century dwelling designed by architect Kirtland K. Cutter and now operated as a house museum with historical exhibits
*Operated by Eastern Wash. State Historical Soc. Open Tues.–Fri. 10–5, Sun. 2–5*

## TACOMA

### ■ FACTOR'S HOUSE, 1845
**Point Defiance Park**
The Factor's House and the granary are the only two original buildings remaining from Fort Nisqually, the communication and supply center for the Hudson's Bay Company's posts on the North Pacific Coast. They have been moved to Point Defiance Park, and the rest of the fort has been reconstructed around them.
*Operated by Metropolitan Park District. Open Tues.–Sun. 8–6; closed Christmas*

## TOPPENISH VICINITY

### FORT SIMCOE STATE PARK
**State Route 220**
One of the two interior Washington Territory military posts established in the fall of 1856 as a result of Indian hostilities. Some of the remaining buildings—the commandant's house, three captain's houses, and a squared-log blockhouse—have been restored and furnished with period pieces.
*Operated by Wash. State Parks and Recreation Comm. Open May–Oct: Wed.–Sun. 9–6*

## TUMWATER

### CAPT. NATHANIEL CROSBY HOUSE, 1858–60
Victorian cottage-style house built among the evergreens overlooking Puget Sound by pioneer Capt. Crosby, the grandfather of singer-actor Bing Crosby. Restored to period, with some original furnishings
*Operated by Daughters of the Pioneers of Wash. Open Thurs. 2–4 and by appointment*

## VANCOUVER

### COVINGTON HOUSE, 1846
**4208 Main St**
Log house built by Richard Covington—English employee of the Hudson's Bay Company of Fort Vancouver—on his land claim five miles east of

*Fort Simcoe Officer's Row*

the city. Moved to its present site *Operated by Vancouver Women's Club. Open June–Aug: Tues., Thurs. 10–4*

*Covington House*

### GRANT HOUSE MUSEUM, 1849
### 1106 E Evergreen Blvd
This two-story log building, presently covered with siding, with column-supported porches and long sloping roof is the oldest in the Vancouver Barracks. It forms part of "Officers' Row" and served for many years as military headquarters and later as the officers' club. Ulysses S. Grant had his office here when he served as a brevet captain in 1852–53.
*Operated by Soroptomist Club of Vancouver. Open Fri.–Wed. 1–4*

*Grant House*

### RED CROSS BUILDING, 1886
### 1310 E Evergreen Blvd
Frame Victorian house, with large porch and peaked tower, located in Officers' Row and formerly the quarters of the commanding officer of Fort Vancouver. Gen. George C. Marshall lived here from 1936 to 1938.
*Operated by American Red Cross. Open by appointment*

*Red Cross Building*

### SLOCUM HOUSE, about 1867
### Sixth and Esther Streets
Frame Victorian house, with front porch supported by columns with fanciful brackets, topped by a cupola and widow's walk. This New England feature made it possible for the builder, Charles W. Slocum, originally of Rhode Island, to have a distant view of the Columbia River. Moved to present site in Esther Short Park
*Operated by "Old Slocum House Theatre Co." Open by appointment*

*Slocum House*

## BETHANY

### ■ ALEXANDER CAMPBELL MANSION, 1793; 1818–23; 1840
**Main Street**
A three-story house originally constructed of oak timbers and hand-cut walnut weatherboarding by John Brown. Here in 1811 Brown's daughter Margaret married Alexander Campbell, chief founder of the Disciples of Christ and Bethany College. During their years of residence Campbell made many alterations and additions to the structure. Furnishings are of the early 1800s, with many items associated with the Campbell family. Also on the grounds are the Campbell study —a small Gothic Revival-style building—a restored one-room schoolhouse, and the Campbell cemetery.
*Operated by Bethany College. Open by appointment*

## CHARLESTON

### GOVERNOR'S MANSION, 1924–25
**1716 Kanawha Blvd**
Beautiful colonial revival-style mansion of red brick designed by Charleston architect Walter Martens. A massive two-story portico supported by Corinthian columns graces the entrance to the structure. Interiors are noteworthy, with some floors of black Belgium and white Tennessee marble, mahogany dual staircases, Aubusson carpets, and an excellent collection of European and American antiques.
*Operated by State of W. Va. Open Fri. 9:30–11:30; closed holidays*

### SUNRISE, 1905
### TORQUILSTONE, 1928
**746 Myrtle Rd**
A magnificent 13-acre estate overlooking the Kanawha River containing two buildings housing museum exhibits, a planetarium, art gallery, live animal fair, nature trail, flower exhibits, workshops and classrooms. Sunrise was built for Gov. William A. MacCorkle, the ninth governor of the state, and named for his ancestral home in Virginia. Torquilstone was designed by Walter Martens for William Goshorn MacCorkle, the governor's son. Remodeled and enlarged 1968–70
*Operated by Sunrise. Open Tues.– Sat. 10–5, Sun. 2–5; closed holidays*

## CHARLES TOWN VICINITY
An annual spring tour of many private homes is held in the historic areas of Charles Town, Martinsburg, Shepherdstown, and Harpers Ferry. Several members of George Washington's family built their homes in this vicinity. One such home is *Harewood* (1770), built by Col. Samuel Washington, brother of George Washington. It was in this house that James Madison and Dolley Payne Todd were married in 1794. For further information contact the Chamber of Commerce or the Jefferson County Historical Soc.

## ELKINS

### ■ GRACELAND HALL (HENRY GASSAWAY DAVIS HOME), about 1894
Three-story structure in the Norman-French style constructed of West Virginia granite. Interiors feature stained-glass windows and ornate fireplaces, one displaying signs of the zodiac. Davis and his son-in-law Stephen B. Elkins founded Davis and Elkins College. Both men were U.S. senators, and Davis was the Vice Presidential candidate in 1904.
*Operated by Davis and Elkins College. Open by appointment*

*Graceland Hall*

## HARPERS FERRY

### ■ HARPER HOUSE, 1775–82
### ■ LOCKWOOD HOUSE (PAYMASTER'S HOUSE), 1848
### ■ MASTER ARMORER'S HOUSE, 1859
**Harpers Ferry National Historical Park**
In 1796 Congress established one of

the first two Federal armories at the confluence of the Potomac and Shenandoah rivers; it was here in 1859 that John Brown led his abortive attempt to capture the arsenal for arms to free the Negro slaves. A number of historic houses have been restored: Harper House, a two-and-a-half-story stone structure, the oldest in Harpers Ferry, was constructed by Robert Harper, who came from Philadelphia to settle here in 1747. Lockwood House is a two-and-a-half-story brick house built as the residence of the paymaster, one of the highest-ranking officials of the U.S. armory. In the winter of 1864–65 Miss Julia Mann, niece of the educator Horace Mann, opened in this house the first school to teach refugee slaves. Storer Normal School, one of the earliest Negro colleges in the country, was begun in 1867 in this building. The Master Armorer's House —a two-story brick structure built just six months before John Brown's raid— is a good example of the type of house the government provided for its officials in the pre-Civil War period. All three houses have period furnishings. *Operated by National Park Service. Open June 15–Labor Day: daily 9–6. After Labor Day–Oct. and Apr. 2–June 4: daily 10–5*

*Harper House*

## HILLSBORO

■ **PEARL S. BUCK BIRTHPLACE,** about 1857
**U.S. Route 219**
Victorian house built of brick with ver-

tical wood siding by Cornelius Johannes Stulting, great-grandfather of the novelist Pearl S. Buck, the only American woman to receive the Nobel Prize for literature. The house is being restored as a cultural center. *Operated by Pearl S. Buck Birthplace Foundation. Hours to be determined*

## MARTINSBURG

■ **BOYDVILLE, about 1810**
**601 S Queen St**
A two-story Georgian-style mansion constructed of stone covered with plaster by Gen. Elisha Boyd. This house was saved by order of Abraham Lincoln when residences of prominent citizens were burned in 1864 in retaliation for the burning of Gov. Bradford's house in Maryland by Confederate forces. Private residence *Operated by Mr. and Mrs. G. Roderick Cheeseman, owners. Open by appointment*

■ **GEN. ADAM STEPHEN HOUSE, completed 1789**
**309 E John St**
Stone house built by the founder of Martinsburg. Gen. Stephen was a Scottish immigrant, a graduate of both the University of Aberdeen and the University of Edinburgh, and a prominent surgeon and soldier of the Virginia militia. The house is being restored and furnished as a museum. *Operated by Gen. Adam Stephen Memorial Assn. Open by appointment*

## PARKERSBURG

**CENTENNIAL CABIN MUSEUM, 1804**
**City Park**
Two-story log cabin built by Henry Cooper 16 years before the town was chartered under its present name. The cabin was moved from its original site in 1911 and serves as a museum, with memorabilia of pioneer days. *Operated by Daughters of the American Pioneers. Open Sun., holidays 1–5, and by appointment*

## POINT PLEASANT

**MANSION HOUSE, 1796–97**
**Tu-endie-wei State Park**
It is said that George Washington

named this town, now a growing resort area near the junction of the Kanawha and Ohio rivers, when he surveyed the area in the late 1740s. Built of hewn logs by Walter Newman, Mansion House is the oldest structure in the Kanawha Valley. Furnished with colonial furniture and relics from the Battle of Point Pleasant (1774)
*Operated by State of W. Va. and Daughters of the American Revolution. Open Apr.–Nov: daily 9–5*

## WHEELING

### MANSION HOUSE MUSEUM, 1835
**Oglebay Park**
Greek Revival mansion containing historical material, with furnishings ranging from the colonial to Victorian periods. Collection of pewter, early Wheeling glass, and china
*Operated by City of Wheeling and Oglebay Institute. Open Mon.–Sat. 9:30–5*

### WILLOW GLEN, 1914–20
**Bethany Pike, Route 88**
Massive sandstone structure built at a cost of $250,000 by wealthy coal owner and merchant Johnson Camden McKinley for his bride, Agra Bennet. Agra, who had been presented to the

British court on her 18th birthday, became the hostess of Wheeling society, and the house became the scene of many gala affairs. Interiors of the house were decorated by Louis Comfort Tiffany. Furnishings include a suite of bedroom furniture presented by the French government to Benjamin Franklin, a dining table that belonged to Mr. and Mrs. Jefferson Davis, and countless curios collected from all over the world.
*Operated by McKinley Estate. Open May–Oct: Tues.–Sat. 11–3, Sun. 1–5. Nov.–Apr: by appointment*

## WHITE SULPHUR SPRINGS

### PRESIDENTS' COTTAGE, 1816
**Greenbriar Hotel**
White cottage with a double gallery has housed several Presidents vacationing at White Sulphur Springs, a fashionable health and pleasure resort since 1778. The cottage served as the summer White House for Martin Van Buren, John Tyler, and Millard Fillmore. Now a furnished house museum
*Operated by Greenbriar Hotel. Open Apr.–Nov: Mon.–Sat. 10–12, 1–4:30. Dec.–Mar: by appointment*

WISCONSIN

## ANTIGO

### FRANCIS A. DELEGLISE CABIN, 1877
**Seventh Avenue and Superior Street**
Log cabin—the oldest in town—was built by Antigo's founder, Francis Augustine Deleglise, a Swiss pioneer. The cabin stands on the lawn of the local museum, which houses a collection of pioneer farm and logging tools and early furnishings.
*Operated by Langlade Co. Historical Soc. Open May–Nov: Tues., Fri. 2–5*

## BARABOO

### SAUK COUNTY HISTORICAL MUSEUM, 1906
**531 Fourth Ave**
English Tudor-style home, built by

the Van Orden family, houses a collection of Civil War relics, Indian artifacts, and some of the Van Orden furnishings. Other displays relate to the Ringling Brothers circus, which had its winter quarters in Baraboo; seven of the original circus buildings are in the city and open to the public.
*Operated by Sauk Co. Historical Soc. Open Memorial Day–Sept. 15: Tues.–Fri., Sun. 2–5*

## BARRON

### BARRON COUNTY SCHOOL MUSEUM
**Highway 8**
Museum complex is made up of a 1910 rural schoolhouse and a pioneer log cabin built in 1880. Restored and furnished with appropriate pieces

Operated by Barron Co. Historical Soc. Open June–Sept: Sat. 10–5, Sun. 12–5

## BELOIT

### BARTLETT MEMORIAL HISTORICAL MUSEUM, 1851
**2149 St. Lawrence Ave**
Architect James H. Hanchett built this limestone house and barn six years before the village took the name Beloit. Now a museum, with Norwegian pioneer furnishings, costumes, and artifacts, and American war relics
*Operated by Beloit Historical Soc. Open Tues.–Fri., Sun. 1–4; closed holidays*

### RASEY HOUSE, 1850
**517 Prospect Ave**
Two-story, three-bedroom cobblestone house erected by Chester Clark, a skilled mason who came from Marion, New York, where cobblestone building was popular. Built by volunteer labor and sold to raise money for Beloit College, whose students gathered the stones for the house. Named for the last owners who furnished the house with Victorian pieces
*Operated by Daughters of the American Revolution. Open by appointment*

*Rasey House*

## BLUE MOUNDS

### LITTLE NORWAY, 1856
**one mile north of U.S. Routes 18 and 151**
Several hewn-oak houses with sod roofs, once a Norwegian pioneer's homestead, have been restored to make up the village, also called Nissedahle, or Valley of the Elves. Rooms are furnished with Scandinavian pio-

neer household items and a large collection of Norwegiana
*Private. Open May–June, Sept.–Oct: daily 9–5. July–Aug: daily 9–7*

## BURLINGTON

### PIONEER LOG CABIN, about 1864
**Echo Park, Highway 30**
Authentic log cabin built by early settlers; restored and furnished with pioneer artifacts
*Operated by Burlington Historical Soc. Open Memorial Day–Labor Day: Sun., holidays 1–4*

## CASSVILLE

### ■ NELSON DEWEY HOMESTEAD, about 1850; 1873
**Nelson Dewey State Park**
Two-story red brick mansion — destroyed by fire and rebuilt in 1873 — was the home of Wisconsin's first governor, Nelson Dewey. Located in a 600-acre state park, the house and outbuildings have been restored and furnished.
*Operated by State Historical Soc. of Wis. Open May–Oct: daily 9–5*

*Nelson Dewey Homestead*

### ■ STONEFIELD VILLAGE, 1890s
**Nelson Dewey State Park**
This village depicts life in a typical turn-of-the-century Midwest farming community. Included among the restored and furnished buildings are a general store, livery stable, cheese factory, and ice-cream parlor.
*Operated by State Historical Soc. of Wis. Open May–Oct: daily 9–5*

WISCONSIN

*Stonefield Village*

## WISCONSIN

## FOND DU LAC

### GALLOWAY HOUSE, 1868
**Pioneer Road**
Victorian country farmhouse, with fine
carved woodwork and stenciled ceilings, is the center of an "outdoor"
museum, which includes a carriage
house, log house, leather shop, and
church. Period furnishings
*Operated by Fond du Lac Co. His-
torical Soc. Open June–Sept: Tues.–
Sun. 1–5*

## FORT ATKINSON

### HOARD HISTORICAL
### MUSEUM, 1865; 1906
**407 Merchants Ave**
Large home built by the Hoard family,
early prominent citizens of the area.
Donated as a museum in 1957; on display is a large collection of local historical memorabilia. Also on the
grounds is the *Dwight Foster Home*,
a frame house built in 1841 by the
community's first settler.
*Operated by City of Fort Atkinson and
Fort Atkinson Historical Soc. Open
Tues., Thurs., Fri. 11–3, Wed., Sat.
8:30–5, and by appointment*

## GREEN BAY

### ■ COTTON HOUSE, 1840s
**2632 S Webster Ave**
Built by Capt. John Winslow Cotton
and considered to be one of the finest
examples of Jeffersonian architecture
in the Midwest; now restored and
shown with period furnishings. On the
grounds is the Baird Law Office, built
in the 1830s by Henry S. Baird, the

first practicing attorney west of Lake
Michigan.
*Operated by Brown Co. Historical
Soc. Open May–Oct: Tues.–Sat. 10–5,
Sun. 2–5*

### HAZELWOOD, 1837
**1008 S Monroe Ave**
Morgan L. Martin, an early Wisconsin
politician, built this one-and-a-half-
story frame frontier house. Martin was
president of the convention held here
which drew up the state's constitution.
Shown with period furnishings, including the table on which the constitution was drafted
*Operated by Neville Public Museum.
Open Apr.–Oct: Tues.–Sat. 10–5, Sun.
2–5*

### ■ TANK COTTAGE, begun 1776
**Fifth Street and Tenth Avenue**
The middle section of this clapboard
house was built by French trader
Francis Roi in the typical French-
Canadian fashion – upright timbers
with twigs woven between and plas-
tered over with a clay-mud mixture.
During the War of 1812, when Judge
Porlier owned the house, it was used
as English headquarters. In 1850 Nils
Otto Tank bought the property and
expanded the house to its present size.
Shown with furnishings, some belong-
ing to the Tank family
*Operated by City of Green Bay. Open
May–Oct: Tues.–Sat. 10–12, 1–5, Sun.
2–5*

## GREENBUSH

### OLD WADE STATE PARK
**Highway 23**
Between 1847 and 1851 Sylvanus

Wade built an inn here on the plank road between Sheboygan and Fond du Lac; he soon added a blacksmith shop. In the 1850s his son-in-law, Charles Robinson, who operated a sawmill, built a home of butternut wood for his family. *Wade House, Butternut House*, the blacksmith shop, and a smokehouse have been restored and authentically furnished. Also included is a carriage museum.
*Operated by State Historical Soc. of Wis. Open May–Oct: daily 9–5*

*Old Wade House*

## HAYWARD

### HISTORYLAND
Complex of reconstructed and renovated buildings represents 300 years of local history from the mid-17th century on. Included are a reconstructed logging camp, a pioneer village with such authentic buildings as a saloon and hotel, and a typical village of the Ojibwa Indians.
*Operated by Historyland. Open June–Labor Day: daily 10–6*

## HILLSBORO

### PIONEER LOG CABIN, about 1900
**Field Memorial Park**
Log cabin built by pioneers of Norwegian origin and shown with typical settlers' furnishings
*Operated by Hillsboro Historical Soc. Open May–Sept: Sun. 2–4. Oct.–Apr: by appointment*

## JANESVILLE

### ■ TALLMAN RESTORATIONS
**440 N Jackson St**
William Morrison Tallman, land speculator and abolitionist, built this fine

26-room Italianate mansion, where Abraham Lincoln was a guest in 1859. Tallman's carriage house is now a museum of local history. A Greek Revival stone house, built in 1842, has been moved to the site. Both homes are restored and furnished.
*Operated by Rock Co. Historical Soc. Open May, Sept.–Oct: Sat., Sun. 11–5. Memorial Day–Labor Day: Tues.–Fri. 1–5, Sat., Sun. 11–5*

*Tallman Restorations*

## JEFFERSON

### AZTALAN MUSEUM
Museum located in an 1852 Baptist church also includes three log houses. The one-room *Pettey Cabin*, built in 1843 by early settlers, features a massive split-rock chimney and pioneer furnishings; the *Loom House*, built in 1849, is now furnished with early tools for spinning and weaving; the *Zickert House*, a two-story log house built about 1867, is furnished as a post-Civil War farmhouse.
*Operated by Lake Mills-Aztalan Historical Soc. Open May–Oct: daily 9–5*

## KAUKAUNA

### GRIGNON HOME, 1835–39
**Augustine Street, Route 2**
Large frame house with classical details, called the "Mansion in the Woods," built by Charles A. Grignon, whose grandfather Pierre founded the first trading post here in 1760. Occupied by the family until 1938, it is shown with the Grignon furnishings.
*Operated by Grignon Home Group. Open May 15–Sept: Tues.–Sun. 11–5 and by appointment*

## LA CROSSE

### HIXON HOUSE, 1857
**429 N Seventh St**
A 15-room frame house built by early settler Gideon C. Hixon, who moved here from Vermont in 1856. House features a cherry wood dining room, ornately carved woodwork, and parquet floors. Occupied by the Hixon family until the early 1960s, it is shown with the family's Victorian furniture. *Operated by La Crosse Co. Historical Soc. Open June–Labor Day: daily 1–5*

## LA POINTE

### MADELINE ISLAND HISTORICAL MUSEUM
This museum is composed of four log structures surrounded by a cedar log fence and is located on an island that was the home of the Chippewa Indians and the base of the Great Lakes fur trade. The main building, one of the last built by the American Fur Company, is furnished as a typical settler's cabin; the *Old Sailor's Home*, also shown with pioneer furnishings, was built as a refuge for any shipwrecked person. The barn and jail house museum collections. *Operated by State Historical Soc. of Wis. Open June 15–Sept. 15: daily 11–4*

*Madeline Island Historical Museum*

## MAUSTON

### BOORMAN HOUSE, 1870
**211 N Union St**
Large brick house built by one of the town's first settlers. Still in use as a private residence; shown with period furnishings and Civil War artifacts *Operated by Mauston Historical Soc. and Edward Pierce, owner. Open July–Sept: Sun. 2–4 and by appointment*

## MENOMONEE FALLS

### MILLER-DAVIDSON HOUSE, 1858
**Country Line Road**
Two-story farmhouse of coursed rubble and limestone with a gable roof; shown with period antiques
*Private. Open May–Oct: Sat., Sun. 1–5, and by appointment*

## MILTON

### MILTON HOUSE, 1844
**junction of State Highways 59 and 26**
This inn, a stagecoach stop built by Joseph Goodrick, is said to be the oldest grout building in the U.S. It features a three-story hexagonal section and a T-shaped wing and is connected to the *Goodrich Log Cabin*, a story-and-a-half settler's home built in 1837. Both are furnished as museums, with Indian and pioneer relics. *Operated by Milton Historical Soc. Open May–Oct. 15: daily 10–5*

## MILWAUKEE

### CHARLES ALLIS ART LIBRARY, 1908
**1630 E Royall Place**
Three-story Tudor-style town house built by Charles Allis, who intended it to become a museum after his death. Shown with the Allis collection of fine art
*Operated by Milwaukee Public Library. Open Tues.–Sun. 1–5, Wed. evg. 7–9:30*

### KILBOURNTOWN HOUSE, 1844
**Estabrook Park**
Greek Revival house built by pioneer Benjamin Church. The wooden frame of the house sits on a brick-filled plaster base, an unusual feature. Partially destroyed by fire, the house—shown with period furnishings—will be reopened to the public when reconstruction is completed.
*Operated by Milwaukee Co. Historical Soc. Restoration in progress*

## MINERAL POINT

### JOSEPH GUNDRY HOUSE 1867
**Pine and Davis Streets**
Large stone mansion with cupola on top and columned porch reminiscent of southern plantation houses; built by

Cornish businessman Joseph Gundry. Shown with period furnishings and museum displays, including a fine mineral collection
*Operated by Mineral Point Historical Soc. Open June–Sept: daily 10–5*

### PENDARVIS HOUSE, about 1828
**114 Shake Rag St**
Two-story house of rock—typical of those built by Cornish miners after the discovery of great mineral deposits here—is now the center of a restoration project. Included are another rock house and a row of dwellings, all modeled after cottages in Cornwall. Furnished with items of local history
*Operated by Neale and Hellum. Open May–Sept: daily 9–12, 1–5*

## NEENAH
### DOTY GRAND LOGGERY, 1847
**Doty Park at East Lincoln Avenue**
One - and - a - half - story squared - log house with a gable roof and recessed porch was built by James Duane Doty, land speculator and politician who served as the second territorial governor of Wisconsin. Shown with Indian relics, the Doty family furnishings, and other items of local history
*Operated by City of Neenah. Open June–Labor Day: Tues.–Fri. 9:30–11:30, 1:30–5, Sat., Sun., holidays 1:30–5*

## NEW GLARUS
### SWISS MUSEUM VILLAGE
**Sixth Avenue and Seventh Street**
Six restored and reconstructed buildings make up this replica of the Swiss settlement founded here in 1845. A log museum houses a collection of Swiss pioneer artifacts.
*Operated by New Glarus Historical Soc. Open May–Oct: daily 9–5*

## OCONTO
### BEYER HOME, about 1860
**917 Park Ave**
Georgian-style Civil War-era mansion is now a museum with Indian and pioneer artifacts and other local historical items. Also on the grounds is a modern annex housing a copper culture Indian exhibit.

*Operated by Oconto Co. Historical Soc. Open Memorial Day–Sept. 15: daily 9–5*

## PLYMOUTH
### JOHN G. VOIGT HOUSE, 1850
**Route 1**
This log house, built by Christopher Meyer, is the oldest one of its kind in Sheboygan County. Restored in 1957 by Elmer Voigt, who named it for his grandson, it is shown with pioneer furnishings.
*Operated by Racine Y.M.C.A. Camp Anokijig. Open June–Aug: Wed.–Sun. 2–5*

## PORTAGE
### OLD INDIAN AGENCY HOUSE, 1832
White clapboard house typical of those built in New England around 1800 was erected by the U.S. government for John H. Kinzie, agent to the Winnebago Indians. Restored in 1932 and shown with Empire furnishings
*Operated by Soc. of Colonial Dames. Open May–Oct: daily 9–5. Nov.–Apr: by appointment*

## PRAIRIE DU CHIEN
### ■ VILLA LOUIS, 1843; 1872
**Villa Louis Road and Bolvin Street**
Hercules Dousman, Wisconsin's first

*Villa Louis*

millionaire, built a frontier Georgian-style mansion here in 1843. A center of political and social life, it was re-modeled as this lavish Victorian mansion by his wife in 1872. Donated as a museum in the 1930s and shown with the family furnishings. Numerous out-buildings on the estate have been restored; the coach house is a museum of early local history.
*Operated by State Historical Soc. of Wis. Open May–Oct: daily 9–5*

## SAUK CITY

### HAHN HOUSE, about 1866
**626 Water St**
Five-room house built into the river-bank; two rooms are on the first floor, and three are on the basement level, which features a built-in stove and oven typical of many German homes. Constructed of red clay brick and now a museum, with furnishings from the 1880s and items of local history
*Operated by Sauk Prairie Historical Soc. Open Memorial Day–Labor Day: Sun., holidays 2–5, and by appointment*

## SHEBOYGAN

### JUDGE TAYLOR HOUSE, 1852
**3110 Erie Ave**
Two-story brick house topped by a cupola built by Judge David Taylor, a prominent pioneer townsman who served on the Wisconsin supreme court (1878–91). For many years the house and surrounding acreage were operated by C.H. Pape as a dairy farm. Now a museum with historical displays
*Operated by Sheboygan Co. Historical Soc. Open Apr.–Sept: Tues.–Sat. 10–5, Sun. 1–5*

## SPRING GREEN

### TALIESIN EAST, begun 1925
Frank Lloyd Wright's rambling house, which he called "not a style" but "in the nature of Style." Added to and altered by him during his lifetime, this was the third house he built here (the first two were destroyed by fire in 1914 and 1924). Now summer head-quarters of the Taliesin Fellowship and Mrs. Wright's residence
*Operated by Frank Lloyd Wright*

*Foundation. Open July–Aug: Mon.–Sat. 10–4, Sun. 12–4*

## SUPERIOR

### PATTISON MANSION, 1890
**906 E Second St**
Modeled after a chateau outside Paris, this 42-room wood-and-sandstone mansion was built by lumberman and pio-neer miner Martin Pattison. Renovated as a museum featuring period furni-ture, Indian relics, and historical items
*Operated by Douglas Co. Historical Museum. Open Tues.–Fri. 10–12, 1–5, Sat. 1–5, Sun. 2–5*

*Pattison Mansion*

## WATERFORD

### HEG MEMORIAL PARK AND MUSEUM, 1837
**South Loomis Road**
Log cabin is shown with pioneer furnishings and other mementos of the early Norwegian settlers. The park is maintained as a memorial to Col. Hans C. Heg, famous for his later-pub-lished Civil War letters written to his family in this Norwegian settlement.
*Operated by Racine Co. Historical Mu-seum and Racine Co. Highway and Parks Dept. Open Memorial Day–Sept. 5: by appointment*

## WATERTOWN

### OCTAGON HOUSE, 1854
**919 Charles St**
Octagonal three-story brick mansion topped by a cupola has doubled-tiered galleries across the façade. Built by pioneer John Richards, it is shown with the original Victorian furnishings. Also on the grounds is the building in which Margarethe Meyer Schurz, wife of Carl Schurz, conducted the first kindergarten in America in 1856.

Operated by Watertown Historical
Soc. Open May–Oct: daily 10–5

## WAUBEKA

### PIONEER VILLAGE, 1840–60
**Hawthorne Hills Park, County Trunk I**
Restored buildings dating from between 1840 and 1860 make up this
village. Dwellings include *Karl Zettler
Half-Timber House*, built 1849, *Michael Ahner Log House*, built 1851 –
both typically German in style – and
the *Halpin Cottage*, a pre-Civil War
frame house. Among the other buildings are a smokehouse and blacksmith
shop. All are furnished with appropriate period pieces.
*Operated by Ozaukee Co. Historical
Soc. Open June–Oct. 15: Wed., Sun.
12–5:30*

## WAUPACA

### HUTCHINSON HOUSE, 1854
**South Park**
Two-story frame house, with a one-
story wing, set in a park and shown
with period furnishings
*Operated by Waupaca Historical Soc.
Open Memorial Day–Labor Day: Sat.,*

Sun., holidays 2–5

## WAUSAU

### YAWKEY HOUSE [MARATHON COUNTY HISTORICAL MUSEUM], 1901
**403 McIndoe St**
Large classical revival house built by
Cyrus C. Yawkey, one of the area's
early lumber barons. Renovated as a
museum in 1952, with exhibits of local
history
*Operated by Marathon Co. Historical
Soc. Open Mon.–Fri. 9–5, Sun. 2–5*

## WAUWATOSA

### LOWELL DAMON HOUSE, 1844–47
**Wauwatosa and Rogers Avenues**
Large frame house begun by wheel-
wright Oliver Damon and completed
three years later by his cabinetmaker
son, Lowell. Built of the native wood
that abounded here, it is typical of the
early houses in the state. Restored by
the local garden clubs and furnished
with period pieces
*Operated by Milwaukee Co. Historical
Soc. Open Wed. 3–5:30, Sun. 1–5*

## BIG HORN

### BRADFORD BRINTON MEMORIAL, 1892; 1923
**Quarter Circle A Ranch**
Built by two Scotsmen, William and
Malcolm Moncreiffe, the main house
and other buildings are typical of the
more prosperous ranches of the Big
Horn area. Bradford Brinton, a native
of Illinois, purchased the ranch house
in 1923, enlarged it to its present 20
rooms, and decorated it with fine furniture and his collection of western art,
Indian handicrafts, books, and historic
documents. The trustees of the estate
have opened the ranch including the
main house to the public on a regular
tour basis.
*Operated by Northern Trust Co., Chi-
cago. Open May 15–Sept. 15: daily
9–5*

## CHEYENNE

### ■ GOVERNOR'S MANSION, 1904
**300 E 21 St**
Red brick Georgian colonial revival
structure built as an executive mansion
and first occupied by Gov. and Mrs.
Bryant B. Brooks (1905–11). Extensively remodeled and refurnished in
1937 with fine reproductions selected
by Gov. and Mrs. Miller. The mansion
features many pieces of Wyoming art –
framed Indian paintbrush dried flower
arrangements, Wyoming jade, and native clay vases – and a library containing works by Wyoming authors. On
display in the dining room is the valuable Wyoming state silver, more than
50 pieces originally commissioned in
1911 by the people of the state for the
battleship U.S.S. *Wyoming*. Guided
tours are available.

*Operated by State of Wyo. Open by appointment*

## CODY

### BUFFALO BILL'S BOYHOOD HOME, 1840
**Buffalo Bill Historical Center, 720 Sheridan Ave**

Frame boyhood home of Buffalo Bill built by his father, Isaac Cody, in Scott County, Iowa, about two miles from Le Claire, and moved from its original site in 1933. It is restored, with some of the original family furnishings, but only the exterior is displayed at present. Also at the center is the Buffalo Bill Museum and Whitney Gallery of Western Art.
*Operated by Buffalo Bill Historical Center. Open June–Aug: daily 7–10. May and Sept: daily 9–9*

*Buffalo Bill's Boyhood Home*

## DOUGLAS VICINITY

### FORT FETTERMAN, 1867
**near junction of La Prele Creek and North Platte River**

A major Army supply post in the 1860s and 1870s, the fort outlived its usefulness with the end of resistance of the Plains Indians and was abandoned in 1882. A civilian center grew up at the site as an outfitting center for ranchers and wagon trains but declined rapidly when the nearby town of Douglas was founded. Today a restored officers' quarters with a museum may be viewed.
*Operated by Wyo. State Archives and Historical Dept. Open May–Sept: Mon.–Sat. 8:30–12, 1–5, Sun. 1–6*

## ELK VICINITY

### ■ CUNNINGHAM CABIN, late 1880s
**Grand Teton National Park**

Log cabin with sod roof possibly built by the hired hands on the Cunningham ranch. The two separate rooms are joined by a common roof; between them is a dogtrot closed at one end. This is typical of the Appalachian-style cabin that moved westward with the frontier and then into the cattle country in Wyoming and Montana. The cabin was the scene of a fierce gunfight in 1893 between two horse thieves and a sheriff's posse from Jackson Hole.
*Operated by National Park Service. Open daily 8–5*

## FORT BRIDGER

### ■ FORT BRIDGER STATE HISTORIC SITE
**U.S. Highway 305**

In 1843 Jim Bridger, most famous of the Rocky Mountain fur traders, and his partner, Louis Vasques, established a trading post on Blacks Fork of the Green River that became a convenient outfitting point on the Oregon Trail to the Pacific Coast. In 1853 the Mormons took over Fort Bridger to aid converts on the trail to Salt Lake City. In 1858 it became an official military post, which it remained until 1890. After its abandonment by the Army, the fort remained a community center and home for the family of long-time resident Judge W.A. Carter, who ran a large livestock operation. In the late 1920s the state of Wyoming acquired the site and now operates a museum, with picnic grounds; the restoration of existing original structures, including the *Judge W.A. Carter Residence*, is now in progress. The house will be open to the public in the near future.
*Operated by Wyo. State Archives and Historical Dept. Open Apr.–Sept. 15: Tues.–Sat. 8–7, Sun.–Mon. 12–7. Sept. 16–Dec. 15: Sat. 8–4, Sun. 12–4*

## FORT LARAMIE

### ■ FORT LARAMIE NATIONAL HISTORIC SITE
**U.S. Highway 26**

In 1834 two traders, William Sublette

and Robert Campbell, built a rude stockade fort near the confluence of the Laramie and the North Platte rivers. When the American Fur Company bought the post in 1836, Fort Laramie became one of the major trading centers in the West. It became an Army post in 1849 and figured prominently in the overland migrations to Oregon and California and in the bloody Indian campaigns. In the late 1870s the fort served as a supply center for the ranchers and homesteaders moving into the region. It was abandoned in 1890 and fell into decay for 50 years until it became part of the National Park Service. Remains of 21 historic buildings may be viewed, including *Old Bedlam* (1849), a four-unit apartment housing bachelor officers, and the *Double Officers' Quarters* (1868), the captain's and post surgeon's family quarters.
*Operated by National Park Service. Open June 15–Labor Day: daily 7–7. After Labor Day–June 14: daily 8–4:30*

## JACKSON

■ **MILLER CABIN, 1898**
**National Elk Refuge**
Two log cabins a few feet apart belonging to a single homesite. The original cabin was the home of Robert A. Miller, chief administrator of the Teton Division of the Yellowstone Timber and Land Reserve. The larger two-storied cabin was built later and was the headquarters for the first major Federal refuge for a large species of wildlife–the wapiti (elk). Thus the house and site are important to the conservation movement and to the founding of the U.S. forest service. Federal officials are working with the Teton chapter of the state historical society to accomplish restoration.
*Operated by U.S. Bureau of Sports, Fisheries, and Wildlife. Restoration in progress*

## MOOSE

■ **BILL MENOR'S HOMESTEAD, about 1892**
**Grand Teton National Park**
Whitewashed log cabin consisting of three rooms built at different times by the builder of the steam-powered ferry that was once the only means of crossing the Snake River in the central Jackson Hole area. Bill Menor's original home is now restored as a museum, and the ferry was refurbished and placed in working order in 1953.
*Operated by National Park Service. Open June 15–Aug: daily 8–5*

## SHERIDAN

■ **SHERIDAN INN, 1893**
**Broadway and Fifth Street**
Three-story frame structure with a piazza and 69 gables in the roof. From 1894 to 1896 Buffalo Bill Cody operated the inn as a hotel catering to sportsmen bound for Big Horn country. Recently restored to its original appearance and operated as a bar and restaurant. The Buffalo Bill bar retains its original features.
*Operated by Mrs. Neltje Kings, owner. Open Mon.–Sat. 10–2*

■ **TRAIL END MUSEUM, 1908–13**
**400 Clarendon Ave**
Ocher brick mansion on a limestone foundation, stonework and brick laid in old Flemish bond pattern, with red tile roof and Flemish-style gables. Built by John B. Kendrick, governor of Wyoming (1915–17) and then U.S. senator until his death in 1933. This "cattle baron's mansion" may well be the finest remaining example of a northern Plains cattle rancher's town house. The first floor is furnished with some of the original pieces, the second has historical exhibits, and the third has a western art gallery.
*Operated by Sheridan Co. Historical Soc. Open afternoons 1–5, evgs. 7–9*

## SOUTH PASS CITY

■ **SOUTH PASS CITY**
**on Willow Creek, 26 miles south of Lander**
A ghost town of the gold-mining era now undergoing restoration. Named for the famous South Pass in the Rocky Mountains, ten miles away, the point where the Oregon Trail crossed the Continental Divide. It was used more than any other route by westbound settlers.
*Open May 15–Oct. 15: daily 8–8*

# ACKNOWLEDGMENTS —
# PICTURE CREDITS

*The editors appreciate the generous assistance provided by many individuals and institutions during the preparation of this book. For space reasons, it would be impossible to list them all; we especially wish to thank the following:*

American Association for State and Local History
William D. Alderson

The American Institute of Architects: Committee on Historic Buildings
F. Blair Reeves
Historic Resources Committee
H. Roll McLaughlin

Daughters of the American Revolution

National Conference of State Historic Preservation Liaison Officers
Dr. Richard W. Hale, Jr.

The National Society of the Colonial Dames of America: National Historical Activities Committee
Mrs. Harry Van Nuys Wade

National Trust for Historic Preservation
Helen Duprey Bullock

Society for the Preservation of New England Antiquities, Inc.
Abbott Lowell Cummings

Sons of the American Revolution

U.S. Department of Interior: National Park Service
Nancy Beinke
Robert G. Ferris
William J. Murtagh

State of Alabama Department of Archives and History
Milo B. Howard

Alaska Historical Library:

Department of Education
R.N. De Armond

Arizona Pioneers' Historical Society
Sidney B. Brinckerhoff

Arkansas History Commission:
Historic Preservation Program
Jack E. Porter

State of California Resources Agency: Department of Parks and Recreation
Allen W. Welts

The State Historical Society of Colorado
Susan A. Nieminen

State of Connecticut Historical Commission
Constance Luyster
William J. Morris

Delaware Department of State: Division of Archives and Cultural Affairs
Emmet T. Calahan

Government of the District of Columbia Executive Office
James G. Banks

Florida Department of State: Bureau of Historic Preservation
J. P. Schuck

Georgia Historical Commission: Historic Sites Survey
William R. Mitchell, Jr.

State of Hawaii Department of Land and Natural Resources
J. M. Souza, Jr.

Idaho State Historical Society
Merle W. Wells

Illinois State Historical Library
John T. Keene